Understanding Government Contract Source Selection

Understanding Government Contract Source Selection

Margaret G. Rumbaugh

.

MANAGEMENTCONCEPTS

8230 Leesburg Pike, Suite 800
Vienna, VA 22182
(703) 790-9595
Fax: (703) 790-1371
www.managementconcepts.com

Printed in the United States of America

Library of Congress Cataloging-in-Publication Data

Rumbaugh, Margaret G.

  Understanding government contract source selection / Margaret G. Rumbaugh.
    p. cm.
  ISBN 978-1-56726-273-5
1. Letting of contracts–United States. 2. Government purchasing–Law and legislation–United States I. Title.
KF850.R86 2010
352.5'3–dc22

2009050410

10   9   8   7   6   5   4   3   2

About the Author

Margaret Rumbaugh has 25 years of experience in government contracts. She is a nationally recognized instructor in acquisition management. She began her career in training as an adjunct professor at the University of Virginia in 1991. Ms. Rumbaugh teaches undergraduate classes in the university's procurement and contract management program.

Ms. Rumbaugh has experience designing, writing, and teaching courses for the intelligence community, defense agencies, civilian agencies, and private industry. She has taught a wide variety of topics, from acquisition planning to contract termination, covering the full spectrum of the acquisition cycle.

As the former national vice president for education and certification of the National Contract Management Association (1997–1998), she was responsible for developing seminars and educational products and overseeing professional certification exams. She has published numerous books and articles with the National Contract Management Association.

As an independent consultant, Ms. Rumbaugh provides acquisition support to government agencies and contractors. In addition to advising on both pre- and post-award matters, she performs technical research and writing and course development and training. Ms. Rumbaugh has experience in both the public and private sectors, beginning her career as a contract specialist for the Navy and working most recently as a contract manager for Fortune 500 defense firms before forming her own consulting company in 1993.

To those who supported my career and encouraged me to write this book, with special thanks to my husband, Jim, and my daughter, Ingrid.

Contents

Preface xix

Acknowledgments xxiii

Chapter 1: The Legislative History of Source Selection 1

The Truth in Negotiations Act 3

    Cost or Pricing Data 3

    Adequate Price Competition 5

    Defective Pricing 6

    The Competitive Range 7

    TINA's Impact on Source Selection 7

The Competition in Contracting Act 9

    CICA Requirements 10

    Exceptions to Full and Open Competition 10

    Planning, Solicitation Requirements, and Protests 11

    CICA's Impact on Source Selection 13

The Procurement Integrity Act 14

    New Rules for Ethical Behavior 14

    The Procurement Integrity Act's Impact on Source Selection 15

The Federal Acquisition Streamlining Act 15

    Emphasizing Commercial Contracting Methods 17

    Using Past Performance as an Evaluation Factor 19

    The Federal Acquisition Computer Network 19

    Amendments to the Truth in Negotiations Act 20

    Best Value Acquisitions 21

    Notifying and Debriefing Offerors 22

    FASA's Impact on Source Selection 23

The Federal Acquisition Reform Act 23

    Efficient Competition 24

    Preaward Debriefing 24

    Commercial Item Amendments 25

    Amendments to the Procurement Integrity Act 26

    FARA's Impact on Source Selection 26

Streamlining the Source Selection Process 27

Chapter Summary 28

Part I: Getting Ready for Competition 33

Chapter 2: Planning the Acquisition 37

Market Research 37

    Market Research Data.. 38

    Market Research Sources... 40

    Documenting Market Research... 41

Acquisition Planning Requirements...43

    The Acquisition Plan 43

    The Source Selection Plan... 49

    The Source Selection Team 51

    The Acquisition Strategy.. 53

Case Study: Inadequate Planning..57

Selling to the Government...58

    Central Contractor Registration.. 59

    Finding Opportunities 61

    General Services Administration Multiple Award Schedule Contracts....... 63

    Developing a Marketing Plan... 66

Methods of Acquisition 67

    Simplified Acquisition Procedures... 68

    Sealed Bidding 69

    Contracting by Negotiation 70

    Commercial Items... 71

Contract Types 72

    Fixed-Price Contracts... 73

    Cost-Reimbursement Contracts.. 74

    Incentive Contracts... 75

    Time-and-Materials Contracts.. 77

    Selecting a Contract Type... 77

Chapter Summary 81

Chapter 3: Writing Evaluation Factors 85

Mandatory Evaluation Factors..86

Common Evaluation Factors 88

    Technical Factors 88

    Management Factors.. 89

    Cost/Price Factors 92

Past Performance Evaluation Factors..95

Using Subfactors 96

Case Study: Unstated Evaluation Factors 97

Selecting Evaluation Factors 99

    Brainstorming Evaluation Criteria 102

    Grouping Evaluation Factors 103

Distinguishing Effective Evaluation Factors 104

    Structuring Evaluation Criteria Using a Work Breakdown Structure 104

    Limiting Evaluation Factors 108

    Writing Evaluation Standards 109

Evaluating Risk 112

    Using an Adjectival Scale for Risk Assessment 114

    Mitigating Risk 115

    Performance Confidence Assessment Technique 115

    Case Study: Risk Assessment 118

Expressing the Relative Importance of Evaluation Factors 119

    Narrative Statements 120

    Numerical Scoring or Weighting 120

Common Problems Associated with Evaluation Factors 124

Chapter Summary 124

Chapter 4: Scoring Plans and Rating Systems 129

The Adjectival Rating System 129

    Case Study: Deviating from a Designated Adjectival Rating System 132

    Case Study: Averaging Adjectives 134

The Color Coding Rating System 136

The Numerical Rating System 139

Combining Scoring Approaches 139

    Case Study: An Inconsistently Applied Scoring Methodology 141

    Case Study: A Deficient Scoring Plan 145

Supporting Rating Systems with Narrative Descriptions 148

Chapter Summary 149

Chapter 5: Writing the Rest of the Solicitation 153

The Uniform Contract Format 154

The Statement of Work 155

    Common Elements of a Statement of Work 157

    Planning and Writing a Statement of Work 159

    Specifying the Contractual Approach 161

Proposal Preparation Instructions (Section L) 168

Organizing Section L...169

Page and Formatting Limits 170

Master Packing List.. 170

Oral Proposals 170

Technical/Management Information 171

Cost/Price Information 171

Past Performance Information 172

Drafting the RFP 173

Reviewing the Final RFP 176

Chapter Summary 180

**Part II: Preparing Proposals and Preparing
for Evaluations... 183**

Chapter 6: Conducting a Pre-Proposal Conference 185

When and Why to Have a Pre-Proposal Conference 185

Topics to Cover at a Pre-Proposal Conference................................187

Planning for a Pre-Proposal Conference 188

Government Considerations 188

Industry Considerations 191

What Happens Next? 195

Chapter Summary 195

Chapter 7: Preparing the Proposal 199

Capture Planning 199

Knowing the Customer 200

Understanding the Program Description.................................... 201

Assessing the Competition...202

Evaluating the Company's Strengths and Weaknesses............... 202

Deciding to Submit a Proposal (Bid/No-Bid)............................ 204

Determining the Win Strategy 207

Teaming Agreements 209

Determining the Structure 211

Designing the Teaming Agreement... 212

Exclusivity and FAR Restrictions on Teaming 214

Key Personnel Considerations...215

Subcontracting Implications 219

Understanding Privity of Contract 219

Understanding Flow-Down Clauses.. 220

Analyzing the RFP...223

Proposal Preparation..225

    Proposal Development Methods 226

    Colorful Reviews 228

    Proposal Submission Tips.. 229

Chapter Summary 230

Chapter 8: Preparing for Proposal Evaluations 235

Selecting Evaluators 235

Case Study: Challenging the Evaluators' Qualifications 236

Training and Orientation...237

    Evaluator Training... 237

    Management Training... 240

Facilities and Security 241

Receiving Proposals 244

    Case Study: Lost Proposal 244

    Determining Conflicts of Interest 246

    Receiving Electronic Proposals 247

    Determining Ineligibility, Debarment, or Suspension Status 248

    Reviewing RFP Compliance 249

    Special Compliance Considerations 253

    Verifying Central Contractor Registration.......................... 253

    Reviewing Representations and Certifications 254

    Late Proposals 254

    Case Study: Late Proposal 255

    Assigning Proposals to Evaluators.................................... 257

Chapter Summary 257

**Part III: Evaluating Proposals and Making
the Award Decision... 261**

Chapter 9: Evaluating Proposals... 265

The Proposal Evaluation Process..266

    Assessing Deficiencies 267

    Assessing Significant Weaknesses..................................... 267

    Assessing Minor Weaknesses... 267

Evaluating Technical/Management Proposal Volumes.................268

    Managing the Evaluation Panel 269

    Conducting the Evaluation 271

    Using Evaluation Forms.. 271

    Case Study: Evaluation Consistency.................................. 273

Evaluating Past Performance 279

Researching Additional Past Performance Information........................ 282

Evaluating Past Performance Information 285

Case Study: Past Performance 288

Evaluating Price or Cost.. 289

Analyzing Price 291

Analyzing Cost 292

Case Study: The Role of the Independent Cost Estimate in
Cost Assessment 299

Evaluating Oral Presentations 303

Scoring Evaluations 305

Case Study: Scoring Methodology 306

Documenting Evaluations 309

Why Document? 310

What to Document 310

Electronic Documentation Issues 312

Case Study: The Importance of Documentation 312

Reaching Consensus 314

The Consensus Process 315

Case Study: Consensus Evaluation Report 317

Chapter Summary 317

Chapter 10: Awarding without Discussions................................**323**

Stating an Intention to Award without Discussions 324

Proposal Weakness and Awarding without Discussions 325

Special Considerations..325

Streamlining the Source Selection Process.............................327

Considering Precedents 327

Case Study: Awarding without Discussions.............................328

Clarifying Proposal Information without Discussions 329

Case Study: Clarifications versus Discussions..........................332

Documenting the Award Decision.......................................333

Notifying Unsuccessful Offerors 334

Chapter Summary 334

Chapter 11: Establishing the Competitive Range **337**

Defining the Competitive Range 337

Communicating with Offerors before Establishing
the Competitive Range 338

Case Study: Making a Competitive Range Determination 340

Limiting the Competitive Range 342

Case Study: Efficient Competition Determination............................343

Case Study: A Revised Competitive Range 344

Case Study: A Competitive Range of One 346

Preaward Debriefing 348

Chapter Summary 350

**Chapter 12: Discussions, Negotiations, and Proposal
Revisions...353**

Distinguishing between Discussions and Negotiations....................353

Planning Negotiations 354

Identifying Topics for Discussion...356

Identifying Significant Weaknesses 356

Identifying Deficiencies...357

Identifying Other Items for Possible Improvement 357

Limits on Discussions 358

Case Study: Adequate Discussions 359

Conducting Negotiations 361

Negotiation Skills...362

Negotiation Styles 363

Revising Proposals..366

Interim Proposal Revisions 366

Final Proposal Revisions..367

Case Study: Misleading Discussions and the Final Proposal Revision 368

Documenting the Negotiation 370

Chapter Summary 372

Chapter 13: Making Trade-Off Decisions....................................375

Comparing Proposals..376

Case Study: Making a Cost/Technical Trade-Off Comparison 378

Exercising Independent Judgment 380

Disagreeing with the Evaluators' Recommendation....................381

Case Study: The SSA Disagrees with the Evaluators' Recommendation... 382

Documenting the Source Selection Decision 385

Case Study: Documenting the Source Selection Decision 387

Chapter Summary 389

Part IV: Completing the Source Selection Process 393

Chapter 14: Conducting Debriefings 395

Why Conduct Debriefings? 397

When to Conduct Debriefings 397

How to Conduct Debriefings 400

Debriefing Methods.. 401

Debriefing Materials 401

Debriefing Attendance 403

Responding to Questions 404

Describing the Source Selection Process and Explaining
Evaluation Results... 404

Attending Debriefings 406

Documenting Debriefings 407

The Protest Clock 408

Case Study: An Untimely Protest...408

Chapter Summary 410

Chapter 15: Filing and Responding to Protests 413

Key Definitions 413

Deciding Whether to File a Protest...415

Identifying Legal Flaws 416

Identifying Prejudice 416

Ensuring an Adequate Business Case.................................... 417

Common Causes for Protest 418

Improper Agency Evaluation.. 418

A Lack of Meaningful Discussions 418

Defective Solicitations.. 419

Improper Exclusion from the Competitive Range 419

A Lack of Cost Realism 419

Agency Bias or Bad Faith 420

Filing a Preaward or Postaward Protests 420

Preaward Protests 421

Postaward Protests.. 421

Protesting to the Agency or the GAO 421

Protesting to the Agency 422

Case Study: Protesting Adverse Agency Action..................... 423

Protesting to the GAO 425

Avoiding a Protest...426

Chapter Summary 428

Appendix I: Sample Proposal Preparation Instructions (Section L) **431**

   L-1. General 431

   L-2. Requirements for Proposal Volumes 432

   L-3. Communication with the Contracting Office...............437

   L-4. Executive Summary Factor Volume Requirements (Volume I)..............437

   L-5. {Factor Name} Factor Requirements (Volume II) 437

   L-6. {Factor Name} Factor Requirements (Volume III) 438

   L-7. Cost Factor Requirements (Volume IV) 438

   L-8. Contract Information Volume Requirements (Volume V) 438

Appendix II: Case Study: Boeing Tanker Protest **439**

   The History...439

   The RFP...440

   Evaluation Factors 441

     Factor 1: Mission Capability 442

     Factor 2: Proposal Risk..443

     Factor 3: Performance Confidence Assessment 444

     Factor 4: Cost/Price 444

     Factor 5: Integrated Fleet Aerial Refueling Assessment 445

   The Proposals 445

   Proposal Evaluations...447

     SSAC Mission Capability Factor Evaluation 449

     Cost/Price Evaluation 449

   The Source Selection Decision.......................................450

   The Protest Decision 451

   Lessons Learned...454

   The Air Force Re-Compete Solicitation 455

     Requirements and Acquisition Strategy 455

     Evaluation Factors..456

   Comparing the Original and New Solicitations 458

Acronyms..**465**

Glossary..**469**

Bibliography..**487**

Index..**501**

Preface

Acquisition professionals with more than ten years' experience can confirm that a metaphorical pendulum in government contracting swings from oversight and restrictions to openness and flexibility and back again.

In the 1980s, the Reagan-era defense buildup led to contracting problems that became front-page stories. This motivated Congress to increase oversight and restrictions. Then, in the 1990s, the Clinton acquisition-reform era reduced oversight and increased flexibility. The pendulum swung through a full cycle in one decade.

After 9/11, the war on terror led to another defense buildup, and the shadow of errors and abuses is creeping over contracting again. Contracting problems such as cost growth and the increased use of sole source exceptions are getting headlines. Although these problems might affect only a minimal amount of transactions, they attract the most press—which gets the attention of Congress.

Now we are entering a new era, and the pendulum could be at the top of its course and making its way back toward more oversight and regulation. For example, in February 2009, Senators Carl Levin and John McCain introduced the Weapon Systems Acquisition Reform Act. Section 203 of this bill reads:

> The Secretary of Defense shall ensure that the acquisition plan for each major defense acquisition program includes measures to maximize competition at both the prime contract level and the subcontract level of such program throughout the life cycle of such program.

In addition, President Barack Obama issued a presidential memorandum on March 4, 2009, requiring the Office of Management and Budget to develop guidance to increase the use of competitive contracts and reduce the use of cost-reimbursement contracts. Change is on the way.

So what does this have to do with source selection? First, the American Recovery and Reinvestment Act (2009) provided billions of dollars to federal agencies to award *competitive* contracts. American taxpayers expect agencies to spend these dollars wisely and to be accountable for their spending. To do this, acquisition personnel must know how to properly conduct a competitive source selection. Conducting a competitive acquisition can be intimidating and complicated. This book walks you through the process and provides advice for both private industry contractors and government agencies.

Second, in this new era, conducting competitive source selections correctly and with fairness and integrity is more important than ever. But this is easier said than done. The acquisition workforce was significantly reduced by acquisition streamlining in the 1990s, and now the number of contracting officers who have experience conducting competitive source selections is limited. How are contracting officers supposed to know what to do? This book will help them along the way.

Finally, acquisition professionals in both government and private industry need to know the laws and regulations that keep changing as the pendulum swings back and forth. These laws establish the requirements for how the government must ensure fair competition and award contracts. This book not only tells you what the laws and regulations require but also explains how to do what is required.

The American Recovery and Reinvestment Act requires transparency, accountability, and textbook accuracy in complying with contracting laws and regulations. Now that sole source acquisitions are receiving greater scrutiny, agencies are conducting more competitive source selections. Acquisition professionals need a current reference book to guide them through the process. Until now, there were no useful textbooks or reference guides on this subject; other books have been written only by lawyers for lawyers.

Understanding Government Contract Source Selection is designed with the acquisition professional in mind and for use as a textbook or a desktop reference guide. This book is unique because it addresses issues of concern to both government and contractor acquisition professionals. Government professionals will learn what contractors consider when deciding to submit a proposal or file a protest. Contractors will learn what it's like to put together a request for proposals (RFP) and evaluate proposals from the contracting officer's perspective.

The process shown in Figure P-1 illustrates the competitive source selection process and lists the chapters in this book that discuss each step in the process. On this flow chart, *G*s indicate the government's responsibilities; the *I*s, actions taken by private industry (contractors).

This book covers the entire acquisition process, from strategy development through contract award. It does not include chapters on contract performance or closeout, which are important parts of the overall acquisition process but are beyond the scope of this text.

Understanding Government Contract Source Selection demystifies the confusing government source selection process, from planning to protest and all the steps in between. It explains each step in the process. Case studies provide further insight, illustrating lessons learned, best practices, and mistakes to avoid. When referring

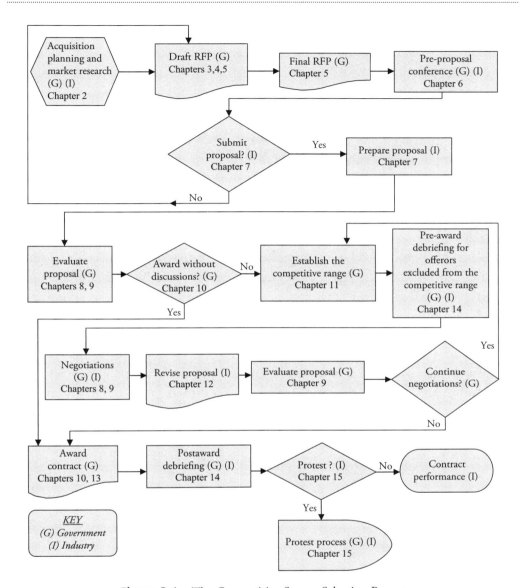

Figure P-1 The Competitive Source Selection Process

to government actions, this text uses the term *contracting officer*; when referring to private industry or contractor actions, the text uses the term *contract manager*.

This book will help government contracting officers:

- Conduct market research
- Prepare the acquisition plan
- Draft the RFP, including evaluation criteria and proposal preparation instructions

- Conduct a pre-proposal conference
- Prepare to receive proposals
- Evaluate proposals.

It will also help private industry contract managers:

- Review a draft RFP and provide comments
- Participate in the pre-proposal conference
- Prepare a proposal complying with RFP requirements
- Negotiate the contract
- Participate in the debriefing.

Although this book provides a comprehensive overview of the competitive source selection process, it is just that: an overview. Government contracting officers must be familiar with their own agencies' acquisition regulation supplements and internal procedures. The suggestions in this text may differ from an agency's internal policies or regulations; if so, readers should follow their agencies' practices. Similarly, private industry contract managers must be familiar with the relevant agency's Federal Acquisition Regulation supplement and internal policies. Company policies might differ from suggestions in this text. Again, readers should follow company rules.

Marge Rumbaugh
South Heidelberg Township, Pennsylvania

Acknowledgments

Writing a textbook can be an impossible undertaking without the support and encouragement of family, friends, and colleagues.

First and foremost, I thank my family for their love, support, and encouragement. My husband Jim has supported my career every step of the way. He suggested I start my own consulting company and didn't complain about late nights taking and teaching classes or traveling across the country. He recommended that I write a book, and here it is. My daughter Ingrid has been supportive, too. She was patient and understanding while I researched, wrote, and edited, sometimes late into the night. It's easy to succeed when you have this kind of support.

In addition, I wish to acknowledge the following professionals for their advice and assistance:

- Rand L. Allen, Esq., partner at Wiley Rein LLP, Washington, D.C.
- Connie Chintall, certified cost estimator/analyst and principal analyst at Chintall Management Consulting, Inc., Warrenton, Virginia
- Michelle Currier, CPCM professor of contract management at the Defense Acquisition University's Norfolk, Virginia, campus
- Tom Reid, Esq., chief problem solver at Certified Contracting Solutions, LLC, Louisville, Colorado
- Michael L. Mixell, Esq., and Sara L. Rubright, Esq., attorneys at Mette, Evans, & Woodside, Wyomissing, Pennsylvania
- Myra Strauss and Courtney Chiaparas, editors at Management Concepts, Vienna, Virginia.

In addition, I'd like to acknowledge the following organizations whose professional support gave me the knowledge and network necessary to write this book:

- The National Contract Management Association
- The University of Virginia's Procurement and Contract Management Program.

Chapter 1

The Legislative History of Source Selection

Many people ask "Why do we have to do this?" during their first competitive source selection. Often, certain procedures are required by law. This chapter explains significant pieces of legislation, and the resulting regulatory framework, that affect competitive negotiated source selections. Occasionally, requirements appear not to make sense or seem overly burdensome, but each step of the acquisition process is backed by some law or regulatory interpretation. Laws and regulations drive this very formal, highly regulated method of spending public money.

Congress lays out the overall structure of and mandates for acquisitions in two primary statutes. The Armed Services Procurement Act of 1947 (10 USC 137) prescribes the general requirements for the Department of Defense (DoD), the National Aeronautics and Space Administration (NASA), and U.S. Coast Guard, while the Federal Property and Administrative Services Act (41 USC 251-260) covers almost all of the rest of the executive branch of the federal government.

The process shown in Figure 1-1 illustrates the competitive source selection process. On this flow chart, *G*s indicate the government's responsibilities; the *I*s, actions taken by industry.

We will discuss the entire acquisition process, from strategy development through contract award. We will not discuss contract performance or closeout, which are important parts of the overall acquisition process but are beyond the scope of this text.

Every aspect of this process has been prescribed by Congress. When Congress perceives that there is a problem related to federal acquisitions, it is often very quick to impose a solution. This is one reason why the process seems extraordinarily complex—and in many respects it is. What must be remembered, however, is

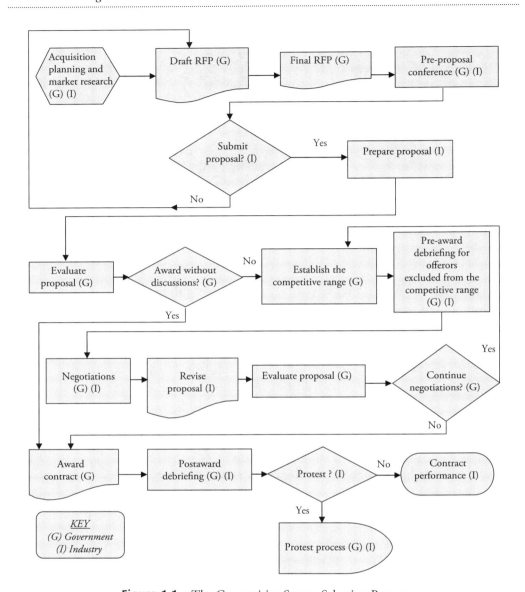

Figure 1-1 The Competitive Source Selection Process

that the public is entitled to great visibility into how its tax dollars are spent, and further, it is entitled to a level of assurance that its money is spent in a fair, equitable, and unbiased manner. Hence the close scrutiny, disclosure, and formalization.

Congress has passed many laws, called *acts*, that affect the way the federal government does business. Some of these acts resulted from studies that were intended to improve the acquisition process, such as the Federal Acquisition Streamlining Act (FASA) and the Federal Acquisition Reform Act. Others were passed in response to heavily publicized horror stories; the Competition in Contracting Act and the Procurement Integrity Act are two examples. In either case, congressional influence on the procurement process is significant.

Even if existing legislation already addresses a situation, Congress sometimes responds to federal acquisition problems by creating additional requirements for the process. The Truth in Negotiations Act and the Procurement Integrity Act are the result of Congress' desire to fix a problem, even though it was already addressed by law or regulation. Let's look at both of these acts and their impact on competitive source selection. We begin with the Truth in Negotiations Act (TINA), which became law in 1962.

THE TRUTH IN NEGOTIATIONS ACT

Many acquisition professionals think that TINA established the requirement for certified cost or pricing data, but this requirement was part of the old Armed Services Procurement Regulation (ASPR) clause number 3-807.3, Certificate of Current Cost or Pricing Data, from 1959. The clause required contractors to certify that the cost or pricing data they were submitting was current.

Regardless, the General Accounting Office (GAO) was concerned that contractors were continuing to overcharge the government, and in 1961 a clause (7-104.29) was added to the ASPR that permitted the government to reduce a contract price if a contractor provided defective cost or pricing data.

Congress passed TINA (Public Law 87-653) in September 1962 because it believed that the government was not receiving factual data from contractors and so was hindered in negotiations. This law is codified at 10 USC 2306 and was initially only applicable to the Department of Defense (DoD), the Coast Guard, and NASA, but Public Law 89-369 made TINA applicable to all executive branch departments and agencies.

Cost or Pricing Data

Cost or *pricing data* are information that prudent buyers and sellers would reasonably expect to have a significant effect on price negotiations and that are true as of the date of price agreement. The contracting officer (CO) and contractor may agree that the data can be accurate as of an earlier date that is as close as practicable to the date of price agreement.

It is important to note that cost or pricing data are factual, not judgmental, and as such, they must be verifiable. While they do not indicate the accuracy of the offeror's judgment about estimated future costs or projections, they do include the data forming the basis for that judgment. Cost or pricing data are more than historical accounting data; they are all the facts that can be reasonably expected to contribute to the soundness of estimates of future costs and to the validity of determinations of costs already incurred. They also include such factors as:

- Vendor quotations
- Nonrecurring costs
- Information on changes in production methods and in production or purchasing volume
- Data supporting projections of business prospects and objectives and related operations costs
- Unit-cost trends, such as those associated with labor efficiency
- Make-or-buy decisions
- Estimated resources to attain business goals
- Information on management decisions that could have a significant bearing on costs.[1]

Submitting cost or pricing data can be a burdensome requirement, especially for large or complex acquisitions. For example, companies must certify that the data is accurate, in accordance with Federal Acquisition Regulation (FAR) 15.406-2. Contrary to what some government personnel assert, this information is *not* typically collected by all companies in the conduct of ordinary business. This is a unique federal government requirement. This is why companies look for exceptions to submitting cost or pricing data.

What exceptions to submitting certified cost or pricing data are available to contractors? Specifically, the government may not ask for cost or pricing data for acquisitions at or below the simplified acquisition threshold. In addition, the contracting officer shall not require a company to submit cost or pricing data to support any action (contracts, subcontracts, or modifications) when any of the following conditions apply:

- The contracting officer determines that prices agreed upon are based on adequate price competition. (Adequate price competition is discussed later in this chapter.)
- The contracting officer determines that prices agreed upon are based on prices set by law or regulation.
- The government is purchasing a commercial item, as defined in FAR 2.101, or any modification to the item, as defined in paragraph (3)(i) of that definition, that does not change the item from a commercial item to a noncommercial item.
- The head of the agency has granted a waiver.
- The action is a contract or subcontract modification for commercial items.

Even if one of these conditions does exist, however, certified data may still be required. For example, the U.S. Air Force KC-X aerial refueling tanker aircraft request for proposals required certified cost or pricing data even though it was a competitive acquisition.[2] Sometimes, high-visibility or high-dollar-value acquisitions require certified cost or pricing data, although more recent changes have restricted contracting officers from automatically requesting certified data.

Adequate Price Competition

Adequate price competition exists when two or more responsible offerors, competing independently, submit priced offers that satisfy the government's expressed requirements. The government will award a contract to the offeror whose proposal represents the best value when price is a substantial factor in source selection. To receive a contract award, the price of an otherwise successful offeror must be reasonable. If the price is found to be unreasonable, the determination of unreasonableness must be factually supported and approved at a level above the contracting officer.[3]

For example, the CO may be faced with an unusual situation where an urgent requirement must be awarded quickly and all of the offerors submitted price proposals that far exceed the government's estimate. The CO could select the "lowest" price proposal but it still would exceed the government's estimate. In this situation the CO must get approval to make the contract award in a timely manner to meet the urgent requirement.

Can there still be adequate price competition if only one offeror submits a proposal? In order for that to occur, the contracting officer must have a reasonable expectation, based on market research or other assessment, that two or more responsible offerors, competing independently, would submit priced offers in response to the solicitation's requirements. In addition, the contracting officer must be able to reasonably conclude that the offer was submitted with the expectation of competition. Indications of expected competition include the following:

- The offeror believed that at least one other offeror was capable of submitting a meaningful offer, and had no reason to believe that other potential offerors did not intend to submit an offer.
- The contracting officer determines that the proposed price is based on adequate price competition.
- The contracting officer's price analysis clearly demonstrates that the proposed price is reasonable in comparison with current or recent prices for the same or similar items, adjusted to reflect changes in market conditions, economic conditions, quantities, or terms and conditions under contracts that resulted from adequate price competition.[4]

For example, the CO may determine after conducting market research that three companies are capable of meeting the requirements and send a request for proposals (RFP) to all three companies. One company is too busy to submit a proposal, and another company doesn't want to enter the federal marketplace. So only one company submits a proposal, but it doesn't know it submitted the only proposal. Thus, the CO may reasonably conclude that the company that submitted a proposal did so anticipating a competitive acquisition. If the proposed price is reasonable, the CO must get approval to award because only one company submitted a proposal.

The CO may, however, need information other than cost or pricing data to support a determination of price reasonableness or cost realism. A contracting officer should only require an offeror to submit cost information other than cost or pricing data when he or she expects that the offeror will be exempted from submitting certified cost or pricing data, but he or she still needs cost information to determine price reasonableness or cost realism. From the data received, the CO should be able to answer the following questions:

- Does the proposed price appear reasonable based on its relationship with estimated costs?
- Are proposed costs realistic for the work to be performed?
- Do proposed costs reflect a clear understanding of contract requirements?
- Are proposed costs consistent with the offeror's technical proposal?[5]

The offeror may submit this data in their company's format.[6] If a company submits cost or pricing data, they must be current, accurate, and complete, or the government may find its pricing data to be defective and seek a price reduction.

Defective Pricing

The government may not know or suspect that the pricing is defective until contract performance begins. After contract award, the government should pay close attention to invoices and performance and compare actual data to the cost proposal.

Factors suggesting cost or pricing data may be defective include:

- A review of current contract performance indicates that the contractor duplicated cost estimates of the current contract.
- The incurred costs are significantly less than projected.
- The data presented during later negotiations are significantly different from data provided for earlier negotiations.
- The budget plans contain data that are different from data submitted in the proposal.

- An estimating system review reveals deficiencies.
- A review of current contract performance indicates that quantity estimates were erroneous because the contractor did not use current information.[7]

The consequences of providing defective pricing data are beyond the scope of this book, but readers should be aware that a defective pricing investigation can lead to investigations by the inspector general, the Defense Contract Audit Agency, or the Department of Justice. If a contractor's pricing information is found to be defective, each invoice it submits may be considered to be a false claim, and additional liability and penalties, both civil (such as fines) or criminal (such as imprisonment), can be levied against the contractor. Thus, if there are any applicable exceptions to submitting certified cost or pricing data, it is advisable for your company to take advantage of them.

The 1986 amendments changed TINA; they required that the government prove that it relied on defective cost or pricing data before it could recover costs that resulted from the defective data. The FASA amendments of 1994 and the Clinger-Cohen Act amendments of 1996 made even more changes. One significant change periodically increased the dollar-value threshold for submitting cost or pricing data. The threshold stands at $650,000 as of June 2009; readers are encouraged to check FAR 15.403-4 for the current threshold. FASA also created a new category of information, "information other than cost or pricing data," as mentioned above.

In addition to the cost or pricing data requirement, TINA also introduced the concept of a competitive range determination.

The Competitive Range

The highest ranked proposals in a negotiated acquisition competition comprise the *competitive range*. The use of a competitive range is one way the government narrows down the field in negotiated acquisitions. Contracting officers must hold discussions with all offerors in the competitive range per Public Law 87-653: "Written or oral discussions shall be conducted with all responsible offerors who submit proposals within a competitive range, price, and other factors considered."[8]

TINA's Impact on Source Selection

The Truth in Negotiations Act had a significant impact on competitive source selection because it established many requirements that are an integral part of source selection today:

- Submitting cost or pricing data
- Determining whether pricing is defective

- Pursuing adequate price competition
- Establishing the competitive range.

Certified cost or pricing data include all facts that prudent buyers and sellers would reasonably expect to significantly affect price negotiations. These facts must be accurate as of the date of the price agreement. Note that facts are verifiable. They are not judgments, projections, or estimates. All facts reasonably available as of the date of the price agreement must be disclosed. Some companies have an unwritten policy of "when in doubt, disclose" when it comes to submitting data because it's safer to disclose information than to withhold it.

An allegation of defective pricing is serious and has serious consequences. FAR 52.215-10 (Price Reduction for Defective Cost or Pricing Data) states in part:

> If any price, including profit or fee, negotiated in connection with this contract, or any cost reimbursable under this contract, was increased by any significant amount because (1)The Contractor or a subcontractor furnished cost or pricing data that were not complete, accurate, and current as certified in its Certificate of Current Cost or Pricing Data; (2) A subcontractor or prospective subcontractor furnished the Contractor cost or pricing data that were not complete, accurate, and current as certified in the Contractor's Certificate of Current Cost or Pricing Data; or (3) Any of these parties furnished data of any description that were not accurate, the price or cost shall be reduced accordingly and the contract shall be modified to reflect the reduction.[9]

Adequate price competition, one exception to submitting certified cost or pricing data, takes advantage of the competitive forces of the marketplace. The presumption in this exception is that competition drives down prices and makes them more reasonable; certified cost or pricing data are thus not needed to establish reasonableness. As we'll see in the next section, encouraging competition for federal government contracts is a recurring theme in federal legislation.

Narrowing the field of competitors by establishing a competitive range helps to speed up the acquisition process by eliminating those vendors that have no chance of receiving the award. The government can then focus on the proposals that have a reasonable chance of being selected for award.

It is interesting to note that in 1962, the philosophy guiding the inclusion of proposals in the competitive range was "When in doubt, keep them in"; now it's "When in doubt, throw them out." This shift was due, in part, to the desires of offerors, especially small businesses. Proposals are extremely expensive endeavors, and if a company no longer has a reasonable chance of overtaking the front runners, it is better for business to stop spending money on a lost cause. Unfortunately, offerors have no way of knowing if this is the case and must rely on the government to use its best judgment.

THE COMPETITION IN CONTRACTING ACT

In 1979, the Commission on Government Procurement recommended that agencies improve competition. This commission planted a seed that was fertilized by procurement scandals in the early 1980s. During this period, the Pentagon's peacetime spending increased significantly. It was purchasing everyday items such as hammers, pliers, coffee makers, and ash trays at inflated prices, which engendered mistrust. Congress determined that lack of competition was the cause of the problem and enacted the Competition in Contracting Act (CICA) in 1984.

The regulations in place at the time already required competition; the Federal Procurement Regulations required "all purchases and contracts, whether by formal advertising [the old way of doing sealed bidding] or by negotiation, [to] be made on a competitive basis to the maximum practicable extent."[10] But before CICA, agencies used the negotiated acquisition method only if formal advertising wasn't practical and if one of 17 exceptions to obtaining competition applied. Therefore, the government still awarded many contracts on a sole source basis.* In 1985, the General Accounting Office asserted:

> All potential contractors should have the opportunity to do business with the government and the right to compete with others equally. Contracts should not be awarded on the basis of favoritism, but should go to those submitting the most advantageous offers to the government. Offering all contractors the opportunity to compete also helps to minimize collusion. In addition, competition is intended to insure that the government pays reasonable prices. The benefits of competition go beyond short-term price advantage. The competitive process provides a means for finding out what is available to meet a particular government need and choosing the best solution. The most important benefits of competition can often be the improved ideas, designs, technology, delivery, or quality of products and services that potential contractors are motivated to produce or develop to obtain government contracts. The chance of winning a government contract or the threat of losing it provides a key incentive for greater efficiency and effectiveness.[11]

---

* Adapted from John Cibinic, Jr., and Ralph C. Nash, Jr., *Formation of Government Contracts* (Washington, DC: George Washington University, 1982), 327. Copyright © 2008 by CCH Incorporated. All Rights Reserved. Reprinted with permission from CCH Incorporated.

CICA Requirements

CICA's requirement for *full and open competition* means that all responsible sources may submit proposals or bids. Not only is competitive procurement the law, it also makes good business sense. Competition can offer cost savings, higher quality, better service, and creative solutions. By advertising requirements to a broad industry base, the government will receive better solutions at reasonable prices. Before CICA, competition was required, but just "to the maximum extent practicable." So if it wasn't practical to have a competitive procurement, it was pretty easy to simply use a sole source.

CICA requires that the government's requirements be *synopsized*, or publicized, in a timely manner. When CICA was passed, synopsis was done through a daily publication called *The Commerce Business Daily* (CBD). Now synopsis is done electronically through the governmentwide point of entry, www.FedBizOpps.gov (short for Federal Business Opportunities). But the objective remains the same: to advertise the government's requirements so that more businesses have an opportunity to compete.

Congress felt so strongly about the importance of competition that it established a new position, the competition advocate, for acquisitions. Each agency is now required to appoint a senior official as its competition advocate. He or she is responsible for challenging barriers to full and open competition and submitting annual reports on competition to Congress.[12]

Finally, CICA requires agencies to use advance procurement planning and market research. Conducting market research to find out which companies can meet the government's requirements can expand the list of potential offerors. The act prohibits the use of noncompetitive procedures based on justifications that rely on funding uncertainties or lack of planning.[13] In other words, CICA prevents agencies from using sole source acquisition just because they didn't plan for their requirements or because funding is about to expire.

Despite the requirement for full and open competition, there are still situations in which it is necessary to conduct a sole source procurement. Sole source acquisitions must be justified using one of the following seven exceptions.

Exceptions to Full and Open Competition

CICA requires that "all responsible sources are permitted to compete."[14] To contract without full and open competition, one of the following exceptions must exist:

- **There is only one responsible source,** and no other supplies or services will satisfy agency requirements. The source must have a unique and innovative concept or unique capability for this exception to apply.[15]

- **The need is of such unusual and compelling urgency** that the government would be seriously injured unless the agency is permitted to limit the number of sources.[16]
- **Industrial mobilization; engineering, developmental, or research capability; or expert services.** This exception applies when it is necessary to maintain a facility, manufacturer, or other supplier in case of a national emergency. It may also be used to establish or maintain an essential capability to be provided by an educational or other nonprofit institution or a federally funded research and development center, or to acquire the services of an expert or neutral person for litigation or dispute.[17]
- **International agreement.** Full and open competition is not required when precluded by the terms of an international agreement or treaty between the United States and a foreign government or international organization.[18]
- **A statute** (such as the Small Business Act or the Javits-Wagner-O'Day Act) **expressly authorizes or requires that the acquisition be made through another agency or from a specified source.**[19]
- **National security.** Full and open competition is not required when disclosing the agency's needs would compromise national security. Requiring access to classified information is not, in and of itself, a justification for using a sole source.[20]
- **Public interest.** When the agency head determines that it is not in the public interest to conduct the procurement with full and open competition, Congress is notified in writing at least 30 days before contract award.[21]

Note that the government is not automatically granted authority for a sole source acquisition just because one of the exceptions applies. Although a contracting officer may conduct an acquisition without using full and open competition when one of the aforementioned conditions exists, he or she is still expected to "solicit offers from as many potential sources as practicable under the circumstances."[22] For example, agencies in the intelligence community still use competitive acquisition, but only vendors that have the appropriate security clearance are considered as potential sources. This is known as a *limited competition*.

Planning, Solicitation Requirements, and Protests

In an attempt to broaden the industrial base from which the government selects contractors, CICA requires that agencies use advance procurement planning and conduct market research, though it does not explain who should do the market research or how it should be done. The current FAR part 10 (Market Research) stems from the Federal Acquisition Streamlining Act, which we'll discuss later in this chapter. And although CICA does not state how agencies should perform acquisition planning, the text in FAR part 7 (Acquisition Planning) is a direct result of CICA requirements.

Not only does CICA require full and open competition, market research, and acquisition planning, it also created requirements for *how* the agency attracts competition. For example, CICA requires that the government:

- Specify its needs and solicit proposals in a manner designed to achieve full and open competition for the procurement
- Develop specifications in such manner as is necessary to obtain full and open competition with due regard to the nature of the property or services to be acquired. [23]

"Specifying needs and soliciting proposals in a manner designed to achieve full and open competition" means that the government must advertise its requirements sufficiently in advance of the proposal due date to give vendors a fair opportunity to compete. In 1985, when CICA was implemented in the FAR, contracting officers were required to "publicize contract actions in order to increase competition, broaden industry participation in meeting government requirements, and assist small business concerns in obtaining contracts and subcontracts."[24] At the time, the government was required to synopsize its requirements at least 15 days before issuing the solicitation, and it had to allow at least 30 days for vendors to submit offers. (These requirements have since been changed.)

CICA also established requirements for how a solicitation should be written. For example, the specifications must permit full and open competition and may include restrictive provisions only to the extent necessary to satisfy the needs of the executive agency or as authorized by law. This requirement addresses the concern of "wiring" an RFP to a particular company. If the specifications are written so that only one company can meet the requirements, it is considered to be "wired." This doesn't fulfill the intent of CICA. To avoid this situation, CICA requires that agencies write specifications in terms of:

- Function, so that a variety of products or services may qualify;
- Performance, including specifications of the range of acceptable characteristics or of the minimum acceptable standards; or
- Design requirements.

CICA also introduced minimum requirements for evaluation criteria. Per 41 USC 253a, they must include a statement of:

A. All significant factors (including price) which the executive agency reasonably expects to consider in evaluating competitive proposals and the relative importance assigned to each of those factors; and

B. A statement that the proposals are intended to be evaluated with, and awards
made after, discussions with the offerors, but might be evaluated and awarded
without discussions with the offerors; and the time and place for submission of
proposals.[25]

Finally, CICA requires agencies to evaluate offers based only on the evaluation criteria
stated in the solicitation. It also introduced the concept of award without discussions
(with the exception of minor clarifications)

> when it can be clearly demonstrated from the existence of full and open competi-
> tion or accurate prior cost experience with the product or service that acceptance of
> an initial proposal without discussions would result in the lowest overall cost to the
> Government.[26]

CICA also added provisions relating to bid protests to Title 31 of the United States
Code, which comprises the entire body of congressional actions. All bills passed
by Congress that become permanent law are *codified*, or placed within a system
for finding and referring to the law. In simple terms, the language is given a section number and placed in one of the titles of the U.S. Code. The laws within are
grouped into similar subject areas; Title 31 covers money and finance.

The Budget and Accounting Act of 1921 is the basic legislation that established the
GAO. The act granted GAO authority to determine the legality of public expenditures. Based on this authority, GAO has ruled on protests filed by interested parties
concerning solicitations, proposed awards, or contracts for property or services.
CICA established an express statutory basis for such decisions. It set strict time
limits for the issuance of bid protest decisions and, in many cases, requires agencies
to suspend, or *stay*, a protested procurement action until the comptroller general
issues a decision. In addition, the act authorizes GAO to award successful protestors their costs of pursuing a protest as well as their costs of preparing bids and
proposals.[27]

CICA's Impact on Source Selection

The effects of CICA on source selection are felt today. They affect the entire acquisition cycle, from planning to solicitation preparation, evaluation, and award.
Now we take for granted that agencies plan for competition, but competition was
not required by law before CICA. The FAR language that requires agencies to list
evaluation factors and their relative importance and to state whether award will
be made with or without discussions came directly from CICA. CICA encouraged
contracting officers to use competitive procedures by requiring agencies to choose

a competition advocate, which added another impediment to contracting on a sole source basis. Finally, CICA also allowed timely protest to stop contract award.

THE PROCUREMENT INTEGRITY ACT

CICA's 1984 debut made acquisition more challenging for agencies and contractors in the mid-1980s. In 1986, the Naval Investigative Service launched a two-year ethics investigation of both government and contractor personnel. The investigation, known as Ill Wind, uncovered corrupt behavior of civilian, military, and contractor personnel within the Department of Defense. The investigation revealed that government officials had awarded contracts to favorite contractors by revealing source selection information; contractors rewarded these officials with bribes and gratuities. Using evidence from court-approved wiretaps and more than two million documents, the Justice Department successfully convicted 70 people.

The acquisition community would never be the same. Congress set forth to make sure a situation like this could never happen again. Despite the existence of other ethics laws and regulations such as the 1978 Ethics in Government Act (P.L. 95-521), the Anti-Kickback Act (18 USC 874), and bribery, graft, and conflict of interest statutes (18 USC 201, 207, and 208), Congress passed another ethics law, the Procurement Integrity Act (P.L. 100-679), in 1988. This act tightened the reins on procurement officials and contractors alike by establishing new rules regarding ethical behavior for government and contractor personnel, including technical staff.

New Rules for Ethical Behavior

The Procurement Integrity Act mandates that during the conduct of any federal agency procurement, no competing contractor or consultant shall knowingly:

- Make any offer or promise of future employment or business opportunity or engage in any discussion of future employment or business opportunity with any procurement official
- Offer, give, or promise to offer or give any money, gratuity, or other thing of value to any procurement official
- Solicit or obtain proprietary or source selection information from any officer or employee of the agency before contract award.

Federal agency procurement officials shall not knowingly:

- Solicit or accept any promise of future employment or business opportunity from any competing contractor or consultant

- Ask for, demand, solicit, accept, receive, or agree to receive any money, gratuity, or other thing of value from any officer, employee, representative, or consultant of any competing contractor
- Disclose any proprietary or source selection information to any individual other than a person authorized by the agency head or contracting officer.

The Procurement Integrity Act goes on to define who is considered a procurement official for purposes of the aforementioned restrictions. A *procurement official* is one who has participated personally and substantially in evaluating proposals, selecting sources, or conducting negotiations in connection with a solicitation and contract. This includes postaward actions such as agreements to modify or extend a contract. Thus, these restrictions apply not only to acquisition/contracting personnel but to technical personnel who help evaluate proposals and negotiate contracts. The Procurement Integrity Act also imposes a requirement on offerors to certify in writing that they have not violated the act.[28]

The Procurement Integrity Act's Impact on Source Selection

The Procurement Integrity Act was intended in part to close a "revolving door": government personnel awarding contracts to a company, then going to work for the same company right after contract award. No procurement official may participate personally and substantially in evaluating, negotiating, awarding, or modifying contracts for a particular contractor for a period of two years before working for that company. Similarly, companies must be careful not to express an interest in hiring a government procurement official. To avoid problems, some companies discourage staff from making even vague statements that could be construed as employment offers. The Procurement Integrity Act also requires annual ethics training that explains the requirements of the law and penalties for noncompliance. Anyone who participates in a source selection should attend this training.

THE FEDERAL ACQUISITION STREAMLINING ACT

Shortly after the Procurement Integrity Act was implemented, section 800 of the National Defense Authorization Act for fiscal year 1991 directed a panel of experts in procurement law and policy from both the public and private sectors to make recommendations on streamlining defense acquisition. The Section 800 Panel's recommendations were the impetus for FASA. The goals of the panel were to:

- Streamline the defense acquisition process and prepare a proposed code of relevant acquisition laws
- Eliminate acquisition laws that were unnecessary for the establishment and administration of the buyer and seller relationships in procurement
- Ensure the continuing financial and ethical integrity of defense procurement programs.

The Section 800 Panel evaluated more than 600 laws and recommended almost 300 for repeal, deletion, or amendment. The panel focused on:

> streamlining (fewer and more understandable laws), the use of commercial items wherever possible, and the implementation of a set of simplified acquisition procedures (reducing the administrative overhead associated with "small" purchases).... which led to several far-reaching changes in the acquisition process.[29]

The panel issued its report in early 1993. President Bill Clinton established a National Performance Review (NPR) led by Vice President Al Gore the same year. NPR's goal was to make federal government functions less expensive and more efficient. The NPR also recommended statutory changes to reform the acquisition system.

Both the Section 800 Panel and the NPR identified existing procurement laws that created barriers to entering the federal government contract marketplace. Competition and innovation were limited by burdensome regulatory requirements unique to the federal government, including:

- Overreliance on outdated specifications and standards
- Restrictive technical data-rights requirements
- Onerous accounting requirements.[†]

The Federal Acquisition Streamlining Act of 1994 sought to address these issues. FASA repealed or substantially modified 225 statutes. The act also introduced new approaches to procurement, including:

- Emphasizing commercial contracting methods
- Using past performance as an evaluation factor
- Using electronic resources in the procurement process, such as the Federal Acquisition Computer Network (FACNET)
- Eliminating burdensome paperwork by amending the Truth in Negotiations Act

---

† James F. Nagle, *A History of Government Contracting*, 2nd ed. (Washington, DC: George Washington University Press, 1999), 512–514. Copyright © 2008 by CCH Incorporated. All Rights Reserved. Reprinted with permission from CCH Incorporated.

- Streamlining the acquisition process by requiring prompt notification of contract award and by conducting debriefings in a timely manner.

Although the effects of FASA are far reaching, this book will focus on those that affect source selection.

Emphasizing Commercial Contracting Methods

FASA expanded the definitions of the terms *commercial item* and *nondevelopmental item*. Before this change, the definition of a commercial item was derived from an exception in the Truth in Negotiations Act. This exception allowed vendors to avoid submitting certified cost or pricing data for commercial items—those items that had established catalog or market prices and were sold in substantial quantities to the general public. Thus, new computers or software updates were not considered commercial items because they hadn't yet been sold in substantial quantities to the general public. This made it difficult for federal agencies to purchase the latest computer technology.

The new definition of *commercial item* from FASA, per FAR 2.101, is:

1) Any item, other than real property, that is of a type customarily used for non-governmental purposes and that—
   a) Has been sold, leased, or licensed to the general public; or,
   b) Has been offered for sale, lease, or license to the general public;
2) Any item that evolved from an item described in paragraph (1) of this definition through advances in technology or performance and that is not yet available in the commercial marketplace, but will be available in the commercial marketplace in time to satisfy the delivery requirements under a Government solicitation;
3) Any item that would satisfy a criterion expressed in paragraphs (1) or (2) of this definition, but for—
   a) Modifications of a type customarily available in the commercial marketplace; or
   b) Minor modifications of a type not customarily available in the commercial marketplace made to meet Federal Government requirements. "Minor" modifications means modifications that do not significantly alter the nongovernmental function or essential physical characteristics of an item or component, or change the purpose of a process. Factors to be considered in determining whether a modification is minor include the value and size of the modification and the comparative value and size of the final product. Dollar values and percentages may be used as guideposts, but are not conclusive evidence that a modification is minor;

4) Any combination of items meeting the requirements of paragraphs (1), (2), (3), or (5) of this definition that are of a type customarily combined and sold in combination to the general public;

5) Installation services, maintenance services, repair services, training services, and other services if such services are procured for support of an item referred to in paragraphs (1), (2), (3), or (4) of this definition, and if the source of such services—

   a) Offers such services to the general public and the Federal Government contemporaneously and under similar terms and conditions; and

   b) Offers to use the same work force for providing the Federal Government with such services as the source uses for providing such services to the general public;

6) Services of a type offered and sold competitively in substantial quantities in the commercial marketplace based on established catalog or market prices for specific tasks performed under standard commercial terms and conditions. This does not include services that are sold based on hourly rates without an established catalog or market price for a specific service performed;

7) Any item, combination of items, or service referred to in paragraphs (1) through (6) notwithstanding the fact that the item, combination of items, or service is transferred between or among separate divisions, subsidiaries, or affiliates of a contractor; or

8) A nondevelopmental item, if the procuring agency determines the item was developed exclusively at private expense and sold in substantial quantities, on a competitive basis, to multiple State and local governments.[30]

Under this expanded definition, items that are not yet available in the commercial marketplace can still be considered commercial items, provided they evolved from an existing commercial item due to advances in technology. This new definition applies well to computer technology updates and computer software upgrades. Also, services can be considered commercial if they are purchased as part of a commercial item package. Such services typically include maintenance agreements that are purchased along with a piece of equipment. For example, when your agency buys a copy machine, its maintenance is considered a commercial service if the copier and service agreement are purchased together.

FASA also made many laws inapplicable to commercial item procurements. This change helped make it easier for traditional commercial companies (those without separate accounting and recordkeeping systems for government contracts) to participate in federal acquisitions. Some firms never competed for government contracts because they were unwilling or unable to set up different divisions just to do business with the government. FAR 12.5 contains the list of laws not applicable to commercial item acquisitions.

Using Past Performance as an Evaluation Factor

FASA also emphasized the evaluation of contractors' past performance. Evaluating past performance is essentially the same thing as evaluating quality. *Past performance information* is relevant information, for future source selection purposes, regarding a contractor's actions under previously awarded contracts. Past performance can include not only federal work, but also work done under state, local, and commercial contracts. New companies without a record of past performance receive a neutral evaluation and will not be deemed nonresponsible when contracting officers make a responsibility determination pursuant to FAR 9.104. Under FASA, past performance evaluation is required for all competitively negotiated acquisitions expected to exceed $100,000. (If past performance information is not evaluated, the contracting officer must document in the contract file why it was not evaluated.)

Because many agencies did not have accurate records of vendors' past performance, they developed past performance surveys, which are part of the RFP package. Offerors ask their customers to complete the (often lengthy) questionnaires before the proposal due date. Then the government's evaluators read the responses and determine the risk of awarding the contract to each offeror based on its past performance. If responses regarding a particular vendor are negative, it is given an opportunity to provide a rebuttal.[31] (Respondents may be concerned about backlash for providing negative information about a company, but by law, the names of the individuals who complete the performance surveys may not be disclosed.)

What past performance information do agencies evaluate? Agencies are interested in a contractor's record of:

- Conforming to specifications and standards of good workmanship
- Forecasting and containing costs on previous cost-reimbursable contracts
- Adhering to contract schedules, including the administrative aspects of performance
- Being reasonable and cooperative, with a commitment to customer satisfaction
- Having a businesslike concern for the interest of the customer.[32]

The Federal Acquisition Computer Network

The Federal Acquisition Streamlining Act also mandated the establishment of the Federal Acquisition Computer Network, which enabled federal agencies and vendors to do business electronically. FACNET was intended to be used primarily for purchases valued above the micropurchase threshold ($2,500 in 1995) up to the simplified acquisition threshold ($100,000 in 1995). Federal officials and others expected to reap many benefits from FACNET, including expanded contracting opportunities for small businesses, increased competition, lower prices for goods and services, reduced contract processing times, simplified procurement processes, and improved federal productivity.

FASA required that FACNET provide (1) widespread public notice of both contracting opportunities and awards; (2) a means for vendors to electronically review, request information on, and respond to solicitations and similar information; and (3) record keeping for each procurement action. The act also required that, if practicable, FACNET provide other capabilities, such as issuing orders under existing contracts and making payments.[33]

Technology, however, quickly surpassed FACNET's capabilities, and in 1997 Congress amended FASA, adding new provisions for electronic commerce (defined as "electronic techniques for accomplishing business transactions," including email, Internet, electronic bulletin boards, purchase cards, and Electronic Data Interchange (see 41 USC 426)). Specifically, the National Defense Authorization Act for fiscal year 1998 expressly mandated that agencies use e-commerce to the maximum extent practicable to buy goods and services. (See also 48 CFR 4.502, which requires the use of e-commerce in government contracting "whenever practicable or cost effective.")[34]

In 2007, Federal Acquisition Circular (FAC) 2005-21 amended the FAR to remove FACNET references. This did not prevent agencies from continuing to use FACNET, but it did serve to recognize alternative technologies and processes agencies were already using. The government now uses www.FedBizOpps.gov as its one-stop virtual marketplace. FedBizOpps lists proposed government procurement actions, contract awards, sales of government property, and other procurement information for acquisitions over $25,000. The information is updated daily. Through this single point of entry, agency buyers can post and amend opportunities, and contractors can search for federal business opportunities.[35]

Amendments to the Truth in Negotiations Act

FASA amended TINA in several significant ways. First, it changed the exceptions to submitting certified cost or pricing data. Companies no longer have to pass the "sold in substantial quantities" test for a commercial item to be exempt from certified cost or pricing data. Vendors offering commercial items, as newly defined in FASA, are generally exempt from submitting certified cost or pricing data. Competition in the commercial marketplace is expected to keep prices fair and reasonable, so certified cost or pricing data is considered unnecessary.

FASA also restricts the circumstances under which contracting officers may require cost or pricing data. The act specifically prohibits contracting officers from requiring cost or pricing data for acquisitions under $500,000 unless the head of the contracting activity states in writing that the data is necessary. A contracting officer may still, however, request certain information related to cost or pricing, such as sales data or prices and quantities for the same or similar items in the commercial marketplace, to determine price reasonableness. The vendor provides this data in its own format.

Contracting officers are expected to purchase supplies and services from responsible sources at fair and reasonable prices. FASA prohibits contracting officers from obtaining more information than is necessary to establish the reasonableness of offered prices. To the extent that TINA permits, contracting officers shall generally use the following order of preference to determine the type of information required:

1. No further information from the offeror if the price is based on adequate price competition.
2. Information other than cost or pricing data; for example:
   a. Information related to prices (e.g., established catalog or market prices), relying first on information available within the Government; second, on information obtained from sources other than the offeror; and, if necessary, on information obtained from the offeror.
   b. Cost information, which does not meet the definition of cost or pricing data.
3. Cost or pricing data. The contracting officer should use every means available to ascertain a fair and reasonable price before requesting cost or pricing data. By law and regulation, contracting officers shall not unnecessarily require cost or pricing data because it leads to increased proposal preparation costs, generally extends acquisition lead time, and wastes both contractor and government resources.[36]

Another implication of FASA's TINA amendments is that the threshold for the mandatory submission of certified cost or pricing data is adjusted every five years. That threshold, provided at FAR 15.403-4, is currently at $650,000.

Best Value Acquisitions

Since 1995, the FAR has allowed contracts to be awarded without discussions to an offeror other than the one whose proposal is priced lowest: "There is no requirement that cost-reimbursement contracts be awarded on the basis of lowest proposed cost, lowest proposed fee, or the lowest total proposed cost plus fee."[37] This concept is known as *best value* acquisition. This change allowed contracting officers to escape the "lowest bid mentality" by freeing agencies to pay more for higher quality. Agencies no longer had to select lower-quality proposals simply because they were the least expensive.

Since then, FAR part 15 has been rewritten; best value is now defined as the expected outcome of an acquisition that, in the government's estimation, provides the greatest overall benefit in response to its requirements.[38] Now, agencies have the flexibility to award a contract to a company offering higher quality at a higher cost, provided they document the rationale for the business judgments and trade-offs made, including the benefits associated with the additional costs.[39]

Notifying and Debriefing Offerors

The acquisition streamlining created by FASA benefits government agencies as well as companies doing business with the government. For example, before FASA, companies sometimes had to wait a long time to find out whether they won or lost contracts. FASA requires agencies to notify unsuccessful offerors about contract award in writing or by electronic means within three days after the date the contract is awarded. This notice need not identify the winning offeror or the contract price. Unsuccessful offerors are given this information in a debriefing.

FASA requires the government to conduct debriefings in a timely manner. In the past, some unsuccessful companies had to file protests in order to find out why they lost; other companies requested debriefings that were never done or were done so late or so poorly that even if there were improprieties in the award of a contract, protesting was no longer an option.

Within three days of notification of award, an unsuccessful offeror may, in writing, request a debriefing. The agency must provide the debriefing within five days of receipt of this request. The debriefing must include all of the following:

- An evaluation of the significant weak or deficient factors in the offeror's proposal
- The overall evaluated cost and technical ratings of both successful and unsuccessful offers
- The overall ranking of all offerors, when a ranking has been developed
- A summary of the rationale for award.

The debriefing may not include point-by-point comparisons with other offerors.[40]

FASA also changed source selection protest procedures. The act defined *day* as a calendar day, not a working day. Agencies are now allowed to take corrective action, including payment of costs to the protester. Agencies were allowed to stay contract performance in the face of a likely protest. Both agency and GAO protests had to be filed within 14 calendar days of learning the basis for the protest, instead of the former ten working days as required by CICA.[41] The timeframe for filing a protest returned back to ten calendar days in 1997.[42]

FASA's Impact on Source Selection

FASA had a significant effect on how the federal government conducts competitive source selections. Because the act expanded the definition of commercial items, the government is able to purchase more products and services faster with fewer regulations. The act's emphasis on past performance helps the government select contractors with an established history of successful contract performance.

FASA also brought federal purchasing into the twenty-first century by introducing and requiring electronic transactions. Although the Internet overtook FACNET, FACNET paved the way to expedited purchasing, which benefited both government and industry.

FASA updated the Truth in Negotiations Act requirements by limiting the circumstances under which certified cost or pricing data is required and increasing the acquisition cost threshold for the submission of such data. These changes help keep the government informed but do not place additional burdens on private industry.

Another of FASA's significant contributions is the concept of best value source selection. Best value allows agencies to award contracts to higher-priced offerors if they are better qualified—a major step in getting higher-quality supplies and services. Finally, FASA helped improve communication between the government and private industry by requiring timely notification of offerors regarding contract award and timely debriefings.

Although these changes improved the acquisition process, Congress didn't stop there. Shortly after the implementation of FASA, on February 10, 1996, Congress passed the Federal Acquisition Reform Act (P.L. 104-106).

THE FEDERAL ACQUISITION REFORM ACT

The Federal Acquisition Reform Act (FARA) was signed into law as part of the National Defense Authorization Act for fiscal year 1996. FARA can be found in Division D of the authorization act. FARA was later dubbed the Clinger-Cohen Act to recognize its sponsors, Rep. William Clinger, chairman of the Government Reform and Oversight Committee, and Sen. William Cohen, chairman of the Governmental Affairs Subcommittee, Oversight of Government Management and the District of Columbia. FARA took the theme of acquisition reform begun by FASA further by introducing new concepts such as *efficient competition*.

Efficient Competition

FARA states that full and open competition must be pursued in a manner that is consistent with the government's need to efficiently fulfill its requirements.[43] This provision does not represent a change from the Competition in Contracting Act, but it caused concerns for small businesses, which feared they could be unfairly excluded from procurements.

Efficient competition is intended to give contracting officers more flexibility to limit the competitive range when they are dealing with large numbers of proposals. Before FARA, competitive ranges comprised proposals that had a reasonable chance of contract award, were acceptable or could be made acceptable through discussions, had deficiencies that could be corrected through discussions, and did not require major revisions to be acceptable. Many offerors' proposals thus fell into the competitive range.

FARA allows the contracting officer to limit the size of the competitive range to the greatest number of proposals that will permit an efficient competition among the most highly rated offerors. Before FARA, questionable proposals were allowed into the competitive range; now, FARA permits the contracting officer to exclude questionable proposals. If a solicitation states that the competitive range can be limited for the sake of efficiency, the contracting officer may determine that the number of proposals that might otherwise be included in the competitive range exceeds the number with which the government can conduct an efficient competition. The contracting officer may then limit the number of proposals in the competitive range.

This determination should depend on the number of offerors initially included in the competitive range and the issues involved in the competitive discussions. For example, it may be possible to efficiently conduct discussions with 20 offerors if the issues are relatively simple. When complex issues are involved, efficient competition may require limiting the competitive range to five firms or fewer. The government should not limit the number of firms arbitrarily (e.g., to five); instead, the government should establish the competitive range after evaluating the proposal ratings and the complexity of the issues involved in the discussions.[44]

Preaward Debriefing

When a contracting officer excludes an offeror that submitted a competitive proposal from the competitive range (or otherwise excludes such an offeror from further consideration before the final source selection decision), the excluded offeror may request in writing a debriefing before award. This request must be made within three days after the date on which the unsuccessful offeror receives notice of its exclusion. The contracting officer shall make every effort to debrief the unsuccessful offeror as soon as practicable, but may refuse a request for a debriefing if it is not in the best interest of the government to conduct a debriefing right away—for example, if time is of the essence. Properly preparing for a debriefing can be time-consuming, so it's reasonable for a contracting officer to want to award the contract before doing the debriefing.

The contracting officer is required to debrief an excluded offeror after award is made only if that offeror requested and was refused a pre-award debriefing. The pre-award debriefing must include the following elements:

- The executive agency's evaluation of the significant elements in the offeror's proposal
- A summary of the rationale for the offeror's exclusion
- An answer to relevant questions posed by the debriefed offeror as to whether source selection procedures set forth in the solicitation, applicable regulations, and other applicable authorities were followed by the executive agency.

The debriefing may not disclose the number or identity of other offerors or information about the content, ranking, or evaluation of other offerors' proposals.[45]

Commercial Item Amendments

FARA also affected source selection in commercial item acquisition. Although FASA changed the definition of the term *commercial item*, FARA made other important improvements. FARA amended TINA to simplify getting exempted from submitting certified cost or pricing data for commercial items. Now there are strict limits on what kind of information a contracting officer may require when purchasing commercial items. Although certified cost or pricing data may not be required, the contracting officer may ask for information on sale prices for the same or similar items that is sufficient to evaluate price reasonableness.[46]

FARA states that certified cost or pricing data shall not be required for commercial items. It also eliminates postaward audit rights for information that commercial suppliers provide instead of certified cost or pricing data. The purpose of this change was to encourage more strictly commercial firms to enter the federal marketplace, thereby increasing competition and lowering prices.

In addition, FARA permits the use of simplified acquisition procedures for contracts up to $5 million when a contracting officer reasonably expects that vendors will offer only commercial items. These simplified acquisitions are exempt from certain Competition in Contracting Act requirements, and the agency may conduct the source selection without a source selection plan or competitive range determination.[47]

Amendments to the Procurement Integrity Act

To further streamline and simplify federal acquisition, FARA amended certain aspects of the Procurement Integrity Act. For example, some of the reporting requirements were repealed for government officials. Former government employees do not need to file a report if they work for a contractor or become a consultant to a defense contractor. Department of Defense procurement officials don't have to report employment contacts made with defense contractors.

FARA retains the act's prohibition on releasing procurement information, but now the restriction applies to anyone who has access to contractor bid or proposal information or source selection information. No person shall "knowingly disclose contractor bid or proposal information or source selection information before the award of a federal agency procurement contract to which the information relates."[48] This amendment focuses on protecting the source selection information, rather than whether or not the person disclosing the information is a source selection official.

FARA also requires agency officials who are participating personally and substantially in a federal agency procurement over the simplified acquisition threshold to report any employment offers and to disqualify themselves from further participation in that procurement if the contractor offers employment. A former official may not accept compensation from a contractor as an employee or consultant within a period of one year after he or she participated in a source selection over $10 million.[49]

FARA's Impact on Source Selection

FARA, like its predecessor FASA, had a major impact on source selection. The concept of efficient competition—limiting the number of proposals in a competitive range—has allowed source selection teams to focus on only the top-rated proposals and to review fewer proposal revisions, streamlining the source selection process.

Pre-award debriefings give offerors a chance to find out why their proposals were eliminated from the competitive range before contract award. Getting this important information earlier in the process can help a vendor submit better proposals in the future and improve its chances of winning contracts.

FARA also made significant changes to commercial item acquisition; notably, it allows the government to use simplified acquisition procedures for contracts up to $5 million. This change allows agencies to bypass some of the burdensome rules that delay contract award, speeding up the acquisition process.

Finally, FARA amended the procurement integrity laws by eliminating some of the certification requirements and focusing on protecting source selection information. Additional reporting requirements were imposed to slow the "revolving door" of federal employees going to work for contractors.

STREAMLINING THE SOURCE SELECTION PROCESS

Chapter 1 explores some of the major statutes that direct federal government source selection procedures. Figure 1-2 summarizes the impact each law has had on source selection.

Now you understand that we have to do many things simply because they are required by law. Contracting officers didn't write the rules to make your life difficult. If contracting officers wrote the rules, they would be much less complicated

Figure 1-2   Summary of Major Laws Affecting Source Selection

Law	Impact on Source Selection
Truth in Negotiations Act (TINA)	• Requires all executive agencies to get certified cost or pricing data in certain circumstances • Permits agencies to get a price reduction for defective cost or pricing data • Requires the presence of adequate price competition for exemption from submitting certified cost or pricing data • Requires contracting officers to hold discussions with offerors in the competitive range.
Competition in Contracting Act (CICA)	• Requires full and open competition unless certain exceptions apply • Identifies seven exceptions to full and open competition • Requires market research and acquisition planning • Requires that specifications foster full and open competition • Requires publicizing requirements to increase competition • Requires that significant evaluation factors be included in the RFP • Requires that award be based only on evaluation criteria stated in the RFP • Permits award without discussion.
Procurement Integrity Act	• Prohibits the government from releasing source selection information before contract award • Restricts procurement officials from seeking or accepting employment from contractors • Prohibits contractors from offering gratuities, gifts, or money to procurement officials • Requires annual ethics training.

Figure 1-2   *(Continued)*

Law	Impact on Source Selection
Federal Acquisition Streamlining Act (FASA)	• Establishes a preference for commercial item acquisition • Emphasizes past performance in source selection • Introduces electronic systems in the procurement process • Eliminates regulatory requirements for simplified and commercial acquisitions • Requires RFPs to identify significant evaluation factors and subfactors and to state whether they are more, as, or less important than cost or price • Permits awarding contracts to other than the lowest-priced proposal (best value) • Requires timely debriefings.
Federal Acquisition Reform Act (FARA) Clinger-Cohen Act	• Introduces the concept of efficient competition to limit the competitive range • Revises the definition of competitive range to include only those proposals that are the most highly rated • Requires pre-award debriefing for companies eliminated from the competitive range • Simplifies commercial item exception to submitting certified cost or pricing data • Permits using simplified acquisition procedures for procurements up to $5 million.

and more efficient. Nonetheless, acquisition reform of the 1990s did help streamline the acquisition process and helped redefine the contracting officer as a business advisor, rather than a paper pusher.

Federal acquisition laws are much like a pendulum on an old clock that methodically swings back and forth. The pendulum moves from more restrictions and oversight (for example, the Truth in Negotiations Act and the Competition in Contracting Act) to more flexibility and less oversight (the Federal Acquisition Streamlining Act and the Federal Acquisition Reform Act). The pendulum will, no doubt, swing back the other way, imposing more rules and more oversight as new horror stories make the news. Something that will get Congress' attention—like the contracting missteps in the wake of the Katrina hurricane disaster—is sure to happen. When it does, watch the pendulum slowly make its way back to restrictions and oversight.

CHAPTER SUMMARY

In this chapter, we explore the history of source selection legislation. Congress has passed a number of laws intended to address federal government contracting problems, beginning with the 1962 Truth in Negotiations Act, which, among other provisions, required executive agencies to get certified cost or pricing data in certain circumstances, allowed agencies to get a price reduction if a contractor submitted defective cost or pricing data, and required the presence of adequate price competition for offerors to be exempt from submitting certified cost or pricing data.

TINA was followed by the Competition in Contracting Act (1984), which required full and open competition, with several exceptions. It also mandated that the government perform market research, publicize requirements to increase competition, include significant proposal evaluation factors in RFPs, and award contracts based only on those factors.

The Procurement Integrity Act (1988) is the next major piece of legislation we review. It added new rules for ethical behavior, including a prohibition on the government's releasing source selection information before contract award and a restriction on procurement officials' freedom to leave the government to work for contractors with whom they have had dealings.

Next, the Federal Acquisition Streamlining Act (1994) emphasized the use of commercial contracting methods and past performance as an evaluation factor. It required the CO to promptly notify offerors of contract award and to conduct timely debriefings, and it introduced the use of electronic systems in the procurement process.

Finally, the Federal Acquisition Reform Act (1996) introduced the concept of efficient competition, revised the definition of *competitive range*, and made pre-award debriefings available to offerors eliminated from the competitive range.

Now that you understand the legislative requirements behind some of the regulations directing source selection, we're ready to move on and learn about the procurement planning process.

NOTES

1 10 *U.S. Code* 2306a(h)(1) and 41 *U.S. Code* 254b; Federal Acquisition Regulation (FAR) 2.101.

2 U.S. Air Force/Air Force Materiel Command, RFP no. FA8625-07-R-6470 (Wright-Patterson Air Force Base, OH: U.S. Air Force/Air Force Materiel Command, January 30, 2007), 86.

3 FAR 15.403-1(c).

4 FAR 15.403-1.

5 Federal Acquisition Institute and the Air Force Institute of Technology, "Cost Analysis," *Contract Pricing Reference Guide*, vol. 3 (Washington, DC: Federal Acquisition Institute, 2005), 107–108.

6 FAR 15.403-3.

7 Federal Acquisition Institute, "Defective Cost or Pricing Data," *Contract Specialist Training Blueprints*, no. 64 (Washington, DC: Federal Acquisition Institute, September 2002).

8 The Truth in Negotiations Act, Public Law 87-653, §2304 (September 10, 1962).

9 FAR 52.215-10.

10 Federal Procurement Regulations §1-1.301-1.

11 U.S. General Accounting Office, *Federal Regulations Need To Be Revised to Fully Realize the Purposes of the Competition in Contracting Act of 1984*, GAO/OGC-85-14 (Washington, DC: U.S. General Accounting Office, August 1985), 1–2.

12 Ibid., 4.

13 U.S. General Accounting Office, *Year End Spending: Reforms Under Way but Better Reporting and Oversight Needed*, GAO/AIMD-98-185 (Washington, DC: U.S. General Accounting Office, July 1998), 9.

14 FAR 2.101.

15 FAR 6.302-1.

16 FAR 6.302-2.

17 FAR 6.302-3.

18 FAR 6.302-4.

19 FAR 6.302-5.

20 FAR 6.302-6.

21 FAR 6.302-7.

22 FAR 6.301(d).

23 41 *U.S. Code* 253a.

24 FAR 5.002 (1990).

25 41 *U.S. Code* 253a.

26 41 *U.S. Code* 253b.

27 U.S. General Accounting Office, *Federal Regulations*, 4.

28 41 *U.S. Code* 423, §27.

29 Defense Systems Management College, *Introduction to Defense Acquisition Management*, 3rd ed. (Fort Belvoir, VA: Defense Systems Management College Press, 1996).

30 FAR 2.101 (1995).

31 Federal Acquisition Streamlining Act of 1994, Public Law 103-355 §1091, codified at 41 *U.S. Code* 401, §2.

32 FAR 42.1501.

33 U.S. General Accounting Office, *Obstacles to Implementing the Federal Acquisition Computer Network*, GAO/NSIAD-97-26 (Washington, DC: U.S. General Accounting Office, January 1997), 1.

34 Rand Allen and Scott M. McCaleb, "E-Contracting in the USA Agency Purchases Are Increasingly Paperless Transactions," February 28, 2000, http://www.wileyrein.com/publications.cfm?sp=articles&id=614 (accessed May 15, 2009).

35 See FAR 5.101 for methods of disseminating information and FAR 5.102 for availability of solicitation requirements.

36 FAR 15.802 (October 1995).

37 FAR 15.605 (October 1995).

38 FAR 2.101.

39 FAR 15.308.

40 Federal Acquisition Streamlining Act of 1994, Public Law 103-355 §1014.

41 U.S. Department of Defense, General Services Administration, and the Administrator for the National Aeronautics and Space Administration, *Federal Acquisition Circular* 90-32 (Washington, DC: U.S. Department of Defense, General Services Administration, and the Administrator for the National Aeronautics and Space Administration, September 18, 1995).

42 *Federal Acquisition Circular* 97-2, 62 RF 51224, September 30, 1997.

43 Federal Acquisition Reform Act, Public Law 104-106 §4101 (February 10, 1996).

44 Federal Acquisition Institute and the Air Force Institute of Technology, "Price Analysis," *Contract Pricing Reference Guide*, vol. 1 (Washington, DC: Federal Acquisition Institute, 1998).

45 Federal Acquisition Reform Act, Public Law 104-106 §4104.

46 Ibid., §4201.

47 Donna S. Ireton and Ronald L. Smith, *Acquisition Reform 1996* (Vienna, VA: National Contract Management Association, 1996), 4-22–4-23.

48 41 *U.S. Code* 423.

49 Ibid.

PART I
Getting Ready for Competition

Getting ready for a competitive source selection can be a daunting task. It helps to follow the adage that advises you to "eat an elephant" one bite at a time. The best way to conduct a competitive source selection is by taking one step at a time, and this book will guide you through that process.

Contracting professionals in both government and industry must prepare themselves for competition, which begins with the request for proposals (RFP) or the proposal itself. Part I covers the initial steps needed to get ready for these stages in the process—the first bite of the elephant.

CHAPTER 2   PLANNING THE ACQUISITION

Chapter 2 explains the planning process—conducting market research and preparing the acquisition plan and source selection plan, if necessary—and offers suggestions to make it less painful.

Chapter 2 covers the following important steps in the planning process:

- Conducting market research
- Understanding acquisition planning requirements
- Selling to the government
- Recognizing the different methods of acquisition
- Understanding contract types.

Conducting market research is an important first step in which both the government and industry participate. The government seeks contracting resources that can meet its requirements, and industry contractors want the government to consider their products and services. This section of Chapter 2 explains how the government conducts market research; what the Federal Acquisition Regulation requires; and how industry participates in the process.

After conducting market research, the government begins the acquisition planning process that includes writing an acquisition plan and/or source selection plan. In this step of the planning process, the government defines its acquisition strategy and decides what source selection method and which contract type to use.

While the government conducts these acquisition planning activities, the industry contractors interested in selling products and services to the government are also busy researching opportunities and developing a marketing plan.

Both government and industry acquisition professionals must understand the different methods of acquisition and the different contract types available. Chapter 2 reviews these essential elements of the acquisition process.

After the government determines the method of source selection and contract type, it writes the RFP's evaluation factors.

CHAPTER 3   WRITING EVALUATION FACTORS

Chapter 3 explains mandatory evaluation factors and the steps involved in selecting evaluation factors; structuring and limiting factors; evaluating risk; and expressing the relative importance of evaluation factors. The chapter also describes how the statement of work (SOW) and the work breakdown structure can be used to establish evaluation criteria; the three basic requirements for writing evaluation factors; and how to limit evaluation factors to those that will actually help discriminate among the submitted proposals.

The government uses the results of its market research to help write relevant evaluation factors. After receiving proposals, it uses the evaluation factors to determine which company should win the contract. Industry contractors use the evaluation factors in their bid/no-bid decision-making process to determine if they have a chance of winning the contract. If the government emphasizes factors a particular contractor has strengths in providing, that company should submit a proposal. On the other hand, if the government emphasizes factors a particular contractor is limited in its ability to provide, that company probably should not submit a proposal.

CHAPTER 4   SCORING PLANS AND RATING METHODS

A *scoring plan* or *rating system* is the internal guideline an agency uses to apply the evaluation criteria and denote the degree to which proposals meet the standards for the non-cost evaluation factors. Chapter 4 explores the various rating and scoring methodologies used by different agencies—e.g., adjectival, color coding, numerical, or a combination of these methodologies. The chapter also discusses the importance of documenting the evaluation with thorough narratives that explain the decision-making process.

Using a scoring plan or rating system helps the government consistently apply evaluation criteria and focus its source selection on the most critical evaluation factors. (This internal guideline is not available to contractors responding to the RFP; rather, the government's requirements are presented to the contractor in the RFP.)

After conducting market research, preparing the acquisition plan and source selection plan, and writing evaluation factors, the government writes the rest of the solicitation.

CHAPTER 5   WRITING THE REST OF THE SOLICITATION

Chapter 5 explains what goes into the rest of the RFP, also called a *solicitation*, including the SOW, the proposal preparation instructions, terms and conditions, evaluation factors and subfactors, instructions to offerors, and other exhibits and attachments.

The Uniform Contract Format helps both the government and industry contractors find important information in the solicitation. It provides a structured approach for formatting information that both parties need to know, so both parties can find it easily. For example, the evaluation factors are always in Section M, and the proposal preparation instructions are always in Section L.

The statement of work is the most important part of the RFP. The SOW drives the market research, evaluation factors, and eventually contract performance. Combined with the evaluation factors, contractors use this information to determine if they should participate in the competition.

Proposal preparation instructions tell offerors what the government wants to see in proposals and how to assemble proposals. Having a consistent format from each offeror facilitates the evaluation process because government evaluators know what to expect in the proposal and where to find particular information.

The contracting officer may decide to release a draft RFP to potential offerors at a pre-solicitation conference. Offerors can review the draft RFP and provide comments to the government. This is an optional but recommended step in the planning process. It not only helps the government fine-tune the RFP, but it also tells interested companies the government's requirements and allows those companies to ask questions before the final RFP is released. Chapter 5 reviews the processes for releasing a draft RFP and conducting a final review of the RFP before releasing it to industry.

Following these planning steps is critical to successfully completing a competitive acquisition. Taking shortcuts in the planning process to save time will most likely cause problems later by effecting poorly written proposals, schedule delays, or protests after contract award. Taking the time to properly plan will help the competitive acquisition process run more smoothly.

Chapter 2

Planning the Acquisition

Let's face it, acquisition planning isn't fun; in fact, some consider it a painful process. Nevertheless, it's mandated by the Competition in Contracting Act. One might compare acquisition planning to getting children to eat vegetables. They might not like it, but it's good for them. Similarly, acquisition planning is actually good for you. Really! It forces you to go through the process step by step and *think* about what you need and how you're going to get it. Once you get past the fact that you have to do something you may not want to, acquisition planning is really not that hard. This chapter explains the planning process and offers suggestions to make it less painful.

During the acquisition planning phase, the government conducts market research and prepares the acquisition plan and source selection plan, if necessary. We'll look at these parts of the planning process in this chapter.

MARKET RESEARCH

Market research is the process of collecting and analyzing information about capabilities within the market that can satisfy an agency's needs.[1] It is the first step in acquisition planning and is essential to designing an acquisition strategy and identifying proposal evaluation criteria. In fact, it should be done before the contracting officer or program manager even begins writing the acquisition plan.

Market research must be done before developing new requirements documents, soliciting offers that exceed the simplified acquisition threshold, and soliciting offers below the simplified acquisition threshold when adequate information is not available and the circumstances justify the cost of conducting market research.[2]

By doing market research, acquisition teams can determine which companies are able to fulfill the government's requirements and can gather information on the customary terms and conditions and typical warranty provisions and financing terms for a particular industry or marketplace.

Recall from the last chapter that the Competition in Contracting Act requires agencies to conduct market research. This requirement, combined with the Federal Acquisition Streamlining Act's emphasis on commercial practices, puts market research at the forefront of any acquisition.

Market research can be used to determine if a commercial item can meet the government's needs and to identify commercial practices that may apply to the acquisition. FAR part 12 requires agencies to acquire commercial items or nondevelopmental items when the government's requirements can be fulfilled with available commercial items.[3]

Market research for complex acquisitions can be intimidating and overwhelming. One approach is to break down each requirement into logical sections. Some use a work breakdown structure as a guide for tackling a project segment by segment. By dividing a complex requirement into smaller sections, the program manager may be able to find commercial components that will satisfy the need even if the end product is not a commercial item.

The results of market research influence the following elements of the request for proposals (RFP):

- Writing the statement of work, performance work statement, or statement of objectives
- Selecting evaluation factors and contracting and source selection methods
- Determining the amount and type of information to request from offerors.

The extent of market research and the degree to which an agency should document the results will vary, depending on such factors as the urgency, estimated dollar value, and complexity of the acquisition, as well as past experience. For less complex acquisitions with a strong procurement history—i.e., previous competitively awarded contracts for the same or similar items, where a well-written SOW along with cost and performance information is available—one person may be able to conduct all the required market research. For more complex requirements or acquisitions for which there is not a strong acquisition history, a team approach may be more successful.

Market Research Data

Acquisitions begin with a description of the government's needs. This description should be specific enough to allow the acquisition team to conduct market research.[4] A well-planned, thoroughly executed market research process yields data on the following, relative to the government's requirements:

- Existing products
- Potential suppliers
- Competitive market forces
- Generalized pricing information
- Available levels of product performance and quality
- Commercial practices
- Support capabilities
- Other organizations' successful acquisition practices.

Because market research can identify so much information about how an industry conducts business, it is the foundation for building an effective solicitation and a successful contract. Not only that, but market research can also:

- Determine whether needs can be met by items available in the commercial marketplace
- Identify commercial practices regarding customizing, modifying, or tailoring items to meet customer needs
- Identify customary industry terms and conditions
- Identify the typical-delivery and logistics-support capabilities of the commercial market
- Ensure maximum and effective use of competitive market forces
- Ensure maximum practicable use of recovered materials and promote energy conservation and efficiency
- Help the agency plan acquisition strategy.

When gathering data on the marketplace's capabilities, the program manager or contracting officer can ask the following specific questions:

- Are there sources capable of satisfying the government's requirements?
- Are commercial items available:
  - That meet requirements without modification
  - That could be modified to meet requirements
  - That could meet requirements if the requirements are modified to a reasonable extent?
- If commercial items are not available, are nondevelopmental items available:
  - That meet requirements without modification
  - That could be modified to meet requirements
  - That could meet requirements if the requirements are modified to a reasonable extent?
- To what extent could commercial items or nondevelopmental items be incorporated at the component level?
- What are customary industry terms and conditions regarding:

- Warranties
- Acceptance
- Inspection
- Buyer financing
- Maintenance support
- Packaging and marking
- Pricing?
- What is the extent of competition in the environment, including:
  - The level of market competition—i.e., how competitive vendors are with each other
  - Sources potentially capable of satisfying requirements—i.e., are there sources that can satisfy the requirements, and how many sources can do so?
  - The amount of competitive pressure on price
  - Quality
  - Product features
  - Speed of technological improvements
  - Energy efficiency
  - Service
  - Support?
- How is the market responding to environmental concerns?
  - Extent of recovered materials used in market products
  - Efficiency standards in the marketplace
  - Market pressures on energy conservation and efficiency.[5]

Market Research Sources

When you consult *Consumer Reports* magazine or ask a neighbor or coworker how he likes a particular product or which contractor she used to finish her basement, you're conducting market research, even if you don't think of it as such. You have a requirement, and you're looking for sources to fulfill that need. Market research for government acquisitions has the same objective.

The Internet is a valuable market research tool, and it's a great place to start. But if you need in-depth information, you might use one or more of the market research techniques listed in FAR 10.002:

- Contacting knowledgeable individuals in government and industry regarding the market's ability to meet requirements.
- Reviewing the results of recent market research undertaken to meet similar or identical requirements.
- Publishing formal requests for information in appropriate technical or scientific journals or business publications.

- Querying the government's interagency databases of contracts and other procurement instruments (available at www.contractdirectory.gov) and other government and commercial databases that provide information relevant to agency acquisitions.
- Participating in interactive, online communication among industry and acquisition personnel and customers.
- Obtaining source lists of similar items from other contracting activities or agencies, trade associations, or other sources.
- Reviewing catalogs and other generally available product literature published by manufacturers, distributors, and dealers. This information may be available online.
- Conducting interchange meetings or holding presolicitation conferences to involve potential offerors early in the acquisition process. For complex acquisitions, these conferences can lead to teaming arrangements.

After conducting market research, the agency may need to refine its requirements. The FAR states:

> If market research indicates commercial or nondevelopmental items might not be available to satisfy agency needs, agencies shall reevaluate the need and determine whether the need can be restated to permit commercial or nondevelopmental items to satisfy the agency's needs.[6]
>
> [....] If market research establishes that the government's need may be met by a type of item or service customarily available in the commercial marketplace that would meet the definition of a commercial item, the contracting officer shall solicit and award any resultant contract using the commercial item acquisition procedures in FAR [p]art 12.[7]

Technical and acquisition staff in government and industry should perform ongoing market research regarding supplies and services that the agency routinely purchases or the company sells. Staying informed about the marketplace and understanding the competitive environment will help ensure that high-quality services or supplies are provided and the government's needs are met.

Documenting Market Research

After collecting the information the agency needs, the contracting officer and program manager must document the market research. Agencies should document the results of market research in a manner appropriate to the size and complexity of the acquisition. The market research report should summarize the research activities. Specifically, the report should, as appropriate:

- Explain the acquisition's background, including its purpose and any special features.
- Identify the market research team members (at a minimum, the buyer and the requirements official).
- Describe the agency's needs, including the functions, performance, or essential physical characteristics of the required goods or services. This section should also summarize any discussions and conclusions reached regarding possible alternatives or modifications to the needs statement or to the potential for trade-off analyses. (See "The Trade-Off Process" later in this chapter.)
- Identify the desired or required schedule for the delivery of the end items, and, if applicable, the relationship of the end items to other acquisitions. (Major acquisitions may include multiple contracts for one large program.)
- Explain the methodology that was used to compile and refine the lists of potential suppliers, including the number of firms that were contacted and a list of the suppliers in the final consideration.
- List the industry sources that were contacted and the types of information obtained from them.
- Summarize the customary industry terms, provisions, and conditions, including payment, freight, delivery, acceptance, and warranties.
- Identify the price ranges discovered, possible reasons for variations, and the potential for determining a fair market price.

The market research report should also include a description of available commercial or nondevelopmental items, along with their respective merits or shortcomings. This summary may also recommend specific contract terms or provisions covering such areas as training, acceptance, and express warranties.[8] If a commercial item cannot meet the government's requirements, an explanation for this determination should be provided.

Once the program manager knows which companies can meet the requirements and has learned about the standard business practices in the marketplace, he or she can begin to refine the requirements document, statement of work, or performance work statement. For many agencies, the next step is writing the source selection plan in addition to or in lieu of an acquisition plan. Unlike the acquisition plan, a source selection plan is not required by law or the FAR. Even though an acquisition plan is required by the FAR, a source selection plan can be used as a substitute if it incorporates the required elements of an acquisition plan, thus satisfying the requirement. Confirm the agency's requirements for a source selection plan or update the acquisition plan to document source selection planning. A written source selection plan is particularly important for a complex negotiated acquisition that will take a long time to complete. Agencies normally do not require source selection plans for less costly acquisitions; the dollar thresholds vary by agency.

ACQUISITION PLANNING REQUIREMENTS

Acquisition planning is the process by which the efforts of everyone responsible for an acquisition are coordinated and integrated through a comprehensive plan for fulfilling the agency's needs. It includes developing the overall strategy for managing the acquisition.[9] Its purpose is to satisfy an agency's needs in the most effective, economical, and timely manner. FAR part 7 states the acquisition planning requirements and provides guidance for developing written acquisition plans.

Acquisition planning should start when an agency identifies a need for supplies or services. It's good practice for the entire acquisition team to work together to develop the acquisition plan. The acquisition team consists of all participants in the acquisition, including representatives of the technical, supply, and procurement communities, the customers they serve, and the contractors that provide the products and services.[10] Technical personnel will be able to suggest sources for market research and identify potential risks. Finance personnel can answer questions about budgeting and funding. Contracting personnel can provide input on acquisition considerations and source selection procedures. If just one person writes the acquisition plan, it will not be balanced and could exclude information that will be important during source selection or contract administration.

The Acquisition Plan

The first part of an acquisition plan describes the big picture: what the requirements are and how the procurement will fulfill them. This part consists of eight sections:

1. **Statement of need.** The first section provides an introduction to the overall acquisition. Summarize the technical and contractual history of the acquisition and how any prior similar acquisitions have shaped potential alternatives. In other words, lessons learned from previous acquisitions could influence the alternatives considered for the current acquisition. The end user of the services or supplies to be acquired writes most of this section. Department of Defense users write a formal mission need statement (MNS) in place of this section.
2. **Conditions affecting the acquisition.** Identifies requirements for compatibility with existing or future programs and any known cost, schedule, or performance constraints.

3. **Cost.** States the cost goals for the acquisition and the rationale for those goals. This section should also identify the life-cycle cost considerations, design-to-cost objectives, and how the contracting officer will apply should-cost analysis.

   Life-cycle cost is the total cost of a system, building, or other product, computed over its useful life. It includes all relevant costs involved in acquiring, owning, operating, maintaining, and disposing of the system or product over a specified period of time, including environmental and energy costs.[11]

   Design-to-cost objectives establish cost elements as management goals to achieve the best balance between life-cycle cost, acceptable performance, and schedule. In this sense, cost is a design constraint during the design and development phases and a management discipline throughout the acquisition and operation of the system or equipment.[12]

   A should-cost analysis is a specialized form of cost analysis and differs from traditional evaluation methods because it does not assume that a contractor's historical costs reflect efficient and economical operation. Instead, a should-cost analysis evaluates the economy and efficiency of the contractor's existing work force, methods, materials, equipment, real property, operating systems, and management. A multi-functional team of government contracting, contract administration, pricing, audit, and engineering representatives conduct should-cost reviews to promote both short- and long-range improvements in the contractor's economy and efficiency, to reduce the cost of contract performance. In addition, by providing a rationale for any recommendations and by quantifying any potential impacts on cost, the government will be better able to develop realistic objectives for subsequent negotiations.[13]

4. **Required capabilities or performance characteristics.** Identifies how these capabilities or characteristics are related to the requirements.

5. **Delivery or performance period requirements.** If the acquisition is urgent, the basis for the urgency and a justification for not providing full and open competition appears in this section. The relationship of this procurement to other procurements is often discussed here.

6. **Trade-offs.** This section discusses the consequences for trade-offs among the cost, performance, and schedule goals. For example, an increase in the budget may increase performance goals. On the other hand, reducing the budget may have a negative effect on performance because the agency can't buy as much. If the schedule is extended, costs may rise to pay for additional overhead and any cost increases over time.

7. **Risks.** Explains technical, cost, and schedule risks and what the agency is doing to reduce these risks. How will the acquisition be affected if the agency can't mitigate the risks? This is a difficult section to write because it forces the agency

to admit that something might go wrong. But in doing so, the agency begins to prepare for that possibility. (Remember, the contracting officer should be prepared—like a good Scout).

8. **Acquisition streamlining.** The final section identifies the acquisition streamlining techniques the contracting officer will use. Acquisition streamlining techniques include a draft RFP, presolicitation conference, or alternative dispute resolution process.

The second part of the acquisition plan is the plan of action. This part details how the contracting officer will conduct the acquisition. It describes sources, the acquisition method, funding, and other considerations.

1. **Sources.** What sources can meet the agency's needs? Small businesses, businesses in historically underutilized areas (HUBZone businesses), small disadvantaged businesses, and women-owned small business concerns should be included in the consideration. This section describes the extent and results of market research conducted and its impact on the acquisition plan. It also uses the information obtained from market research to identify companies that can meet the requirements. The program manager and end user lead the writing of this section.

2. **Competition.** How will the contracting officer promote and sustain competition throughout the acquisition? If full and open competition is not conducted, why not? What is the statutory authority for the exemption to full and open competition? How will competition be promoted and sustained for spare and repair parts? This section describes how subcontract competition is sustained throughout the acquisition, if applicable. What barriers exist to increasing competition, and how will the contracting officer overcome them? The program manager and contracting officer lead the writing of this section.

3. **Source selection procedures.** This section describes source selection procedures for the acquisition, including the timing for submitting and evaluating proposals. How do evaluation factors relate to the acquisition objectives? The contracting officer leads the writing of this section.

4. **Acquisition considerations.** This section identifies the contract type contemplated and any options or special contracting methods the contracting officer might use. What special clauses, solicitation provisions, or FAR deviations apply? Will the agency lease or purchase special equipment? The contracting officer leads the writing of this section, with support from other members of the acquisition team.

5. **Budgeting and funding.** This section provides budget estimates and explains how the agency came up with the numbers. What is the schedule for getting the funds the agency needs for the procurement? This section is developed by the budget and finance office, with support from other members of the acquisition

team. The business manager leads the writing of this section, with input from the program manager and contracting officer.

6. **Product or service description.** This section explains how the program manager determined the performance standards for the acquisition and describes the performance-based acquisition methods used. This section could be written by the technical lead or program manager and end user, with support from other members of the acquisition team.

7. **Priorities, allocations, and allotments.** When an urgent requirement demands a short delivery or performance schedule, this section is used to explain how the Defense Priorities and Allocations System (DPAS) will be used to fulfill the requirement. See FAR 11.6 for DPAS applicability. The program manager and contracting officer lead the writing of this section.

8. **Contractor versus government performance**. If applicable, address contractor versus government performance, the policy outlined in Office of Management and Budget (OMB) Circular A-76, as discussed in FAR 7.3. The longstanding policy of the federal government has been to rely on the private sector for needed commercial services. Thus, government agencies shall identify all activities performed by government personnel as either commercial or inherently governmental and conduct a competition to determine if government personnel should perform a commercial activity.[14] The program manager and contracting officer lead the writing of this section.

9. **Inherently governmental functions.** Contractors may not perform inherently governmental functions; this section ensures that inherently governmental functions are not performed by contractors. FAR 7.503 lists examples of inherently governmental functions. Specifically, the following tasks related to source selection are considered inherently governmental:

    a. Determining what supplies or services are acquired by the government
    b. Participating as a voting member on a source selection board
    c. Determining whether contract costs are reasonable.

    The program manager and contracting officer lead the writing of this section.

10. **Management information requirements.** This section describes the management system the government will use to monitor the contractor's effort—specifically, the methodology the agency will use to analyze the data and assess contract performance. It also states whether earned value will be used to measure performance. The program manager and contracting officer lead the writing of this section.

11. **Make or buy.** The prime contractor is responsible for managing contract performance, including administering subcontracts as necessary to ensure the

lowest overall cost and technical risk to the government. A *make-or-buy program* is part of a contractor's written plan identifying the major deliverables produced or performed by the prime contractor and those that will be subcontracted to other vendors.[15] When a contract requires a make-or-buy program, the government may reserve the right to review and agree on the make-or-buy program to ensure reasonable prices and satisfactory performance.[16] Previous contracts for the same or similar items provide some input on the efficacy of make-or-buy programs. The contracting officer leads the writing of this section.

12. **Test and evaluation.** This section describes the government and contractor test programs for each major phase of a large system acquisition. Market research provides some information about contractor test programs. The program manager and end user lead the writing of this section.

13. **Logistics considerations.** This section describes the assumptions for contractor or agency support for start-up and throughout the life of the contract, including maintenance, servicing, and distribution of commercial items. What are the government's reliability, maintainability, and quality assurance requirements, and are they covered under available warranties? Market research should provide insight into a company's warranties. Any requirements for contractor data and data rights, along with its estimated cost and how the data will be used, should be included in this section. See FAR subpart 27.4 for regulations regarding data rights.

14. **Government property.** This section lists any property that will be furnished to contractors, including materials and facilities, and states when the property will be available with regard to the acquisition schedule. If government-furnished property is not available when it is needed, performance schedules and cost estimates may be affected, so it's better to know in advance if the property will really be available when the agency needs it. If government property will not be available as needed, the contracting officer documents alternative actions—plan B—in this section. The program manager and end user lead the writing of this section.

15. **Government-furnished information.** This section discusses any government information required for proposal preparation or contract performance, such as manuals, drawings, and test data. Any additional controls to monitor access and distribution of certain information, such as technical data, specifications, maps, or building designs, are described here. This information is generally accessible through the Federal Technical Data Solution. The program manager and end user lead the writing of this section.

16. **Environmental and energy conservation objectives.** This section describes the environmental and energy conservation objectives and the environmental requirements, if applicable, associated with the acquisition. (FAR part 23 details

acquisition policies for protecting and improving the quality of the environment.) Will an environmental assessment be performed or an environmental
impact statement prepared? How will environmental issues be resolved? The
program manager and end user lead the writing of this section.

17. **Security considerations.** This section is applicable to acquisitions that deal
with classified matters. It explains how adequate security measures will be
established, maintained, and monitored. If the acquisition is for information
technology, how will the agency's information security requirements be met?
If the contractor will require routine physical access to a federally controlled
facility or information system, how will the agency's requirements be met for
personal identity verification of contractors? (See FAR 4.1300 for regulations
on personal identity verification of contractor personnel.) The program manager and contracting officer lead the writing of this section with input from the
security office.

18. **Contract administration.** This section describes how the contract will be
administered. If the contract is for services, how will the contracting officer
enforce inspection and acceptance of the services in accordance with the performance criteria in the statement of work? The contracting officer leads the
writing of this section.

19. **Other considerations.** In this section, the contracting officer and program
manager explain any standardization concepts, the industrial readiness program,
the Defense Production Act, the Occupational Safety and Health Act, foreign
sales implications, and any other matters applicable to the acquisition plan that
are not covered elsewhere.

20. **Milestones for the acquisition cycle.** This section addresses the following
phases of the acquisition cycle:
    a. Acquisition plan approval
    b. Development of the statement of work
    c. Development of specifications
    d. Development of data requirements
    e. Completion of the acquisition package
    f. Purchase request
    Justification and approval for other than full and open competition and approval
    of determination and findings, if applicable. A *determination and finding* is a
    document signed by an authorized government official justifying a decision to
    take a certain action; it is expressed in terms of meeting the regulatory require-
    ments of the situation.
    g. Synopsis of the solicitation
    h. Determination of draft RFP and final RFP release dates
    i. Development of proposal evaluation schedule
    j. Development of negotiation schedule

k. Contract preparation, review, and clearance

l. Estimated contract award date.

The milestones section illustrates the effects of acquisition planning on the entire acquisition cycle. The dates established in the acquisition plan set the expectations for both government and industry. If contract award is significantly delayed, this affects not only the contractor's efforts, including the validity of its cost estimates and the availability of personnel and materials, but also the availability of government funding and government-furnished property. On the other hand, pushing to meet an unrealistic schedule can, for example, result in a poorly written RFP that is not properly reviewed. An unclear or inaccurate RFP can yield proposals that do not address the government's real requirements. These proposals will lengthen negotiation time and delay contract award. Rushing through the process doesn't necessarily yield a quality contract.

The contracting officer and program manager must think through the potential risks, consequences, and mitigation plan when developing the acquisition plan. When an unexpected event affects the schedule, they should be able to respond quickly to minimize potential problems. If the contracting officer or program manager pretends that nothing could possibly go wrong—and something inevitably will—then they'll waste valuable time trying to find a solution that should have been addressed in the acquisition plan.

Seldom does the same team that wrote the acquisition plan complete contract close-out, so the acquisition plan serves as a roadmap for the contracting officer who will close out the contract. The acquisition plan should provide guidance for a seamless transition between you and those who take over your job when you move on. Too often, government personnel get important historical information from the contractor, because no one is left on the program who knows what happened and what was planned. This is not a good management strategy, but it can be avoided with a thorough acquisition plan. This is why acquisition planning and tracking is really worth the time and effort.

Now that you understand how to put together an acquisition plan, we'll discuss the development of the source selection plan. The acquisition plan is a top-level version of the source selection plan. The source selection plan covers many of the same topics, but from a different angle and in greater depth.

The Source Selection Plan

Documenting key elements of the source selection is an important part of the planning process. This documentation can be done either in a separate source selection plan (SSP), if required by the agency, or as a supplement to the acquisition plan. The source selection plan should discuss the acquisition strategy, including the requirements, expected competition, and the method of procurement.

Johnnie E. Wilson writes, "The source selection plan serves several purposes, including:

- Defining a specific approach for soliciting and evaluating proposals
- Describing the evaluation factors and subfactors, their relative importance, and the methodology used to evaluate proposals
- Providing essential guidance to the RFP authors, especially about putting together sections L (proposal preparation instructions) and M (evaluation factors) of the solicitation
- Serving as a charter and guide for the source selection team on the roles of the members and the conduct of the entire source selection from proposal evaluation, through the cost/price/technical trade-off, award decision, and debriefing."[17]

Suggested topics to be covered in a source selection plan include the following:

- A description of what the agency is buying.
- Goals of the acquisition.
- A description of the source selection organization, including a listing of individuals recommended for membership and their titles or functional areas.
- A description of presolicitation activities, including market research, the development of the sources-sought synopsis and draft RFP, and the pre-proposal conference. A sources-sought synopsis is issued before the solicitation and is typically published for market research purposes.
- Evaluation procedures, including whether award will be made based on the identified lowest priced technically acceptable offer or on a trade-off evaluation.
- Proposed evaluation factors and subfactors, their relative importance, and associated standards. The relative importance of the following factors should be identified, as applicable:
  - Price or cost
  - Technical proficiency
  - Management
  - Past performance.
- The proposed acquisition strategy, including anticipated contract type.
- The schedule of events, including key events and the projected dates for completion. Key events should include such activities as:
  - Issuing the solicitation
  - Receiving proposals
  - Completing proposal evaluation

- Making the source selection decision
- Preparing the contract for signature
- Completing contract award.

The Source Selection Team

The source selection authority (SSA) is the decision maker who approves the source selection plan and the acquisition plan and is responsible for conducting the entire source selection process, encompassing proposal solicitation, evaluation, and contract award.[18] The SSA has, subject to law and applicable regulations, full responsibility and authority to select the source for award. In carrying out these responsibilities, the SSA:

- Reviews and approves the source selection plan (SSP)
- Provides executive oversight of the source selection process and results to ensure that the source selection evaluation team (SSET) follows the evaluation process described in the SSP
- Authorizes access to or release of source selection records
- Authorizes the release of the request for proposal
- Approves the exclusion of offerors from the competitive range
- Approves entering into discussions with offerors in the competitive range, if required
- Determines whether it is appropriate to make award based on initial offers
- Ensures that the evaluation criteria are limited to the key discriminators; and
- Selects the winning proposal(s) and documents the supporting rationale in the source selection decision document.

The source selection team is charged with working to thoroughly understand the evaluation procedures and criteria. Members of the source selection team may not have a vested interest in the outcome of the source selection process, nor any economic, social, or intellectual conflict of interest concerning the matters discussed during the source selection process. All members of the source selection team must:

- Execute nondisclosure agreements and conflict of interest statements
- Possess the knowledge and perception to competently evaluate proposals
- Understand their roles and responsibilities in the evaluation process, including their obligation to be fair and impartial
- Clearly record their impartial individual evaluations and ensure the accuracy of summary evaluations
- Defend, in fair debate with their peers, the rationale for their decisions

- Prevent the release of source selection information to anyone not authorized to receive it.[19]

An *ombudsman* is an agency employee who investigates concerns or complaints about source selections, such as potential conflicts of interest or improper activities. The ombudsman may be a senior staff member from outside the program office and the program approval chain. He or she is responsible for providing an unbiased, nonattributable avenue of communication for source selection personnel and offerors to submit acquisition-related issues, concerns, or grievances. In other words, if someone contacts the ombudsman, the information the ombudsman receives is not attributed to the person who initiated the contact.

The composition of the SSET or source selection team (SST) is customized for each acquisition. For example, some acquisitions may not have a security panel. Other acquisitions may combine the cost and contract panels. The structure of the source selection team depends on the nature of the acquisition and the agency's regulations. Figure 2-1 illustrates a sample source selection team. Some agencies may use different terminology, but the elements are similar.

The source selection team structure shown in Figure 2-2 includes a senior-level source selection council (SSC), which may also be called a source selection advisory council. In some agencies, SSCs offer advice and an additional level of independent review for high-dollar or high-visibility acquisitions. An SSC may be composed of senior government personnel, including a senior contracting officer, selected by the SSA. SSC members do not participate in the source selection evaluation. Instead, the SSC conducts an independent review of the source selection evaluation results and recommendations, and presents its findings to the SSET and SSA.

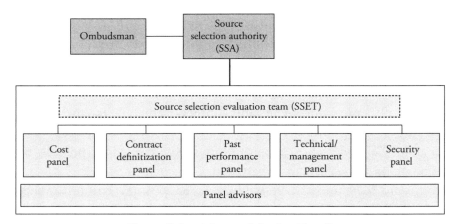

Figure 2-1   A Source Selection Team[20]

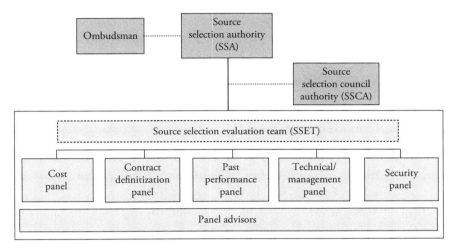

Figure 2-2 The Source Selection Council[21]

Source selection teams should decide whether or not the source selection plan should be marked and protected as source selection information (SSI), in accordance with FAR 2.101 and 3.104. The source selection team and the legal office should make this decision together. Per the U.S. Air Force's *Source Selection Plan Guide*, source selection teams

> should consider whether disclosure of information in the SSP would jeopardize the integrity or successful completion of the acquisition to which the information relates, and whether such information has previously been made available to the public or otherwise disclosed publicly. Openly sharing source selection plan information, evaluation factors and criteria demystifies the source selection process. Moreover, it helps offerors decide whether or not to submit a proposal confident they understand not only the requirement but also the proposal evaluation procedures.[22]

The Acquisition Strategy

One of the first steps in designing an acquisition strategy is to determine which evaluation methodology on the best value continuum to use: lowest price technically acceptable (LPTA) or trade-off. *Best value* means the expected outcome of an acquisition that, in the government's estimation, provides the greatest overall benefit in response to the requirements.[23] An agency can obtain best value in negotiated acquisitions by using one or a combination of source selection approaches.

In different types of acquisitions, the relative importance of cost or price may vary. For example, in acquisitions for which the requirement is clearly definable and the risk of unsuccessful contract performance is minimal, cost or price may play a dominant role in source selection. The less definitive the requirement, the more development work required, or the greater the performance risk, the more technical or past performance considerations may play a dominant role in source selection.[24] In either case, the evaluation factors and significant subfactors must be identified in the RFP. Let's examine how to decide which method of negotiated acquisition to use: LPTA or trade-off.

The Lowest Price Technically Acceptable

A *lowest price technically acceptable proposal* is a proposal that offers the best price to the government after minimum technical requirements have been met. The lowest price technically acceptable source selection process is appropriate when best value is expected from the technically acceptable proposal with the lowest evaluated cost.

Proposals are evaluated for acceptability but are not ranked based on non-cost/price factors. The RFP must specifically state that award will be made on the basis of the lowest evaluated price, as long as the proposal meets or exceeds the acceptability standards for non-cost factors.[25] All factors are evaluated using the "go/no-go" decisional rule. This rule works like a pass/fail grading system. A proposal will receive a "go," or an acceptable rating, if it meets all aspects of the standard for evaluation. A proposal will receive a "no-go," or unacceptable rating, if one or more elements of the offeror's proposal do not meet the minimum requirement of the standard of evaluation.

Price or cost must *always* be an evaluation factor when using either LPTA or trade-off methods. Sometimes, the government cannot predict cost performance or provide data for the offeror's cost estimation. The risk to the offeror may be unusually high, or the government may demand very high qualifications or experience that a low-cost offeror may not have.

For other acquisitions, the LPTA process may be the most appropriate methodology. It works when the government's requirements are not complex and the technical and performance risks are minimal, such as acquisitions in which service, supply, or equipment requirements are well defined, but discussions may be necessary. The LPTA method also "may be used in situations where the agency would not realize any value from a proposal exceeding the minimum technical requirements."[26] In such a case, the agency establishes certain standards that a proposal must meet to be considered technically acceptable. The award must then be made to the offeror whose proposal has met the technical requirements, even if just marginally, and is priced lowest.

Johnnie E. Wilson writes:

> The lowest price technically acceptable process is similar to a sealed bid approach in that award is made to the acceptable offeror with the lowest evaluated cost or price. The major

difference is that the contracting officer can have discussions with offerors before source selection to ensure they understand the requirements and to determine acceptability. Tradeoffs are not permitted and no additional credit is given for exceeding acceptability. Proposals are evaluated, however, to determine whether they meet the acceptability levels established in the solicitation for each non-cost evaluation factor and subfactor.[27]

Table 2-1 compares the LPTA with the trade-off acquisition method.

The Trade-Off

Using the trade-off approach to source selection allows an agency to select the most significant factors for emphasis—cost or price as well as non-cost factors—and allows the government to award the contract to a company that did not submit the lowest price. It is appropriate to use the trade-off process when it may be in the best interest of the government to consider awarding a contract to an offeror whose proposal is not the lowest priced nor the highest rated technically. This process was called "best value" before the FAR part 15 rewrite in 1997.

The RFP for a procurement using the trade-off process must state whether all evaluation factors other than cost or price, when combined, are significantly more important than, approximately equal to, or significantly less important than cost or price. The perceived benefits of the higher-priced proposal must merit the additional cost, and the agency must document the rationale for making the trade-off.[28]

Wilson urges agencies to "always consider the strengths and potential pitfalls of using a trade-off process to ensure that it is consistent with the agency's overall acquisition strategy."[29] For some acquisitions, the trade-off process is the most effective option and results in the best value to the government. It should be used when it is in the government's best interest to consider awarding the contract to other than the lowest-priced offeror. The trade-off process is particularly appropriate if:

Table 2-1   LPTA and Trade-Off Comparison[30]

	If…	**Then…**
Example 1	The government's needs can be met by any offeror that meets the minimum requirements for technical acceptability, and the procurement is straightforward and uncomplicated with few or no problems encountered in satisfying past government requirements …	The lowest price technically acceptable proposal approach may be best.
Example 2	The government's requirements are difficult to define, are complicated, or have been historically troublesome, and there is a reason to pay more money to select a more advantageous proposal …	The trade-off approach may be best.

- The government's requirements are difficult to define, complex, or historically troublesome.
- There is more than one possible acceptable solution for meeting the government's needs.
- The agency expects measurable differences between proposals in the design, performance, quality, reliability, or supportability.
- The services being procured are not clearly defined, or highly skilled personnel are needed to perform them.
- The agency is willing to pay extra for capability, skills, reduced risk, or other non-cost factors if the added benefits are worth the premium.

In trade-off acquisitions, evaluation factors other than price are often given more weight. These factors are especially important when there is a high technical risk and thus a stronger imperative to reduce the risk by selecting an offeror with superior technical capabilities. As a general rule, the higher the risk, the greater the emphasis on technical factors over price.

Using the trade-off process, the agency evaluates both cost (or price) and non-cost factors and awards the contract to the offeror whose proposal represents the best value based on the evaluation criteria. This process requires the source selection authority to make trade-offs as he or she considers each proposal's non-cost strengths and weaknesses, risks, and cost (or price). The SSA selects the successful offeror by considering these trade-offs and using his or her business judgment to choose the proposal that represents the best value.

Common Elements of LPTA and Trade-Off Source Selection

Although there are differences between the way the government evaluates proposals using the trade-off and LPTA methodologies, there are common elements between them. For example, in both source selection methods, contracting officers must:

- Make the RFP available through the governmentwide point of entry at http://www.fedbizopps.gov.[31]
- Use the uniform contract format when writing the RFP.[32]
- List all evaluation factors and significant subfactors that will affect contract award and their relative importance.[33]
- Evaluate proposals in accordance with the evaluation criteria stated in the RFP.[34]
- Award without discussions (if permitted by the solicitation) when appropriate. Otherwise, conduct discussions with offerors in the competitive range.[35]
- Select the proposal for contract award that represents the best value.[36]

Next, we'll examine a case study related to acquisition planning and market research. Recall that acquisition planning requires an agency to explain how it will promote and sustain competition or, if the agency is using a sole source exception, to discuss why it did not compete the requirement.[37] What happens if the agency wants to award a sole source contract and does not consider a competitor's product?

CASE STUDY: INADEQUATE PLANNING

eFedBudget Corporation protested the proposed award of a contract on a sole source basis to RGII Technologies, Inc., pursuant to presolicitation notice No. B-P-06, issued by the Department of State (DOS), for continued implementation, maintenance, enhancement, and support for DOS's worldwide budget and planning software systems. The protester asserted that the agency's decision to procure the software services on a sole source basis was improper. Specifically, the protester argued that

- The required justification and approval (J&A) was deficient.
- The agency unreasonably refused to consider the protester's approach of developing a nonproprietary software system.
- The need for the sole source procurement arose from the agency's lack of advance planning.[38]

Although the J&A stated that "licensing restrictions dictate that only RGII Technologies can do this work," it identifies no actions the agency had considered taking to remove or overcome any barriers to future competition resulting from the restrictive license, such as purchasing additional, broader license rights. The J&A notes only that RGII is "assessing the ability" to license other vendors to operate its software, and that the agency "will consider other application, maintenance, and support options based on the degree of success RGII achieves in these endeavors."

The Government Accountability Office's (GAO) decision in response to the protest stated that:

> CICA permits noncompetitive acquisitions in certain circumstances, such as when the services needed are available from only one responsible source. When an agency uses noncompetitive procedures, it is required to execute a written J&A with sufficient facts and rationale to support the use of the cited authority.... Our review of an agency's decision to conduct a sole-source procurement focuses on the adequacy of the rationale and conclusions set forth in the J&A. As a result, an agency's decision in this regard is not generally questioned by the GAO so long as the J&A sets forth reasonable justifications for the agency's actions....

Moreover, an agency has broad discretion to determine its needs and the method for accommodating those needs.... Use of noncompetitive procedures is not justified, however, where the agency created the need for the sole-source award through a lack of advance planning.

According to GAO,

> the agency had produced no record of any steps that it had taken to end its reliance on the services of the incumbent to maintain the existing software systems; in fact, this latest proposed sole-source award had a potential term of 5 years. It is possible, for example, that the agency could purchase additional rights to the proprietary software in order to promote competition.
>
> Under the circumstances here—where the agency ceded substantial rights in the software created by RGII under the development contract, and where there is no indication that the agency has explored the possibility of acquiring additional rights from RGII, GAO stated that, to satisfy its obligation to engage in reasonable advance planning and to promote competition, the agency was required to consider whether the costs associated with a purchase of additional license rights, or some other alternative, outweighed the anticipated benefits of competition.

GAO recommended that the agency "conduct a documented cost/benefit analysis reflecting the costs associated with obtaining competition, either through purchasing additional rights to the proprietary software or some other means, and the anticipated benefits." If the cost/benefit analysis "reveal[ed] a practicable means to obtain competition," GAO further recommended that the agency proceed with a competitive procurement.[39]

This case illustrates the importance of advance acquisition planning and market research. The Competition in Contracting Act states that lack of advance planning is not an adequate justification for using a sole source exception. Furthermore, agencies must plan for future competition even if a sole source procurement is appropriate now. Conducting thorough market research into other companies' capabilities should highlight potential competitors.

Up to this point, the chapter explained the government's responsibilities in acquisition planning and strategy. While the government develops the acquisition strategy, companies must know how to sell their products and services to the government. The next section explains how this is done.

SELLING TO THE GOVERNMENT

Government employees aren't the only ones subjected to the planning process. Potential contractors have to go through a maze of paperwork and learn confusing acronyms just for the possibility of winning a government contract. This section explains some of the basic steps of getting started in government contracting.

Central Contractor Registration

To compete in federal government source selections, one of the first things a company must do is register with the Central Contractor Registration (CCR). CCR is the primary registrant database for the federal government. The database collects, validates, stores, and disseminates data in support of agency acquisition missions, including federal agency contracts and assistance awards. (*Assistance awards* include grants, cooperative agreements, and other forms of federal assistance.) Whether they are applying for assistance awards, contracts, or other business opportunities, all entities are considered *registrants*.

According to the FAR, prospective contractors must be registered in the CCR database before a contract or agreement is awarded to them, except when:

- A governmentwide commercial purchase card is used as both the purchasing and payment mechanism
- The contract is classified, and registering in the CCR database or using CCR data could compromise classified information
- The contract is awarded by a deployed contracting officer in the course of military operations
- The contract is awarded by a contracting officer conducting emergency operations, such as responding to natural or environmental disasters
- The contract is awarded to support unusual or compelling needs
- The contract is awarded to a foreign vendor for work performed outside the United States
- The acquisition is a micropurchase, and electronic funds transfer will not be used.[40]

Both current and potential federal government contractors have to register in CCR in order to receive a contract award by the federal government. Companies must complete a one-time registration in which they provide basic information relevant to procurement and financial transactions. They must update or renew their registration at least once a year to maintain an active status. In addition, entities (including private nonprofits, educational organizations, and state and regional agencies) that apply for assistance awards from the federal government through www.grants.gov must now register with CCR. Note that registration does not guarantee that a company will receive a contract; it only qualifies it to do so.

CCR validates the registrant's information and electronically shares the secure and encrypted data with the federal agencies' finance offices to facilitate paperless payments through electronic funds transfer (EFT). Additionally, CCR shares the data with federal government procurement and electronic business systems. Note that any information provided in a company's registration may be shared with authorized federal government offices.[41] Registrants must also provide a release to the IRS that permits CCR to validate that the company is properly registered to pay its taxes.

Companies or individuals can complete the registration online at http://www.ccr. gov/default.aspx. CCR registrants are required to submit certain types of detailed information on their companies. CCR also requests additional, non-mandatory information. The *CCR User's Guide* (http://www.ccr.gov/handbook.aspx) defines and details specific informational requirements.[42]

The following is a list of basic information required to complete the CCR registration process:

- **Data Universal Numbering System (DUNS) number:** A unique nine-character identification number provided by the commercial company Dun & Bradstreet (D&B). Call D&B at 1-866-705-5711 or visit the D&B website at http://fedgov. dnb.com/webform if your company does not have a DUNS number.
- **Legal business name and doing business as (DBA) name:** Enter the legal name by which the company is incorporated and pays taxes. If the company commonly uses another name, such as a franchise, licensee name, or an acronym, include that in the DBA space below the legal business name. The company's legal business name as entered on the CCR registration must match the legal business name at Dun & Bradstreet, which must, in turn, match any state registrations. Make sure to include "Inc." or "LLC," etc., if those designations are part of the company's legal business name.
- **U.S. Federal Tax Identification Number (TIN):** A nine-digit number which is either an Employer Identification Number (EIN) assigned by the Internal Revenue Service (IRS) (http://www.irs.gov/businesses/small/article/0,,id=98350,00.html) or a Social Security number (SSN) assigned by the Social Security Administration (SSA) (www.ssa.gov). If you do not know your TIN/EIN, contact the IRS at 1-866-255-0654. If you operate as an individual sole proprietorship, you may use your Social Security number.
- **Business start date:** Enter the date the business was formed or established. This may be used to distinguish your firm from others with similar names.
- **Fiscal year end date:** Enter the day on which the company closes its fiscal year. For example, if the company uses the calendar year, enter 12/31.
- **Average number of employees, including all affiliates:** This information is passed to SBA in order to calculate the company's business size using SBA's official

size standards for your industry. Enter the average number of persons employed for each pay period over the firm's latest 12 months, including people employed by the parent organization, all branches, and all affiliates worldwide.

- **Average annual receipts, including all affiliates:** Receipts means *total income* (or in the case of a sole proprietorship, gross income) plus *cost of goods sold*, as these terms are defined and reported on Internal Revenue Service tax return forms. Receipts are averaged over a concern's latest three completed fiscal years to determine its average annual receipts.[43]

- **North American Industry Classification System (NAICS) code number:** NAICS (pronounced *nakes*) was developed as the standard for use by federal statistical agencies in classifying business establishments for collecting, analyzing, and publishing statistical data related to the business economy of the U.S. NAICS was developed under the auspices of the Office of Management and Budget (OMB) and adopted in 1997 to replace the old Standard Industrial Classification (SIC) system.

- **Commercial and Government Entity (CAGE) Code:** A five-character ID number used extensively within the federal government. The CAGE Code is used to support a variety of mechanized systems throughout the government and provides a standardized method of identifying a given facility at a specific location. The code may be used for a facility clearance, a preaward survey, an automated bidders list, identification of debarred bidders, and fast pay processes, among other functions.

Finding Opportunities

The government isn't the only party that conducts market research in the acquisition process. Companies must make their products and services known to agencies, too. Part of a company's marketing charge is to find out which federal agencies need the products or services it provides. Gathering information about the federal target market should be your first step towards increasing federal sales. There are five sources that provide important data about potential federal customers.

Federal Procurement Data Systems

The Federal Procurement Data Center (FPDC), part of the U.S. General Services Administration (GSA), operates and maintains the Federal Procurement Data System (FPDS; www.fpdc.gov). The FPDS is the central repository of statistical information on federal contracting. The system contains detailed information on contract actions over $25,000 and summary data on procurements of less than $25,000. Executive branch departments and agencies award more than $200 billion annually for goods and services, and this system can identify who bought what, from whom, for how much, when, and where. By searching this database, companies can find potential customers. If you learn that a particular agency contracted for a service that your company can provide, contact the agency to discuss how your firm can meet its requirements.

FedBizOpps

The governmentwide point of entry for procurement opportunities, FedBizOpps or FBO (Federal Business Opportunities; www.fedbizopps.gov), which is managed by GSA, is the single source for federal government procurement opportunities over $25,000. Vendors do not have to register, nor do they need a username and password, to begin using FedBizOpps. For vendors, the FedBizOpps system offers:

- The ability to browse active procurement notices by posted date, classification code, business set-aside type, and awards for a particular agency, office, or location.
- The ability to search for procurement notices through the use of the FedBizOpps synopsis/award search page.
- An email notification service (vendor notification service) that allows vendors to receive daily email notifications of procurement notices by agency, office, or location, procurement classification code, set-aside type, or place of performance ZIP code.
- An interested vendors module (bidder's list) to promote teaming opportunities for vendors.
- An FBO data feed file, which provides daily posting data in HTML format. The data feed file is available free of charge from the FBO FTP site at www.fedbizopps. gov. The file follows the naming convention "FBOFeedyyyymmdd" and includes all eight types of synopses: presolicitation, modification to a previous notice, award, sources sought, foreign government standard, sale of surplus property, special notice, and combined synopsis/solicitation.

By signing up to automatically receive procurement information, vendors can react more quickly to procurement opportunities because they are better informed. Vendors can also search procurements by solicitation number, date, procurement classification code, and agency for active or archived solicitations. Currently, 140,000 registered vendors receive email notifications from FedBizOpps about opportunities; roughly 50,000 e-mails are sent out daily. Fifty-one agencies (or 17,400 contracting officers/specialists) currently post opportunities on FedBizOpps.

Commerce Business Daily

Although FedBizOpps has replaced the Commerce Business Daily (CBD; http://cbdnet.access.gpo.gov) as the notification site for procurements over $25,000, the CBD is still a valuable marketing resource. The CBD website contains historical information about government agency purchases. You can find out which potential customers have bought your services in the past and even get an idea of when their existing contracts may expire.

Military Installations

Military installations offer huge opportunities for businesses. The trick to finding these opportunities is locating the right program office. Start with Armed Forces Network's (www.armedforces.net) list of military installations worldwide, then narrow your search by region, state, and activity.[44]

Long Range Acquisition Estimate

The Long Range Acquisition Estimate (LRAE) is a searchable database that covers projected U.S. Air Force RFPs. It includes information on buying activities, estimated dollar amounts, award dates, points of contact and contact information, and other information potential suppliers need to formulate marketing strategies. The LRAE can be found at http://safsbadmin.mysite4now.net/opportunities/lraesearch.aspx.

General Services Administration Multiple Award Schedule Contracts

A great way for companies to get experience in federal government contracting is to pursue a General Services Administration Multiple Award Schedule contract. Under the GSA Schedules (also referred to as Multiple Award Schedules and Federal Supply Schedules) Program, GSA establishes long-term governmentwide contracts with commercial firms. GSA Schedule contractors supply more than 11 million commercial products and services, which the government can order directly from the contractors or through the GSA Advantage!® online shopping and ordering system.

To become a GSA Schedule contractor, a vendor must first submit an offer in response to the applicable GSA Schedule solicitation. GSA awards contracts to responsible companies offering commercial items at fair and reasonable prices that fall within the generic descriptions in the GSA Schedule solicitations. Contracting officers determine whether prices are fair and reasonable by comparing the prices/discounts that a company offers the government with the prices/discounts that the company offers to commercial customers. This negotiation strategy is commonly known as *most favored customer pricing*. In order to make this comparison, GSA requires offerors to furnish commercial price lists and disclose information regarding their pricing/discounting practices.

GSA offers a great deal of assistance to its commercial partners through two programs: the GSA Marketing Partnership and GSA Advantage!®.

The GSA Marketing Partnership

The GSA Marketing Partnership (http://www.gsa.gov/marketingpartnership) is a free service offered by the GSA's Office of Marketing and Business Development. Participation ensures the success of Schedule contractors in building identification and increasing sales. The website offers information about Schedule Program enhancements, shows, expos, and various marketing opportunities. Participating in GSA's shows will help your company sell to the government, increase your customer base, and penetrate overseas federal and military markets. In addition, you can download the GSA Starmark logos, GSA SmartPay® logos, and the GSA Advantage!® logos at the partnership website. Using these logos in your printed and online communications will promote your status as a GSA Schedule contractor.

GSA Advantage!®

GSA Advantage!® (www.gsaAdvantage.gov) is an online electronic shopping and ordering system. It provides online access to several thousand contractors and millions of products and services. It allows federal agencies to search for products and services using keywords, national stock numbers, contract numbers and vendor names; compare features, prices, and delivery options; and place orders electronically.

Products and services under contract must be posted on GSA Advantage!®—in other words, participation in GSA Advantage!® is mandatory for Schedule holders. See Clause I-FSS-597 in any GSA Advantage!® solicitation for more details.[45] Every Schedule contract holder is represented by either a product or service listing or a text description of the company's offerings. When your company submits its GSA Advantage!® information, make sure that the text contains keywords that customers may be using to search the site. Note also the holding of GSA Schedule contractor status requires regular and constant contract administration—e.g., meeting requirements during contract performance, submitting proper invoices, and conducting contract closeout as required by the contract, as well as filing of periodic reports on sales. If a company fails to do so, it can lose the Schedule.

Small Business Opportunities

Another way companies get started in federal government contracting is through the Small Business Administration's special contracting opportunities. The Small Business Administration (SBA) has procurement center representatives (PCR) who work with federal agencies to identify prime contracting opportunities, reserve procurements for competition among small business concerns, provide small business sources to federal buying agencies, and counsel small firms.

SBA's commercial marketing representatives (CMR) conduct compliance reviews of prime contractors, counsel small businesses on how to obtain subcontracts, conduct matchmaking to facilitate subcontracting to small businesses, and provide orientation and training on the government's Subcontracting Assistance Program for both large and small businesses. To find the PCR or CMR representative servicing your company's area, go to www.sba.gov/aboutsba/sbaprograms/gc/contacts/gc_pcrd1.html.

Small Disadvantaged Business Certifications enable qualified firms to gain access to federal prime contracting and subcontracting opportunities. To qualify, a business must be at least 51 percent owned and controlled by one or more individuals who are socially and economically disadvantaged. Contracting officers and prime contractors may query Central Contractor Registration and the Dynamic Small Business Search for potential contractors that can help fulfill their goals.

There are several self-certification programs in which the small business certifies on the representations and certifications portion of the RFP and on a federal contract that it meets the requirements of that program. These programs are:

- **Service-disabled veteran-owned small business.** The federal government has established special procurement opportunities for service-disabled veterans. Under certain conditions, contracting officers may award a sole source or set-aside contract to a small business owned and controlled by a service-disabled veteran. To determine whether your business is eligible, contact your local veteran's business development officer in the nearest SBA district office (go to http://www.sba.gov/localresources for contact information), or contact the SBA's Office of Veterans Business Development (see http://www.sba.gov/vets for more information).
- **Veteran-owned small business.** A *veteran-owned small business* is defined as one which is at least 51 percent owned and controlled by one or more veterans, or, in the case of any publicly owned business, at least 51 percent of the stock is owned by one or more veterans, and the management and daily business operations are controlled by one or more veterans. If your company is a small business that meets the definition of veteran-owned, it can self-certify on a proposal for a contract. The Department of Veterans Affairs has authority to conduct

veteran-owned business set-asides for its own procurements. For information on VA programs, go to www.va.gov. For information on SBA's programs and services for veterans, contact the SBA's Office of Veterans Business Development (visit http://www.sba.gov/vets for more information).

- **Woman-owned small business.** The federal government has established a governmentwide goal for participation by small businesses owned and controlled by women. Not less than 5 percent of the total value of all prime contract and subcontract awards for each fiscal year shall be made to woman-owned small businesses. A *woman-owned small business* is defined as one that is at least 51 percent owned and controlled by one or more women, or, in the case of any publicly owned business, at least 51 percent of the stock is owned by one or more women, and the management and daily business operations are controlled by one or more women. If your company submits a proposal for a federal contract, it can self-certify that it is a woman-owned small business. For more information on SBA's programs and services for women entrepreneurs, go to http://www.sba.gov/aboutsba/sbaprograms/onlinewbc.

Agencies have a strong incentive to look for qualified small businesses when awarding contracts. Contract managers should therefore apply for the formal certifications and self-certifications for which their companies qualify. Federal agencies' Offices of Small and Disadvantaged Business Utilization have specialists to assist small businesses. Go to http://www.osdbu.gov/offices.html for more information.[46]

Developing a Marketing Plan

After your company identifies agencies that need its products or services, the next step is to put together a plan that describes how the company can meet their requirements. Just as a federal agency must write an acquisition plan if it wants a procurement to succeed, your company should develop a marketing plan.

First, the contract manager must understand how the company can fulfill the agency's needs. Many companies like to meet with agency personnel to discuss their products or services. Before meeting a potential customer, the contract manager should compile a list of the company's previous clients and be able to clearly and concisely answer these questions:

- What is the agency's mission?
- Which department in the agency has a requirement for your firm's product or service?
- How can your company help the agency meet its goals and objectives?
- What features do your products or services have that attracted customers to your company?

Once you understand the value your company can provide, create a plan that will show the agency why it should buy your product or services.

- Research information on the agency's budgets. The Budget Analyst website (www.budgetanalyst.com) is a good starting point.
- Understand the agency's mission and goals, and match your company's products and services to the agency's mission.
- Research GAO Reports on the agency you're targeting to see what kind of issues or problems it has had in the past. Be prepared to explain how your company can help the agency avoid that issue or solve that problem. GAO Reports are available at http://www.gpoaccess.gov/gaoreports/index.html.
- Get the agency's organization chart and develop a plan for calling agency staff— i.e., who will call whom? For example, if someone in the company already knows the contracting officer or program manager, it makes sense for that person to initiate the call or introduce the appropriate parties.

Now that you understand the planning process for both government and industry, let's discuss the methods of acquisition and contract types available.

METHODS OF ACQUISITION

Different acquisition methods are used to accommodate different requirements. There is often more than one way to do things, so contracting officers must understand different acquisition methods so the agency's requirements can be met in the most effective manner. The federal government uses three primary methods of acquisition:

1. Simplified acquisition procedures (FAR part 13)
2. Sealed bidding (FAR part 14)
3. Contracting by negotiation (FAR part 15).

Each of these three methods may be modified if the acquisition involves the purchase of commercial items as defined by law and regulation. Commercial acquisitions are sometimes viewed as a fourth acquisition method, but there are only three authorized methods of acquisition. The rules for each of the three methods also govern commercial item procurements, but they are simplified, in an effort to encourage broader participation by commercial contractors in federal acquisitions.

How does the agency decide which method to use for a given procurement? It must consider the acquisition's purpose, objective, or mission. Another consideration is maximizing competition. Some methods of acquisition lend themselves to more competition. Generally, the less complex the solicitation and method of acquisition, the more companies are interested in competing. Commercial item procurements, no matter which of the three acquisition methods are used, are simpler and faster because certain laws aren't applicable.

In addition, the contracting officer must consider the requirement's complexity. Sometimes it makes sense to use negotiation as an acquisition method when discussions are required for complex requirements.

Simplified Acquisition Procedures

FAR part 13 establishes policies and procedures for simplified acquisitions. There are three different ways to use simplified acquisition procedures: (1) commercial purchase card, (2) purchase orders, and (3) Blanket Purchase Agreements (BPA). The simplified acquisition threshold is currently $100,000. If the purchase is for supplies or services that are used to support a contingency operation or to facilitate defense against or recovery from nuclear, biological, chemical, or radiological attack, the threshold is $250,000 for any contract to be awarded and performed, or purchase to be made, inside the United States, and $1 million for any contract to be awarded and performed, or purchase to be made, outside the United States.[47] There is also a special authority for commercial item acquisitions over the $100,000 simplified acquisition threshold and under $5.5 million. See FAR 13.5 for a description of the test program for certain commercial items.

The primary purposes of the simplified acquisition procedures are to:

- Reduce administrative costs
- Improve opportunities for small, small disadvantaged, woman-owned, veteran-owned, HUBZone, and service-disabled veteran-owned small businesses to obtain a fair proportion of government contracts
- Promote efficiency and economy in contracting
- Avoid placing unnecessary burdens on agencies and contractors.[48]

The governmentwide commercial purchase card is the preferred method for making and paying for micropurchases. The micropurchase threshold is generally $3,000. For construction acquisitions subject to the Davis-Bacon Act, the threshold is $2,000, and for acquisitions of services subject to the Service Contract Act, the threshold is $2,500. These thresholds may change, so readers are advised to check FAR 2.101 for the current micropurchase thresholds.

Solicitations under simplified acquisition procedures may require companies to submit either a quotation or an offer. The primary type of solicitation used under simplified acquisition procedures is the request for quotations (RFQ).

Contracting professionals are responsible for choosing the appropriate method of solicitation (electronic commerce, verbal, or written) and for establishing the time frame for issuing the solicitation and receiving quotations or offers. The contracting officer also has to decide which clauses and provisions to include in the solicitation.

When contracting officers request quotations, they should notify potential vendors of the basis on which award will be made, such as price alone or price, past performance, and quality. Contracting officers have broad discretion in determining the evaluation procedures and may draw from those described in FAR parts 14 and 15. However, these procedures are not mandatory. For example, developing formal evaluation plans, establishing a competitive range, and holding discussions are not required. The contracting officer must evaluate the quotations based on what is established in the RFQ.[49]

Keep in mind that a quotation is *not* an offer and cannot be accepted by the government to form a binding contract. When the government issues an order in response to a supplier's quotation, therefore, it does not establish a contract. The order is an offer by the government to the supplier to buy certain supplies or services based on specified terms and conditions. A contract is established when the supplier accepts the offer, either formally, by signing the purchase order, or by initiating performance.[50]

Sealed Bidding

Sealed bidding is an acquisition method in which the government issues an invitation for bid (IFB). The IFB is publicized by distributing it to prospective bidders, posting it in public places, and posting it on the FedBizOpps website. Sufficient time must be allowed between the time the IFB is publicized and bids are opened publicly to enable prospective bidders to prepare and submit bids.

An IFB should describe the government's requirements clearly, accurately, and completely. Unnecessarily restrictive specifications or requirements that might unduly limit the number of bidders are prohibited. The invitation includes all documents (whether attached or incorporated by reference) furnished to prospective bidders for bidding purposes.[51]

Agencies must use a fixed-price contract for sealed bidding.[52] A pre-bid conference may be used, generally for a complex acquisition, as a means of briefing prospective bidders and explaining complicated specifications and requirements to them as early as possible after the invitation has been issued and before the bids are opened. The pre-bid conference should never be used as a substitute for amending a defective or ambiguous invitation.[53]

To be considered for award, a bid must comply in all material respects with the invitation for bids. Such compliance enables bidders to stand on an equal footing and maintain the integrity of the sealed bidding system. Bidders are responsible for submitting bids and any modifications or withdrawals in time to reach the government office designated in the invitation for bid by the time specified in the IFB. They may use any transmission method authorized by the IFB (such as regular mail, email, or facsimile). If no time deadline is specified in the IFB, the deadline is 4:30 p.m. (local time for the designated government office) on the date that bids are due.[54]

The bids are publicly opened, and the award is made based on price or price-related factors without any discussions or negotiations. Award can be made only to an offeror whose bid conformed to the invitation. The contracting officer must award the contract within the time frame for acceptance specified in the bid to the responsible bidder whose bid will be most advantageous to the government, considering only price and the price-related factors stated in the IFB.[55]

Sealed bidding should be used when all of the following conditions exist:

- The specifications are precise enough to permit price and price-related factors to be the determining criteria for award.
- There's enough time for soliciting, submitting, and evaluating sealed bids.
- The award will be made on the basis of price and other price-related factors.
- It is not necessary to conduct discussions with the responding bidders about their bids.
- There is a reasonable expectation of receiving more than one sealed bid.[56]

Contracting by Negotiation

If sealed bidding is not appropriate for a particular acquisition, contracting officers use the competitive negotiated method.[57] When contracting by negotiation, contracting officers have much more flexibility than with other acquisition methods because they can select from all of the available contract types, conduct discussions (negotiations), and evaluate factors other than price.

An agency gets best value in negotiated acquisitions by using any one or a combination of source selection approaches. In different types of acquisitions, the relative importance of cost or price may vary. For example, in acquisitions for which the requirement is clearly definable and the risk of unsuccessful contract performance is minimal, cost or price may play a dominant role in source selection. The less definitive the requirement, the more development work required, or the greater the performance risk, the more technical or past performance considerations may play a dominant role in source selection. This process is called the *best value continuum*.[58]

In a negotiated acquisition, the contracting officer uses a request for proposals to communicate government requirements to potential offerors and to solicit proposals. RFPs for competitive acquisitions describe the:

- Government's requirements
- Anticipated terms and conditions that will apply to the contract
- Information required to be in the offeror's proposal
- Factors and significant subfactors that will be used to evaluate the proposal and their relative importance.[59]

With negotiated acquisition, contracting officers can choose from two methods that were discussed earlier in this chapter: the trade-off procedure or the lowest priced technically acceptable procedure.

Commercial Items

As discussed in the first chapter, the Federal Acquisition Streamlining Act changed the definition of commercial items, giving the government greater flexibility. Agencies conduct market research to determine if commercial items are available that can meet their requirements. The government's policy is to purchase commercial items when they are available to meet the agency's needs.[60]

The FAR states that contracting officers "shall" (meaning that if the item meets the definition of *commercial item*, there is no discretion) use the policies unique to commercial items in FAR part 12, along with the policies and procedures in FAR parts 13 (simplified acquisition), 14 (sealed bidding), and 15 (negotiation). Thus, a commercial item purchase will use one of the three proscribed methods of acquisition, modified as permitted for commercial items.

The Small Business Act and the Office of Federal Procurement Policy Act require that agencies make notices of proposed contract actions available to prospective offerors.[61] This notification action is called *synopsis*, and it is typically a separate step in the process. The FAR, however, provides a streamlined method for soliciting and evaluating commercial items. The streamlined procedures may combine the synopsis and solicitation into a single document. Because the synopsis and solicitation are combined, it isn't necessary to publicize a separate synopsis 15 days before issuing the solicitation.[62] The solicitation response time may also be less than 30 days for commercial item acquisitions, but contracting officers must consider the circumstances of the individual acquisition, such as complexity and urgency, when establishing the due date.[63] While the FAR sets forth solicitation provisions and contract clauses for commercial items,[64] contracting officers may tailor the terms and conditions to reflect the specific market for that acquisition.[65]

Commercial item contracts must be firm fixed-price or fixed-price with an economic price adjustment.

CONTRACT TYPES

Acquisition professionals in government and industry may choose from a wide selection of contract types to get the flexibility they need when acquiring supplies and services. Contract types vary according to the degree and timing of the responsibility assumed by the contractor for the costs of performance and the amount and nature of the profit incentive offered to the contractor for achieving or exceeding specified standards or goals.

There are two broad categories of contract types: fixed-price contracts and cost-reimbursement contracts. A *fixed-price contract* stipulates a fixed sum of money to be paid the contractor as consideration for performance. The contractor is obligated to deliver an acceptable product or services for the agreed-to price, no matter how much it costs the contractor to perform the work.

Under a *cost-reimbursement contract*, the government reimburses the contractor for the reasonable, allowable, and allocable costs of performance as or after they are incurred. The contractor is only obligated to make a "good faith" effort within the estimated cost and may not continue performance once the money runs out.

Specific contract types range from firm fixed-price, in which the contractor has full responsibility for the performance costs and resulting profit (or loss), to cost-plus-fixed-fee, in which the contractor has minimal responsibility for the performance costs, and the negotiated fee (profit) is fixed. In between these extremes are various kinds of incentive contracts, under which the contractor's responsibility for the performance costs and the profit or fee incentives offered are tailored to the uncertainties of contract performance.[66]

Four contract types deserve more detailed attention here:

- Fixed-price contracts
- Cost-reimbursement contracts
- Incentive contracts
- Time-and-materials contracts.

Fixed-Price Contracts

In fixed-price contracts, there is a firm price, or in some cases, an adjustable price. Fixed-price contracts with an adjustable price may include a ceiling price, a target price (including target cost), or both. Unless otherwise specified in the contract, the ceiling price or target price can be adjusted only by applying a contract clause that allows an equitable adjustment or other price revision under stated circumstances. In appropriate circumstances, a fixed-price redeterminable contract may be used with either prospective or retroactive features. Redeterminable contracts permit the parties to adjust or redetermine the prices. This adjustment may be made prospectively at predetermined times during contract performance (see FAR 52.216-5) or retroactively within a specified time after contract delivery (see FAR 52.216-6).

The price of a firm fixed-price (FFP) contract may not be adjusted during contract performance. This contract type places the risk and full responsibility for all costs and resulting profit or loss on the contractor. It also provides maximum incentive for the contractor to control costs and perform effectively and imposes a minimum administrative burden on government oversight. A firm fixed-price contract is suitable for acquiring commercial items or other supplies or services based on reasonably definite functional or detailed specifications, and when the contracting officer can establish fair and reasonable prices at the outset, such as when one of these conditions is met:

- There is adequate price competition.
- There are reasonable price comparisons with prior purchases of the same or similar supplies or services made on a competitive basis or supported by valid cost or pricing data.
- Available cost or pricing information permits realistic estimation of the probable costs of performance.
- Performance uncertainties can be identified, reasonable estimates of their cost impact can be made, and the contractor is willing to accept a firm fixed price that represents assumption of the risks involved.[67]

Another type of fixed-price contract is a fixed-price contract with an economic price adjustment (EPA). This type of contract allows the contract price to be adjusted upward and downward when specified contingencies occur. Economic price adjustments are of three general types:

1. **Adjustments based on established prices.** These price adjustments are based on increases or decreases from an agreed-upon level in published or otherwise established prices of specific component items or the contract end items.

2. **Adjustments based on actual costs of labor or material.** These price adjustments are based on increases or decreases in specified costs of labor or materials that the contractor actually experiences during contract performance. Note that this provision may not be used to protect against performance risk from inaccurately estimating the *amount* of labor or materials required, but only the *cost* of the proposed amount of labor or materials needed.

3. **Adjustments based on cost indexes of labor or materials.** These price adjustments are based on increases or decreases in labor or material cost standards or indexes (such as the cost index for gold) that are specifically identified in the contract.

Contracting officers use a fixed-price contract with economic price adjustment when serious doubt exists about the stability of market or labor conditions that will exist during an extended period of contract performance. This type of contract is also appropriate when major contingencies (that would otherwise be included in the contract price) can be identified and covered by a price adjustment clause in the contract. Price adjustments based on established prices should normally be restricted to industry-wide contingencies. Price adjustments based on labor and material costs should be limited to contingencies beyond the contractor's control.[68]

Cost-Reimbursement Contracts

Cost-reimbursement contracts pay allowable incurred costs to the extent prescribed in the contract. The estimated total cost is used to obligate funds and establish a ceiling that the contractor may not exceed (except at its own risk) without the approval of the contracting officer. Cost-reimbursement contracts are suitable for use only when uncertainties associated with contract performance do not permit costs to be estimated with sufficient accuracy to use any type of fixed-price contract.

A cost-reimbursement contract may be used only when the contractor's accounting system is adequate for determining costs applicable to the contract, and appropriate government surveillance during performance provides reasonable assurance that the contractor is using efficient methods and effective cost controls. Contracting officers may not use cost-reimbursement contracts for commercial item acquisitions.[69]

One popular type of cost-reimbursement contract is the cost-plus-fixed-fee (CPFF) contract. CPFF is a cost-reimbursement contract that pays the contractor a negotiated fee that is fixed at contract award. The fixed fee does not vary with actual cost, but may be adjusted as a result of contract changes. This contract type enables acquisitions that might otherwise present too great a risk to contractors, but it gives the contractor only a minimum incentive to control costs.

Contracting officers may use a cost-plus-fixed-fee contract when the contract is for performing research, preliminary exploration, or study, and the level of effort required is unknown. CPFF contracts can also be used for development and test when using a cost-plus-incentive-fee (CPIF) contract is not practical.

A cost-plus-fixed-fee contract may take one of two basic forms—completion or term.

The *completion* form describes the scope of work by stating a definite goal or target and specifying an end product. This form of contract normally requires the contractor to complete and deliver the specified end product (e.g., a final report on research that accomplished the goal or target) within the estimated cost, if possible, as a condition for payment of the entire fixed fee. If the contractor can't complete the work within the estimated cost, however, the government may require the contractor to complete performance by increasing the estimated cost without increasing the fee.

The *term* form describes the scope of work in general terms and obligates the contractor to devote a specified level of effort for a stated time period. If the government considers performance satisfactory, the fixed fee is payable at the end of the stated period, after the contractor shows that it expended the specified level of effort during contract performance. If the contract is renewed for additional periods of performance, that is considered a new acquisition that involves new cost and fee arrangements.

Because the contractor assumes different obligations and risk depending on whether the term or completion form of CPFF contract is used, the government prefers the completion form whenever the work, or specific milestones for the work, can be defined well enough to permit the contractor to develop estimates within which they will complete the work. Term form CPFF contracts require contractors to provide a specific level of effort within a definite time period.

Agencies should avoid using a cost-plus-fixed-fee contract when developing major systems once preliminary exploration, studies, and risk reduction have indicated a high degree of probability that the development is achievable and the government has established reasonably firm performance objectives and schedules.

Before awarding a cost-plus-fixed-fee contract, the contracting officer must first analyze the proposal per FAR 15.404 and ensure that the contractor has an adequate accounting system and the government has an appropriate surveillance system in place to ensure that the contractor is performing efficiently.[70]

Incentive Contracts

Incentive contracts may be used when a firm fixed-price contract is not appropriate and the required supplies or services can be acquired at lower costs and, in certain instances, with improved delivery or technical performance, by relating the amount of profit or fee payable under the contract to the contractor's performance. Incentives may include cost, performance, or delivery incentives, or any combination of the three. Incentive provisions can be included in both fixed-price and cost-type contracts.

Incentive contracts are designed to obtain specific acquisition objectives by

- Establishing reasonable and attainable targets that are clearly communicated to the contractor
- Including appropriate incentive arrangements designed to motivate contractor efforts that might not otherwise be emphasized and to discourage contractor inefficiency and waste.

When predetermined formula-type incentives on technical performance or delivery are included, increases in profit or fee are provided only for achievement that surpasses the targets, and decreases are provided for if targets are not met. The incentive increases or decreases are applied to performance targets rather than minimum performance requirements.[71]

Award-fee contracts are also a type of incentive contract. A cost-plus-award-fee (CPAF) contract is a cost-reimbursement contract that provides for a fee consisting of a base amount fixed at inception of the contract and an award amount that the contractor may earn in whole or in part during performance. The award amount should sufficiently motivate excellence in such areas as quality, timeliness, technical ingenuity, and cost-effective management. The amount of the award to be paid is determined by the government's subjective judgment of the contractor's performance in terms of the criteria stated in the contract. This determination and the method for determining the award fee are unilateral decisions made solely at the discretion of the government. Award-fee plans, which may be renegotiated on a periodic basis as the needs of the program change, are usually developed for award-fee contracts.

Contracting officers use a CPAF contract when the work required does not permit establishing a predetermined, objective incentive target for cost, technical performance, or schedule. A CPAF contract can also be used if it enhances the likelihood of meeting acquisition objectives, because this contract type effectively motivates the contractor toward exceptional performance and gives the government the flexibility to evaluate both actual performance and the conditions under which it was achieved. Contracting officers need to consider the additional administrative effort and cost required to monitor and evaluate performance in a CPAF contract.

A contractor is evaluated at regular intervals while performing a CPAF so that the government can give feedback on the quality of its performance and the areas in which it expects improvement. Generally, the contractor is paid part of the fee during each evaluation period. Thus, by inducing the contractor to improve poor performance or to continue good performance, the award fee acts as an effective incentive. The award-fee criteria and rating plan should motivate the contractor to improve performance in the areas noted as needing improvement, but not at the expense of at least minimum acceptable performance in all other areas.

Contracting officers may not award a CPAF contract unless the contractor has an adequate accounting system and the government has appropriate surveillance systems in place to ensure efficient and effective cost controls.[72]

Time-and-Materials Contracts

Another type of contract that doesn't fit into the fixed-price or cost-reimbursement categories is the time-and-materials (T&M) contract. A *time-and-materials contract* allows the government to purchase supplies or services on two bases: direct labor hours at a fixed hourly rate and the cost of materials. The direct hourly rate includes wages, overhead, general and administrative expenses, and profit. The material expenses are reimbursed based on their actual cost.

A time-and-materials contract may be used only when it is not possible to estimate accurately the extent or duration of the work or to anticipate costs with any reasonable degree of confidence at contract award. A time-and-materials contract provides no positive profit incentive to the contractor for cost control or labor efficiency. Appropriate government surveillance of contractor performance is therefore required to give reasonable assurance that efficient methods and effective cost controls are being used.

By now, you can see that some contract types are riskier to the government; other contract types are riskier to the contractor. Figure 2-3 illustrates the relationship between risk and contract type for both government and contractor.

Note that firm fixed-price contracts have the least risk for the government, but the most risk for the contractor. Similarly, time-and-materials contracts have the least risk for the contractor but the most for the government. This risk relationship makes selecting a contract type challenging.

Selecting a Contract Type

How do you know which type of contract will work best for your procurement? There are a lot of different ways the contracting officer can go about choosing a contract type. The contract type is generally selected by negotiation, although agencies

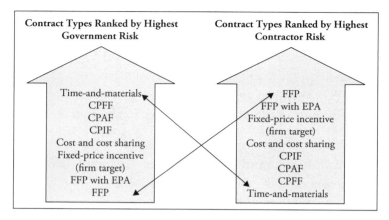

Figure 2-3 Contract Type Risk Ranking

will recommend or suggest a contract type in the RFP. Negotiating the contract type and negotiating prices are closely related, and contract type and price should be considered together. The objective is to negotiate a contract type and price (or estimated cost and fee) that will result in reasonable contractor risk and provide the contractor with the greatest incentive for efficient and economical performance.

Agencies use a firm fixed-price contract emphasizing profit, for example, when the risk involved is minimal or can be predicted with an acceptable degree of certainty. When a reasonable basis for firm pricing does not exist, however, contracting officers must consider other contract types and direct negotiations toward selecting a contract type (or combination of types) that links profit to contractor performance.

The FAR discourages using a cost-reimbursement or time-and-materials contract type over an extended period of time. Experience with a particular product or service provides a basis for firmer pricing.[73]

Sealed bidding requires firm fixed-price contracts or fixed-price contracts with economic price adjustment. Contracts negotiated under FAR part 15 may be of any type or combination of types that will promote the government's interest, except the cost-plus-a-percentage-of-cost system. That contract type is prohibited.[74]

Selecting a contract type that is inappropriate for a particular acquisition can cause severe performance problems or lead to a default termination. For example, using a firm fixed-price contract when the circumstances call for a cost-reimbursement contract will put pressure on the contractor to either propose a very high price to protect itself or perhaps deliver an inadequate product for the agreed-upon price.

The U.S. Navy's A-12 aircraft contract is an infamous example of selecting the wrong contract type. In 1984, the navy awarded two teams fixed-price contracts for concept formulation and demonstration validation. Even though the initial contract results from the concept formulation phase indicated that the design was immature, the navy awarded McDonnell Douglas and General Dynamics a full-scale engineering and development contract to develop the A-12, a stealth aircraft.

In 1990, the contracting team informed the navy that the schedule for first flight had slipped significantly and that it couldn't absorb a contract ceiling overrun or meet some performance specifications. The navy terminated the contract for default in 1991.[75] The claims court ruled that the termination for default was improper and converted it into a termination for the convenience of the government.[76] The government appealed the decision, and after several years of appeals, the U.S. Court of Federal Claims ruled in favor of the government, stating:

> The Government can point to reasons in retrospect why plaintiffs were not making the progress that some officials hoped and perhaps expected. So long as those reasons form a rational basis for a reviewing court to uphold defendant's decision to terminate, the court must do so.[77]

Boeing (which now owns McDonnell Douglas) appealed to the United States Court of Appeals for the Federal Circuit on May 4, 2007; we still await the result. The lesson learned from this contract, even though it's been litigated longer than it was performed, is that selecting the correct contract type can mean the difference between success and failure.

There are many factors that the contracting officer should consider when selecting and negotiating the contract type, including:

- **Price competition.** Normally, effective price competition results in realistic pricing. A contract type that shifts too much risk to the contractor may reduce the level of or amount of competition. If an RFP poses too much risk, companies may not submit proposals, thereby reducing the amount of competition.
- **Price analysis.** Price analysis, with or without competition, may provide a basis for selecting the contract type. Contracting officers should carefully consider the degree to which price analysis can provide a realistic pricing standard.
- **Cost analysis.** In the absence of effective price competition, and if price analysis is not sufficient, the offeror's and government's cost estimates provide the bases for negotiating contract pricing arrangements. It is essential to identify and evaluate the uncertainties involved in performance and their possible impact upon costs, so that the contracting officer can negotiate a contract type that places a reasonable degree of cost responsibility upon the contractor.
- **Type and complexity of the requirement.** The government usually assumes more risk in contracts with complex requirements, particularly those unique to the government. This is especially true for complex research and development

contracts, when performance uncertainties or the likelihood of changes makes it difficult to estimate performance costs in advance. As a requirement recurs or as quantity production begins, the cost risk should shift to the contractor, and the contracting officer should consider a fixed-price contract.

- **Urgency of the requirement.** If urgency is a primary factor, the government may choose to assume a greater proportion of risk, or it may offer incentives to ensure timely contract performance.
- **Period of performance or length of production run.** In times of economic uncertainty, contracts extending over a relatively long period may require economic price adjustment terms.
- **Contractor's technical capability and financial responsibility.** A contractor that must hire the necessary personnel or that suffers from high employee turnover may not be able to perform under some contract types. A contractor experiencing financial difficulty may not have the resources to purchase required supplies or meet payroll for contract performance.
- **Adequacy of the contractor's accounting system.** Before agreeing on a contract type other than firm fixed-price, the contracting officer must be certain that the contractor's accounting system will permit timely assembly of all necessary cost data in the form required by the proposed contract type. This factor may be critical if the contract type requires price revision during contract performance, or if the parties are considering a cost-reimbursement contract, and all current or past experience with the contractor has been on a fixed-price basis.
- **Concurrent contracts.** If performance under the proposed contract involves concurrent operations under other contracts, the contracting officer should consider the impact of those contracts, including their pricing arrangements. For example, companies must have an accounting system that can differentiate between charges incurred on fixed-price and cost-reimbursement contracts so that mischarging does not occur.
- **Extent and nature of proposed subcontracting.** If the contractor proposes extensive subcontracting, the contracting officer should select a contract type reflecting the actual risks to the prime contractor.
- **Acquisition history.** As the contractor gains experience in providing the products or services required, it is exposed to less risk, so a fixed-price contract may be appropriate for follow-on acquisitions. More definite product or service descriptions also reduce risk, and facilitate the use of a fixed-price contract type.[78]

There are so many factors to consider before selecting a contract type, it's no wonder that there are occasionally mismatches between the acquisition and the contract type. Keep in mind, however, that the contract type is negotiable. The contract type the government suggests in the RFP is a recommendation, not a requirement. An offeror may propose another contract type and explain in its proposal why the alternative makes more sense from a risk or performance standpoint. Sometimes, the parties determine to change the contract type during contract performance. In any case, the contracting officer must document why he or she selected a particular contract type.[79]

CHAPTER SUMMARY

Chapter 2 explains the essential tasks government agencies and potential offerors perform when planning for a federal acquisition. First, for most procurements, agencies must perform market research. We discuss the types and sources of market research data and detailed how to document data once it is collected.

Next, the agency writes an acquisition plan and a source selection plan, which guide the acquisition strategy. Depending on their requirements, agencies can choose one of two basic acquisition strategies: awarding to the lowest-priced technically acceptable offeror or awarding to another offeror based on factors unrelated to cost or price.

Switching to industry's perspective, we discuss the elements of selling to the government. The chapter details the essential Central Contractor Registration process and offers guidance on finding federal business opportunities for businesses of any size and those new to federal contracting. We also offer suggestions for developing a marketing plan.

Finally, the chapter covers four methods of acquisition (simplified acquisition, sealed bidding, contracting by negotiation, and contracting for commercial items) and details the requirements for each. It also explains the four basic contract types—fixed-price, cost-reimbursement, incentive, and time-and-materials—and suggests factors to consider when selecting a contract type.

NOTES

1 Federal Acquisition Regulation (FAR) 2.101.

2 FAR 10.001.

3 FAR 12.101.

4 FAR 10.002.

5 Margaret G. Rumbaugh and Mark J. Lumer, *The Brave New World of Market Research* (Vienna, VA: National Contract Management Association, 1996), 3-10–3-14.

6 FAR 10.002(c).

7 FAR 10.002(d).

8 Rumbaugh and Lumer, 3-20–3-21.

9 FAR 2.101.

10 FAR 1.102.

11 Office of Management and Budget, "Value Engineering," *OMB Circular* A-131 (Washington, DC: Office of Management and Budget, May 21, 1993).

12 FAR 2.101.

13 FAR 15.407-4

14 "Performance of Commercial Activity," *OMB Circular* A-76, May 29, 2003.

15 FAR 2.101.

16 FAR 15.407-2.

17 Johnnie E. Wilson, *Best Value Source Selection* 715-3 (Alexandria, VA: Army Materiel Command, 1998), 8.

18 FAR 15.303.

19 National Reconnaissance Office Source Selection Plan Template version 1.6 October 2006 pg 5.

20 National Reconnaissance Office Source Selection Plan Template version 1.6 October 2006 pg 4.

21 National Reconnaissance Office Source Selection Plan Template version 1.6 October 2006 pg 5.

22 Air Force Materiel Command, *Source Selection Plan Guide* (Dayton, OH: Air Force Materiel Command, March 2005), iv.

23 FAR 2.101.

24 FAR 15.101.

25 FAR 15.101-2.

26 Claude M. Bolton, Jr., *Army Source Selection Manual* (Washington, DC: Office of the Assistant Secretary of the Army for Acquisition, Logistics and Technology, 2007), 4.

27 Wilson, 6.

28 Federal Acquisition Institute, *Source Selection Text Reference* (Washington, DC: Federal Acquisition Institute, 1993), 3-27.

29 FAR 15.101-1.

30 Wilson, 4.

31 FAR 5.102.

32 FAR 15.204-1.

33 FAR 15.101-2 and 15.101-2.

34 FAR 15.305.

35 FAR 15.306.

36 FAR 15.302.

37 FAR 7.105(b)(2).

38 U.S. Government Accountability Office, "eFedBudget Corporation," B-298627 (Washington, DC: U.S. Government Accountability Office, November 15, 2006).

39 Ibid.

40 FAR 4.1102.

41 Central Contractor Registration, *Central Contractor Registration Handbook* (Washington, DC: Central Contractor Registration, September 2008), 1.

42 Central Contractor Registration website, http://www.ccr.gov/Default.aspx (accessed October 10, 2008).

43 Central Contractor Registration, *Central Contractor Registration Handbook*, 7–10.

44 U.S. General Services Administration, *A Guide: How to Market to the Federal Government,* June 2009, http://www.gsa.gov/Portal/gsa/ep/contentView.do?contentType=GSA_DOCUMENT&contentId=17212&noc=T (accessed August 20, 2009).

45 Ibid.

46 U.S. Small Business Administration, *Opening Doors: Small Business Opportunities in Federal Government Contracting*, http://www.sba.gov/idc/groups/public/documents/sba_homepage/serv_pub_contracting.pdf (accessed August 20, 2009).

47 FAR 2.101.

48 FAR 13.002.

49 FAR 13.106-2.

50 FAR 13.004.

51 FAR 14.101.

52 FAR 14.104.

53 FAR 14.207.

54 FAR 14.301.

55 FAR 14.408-1.

56 FAR 6.401.

57 FAR 6.102.

58 FAR 15.101.

59 FAR 15.203.

60 FAR 12.101.

61 FAR 5.201.

62 FAR 12.603.

63 FAR 5.203.

64 FAR 12.301.

65 FAR 12.302.

66 FAR 16.101.

67 FAR 16.202.

68 FAR 16.203.

69 FAR 16.301.

70 FAR 16.306.

71 FAR 16.401.

72 FAR 16.405.

73 FAR 16.103.

74 FAR 16.102.

75 Herbert L. Fenster, "The A-12 Legacy: It Wasn't an Airplane—It Was a Train Wreck," *U.S. Naval Institute Proceedings* 125 (Annapolis, MD: U.S. Naval Institute, February 1999). Copyright © 1999 U.S. Naval Institute/www.usni.org. Reprinted from *Proceedings* with permission.

76 *McDonnell Douglas Corp. v. United States of America*, 35 Fed. Cl. 358 (1996).

77 *McDonnell Douglas Corp. and General Dynamics Corp. v. United States of America*, no. 91-1204C (Fed. Cl. 1998).

78 FAR 16.104.

79 FAR 16.103.

Chapter 3

Writing Evaluation Factors

Recall from Chapter 2 that evaluation factors and subfactors, and the determination of their relative importance, are part of the source selection plan. The evaluation factors and their relative order of importance illustrate the government's priorities. For example, if the most important evaluation factor is price, that means the agency is not willing (or able) to pay more for higher quality.

In every RFP, the contracting officer (CO) must include the evaluation criteria and state the relative order of importance for each criterion. This chapter will help the reader understand the mandatory evaluation factors and explains the steps involved in selecting evaluation factors, structuring and limiting factors, evaluating risk, and expressing the relative importance of the evaluation factors.

Reading and understanding the statement of work (SOW) is the first step in establishing evaluation criteria. The evaluation factors must address the SOW requirements. The work breakdown structure (WBS) is also a helpful tool for writing evaluation criteria.

The evaluation factors must support meaningful comparison and discrimination between and among competing proposals.[1] How does the CO do that? There are three basic requirements for writing evaluation factors:

1. **The factor must be a variable**—that is, there must be a reasonable expectation of variance among offerors.
2. **The variance must be measurable.** This does not mean that it must be quantifiable. Qualitative measurements are equally valid.
3. **The factor must be determinant.** The Comptroller General has stated in several decisions that a particular evaluation factor is valid only if the agency's needs warrant a comparative evaluation of the area the factor addresses. The FAR reinforces this by stating that an award decision is based on evaluation factors and significant subfactors that are tailored to the acquisition.[2] The simplest way to

evaluate if the factor is determinant is to ask, "Is the government willing to pay more for higher quality relative to this factor?"[3]

After selecting the evaluation factors, the evaluation team must structure them in a meaningful way to support the acquisition's objectives as stated in the acquisition and source selection plans. Part of the structuring process is limiting the evaluation factors to those that will actually discriminate among the proposals submitted and eliminating the factors that will not.

Another aspect of source selection that is part of determining the evaluation factors is deciding how the agency will evaluate risk. We will review various approaches to evaluating risk later in this chapter.

Finally, the evaluation team must state the relative importance of the evaluation factors and subfactors, per FAR 15.304(e).

Now, let's examine the details of how to write evaluation factors. We'll start by describing the evaluation factors required by the FAR.

MANDATORY EVALUATION FACTORS

Although each agency has a great deal of flexibility in determining evaluation factors and their relative importance, the FAR states that there are four required evaluation factors:

- Price or cost to the government (required by the Competition in Contracting Act)
- Quality of the product or service (required by the Armed Services Procurement Act)
- Past performance (required by the Federal Acquisition Streamlining Act)
- Small business participation for acquisitions over $550,000 (required by the Small Business Act).

First, the government must evaluate price or cost for every source selection. Price (or cost) does not have to be the most important factor, but the government must take it into consideration before making the award.

Second, contracting officers must evaluate the quality of the product or service for every source selection by considering offerors' past performance, compliance with solicitation requirements, technical excellence, management capability, personnel qualifications, and prior experience.

Third, the government also must evaluate offerors' past performance for all negotiated competitive acquisitions expected to exceed the simplified acquisition threshold, unless the CO documents why past performance isn't an appropriate evaluate factor.

Finally, for unrestricted acquisitions expected to exceed $550,000 ($1,000,000 for construction), the government evaluates the extent to which small disadvantaged business concerns participate in contract performance.[4] Agencies may consider the following when developing the small disadvantaged business (SDB) evaluation factor:

- The extent to which SDB companies are specifically identified as potential offerors
- The extent of commitment to using SDB companies (For example, enforceable commitments are to be weighted more heavily than non-enforceable ones.)
- The complexity and variety of the work SDB companies are to perform.
- The realism of the SDBs' proposals for the current acquisition.
- Past performance of offerors in complying with subcontracting plan goals for SDB companies and monetary targets for SDB participation
- The extent of participation of SDB companies in terms of the value of the total acquisition.[5]

Some acquisitions might involve *bundling*, which means consolidating two or more requirements for supplies or services, previously provided or performed under separate smaller contracts, into a solicitation for a single contract. This single contract might be unsuitable for small business concerns due to any of the following factors:

- The diversity, size, or specialized nature of the performance elements specified
- The aggregate dollar value of the anticipated award
- The geographical dispersion of the contract performance sites
- Any combination of the above.[6]

When a solicitation involves bundling that offers a significant opportunity for subcontracting, the contracting officer must include a factor to evaluate past performance, indicating the extent to which the offeror attained applicable goals for small business participation under contracts that required subcontracting plans. This helps make up for the possibility that small businesses might not be able to compete for the larger, bundled contract. The contracting officer must also include proposed small business subcontracting participation in the subcontracting plan as an evaluation factor.

Another FAR requirement with regard to evaluation criteria pertains to telecommuting. Some companies permit their employees to telecommute, and agencies shall not discourage a contractor from allowing its employees to telecommute while performing government contracts. However, the agency may prohibit an offeror from allowing its employees to telecommute if the contracting officer determines that the requirements of the agency, including security requirements, cannot be met if the contractor permits telecommuting. The contracting officer must document the basis for the determination in writing and state the prohibition and address the evaluation procedures in the solicitation. When telecommuting is allowed, agencies may not downgrade an offer because it proposes telecommuting.[7]

Now that you understand the FAR requirements for evaluation factors, we'll discuss how to select evaluation factors for each competitive source selection. In addition to the factors required by the FAR, most agencies include technical and management factors in the source selection plan and RFP that are used to evaluate the quality of the proposed products and services.

The next section discusses the typical evaluation factors and the information that might be included in proposals when an RFP uses those evaluation factors.

COMMON EVALUATION FACTORS

Although evaluation factors are tailored to each acquisition, agencies tend to focus on the same broad categories: technical, management (including key personnel and security), cost or price, and past performance.

Agencies typically use technical or management evaluation factors to measure quality. Agencies evaluate cost or price for reasonableness, and some agencies also examine cost realism and completeness. Evaluating key personnel is especially important in services acquisition. The past performance evaluation is a predictor of future performance.

Technical Factors

An offeror's technical proposal describes how well it understands the statement of work and the RFP requirements. The evaluation team reads and analyzes the technical proposal to evaluate the offeror's comprehension of the requirements set forth in the RFP. Although costs are analyzed separately from the technical proposal, they may signify the offeror's understanding of the resources, personnel, and material required to perform the contract. Accordingly, technical evaluators should have access to the cost proposal or portions of the cost proposal to help determine how well the offeror understands the RFP's requirements.

Reviewing the cost information may also help evaluators assess the offeror's approach to performing the work. Evaluators can take into account a proposal's cost realism, or lack thereof, as part of their assessment of each offeror's technical understanding. Also, an offeror's justification or rationale for proposed costs can give technical evaluators insight into how well it understands the work to be performed.

A factor, by itself, may be too broad to measure key aspects of the proposal, so the contracting officer may have to develop two or more subfactors for a given evaluation factor. For example, a factor such as *technical approach* for a computer system acquisition may be broken down into three subfactors: *hardware installation plan*, *software installation plan*, and *network services and maintenance plan*. [8]

Similarly, a subfactor may be divided into various related elements. For example, *technical approach* could be subdivided as follows:

1. Technical approach
   1.1. Use of technology
   1.2. Industry standards and best practices
   1.3. Customer service
   1.4. Standardized technical processes
   1.5. Definitions.

Technical subfactors agencies may use include, but are not limited to:

- Understanding the requirements
- Technical innovation or use of technology
- Technical approach or methodology
- Quality control
- Standardized technical processes
- Customer service
- Safety and accident prevention measures
- Use of special materials
- Industry standards and best practices.

Usually, the technical personnel are the most qualified to recommend the factors and subfactors they need to satisfy the acquisition's objectives. We'll examine the details of technical proposal evaluation in Chapter 9.

Management Factors

An offeror's management proposal identifies its plan for efficiently managing the work proposed in its technical proposal. A management proposal may cover the vendor's proposed organizational structure and essential management functions and how it will integrate these management functions. The organizational structure described in a management proposal outlines the offeror's internal operations and lines of authority, as well as its external interfaces and relationships with the government, major subcontractors, and associate contractors. When a management proposal is properly prepared, evaluators can determine the project manager's authority, the project manager's relationship to the next echelon of management, and the project manager's command of company resources. The management proposal also identifies schedules necessary for the logical and timely completion of work, along with a description of the offeror's work plan.

Management evaluation factors assess how the project will be controlled. Depending on the agency's specific needs, the contracting officer may wish to include typical subfactors that evaluate each offeror's control and accounting procedures, organizational schemes, subcontracting plans, reporting procedures, or special security arrangements. Increasingly, quality control (QC) measures are included as a key subfactor.

Also, evaluators should assess the personnel and facilities resources proposed by each offeror. The management proposal should help evaluators answer these questions:

- Does the offeror propose the proper skill mix and number of people necessary to do the work?
- Does the offeror propose facilities and, where required, special test equipment suitable and adequate to assure timely performance of the work?

If the offeror does not have adequate resources internally, does it have a demonstrated ability to acquire them through subcontracts or otherwise?

Management subfactors might include:

- Key personnel
- Security
- Subcontract management
- Property management
- Safety and accident prevention programs
- Procurement systems
- Continuous process improvement
- Reports and procedures
- Environmental compliance.

Key personnel and security subfactors warrant special attention here.

Key Personnel Subfactors

The RFP must identify specific key personnel positions considered most important for successful contract performance. This is particularly significant for services contracts. Key personnel can include technical, management, operational, and administrative personnel. The proposal preparation instructions must identify resume requirements, such as including the experience and education of each key person and specifying the number of pages. The RFP should state the minimum requirements and whether or not the agency will favorably evaluate proposals that exceed the minimum. Consider the following issues before writing key personnel requirements:

- **Be careful about minimums.** Does the agency really need a project manager with a PhD and 20 years' experience? How would the source selection team evaluate an otherwise "perfect" candidate with two master's degrees?
- **Do market research regarding key personnel salaries.** Is the agency familiar with the salary range for an individual with the desired level of education and experience in the geographic area in question? If the market research isn't current, offerors' cost proposals might surprise the contracting officer.
- **Make sure experience expectations are realistic.** For example, don't ask for someone with 15 years of experience in the Microsoft Visual C# programming language, because the language hasn't been around that long.

Some agencies have specific key personnel clauses that require offerors to identify by name key personnel who will work on the contract. Under one of these clauses, removing or replacing key personnel generally requires advance notification, and the agency must approve the replacement in advance. The candidate replacement must meet the experience and education criteria the agency established for that position.

Agencies have to remember that they're not guaranteed an individual, but a set of qualifications.[9] For example, a company may have proposed Sue Blue as the program manager, but because of a delay in contract award, Sue Blue was assigned to work on another contract. Instead, Gene Green, who has the same level of experience and education as Sue Blue, will perform in her stead. Companies generally do not like to have their highly experienced and educated personnel charge an overhead account while awaiting contract award. If a company wins a contract from another agency while waiting to find out whether it will be awarded your agency's contract, some of the key personnel the company proposed may be placed on the other contract. This isn't bait and switch; it's business. To avoid the perception of bait and switch, some companies specifically state an expiration date for the availability of the key personnel named in their proposals. Typically, this expiration date is between 90 and 180 days after the proposal due date.

Security Subfactors

Offerors' security capabilities are usually evaluated for acquisitions involving classified material. Some contracts can be performed only by companies that have or can get the appropriate facility and personnel clearances. Facility clearances are necessary when contract performance requires the contractor to be able to store classified material at its facility. If the RFP contains classified information, the offeror may need to write the proposal in a cleared facility. Personnel clearances are required when contractor personnel need access to classified material during contract performance.

Agencies typically evaluate security first. If a company does not pass the agency's security evaluation, it is not eligible for award. Security is typically evaluated on a pass/fail basis. Agencies should ask the following questions about each offeror:

- Does the company have the required facilities and clearances?
- How many key personnel are already cleared?
- What is the offeror's approach for ensuring and maintaining compliance with and staying abreast of changes in the National Industrial Security Program Operating Manual?
- How has it performed in the past with regard to security training and reporting breaches?

Sometimes, a company may not need to have all of the personnel cleared on day one of contract performance, but in any case all contract parties should take into consideration the lengthy security clearance process, which can last six months or more, depending on the level of clearance required.[10]

We'll examine the details of the management proposal evaluation in Chapter 9.

Cost/Price Factors

The Competition in Contracting Act (CICA) requires that agencies include price or cost to the government as an evaluation factor in every source selection. Cost-related factors and considerations will vary depending on the type of contract. Regardless of contract type, however, cost reasonableness must always be a consideration, because the FAR requires that the government award contracts at prices or costs that are fair and reasonable.[11] The RFP must describe how evaluators will conduct cost or price analysis in accordance with FAR 15.404.

For fixed-price contracts, section M of the solicitation explains how the evaluators will analyze proposed prices. For cost-reimbursable contracts, section M states how evaluators will evaluate individual cost elements. For example, in acquisitions for which the requirement is clearly definable and the risk of unsuccessful contract performance is minimal, cost or price may play a primary role in source selection. The less definitive the requirement, the more development work required, or the greater the performance risk, the more technical or past performance considerations may play a primary role in source selection.

Cost analysis is the review and evaluation of the separate cost elements and profit in an offeror's or contractor's proposal (including cost or pricing data or information other than cost or pricing data), and the application of judgment to determine how well the proposed costs represent what the cost of the contract should be, assuming reasonable economy and efficiency. The government may use various cost analysis techniques and procedures to ensure a fair and reasonable price, given the circumstances of the acquisition. Such techniques and procedures include the following:

- Verifying cost or pricing data and evaluating cost elements, including:
  - Determining the necessity for, and reasonableness of, proposed costs, including allowances for contingencies
  - Projecting the offeror's cost trends, on the basis of current and historical cost or pricing data
  - Determining the reasonableness of estimates generated by appropriately calibrated and validated parametric models or cost-estimating relationships
  - Applying audited or negotiated indirect cost rates, labor rates, and cost of money or other factors. The cost of money rate for any cost accounting period is the arithmetic mean of the interest rates specified by the Secretary of the Treasury pursuant to Public Law 92-41 (85 Stat. 97). Where the cost of money must be determined on a prospective basis, the cost of money rate is based on the most recent available rate published by the Secretary of the Treasury.[12]
- Evaluating the effect of the offeror's current practices on future costs. In conducting this evaluation, the contracting officer shall ensure that the effects of inefficient or uneconomical past practices are not projected into the future. In pricing the production of recently developed complex equipment, the contracting officer should perform a trend analysis of basic labor and materials, even in periods of relative price stability.
- Comparing costs proposed by the offeror for individual cost elements with:
  - Actual costs previously incurred by the same offeror
  - Previous cost estimates from the offeror or from other offerors for the same or similar items
  - Other cost estimates received in response to the government's request
  - Independent government cost estimates by technical personnel
  - Forecasts of planned expenditures
  - Time phasing of costs for long-term contracts (to determine the effect of inflation)
  - Total contract value and supporting documentation.
- Verifying that the offeror's cost submissions are in accordance with the contract cost principles and procedures in FAR part 31 and, when applicable, the requirements and Cost Accounting Standards. Cost Accounting Standards are accounting

requirements designed to achieve uniformity and consistency in the cost accounting practices governing measurement, assignment, and allocation of costs to contracts with the United States government. See FAR Part 30 for applicability.

- Determining whether any cost or pricing data that are needed to make the contractor's proposal accurate, complete, and current have not been submitted or identified in writing by the contractor. If any such data is missing, the contracting officer shall attempt to obtain them and will then negotiate, either using them or making satisfactory allowance for the incomplete data.

- Analyzing the results of any make-or-buy program reviews in evaluating subcontract costs.[13]

A cost realism analysis is different from a cost analysis. A *cost realism analysis* is the process of independently reviewing and evaluating specific elements of each offeror's proposed cost estimate to determine whether the estimated proposed cost elements are realistic for the work to be performed, reflect a clear understanding of the requirements, and are consistent with the unique methods of performance and materials described in the offeror's technical proposal.[14] Some agencies evaluate realism by assessing the comparability of the proposed costs with the proposed scope of work and effort. Cost realism includes the validity of the costs and the government's confidence in the offeror's ability to perform the work within the cost estimate. Cost realism, or lack thereof, contributes to the agency assessment of how well the offeror understands the work required.

Thus, cost realism analysis and detailed cost analysis are different and can produce different results. A cost analysis could produce a determination that the proposed costs are reasonable for what the offeror proposes to do, while a cost realism analysis could indicate that the same offeror's proposed costs are not realistic because they don't match the proposed technical approach and the government requirement. In a cost analysis, the government evaluates detailed labor rates, labor categories, and projected rates to determine if they're reasonable. Cost realism evaluates the same costs in a different way. In cost realism analysis, the agency evaluates labor rates along with the level of the proposed personnel to determine if an employee at that level and labor rate can meet the government's requirement by doing the work proposed in the technical proposal.[15] In some cases, the offeror may propose too many senior personnel and not enough junior-level personnel to accomplish the work.

In addition to reasonableness and realism, some agencies also evaluate completeness of the cost proposal. The completeness evaluation assesses whether the offeror has provided cost data for all of the RFP's SOW requirements. The scope of work proposed may be compared with the SOW to determine whether all expected costs are included. To facilitate this evaluation, the cost proposal should trace the cost elements to the SOW requirements. The objective of the completeness evaluation is to provide the source selection authority (SSA) with the information he or she needs to select a contractor that is able to successfully perform all of the work at a reasonable cost.

We'll examine the details of cost proposal evaluation in Chapter 9.

PAST PERFORMANCE EVALUATION FACTORS

Recall from Chapter 1 that the Federal Acquisition Streamlining Act requires the government to include past performance as an evaluation factor. Past (and present) performance information is used to predict whether an offeror can fulfill the agency's current requirements. A past performance assessment evaluates the quality of the offeror's performance on current or completed contracts, allowing the government to determine the likelihood that the offeror will be able to successfully fulfill the agency's requirements.

The evaluation considers work comparable in size and scope to or related to the work required in the RFP. The RFP should solicit from offerors references to contracts they performed that were of similar size, scope, and magnitude to the work required in the RFP. The past performance evaluation should assess technical, cost, schedule, and management factors and focus on the risk areas identified in the acquisition plan.

In conducting a past performance evaluation, the government may use information provided in the offeror's proposal and data obtained from other sources. Often, agencies include a questionnaire in the RFP that offerors ask past and current customers to complete and return directly to the government. Contracting officers also may query past performance databases within their own agency or others.

Some agencies do not score the past performance volume (proposals are typically submitted in major sections called *volumes*), but use an adjectival or risk rating to evaluate past performance. In either case, section M of the solicitation should identify the rating system that will be used for past performance. The following describes past performance adjectival definitions that may be used in section M:

- **Excellent.** The offeror's performance has been exemplary. Past contract work was completed in a timely, efficient, and economical manner. Problems were very minor and had no adverse effect on overall performance. The offeror's experience is highly relevant to this procurement. Based on the offeror's performance record, there is a very high level of confidence that the offeror will successfully perform the required work.

- **Very good.** The offeror's performance has been very effective, and it was fully responsive to contract requirements, accomplishing them in a timely, efficient, and economical manner. Only minor problems existed, with little identifiable effect on overall performance. The offeror's experience is very relevant to this procurement. Based on the offeror's performance record, there is a high level of confidence that the offeror will successfully perform the required work.
- **Good.** The offeror's performance has been effective, and it was fully responsive to contract requirements. There were some problems, but they had little identifiable effect on overall performance. Its experience is relevant to this procurement. Based on the offeror's performance record, there is confidence that the offeror will successfully perform the required work.
- **Fair.** The offeror has met or slightly exceeded minimum acceptable standards, and its results have been adequate. There were some problems, with identifiable but not substantial effects on overall performance. The offeror's experience is at least somewhat relevant to this procurement. Based on the offeror's performance record, there is low confidence that the offeror will successfully perform the required work. Changes to the offeror's existing processes may be necessary in order to meet contract requirements.
- **Poor.** The offeror has not met minimum acceptable standards in one or more areas. There were problems in one or more areas that adversely affected overall performance. Based on the offeror's performance record, there is very low confidence that the offeror will successfully perform the required work.
- **Neutral.** The offeror does not have a record of relevant past performance, or information on past performance is not available. Offerors without past performance history may not be evaluated favorably or unfavorably (see FAR 15.305(a)(2)(ii) and (iv)).[16]

Now that readers understand the typical evaluation factors used in source selection, let's discuss how to use subfactors to help organize the evaluation process.

USING SUBFACTORS

A subfactor represents an important element of a primary evaluation factor. It is needed to explain the meaning and significance of the primary factor. Peter S. Cole writes, "A significant subfactor is one that could make a difference as a discriminator in the overall evaluation."[17] *Discriminators* are the elements in a proposal that differentiate one company's approach from another's.

FAR 15.304(b) requires that the contracting officer identify only significant subfactors in the RFP. This subjective restriction leads to the possibility of using unstated subfactors in the evaluation process, and doing so opens the door to potential protests from offerors. The case study below illustrates how unstated subfactors can lead to a protest.

CASE STUDY: UNSTATED EVALUATION FACTORS

Mnemonics, Inc., protested when the Department of the Army excluded its proposal from the competitive range based on unstated evaluation factors. Per Government Accountability Office (GAO) decision B-290961,

> The solicitation provided that proposals would be evaluated on the basis of technical, business, and past performance factors, and that technical factors were "of paramount importance."… Section M of the solicitation listed 17 technical evaluation factors, and explained that 14 of these 17 factors would be evaluated on a "pass/fail" basis. Then the proposals would be subjectively "graded" under the [three] remaining technical factors. … The solicitation also provided that an evaluation of "proposal risk" would be integrated into the rating of each technical evaluation factor.

Despite the pass/fail statement in the RFP, the agency also performed a qualitative assessment of proposal "strengths," "weaknesses," and "deficiencies" related to each of the 14 pass/fail factors.

> While acknowledging that Mnemonics' proposal met every stated requirement under each of the "pass/fail" factors, the agency evaluated Mnemonics' proposal as reflecting certain "weaknesses" and "deficiencies" under these factors. Most significantly, the agency assessed a "major deficiency" in evaluating Mnemonics' proposal under one of the "pass/fail" factors.
>
> [Although agencies have broad discretion to select the evaluation criteria,] they are required to disclose all evaluation factors and significant subfactors, along with their relative importance, in order for offerors to meaningfully compete on an equal basis. … An agency may not induce offerors to prepare and submit proposals based on one premise, then make source selection decisions based on another. … Accordingly, once offerors are informed of the evaluation criteria against which proposals will be evaluated, the agency must adhere to the stated criteria, or inform all offerors of all significant changes… Offerors are provided an opportunity to amend their proposals based on these changes.
>
> Here, the agency clearly advised offerors that proposals would be evaluated under 14 of the 17 technical evaluation factors based on an objective assessment as to whether or not they met the stated performance requirements. The agency's stated basis of evaluation for these factors was specifically described in contrast to the subjective grading by which the remaining three technical factors would be evaluated. Notwithstanding these publicly stated ground rules for the competition, the agency proceeded to make

qualitative distinctions between the two proposals based on factors which were neither disclosed, nor reasonably subsumed within the stated requirements.

Despite the undisputed fact that Mnemonics' proposal met the solicitation's stated requirements, the agency concluded that one aspect of Mnemonics' proposal rendered its proposal "deficient" because this approach was "a significant departure from the intent of the government." … On this basis alone[,] the GAO found that the agency applied an unstated evaluation factor. The agency asserts that, by advising offerors of the agency's intent to perform a "proposal risk" assessment, the agency fulfilled its obligation to disclose all of the evaluation criteria that it subsequently applied.

The comptroller general disagreed, asserting,

While agencies are not required to identify each and every individual element encompassed within a stated evaluation factor/subfactor, unstated individual elements must be reasonably subsumed within the stated factors/subfactors. This was not the case here. Specifically, nothing in the solicitation's stated requirements reasonably put offerors on notice that a proposal would be evaluated as contrary to the "intent of the government" and that such a proposal would be evaluated as containing a "major deficiency."

Additionally, the agency's assessment of "strengths" under the "pass/fail" evaluation factors was inconsistent with the solicitation statement that proposals would be evaluated against the stated performance requirements on a "pass/fail" basis. Nothing in the solicitation reasonably notified offerors that, in addition to evaluating whether or not a proposal met the stated "pass/fail" requirements, proposals would be credited with "strengths" for exceeding those requirements in various undisclosed ways. Offerors whose proposals were excluded from the competitive range might have proposed enhancements had they been advised of the agency's intent in this regard.

The GAO decision concluded that the "agency's failure to disclose its intent created an unfair competition." The additional adjectival ratings beyond the pass/fail scenario described in the RFP constituted an unstated subfactor. This unstated subfactor was significant because it was a discriminator, leading to excluding Mnemonics from the competitive range.[18]

Cole writes,

Over the years, the Comptroller General has ruled that two things should be considered with respect to unstated evaluation subfactors:

1. A subfactor, significant in terms of its relative importance in the evaluation, must be identified in the RFP. A significant subfactor is a discriminator, in that its assessment could make a difference in the evaluation results.

2. A subfactor inherently related to the prime factor, to the extent that offerors could reasonably be expected to anticipate that the subfactor would be evaluated, need not be specifically identified in the RFP.

Although the comptroller general states that agencies are not required to reveal such subfactors, the contracting officer is not prohibited from doing so. Cole notes, "Failing to list subfactors not only leaves the primary evaluation factor incomplete, but makes the acquisition subject to potential protest for unstated evaluation subfactors."[19]

Now that readers understand typical evaluation factors and subfactors, let's explain *how* an agency selects them. The government has a great deal of flexibility regarding its use of these factors.

SELECTING EVALUATION FACTORS

Although the FAR identifies required evaluation factors, *how* the agencies use these factors varies with each agency and with each acquisition within an agency. The evaluation team should select evaluation criteria that reflect key attributes relevant to the acquisition and that are expected to allow a reasonable level of discrimination between offerors. When establishing evaluation factors, the evaluation team should ask two questions:

- What are the critical areas of the statement of work that we need to evaluate to determine if an offeror can perform the contract?
- What information do we need from an offeror to evaluate its proposal?

The answers to these questions form the preliminary basis for determining the RFP's evaluation criteria.[20] Of course, the evaluation factors the contracting officer selects depend on the specific nature of the acquisition. Because all acquisitions vary, it is not a good idea to just copy evaluation factors from similar acquisitions.

Effective evaluation factors are:

- **Consistent.** The technical evaluation factors must agree with the statement of work or specifications. The statement of work or specifications must accurately identify the agency's requirements, and in turn, the evaluation factors establish the basis for how the agency will measure each offeror's proposal against these requirements. Tracking or checking evaluation factors against the statement of work is called *mapping*.
- **Limited in number.** Avoid the temptation to generate too many evaluation factors. A large number of factors dilutes the relative importance of the most important ones. Also, having a very large number of factors may lead to overlap and increase the time it takes to complete proposal evaluations. Delete the factors that

are not important enough to influence the source selection. Remember to allow sufficient time in the schedule to evaluate each factor.

- **Independent.** Evaluation factors must not overlap one another. For example, "evidence of successful completion on similar projects" and "applicable project experience" are nearly the same factor. Eliminate or consolidate factors that assess the same thing.

- **Relevant.** An evaluation factor may be valid (meaning that it measures what it is supposed to measure) without being relevant to the source selection. For example, in a source selection for services, it doesn't make sense to ask for experience in manufacturing. To determine relevance of the factor ask, "Does this factor really impact the evaluation?"[21]

After compiling a list of candidate evaluation criteria, the team should review the criteria to make sure they really belong in the source selection. It is important not to take any evaluation factor at face value. The contracting officer must ensure that each evaluation factor or subfactor is critiqued and analyzed to ensure that it is reliable, valid, and relevant. Per the Federal Acquisition Institute:[22]

- **Check for reliability.** A reliable factor is one which can be applied consistently by the source selection evaluators in a uniform manner to rate each proposal the same way with minimum variation among the evaluators. If two evaluators provide widely different ratings to the same factor on the same proposal, it could mean there's a problem with that factor. A major problem with the reliability of an evaluation factor or subfactor is that the language used to describe it may be subject to different interpretation. For this reason, be careful to avoid using language that is vague, ambiguous, or subject to different interpretation by evaluators. For example, the following words and phrases do not belong in evaluation criteria.

  - *Any, either, and/or*
  - *As needed, as required*
  - *Satisfactory* (unless defined).

Check for validity. A valid factor is one that measures what it is supposed to measure. For example, if there is a 'subcontract management' evaluation factor in the management area, then evaluating the subcontractor's past performance is not a valid measurement of the prime's subcontract management. Although evaluating a subcontractor's past performance is valid for the past performance volume, it doesn't answer the risk of how well the prime contractor manages subcontractors. There needs to be a logical connection between the evaluation factor and the risk the agency needs to mitigate or the acquisition priority it needs to emphasize. The factor should be predictive of an offeror's ability to satisfy the government's requirement.

- **Check for relevance.** A relevant factor is one that belongs in the source selection. For example, if the agency will award a contract for computer programming, the contracting officer should question the relevancy of an evaluation factor that is not related to computer programming.

Developing evaluation criteria should be a group effort for the evaluation team. The evaluators should participate in developing the criteria because they will be the ones making judgments about the proposals. Thus, their acceptance and understanding of the criteria and standards are very important.

Before developing the evaluation criteria, the evaluation team should review the goals identified in the acquisition plan. After reviewing the acquisition's goals and the statement of work, the evaluation team begins outlining potential evaluation criteria. Generally, the evaluation team separates evaluation criteria into two main groups: cost and non-cost. Figure 3-1 illustrates the structure using this approach.

Evaluation criteria should be tailored to the specific characteristics of a program, and only those that will affect the source selection decision should be included. For example, if the market research shows that all prospective offerors have established facilities and are producing high-quality products, then evaluating an offeror's facilities and production processes isn't going to help your team differentiate the proposals. In this case, facility and product quality are not effective discriminators.

To determine what to evaluate, go back to the acquisition plan's risk assessment. Here, the contracting officer can apply the results of the painful planning process to something that really matters: evaluation criteria. If the risk assessment indicates that the subcontractor management risk is high, then subcontractor management should be included as evaluation criteria in the management and past performance evaluation. Focus on "evaluation factors and significant subfactors that point out the differences rather than the similarities between the proposals."[23] One way to assess a potential evaluation factor is to ask: "Will superiority in this factor provide value to the government, and are we willing to pay more for that superiority?"[24]

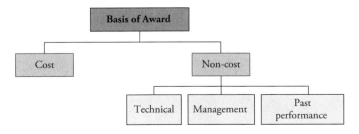

Figure 3-1 Evaluation Criteria Structure

Beware of the temptation to copy and paste evaluation criteria from another RFP, even if the criteria are for a similar requirement. As market research should show, since that RFP was issued, it's probable that technology or the economy has changed; new companies may have entered the marketplace, or perhaps companies have left the marketplace or merged. Any of these events will affect the competition and thus the evaluation criteria, even if the requirement is similar to an old one.

Brainstorming Evaluation Criteria

One method used to select evaluation criteria is gathering the key players in the same room to brainstorm potential criteria. The possible criteria are then categorized into logical groups. The following are effective brainstorming methods for selecting evaluation criteria:

- **Use sticky notes to collect ideas about potential criteria.** Participants propose evaluation factors by writing each one on a note and sticking the notes on a flip chart or wall. This activity continues until participants don't have any more ideas. One advantage of this method is that it's anonymous. It also prevents a strong personality from taking over and dictating to the group; using this method, everyone's ideas have equal weight.
- **Round robin** is a simple method in which each person in turn calls out an idea, and a recorder writes down all of the suggestions. This method may not work as well if some participants have strong personalities or are very shy and won't call out their ideas. Some of the benefits of brainstorming will be lost if the shy people won't participate or are bullied by the strong personalities. To avoid this, some groups use a random call method, in which a facilitator randomly calls on individuals to contribute ideas. Some participants don't like this method because it puts them on the spot.

Some agencies use electronic collaborative software to collect ideas. The evaluators and acquisition team members participating in the evaluation criteria selection process type in potential evaluation criteria, and then they categorize the ideas into logical groups. This method is also anonymous and has the added advantage of making documentation easier because the participants type the data directly into the computer.

No matter what method the team uses, members should hold comments and criticisms until the group documents all of the proposed evaluation criteria. Experienced group facilitators can encourage a fast pace to foster high energy and an "anything goes" environment. A fast pace minimizes time for self-evaluation and self-censorship. At this early stage, collecting a long list of potential criteria is a good thing. We'll discuss limiting the evaluation criteria later in this chapter.

Grouping Evaluation Factors

At this stage, the evaluation team discusses the ideas collected, merges duplicate ideas, and discards ideas that are not important or are not discriminators. The next step is to create categories or groupings of factors. Begin by selecting an idea that represents an overarching concept, such as program management. Under this category, place other ideas that are related, such as subcontract management. Continue to create categories as needed to store ideas. Some typical categories might be hardware, software, transition, key personnel, systems engineering, software development, planning, and resources.

After the evaluation team determines the main categories for the evaluation criteria, the next step is to arrange them. Continuing with the example above, the evaluation team might take hardware and software and put them into a group called "computer." Engineering and transition are put into a group called "system integration." Computer and system integration are placed into a group called "technical/ management." Finally, planning and resources are grouped under a category called "program management." Using this method helps to create a hierarchical model of evaluation areas, items, and factors, as shown in Figure 3-2.

As stated above, the SOW is the basis for the evaluation criteria. Thus, there should be at least one evaluation factor or significant subfactor for each supply item, service, or specification for which the agency wants to distinguish the advantages and disadvantages among the proposals. Ask yourself, "Is there an evaluation factor to evaluate this requirement?" If not, the contracting officer must generate an evaluation factor or significant subfactor. All requirements must be evaluated, but a single factor can cover multiple requirements (or aspects of the requirements). For example, if the SOW calls for delivery of a service, is there an evaluation factor to measure how well, how soon, or how frequently that service will be provided?

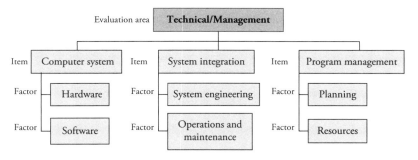

Figure 3-2 Evaluation Criteria Model

In addition, the contracting officer should make sure the evaluation factors are consistent with the solicitation requirements. For example, if an evaluation factor calls for "offeror experience," check the SOW to make sure the requirement for such experience is justified. Ask yourself, "What are the likely problem areas in this type of procurement?" Does it require new or untried technology? Will it be hard to manage? Is it difficult to predict costs or performance? [25]

Now let's explore how to structure evaluation factors in a logical manner and limit them to the ones that have the most impact.

DISTINGUISHING EFFECTIVE EVALUATION FACTORS

Effective evaluation factors distinguish meaningful differences between proposals. So how does the evaluation team determine which potential evaluation factors are going to be the most effective?

Structuring Evaluation Criteria Using a Work Breakdown Structure

Some organizations use a work breakdown structure to help describe the evaluation factors. A WBS is developed by subdividing a process, product, project, or service into its major work elements. It is a hierarchical approach to describing the elements of a project. Each major element is then broken down into smaller and smaller elements. A WBS defines the total effort and shows participants the big picture by defining the contract's objectives as tangible, measurable deliverables. The WBS thus becomes the principal communication tool for both government and industry. Structuring the evaluation criteria using a WBS helps ensure that the evaluation team addresses all of the contract's major elements. The contracting officer may also want to use the WBS to structure the proposal preparation instructions for the offeror's cost volume.

Figure 3-3 illustrates a sample work breakdown structure for an acquisition training class.

The top box in Figure 3-3 symbolizes the ultimate product or service required: the training class itself. The four numbered boxes below the top box represent the major components that make up the end product or service:

1. Developing course materials
2. Preparing instructors
3. Managing facilities and logistics
4. Managing the project.

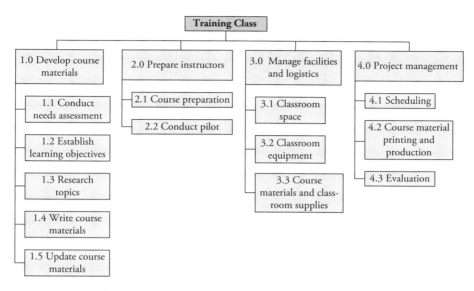

Figure 3-3   Sample WBS: Acquisition Training Class

These four components can be divided into overarching technical and management evaluation criteria:

- Technical
  - Developing course materials
  - Preparing instructors
- Management
  - Managing facilities and logistics
  - Managing the project.

The next step is to establish evaluation factors for these major components of the project. The elements shown below each component further subdivide the effort into discrete tasks. In Table 3-1, each of these four WBS components is matched up with typical evaluation factors—cost, quality, and past performance—for both technical and management factors.

Now let's categorize the possible evaluation factors into logical groupings: cost, quality, and past performance. First readers can see that reasonable, complete, and realistic cost spans all of the major WBS elements, so it makes sense to combine it into one overarching cost evaluation factor. Similarly, past performance spans all of the WBS elements, so it can also be its own evaluation factor.

Next, let's consider what's left over: the quality factors. Although quality is an evaluation factor for both technical and management areas, they can be separated into technical quality and management quality or kept together. If the acquisition is complex, requiring

Table 3-1 Sample Evaluation Factors for Acquisition Training Class

Technical Factors	Cost	Quality	Quality	Past Performance
Developing course materials	Reasonable, complete, and realistic cost.	Course material must be current and accurate, including agency policies and FAR citations.	Updating and revising the course materials to stay current with regulatory changes.	Past experience in delivering acquisition training on a nationwide scale.
Instructors	Reasonable, complete, and realistic cost.	Instructors know agency acquisition regulations and policies.	Instructors can teach using student-centered instructional techniques.	Instructor past performance in acquisition training as determined from actual student evaluations.

Management Factors	Cost	Quality	Quality	Past Performance
Managing the project	Reasonable, complete, and realistic cost.	Established process for identifying and correcting performance problems.	Demonstrated effectiveness in evaluating instructor performance	Past performance in managing a program of similar size and scope.
Managing facilities and logistics	Reasonable, complete, and realistic cost.	Demonstrated ability to obtain adequate classroom space.	Demonstrated effectiveness in printing and delivering course materials.	Experience ensuring classrooms have necessary supplies.

separate technical and management proposal volumes, then the quality evaluation factors can be separated into technical quality and management quality. If, on the other hand, the acquisition is less complex where the technical and management proposal volumes are combined, then these evaluation factors may be grouped into a single factor called *quality.*

The source selection evaluation team should link these non-cost evaluation criteria to the critical aspects of the acquisition—the high-value and high-risk areas. (These critical areas should be documented in the acquisition plan.) If we structure this using an outline, it would look like Figure 3-4.

Figure 3-5 takes a graphical approach to correlating the WBS to evaluation factors.

Now that readers understand how to link the evaluation factors to the WBS, the next step is to decide if the agency really needs all of the factors. Remember: More isn't better. More evaluation factors can dilute the importance of the ones that really matter, so it's important to take the time to narrow the field down to the most critical.

1. Cost
   1.1.   Reasonable
   1.2.   Complete
   1.3.   Realistic

2. Past performance
   2.1.   Experience delivering acquisition training on a nationwide scale
   2.2.   Instructor past performance as documented in actual student evaluations
   2.3.   Managing a program of similar size and scope
   2.4.   Experience ensuring classrooms have necessary supplies

3. Technical
   3.1.   Course material is current and accurate
   3.2.   Updating and revising the course material to stay current with regulatory changes
   3.3.   Instructors are familiar with agency acquisition regulations and policies
   3.4.   Instructors use student-centered instructional techniques

4. Management
   4.1.   Project management
          4.1.1.   Established process for identifying and correcting performance problems
          4.1.2.   Demonstrated effectiveness evaluating instructors
   4.2.   Facilities and logistics
          4.2.1.   Demonstrated ability to obtain adequate classroom space
          4.2.2.   Demonstrated effectiveness in printing and delivering course material

Figure 3-4   Correlating the WBS to Evaluation Factors

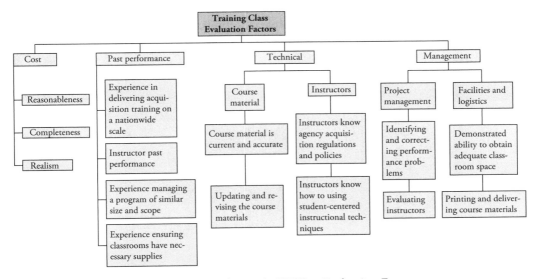

Figure 3-5   Correlating the WBS to Evaluation Factors

Limiting Evaluation Factors

Once the evaluation team selects the evaluation criteria, it must review the criteria and limit the final selection to those that are critical to the acquisition. Evaluating every possible risk will bog down the process and dilute the importance of the essential criteria.

Use the risk analysis in your acquisition plan to decide which evaluation criteria to include. Identify the risks that could have a significant effect on contract performance, and plot them according to their likelihood of occurrence and their impact on program success. Figure 3-6 illustrates this approach.

The *x*-axis depicts the likelihood of a risk occurring, and the *y*-axis depicts the effects on contract performance if this risk should occur. Risks with the highest probability of occurrence should be plotted in the upper right quadrant; the least probable risks, on the left side of the graph. Plot high-impact risks with a low likelihood of occurrence in the upper left quadrant. Plot low-impact risks with a low likelihood of occurrence in the lower left quadrant. There will always be risks, such as technological failure, that could have a catastrophic effect on contract performance, but how likely is it that this will actually happen? Such an event would have a major impact on contract performance, but because the possibility that it will actually occur is minimal, the plot is on the upper left—the low likelihood—part of the graph.

After you have plotted the risks, focus on the ones that are in the upper right quadrant or the right side of the upper left quadrant. These risks are the ones that would have a major impact on contract performance and that are most likely to occur. They fall into the shaded area on the graph. These risks are good candidates for evaluation criteria, as are risks that are related. Evaluation factors can address groups of smaller risks. The contracting officer may eliminate any evaluation criteria that address the outliers—risks that are unlikely and those that would not have a significant effect on contract success.

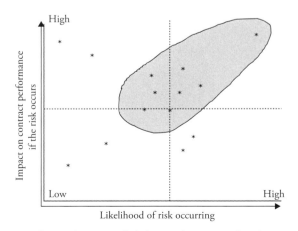

Figure 3-6   Probability and Impact of Risk

How can evaluators determine if offerors have adequately addressed the evaluation factors in their proposals? That's where standards come in. Evaluators use standards to measure each proposal against a set baseline.

Writing Evaluation Standards

The agency's proposal evaluators must determine the relative merit of each proposal with regard to the evaluation factors. Many agencies use standards to accomplish this objective in a consistent manner. *Standards* are the baseline against which an agency evaluates offerors' proposals to determine their acceptability and value. Evaluation standards provide consistent guides to help evaluators measure how well a proposal addresses each factor identified in the solicitation. Standards also require evaluators to evaluate proposals against uniform objectives rather than against other proposals. The use of evaluation standards minimizes any inadvertent bias that may occur from comparing proposals against each other. Applying evaluation standards has the added advantage of promoting consistency by ensuring that the evaluators judge each proposal against the same baseline.

Standards can be qualitative or quantitative. A *quantitative standard* relates to a measurement of quantity. For example, buying specialized equipment might require applying a quantitative standard if the equipment's speed or volume is critical to meeting the agency's requirements. The following language describes a quantitative standard applied to a hypothetical technical factor called "operating speed":

> This standard is met when the pump can pump 500 gallons per minute for a period of at least five hours of continuous operation without shutting down or requiring operator maintenance during an acceptance test.

If the pump cannot produce 500 gallons per minute, then it fails to meet the standard. A pump that meets the operating speed requirement could be awarded a satisfactory rating. A pump that exceeds the minimum operating speed could be awarded extra points or a greater degree of merit.

On the other hand, a *qualitative standard* relates to quality or kind. It does not relate specifically to quantity. The following language describes a qualitative standard applied to a hypothetical factor called "compliance with quality control program":

> This standard is met when the offeror provides evidence of a functioning quality control (QC) program. The offeror's QC program may be subject to a formal evaluation or random audit by representatives from this agency's office of quality assurance. This agency will use the American National Standards Institute's general requirements for a quality control program to evaluate the offeror's QC program.

Another example of a qualitative standard might be for experience in hazardous waste training:

> This standard shall be met when the offeror provides evidence of a documented in-house training program for the handling, transport, and disposal of hazardous waste in accordance with EPA and state guidelines and regulations.[26]

While quantitative standards are easier to develop because of their definitive nature, qualitative standards are commonly used for source selection. Quantitative standards are usually included in hardware and software acquisitions, and qualitative standards are commonly used in service acquisitions.

The evaluation team should consider the following guidelines when developing standards for each evaluation factor:

- Each standard should contain only one metric or measurement. Multiple metrics in one standard can cause confusion and misinterpretation by the evaluators. Hint: if the standard contains the word "and," it probably has more than one metric.
- A description of a standard should specify a target performance level that the proposed solution must achieve.
- Do not write a standard that is so high that no proposal can meet it. Likewise, do not write a standard that all proposals will exceed.
- Avoid overly general standards; they make obtaining consensus among evaluators very difficult.
- Do not write standards that allow an offeror to meet the standard merely by addressing the topic in its proposal. For example, a standard should not merely require offerors to submit staffing plans in their proposals. If all offerors include a staffing plan, then everyone meets the standard, but the standard would not allow for meaningful discrimination between the proposals because it does not address the *quality* of the staffing plan.
- Standards are not normally included in a solicitation, though doing so is not prohibited by regulation. Including standards in an RFP gives offerors a "recipe"; some may write a proposal to the standards, even if they cannot actually perform at that level.
- Standards should be used only to evaluate the acceptability of a proposed solution to a stated requirement, not to create a new requirement.

Writing standards is a challenging part of source selection. Previous source selection plans might provide guidance on standards that can be tailored to the current acquisition. Again, avoid the temptation to copy and paste from another source selection plan.

Determining what constitutes "meets the standard" is very difficult. It's a good idea to have evaluators help write the standards so they understand what the standards mean before they must apply them.

The following examples include typical evaluation factors and standards for assessing offerors' personnel, program management, and past performance.

1. **Personnel factor.** This factor addresses the suitability of the personnel that the offeror has proposed and its plans for continuing to provide and manage a qualified workforce.

   1.1. **Skill mix standard.** This standard is met when the offeror proposes and justifies a cadre of personnel whose skills, expertise, and experience are appropriate for meeting the requirements of the SOW.

   1.2. **Providing qualified personnel standard.** This standard is met when the offeror has an acceptable approach for providing personnel who have the minimum skills and qualifications required to meet SOW and other program requirements.

2. **Program management factor.** This factor evaluates the quality of the offeror's response and the evidence of the extent to which the offeror's proposal will help achieve the program office's objectives and help it accomplish its mission.

   2.1. **Program management planning standard.** This standard is met when the offeror demonstrates the ability to develop and execute program tasks required in the SOW in accordance with a detailed program management plan. The offeror should show the ability to reallocate resources or recommend modifications as necessary to best achieve required capabilities using the time and resources available.

   2.2. **Customer service orientation standard.** This standard is met when the offeror provides evidence of the ability to be accessible and responsive in managing the contract. The offeror's proposed approaches to resolving problems, interacting with government contract and program management officials, and providing timely information about the management and performance of its contract should be examined.

   2.3. **Managing subcontractors standard.** This standard is met when the offeror provides a subcontractor management plan that describes the roles and responsibilities of each subcontractor and independent consultant. The plan should detail the management mechanisms that will promote effective communication with subcontractors and that will ensure the subcontractors' technical contribution to the program.

3. **Past performance factor.** This factor assesses the offeror's performance on contracts (current or completed within the last three years) of similar size and scope to the work that will be performed under this contract. Based on the quality of

the offeror's past or current work, the government establishes its level of confidence that the offeror will be able to successfully fulfill the agency's objectives. The following points will be considered in assessing the offeror's ability to perform the contract successfully:

3.1. **Management performance standard.** The offeror's past performance on similar, relevant efforts must indicate that those efforts were managed well within cost and schedule, with risk effectively mitigated, and that all requirements were met as proposed.

3.2. **Technical performance standard.** The offeror shall demonstrate that past performance and experience on similar, relevant efforts resulted in providing services that met the technical requirements of the contract.

3.3. **Cost control performance standard.** The offeror's past performance and experience on similar, relevant efforts must show that it was able to manage and control costs within the negotiated contract value, provide accurate and timely cost estimates and reports, and provide a cost plan consistent with the requirements outlined in the SOW.[27]

When evaluating proposals, evaluators assess individual proposals against each standard to determine if each proposal meets the standard, is above the standard, or is below the standard. Grading the strengths and weaknesses allows for finer distinctions. Many agencies use plusses and minuses to designate the degree to which a proposal exceeds or falls below the standard; see Table 3-2 for an example of this grading system.

EVALUATING RISK

After evaluators have determined how well the proposals meet the requirements, there's another element to consider: the risk that a company cannot do what it promises in its proposal. *Risk* is a measure of the inability to achieve overall program objectives within defined cost, schedule, and technical constraints. It has

Table 3-2   Grading Proposals against Evaluation Standards

Strengths	Weaknesses
+ Minor strength: Slightly above standards/expectations.	− Minor weakness: Slightly below standards/expectations.
++ Major strength: Clearly above standards/expectations.	−− Major weakness: Clearly below standards/expectations.
+++ Significant strength: Significantly above standards/expectations.	−− Significant weakness: Significantly below standards/expectations.

two components: (1) the *probability* of failing to achieve a particular outcome and (2) the *consequences/impacts* of failing to achieve that outcome. For processes, risk is a measure of the difference between actual performance of a process and the known best practice for performing that process.[28]

There are many types of risk to consider in a source selection: technical, cost, schedule, proposal, and performance risk.

- **Technical risk.** This is the risk associated with the design and production of the offeror's solution. It affects the level of performance necessary to meet the requirements. The contractor's and subcontractors' design, test, and production processes influence the technical risk and the nature of the product.
- **Cost risk.** This is the risk associated with the ability of the program to achieve its life cycle cost objectives. Two risk areas that affect cost are:
  - The accuracy and reasonableness of the cost estimates and objectives
  - The risk that program execution will not meet the cost objectives as the result of failure to handle cost, schedule, and performance risks.
- **Schedule risk.** These risks are those associated with the adequacy of the time estimated and allocated for developing, producing, and fielding the system. Two risk areas that affect schedule are:
  - The accuracy and reasonableness of the schedule estimates and objectives
  - The risk that program execution will fall short of the schedule objectives as a result of failure to handle cost, schedule, or performance risks.[29]
- **Proposal risk.** This refers to the risk associated with the offeror's proposed approach to meeting the government's cost, schedule, and performance requirements. Evaluating proposal risk includes assessing the proposed time and resources and recommended adjustments. This assessment is done according to the definitions and evaluation standards developed for the source selection.[30]
- **Performance risk.** A performance risk assessment evaluates the contractor's past and present performance record to establish a level of confidence in the contractor's ability to perform the proposed effort. This evaluation is not limited to technical issues and may include assessing the company's financial viability.[31]

Typically, past performance data from similar contracts are the data source for the performance risk rating. At a minimum, the solicitation should clearly state that the agency will conduct a performance risk assessment based on the past performance of the offerors and their proposed major subcontractors as it relates to the probability of successfully performing the solicitation requirements. The solicitation should also clearly describe the approach evaluators will use to evaluate past performance. The RFP must explain:

- What past performance information the agency will evaluate
- How the agency will evaluate the past performance
- The weight or relative importance of past performance compared with other evaluation factors and subfactors
- How the agency will evaluate offerors with no past performance history.

Agencies should tailor the amount of information they request from offerors to the circumstances of the acquisition. The amount should be reasonable and should not impose excessive burdens on offerors or evaluators. In conducting the performance risk assessment, the government may use data provided by the offeror and data obtained from other sources. While the government may elect to consider data obtained from other sources, the burden of providing thorough and complete past performance information rests with the offeror.

The proposal submission instructions must, as a minimum, instruct offerors to submit recent and relevant information concerning contracts and subcontracts (including federal, state, and local government and private industry) that demonstrates their ability to perform the proposed effort.

Using an Adjectival Scale for Risk Assessment

Table 3-3 illustrates one way to assess risk: using an adjectival scale that correlates past performance with risk level. Note that the higher the rating on the left, the lower the risk on the right.

Table 3-3   Adjectival Risk Evaluation Scale[32]

Adjective	Definition	Associated Risk Level
Excellent	Essentially no doubt exists that the offeror will successfully perform the required effort based on its performance record.	Very low
Good	Little doubt exists that the offeror will successfully perform the required effort based on its performance record.	Low
Adequate	Some doubt exists that the offeror will successfully perform the required effort based on its performance record.	Moderate
Marginal	Significant doubt exists that the offeror will successfully perform the required effort based on its performance record.	High
Poor	It is extremely doubtful that the offeror will successfully perform the required effort based on its performance record.	Very high
Unknown	The offeror has little or no relevant past performance history upon which to base a meaningful performance risk prediction.	=Unknown

Mitigating Risk

Effective risk assessment is important for ensuring a successful best value source selection. Certain risks may be inherent in a program by virtue of the program objectives relative to the available technology. Risks may arise from any one of the following factors, or a combination of them:

- The proposed technical approach
- The proposed manufacturing plan
- The proposed materials, processes, and equipment
- The proposed costs, schedules, and economic impacts associated with the approach.

In major programs, certain risks may already exist when the agency releases the RFP. In this case, the agency should ask for a risk mitigation plan in section L of the RFP and should identify how it will evaluate the risk mitigation plan in section M of the RFP. This approach gives offerors an opportunity to identify how they can manage the inherent risk, and the agency can then evaluate each offeror's approach. The risk assessment should address the acceptability of the proposed solution, rather than placing undue emphasis on the existence of a risk. When assessing the solution, evaluators must consider both the approach proposed and the alternatives available to manage the risks. Evaluation teams should ensure that the cost/price team is aware of the risk and should help the team determine any resulting cost impact.[33]

Performance Confidence Assessment Technique

Another approach to assessing risk is the performance confidence assessment technique, which the U.S. Air Force requires for acquisitions over $100 million. This technique evaluates the government's confidence in the offeror's ability to fulfill the solicitation requirements while meeting schedule, budget, and performance quality constraints (see Table 3-4). The past performance evaluation considers each offeror's demonstrated record of performance in supplying products and services that meet users' needs. The performance confidence rating is normally an overall rating determined after aspects of the offeror's recent past performance, particularly those that are relevant to the mission capability subfactors and cost or price, are evaluated.[34] This integrated performance confidence assessment rating is based on combined recency, relevance, and performance ratings for each of the projects.

Offerors without a record of relevant past performance or for whom information on past performance is not available or is so sparse that no confidence assessment

Table 3-4 Performance Confidence Assessment Ratings[35]

Rating	Description
Substantial confidence	Based on the offeror's performance record, the government has a high expectation that the offeror will successfully perform the required work.
Satisfactory confidence	Based on the offeror's performance record, the government has an expectation that the offeror will successfully perform the required work.
Limited confidence	Based on the offeror's performance record, the government has a low expectation that the offeror will successfully perform the required work.
No confidence	Based on the offeror's performance record, the government has no expectation that the offeror will be able to successfully perform the required work.
Unknown confidence	No performance record is identifiable, or the offeror's performance record is so sparse that no confidence assessment rating can be reasonably assigned.

rating can be reasonably assigned will not be evaluated favorably or unfavorably on past performance. They will receive an "unknown confidence" rating for the past performance factor.

A strong record of relevant past performance may be considered more advantageous to the government than an "unknown confidence" rating. Likewise, a more relevant past performance record may receive a higher confidence rating and be considered more favorably than a less relevant record of favorable performance.[36]

The U.S. Navy uses a similar approach: the level of confidence assessment rating (LOCAR). The government will assign a LOCAR to the capability of each acceptable offeror. The LOCAR is based on an evaluation of relevant corporate experience, personnel resources, past performance and the offeror's understanding of the work. The following is an excerpt from a Navy RFP that describes the LOCAR process:

> The Government will award this contract to the offeror submitting an acceptable proposal that represents the best overall value to the Government based on the Level of Confidence Assessment Rating (LOCAR) process. The government will use our assessment of your capability to develop a LOCAR. The LOCAR will reflect our subjective assessment of the likelihood that you will keep your promises to comply with the terms and conditions of this solicitation. Our LOCAR will be an important consideration in the source selection decision.

Table 3-5 shows the rating scale for the LOCAR.

Table 3-6 shows a sample rating scenario for five offerors.

The government will use the LOCAR to determine which proposal represents the best overall value. Table 3-7 shows the rating process used to establish best overall value.

Table 3-5 LOCAR Rating Scale

Less confident (less likely to succeed)	Neutral (equally likely to succeed or fail)	More confident (more likely to succeed)	Most confident (most likely to succeed)
Low − / Low / Low +	Moderate	High − / High	High +

Table 3-6 Sample LOCARs Indicating Offeror Capability

Offeror	Under-standing of the work	Transition plan	Imple-mentation plan	Personnel resources	Relevant corporate experience	Past per-formance	LOCAR
A	Excellent	Excellent	Excellent	Good	Good	Good	High +
B	Good	Excellent	Good	Good	Good	Good	High
C	Good	None	Good	Poor	Good	Good	Moderate
D*							None
E	Poor	Good	Poor	Good	Poor	Poor	Low+

*Offeror D's submission is unacceptable, so no LOCAR is assigned.

Table 3-7 LOCAR and Best Overall Value

Offeror	LOCAR	Price/cost and fee (based on cost realism evaluation)
A	High +	$52 million
B	High	$49 million
C	Moderate	$56 million
D*	None	$54 million
E	Low+	$53 million

* Offeror D's submission is unacceptable, so no LOCAR is assigned.

The government makes a series of paired comparisons between the offerors, trading off the differences in the non-price factors against the difference in most probable cost and proposed fees between the members of each pair.

If, in any paired comparison of any two offerors, one offeror has both the higher LOCAR and the lower price, then that offeror is the best overall value. If one offeror has the higher LOCAR and the higher price, then the government must decide whether the margin of the higher LOCAR (indicating a greater probability of success) is worth the higher price. The government will continue to make paired comparisons in this way until it decides which offeror represents the best value.[37]

Case Study: Risk Assessment

Colmek Systems Engineering, Inc., protested the Navy's award of a contract to RD Instruments (RDI) for the production, delivery, and support of an underwater imaging system to be used by the Navy's explosive ordnance disposal forces. Colmek argued that the Navy improperly evaluated its proposal.

The Navy assigned a LOCAR to each offeror's capability (including relevant experience and past performance) using a scale that indicated the degree of confidence the Navy had in each firm's ability to succeed. The level of confidence rating was subjective. It reflected the degree to which the Navy believed an offeror was likely to keep the promises it made in its offer. The Navy also determined each offeror's expected value by multiplying its technical approach score by its LOCAR. The expected value was expressed as a percentage. The results of the Navy's evaluation of Colmek's and RDI's proposals are shown in Tables 3-8 and 3-9.

To determine which offeror represented the best value to the government, the Navy made a series of paired comparisons among the offerors, trading off the differences in the non-price factors against the difference in most probable price between the offerors. If the offeror with the higher expected value had the higher price, the Navy had to decide whether the margin of higher expected value was worth the higher price.

Table 3-8   Navy Case Study Scoring

	Colmek	RDI
Technical approach	74	97.5
Summary (10 points)	4	9.88
Pre-production and production evaluation (30 points)	19	29.75
Production plan (25 points)	19.5	23.23
Supply support (20 points)	17.5	19.88
Engineering services (15 points)	14	14.75
LOCAR determination/offeror capability	.81	.95
Relevant experience	Satisfactory	Excellent
Past performance	Excellent	Good

Table 3-9   Navy Case Study Expected Value

	Promised value	Multiplied by	LOCAR	Equals	Expected value	Evaluated cost/ price
Colmek	74.00 percent	x	.81	=	60 percent	$6,743,935
RDI	97.50 percent	x	.95	=	93 percent	$8,613,493

The source selection authority reviewed these findings and noted that RDI offered 33 more points of expected value, which meant, according to the SSA, that the Navy was "33 percent more confident" that RDI would perform successfully than Colmek. She also noted that the price difference between the two offerors was $1,869,558, or 21.7 percent.

The SSA considered the effort to be very complex, requiring significant technical expertise and understanding. She explained that RDI's technical proposal contained very few weaknesses and many strengths, resulting in its 97.5 percent promised value. On the other hand, Colmek's technical proposal had several weaknesses and very few strengths, resulting in its 74 percent promised value. RDI also had extensive relevant experience in manufacturing handheld systems; Colmek had no experience in manufacturing similar systems.

The SSA concluded that paying an additional $56,653.27 per expected value point over a ten-year period was worth the additional technical and experience capability the Navy would obtain from RDI, and that RDI's offer thus represented the best value to the government. Colmek's protest was denied.[38]

EXPRESSING THE RELATIVE IMPORTANCE OF EVALUATION FACTORS

To submit accurate, realistic proposals, offerors need to understand the criteria against which the government will evaluate their proposals. As required by the FAR, the government must tell potential offerors how important each evaluation factor is relative to the other evaluation factors.[39] All factors and significant subfactors that will affect contract award, as well as their relative importance, must be clearly stated in the solicitation. The agency must also indicate the relative importance of cost or price and non-cost factors in both the solicitation and the weights or priority statements in the source selection plan.

Agencies generally do not score cost/price evaluations because of possible distortions that may occur when converting cost/price proposal analyses into scores. But, just like all other factors and subfactors, cost/price must be weighted to indicate its importance relative to the other evaluation factors and subfactors and to the overall evaluation. The circumstances of a particular acquisition will dictate how important cost/price is in satisfying the requirement.[40]

The RFP must state, at a minimum, whether all evaluation factors other than cost or price, when combined, are:

• Significantly more important than cost or price
• Approximately equal to cost or price
• Significantly less important than cost or price.[41]

The relative importance of evaluation factors and subfactors is usually presented in descending order of importance. However, simply listing the factors in descending order of importance is not sufficient when some factors are significantly more important than others. You must include a more specific expression of their relative importance. You can do this by providing a narrative statement, evaluation weights, a numerical score, or a combination of these in the RFP.

Narrative Statements

Cole writes that narrative statements should be used "only if the relationships between the factors are simple [and] easy to understand and when there are few factors to consider."[42] For example, "Factor A is three times as important as factor B. Factor B is twice as important as factor C. All subfactors are of equal importance." When there are several evaluation factors and subfactors, or the relationships are complex, using narrative statements can be problematic. The statements become confusing and may not effectively communicate the agency's intentions. For example, the following is a complicated and confusing narrative:

> Criteria I and IV are of equal importance, and each are of greater weight [than] criteria II and III, [which] are of less importance and are of equal weight. Individually, criteria I and IV are 1.5 times the weight of criteria II and III individually. Subcriteria I.A is of greatest weight and is twice as important as subcriteria I.D, which is of least importance. Subcriteria I.B is of slightly less importance than subcriteria I.A, and subcriteria I.C is of slightly greater importance than subcriteria I.D.[43]

Convoluted descriptions may cause offerors to misunderstand the importance of the factors. Offerors may not adequately address important aspects of the requirement in their proposals because of the way the agency explained the relative importance of the evaluation criteria. Offerors should not have to guess what is important in a solicitation. Although some hard-liners may believe that if the offeror really understood the customer, then it would *know* what is important to the customer, this belief is not supported by law and regulation.

Figure 3-7 illustrates examples of different kinds of narrative priority statements.

Numerical Scoring or Weighting

If there are several evaluation factors or subfactors, an effective way to describe their relative importance is through numerical scores or weights. *Numerical weighting* involves assigning relative importance to evaluation criteria using points or percentages. Numerical scores or weights most precisely describe the relative importance of

---

Example 1: Best Value Priority Statement

The government will make award to the responsible offeror(s) whose offer conforms to the solicitation and is most advantageous to the government, cost or price and technical factors listed below considered.

The technical evaluation factors listed below are in descending order of importance:

1. Past performance on similar projects
2. Management approach
3. Experience on similar projects
4. Qualifications of key personnel.

Price is less important than the combined weight of the technical factors listed above.

Example 2: Lowest Price Technically Acceptable Priority Statement

The government will make award to the offeror(s) submitting the lowest price technically acceptable proposal. In order to be considered technically acceptable, proposals must meet the following minimum requirements:

1. **Experience on similar contracts.** The offeror must demonstrate that it has successfully performed at least three similar contracts within the past three years.
2. **Technical specification requirements.** The offeror must demonstrate that the product offered complies with the mandatory technical requirements described in the statement of work.

Note: There is no relative importance for go/no-go factors.

Example 3: Descending Order of Importance

The government will make award to the responsible offeror(s) whose offer conforms to the solicitation and is most advantageous to the government, cost or price and technical factors listed below considered. The evaluation factors listed below are in descending order of importance:

1. Past performance on similar projects
2. Management approach
3. Experience on similar projects
4. Qualifications of key personnel
5. Price/cost.

Figure 3-7 Solicitation Priority Statements[44]

evaluation factors and subfactors, which helps offerors address the items of importance in their proposals without guesswork.

The numerical weights themselves are rarely disclosed in the solicitation, but doing so is not prohibited. Some argue that providing the weights in the RFP will open the door to protests or limit the government's flexibility in the evaluation process. In order for the competitive process to be most effective, however, offerors must be fully informed about how the government will evaluate their proposals. Specifically stating the evaluation weights does this rather clearly. If the numerical weights are not noted in the solicitation, narrative statements should be used to describe the evaluation criteria. If this information is not

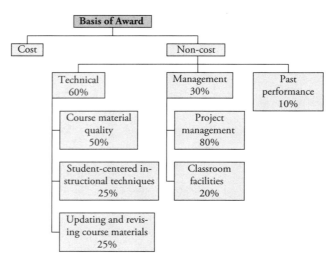

Figure 3-8 Weighted Evaluation Criteria Model

provided at all or is vague or ambiguous, misunderstandings—which can lead to protests—may arise.[45]

Figure 3-8 extends the training class example illustrated in Figure 3-3. In this example, there are three non-cost evaluation factors: technical is 60 percent, management 30 percent, and past performance 10 percent. One subfactor under technical, *course material quality*, is 50 percent. The other two subfactors, *student-centered approach* and *updating course materials*, are 25 percent each. The two subfactors under management, however, are weighted differently. Project management is significantly more important (80 percent) than classroom facilities (20 percent).

The relative importance of cost/price may be weighted or unweighted. If cost is a significant factor in an evaluation, it should be weighted. However, weighting the cost/price factor may have an unintended consequence: It may reduce the value of the technical factors and unreasonably inflate the value of the lowest-priced proposal. Table 3-10 shows how weighting the cost factor may dilute the technical factor. In this example, technical factors are weighted at 70 percent; cost, at 30 percent. The agency received two proposals. The evaluated cost of company A's proposal is $387,000, and it received a technical score of 92 points. The evaluated cost of company B's proposal is $193,500, and it received a technical score of 69 points. Company B has the lower evaluated price, but has a much lower technical score.

In this scenario, company B receives 30 points for having the lowest evaluated cost, because cost is weighted at 30 percent. Reviewing the total score after applying

Table 3-10 The Effect of Weighting the Cost Factor[46]

Proposal	Evaluated cost	Cost score (30 percent of points)	Technical points	Weighted technical score (70 percent of points)	Total score (cost score + technical score)
A	$387,000	15	92	64.4	79.4
B	$193,500	30	69	48.3	78.3

the weights, it looks as if the proposals are essentially equal. If award is made on the lowest price technically acceptable basis, company B would win for having the lowest evaluated cost. If, on the other hand, award is made on the trade-off basis, the source selection authority must determine whether the technical difference between companies A and B is worth the price premium of $193,500 (the difference between the evaluated cost of company A and B's proposals.) Thus, the technical superiority of company A is reduced by applying a weighted cost formula.

A weighted cost evaluation factor is especially risky when an offeror might try to buy in to win the contract. *Buying in* occurs when an offeror submits an unusually low price in order to receive an award. Why would an offeror do this? To get its foot in the door of a particular agency. The offeror may be willing to take a loss on the assumption that it will make up for it through contract change proposals.

It's not advisable to establish a high weight for the cost factor because it can blur the differences between proposals. Remember that the purpose of conducting an evaluation is to identify the discriminators between proposals. The results of your market research should show whether your offerors' estimates will be accurate and similar. If this is likely, then it may be appropriate to use a weighted cost factor. If there will probably be a lot of variability in the pricing, then it may be more effective to evaluate cost/price without weighting.[47]

We recommend using cost/price as an unweighted factor when technical factors are more important than cost. This separates pricing considerations from the technical considerations and allows evaluators to concentrate on the technical aspects of the proposals. This approach works best, of course, with the trade-off method. After the evaluators rate and rank the technical proposals, the results are compared with each proposal's evaluated cost, and the SSA conducts a cost/technical trade-off assessment to determine which proposal offers the best value. When technical proposals are similar in quality, then cost becomes a more significant discriminator between proposals and may become the determining factor in contract award.[48]

Table 3-11 Evaluation Factors: Problems and Solutions[49]

If...	Then ...
An evaluation factor's (or standard's) wording is vague or ambiguous (if the evaluation panel members do not agree on the meaning, it may be ambiguous) ... **or** The language describing the factor or standard does not establish what is minimally acceptable ...	Rewrite the terminology to define what the language means and how it will be applied to evaluate proposals, or delete the ambiguous factor or standard. All evaluation panel members must agree on the meaning so that they can apply the terms consistently during the evaluation. Examples of ambiguous terms are "similar," "comparable," "satisfactory," and "substantial."
The description of the factor does not clearly indicate the elements or subfactors that are needed ...	Rewrite the evaluation factor to clearly indicate the elements or subfactors required.
The importance assigned to each factor or subfactor does not accurately reflect its relative importance and relationship with other factors or subfactors ...	Review and revise the relative importance so that it reflects how the evaluation team will evaluate the proposals.
There are duplicate factors for one requirement ...	Revise the factors so that they evaluate distinct aspects of the requirement, or delete the duplicate factor.
The evaluation factors seem overly complex or are difficult to apply without assistance from nongovernment advisors ...	Simplify the evaluation factors or obtain assistance from outside advisors, providing that there is no conflict of interest.

COMMON PROBLEMS ASSOCIATED WITH EVALUATION FACTORS

Evaluation criteria are weakened by the following common errors:

- Vague or ambiguous language
- Inconsistency between the SOW and proposal preparation instructions (For example, the SOW might require a training plan, but there's no corresponding requirement in the proposal preparation instructions about what to include in the training plan.)
- Absence of any relationship between an evaluation factor and the SOW
- Missing elements, such as missing standards or measures of relative importance
- Mathematical errors; for example, the weights of subfactors exceed the total points allocated for the factor.

Table 3-11 suggests remedies for weak evaluation factors.

CHAPTER SUMMARY

Chapter 3 explains the importance of writing effective evaluation criteria. The required evaluation factors are price or cost to the government; quality of the product or service; past performance; and small business participation.

The typical evaluation factors are technical, management (key personnel and security), cost or price, and past performance. After selecting the primary evaluation factors, the government determines if it needs subfactors. A subfactor represents an important element of a primary evaluation factor and is used to explain the meaning and significance of the primary factor. The solicitation must disclose all evaluation factors and significant subfactors.

Evaluation factors can be structured and limited to focus on those elements that are critical to the acquisition. Agencies should review the risk analysis documented in the acquisition plan to decide which evaluation criteria to include. Identify the risks that could have a significant effect on contract performance. The evaluation factors used in the solicitation should reflect the risks that have the greatest impact on the contract and have the highest likelihood of occurrence.

Many agencies use evaluation standards to help keep evaluators focused on a baseline to assess proposal's suitability. *Standards* are the baseline against which an agency evaluates offerors' proposals to determine their acceptability and value. Using evaluation standards helps to provide a consistent guide so evaluators can measure how well a proposal addresses each factor identified in the solicitation.

A contract without risk does not exist, but we can't ignore the possibility of problems occurring either. Typical risks include technical, schedule, cost, performance, and proposal risk. Evaluating risk is a way to assess the government's confidence that an offeror can complete the work proposed. Another method of evaluating risk is the performance confidence assessment technique or the level of confidence assessment rating.

Finally, the agency needs to express the relative importance of evaluation factors so that offerors understand what their requirements are. The solicitation must clearly state all factors and significant subfactors that will affect contract award, as well as the relative importance of each.

NOTES

1 Federal Acquisition Regulation (FAR) 15.304(b).

2 FAR 15.304(a).

3 Federal Acquisition Institute, *Source Selection Text Reference* (Washington, DC: Federal Acquisition Institute, 1993), 115.

4 FAR 15.304.

5 FAR 19.1202-3.

6 FAR 2.101.

7 FAR 7.108.

8 Federal Acquisition Institute, 125.

9   Peter S. Cole, *How to Evaluate and Negotiate Government Contracts* (Vienna, VA: Management Concepts, 2001), 85–91.

10 Ibid., 97–99.

11 FAR 15.404-1.

12 Cost Accounting Standard, 414.

13 FAR 15.404-1(c).

14 FAR 15.404(d).

15 Cole, 68.

16 National Aeronautics and Space Administration, *Source Selection Guide* (Washington, DC: National Aeronautics and Space Administration, June 2007), 24–28.

17 Cole, 30.

18 U.S. Government Accountability Office, "Mnemonics, Inc.," B-290961 (Washington, DC: U.S. Government Accountability Office, October 28, 2002).

19 Cole, 33.

20 Ibid., 21.

21 Federal Acquisition Institute, 114.

22 Federal Acquisition Institute, 128–129.

23 Cole, 22.

24 Defense Information Systems Agency, *Source Selection Deskbook* (Arlington, VA: Defense Information Systems Agency, May 2003), 12.

25 Ibid., 117–118.

26 Ibid., 126–127.

27 Chantilly, VA: National Reconnaissance Office Acquisition Center of Excellence, May 2006, pp. 6–8.

28 Defense Acquisition University, *Risk Management Guide for DoD Acquisition*, 5th ed. (Washington, DC: Defense Acquisition University, June 2003), B-5.

29 Ibid., B-6.

30 Ibid., 46–47.

31 Ibid., 47.

32 Johnnie E. Wilson, *Best Value Source Selection* 715-3 (Alexandria, VA: Army Materiel Command, 1998), D-6.

33 Harold V. Hanson, *NAVSEA Source Selection Guide* (Washington, DC: U.S. Naval Sea Systems Command, 2001), 23.

34 U.S. Air Force, "Source Selection," *Mandatory Procedure* MP5315.3 (Washington, DC: U.S. Air Force, March 2009).

35 U.S. Air Force, Mandatory Procedure MP 5315.3.

36 U.S. Air Force/Air Force Materiel Command, Draft RFP no. FA8903-09-R-8374 (Wright-Patterson Air Force Base, OH: U.S. Air Force/Air Force Materiel Command, March 3, 2009).

37 U.S. Navy, Naval Air Systems Command, RFP no. N00421-08-R-0042 (April 21, 2008).

38 U.S. Government Accountability Office, "Colmek Sys Eng'g," B-291931.2 (July 9, 2003).

39 FAR 15.304(e).

40 Wilson, 12.

41 FAR 15.304(e).

42 Cole, 104.

43 Ibid., 105.

44 Ibid., 107.

45 Washington, DC: Federal Acquisition Institute, 1993, 138–139.

46 Ibid., 116–117.

47 Ibid., 119.

48 Ibid., 120.

49 Adapted from Federal Acquisition Institute, 130.

Chapter 4

Scoring Plans and Rating Systems

The FAR does not specify how agencies should score proposals, so contracting officers have a lot of flexibility in doing so. A *scoring plan* or *rating system* is the internal road map an agency uses to apply the evaluation criteria. Each agency uses a different scoring plan; sometimes there are variations between an agency's divisions or departments. The plan uses a scale of words, colors, numbers, or other indicators to denote the degree to which proposals meet the standards for the non-cost evaluation factors.

The particular scoring method an agency uses is less important than are:

- The consistency with which the evaluators apply the selected method to all competing proposals
- The thoroughness of the narrative used to support the rating.[1]

The most commonly used rating systems are:

- Adjectival
- Color coding
- Numerical
- A combination of these systems.

THE ADJECTIVAL RATING SYSTEM

Agencies frequently use adjectival ratings to score or rate proposals because this method is flexible. The adjectives used indicate the degree to which the proposal meets the standard for each factor evaluated. After reading and evaluating a proposal, the evaluator assigns an appropriate adjectival rating to each factor and significant subfactor. Adjectival systems may be used alone or in connection with other rating systems.[2]

Typically, agencies provide a narrative definition for each rating so that evaluators have a common understanding of how to apply the rating[3] and can do so consistently. Table 4-1 illustrates one way to use an adjectival scoring method.

Table 4-2 shows a sample adjectival rating scale specifically designed for evaluating technical/management factors and past performance. A proposal need not have all of the characteristics listed in the narrative for each adjectival rating in order to receive that rating. Evaluators should rely on their judgment as well as the narrative descriptions when assigning ratings.

Table 4-1 Sample Adjectival Rating Method[4]

Adjective	Definition
Outstanding	A proposal that satisfies all of the government's requirements, with extensive detail indicating the feasibility of the approach and a thorough understanding of the problems. The proposal has numerous significant strengths that are not offset by weaknesses. The proposal has an overall low degree of risk.
Good	A proposal that satisfies all of the government's requirements, with adequate detail indicating a feasible approach and an understanding of the problems. The proposal has some significant strengths or numerous minor strengths that are not offset by weaknesses. The proposal has an overall low to moderate degree of risk.
Acceptable	A proposal that satisfies all of the government's requirements, with minimal detail indicating a feasible approach and a minimal understanding of the problems. The proposal has an overall moderate to high degree of risk.
Marginal	A proposal that satisfies all of the government's requirements, with minimal detail indicating a feasible approach and a minimal understanding of the problem. The proposal has an overall high degree of risk.
Susceptible to being made acceptable	An approach which, as initially proposed, cannot be rated "marginal" because of at least one minor error, omission, or deficiency, which can be corrected without a major rewrite or proposal revision. (Note that this rating cannot be a final rating. The final rating must either be "marginal" or higher or "unacceptable.")
Unacceptable	A proposal that contains at least one major error, omission, or deficiency that indicates a lack of understanding of the problems. The approach cannot be expected to meet requirements or involves a very high risk. None of these conditions can be corrected without a major rewrite or proposal revision.

Table 4-2   Adjectival Rating Method for Technical/Management and Past Performance[5]

Adjective	Technical/management definition	Past performance definition
Outstanding	An outstanding proposal has the following characteristics: • The proposed approach indicates an exceptionally thorough and comprehensive understanding of the program goals, resources, schedules, and other aspects essential to performance of the program. • The proposal contains major strengths, exceptional features, or innovations that should substantially benefit the program. • There are no weaknesses or deficiencies. • The risk of unsuccessful contract performance is extremely low.	The offeror's performance of previously awarded relevant contracts met contractual requirements and exceeded many to the government's benefit. The company performed with very few or very minor problems, for which corrective actions taken were, or are expected to be, highly effective. Performance of completed contracts was either consistently of the highest quality or exhibited a trend toward becoming so. The offeror's past performance record leads to an extremely strong expectation of successful performance.
Good	A good proposal has the following characteristics: • The proposed approach indicates a thorough understanding of the program goals and the methods, resources, schedules, and other aspects essential to the performance of the program. • The proposal has major strengths or minor strengths that indicate the proposed approach will benefit the program. • The weaknesses, if any, are minor and are more than offset by strengths. • The risk of unsuccessful performance is very low.	The offeror's performance of previously awarded relevant contracts met contractual requirements and exceeded some to the government's benefit. The company performed with some minor problems, for which corrective actions taken were, or are expected to be, effective. Performance of completed contracts was either consistently of high quality or exhibited a trend toward becoming so. The offeror's past performance record leads to a strong expectation of successful performance.
Satisfactory	A satisfactory proposal has the following characteristics: • The proposed approach indicates an adequate understanding of the program goals and the methods, resources, schedules, and other aspects essential to the performance of the program. • The proposal has few, if any, exceptional features to benefit the program. • The risk of unsuccessful performance is low. • The weaknesses are generally offset by strengths.	The offeror's performance of previously awarded relevant contracts met contractual requirements. The company performed with some problems, for which corrective actions taken by the contractor were, or are expected to be, effective. Performance of completed contracts was consistently of adequate or better quality or exhibited a trend toward becoming so. The offeror's past performance record leads to an expectation of successful performance.

Table 4-2 (*Continued*)

Adjective	Technical/management definition	Past performance definition
Marginal	A marginal proposal has the following characteristics: • The proposed approach indicates a superficial or vague understanding of the program goals and the methods, resources, schedules, and other aspects essential to the performance of the program. • The proposal has weaknesses that are not offset by strengths. • The risk of unsuccessful contract performance is moderate.	The offeror's performance of previously awarded relevant contracts did not meet some contractual requirements. The contractor's performance reflected some serious problems, for which the contractor either failed to identify or implement corrective actions in a timely manner, or for which the corrective actions implemented or proposed to be implemented were, or are expected to be, only partially effective. Performance of completed contracts was consistently of mediocre quality or exhibited a trend toward becoming so. The offeror's past performance record leads to an expectation that successful performance might be difficult to achieve or that it can occur only with increased levels of government management and oversight.
Unsatisfactory	An unsatisfactory proposal has the following characteristics: • The proposed approach indicates a lack of understanding of the program goals and the methods, resources, schedules, and other aspects essential to the performance of the program. • There are numerous weaknesses and deficiencies. • The risk of unsuccessful performance is high.	The offeror's performance of previously awarded relevant contracts did not meet most contractual requirements, and recovery, if any, did not occur within the period of performance. The contractor's performance reflected serious problems for which the offeror either failed to identify or implement corrective actions or for which corrective actions were mostly ineffective. Performance of completed contracts was consistently of poor quality or exhibited a trend toward becoming so. The offeror's past performance record leads to a strong expectation that successful performance will not be achieved or that it can occur only with greatly increased levels of government management and oversight.
Neutral	Not applicable	The offeror lacks a record of relevant or available past performance history. Based on this, there is no expectation of either successful or unsuccessful performance.

Case Study: Deviating from a Designated Adjectival Rating System

Trajen, Inc., and Maytag Aircraft Corporation protested the award of a contract to LB&B Associates, Inc., for services at various naval facilities. The purpose of the solicitation was to award a fixed-price contract for labor, management, and equipment to operate five fuel terminals. Proposals were to be evaluated on the basis of operational capability, past performance, price, and socioeconomic/subcontracting.

The RFP stated that the following adjectival rating scale would be used:

- Exceptional
- Very good
- Satisfactory
- Marginal
- Unsatisfactory.

However, the technical evaluation team actually evaluated proposals using three adjectival ratings with a corresponding point value:

- Exceptional (3)
- Average (2)
- Marginal (1).

Evaluators considered technical factors to be more important than price.

The contracting officer (CO), as the source selection authority (SSA), reviewed the technical evaluation team's consensus evaluations of each proposal and performed a price-technical trade-off. The evaluation results are summarized in Table 4-3.

According to the Government Accountability Office (GAO) decision on the protest, "The SSA concluded that LB&B's superior technical proposal … more than offset the other offerors' lower prices." Trajen and Maytag protested, arguing that the evaluation was flawed because the agency did not follow the evaluation scheme outlined in the RFP; while the RFP provided for an evaluation using five adjectives, the technical evaluation team used only three adjectives.

Per the GAO decision:

> In reviewing a protest of an agency's proposal evaluation, [the GAO will only determine if] the agency acted reasonably and consistent with the terms of the RFP, applicable statutes and regulations.… When considering the ratings assigned by an agency to an offeror's proposal, [the GAO has] consistently taken the position that evalua-

Table 4-3 Trajen and Maytag Case Study Evaluation Results

Evaluation factor	Maytag	Trajen	LB&B
Operational capability	Average (44)	Average (42)	Exceptional (66)
Past performance	Very good	Very good	Exceptional
Socioeconomic/subcontracting	Exceptional	Exceptional	Exceptional
Price	$30,511,080	$29,985,000	$33,309,107

tion ratings, be they adjectival, numerical, or color, are merely guides for intelligent decision-making in the procurement process.

The agency's use of three adjectives instead of the five stated in the RFP had no prejudicial impact on the evaluation. In this regard, all proposals were evaluated under the same scheme and the evaluation was not based solely on the adjectives; each of the nine subfactors had an individual weight that was multiplied by the numerical score assigned by the individual and consensus evaluations as well as supporting narratives.... To the extent that a greater number of adjectives would operate to provide more precise differentiation among proposals, the numerical scoring of the proposals provided that differentiation. With a score of 66 points, LB&B's proposal was considered to be mid-exceptional, and the protesters' scores placed them in the mid-average range.

The decision continues, "Regardless of the adjectives applied, the relative standing of the offerors' proposals would remain the same, with LB&B's proposal rated significantly higher than either of the protester's." The GAO also noted "that the source selection was not merely based on the adjectival or numerical ratings; the SSA specifically considered the narrative comments in the consensus evaluations and weighed the advantages of various aspects of LB&B's proposal over the others." The GAO concluded "that the agency's failure to use all five of the adjectives identified in the RFP was unobjectionable." The protest was denied.[6]

This case illustrates that an agency has a great deal of flexibility in designing the scoring plan and may even deviate from the scoring plan as long as the resulting evaluation is reasonable and done consistently for all offerors.

Now, let's review another case study about the adjectival scoring method. This case deals with how the evaluators reach a consensus by averaging the adjectival scores.

Case Study: Averaging Adjectives

Chapman Law Firm, LPA, protested the award of a contract to Harrington Moran Barksdale, Inc., (HMBI) under a request for proposals issued by the Department of Housing and Urban Development (HUD) for marketing and management services.

According to the GAO decision on the protest,

The solicitation provided for a "best value" evaluation based on price and the following technical factors (in descending order of importance):

- Management capability/quality of proposed management plan
- Past performance
- Experience

- Proposed key personnel
- Subcontract management
- Small business subcontracting participation.

Price was significantly less important than the technical factors, which were rated using an adjectival scale of excellent, good, fair, marginal and unacceptable.

HUD received several proposals. Chapman's and HMBI's were among those included in the competitive range. The evaluation results are summarized in Table 4-4.

After multiple rounds of discussions and receiving final proposal revisions (FPR), the technical evaluation panel recommended HMBI for award as the firm submitting the best value proposal. The contracting officer concurred and made award to HMBI.

In its protest, Chapman asserted that, based on its ratings (in order of importance), its proposal should have been rated "good," rather than "fair," overall. The GAO disagreed with this argument. First, the GAO did not see anything

objectionable in a final adjectival rating of fair, given that three of the four most important factor ratings were fair. In any case, Chapman attaches unwarranted weight to the adjectival ratings. Such ratings are not binding on the source selection official but, rather, serve only as a guide to intelligent decision making.... Here, the record demonstrates that HUD's comparison of the proposals and award decision were based, not on a mechanical application of the overall ratings, but on the underlying qualitative merits of the proposals. This being the case, arriving at a different "average" adjectival rating—good, instead of fair, as Chapman claims its proposal should have been rated— for the proposal's overall rating would have had no effect on the award decision.

The protest was denied.[7]

Table 4-4   HUD Case Study Evaluation Results

Evaluation factors	Chapman	HMBI
Overall	Fair	Good
Management	Fair	Good
Past performance	Good	Good
Experience	Fair	Good
Key personnel	Fair	Good
Subcontract management	Good	Good
Small business plan	Excellent	Good
Price	$147,776,750	$177,697.00

THE COLOR CODING RATING SYSTEM

The color coding system uses colors to indicate the degree to which an offeror's proposal meets the standard for each factor evaluated. Like the adjectival method, color coding is a flexible system. Agencies use different colors and definitions for each color, but generally, "blue" is the highest possible rating, and "red" the lowest possible rating, and the colors in between vary.

Let's look at some examples of a color rating system. The first example uses six different colors and integrates the past performance assessment with the color score. Table 4-5 illustrates this kind of color rating method.

As shown in Table 4-6, the U.S. Army uses six different colors for its rating scale and includes a corresponding adjective for each rating. The risk rating is integrated into the narrative, but past performance is evaluated separately. The narrative is the same as that used in Table 4-1, the first example of the adjectival rating method in this chapter. The Army assesses strengths, weaknesses, and deficiencies in determining which rating applies to a proposal. Evaluators must support their ratings by writing evaluation narratives stating strengths, weaknesses, and deficiencies.

The U.S. Air Force uses only four colors, though it also combines the colors with adjectival ratings, as illustrated in Table 4-7. The description provides specific guidance to evaluators by explaining how strengths and weaknesses should be used to determine the rating. Like the Army approach shown in Table 4-6, this approach requires evaluators to write specific evaluation narratives listing strengths, weaknesses, and deficiencies to justify their ratings.

Although the adjectival and color coding systems may be more difficult to use because they are subjective, they may be the most effective. Admittedly, applying the color codes can be challenging. Achieving consensus may be difficult if, for example, the technical factor is weighted at 50 percent and is rated acceptable ("green"), and past performance is weighted at 40 percent and is rated exceptional ("blue"). Unfortunately, no simple process exists to help the evaluators reach a consensus rating. The evaluators must assess the collective impact of evaluation subfactors on each factor, then assess all of the evaluation factors as they relate to each other under the weighting methodology identified in the solicitation.

This is a complex process that requires evaluators to thoroughly understand the strengths and weaknesses of each individual proposal as they relate to the evaluation

Table 4-5 Defense Information Systems Agency Color Rating Method[8]

Color	Technical capability	Strengths	Weaknesses	Past performance
Blue	The proposal exceeds requirements and clearly demonstrates the offeror's capability to deliver exceptional performance.	The proposal has numerous strengths that are of direct benefit to the government.	Weaknesses are considered insignificant and have no apparent impact on the program.	Highly relevant/ very recent past performance in all identified past performance efforts; excellent performance ratings.
Green	The proposal is satisfactory; the offeror is capable of meeting performance requirements.	Some strengths exist that are of benefit to the government; the strengths clearly offset weaknesses.	A few weaknesses exist; they are correctable with minimal government oversight or direction.	Relevant/ somewhat recent past performance in all identified past performance efforts; acceptable performance ratings.
Yellow	The proposal is minimally adequate; the offeror is most likely able to meet performance requirements.	Few strengths exist that are of benefit to the government; the strengths do not offset the weaknesses.	Substantial weaknesses exist that may impact the program; they are correctable with some government oversight and direction.	Somewhat relevant/ not very recent past performance; mostly acceptable performance ratings.
Orange	The proposal is inadequate; it is doubtful whether the offeror can meet performance requirements.	Few, if any, strengths exist that are of benefit to the government; the weaknesses clearly offset the strengths.	Weaknesses exist that adversely impact the program; they are correctable with significant government oversight and direction.	Little relevant past performance identified; mostly unacceptable performance ratings.
Red	The proposal is highly inadequate; the offeror cannot meet performance requirements.	There are no beneficial strengths.	Numerous weaknesses exist that are so significant that a proposal rewrite is not feasible within a suitable timeframe.	Little relevant past performance identified; almost all unacceptable performance ratings.
White	Not used.	Not used.	Not used.	The offeror completely lacks relevant performance history, or past performance is unavailable, not due to the offeror's failure to provide information.

Table 4-6 U.S. Army Color and Adjectival Rating Method[9]

Adjective	Color	Description
Outstanding	Blue	A proposal that satisfies all of the government's requirements, with extensive detail indicating the feasibility of the approach and a thorough understanding of the problems. The proposal has numerous significant strengths that are not offset by weaknesses. The proposal has an overall low degree of risk.
Good	Green	A proposal that satisfies all of the government's requirements, with adequate detail indicating a feasible approach and an understanding of the problems. The proposal has some significant strengths or numerous minor strengths that are not offset by weaknesses. The proposal has an overall low to moderate degree of risk.
Acceptable	Yellow	A proposal that satisfies all of the government's requirements, with minimal detail indicating a feasible approach and a minimal understanding of the problems. The proposal has an overall moderate to high degree of risk.
Marginal	Orange	A proposal that satisfies all of the government's requirements, with minimal detail indicating a feasible approach and a minimal understanding of the problem. The proposal has an overall high degree of risk.
Susceptible to being made acceptable	Pink	An approach which, as initially proposed, cannot be rated "marginal" because of at least one minor error, omission, or deficiency, which can be corrected without a major rewrite or proposal revision. (Note that this rating cannot be a final rating. The final rating must either be "marginal" or higher or "unacceptable.")
Unacceptable	Red	A proposal that contains at least one major error, omission, or deficiency that indicates a lack of understanding of the problems. The approach cannot be expected to meet requirements or involves a very high risk. None of these conditions can be corrected without a major rewrite or proposal revision.

criteria and standards in order to reach consensus. Keep in mind that evaluators' written narratives are important not only at this point in the acquisition process. They are also used to make other decisions during the source selection process, such as determining the competitive range.[10]

Table 4-7 U.S. Air Force Mission Capability Technical Ratings[11]

Color	Adjective	Description
Blue	Exceptional	Exceeds specified minimum performance or capability requirements in a way beneficial to the government. A proposal must have one or more strengths and no deficiencies to receive a blue rating.
Green	Acceptable	Meets specified minimum performance or capability requirements. A proposal must have no deficiencies to receive a green rating but may have one or more strengths.
Yellow	Marginal	There is doubt about whether an aspect of the proposal meets specified minimum performance or capability requirements, but any such uncertainty is correctable.
Red	Unacceptable	Fails to meet specified minimum performance or capability requirements. The proposal has one or more deficiencies and is not awardable.

THE NUMERICAL RATING SYSTEM

The numerical system assigns point scores (such as 0 to 10, 0 to 100, or 0 to 1,000) to rate proposals. This rating system generally allows for more rating levels and thus may appear to give more precise distinctions of merit.

Numerical systems, however, can have drawbacks; their apparent precision may actually obscure the strengths, weaknesses, and risks that support the numbers. Per the Department of Energy's *Source Selection Guide*, unlike adjectival and color coding systems,

> numeric systems can provide a false sense of mathematical precision that can be distorted depending upon the evaluation factors and the standards used. For example, if a standard indicated there could be no weaknesses, a very minor weakness in a proposal would force assignment of the next lower level rating. This would potentially cause a significant mathematical difference in the proposal rating.[12]

Hence, some organizations do not permit the use of numerical rating systems.[13]

The National Aeronautics and Space Administration (NASA) uses numerical weights and scores for its "mission suitability" evaluation factor. This factor indicates the merit or excellence of the work to be performed or product to be delivered. It includes, as appropriate, both technical and management subfactors. Mission suitability is numerically weighted and scored on a 1,000-point scale.[14] The evaluation factors might, for example, be divided into four subfactors, all of which add up to 1,000 possible points:

1) Understanding the requirements of the statement of work (275 points)
2) Technical approach to representative task orders (275 points)
3) Management plan (400 points)
4) Safety and health (50 points).[15]

The Environmental Protection Agency also uses a numeric system. A sample of its rating system is shown in Table 4-8.

COMBINING SCORING APPROACHES

Some agencies use a combination approach to scoring that includes colors, numbers, and adjectives. The evaluator can assign a numerical score or color rating to the proposal by applying the definitions provided. This approach provides flexibility for those who might prefer a definitive numerical approach and for those who prefer the more general color-based or adjectival approach.

Table 4-8 EPA Numeric Scoring Plan[16]

Value	Descriptive statement
0	The factor is not addressed, or is addressed in a way that is totally deficient and without merit.
1	The factor is addressed, but there are deficiencies or weaknesses that can be corrected only by major or significant changes to relevant portions of the proposal, or the factor is addressed so minimally or vaguely that there are widespread information gaps. In addition, because of the deficiencies, weaknesses, or information gaps, the technical evaluation team has serious concerns about the offeror's ability to perform the required work.
2	Information related to the factor is incomplete, unclear, or indicates an inadequate approach to, or understanding of, the factor. The technical evaluation team believes there is a question as to whether the offeror would be able to perform satisfactorily.
3	The response to the factor is adequate. Overall, it meets the specifications and requirements, such that the technical evaluation team believes that the offeror could perform to meet the government's minimum requirements.
4	The response to the factor is good, with some superior features. Information provided is generally clear, and the demonstrated ability to accomplish the technical requirements is acceptable, with the possibility of more than adequate performance.
5	The response to the factor is superior in most features.

To arrive at the numerical score for each factor, the evaluator considers the offeror's proposed approach, evaluates the proposed approach in relation to the evaluation standards, assigns an appropriate score, and writes a narrative explanation for that score. This approach is illustrated in Table 4-9.

The Department of Energy (DOE) uses a different number scale and different colors, adjectives, and definitions for its combined scoring approach, illustrated in Table 4-10.

NASA uses an adjectival and numerical scale to evaluate its 1,000-point mission suitability factor.[17] The adjectives, definitions, and percentile ranges the agency uses are shown in Table 4-11.

A numerical rating system can also be used to score how close a cost proposal is to the government's independent cost estimate. When contracting on a cost-reimbursement basis, the agency conducts a cost realism analysis under the cost factor. NASA uses a structured approach to proportionally adjust technical mission suitability scores based on the degree of assessed cost realism. According to NASA's *Source Selection Guide*, this method of cost proposal rating:

• Establishes a threshold at which mission suitability adjustments would start. The threshold should reflect the acquisition's estimating uncertainty—the higher the degree of estimating uncertainty, the higher the threshold.

Table 4-9 Combined Color, Numerical, and Adjectival Scoring Method[18]

Color rating	Numerical score	Adjectival rating	Definition
Blue	10–9	Exceptional	The offeror's proposal demonstrates an exceptional understanding of the requirements, and the approach is of superior quality. Two or more significant strengths exist. There are no major or significant weaknesses, and no deficiencies exist.
Teal	8–7	Good	The offeror's proposal demonstrates a good understanding of the requirements, and the approach is of good quality. Strengths clearly outbalance any weaknesses that exist. There are no significant weaknesses and no deficiencies.
Green	6–4	Satisfactory	The offeror's proposal demonstrates an acceptable understanding of the requirements, and the approach is of satisfactory quality. There may be strengths or weaknesses, and the strengths balance the weaknesses. No deficiencies exist.
Yellow	3–2	Marginal	The offeror's proposal demonstrates a marginal understanding of the requirements, and the approach is of poor quality. There may be significant weaknesses or deficiencies. The weaknesses outweigh the strengths.
Red	1–0	Unsatisfactory	The offeror's proposal does not demonstrate an understanding of the requirements, and the approach is of unacceptable quality. There are significant weaknesses or deficiencies. The weaknesses negate any strengths.

- Affects a significant number of points to induce realistic pricing. *Points* refers to the point adjustment NASA assigns for the difference from the internal government cost estimate illustrated in Table 4-12. If NASA assigns a high enough point adjustment for unrealistic pricing, then companies are more likely to submit a realistic cost proposal.
- Allows for a mission suitability point adjustment based on the percentage difference between proposed and probable cost, as shown in Table 4-12.

Case Study: An Inconsistently Applied Scoring Methodology

The United States Agency for International Development (USAID) issued an RFP for assistance with the agency's Market Chain Enhancement Program in Haiti. Fintrac, Inc., protested the award to Citizens Network for Foreign Affairs (CNFA).

Table 4-10 DOE Combined Numerical, Adjectival, and Color Rating Scale[19]

Numerical score	Adjectival rating	Color rating	Definition or standard
10	Excellent	Blue	The proposal demonstrates an excellent understanding of requirements and has an approach that significantly exceeds performance or capability standards. It has exceptional strengths that will significantly benefit the government.
8	Good	Green	The proposal demonstrates a good understanding of requirements, and the approach exceeds performance or capability standards. It has one or more strengths that will benefit the government.
5	Satisfactory	Yellow	The proposal demonstrates an acceptable understanding of requirements, and the approach meets performance or capability standards. The solution is acceptable. There are few or no strengths.
3	Marginal approach	Amber	The proposal demonstrates a shallow understanding of requirements and only marginally meets performance or capability standards necessary for minimal but acceptable contract performance.
0	Unsatisfactory	Red	The proposal fails to meet performance or capability standards. Requirements can only be met with major changes to the proposal.

Table 4-11 NASA Adjectival and Percentile Rating Scale[20]

Adjectival rating	Definition	Percentile range
Excellent	The proposal is comprehensive and thorough with exceptional merit and one or more significant strengths. No deficiencies or significant weaknesses exist.	91–100
Very good	The proposal has no deficiencies and demonstrates overall competence. One or more significant strengths exist, and strengths outweigh any weaknesses.	71–90
Good	The proposal has no deficiencies and shows a reasonably sound response. There may be strengths, weaknesses, or both. As a whole, weaknesses are not offset by strengths but do not significantly detract from the offeror's response.	51–70
Fair	The proposal has no deficiencies and has one or more weaknesses. The weaknesses outweigh any strengths.	31–50
Poor	The proposal has one or more deficiencies or significant weaknesses that demonstrate a lack of overall competence or would require a major proposal revision to correct.	0–30

Table 4-12   Adjusting Mission Suitability Scores[21]

Difference in cost of services	Difference in cost of hardware development	Point adjustment
+/- 5 percent	+/- 30 percent	0
+/- 6 to 10 percent	+/- 31 to 40 percent	-50
+/- 11 to 15 percent	+/- 41 to 50 percent	-100
+/- 16 to 20 percent	+/- 51 to 60 percent	-150
+/- 21 to 30 percent	+/- 61 to 70 percent	-200
+/- more than 30 percent	+/- more than 70 percent	-300

As documented in the GAO protest decision B-311462.2; B-311462.3, the RFP, issued in March 2007, "sought proposals to provide economic development assistance to Haiti.... The RFP stated that offerors would be evaluated on the basis of six evaluation factors," which were listed in descending order of importance. But it "also assigned specific points to the factors [,which were] inconsistent with the 'descending order of importance' evaluation scheme." Table 4-13 shows the scoring methodology used.

According to the decision,

> Under each of the technical evaluation factors, other than personnel, the RFP identified a number of subfactors.... With respect to costs, the RFP stated that cost would be evaluated for reasonableness, allowability, allocability, and cost realism.... The solicitation also stated that for purposes of the selection decision, "all technical evaluation factors, when combined, are significantly more important than cost."

After releasing the RFP, USAID amended the solicitation, stating that "it would use the point scores to establish the relative importance of the [evaluation] factors."

Table 4-13   Scoring Methodology Case Study Evaluation Factors

Evaluation factor	Points
Technical approach	25
Personnel	20
Corporate capability	10
Work and milestone plan	35
Past performance	10

USAID received proposals from six offerors, including Fintrac and CNFA, the awardee. USAID advised Fintrac that its proposed salaries were not realistic because they were lower than the prevailing market rate. USAID was concerned that it would not find suitable candidates for the work at such low salaries. USAID also advised Fintrac that its proposal had a significant weakness because it did not meet all of the SOW requirements.

When evaluating the final proposal revisions, USAID weighted the evaluation factors as indicated in the solicitation amendment. Table 4-14 shows the original evaluation results.

"USAID concluded that the technical proposals were essentially equal[, and] the difference between the proposed costs became the primary discriminator." Given the lower proposed costs of CNFA's proposal, USAID awarded the contract to CNFA. It is important to note that CNFA is a not-for-profit and did not propose a fee.

Fintrac filed a protest in April 2008 and, as a result, the agency reevaluated the proposals. "During the course of the reevaluation, the CO concluded that the initial scoring methodology of weighting subfactors in descending order of importance was inconsistent with the solicitation." The CO instructed the technical evaluators to weight the subfactors equally. "Despite this change, the offerors were not permitted to revise their proposals." The new scoring methodology raised CNFA's technical score to 89.6 and lowered Fintrac's to 84.7. The most probable cost remained the same. In June 2008, USAID awarded the contract to CNFA, and Fintrac filed another protest in July 2008. Table 4-15 illustrates the reevaluation results.

Fintrac challenged the reasonableness of USAID's evaluation of technical and cost proposals. Fintrac argued that during the reevaluation, USAID improperly changed the weights applied to the technical evaluation subfactors. Fintrac also argued "that the revised scoring methodology was inconsistent with the terms of the solicitation.

The RFP set forth two conflicting bases for evaluating technical proposals:

> On the one hand, it stated that the factors were listed in descending order of importance; on the other hand, it identified point scores for factors that were inconsistent with a scheme of descending weight. USAID clarified this ambiguity in [an

Table 4-14   USAID Case Study Original Evaluation Results

	CNFA	Fintrac
Technical score	89 points	88.1 points
Most probable cost	$23,999,834	$25,687,783

Table 4-15 USAID Case Study Reevaluation Results

	CNFA	**Fintrac**
Technical score	89.6 points	84.7 points
Most probable cost	$23,999,834	$25,687,783

amendment] to the solicitation, stating that the point scores established the weight for the evaluation factors.

USAID also concluded that the scoring methodology for the technical evaluation subfactors was flawed, and "although the RFP was silent as to the weight of the subfactors, the agency had weighted them in descending order of importance." The CO therefore instructed the evaluators to give equal weight to the subfactors for the reevaluation after the first protest.

GAO asserted,

Solicitations must advise offerors of the basis upon which their proposals will be evaluated…. Contracting officials may not announce in the solicitation that they will use one evaluation scheme and then follow another without informing the offerors of the changed plan and providing them an opportunity to submit proposals on that basis…. Although the solicitation initially contained a patent ambiguity regarding the weights accorded to the evaluation factors, this ambiguity was resolved in [an amendment] to the RFP.

The RFP, however, was silent as to the weight of the subfactors. The GAO has recognized that "where a solicitation does not disclose the relative weight of the evaluation factors or subfactors, … they should be considered approximately equal in importance or weight."

GAO argued that a "protester's mere disagreement with the agency's judgment in its evaluation of the relative merit of competing proposals does not establish that the evaluation was unreasonable." The protest was denied.[22]

This case illustrates that an agency can make an error in the RFP's scoring plan and can then correct it during the solicitation process. It's also important to note that if a solicitation does not disclose the relative weight of the evaluation factors or subfactors, they should be considered approximately equal in importance or weight.

Case Study: A Deficient Scoring Plan

GAP Solutions, Inc., (GAP) protested the award of a contract to Total Solutions, Inc., under a request for proposals issued by the Centers for Disease Control and

Prevention (CDC) for domestic technical, operational, and professional services. GAP stated that the technical evaluation scheme used by the agency failed to highlight the distinctions among the proposals.

Per GAO decision B-310564,

> The RFP advised that the agency intended to make award on a "best value" basis, with technical factors being given greater consideration than price. The RFP further advised, however, that, if the technical proposals were determined to be essentially equal, price would govern the agency's source selection decision. For evaluation purposes, the RFP provided that proposals would be scored using a 420[-]point scale, with 100 points allocated to the evaluation of the proposal overall, 100 points allocated to the offerors' responses to each of three task orders, and 20 points allocated to past performance.... The 100 points allocated to the proposal overall were equally divided among four subfactors: technical approach/understanding of the requirement, personnel expertise/management plan, corporate experience/capabilities, and financial capabilities.

After evaluating the final proposal revisions, the agency assigned the proposals the scores shown in Table 4-16:

Finding that all four competitive range proposals were technically acceptable, the agency made award to Total Solutions on the basis of its low price. After receiving a debriefing, GAP Solutions protested to the GAO.

GAP asserted:

> The agency's proposal scoring scheme was flawed in that it essentially "negated" the technical distinctions among the proposals. In this respect, the record shows that the agency evaluated proposals by assigning numeric scores between 0 and 5 points for each of the 13 evaluation subfactors, and then multiplied the raw score by the weight assigned to each of the subfactors to arrive at weighted scores. According to the protester, because all of the acceptable proposals (that is, proposals that it

Table 4-16   CDC Case Study Evaluation Results

Offeror	Technical score/ percentage of available points	Adjectival rating	Price
Offeror A	325 / 77.38 percent	Technically acceptable	$563,292.00
GAP Solutions	322.5 / 76.79 percent	Technically acceptable	$387,997.20
Offeror B	318.33 / 75.79 percent	Technically acceptable	$398,429.32
Total Solutions	314.16 / 74.8 percent	Technically acceptable	$380,105.68

describes as likely to have been included in the competitive range) would in practice be assigned raw numeric scores of either 3 or 4, the effect was to artificially narrow the range of possible total scores, such that it would appear from the numeric scores that all of the proposals were technically equal. According to the protester, this effectively left the source selection to be based on low price rather than on technical considerations which were to have received paramount consideration under the terms of the RFP.

The GAO ruled that this argument was without merit, stating:

> It is well established that ratings, be they numerical, adjectival, or color, are merely guides for intelligent decision making in the procurement process.

> Where the evaluators and source selection official reasonably consider the underlying bases for the ratings, including advantages and disadvantages associated with the specific content of competing proposals, in a manner that is fair and equitable and consistent with the solicitation, a protester's disagreement over the actual adjectival or numeric ratings assigned essentially is inconsequential in that it does not affect the reasonableness of the judgments made in the source selection decision.

> The record here shows that the agency performed an evaluation of the proposals consistent with the RFP evaluation factors and prepared detailed narrative materials reflecting the evaluators' findings.... The record also shows that those findings were specifically considered in detail by the agency's source selection official in making the agency's award decision. Indeed, because the scoring was so close among the four proposals, the source selection official expressly queried the evaluators "to determine if there was a proposal that contained technical aspects that would clearly set it apart from any of the other ones." The technical panel concluded that no proposal had technical advantages or discrepancies that would set it apart from the other proposals and, as a result, the proposals were determined to be technically equal.

> GAP does not challenge any of the agency's underlying substantive findings with respect to the relative merits of the competing proposals. [The protester did not, for example,] allege that the agency unreasonably failed to identify strengths that were present in its proposal or unreasonably identified weaknesses that were not present; nor [did] it challenge the agency's underlying findings with respect to the other proposals in the competitive range, including the awardee's. [Moreover, GAP did not allege or demonstrate] that it should have been assigned higher numeric scores, or that the awardee should have been assigned lower numeric scores, based upon the strengths or weaknesses identified by the agency in its evaluation.

"Given the absence of any substantive challenge to the agency's detailed narrative evaluation findings," the GAO had no basis to question the agency's evaluation results. The protest was denied.[23]

This case demonstrates that when an agency evaluates proposals in a reasonable manner and considers the basis for the evaluators' ratings along with the advantages and disadvantages of each proposal, the actual adjectival or numeric ratings assigned are inconsequential and don't affect the reasonableness of the source selection authority's decision.

SUPPORTING RATING SYSTEMS WITH NARRATIVE DESCRIPTIONS

Proposal evaluators must support adjectival, color, or numerical ratings with narrative statements that explain or justify the given score. Narrative statements describe to the source selection authority all of a proposal's relative strengths, weaknesses, and risks relative to the evaluation criteria in a way that adjectives, colors, and numbers alone cannot. Thus, they help to provide a reasonable and rational basis for the selection decision.[24]

Narratives are required when:

- The evaluators apply evaluation standards
- The evaluation team compares proposals
- The source selection authority conducts a cost/technical trade-off.

The contracting officer also needs the detailed information on strengths and weaknesses to debrief unsuccessful offerors, per FAR 15.506(d). So do contracting and legal personnel, to defend against any protests that might be filed with the agency or the GAO.[25]

It is helpful to provide specific proposal page references in narratives; this will make it easier to discuss the proposals in consensus sessions. Providing references to specific pages in an offeror's proposal also helps when preparing for debriefings because companies want to understand how to improve their proposals for the next competition.

In their narratives, evaluators must list and justify proposal strengths and weaknesses for each factor based on all evaluation standards.

- A *strength* is an aspect of an offeror's proposal that exceeds the standard.
- A *significant strength* is a strength that is an outstanding or exceptional aspect of an offeror's proposal. It has merit and exceeds specified performance or capability requirements in a way that is advantageous to the government and either will be included in the contract or is inherent in the offeror's process.
- A *weakness* is a flaw in a proposal that increases the risk of unsuccessful contract performance.
- A *significant weakness* in a proposal is a flaw that appreciably increases the risk of unsuccessful contract performance.

Table 4-17   Degrees of Strength and Weakness[26]

Strength		Weakness	
+	Slightly above standards/expectations	-	Slightly below standards/expectations
++	Clearly above standards/expectations	--	Clearly below standards/expectations
+++	Significantly above standards/expectations	---	Significantly below standards/expectations

If a proposed approach exceeds the evaluation standard, the evaluator records a strength and assigns a degree to that strength (see Table 4-17). Likewise, if a proposed approach is below standards, the evaluator documents the weakness and assigns the appropriate degree to that weakness. If an evaluator does not fully understand what the offeror proposes because the proposal does not have sufficient information, that aspect of the proposal is considered to be below the standard. If a proposed approach meets government expectations, it is assigned a "meets standards" rating and does not require justification; however, evaluators may include a statement to support their "meets standard" assessment.

The degree of a strength or a weakness is a subjective determination based on the evaluator's reasoned judgment, and it must be supported by the narrative. Before evaluating proposals, the evaluation team should have a common understanding of the expectations for each of the evaluation standards.

Evaluators must use the evaluation factors from the RFP to make a consistent and integrated assessment of each offeror's ability to satisfy the requirements of the solicitation. They should individually evaluate the proposals against the requirements of the solicitation—not evaluate the merits of one proposal against another. Each evaluator's narrative creates a record that demonstrates that the evaluation was fair, comprehensive, and performed in accordance with the solicitation and source selection plan.[27]

Narratives must be specific and thorough yet concise, because they are used extensively during the factor group consensus process (see Chapter 9 for a detailed discussion of the consensus process), to prepare panel reports, and for SSA briefings and unsuccessful offeror debriefings.[28]

CHAPTER SUMMARY

Chapter 4 explores the various rating and scoring methodologies used by different agencies. Agencies have a great deal of flexibility in setting up and applying the rating scales for a source selection. Agencies typically use adjectival, color, numerical, or a combination of them.

Agencies frequently use adjectival ratings to score or rate an offeror's proposal because it has a great deal of flexibility. The adjectives indicate the degree to which the proposal meets the standard for each factor evaluated. Adjectives used may include *outstanding, good, acceptable, marginal,* or *unsatisfactory.*

Another method for scoring proposals is the color coding rating scale. The color coding system uses colors to indicate the degree to which the offeror's proposal meets the standard for each factor evaluated. Like the adjectival method, color coding provides a flexible system. Agencies use different colors and definitions for what each rating means. Generally, blue is the highest possible, and red is the lowest possible; but the colors in between vary.

Numeric scoring is another way to rate proposals. The numerical system assigns point scores (such as 0 to 10, 0 to 100, or 0 to 1,000) to rate proposals. This rating system generally allows for more rating levels and thus may appear to give more precise distinctions of merit. However, numerical systems can have drawbacks as their apparent precision may obscure the strengths, weaknesses, and risks that support the numbers.

Some agencies use a combination approach to scoring, using colors, numbers, and/or adjectives. The evaluator can assign a number or color to the proposal by applying the definitions provided. This approach provides flexibility for those who might prefer a definitive numerical approach and those who prefer the more general color or adjectival approach.

Regardless of the scoring method used, the important thing is to document the evaluation with thorough narratives that explain the decision making process. The evaluator's written narrative is used in conjunction with a rating system to indicate a proposal's strengths, weaknesses, and risks. Evaluators must support an adjectival, color, or numerical rating with narrative statements that explain or justify the given score. Narrative statements can describe the proposals' relative strengths, weaknesses, and risks to the source selection authority in a way that adjectives, colors, and numbers alone cannot.

The chapter's case studies illustrate that an agency's source selection evaluation plan is an internal agency guideline and that failure to adhere to such a plan does not provide a valid basis for protest. It is the evaluation scheme in the RFP, not internal agency documents, to which an agency is required to adhere in evaluating proposals and in making the source selection.[29]

NOTES

1 Harold V. Hanson, *NAVSEA Source Selection Guide* (Washington, DC: U.S. Naval Sea Systems Command, 2001), 23.

2 U.S. Department of Energy, *Source Selection Guide* (Washington, DC: U.S. Department of Energy, 2005), 11.

3 Johnnie E. Wilson, *Best Value Source Selection* 715-3 (Alexandria, VA: Army Materiel Command, 1998), 8.

4 Claude M. Bolton, Jr., *Army Source Selection Manual* (Washington, DC: Office of the Assistant Secretary of the Army for Acquisition, Logistics and Technology, 2007), 4.

5 Adapted from Hanson, 14–17.

6 U.S. Government Accountability Office, "Trajen, Inc.; Maytag Aircraft Corporation," B-296334; B-296334.2; B-296334.3; B-296334.4 (July 29, 2005).

7 U.S. Government Accountability Office, "Chapman Law Firm, LPA," B-293105.6; B-293105.10; B-293105.12 (November 15, 2004).

8 Defense Information Systems Agency, *Source Selection Deskbook* (Arlington, VA: Defense Information Systems Agency, May 2003), 15.

9 Bolton, 20.

10 U.S. Department of Energy, 11.

11 U.S. Air Force, "Source Selection," *Mandatory Procedure* MP5315.3 (January 2009), 10–11.

12 Ibid.

13 Wilson, 13.

14 National Aeronautics and Space Administration, *NASA FAR Supplement* 1815.300-70(a)(1)(ii) (Washington, DC: National Aeronautics and Space Administration).

15 U.S. Government Accountability Office, "ASRC Research & Technology Solutions, LLC," B-400217; B-400217.2 (August 21, 2008), 2.

16 U.S. Environmental Protection Agency, *EPA Acquisition Regulation* 1515.305-70 (Washington, DC: U.S. Environmental Protection Agency).

17 National Aeronautics and Space Administration, *NASA FAR Supplement* 1815.304-70 (Washington, DC: National Aeronautics and Space Administration).

18 National Reconnaissance Office, *Source Selection Manual* N87 (Chantilly, VA: National Reconnaissance Office, 2008), 32.

19 U.S. Department of Energy, 13.

20 National Aeronautics and Space Administration, *Source Selection Guide* (Washington, DC: National Aeronautics and Space Administration, June 2007), 41.

21 Ibid., 43.

22 U.S. Government Accountability Office, "Fintrac, Inc.," B-311462.2; B-311462.3 (October 14, 2008).

23 U.S. Government Accountability Office, "Gap Solutions, Inc.," B-310564 (January 4, 2008).

24 Wilson, 13.

25 U.S. Department of Energy, 14.

26 National Reconnaissance Office, 31.

27 Hanson, 8.

28 National Reconnaissance Office, 31.

29 U.S. Government Accountability Office, "Base Technologies, Inc.," B-293061.2; B-293061.3 (January 28, 2004).

Chapter 5

Writing the Rest of the Solicitation

This chapter explains what goes into the rest of a request for proposals (RFP), also called a *solicitation*, including the statement of work and the proposal preparation instructions. Although it seems backwards, evaluation teams should prepare the evaluation criteria (section M) before the proposal preparation instructions (section L). This approach helps ensure that the agency gets the information it needs from offerors in order to evaluate the proposals. The agency can't write the proposal preparation instructions until it knows what it's going to evaluate. The proposal preparation instructions tell the offeror to provide the necessary information to meet the requirements established by the evaluation criteria. That's why the agency must write the evaluation criteria first.

All the parts of a solicitation must work together to communicate the government's requirements to potential offerors. The RFP provides all the information the offeror must have to understand what the government needs, the acquisition method, and the evaluation criteria, including:

- The statement of work or performance work statement
- The terms and conditions
- Evaluation factors and significant subfactors and the relative importance of the factors and subfactors
- Instructions to offerors, including whether the government might award without discussions, and other exhibits and attachments.

Once the contracting officer (CO) completes the RFP's major elements, he or she may decide to release a draft RFP to potential offerors for comment. Later in this chapter, we'll review the process for using a draft RFP and the important preliminaries before releasing the final RFP.

Table 5-1 Uniform Contract Format

Section	Title
Part I—The schedule	
A	Solicitation/contract form
B	Supplies or services and prices/costs
C	Description/specifications/statement of work
D	Packaging and marking
E	Inspection and acceptance
F	Deliveries or performance
G	Contract administration data
H	Special contract requirements
Part II—Contract clauses	
I	Contract clauses
Part III—List of documents, exhibits, and other attachments	
J	List of attachments
Part IV—Representations and instructions	
K	Representations, certifications, and other statements of offerors or respondents
L	Instructions, conditions, and notices to offerors or respondents
M	Evaluation factors for award

THE UNIFORM CONTRACT FORMAT

The uniform contract format (UCF) helps agencies and offerors find answers to questions about an acquisition. The same information always appears in the same section for each RFP, regardless of the requirement. Table 5-1 illustrates the uniform contract format.

The UCF consists of the following sections:

A. **Solicitation/contract form.** Optional Form (OF) 308: Solicitation and Offer – Negotiated Acquisition; Standard Form (SF) 33: Solicitation, Offer and Award; the agency equivalent; or plain paper format can be used.

B. **Supplies or services and prices/costs.** Generally, the OF 336: Continuation Sheet or agency equivalent is used. Include a brief description of each line item, including item number, national stock or part number (if applicable), and name or short title, and quantity.

C. **Description/specifications/statement of work.** Include any description or specifications needed to describe the government's requirements in addition to the information in section B.

D. **Packaging and marking.** Detail packaging, packing, preservation, and marking requirements (if any).

E. **Inspection and acceptance.** Include inspection, acceptance, quality assurance, and reliability requirements.

F. **Deliveries or performance.** Specify requirements for time, place, and method of delivery or performance of the contract.

G. **Contract administration data.** Include any required accounting and appropriation data and any required contract administration information or instructions other than those on the solicitation form.

H. **Special contract requirements.** State any special contract requirements not included elsewhere. Be sure these requirements do not conflict with other requirements.

I. **Contract clauses.** Include clauses required by law, the FAR, agency regulations, or other requirements that are not included elsewhere.

J. **List of attachments.** List the title, date, and number of pages for each attached document, exhibit, or other attachment. For complex acquisitions, the requirements document is typically included in this section.

K. **Representations, certifications, and other statements of offerors or respondents.** Include provisions that require representations, certifications, or submission of other offeror information.

L. **Instructions, conditions, and notices to offerors or respondents.** Insert solicitation provisions and other information and instructions not required elsewhere that will guide offerors in preparing proposals. Prospective offerors may be instructed to submit proposals or information in a specific format or in severable parts, frequently called *volumes*, to facilitate evaluation. The instructions may specify further organization of proposal or response parts. For example, there may be specific guidelines for the organization or submission of administrative, management, technical, past performance, and cost or pricing data or information other than cost or pricing data.

M. **Evaluation factors for award.** Identify all significant factors and any significant subfactors that will be considered in awarding the contract and their relative importance. Describe the relative importance of cost or price and other factors by inserting one of the phrases in FAR 15.304(e).[1]

THE STATEMENT OF WORK

(Note: Much of the material in this section is based on the Department of Health and Human Services *Project Officers' Contracting Handbook.*)

The statement of work (SOW) is the single most critical document in the acquisition process. It must define requirements in clear, concise language, identifying specific work the contractor must accomplish. It also defines the respective responsibilities of the government and the contractor and provides an objective measure so that both the government and the contractor will know when the work is complete and payment is due. In performance-based acquisitions, the SOW is called the performance work statement (PWS). It states the technical, functional, and performance characteristics of the work to be performed. In this section we will use the terms *SOW* and *PWS* synonymously, unless noted otherwise.

The agency must carefully word the SOW because it will be read and interpreted by a variety of people in both government and industry, such as the program manager, contract manager, cost estimators, and technical personnel. If the SOW does not state exactly what the agency needs, or does not state the requirements precisely, the contracting officer and contractor will face contract administration problems during performance. Ambiguous statements of work often result in unsatisfactory contractor performance, delays, disputes, changes, and higher contract costs. If there's any ambiguity or confusion about what the agency requires, potential offerors should ask for clarification during the draft RFP process or proposal preparation process.

In the event of a dispute or protest, the SOW may be reviewed by an administrative board, GAO, or the courts for interpretation. These interpretations represent what an objective third party thinks is the document's intent. Generally speaking, the court or board will not concern itself with what the author intended to express, but will look at what it did express. This determination is usually made solely on the basis of the words used and the context in which they appear. Keep in mind that the comptroller general and the courts generally interpret ambiguous requirements against the drafter. If the government wrote the document (such as a statement of work), then the fault for the ambiguity rests with government. If, on the other hand, the contractor wrote the document (such as a performance work statement), then the fault for the ambiguity rests with the contractor.

The SOW affects the entire acquisition cycle:

- It determines the contract type.
- It influences the number and quality of proposals received.
- It serves as a baseline against which to evaluate proposals and contractor performance after award.

Thus, the SOW is the key element in shaping and directing all three stages of the acquisition cycle: solicitation, evaluation, and postaward administration.

In the presolicitation phase, the SOW establishes the parameters of the government's requirements so that the program manager and contracting officer can determine the best way to accomplish them. It guides the market research that impacts the other stages of the acquisition process. Therefore, the SOW not only articulates the program objectives, it also establishes the minimum requirements for performing the work.

In the solicitation, evaluation, and award phase, the SOW communicates the agency's requirements to prospective offerors. At this stage, the SOW guides the offerors on the content of their technical proposals. When a contract is awarded, the SOW becomes part of the contract between the two parties, stating what the contractor proposed and the government accepted. Therefore, the statement of work defines not only the scope of work, but also the details, including tasks the contractor must undertake, types or stages of work, number and type of personnel, the sequence of work, and reporting requirements.

In the postaward stage, the SOW provides the mechanism for defining the work or supplies that are to be produced and the deadlines for producing them. To be effective at this stage, the SOW should provide a guide for monitoring the progress of work by specifying what supplies the contractor should deliver or tasks the contractor should accomplish at specific times during the course of the contract. The SOW also should describe the desired supplies or results of the work effort and set standards for contractor performance.

Common Elements of a Statement of Work

Because each acquisition is unique, each SOW must be tailored to the project's requirements and mission. The SOW's elements will vary with the objective, complexity, size, and nature of the acquisition. But in general, an SOW should include the following topics, as applicable:

1. **Background.** This section describes the requirements in general, nontechnical terms and explains why the agency is undertaking the acquisition and how it relates to past, current, or future projects. Include a summary of statutory program authority and any regulations that may apply. Discuss effective techniques from previous efforts, as well as unsuccessful efforts and what the agency is doing differently to ensure success.

   A statutory program authority is a program that is required by statute. For example, the Commerce Department established an International Buyer Program to bring international buyers together with U.S. firms by promoting U.S. trade shows in industries with high export potential. This program is required by statute which states in part: "In order to facilitate exporting by United States businesses, the Secretary of Commerce shall provide assistance for trade shows in the United States which bring together representatives of United States businesses seeking to export goods or services produced in the United States and representatives of foreign companies or governments seeking to buy such goods or services from these United States businesses."[2]

2. **Project objectives.** This section provides a succinct statement of the acquisition's purpose. It should outline the results that the government expects and may also explain the program's benefits.

3. **Scope of work.** This section is an overall, nontechnical description of the work to be performed. It expands on the project's objectives, but does not detail all of the work required. The various phases of the project are identified and summarized, as are specific objectives, time limits, special provisions, or other limitations. This information must be consistent with the detailed requirements. Summarize the contractor's responsibilities along with the expected results or deliverables.

4. **Detailed technical requirements.** This section explains precisely what is expected of the contractor during contract performance. It describes the specific tasks and phases of the work and specifies the total effort each task or phase should receive. Include considerations that may guide the contractor in analyzing the requirement, designing a solution, or dealing with specific work issues or risks. Specify the requirements (such as training, computer modeling, testing, or verifying), and indicate the scope of each. For example, include the parameters of tests and the criteria governing how many designs or tests are required. Also identify any budgetary, environmental, security, or other constraints. If more than one approach is possible, and the agency prefers a specific approach, then the agency must identify the preferred approach in this section. If a particular approach is not specified, state the criteria the agency will use to determine which of the alternative approaches is best.

5. **Deliverables.** Clearly identify the deliverables the agency requires under the contract, and detail the criteria for accepting the deliverables. Delivery or completion deadlines can be expressed by calendar date, or a certain number of days from the date of contract award may be allowed. When using the latter method, contracting officers should state whether the days counted are work days or calendar days.

6. **Reporting schedule.** In this section, specify how the contractor should show that it has fulfilled its obligations. Define how the contractor can demonstrate progress and compliance with the requirements and present any problems it may have encountered. It is important to require the contractor to prepare and submit technical and financial progress reports, as they help the contracting officer keep track of the contractor's progress. Reports should correlate costs incurred and the degree of contract completion.

Agencies typically require monthly or bimonthly progress reports. Specify the topics that must be covered in the reports, the report format, the number of copies the contractor should submit, and to whom they should be submitted. Clearly identify the criteria to be used by the agency for accepting the report. Don't ask for more information than the agency needs or for more copies of the report than necessary for only the personnel who will actually read it. Requiring unnecessary information or copies of the report will only increase costs.

7. **Special considerations.** In this section, include any information that does not fit neatly or logically into one of the other sections. For example, in complex acquisitions, a program may be composed of several contracts. Contractors may have to work together to ensure program success but may not have a contractual relationship with each other. The agency must explain any special relationships between the contractor and other contractors also working for the government with whom they may work.

8. **References.** Provide a detailed list and description of any studies, reports, and other data referred to elsewhere in the statement of work. The agency should describe, cite, and cross-reference each document to the applicable part of the work statement. If documents are limited or are not included in the RFP, the agency should tell offerors where they can get a copy or when and where the documents will be available for review. Examples of references include memoranda, technical reports, scholarly studies, articles, specifications, and standards.

   Be careful not to incorporate too many references. They may be interpreted as requirements by the offerors, which can lead to cost increases. Only include references that are critical to successful completion of the work at hand. The RFP should state whether these documents are contractually binding or are used only for guidance.

Planning and Writing a Statement of Work

Because the SOW is the most influential document in an acquisition, the agency must plan and write it carefully. The SOW expresses what the contractor must accomplish and determines whether the government receives the supplies or services it needs. The first step in writing a successful SOW is planning.

Carefully planning the SOW will save time in the writing phase and will make it possible to develop a concise RFP. The first step in this planning process is determining the project's objectives. This involves developing clear statements about why the agency is undertaking the acquisition and what it hopes to achieve. Such statements are critical: It is impossible to communicate a requirement to potential offerors unless the agency clearly states the requirement.

Once the agency states the project's objectives, the next step is for the project manager to meet with the contracting officer, who will help lay out the requirements for the acquisition and the schedule of events that must occur in order to award the contract by a specific date. The contracting officer can also identify applicable regulations and in-house experts who may be able to help complete the acquisition.

The next step is to determine all of the individual requirements the contractor must fulfill for the agency to meet its objectives. Requirements that must be considered at this stage include:

1. **Deliverables and performance standards**
   1.1. What supplies/services are required?
   1.2. Who will use the supplies and how?
   1.3. What performance/accuracy standards can the agency specify for the supplies or services?
2. **Personnel**
   2.1. What level of staffing should the contractor provide?
   2.2. What qualifications must the contractor's staff have?
   2.3. What qualifications/experience should the contractor have?
   2.4. What education and/or certifications should the personnel have?
3. **Methodology**
   3.1. What is the appropriate methodology for performing the work?
   3.2. Are there alternative methodologies, and are these alternatives acceptable?
   3.3. What stages/phases does the project have?
4. **Schedule**
   4.1. When does the agency need the project completed?
   4.2. How long should the project take?
   4.3. What is the schedule for the deliverables?
5. **Location**
   5.1. Where should the performance take place?
   5.2. Is travel required? If so, where and how often?

Once the acquisition team lists all of the requirements, the contracting officer and program manager arrange them into a logical sequence. While listing the requirements, it may be helpful to do some background reading. Collect and analyze previous documents and contract deliverables that impact the requirements, including:

- Documents that discuss overall program goals and objectives of related or similar programs
- Reports, manuals, or other deliverables produced in the past
- Statements of work developed for similar projects
- Previous contracts, to determine what modifications were added.

Review governmentwide or departmental regulations, policy directives, or administrative memoranda that apply to the type of acquisition under consideration. Consult with other program personnel to get additional views on the project and its objectives and requirements. Consult the end users to find out what they really need and how soon they need it.

At this stage, it is important to decide if the complexity of the project requires advice from technical specialists or help from additional writers. If so, identify the personnel needed and specify the areas that each should address.

Specifying the Contractual Approach

Once the contracting officer has stated the project objectives and listed the requirements, he or she can begin identifying the contractual approach. This process requires the CO to decide if the SOW should be a detailed design-oriented requirements document, a performance-oriented requirements document, or a combination, and whether the contract should be done on a completion or a level-of-effort basis (see "Term vs. Completion Statements of Work" later in this chapter).

Each of these decisions is discussed in more detail below, but as the CO makes these decisions, a few points should be kept in mind. The project's objectives affect how much flexibility the contractor has in planning its approach to the work. An SOW may be broad and general or specific and detailed. But whether an SOW is loose or tight, simple or complex, certain general principles apply. The SOW:

- Should neither be so narrow as to restrict the contractor's efforts nor so broad as to permit the contractor to explore or undertake work in areas that have little relationship to the stated contract tasks.
- Must define the contractor's obligations and be definitive enough to protect the government's interests.
- Should give the contractor sufficient guidance to be able to perform the work required. It should provide a clear, unambiguous, and complete basis for effective and efficient performance. Keep in mind that the government may not provide relatively continuous supervision and control over the contractor personnel, or the contract may be interpreted as a personal services contract.[3]

A personal services contract is characterized by the employer-employee relationship it creates between the government and the contractor's personnel. The government is normally required to obtain its employees by direct hire under competitive appointment or other procedures required by the civil service laws. Obtaining personal services by contract, rather than by direct hire, circumvents those laws unless Congress has specifically authorized acquisition of the services by contract.

Specifying Requirements

An SOW may be a detailed design-oriented requirements document, a performance-oriented requirements document, or a combination of both. A *detailed design-oriented requirements document* describes the work in terms of *how* the contractor accomplishes work, or it specifies the number of hours allowed for the work. A detailed design might include specific materials, parameters, and methods a contractor must use to deliver a project or service to the government. When the government requires specific materials and methods, then the government is responsible for the results. The contractor must follow the specified steps, but the government is responsible for ensuring that following these steps will produce the desired result. For example, if the government issues a detailed design-oriented document for a testing program, the contractor implements the program specified but is not responsible for the validity or usefulness of the test results.

A *performance-oriented requirements document*, on the other hand, does not limit a contractor to providing a specific product or service. It describes the work in terms of the required output, rather than how the work should be done or the number of hours that must be delivered.[4] It explains the objectives the contractor must accomplish, the end goal, or the desired achievement, including all pertinent information needed to prepare a proposal. For example, a performance work statement for a training course might specify the skills to be taught and the level of skill that participants must have upon course completion. It is then the offeror's responsibility to specify in its proposal how it will fulfill these objectives.

As a general rule, it is best to place maximum responsibility for performance on the contractor because the contractor is being hired for its expertise and ability to perform. However, the cost of the contract may be higher if the contractor must determine the proper approach and methods. Consequently, if the program office or agency believes it has devised a good method for accomplishing its objectives, the cost benefit of specifying this method in the SOW should be weighed against the risk that offerors might know even better methods. Market research conducted during the acquisition planning phase should yield insights into the methods companies are currently using and how well they would meet the government's needs.

Often SOWs use a combination of detailed design-oriented and performance-oriented requirements. If the agency uses such a combination, it must be certain that the contractor can achieve the required result by following the government's requirements documents. Per FAR part 11, requirements should be stated in terms of:

- Functions to be performed
- Performance required
- Essential physical characteristics.

The contracting officer's technical representative must also define requirements in terms that enable and encourage the offerors to supply commercial or nondevelopmental items.[5]

FAR 37.602 provides guidance on using performance work statements (PWS). Essentially, they must describe the work in terms of the required results rather than either how the work is to be accomplished or the number of hours to be provided. A PWS should:

- Enable assessment of work performance against measurable performance standards
- Rely on the use of measurable performance standards and financial incentives in a competitive environment to encourage competition and to develop and institute innovative and cost-effective methods of performing the work.[6]

Quality assurance surveillance plans (QASP) must be developed when acquiring services using a performance-based work statement. The plans should be written in conjunction with the performance work statement and should specify all work requiring surveillance and the method of surveillance.[7] These plans should recognize the responsibility of the contractor to carry out its quality control obligations and must contain measurable inspection and acceptance criteria corresponding to the performance standards contained in the PWS. QASPs must focus on the level of performance required by the PWS rather than on the methodology used by the contractor to achieve that level of performance.

Distinguishing Term from Completion Statements of Work

Chapter 2 discusses different contract types and introduced the concept of term and completion contracts. It is important to understand the distinction when writing a statement of work. A *term* or *level-of-effort acquisition* requires that the contractor furnish a report on technical effort during the period of performance, while *completion acquisitions* require the contractor to develop a tangible end item that is designed to meet specific performance characteristics.

A term or level-of-effort SOW is appropriate for research when the government is seeking to gather general information. A term or level-of-effort statement of work may only require that a specific number of labor-hours be expended without requiring a final product. For example, a level-of-effort SOW might entail providing a certain level of maintenance services or technical support.

A completion-type SOW is appropriate for development work when the government already knows that it is feasible to produce a certain end item. Completion statements of work may describe what is to be achieved through the contracted effort, such as developing new methods, new end items, or other tangible results.

For example, a completion requirement might entail delivering a final study report, submitting test results, or developing and delivering documentation on a computer program.

Whichever method is selected, the SOW should be definitive and precise. In describing an end item, for example, be specific about the characteristics it must possess and the standards it must meet. In a level-of-effort SOW, where results of the effort are not measurable, be specific about the goals and directions toward which the contractor is to deploy resources.

Phasing Contracts

Individual research, development, or demonstration projects frequently lie well beyond the present state of the art and entail procedures and techniques of great complexity and difficulty. Under these circumstances, a contractor, no matter how carefully selected, may be unable to deliver the desired result.

Moreover, the job of evaluating the contractor's progress is often difficult. Such a contract is frequently divided into stages or phases, each of which must be completed and approved before the contractor may proceed to the next stage or phase. When the agency can identify phases of work, the statement of work should explain the phasing, and the RFP should require offerors to submit proposed costs by phases. The resultant contract will reflect costs by phases, require the contractor to identify incurred costs by phases, establish delivery schedules by phase, and require the written acceptance of each phase before starting the next phase.

Phasing makes it necessary to develop certain methods and controls, including reporting requirements for each phase of the contract and factors for evaluating the reports the contractor submits, which will provide necessary data for making decisions relative to all phases. A phased contract may include stages of accomplishment such as research, development, demonstration, or validation. Within each phase, there may be a number of tasks that should be included in the statement of work.

Phasing should not be used for projects in which several tasks must proceed simultaneously, because if each task is made a separate phase, progress will be blocked by lack of data.

Outlining Statements of Work

Once the agency clearly states the individual requirements for accomplishing the project objectives and identifies the contractual approach, the next step is to outline the SOW. An outline provides a structure for the document and saves a great deal of writing time. A detailed outline makes it easier to focus on content and to spot inconsistencies, redundancies, and gaps that may need to be filled. It also provides a clear picture of the interrelationship among ideas and the most logical order in which to present them. This can best be done by developing a work breakdown structure (WBS) for the contemplated effort. We briefly discussed the work breakdown structure in Chapter 3, where we explained structuring and limiting evaluation criteria.

Once the program manager has written the outline, write a first draft. Remember that the purpose is not to create an entertaining piece of literature, but to express a need and to state requirements such that potential offerors understand what the agency is looking for and can respond. In general, the object in writing a first draft is to get the ideas down on paper. Follow the outline, and write one part at a time. Write as much as possible at a time, but don't try to revise the first draft as it is being written. Include enough detail to communicate clearly with the reader. Explain and illustrate points wherever it is necessary to convey the correct meaning.

Revising Statements of Work

When the first draft is finished, the program manager must rewrite and revise it. The writer should read the statement of work several times, revising and clarifying each time. The first time, the writer should check only the content, asking the following questions:

- Does the SOW contain sufficient information?
- Do I need to provide more examples to clarify the objectives?
- Have I included too much material?
- Does the writing reflect sound reasoning?

During the second review, check the organization of the SOW, asking the following questions:

- Is the subject stated clearly?
- Does the document flow logically?
- Is the connection between sections clear?
- Are there any gaps that need to be filled?

During the third reading, check the sentence structure and grammar. The next part of this section provides suggestions on what to look for during the third reading.

Continue this process by revising the SOW until the document is logical and readable, conveys exactly what is required of the contractor, and emphasizes the critical elements. One of the best ways of determining whether an SOW meets the document's objectives is to have it reviewed by someone else in the program office. Writers often have trouble critiquing their own writing because they tend to read into their own work what they intended it to say instead of what it actually says.

Writing Clear, Effective Statements of Work

The basic purpose of all writing is to convey a meaning to a reader. The quality and clarity of the writing will determine whether that purpose is accomplished. If the writing is unclear, the reader will not understand the message; if it is wordy, the reader will waste time trying to determine the meaning and may misinterpret it. If the language is unfamiliar or too technical, the reader may misunderstand or lose interest. Following is a list of writing suggestions.

- **Use simple, direct, and clear language.** Use short, clear, well-understood words. Avoid technical language unless its meaning is well understood or unless it is defined in the statement of work itself. Avoid words with multiple meanings and vague words such as *reasonable* or *et cetera* (*etc.*).
- **Use active verbs.** Passive verbs are vague. For example, say "The contractor shall perform," not "It shall be performed," because the latter doesn't define *who* will perform the work. This is particularly important in research and development acquisitions, in which many of the contractor's activities depend on the government supplying certain information first.
- **Use adjectives carefully.** Many times, adjectives make meanings vague instead of adding clarity. For example, using adjectives such as *workmanlike, successful, substantial*, and *reasonable* to modify the description of work the contractor is to perform tends to decrease the contractor's obligation because the adjectives are subject to interpretation. For example, how much is substantial, and who decides if the deliverable is substantial enough for acceptance? It's better to be specific and clear rather than vague and subjective.
- **Use language consistently.** Do not change a word or phrase unless a change in meaning is intended. The same words and phrases must be used consistently when describing the same requirement. It is confusing if an opening is referred to as a *gap* in one section and an *aperture* in another section.
- **Use *and/or* sparingly.** The phrase *and/or* is confusing, and it should not be used unless necessary. This is one situation in which the rule of using as few words as possible can be ignored. For example, if the SOW says, "The contractor shall supply A, B, and/or C," is the firm in compliance if it supplies A and C? Or can it merely supply C, under the assumption that *and/or* meant that supplying C was sufficient? If the writer really means that the contractor has the choice of supplying any or all of the three items, it is better to say, "The contractor shall supply A, B, or C; all of them; or any combination of them."

Confusing SOW Elements

In addition to the specific language pitfalls mentioned above, there are certain elements in the SOW that often cause confusion.

- **Time.** One of the big problems when writing an SOW is specifying when something must be done. It is best if the obligation is made certain: "On February 1, the contractor shall submit a report." But sometimes the submission of that report will depend on other contingencies. One of the most annoying contingencies is uncertainty about the date the contractor is to start work or is permitted by the government to start work. When using language such as "Deliver within 90 calendar days...", be sure to specify the date from which the 90 days will be counted. Avoid phrasing like "90 days from the award of the contract," because this is ambiguous. "Award" might mean the date the government decided who the contractor would be, the date the contracting officer approved the selection of the contractor, or the date the contract was signed. To avoid this kind of ambiguity, say "90 days from the *effective date of the contract*." The "effective date" is a definitive date, such as November 2, 2010, and stating a specific date gives a firm base from which to start.

- **Personnel references.** Sometimes an SOW requires that the contractor deliver a report or invoice to a certain person. Generally, it is better to specify this person by title rather than by name because personnel can change.

- **Incorporation by reference.** Often, an agency needs to incorporate other documents into the SOW, such as previous studies or reports. When this is done, the government should completely identify the incorporated document by date, title, and revision number, if applicable. The government must specifically state where an offeror can obtain the document if it is not attached. If standard tables are incorporated, the author should be clear about which tables and revision date have been used and should know exactly what the tables say. Again, the government must specify whether these documents establish contractual requirements required for compliance or are provided only for reference or guidance.

- **Agreements to agree.** Be careful about "agreeing to agree" on some significant points. If "the model is to be painted a color to be mutually agreed upon," and the author of the SOW really does not care what color it is, then no harm is done. But if the color is actually significant, the matter should not be left open.

- **Theoretical discussion.** Sometimes theoretical discussion is included in an SOW, with confusing results. If it is necessary to include scientific background or theoretical reasons for doing the work, the author should try to do this in a separate part of the SOW so that there will be a clear line of demarcation between the "why" and the "what." Ideally, an SOW should consist of a description of work, not theoretical discussion. The inclusion of the latter may have the effect of modifying the instructions, so that the contractor is given a *reason* for not performing in accordance with the author's wishes or for doing something that was not desired.

- **Government obligations.** Be specific about describing what the government is supposed to do. Frequently, a contractor's obligation to perform depends on what the government does first. If the government does not perform its part, the contractor will be excused from performing. If it appears that the government did not perform, then the contractor will have the foundation for a dispute.

This situation may arise if it is not sufficiently clear what the government is to do and when. For example, the phrase "Based on information supplied by the government, the contractor shall..." leaves open what information the government should supply. It could be a great deal; it could be very little. There is no way of knowing whether it is significant or not, costly or inexpensive. There is no way of determining when the government will supply this information. But the contractor is in a position at any time to claim that whatever the necessary information was, the firm did not have it. Furthermore, the contractor is in a position to claim that even if it did get what it needed, it did not get it soon enough.

State precisely the kind of information the government will supply, and when. Limit the obligation to supplying information or services that are readily available to the government. Do not agree to give information or services that the government does not have or that may cost a great deal to get.[8]

PROPOSAL PREPARATION INSTRUCTIONS (SECTION L)

Proposal preparation instructions, which appear in section L of a solicitation, provide offerors with directions for preparing responses to the requirements. Section L must explain:

- The methods by which offerors should submit their proposals
- The requirements for addressing the specific areas the agency will evaluate and score or rate during source selection.[9]

There must be a link between the statement of work, each evaluation factor and subfactor (which appears in section M), and the proposal preparation instructions. If the contracting officer cannot map the solicitation requirements, factors and subfactors, and the proposal preparation instructions, the contracting officer must correct the conflict before releasing the RFP or draft RFP.

It's important that the solicitation request only the information needed to evaluate proposals against the evaluation factors and subfactors. Never ask for information the agency will not evaluate.[10] Contracting officers must try to avoid requiring offerors to submit large amounts of information. Not only do evaluators have to read and evaluate everything they receive, but if the requirements are too rigorous, potential offerors might not submit a proposal and may choose to pursue a less costly opportunity elsewhere. Requiring lengthy proposals not only increases the government's costs to perform the evaluation, in terms of personnel and facilities required to evaluate the proposals, but also extends the time it takes to evaluate all of the proposals. To simplify proposal preparation and to make the evaluation process easier, the contracting officer might consider imposing a realistic limit on the number of pages and foldouts.

In short, offerors should submit proposals that detail their approach for accomplishing the work required in the solicitation. Proposals should be clear, coherent and detailed enough for evaluators to assess them against the evaluation criteria. Proposals must also include convincing rationale for claims made within. The government does not want unnecessarily elaborate proposals. They need only to be a complete response to the RFP.

Specific, clear proposal preparation instructions also can simplify the evaluators' job. For example, if all offerors' proposals are formatted identically, evaluators will be able to read and assess them more quickly. Many agencies accept proposals in electronic form to help automate the evaluation process. Regardless of the form accepted, the instructions for preparing and submitting proposals must:

- Be clearly and precisely stated
- Be keyed to the evaluation factors and subfactors
- Describe the type, scope, content, and format of the information to be submitted
- Describe the order in which proposal responses and materials are to appear
- Be limited to the information needed to do the evaluation.[11]

Section L also provides the address to which proposals should be submitted and the due date and time. Offerors should note that if the RFP does not specify a time, the deadline for receipt is 4:30 p.m. local time per the FAR.[12]

ORGANIZING SECTION L

An effective way to organize section L is to group the proposal preparation instructions by the evaluation factor or subfactor under which evaluators will assess the requested information. If section L is structured this way, it will correlate to the sequence of evaluation factors and subfactors in section M. This increases the probability that offerors will format their proposals uniformly and facilitates efficient and effective evaluation. A sample section L is provided in Appendix 1. This format can be adapted as necessary.

Typically, proposal preparation instructions set standards for:

- Page and formatting limits
- The master packing list
- Oral proposals
- Technical/management information
- Cost/price information
- Past performance information.

Page and Formatting Limits

Section L establishes the page limitations for proposals. These should be firm limits, not guides. When determining page limits, the contracting officer should carefully consider the minimum number of pages an offeror will need to adequately address the RFP requirements. If the page limitations do not apply to certain portions of the proposal, this should be stated clearly. For example, the cost volume does not have any page limits. Section L should also mandate font size, margin size, the formatting of unnumbered section dividers, and whether foldouts on paper larger than 8 1/2 x 11 inches are allowed.

Because cost volumes do not have page limits, an offeror may put extra technical information in the cost volume to circumvent the established page limits. The contracting officer must make clear that pages submitted in excess of the limitation will not be evaluated and will be returned to the offeror with a letter citing the applicable RFP provision.

Master Packing List

For complex acquisitions, the proposal preparation instructions should instruct offerors to place a master packing list and all electronic proposals in the first box ("box 1") they submit. The master packing list should identify all proposal volumes by copy number and box number. This requirement will make it easier and more efficient to unpack and log in the proposals when they arrive.

Government agencies are increasingly requesting electronic submissions. Contracting officers must specify the file format and software version they will use to read the files.

Oral Proposals

Oral proposals may be substituted for, or augment, written proposal information. Substituting an oral presentation for portions of a proposal can be an effective way to streamline the source selection process. If the agency will accept oral proposals, consider establishing guidelines for the following elements:

- Time limits
- Record keeping (e.g., audio, video, and transcripts)
- Number of presentation slides
- Font size on slides
- Number and type of participants
- Extent and nature of the information exchanged
- Number and length of breaks.

Section L should also state whether presentations will constitute discussions as defined in FAR 15.306(d) and whether offerors should cover price or cost and fee in presentations. Finally, it should describe the facilities available at the presentation site.

Of course, the complexity of the procurement will determine how the oral presentations will be structured. The solicitation should require the offeror to provide a listing of names and position titles of all presenters and copies of all slides and other briefing materials used in its presentation. It is preferable that such materials be submitted to the evaluation team before the presentation to permit the evaluators to familiarize themselves with the information. Materials referenced in a presentation but that are not an actual part of the presentation must not be accepted or used in evaluations.[13]

Technical/Management Information

For the technical/management volume, section L should request very specific information correlating with each of the evaluation factors and subfactors. This information should also map to the statement of work. For example, if the source selection plan identified inherent technical risks, offerors could be asked to include a risk mitigation plan in their proposals or asked to identify risk areas and discuss their proposed approaches to minimize their impact. Or, if the evaluation factors listed in section M address the qualifications of key personnel, the resume requirements must be stated in section L.

Cost/Price Information

Section L provides detailed instructions on how cost information should be presented and includes electronic spreadsheet cost templates. However, the contracting officer shall not require offerors to submit cost and pricing data when adequate price competition exists.[14] The contracting officer should request information other than cost and pricing data only to the extent necessary to analyze costs. Examples of information other than cost and pricing data include catalog pricing, market prices compiled from market research, or evidence of the lowest prices charged to other customers for similar products or services.[15]

Section L should explain how offerors should organize cost information. For example, requesting that the offeror map cost data to the work breakdown structure simplifies cost analysis. If the cost evaluators will use an automated cost model, then the contracting officer may require offerors to submit the cost volume electronically and in hard copy. State the electronic submission requirements, and identify the order of precedence if there is a conflict between the electronic and paper versions.

Past Performance Information

Section L should seek to obtain information regarding offerors' and major subcontractors' (the RFP should define "major subcontractor") relevant past performance in areas including technical performance, contract management, cost performance, schedule, safety and health, and environmental compliance. Each offeror should provide detailed information on a prescribed number of contracts (performed by the same company element proposing to perform the current procurement action) that the offeror believes to be most similar in size, scope, and complexity to the impending contract. For the sake of evaluation efficiency, consider limiting the number of past performance references to be provided by the offerors.

Section L should also specify the process to be used by the offeror in submitting customer references. For example, the contracting officer may require the past performance volume to be submitted before the other proposal volumes. By requesting the past performance volume first, the agency can begin checking past performance references and can pursue other sources of past performance information. Because evaluating the past performance volume is so time-consuming, requesting this information first also permits agencies to begin this evaluation before receiving technical and cost proposals. By timing the proposal submissions this way, the past performance evaluation should be completed around the same time as the technical and cost evaluations.

Offerors could develop a matrix listing each relevant past contract, relating the contracts to critical functions of the current SOW. The RFP should provide very specific instructions on creating such a matrix, including instructing offerors to insert

Table 5-2 Past Performance Matrix

Company XYZ past performance	Customer name	Contract number and period of performance	Point of contact name and phone number
Past experience in delivering acquisition training on a nationwide scale	Chintall Management Consulting, Inc.	CMC 2007-01 January 5, 2007– January 6, 2008	Connie Chintall 540-555-1212
Instructor past performance in acquisition training as determined from actual student evaluations	Certified Contracting Solutions, LLP	CCS 2008-06 June 6, 2008– July 6, 2010	Tom Reid 303-555-1212
Past performance in managing a program of similar size and scope	WileyRein, LLP	WRF 2007-05004 May 4, 2007– May 30, 2010	Rand Allen 202-555-1212
Experience ensuring classrooms have necessary supplies	Defense Acquisition University	DAU4Me-06-C-1234 October 1, 2006– September 30, 2008	Michelle Currier 757-555-1212

the appropriate contract number in a column and to list the number of personnel in each functional area.[16]

For large or complex acquisitions, a company may have relevant past performance from an element of a particular contract, even if the overall contract effort is not relevant. Allowing offerors to map past performance information by WBS element is one way to encourage the submission of focused past performance data.

Using the WBS example from Chapter 3, Table 5-2 illustrates an example past performance matrix. In this example, the agency would state the information it requires in the shaded areas. The offeror would then fill in the white spaces providing past performance references, including the customer name, contract number, and point of contact for each of the WBS areas.

DRAFTING THE RFP

A draft request for proposal (DRFP) is the initial informal document that explains the government's requirements to industry and requests questions, comments, suggestions, and corrections that may improve the final RFP. It is sent to potential offerors early in competitive acquisitions.

A DRFP need not include all of the sections of the final RFP, but should contain as much as possible of the "business" sections, which will help companies provide meaningful feedback. The DRFP should include the following elements, at a minimum:

- Section L (instructions to offerors)
- Section M (evaluation criteria)
- The statement of work.

No rule exists regarding when an agency should provide the DRFP to potential offerors for review and comment. It is a good idea for an agency to allow sufficient time to develop a thorough DRFP and for companies to make meaningful comments, as well as enough time for the agency to review the comments and incorporate them as appropriate into the final RFP. It is a waste of time to issue a DRFP without taking into consideration helpful suggestions.

Industry feedback on a DRFP may

- Point out ambiguities
- Identify cost drivers that could be reduced
- Identify contract requirements that are not cost effective
- Suggest ways to improve system performance
- Suggest ways to reduce life cycle costs[17]
- Identify potential commercial solutions if requirements are slightly altered.

However, a draft RFP should not be used to clean up the RFP before release. Don't use potential offerors as proofreaders. Instead, issue the draft RFP in as complete and accurate a form as possible. A more comprehensive DRFP will better help potential offerors understand what the agency needs and how the agency will evaluate their proposals.

When releasing a DRFP, the contracting officer should ask that potential offerors identify unnecessary or inefficient requirements. If the DRFP contains government-unique standards, invite prospective offerors to identify alternatives—voluntary consensus standards that meet the requirements.[18] The contracting officer may request comments on the following elements of the DRFP:

- Safety or occupational health
- Security (including information technology security)
- Environmental concerns
- Use of government-furnished property
- Quality assurance

- Export control—The Arms Export Control Act (22 U.S.C. 2778) provides the authority to control the export of defense articles and services, which includes Foreign Military Sales and Military export control items.
- Other programmatic risk issues associated with performing the work.

When issuing a DRFP, the contracting officer should advise prospective offerors that the DRFP is not a solicitation, and the agency is not yet requesting proposals. The contracting officer may consider placing this phrase on the DRFP's cover: "This draft RFP is not a solicitation but is issued as an acquisition planning tool and as a means of soliciting industry comments for use in developing a future formal solicitation." Figure 5-1 offers more suggestions for drafting the RFP.

Upon receiving the comments, the CO should summarize the significant comments, and how the agency responded to those comments, in the final RFP.[19] A word of caution to contracting officers: Be careful about incorporating all suggestions from all offerors. Often, offerors will make recommendations about changing an aspect of the RFP (the statement of work or evaluation factors) to favor their own companies. Make changes to the RFP that are in the government's best interest

---

Do

- Schedule enough time in the draft RFP process to allow companies to thoughtfully review the document and provide meaningful feedback.
- Schedule enough time in the draft RFP process to allow the government to thoughtfully review industry comments and make changes to the final RFP.
- Establish a configuration control process for the draft RFP and final RFP to avoid having multiple working versions of these documents at the same time.
- State a clear cutoff date for accepting questions or comments on the draft RFP that is early enough for the agency to answer the questions and make revisions to the RFP without affecting the scheduled final RFP release date.
- Conduct a final RFP review to ensure consistency between the SOW, section M (evaluation factors), and section L (proposal preparation instructions).

Don't

- Ignore questions from industry about the draft RFP. Companies' questions may point out an ambiguity or error in the proposal preparation instructions. Clarifying such concerns before releasing the final RFP streamlines the evaluation process.
- Issue the final RFP before it's ready just to meet a schedule. Review it early and often until ambiguities have been clarified.
- Discourage questions about the final RFP. Revising the draft RFP may lead to new ambiguities or inconsistencies. Don't prevent offerors from bringing this to your attention, only to discover during proposal evaluation that there is a problem.

Figure 5-1   Tips for Drafting the RFP

and support the acquisition's objectives. (Go back to the acquisition plan and review the acquisition's objectives, if necessary.) Before making any changes, the contracting officer should ask: "Will making this change provide a better product or service to the end user?"

After making changes to the draft RFP, go back through the document one last time to make sure all parts are consistent with each other. This is the next step before releasing the RFP: the final RFP review.

REVIEWING THE FINAL RFP

Conducting a final RFP review is an important step that ensures clarity, thoroughness, and consistency between all of the RFP parts. It's a good idea for an objective person who has not worked on the RFP to review the final document before release. His or her fresh eyes will find inconsistencies or errors that those familiar with the document would miss, simply because they've seen it so many times. Some agencies ask consultants who have experience in both government and industry to review the final RFP. This practice is acceptable, provided the consultant signs a nondisclosure agreement and is not competing in or does not have a financial interest in the outcome of the source selection. Some agencies also require such consultants to file a financial disclosure statement.

The RFP reviewer should consider the following questions when conducting the final review:

- Does the statement of work clearly and concisely state the requirements without ambiguity?
- Are all deliverables identified, including the schedules for and frequencies of deliveries?
- Does section L request the minimum information required to evaluate proposals in accordance with section M criteria?
- Will evaluators use all of the information requested in section L? Don't request information from offerors that won't be evaluated.
- If offerors will make oral presentations, does the RFP explain the process, including when and where the oral presentations will take place, time limits, limits on written materials presented, who can make the presentation, equipment available for presentations, and the formats that are supported by equipment and permitted for review (such as overheads or PowerPoint slides)?
- Does the RFP explain how offerors should organize their proposals, including specifying the information to be included in each volume?
- Are maximum page limits set forth for non-cost volumes?

- Does section L specify page size, font size, and format limitations?
- Does section L specifically require offerors to include relevant past performance information pertaining to subcontractors, teaming partners, key personnel, and predecessor companies?
- Does section L ask the offeror to explain why each past performance reference is relevant to the impending acquisition?
- Does section M repeat any information from section L? Specifically, section M language should not give instructions to offerors on what to provide as part of their proposals; this information belongs in section L.
- Does each factor and subfactor in section M have corresponding proposal preparation instructions in section L that state the specific information the offeror must submit?
- Are the evaluation criteria in section M identical to the criteria approved in the source selection plan?
- Are all factors and significant subfactors that will affect contract award and their relative importance stated clearly in the solicitation, and is the relative importance of the factors addressed in accordance with FAR 15.304(d)?
- Is the relative importance of cost (significantly more important, equal, or significantly less important) to all other non-cost factors combined stated, as required by FAR 15.304(e)?
- Does the RFP clearly state how the agency will rate proposals (pass/fail, or with numerical ratings, adjectival ratings, color ratings, risk ratings, or by confidence assessment). (See Chapter 3, "Performance Confidence Assessment Technique," for more information.)
- Do the evaluation criteria reflect the most important aspects of the statement of work?
- Will the evaluation criteria discern salient differences between the proposals?
- Have any FAR provisions or clauses changed since the draft RFP was released? Check for updates to make sure the final RFP is current.
- Are all attachments complete and up to date? Check to make sure that all of the pages are included.
- Are the contents of the solicitation consistent with what's listed on Standard Form 33, Solicitation, Offer and Award (Figure 5-2)?

Some agencies develop a matrix—a sort of a table of contents for the RFP—that shows where in sections L and M certain content is covered. Give potential offerors a copy of the matrix (make it part of the solicitation) as a reference tool to help them with proposal preparation. This approach establishes the linkage between sections L and M, which helps explain how all parts of the proposal will be used in the evaluation process.[20] The contracting officer may also want to map the RFP sections to the SOW and the WBS. Table 5-3 illustrates such a matrix.

SOLICITATION, OFFER AND AWARD		1. THIS CONTRACT IS A RATED ORDER UNDER DPAS (15 CFR 700)		RATING	PAGE	OF	PAGES

2. CONTRACT NUMBER	3. SOLICITATION NUMBER	4. TYPE OF SOLICITATION	5. DATE ISSUED	6. REQUISITION/PURCHASE NUMBER
		☐ SEALED BID (IFB) ☐ NEGOTIATED (RFP)		

7. ISSUED BY	CODE	8. ADDRESS OFFER TO *(If other than Item 7)*

NOTE: In sealed bid solicitations "offer" and "offeror" mean "bid" and "bidder".

SOLICITATION

9. Sealed offers in original and _____ copies for furnishing the supplies or services in the Schedule will be received at the place specified in Item 8, or if handcarried, in the depository located in _____ until _____ local time _____

(Hour) *(Date)*

CAUTION - LATE Submissions, Modifications, and Withdrawals: See Section L, Provision No. 52.214-7 or 52.215-1. All offers are subject to all terms and conditions contained in this solicitation.

10. FOR INFORMATION CALL:	A. NAME	B. TELEPHONE *(NO COLLECT CALLS)*			C. E-MAIL ADDRESS
		AREA CODE	NUMBER	EXT.	

11. TABLE OF CONTENTS

(X)	SEC.	DESCRIPTION	PAGE(S)	(X)	SEC.	DESCRIPTION	PAGE(S)
		PART I - THE SCHEDULE				PART II - CONTRACT CLAUSES	
	A	SOLICITATION/CONTRACT FORM			I	CONTRACT CLAUSES	
	B	SUPPLIES OR SERVICES AND PRICES/COSTS				PART III - LIST OF DOCUMENTS, EXHIBITS AND OTHER ATTACH.	
	C	DESCRIPTION/SPECS./WORK STATEMENT			J	LIST OF ATTACHMENTS	
	D	PACKAGING AND MARKING				PART IV - REPRESENTATIONS AND INSTRUCTIONS	
	E	INSPECTION AND ACCEPTANCE			K	REPRESENTATIONS, CERTIFICATIONS AND OTHER STATEMENTS OF OFFERORS	
	F	DELIVERIES OR PERFORMANCE					
	G	CONTRACT ADMINISTRATION DATA			L	INSTRS., CONDS., AND NOTICES TO OFFERORS	
	H	SPECIAL CONTRACT REQUIREMENTS			M	EVALUATION FACTORS FOR AWARD	

OFFER *(Must be fully completed by offeror)*

NOTE: Item 12 does not apply if the solicitation includes the provisions at 52.214-16, Minimum Bid Acceptance Period.

12. In compliance with the above, the undersigned agrees, if this offer is accepted within _____ calendar days *(60 calendar days unless a different period is inserted by the offeror)* from the date for receipt of offers specified above, to furnish any or all items upon which prices are offered at the price set opposite each item, delivered at the designated point(s), within the time specified in the schedule.

13. DISCOUNT FOR PROMPT PAYMENT *(See Section I, Clause No. 52.232-8)*	10 CALENDAR DAYS (%)	20 CALENDAR DAYS (%)	30 CALENDAR DAYS (%)	CALENDAR DAYS (%)

14. ACKNOWLEDGMENT OF AMENDMENTS *(The offeror acknowledges receipt of amendments to the SOLICITATION for offerors and related documents numbered and dated)*:	AMENDMENT NO.	DATE	AMENDMENT NO.	DATE

15A. NAME AND ADDRESS OF OFFEROR	CODE	FACILITY	16. NAME AND TITLE OF PERSON AUTHORIZED TO SIGN OFFER *(Type or print)*

15B. TELEPHONE NUMBER			15C. CHECK IF REMITTANCE ADDRESS IS ☐ DIFFERENT FROM ABOVE - ENTER SUCH ADDRESS IN SCHEDULE.	17. SIGNATURE	18. OFFER DATE
AREA CODE	NUMBER	EXT.			

AWARD *(To be completed by Government)*

19. ACCEPTED AS TO ITEMS NUMBERED	20. AMOUNT	21. ACCOUNTING AND APPROPRIATION

22. AUTHORITY FOR USING OTHER THAN FULL AND OPEN COMPETITION: ☐ 10 U.S.C. 2304(c) ( ) ☐ 41 U.S.C. 253(c) ( )	23. SUBMIT INVOICES TO ADDRESS SHOWN IN *(4 copies unless otherwise specified)*	ITEM

24. ADMINISTERED BY *(If other than Item 7)*	CODE	25. PAYMENT WILL BE MADE BY	CODE

26. NAME OF CONTRACTING OFFICER *(Type or print)*	27. UNITED STATES OF AMERICA *(Signature of Contracting Officer)*	28. AWARD DATE

IMPORTANT - Award will be made on this Form, or on Standard Form 26, or by other authorized official written notice.

AUTHORIZED FOR LOCAL REPRODUCTION
Previous edition is unusable

STANDARD FORM 33 (REV. 9-97)
Prescribed by GSA - FAR (48 CFR) 53.214(c)

Figure 5-2 Standard Form 33—Solicitation, Offer, and Award

Table 5-3   RFP Compliance Matrix[21]

Requirement	Section L Paragraph	Section M Paragraph
Volume I: Executive Summary	3.0	N/A
	3.1	N/A
	3.2	N/A
Volume II: Mission Capability	4.0	N/A
	4.1	N/A
	4.2	N/A
Subfactor 1: Key system requirements	4.2.2	N/A
Subfactor 2: System integration and software	4.2.3	N/A
Subfactor 3: Logistics	4.2.4	N/A
	4.2.4.2	2.2.3
Manpower and personnel	4.2.4.3	N/A
Supportability	4.2.4.5	2.2.3
	4.2.4.5.1	2.2.3
Data management	4.2.4.6	2.2.3
Supply support	4.2.4.7	N/A
Training	4.2.4.9	2.2.3
Subfactor 4: Program management	4.2.5	N/A
	4.2.5.1	2.2.4
SOW	4.2.5.2	2.2.4
Integrated master plan	4.2.5.3	2.2.4
Integrated master schedule	4.2.5.4	2.2.4
Cost reporting	4.2.5.6	2.2.4
Integrated risk management	4.2.5.7	2.2.4
Small business	4.2.5.8	2.2.4
Manufacturing and subcontract management	4.2.5.9	N/A
Test and evaluation	4.2.5.10	2.2.4
Subfactor 5: Tech maturity and demonstration	4.2.6	2.2.5
Proposal risk	4.3	2.3
Volume III: Past Performance	5.0	2.4
	5.1	2.4
	5.2	2.4
	5.3	2.4
	5.4	2.4
	5.5	2.4

Table 5-3 (*Continued*)

Requirement	Section L Paragraph	Section M Paragraph
Volume IV: Cost	6.0	2.5
	6.1	2.5
Volume VI: Contract Documentation	8.0	N/A
	8.1	N/A
	8.2	N/A
	8.3	N/A
Volume VII: Oral Presentation	9.0	

CHAPTER SUMMARY

Chapter 5 explains the importance and use of the uniform contract format (UCF). The UCF helps agencies and offerors find answers to questions about an acquisition. The same information always appears in the same section for each RFP, regardless of the requirement.

The statement of work (SOW) is the most important part of the RFP. Not only must it define requirements in clear, concise language, identifying specific work the contractor must accomplish, but it must also define the respective responsibilities of the government and the contractor. It provides an objective measure so that both the government and the contractor will know when the work is complete and payment is due.

In performance-based acquisitions, the SOW is called the *performance work statement* (PWS). The PWS states the technical, functional, and performance characteristics of the work the contractor must perform.

The common elements of the SOW are the background, project objectives, scope of work, detailed technical requirements, deliverables, reporting schedule, special considerations, and references. Using simple, clear language and active verbs helps to effectively communicate the requirements. Avoiding confusing references to requirements and due dates also ensures clarity.

Proposal preparation instructions, which appear in section L of a solicitation, provide offerors with directions for preparing responses to the requirements. The statement of work must link to the evaluation factors and subfactors, which appear in section M, and the proposal preparation instructions, in section L.

After the RFP is reasonably complete, contracting officers may release a draft RFP (DRFP) for industry review and comment. This practice can help to streamline the acquisition by including industry feedback in the process. A DRFP need not include all of the sections of the final RFP, but it should contain as much information as possible in the "business" sections, which will help companies provide meaningful feedback. The DRFP should include the following elements, at a minimum: section L (instructions to offerors), section M (evaluation criteria), and the statement of work.

Finally, agencies should conduct a final review of the RFP before releasing it to industry. Conducting a final RFP review is an important step that ensures clarity, thoroughness, and consistency between all of the RFP parts. It's a good idea to ask someone who has not worked on the RFP to review the final draft before release. His or her fresh eyes could find inconsistencies or errors that those more familiar with the document might miss.

After the RFP is ready, the next step is to conduct a pre-proposal conference. Some agencies release the final RFP at the pre-proposal conference. Chapter 6 explains what typically happens at this conference.

NOTES

1 Federal Acquisition Institute, "Solicitation Preparation," *Contract Specialist Training Blueprints*, no. 20 (Washington, DC: Federal Acquisition Institute, September 2002).

2 U.S. Government Accountability Office, *Federal Register* 74.166 (August 28, 2009) and 15 USC 4724.

3 Federal Acquisition Regulation (FAR) 37.104(c)(2).

4 FAR 37.602(b).

5 FAR 11.002.

6 FAR 37.602.

7 FAR 46.401.

8 U.S. Department of Health and Human Services, *DHHS Project Officers' Contracting Handbook* (Washington, DC: U.S. Department of Health and Human Services, 2003), III-16–III-29.

9 Federal Acquisition Institute, *Source Selection Text Reference* (Washington, DC: Federal Acquisition Institute, 1993), 39.

10 Claude M. Bolton, Jr., *Army Source Selection Manual* (Washington, DC: Office of the Assistant Secretary of the Army for Acquisition, Logistics and Technology, 2007), 14.

11 Johnnie E. Wilson, *Best Value Source Selection* 715-3 (Alexandria, VA: Army Materiel Command, 1998), 15.

12 FAR 15.208(a).

13 U.S. Department of Energy, *Source Selection Guide* (Washington, DC: U.S. Department of Energy, 2005), 29–30.

14 FAR 15.403-1(b).

15 Federal Acquisition Institute and the Air Force Institute of Technology, *Contract Pricing Reference Guide*, vol. 1, "Price Analysis" (Washington, DC: Federal Acquisition Institute, 2005), 105.

16 National Aeronautics and Space Administration, *Source Selection Guide* (Washington, DC: National Aeronautics and Space Administration, June 2007), 28–29.

17 Harold V. Hanson, *NAVSEA Source Selection Guide* (Washington, DC: U.S. Naval Sea Systems Command, 2001), 19.

18 For more information, see FAR 11.101 and "Federal Participation in the Development and Use of Voluntary Consensus Standards and in Conformity Assessment Activities," *OMB Circular* A-119 (e.g., industry standards such as ISO-9000/9001).

19 National Aeronautics and Space Administration, 25.

20 Bolton, 15.

21 Adapted from U.S. Air Force/Air Force Materiel Command, RFP no. FA8625-07-R-6470, Section L, Attachment 1 (Wright-Patterson Air Force Base, OH: U.S. Air Force/Air Force Materiel Command, January 30, 2007).

PART II

Preparing Proposals and Preparing for Evaluations

At this stage in the acquisition cycle, the government has issued a draft request for proposals (RFP) and has made any necessary revisions before releasing the final RFP. Part II explains how pre-proposal conferences are typically conducted; how offerors can prepare for and write proposals; and how the government can prepare to evaluate offeror proposals once submitted.

The pre-proposal conference is an optional but important step to enhance communication between government and industry offerors. After this conference, the industry side of the acquisition becomes the focal point in the process while offerors prepare for and write their proposals. In the meantime, the agency must shift gears from writing the solicitation to preparing for its evaluation of proposals.

CHAPTER 6   CONDUCTING A PRE-PROPOSAL CONFERENCE

After the RFP is complete, the government agency may conduct a pre-proposal conference. The pre-proposal conference is an important step in improving communications between the government agency and industry offerors. It gives the potential offerors an opportunity to ask questions, learn more about the agency's source selection process, and begin assembling a project team.

This opportunity to answer questions posed by potential offerors and explain how the agency's source selection process will work will help the government ensure that submitted proposals address its requirements and needs. It will also enhance the government's understanding of industry capabilities.

CHAPTER 7   PREPARING THE PROPOSAL

After potential offerors receive the RFP, they have important decisions to make, such as whether to submit a proposal, and if so, how to write the proposal so it wins the contract. Chapter 7 explains important aspects of competing in the federal marketplace, including assessing the competition, establishing teaming partners, and analyzing the RFP.

Once the government issues the final RFP, the companies submitting a proposal become the primary participants in the acquisition process. The proposal-writing process can be intimidating, especially for those vendors new to federal government acquisition. Chapter 7 explores how companies prepare proposals.

CHAPTER 8   PREPARING FOR PROPOSAL EVALUATIONS

Although the solicitation is the focal point of any acquisition, the agency is not done getting ready for competition when the RFP is complete. The next step is to get ready to evaluate proposals. Depending on the size and scope of the acquisition, agencies can spend considerable time preparing for evaluations.

While offerors are preparing proposals, agencies should train proposal evaluators, providing background and other important information, including agency objectives, evaluation factors, and the proposal requirements. Evaluators should know what to look for in submitted proposals, how to interpret what they find, and the procedures for documenting their findings.

Chapter 8 explains the process of receiving proposals, selecting and assigning proposals to evaluators, and providing evaluators' orientation training sessions. In addition, the chapter discusses the typical facilities and security needed for the evaluation process.

Chapter 6

Conducting a Pre-Proposal Conference

This chapter explains how to conduct and participate in a pre-proposal conference. The pre-proposal conference is an important communication opportunity for both government and industry. The FAR encourages agencies to engage in such exchanges with industry before they receive proposals, as long as they are consistent with procurement integrity requirements. The purpose of exchanging information is to improve potential offerors' understanding of government requirements and the government's understanding of industry capabilities. This allows potential offerors to determine if or how they can satisfy the government's requirements. It also enhances the government's ability to obtain quality supplies and services at reasonable prices and increases efficiency in proposal preparation, evaluation, negotiation, and contract award.[1]

Note that we use the term *pre-proposal conference* instead of *bidder's conference* to be consistent with terminology used in negotiated acquisitions. Technically, a bidder's conference is conducted before an invitation for bid is released.

WHEN AND WHY TO HAVE A PRE-PROPOSAL CONFERENCE

Acquisition teams have a lot of flexibility in scheduling a pre-proposal conference. Some hold the pre-proposal conference early in the process and release the draft RFP at the conference. Others prefer to hold the pre-proposal conference after comments from the draft RFP have been incorporated into the final RFP, then release the final RFP at the conference. In either case, agencies should publicly announce the conference date, time, and location so that all interested parties and potential offerors have an opportunity to attend. Some agencies conduct shorter one-on-one conferences rather than large group conferences. The important thing is to keep the lines of communication open to exchange information.

An early exchange of information among industry and the program manager, contracting officer (CO), and other participants in the acquisition process allows the parties to identify and resolve concerns regarding the acquisition strategy, including proposed contract type, terms and conditions, and acquisition planning schedules; the feasibility of the requirement, including performance requirements, statements of work, and data requirements; the suitability of the proposal instructions and evaluation criteria, including the approach for assessing past performance information; the availability of reference documents; and any other industry concerns or questions.[2]

When the government wishes to clarify certain issues, or potential offerors need more information before making a decision about submitting a proposal, holding a pre-proposal conference is advisable. A pre-proposal conference is likely to be most beneficial when there have been significant questions about a solicitation or when the final solicitation incorporates significant changes from a previously released draft solicitation.[3]

The nature of the government's requirement and the nature of the competition also influence the decision to hold a pre-proposal conference. Review the results of the market research conducted to determine if new companies are likely to compete or if complex teaming arrangements are necessary to form an effective team. If either of these conditions exists, it's advisable to have a pre-proposal conference.

In sum, the following factors often drive the decision to conduct a pre-proposal conference:

- To explain a complex requirement or complex technical evaluation factors
- When potential offerors' questions suggest that key terms and conditions in the solicitation are vague, ambiguous, or unattractive to industry
- To highlight or explain changes in a longstanding requirement
- When there has been a long period of time between awards
- To allow offerors an opportunity to physically inspect work sites or property to be furnished by the government
- To disseminate additional background data
- When the statement of work puts exceptional demands on a contractor's capability
- When there are complications involving access to classified material.[4]

Pre-proposal conferences may be only an hour long for less complex requirements or may last an entire day for complex acquisitions. If a site survey is included in the pre-proposal conference, it may take more than a day. Agencies should allow enough time to cover the topics to be discussed and allow for questions and answers.

TOPICS TO COVER AT A PRE-PROPOSAL CONFERENCE

The agency sets the agenda and leads the discussion at a pre-proposal conference. The following suggested agenda includes the essential topics to be covered.

- Describe the background of the acquisition and key program interfaces.
- Explain the acquisition strategy and life cycle considerations as well as the acquisition objectives.
- Introduce the contracting officer, program manager, and ombudsman (if assigned), and provide contact information for the CO and ombudsman.
- Describe the contract's scope and agency's requirements.
- Summarize the tasks and deliverables.
- State the expected period of performance.
- Explain the contract type and other contractual considerations, such as special contract clauses.
- Discuss oral presentation information (if applicable).
- Describe the proposal evaluation process for:
  - Technical/management area
  - Oral presentations (if applicable)
  - Past performance area
  - Cost/price area
  - Security.
- State the solicitation and contract award schedule.
- Explain all details of the work statement and specifications.
- Clarify instructions for completing the proposal.
- Allow offerors to ask questions and receive answers.
- Stress the importance of significant elements of the solicitation.
- Receive written questions from the audience.[5]
- Discuss ethics requirements.

Procurement Integrity Act reminders should also be issued to the source selection team and the pre-proposal conference participants. Reminding everyone of the law's requirements could be an agenda item at the pre-proposal conference. If some attending companies are new to federal procurement, they may not be familiar with the requirements and could try to communicate inappropriately with source selection personnel. For example, a company may try to communicate directly with the program manager or contracting officer's technical representative instead of the contracting officer, or it might invite agency contracting personnel to use the company's front row seats at a sporting event.

PLANNING FOR A PRE-PROPOSAL CONFERENCE

If you know in advance that you're going to conduct a pre-proposal conference, the announcement should be made in the draft request for proposal (DRFP). Generally, the announcement should include information on the nature and scope of the conference and the time and place of the conference. If possible, include a copy of the agenda and request that interested parties submit written questions in advance.

Some agencies ask for written questions before the conference so they have time to develop thorough answers and explain them at the conference. Companies may prefer to submit questions in writing for the sake of anonymity, rather than having a representative ask a question in person at the conference where competitors are present.

Fully answer potential offerors' questions by referring the questions to subject matter experts: Technical representatives should answer technical questions; the contracting officer, contract questions; and the cost/price analyst, pricing questions. Prepare consolidated responses to questions on business terms and conditions after considering comments from technical personnel. Review the answers as a whole for clarity and accuracy before the conference.[6]

For complex or high-visibility acquisitions, the contracting officer may conduct a dry run before holding the conference. The purpose of a dry run is to make sure that everyone understands their roles and what they'll say before the actual event. Test the equipment and make sure everything you'll need, such as computer projection equipment, is there and is working properly.

GOVERNMENT CONSIDERATIONS

Government participants in the pre-proposal conference should include

- The evaluation team
  - The program manager
  - The contracting officer
  - Cost/price analysts
- The ombudsman (if applicable)
- A recorder.

The agency may also invite specialists from other government agencies to participate, such as:

- The Small Business Administration
- The Defense Contract Management Agency

- The Defense Contract Audit Agency
- Any agency that might make use of the contract vehicle being awarded.

Representatives from these agencies may participate in the conference if they will play a role in the evaluation.

Be prepared to use the pre-proposal conference to answer difficult questions about the acquisition strategy. It's important for potential offerors to understand the basis for the acquisition strategy decisions, such as:

- Why is or isn't the acquisition set aside for small business?
- Why is the agency directing offerors to use a specific subcontractor?
- Why are exclusive teaming arrangements permitted or prohibited?

If these issues are properly addressed at the pre-proposal conference, the government may consider offerors to be fully informed about them. If a company wishes to protest an issue raised at the pre-proposal conference, it has only ten calendar days to do so. This time limit is called a "protest clock." Once a company learns about an issue, the protest clock has officially started. (This and other rules for protest are discussed at length in Chapter 15.)

For example, the agency may make a statement at the pre-proposal conference that is controversial, such as prohibiting exclusive teaming arrangements or permitting consultants to help with the source selection. If a company wants to protest the prohibition, then it must do so within ten days of learning about it at the pre-proposal conference. The company cannot wait to see if it wins the contract because that decision would be made past the ten-day restriction. By disclosing controversial issues early, and thereby starting the protest clock, the agency puts the companies on notice about what they can expect. Some companies are hesitant to file a protest this early in the acquisition process because it might jeopardize the competition. To the agency, this is an added advantage of getting controversial issues out of the way early.

An agency may amend an RFP to clarify it, or questions received during the pre-proposal conference may result in changes to the RFP.[7] But if any of the terms and conditions or requirements of the solicitation were changed in the RFP, the CO must issue a formal solicitation amendment. Many agencies begin a pre-proposal conference with a statement such as, "The remarks and explanations at the conference will not qualify the terms of the RFP. Solicitation terms and specifications will not change unless the solicitation is amended in writing."[8] Thus, potential offerors may not interpret verbal statements made at the conference as solicitation amendments. It's essential that industry participants understand this, especially if companies new to the government marketplace are participating.

After releasing the final RFP, the contracting officer must be the focal point of any exchange with potential offerors. When specific information about the acquisition necessary for preparing proposals is disclosed to one or more potential offerors, that information must be made available to the public as soon as practical, but no later than the next general release of information, in order to avoid creating an unfair competitive advantage. Per FAR 15.201, "When conducting a presolicitation or pre-proposal conference, materials distributed at the conference should be made available to all potential offerors, upon request."[9] Information provided to a potential offeror in response to its request, however, must not be disclosed if doing so would reveal the potential offeror's confidential business strategy. This information is protected under FAR 3.104 and FAR 24.2.

The agency generally provides a written summary of the questions answered during the conference in the record of conference proceedings, which is provided to all attendees and is made available to those who weren't able to be there. The proceedings should also include a list of participants (government and industry), the agenda, and any briefing materials presented. As soon as possible after the pre-proposal conference, the contracting officer should ensure that all potential offerors receive the written record of the conference proceedings, including any new material provided, and should make certain that all questions have been addressed.

For larger acquisitions, some agencies post the proceedings online or set up a library or reading room. A *contractor library* is a resource center for offerors to help them prepare their responses to an RFP. The library or reading room may be web-based, a walk-in reading room, or both.[10] It may offer access to reference documents, specifications, operational concepts, integration plans, organizational charts, master schedules, configuration management systems, as well as pre-proposal conference agendas, briefing charts, questions, and answers.[11]

Potential offerors attend the pre-proposal conference to get as much information as possible about the acquisition. The conference also fosters networking and teaming opportunities for both existing and new offerors. Attendees have the opportunity to learn who their competitors are, meet new competitors, and note which traditional competitors chose not to attend. Becoming familiar with the competition helps offerors better position themselves, strategically speaking, to participate in the solicitation.[12]

Typically, industry attendees include a contracting representative and a technical representative, usually a proposal manager, program manager, or capture manager. However, some companies prefer to send other representatives, such as senior marketing personnel. If it's a large acquisition, attendees may include major subcontractors'

- Release information to all potential offerors on a fair and equitable basis in accordance with regulatory and legal restrictions.
- Establish clear ground rules for the conduct, timing, and documentation of any one-on-one meetings to ensure potential offerors are given equal access to information needed to prepare proposals.
- Protect any proprietary information that you are given access to during this process.
- Request contracting advice and legal counsel if any questions arise about pre-proposal exchanges.[13]
- Do not discuss source selection information, such as the evaluation standards, at the pre proposal conference.[14]

Figure 6-1   Pre-Proposal Conference Tips for Government Participants

staff. Some agencies must limit the number of attendees per offeror or offeror team at the pre-proposal conference due to space constraints, but it's important to allow as many participants as possible to encourage communication. If necessary, consider running two sessions to accommodate as many offerors as possible. Figure 6-1 offers more suggestions on holding a pre-proposal conference.

INDUSTRY CONSIDERATIONS

At pre-proposal conferences, companies may be cautious about asking questions for fear of revealing too much information about their planned technical approach or potential weaknesses. Because all questions and answers are made available to all offerors, a company's questions about an RFP should be asked in a way that does not disclose the company's proprietary or confidential information.

Government contracts are more complicated than commercial contracts. Vendors usually work with a single point of contact when selling products or services to a commercial entity. In government contracting, companies must know three important players: the agency's technical representative or program manager, the budget or finance officer, and the contracting officer. Developing long-term relationships with these decision makers helps an offeror show the government that its company is trustworthy and can perform the contract on time and within budget.[15]

While establishing relationships is helpful to both parties, vendors must keep in mind that presenting information briefings or getting face time with a program manager, budget officer, or contracting officer does not give their companies an advantage in source selection. A vendor's proposal—not its marketing manager or program manager—determines contract award.

This doesn't mean, however, that a vendor should not get to know the customer better or shouldn't work to understand its requirements. In fact, potential offerors should take every opportunity to get information about the government's requirements, and it's important to have the right people gather the information. For example, if there is a pre-proposal conference or other forum for information exchange between the government and industry, your program manager and contracts people, not just your marketing manager, should attend.[16] Companies should bring personnel with technical, contracts, financial, quality, property, and safety requirements expertise, or any other type of expertise required to understand specific issues related to the acquisition.

The agency should take into consideration the acquisition's complexity and teaming arrangement potential when determining how many industry representatives will be allowed to attend. If the agency states an attendance limitation, offerors should strive to abide by that request. After all, if an offeror can't follow the agency's instructions regarding the number of people allowed to attend the pre-proposal conference, how can the agency have any confidence that the offeror will follow the contract's requirements?

Before the presolicitation conference, offerors should make sure to thoroughly read the draft RFP, if it was issued in advance. Offerors don't want to ask a question that the draft RFP answers. Prepare a compliance matrix that maps the statement of work to section L proposal preparation instructions and section M evaluation criteria, if one wasn't provided in the draft RFP. Refer to Figure 5-3 for a sample compliance matrix. If an element doesn't map, ask about the conflict at the conference. For example, if section L requires offerors to submit a training plan, but section M does not contain corresponding evaluation criteria for the plan, the offeror should find out how the agency will evaluate the plan.

If an offeror does not have an organization chart for the agency, it should download one from the agency's website. It's important to know who's who in the agency, even though the offeror will not get extra credit for face time. It is still important to know who might be involved in the source selection. An offeror's proposal should demonstrate an understanding of the requirement in a way that the evaluators can follow, and sometimes it helps to know the evaluators. For example, some people prefer looking at graphics to reading text. If this is true of the evaluators who will review the proposal, it will make their job easier to submit a proposal with as many graphics as appropriate.

Offerors may know a potential evaluator's preferences from having worked with the agency in the past. Some agencies will include evaluators at the pre-proposal conference. Other agencies prefer to keep evaluator identities anonymous. Companies will nevertheless try to figure out who will be on the evaluation team based on any prior history with the agency. If a company knows or suspects someone is an evaluator, it can adjust its proposal accordingly. In the end, it's a guessing game. Of course, evaluators still must follow the criteria detailed in the RFP when assessing proposals, but it does not hurt to simplify the process.

An offeror's goal in attending the pre-proposal conference should be to leave with answers to the following questions:

- What is the purpose of this program?
- Who is/are the customer(s)?
- Who is/are the end user(s)?
- How does this program fit into the agency's mission?
- Are there related, similar, or competing programs?
- Who are the principal players in this program?
- How does this program fit into our company's strategic plan?
- What are the agency's acquisition priorities?
- Who are the key agency decision makers, both internal and external?
- What are the contract milestones?
- Are the agency's milestones consistent with what is stated in the solicitation document?
- Are the milestones realistic or politically motivated? What is the critical path—i.e., which activities, when delayed, have an impact on the total project schedule?
- What other programs have a potential impact on this program?
- What other programs does this acquisition impact?
- Are there any (budget, technical, political) constraints on this program? [17]

The agency isn't the only organization that should conduct market research. Potential offerors should do market research on the agency's recent acquisitions of a similar size and scope to try to find the answers to the following questions:

- How is this acquisition similar to or different from other recent procurements?
- If this is a follow-on contract, who are the incumbent contractor and subcontractors?
- What is our company's history with this agency?
- Who are the potential competing offerors?
- What specialized resources are necessary to perform this program? Do we have them, or can we obtain them?
  - Personnel
  - Materials
  - Facilities/equipment

- Financial
- Information technology
- Will we need to team with another company to submit a successful proposal?
  - Do we know who potential team members would be?
  - Should we seek out potential teammates at the pre-proposal conference?
- What could jeopardize program success?
  - Cost
  - Schedule
  - Specifications
  - Quality
  - Resources
  - Management
- Do we know how to accurately estimate costs for this effort?
- Do we know the customer's funding profile and sources of funding?
- Do we know how this acquisition could financially benefit our company?
- Do we know the financial risks?
- What cost-control measures will be required?[18]

After preparing for the pre-proposal conference, what should offerors do at the actual conference? The answer depends on whether the offeror is going to pursue the contract alone; the offeror has already assembled a team to fulfill the contract; or the offeror is looking for potential teammates.

Some companies prefer a low-profile approach and attend the pre-proposal conference primarily to get information about who else is there. Their staffers collect business cards to get a better idea of who the competition is and pay careful attention to who talks to whom, trying to figure out who might be teaming with whom and who is still looking for teaming partners. These vendors seldom ask questions and will watch how attendees react when anonymous questions are read aloud to try to determine who asked the question.

Vendors looking for teaming partners could use the pre-proposal conference as a networking opportunity to find potential partners. Remember to bring plenty of business cards and corporate literature to share that emphasizes how your company can help meet the requirements. Teaming agreements will be discussed in more detail in the next chapter, but for now, readers should keep in mind that the pre-proposal conference is often a launching point for establishing teaming relationships.

In any case, all companies should use the conference as an opportunity to clarify technical and business-related questions as much as possible.

WHAT HAPPENS NEXT?

If the contracting officer has already received comments on the draft RFP (if one was issued) and has incorporated them into the final RFP, the agency may choose to issue the final RFP at the pre-proposal conference. It can also be released a couple of weeks before the conference. No matter when it is released, the final RFP must be issued in accordance with the policies and procedures in FAR 5.102, FAR 19.202-4, and FAR part 6.[19] After releasing the solicitation, the contracting officer is the focal point of any exchange with potential offerors.

Whenever the final RFP is released, make sure that all of the sections map: that the statement of work is consistent with the evaluation criteria and that the proposal preparation instructions support the evaluation criteria.

CHAPTER SUMMARY

Chapter 6 explains how to use a pre-proposal conference to disseminate information to potential offerors and to collect information about the agency's acquisition requirements. The pre-proposal conference is an important tool for both government and industry to exchange information about the acquisition.

The FAR encourages agencies to engage in such exchanges with industry before they receive proposals, as long as the conferences are consistent with procurement integrity requirements. The purpose of exchanging information is to improve potential offerors' understanding of government requirements and the government's understanding of industry capabilities. This allows potential offerors to determine if or how they can satisfy the government's requirements.

Factors that influence whether contracting parties should hold a pre-proposal conference include:

- Complex requirements or complex technical evaluation factors
- Key terms and conditions in the solicitation that are vague, ambiguous, or unattractive to industry
- Changes in a longstanding requirement
- The need for physical inspections of worksites or property furnished by the government
- The need to disseminate additional background data.

Potential offerors also have to be prepared for a pre-solicitation conference. Before the pre-solicitation conference, offerors should make sure to thoroughly read the draft RFP. They should also prepare a compliance matrix that maps the statement of work to proposal preparation instructions in section L and evaluation criteria in section M, if one wasn't provided in the draft RFP. Company representatives attending a pre-solicitation conference should focus on learning about:

- The purpose behind the solicitation
- The customer
- The end user
- How this program fits into the agency's mission and related, similar, or competing programs
- The principal players in the agency's relevant programs
- How the contract work fits into the offeror's strategic plan
- The agency's acquisition priorities
- Contract milestones.

What does a potential offeror do after the pre-proposal conference? Chapter 7 explains private industry's role in the acquisition process.

NOTES

1 Federal Acquisition Regulation (FAR) 15.201.

2 Ibid.

3 National Aeronautics and Space Administration, *Source Selection Guide* (Washington, DC: National Aeronautics and Space Administration, June 2007), 33.

4 U.S. Department of Energy, *Source Selection Guide* (Washington, DC: U.S. Department of Energy, 2005), 6.

5 Ibid., 6–7; National Reconnaissance Office, *Source Selection Manual* N87 (Chantilly, VA: National Reconnaissance Office, 2008), 24.

6 Federal Acquisition Institute, "Pre-Quote/Pre-Bid/Pre-Proposal Conferences," *Contract Specialist Training Blueprints*, Unit 22 (Washington, DC: Federal Acquisition Institute, October 2003).

7 National Aeronautics and Space Administration, 34. See also FAR 15.206(e).

8 Federal Acquisition Institute.

9 FAR 15.201.

10 U.S. Department of Energy, 7.

11 *Source Selection Manual* N87, 23.

12 *Source Selection Manual* N87, 25.

13 Johnnie E. Wilson, *Best Value Source Selection* 715-3 (Alexandria, VA: Army Materiel Command, 1998), 7.

14 Federal Acquisition Institute.

15 Thomas Reid, "Exactly Who Is the Government Customer?" *Contract Management* 46 (Ashburn, VA: National Contract Management Association, December 2006), 8–13.

16 Deanna J. Bennett, "A Program Manager Talks: What Contractors Should Know," *Acquisition Review Quarterly* (Fort Belvoir, VA: Defense Acquisition University, Fall 1997), 435–436.

17 Daniel M. Jacobs, *The Program/Contract Definition Document* (Warrenton, VA: Federal Market Group, 1999), 1–3.

18 Ibid., 8.

19 FAR 15.205.

Chapter 7

Preparing the Proposal

Receiving the final RFP marks an important milestone in the acquisition process. Now the companies that will submit a proposal in response to the RFP are the primary participants. Beginning the proposal-writing process can be intimidating, especially for those vendors new to federal government acquisition. As we've seen in the preceding chapters, government acquisition is a formal process, so companies that have a structured approach to responding to the RFP may be more likely to be successful. Chapter 7 explores how companies prepare proposals.

Both government and industry have program managers. To avoid confusion of these terms in this chapter, *proposal manager* will designate the company's program manager.

CAPTURE PLANNING

Capture planning is a life cycle process used by both small and large businesses that ensures consistency and discipline in the aggressive pursuit and winning of contracting opportunities.[1] The foundation of capture planning is focusing on the customer's business problem or objective. It is intended to win new business by creating mutually beneficial offers that solve the customer's problems and meet the company's profitability and risk requirements.

Capture planning produces proposals that are customer focused, designed to meet or exceed the customer's requirements. This approach allows the vendor to focus on offering its best solution and also helps the company identify alternatives that are better than what the customer may have expected.[2]

Figure 7-1 illustrates what a capture planning file cabinet might look like. The company should start setting up the capture plan folders before the pre-proposal conference. By starting early, contract managers will know ahead of time what information they must gather at the conference.

Customer
Program manager
Organization chart
Source selection process and personnel
History with customer
Agency view of company

Program description
Requirement description
Scope of work
Related programs
Contract type
Prime contractor's role
Subcontractor's role
Schedule
Funding amount

The competition
Expected competitors
Competitors' proposal managers
Competitor legacies
Known teaming relationships
Strengths and weaknesses
Rate structures
Competitors' reputations

Our strengths and weaknesses
Reputation with customer
Past performance history
Knowledge of customer and program
Comparison of rate structures
Personal relationships
Technical approach
Conflicts of interest
Commitment to win
Level of proposal activity
Requisite technical skills

Proposal submission decision
Resources available for proposal preparation
  and contract performance
Allocation of proposal funds required
Do we have the technical skills required?
Competition strengths and weaknesses
Contract type
Win probability
Timing

Win strategy
How can we be the best technically and
  offer the lowest price?
Does the proposal team understand the
  requirements?
Do we have a strong, competitive team?
Is our pricing strategy sound?
Are key personnel involved?
Have we applied our best resources?
Have we fixed all our weaknesses?
Have we countered all competitive
  strengths?
Ghosting possibilities?

Figure 7-1   Capture Planning File Cabinet[3]

KNOWING THE CUSTOMER

The first capture planning folder is for the customer; a company's capture planning efforts should always focus on the customer. The customer folder could be for an entire agency or for a specific program. Depending on the company's history with the agency, it may already have an organizational chart for the agency and know who the program manager is for this solicitation. If the company has existing contracts with the agency, it is already familiar with the agency's source selection process. If not, the contract manager will find out who the program manager will be and will learn about the source selection process for the acquisition at the pre-proposal conference.

A summary of the customer and its requirements should be placed in the folder. Next, include documentation of the company's history with the customer. First, list completed contracts, including contract type, dollar value, and noteworthy accomplishments. If there were problems, document them and how the company overcame them; this information may be useful if required for the past performance volume. The company should also be able to state what they did to ensure the problems do not recur. Finally, list current contracts with the agency, along with the contract details listed above.

The next step is to determine how the agency views the company's performance. This task can be challenging but is an important part of the process. Contract managers can get this data from past performance assessments of completed contracts or program reviews. Award-fee assessments also contain this information (see Chapter 2, "Incentive Contracts"). It's important to document both the good and the bad—the customer certainly will. Don't gloss over problems because your company will have to address them in the past performance volume of the proposal anyway. Contract managers and proposal managers should identify the issues and discuss how the company solved any problems or mitigated their effects.

Before using any past customer as a reference, call the customer first to ask if it is comfortable giving a reference. Sometimes, making a blind call to verify whether a customer will give a positive reference can help. Keep a database or other file containing customer contact information. Remember that people move, change jobs, and retire. Keep this file current.

Understanding the Program Description

The next file in the capture planning filing cabinet is the program description. This folder contains detailed information about the customer's requirement. The company's proposal manager or contract manager might be able to begin working on this folder early if the company has an ongoing relationship with the agency. For example, the company's proposal manager can identify related programs and the company's history with any of them. The program manager and contract manager can find most of the program description elements in the draft RFP (if one was issued), such as the description of the requirement and the scope of work, contract type, and schedule. If not, look for details at the pre-proposal conference.

The company should describe the agency's requirement in terms of what it means to the agency and to the company. This description will serve as the basis for decisions about proceeding with the proposal and allocating resources to the proposal preparation process.[4] Additional information about the program comes from attending the pre-proposal conference. For example, the contract manager might learn about the agency's funding profile and the contract type and schedule at the pre-proposal conference.

ASSESSING THE COMPETITION

The next folder in the capture planning filing cabinet assesses the competition. Companies with a lot of experience in the federal contracting marketplace probably already have an idea of who the potential competition may be. Contract managers can get information about potential competition at the pre-proposal conference simply by identifying which companies are or are not in attendance. They can then consider potential teaming relationships and which company might lead the effort as the prime contractor.

After collecting this information, the company can begin to conduct an honest assessment of its competitors' legacy with the agency, including their strengths and weaknesses. What is their reputation with the agency? What is their history with the program office, and how have they performed on similar contracts with other agencies? If one or more competitors have significant strengths, acknowledge them here. This will help you determine how your company will counter them in the proposal.

Once the competition assessment is complete, it's time to move on to the next file, in which you evaluate your own company's strengths and weaknesses. In today's contracting environment, teaming among competitors is very common. Your company may have direct knowledge of a competitor's strengths and weaknesses from a prior team arrangement. If so, the competitor knows your company as well as you know it. It may try to counter your company's weaknesses in its own proposal, and your company must be prepared to promote its strengths.

Evaluating the Company's Strengths and Weaknesses

Honestly evaluating your company's strengths and weaknesses is an important part of the capture planning process. To determine whether your company has a real chance of winning the contract, the proposal manager needs to know if your company's strengths can meet or exceed the government's requirements. If your company has a weakness, it may want to identify a team member who can counter that weakness. As part of the strengths and weaknesses assessment, ask the following questions about your company:

- What is your company's reputation with the customer?
- What is the company's documented past performance history?
- How well does the company know the customer and the program requirements?
- Does the company have the requisite technical skills to complete the work?
- How competitive are your company's rates?
- What is the company's technical approach to winning the contract?
- Do you need to team with another company to make up any capability gaps? (Teaming will be discussed in detail later in this chapter.)

Another part of the strengths and weaknesses assessment is determining if the company has a conflict of interest with ongoing programs. For example, a contractor that provides systems engineering and technical direction for a system but does not have overall contractual responsibility for its development, integration, assembly, checkout, or production should not be awarded a contract to supply the system or any of its major components, or be a subcontractor or consultant to a supplier of the system or any of its major components.[5] Or, if a contractor prepares and furnishes complete specifications for nondevelopmental items to be used in a competitive acquisition, that contractor shall not be allowed to furnish these items, either as a prime contractor or as a subcontractor, for a reasonable period of time including, at least, the duration of the initial production contract. This requirement exists in order to avoid a situation in which a contractor drafts specifications favoring its own products or capabilities. In this way, the government can be assured of getting unbiased advice on the content of the specifications and can avoid allegations of favoritism in the award of production contracts.[6]

Sometimes agencies use consultants to assist with the evaluation process. Contracts for evaluating offers for products or services should not be awarded to a contractor that will evaluate its own offers for products or services, or those of a competitor, without proper safeguards to ensure objectivity to protect the government's interests.[7]

See Federal Acquisition Regulation (FAR) 9.505 for more information about organizational conflicts of interest and FAR 9.508 for additional scenarios. If a company plans to submit a proposal but a potential conflict exists, it may wish to advise the contracting officer or develop an internal mitigation plan. The mitigation plan documents how the company will ensure that the potential conflict of interest does not turn into an unfair competitive advantage. It might cover interdivisional separation, firewalls, or other activities that separate those with prior knowledge of the information that creates the competitive advantage from those who will be working on the proposal and the resulting program. For very large companies with multiple divisions or lines of business, there may be a conflict of interest for one division but not another. In this situation, the company has to keep the divisions completely separated from proposal preparation through contract completion.

After completing the strengths and weaknesses assessment, the company is ready to make a decision about submitting a proposal.

Deciding to Submit a Proposal (Bid/No-Bid)

Now that the company has compiled folders on the customer, the program description, the competition, and the company's strengths and weaknesses, it must decide if it is really going to submit a proposal. This decision is typically called a *bid/no-bid decision*, even in the negotiated acquisition environment. This folder in the capture planning filing cabinet documents the proposal submission decision. In making this decision, a company should ask the following questions:

- Does the company have the resources necessary to submit a successful proposal?
- Does the company have the requisite technical skills required?
- Can the company counter the competition's strengths?
- Is the company capable of managing the contract? If it's a cost-reimbursement contract, can the company's accounting system segregate costs?

Gregory A. Garrett recommends a ten-point approach a company can use to evaluate the elements of a contracting opportunity and conduct an honest assessment of its ability to perform the contract work.

1. **Corporate direction match.** This refers to how consistent an opportunity is with your company's core business. Your company has a much higher probability of winning contracts and successfully delivering when an opportunity is consistent with its core business and strategic direction.
2. **Competitive environment.** Is your company or your competitor perceived by the customer as the solution leader? Opportunities for which the customer perceives your company as the leader and the favored supplier (for reasons other than price) are highly desirable.
3. **Revenue value.** What is the dollar value of the opportunity? It's important to distinguish small- from large-revenue opportunities. Companies have business goals, including how much money (revenue) they need or want to make. If the company is unlikely to meet its revenue goals, then it should pursue large-revenue opportunities. On the other hand, if the company has already met its

revenue goals, then it has more liberty to pursue small-revenue opportunities. Your company must develop a best estimate and focus on near-term revenues, such as those likely to come in the first year of the contract. This estimate should be addressed in the context of your company's size and the typical size of new opportunities the company is pursuing.

4. **Potential profitability.** What is the likely profit margin, given the competitive environment and what it will take to win the contract? Many companies have guidelines regarding the profitability of new opportunities, which serve as the basis for assessing the probable size of profit margins. Don't estimate profit margins on future business, but focus on the near term.

5. **In-house content.** How much of the work will be done by your company? Many times, new business requires teaming or subcontracting to win the contract, but most of the effort should come from within your company.

6. **Future business potential.** How will this opportunity impact additional business beyond the scope of this RFP? For example, will winning this contract provide a way to win even more business with this or another agency, or will it protect an existing line of business? What is the degree to which specific, identifiable future business depends on winning this contract? (Alternatively, will performing this work create an organizational conflict of interest that will preclude participation in future work?)

7. **Proposal preparation resources.** Does your company have the resources required to submit a successful proposal? How will pursuing this contract impact its ability to pursue other opportunities? All companies have resource constraints, so they must consider the opportunity cost of not pursuing other opportunities they may have a better chance of winning. On the other hand, what is the cost of leaving assets idle until that opportunity arises?

8. **Probability of success.** What is the likelihood that your company will win the contract over one of your competitors?

9. **Collateral benefit.** What is the degree to which pursuing this opportunity will improve your company's existing skill level or develop new skills that will help it win future business?

10. **Overall strategic value.** What is the need to win this contract, considering all of the aforementioned opportunity elements along with other relevant aspects of the competitive environment?

These ten opportunity elements must be balanced against ten risk elements:

1. **Customer commitment.** Has the customer demonstrated a solid commitment to implementing the program? Has it identified and allocated the necessary personnel, resources, and funding?

2. **Corporate competence.** Does your company have experience in similar projects? The more experience, the lower the risk.

3. **External obstacles.** What roadblocks exist that are beyond your company's control or your customer's control? For example, congressional involvement in the procurement could jeopardize funding or establish requirements that the agency doesn't really want.

4. **Opportunity involvement.** How much influence did your company or your competitors have in establishing the requirements? There's a fine line between influencing a requirement and establishing or writing a requirement. For example, a company with an existing contract (the incumbent) may influence a re-compete or follow-on solicitation. Although this situation might create a competitive advantage for the incumbent, it's not an unfair competitive advantage or a conflict of interest.

5. **Solution maturity.** How much does your company's proposed solution use existing mature technology versus newer technology? Mature products tend to have lower risk than do untested state-of-the-art solutions. The level of risk also depends on the agency's evaluation criteria. For example, if the evaluation criteria state the agency is looking for an innovative approach or state-of-the-art solution, then it may be willing to accept more risk. On the other hand, if the evaluation criteria state that the agency is looking for standardized or established processes, then it may be more averse to a newer, riskier approach.

6. **Period of performance.** How long is the contract, and how will it fit in with other work your company currently has? The longer the period of performance, the higher the likelihood of changes in personnel (yours and the agency's), funding availability, and technology. Also consider schedule realism: Can your company realistically perform the work within the desired or required schedule?

7. **Delivery schedule.** A schedule dictated by the agency is more risky than one your company proposes. A flexible schedule poses less risk than a firm schedule without any slack. An extremely long schedule may have pricing implications for supplies and subcontracts, which can also increase risk.

8. **Resource coordination.** How many divisions or departments in your company would play a role in completing the contract? When more internal groups are involved, more coordination is required, and there is an increased chance of miscommunication or disconnection. For example, one group might assume another group is working on an issue without confirming, and then the problem doesn't get addressed at all. Coordinating outside suppliers and subcontractors introduces even more risk because you have less control over another company's communication process.

9. **Penalties.** What penalties are involved with this effort? Will the contract have a liquidated damages clause that applies if work is not delivered in a timely

manner? (Cost-reimbursement contracts have a cost ceiling; although it is not technically a penalty, contractors exceed that ceiling at their own risk. Companies new to government contracting need to be aware of this risk and plan accordingly).

10. **Overall feasibility.** What is the likelihood of successfully performing this contract and getting an excellent performance evaluation upon completion? What is your company's history with the customer? How well have past contracts with the agency gone? If the project is complex, and the customer doesn't have a good track record of supporting the effort, there is a high risk of problems during performance.[8]

Companies can use several approaches to decide whether to submit a proposal. Some are quantitative, using a rating scale to assess the opportunity and risk elements discussed above. Or a company can use a subjective approach and evaluate possible risks and rewards for each opportunity, then direct resources to those opportunities that have the highest probability of success. One approach that works well is to put together a *capture team* of professionals with experience in sales, business development, accounting or finance, technical, project management, proposal or capture management, legal, and of course, contracts. The capture team would conduct the capture planning activities. Figure 7-2 suggests individuals who might compose the team, along with departments from which additional team members may be selected.

Determining the Win Strategy

If the company decides to submit the proposal, the next folder in the capture planning filing cabinet should be the win strategy file. In a recent study, the average company won less than 18 percent of the dollars it bid on, while three companies won more than 60 percent, and one company consistently won more than 80 percent. These top performers differed not only in performance but in their

Figure 7-2 Capture Team Organization[9]

business development process. Specifically, they were significantly more selective about the opportunities they pursued and how they used capture teams.[10] Once the company understands the customer's needs and the evaluation criteria and decides to submit a proposal, it must develop a solution that meets the customer's needs and fulfills the evaluation criteria.

For example, if the evaluation criteria emphasize technical superiority, then your company's solution should offer technical excellence at a reasonable price. If, on the other hand, the agency is looking for the lowest price technically acceptable proposal, then your company's solution should emphasize price reasonableness while still fulfilling the technical requirements. It's a difficult balancing act, but your company must focus on meeting the agency's requirements to have an effective win strategy.

Another important element of a successful win strategy is making sure the entire proposal team understands the requirements. The entire team must also work toward meeting them. This can be a challenge on large or complex contracts; frequent team meetings are important so that everyone stays on point. The capture team needs to agree on the technical solution and must communicate it effectively in the proposal. Disagreements can lead to conflicts or ambiguities in the proposal, which will make the proposal hard to evaluate and the technical solution look less desirable to evaluators. Building a strong team to write the proposal and execute the contract is critical to a successful win strategy.

Even if the evaluation criteria state that technical factors are more important than cost, price reasonableness is always an evaluation factor. Having a sound pricing strategy is only part of the picture. The company needs to understand the customer's budget and priorities. Does the agency have enough funding for the work? Funding issues play a role in determining a pricing strategy. Subcontractors and suppliers also affect proposal pricing, so they need to be kept informed about the technical solution to which they're contributing and any budgetary limits or thresholds your company has imposed for their portion of the work. Subcontractors and suppliers need to be conscientious about reasonable prices when submitting their part of the effort to the prime contractor. An overpriced subcontract or component can have a negative effect on the overall price reasonableness determination. Keeping the lines of communication open is another important part of a win strategy.

Win strategies often focus on contract or product life cycle issues. For example, will spending more money early in the development stage save production costs later? Will a proposed change in materials increase producibility, reliability, or maintainability costs? Even if future production or maintenance is not part of the instant contract, giving attention to such factors in the proposal can be an effective win strategy.

The final aspects of the win strategy are probably the most difficult to tackle. Has your company allocated the best resources to this proposal? It's not always practical to pursue every possible opportunity. If the company can't commit the necessary resources to prepare a quality proposal, will it have the resources to perform the work? Sometimes it makes more sense to pass on an opportunity in order to reserve the resources for an opportunity your company has a better chance of winning.

If the company decides to allocate its best resources to submit a quality proposal, then it must work to address its weaknesses and counter its competitors' strengths. This is where an honest assessment of the company's strengths and weaknesses, along with its competitors', fits in. If the company can't overcome its weaknesses or the competitor's strengths are significant, then it might consider teaming or subcontracting to compensate.

TEAMING AGREEMENTS

The FAR defines a *contractor team arrangement* as an agreement in which two or more companies form a partnership or joint venture to act as a potential prime contractor, or a potential prime contractor agrees with one or more other companies to have them act as its subcontractors under a specified government contract or acquisition program.[11] Teaming arrangements, regardless of the nature of the legal relationship created, are of limited duration and are usually targeted at a specific opportunity.

The FAR goes on to explain that contractor team arrangements may be desirable from both a government and industry standpoint in order to enable the companies involved to complement each other's unique capabilities and offer the government the best combination of performance, cost, and delivery for the system or product being acquired. Contractor team arrangements may be particularly appropriate for complex research and development acquisitions but may be used for other appropriate acquisitions, including production.[12]

Before entering a teaming arrangement, companies must ask themselves the following questions:

- What are my company's goals in pursuing this teaming arrangement?
  - What is the purpose of the team?
  - Are the company's interests long term or short term?

- • What is the company willing to give up in order to execute the teaming agreement?
  - • What kind of proprietary data or technical knowledge is the company willing to exchange with its teammate?
- • How much do we know about our potential teammate?
  - • Is the company responsible and solvent?
  - • How can the company protect itself in the event that the teammate cannot perform?
  - • Where else could the company go for the supplies or services?
- • How will the customer react to this teaming arrangement?
  - • Will the team enhance our company's ability to win the contract?[13]

The companies involved normally form a contractor teaming agreement before submitting the proposal, but they may enter into an arrangement later in the acquisition process, including after contract award. The government will recognize the integrity and validity of contractor team arrangements, *provided* the arrangements are identified and company relationships are fully disclosed in an offer or, for arrangements entered into after submission of an offer, before the arrangement becomes effective. The government does not normally require or encourage the dissolution of contractor team arrangements.[14]

Because teaming arrangements create a temporary association between potential competitors, the parties must protect their competitive interests while creating a viable team to win the contract. Companies should be able to answer the following questions about issues typically encountered when creating a teaming agreement:

- • Does the prime expect the subcontractor to be exclusive to its company, or can the subcontractor work with a competitor on the same contract?
- • How will the team determine performance and technical issues? What work will each party perform?
- • Will there be an exchange of proprietary data that would require signing nondisclosure agreements? Will firewalls or other mechanisms be created to insulate the data?
- • How will the parties conduct inspection and acceptance?
- • What is the fee or profit split?
- • Who has primary or sole responsibility for communicating with the ultimate customer?

Teammates must address these issues before beginning proposal preparation efforts. Another element of establishing teaming arrangements is determining how to structure the relationship.

Determining the Structure

Once parties decide to work together, they need to determine the right structure for the arrangement: joint venture, or prime contractor and subcontractor relationship. Federal antitrust laws may restrict establishing a joint venture, so the parties should consult legal counsel before entering into such a relationship.

Joint Ventures

In a *joint venture*, the parties jointly own and manage either a partnership or a corporation established for the express purpose of entering into a contract with a customer. Because the joint venture has privity of contract with the customer, neither party on its own has that relationship. Unlike a prime contractor–subcontractor relationship, each party has an equal say in making decisions about the project—limited, of course, to a decision-making process agreed to by the parties to the joint venture. Thus, a joint venture has an advantage over a prime contractor–subcontractor relationship: The parties share the risks and profits of the venture in proportion to their investment. This may lead to a stronger, more unified team.

Not all joint ventures are set up as a corporation, but when they are, one advantage of the arrangement is that corporations have limited liability. The parties to the joint venture are liable only to the extent of their investment in the joint venture.

Prime Contractor-Subcontractor Relationships

In a *prime contractor-subcontractor relationship*, the prime contractor is the only party that has privity of contract with the customer. The parties operate under separate contracts with potentially different terms, risks, and obligations. This flexibility permits the parties to negotiate contractual arrangements that are tailored to their own specific needs.[15]

Although the prime contractor is fully responsible for contract performance, a teaming agreement is also a documented legal relationship, and potential subcontractors should expect the prime to live up to its teaming obligations. Let's look at a case in which this didn't happen.

Case Study: Subcontractor Teaming

In the case of *EG&G Inc. v. the Cube Corp* (Cube), Cube, as the prime contractor, was sued by EG&G, its subcontractor, for failure to live up to the terms of their teaming agreement. The central issue was whether the teaming agreement and supporting documentation bound the parties inextricably together, and whether the subcontractor could seek specific performance under the teaming agreement, rather than merely suing for monetary damages if the prime failed to live up to the terms of the teaming agreement. As the prime contractor, Cube argued that the teaming agreement did not constitute a contract; rather, it was merely an "agreement to agree."

The judge disagreed with Cube's position and found that all of the necessary particulars of a contract were in place. The judge ruled that the subcontractor was entitled to obtain specific performance from the teaming agreement. The court found that the prime contract was awarded to Cube partly on the basis of EG&G's experience. When Cube sought to negotiate the subcontract after the prime contract was awarded, however, it sought to cap EG&G's allowable indirect cost rates and to include a blanket termination-for-convenience clause, stating that Cube could terminate the subcontracting relationship at any time, without first being terminated itself by the customer. EG&G refused to accept these additional provisions, and when discussions broke down, it brought suit.

The judge found that the two disputed terms (the cap on allowable indirect cost rates and the termination-for-convenience clause) were never part of the original agreement and held that the teaming agreement's central terms were clear and definite enough to permit the court to award specific performance.[16]

This case is noteworthy because it is the first case in which a subcontractor was successful in suing to enforce a teaming agreement, although one wonders how well the parties worked together after the fact. This case signals the need for both prime contractors and subcontractors to exercise great care in negotiating teaming agreements.[17]

Designing the Teaming Agreement

After determining the structure of the teaming arrangement, the parties need to formally establish their working relationship in a teaming agreement. Teaming agreements typically cover the following:

- A statement of purpose, including a discussion of the nature of the teaming relationship
- The work share split
- The process defining how the parties will exchange information and handle proprietary information
- The expectations for the standards of performance and payment
- The term and termination
- The key personnel (if any—sometimes the RFP does not require key personnel)

The statement of purpose identifies the government program or the contract the parties are pursuing. The parties should also define the nature of the teaming relationship. Typical questions the parties should ask and answer about the relationship include:

- Is there an exclusive relationship between the parties?
- May the prime contractor look for other teammates offering the same supplies or services?
- Does the subcontractor have any influence concerning other teammates added to the team? (For example, the prime contractor may expect the subcontractor to do all of the subcontracted work on its own and prohibit the subcontractor from using other companies to complete the effort. Or, the subcontractor might have an exclusivity policy where it insists it's the only company to do a certain portion of the work).
- Will the subcontractor be allowed to submit a proposal with another prime contractor, thereby increasing its chances of getting a contract?
- How much proposal preparation support does the prime expect of the subcontractor? If the subcontractor will perform a major portion of the work, the prime may expect it to write major sections of the proposal for that portion of work. Other primes prefer to retain control of the entire proposal preparation effort.
- Upon contract award, what share of the work would the subcontractor receive, and how quickly will the subcontract be executed?
- How will the parties communicate with the government customer?

Sometimes a prime contractor entices a subcontractor into a teaming arrangement in order to compensate for the prime's weaknesses, only to offer the subcontractor limited work after contract award. Some subcontractors insist on a guarantee of a certain percentage or dollar value of work upon contract award. The prime contractor may be hesitant to make such a guarantee and may want to maintain flexibility in the event the subcontractor does not perform well.

The parties must document how they will handle proprietary data. Many prime-sub relationships begin with a nondisclosure agreement. Such an agreement prohibits the parties from using or disclosing information except for purposes of writing the proposal or performing the subsequent contract and subcontract. Executing a nondisclosure agreement would prevent one party from using the other's technology on another proposal. A nondisclosure agreement can also prohibit the disclosure of information about a specific government customer and the company's history with that customer.

Identifying standards of performance helps to reduce risk for both parties. During the proposal preparation phase, each party is expected to expend reasonable effort to prepare and submit the proposal. Then, the parties must determine how the proposal review process will work. Will the subcontractor have an opportunity to review the entire proposal before it's submitted? What is the subcontractor expected to do during negotiations, oral presentations, or subsequent proposal revisions? Each party typically pays for its own bid and proposal expenses, including negotiation support, and subcontractors are not usually given access to all of the prime contractor's cost or pricing data.

The term and termination portion of the teaming agreement states the period during which it is effective. Teaming agreements typically terminate upon award of the subcontract or if the customer cancels the solicitation. There may also be a time limit of a certain number of years.

Finally, teaming agreements should identify key personnel. Recall from Chapter 3 that the proposal preparation instructions and evaluation criteria may identify key personnel requirements. Team members must determine which company will provide which key personnel.

Exclusivity and FAR Restrictions on Teaming

Please note that some companies look for or expect exclusive teaming partners. An exclusive teaming arrangement is created when two or more companies agree in writing, through understandings, or by any other means to team together and further agree not to team with any competitors for that contract.[18] The contract manager must know if the company—his or her own company or a potential prime or subcontractor—is willing or able to enter an exclusive arrangement. If a prime contractor expects its subcontractors to be exclusive, the prime needs to state that expectation in the teaming agreement. Similarly, if a subcontractor has a policy of never executing exclusive teaming agreements, it needs to notify the prime contractor of that fact. Note also that certain agencies may prohibit exclusive teaming arrangements because they have a negative effect on competition. Companies must know the policies of the agency releasing the RFP before agreeing to an exclusive teaming arrangement.

There are additional limitations companies need to be aware of before entering into teaming agreements. For example, per FAR 9.604, companies may not establish "team arrangements in violation of antitrust statutes" and may not limit the government's rights to do the following:

- "Require consent to subcontracts
- Determine, on the basis of the stated contractor team arrangement, the responsibility of the prime contractor

- Provide to the prime contractor data rights owned or controlled by the government
- Pursue its policies on competitive contracting, subcontracting, and component breakout after initial production or at any other time
- Hold the prime contractor fully responsible for contract performance, regardless of any team arrangement between the prime contractor and its subcontractors."[19]

KEY PERSONNEL CONSIDERATIONS

If the RFP requires identification of key personnel, companies must make sure that personnel they're proposing are available to work on this effort. Companies should be careful about the temptation to "bait and switch" regarding key personnel. The term *bait and switch* generally refers to an offeror's misrepresentation in its proposal of the personnel that it expects to use during contract performance. Where such a misrepresentation materially influences an agency's evaluation of an offeror's proposal, it undermines the integrity of the competitive procurement system and generally provides a basis for proposal rejection or termination of a contract award based upon the proposal.

To demonstrate a "bait and switch," a protester must show not only that personnel other than those proposed are performing the services—the "switch"—but also that:

- The awardee stated in its proposal that it would rely on certain specified personnel to perform the services,
- The agency relied on this representation in evaluating the proposal, and
- It was foreseeable that the individuals named in the proposal would not be available to perform the contract work.

Each of these three elements must be present to establish the "bait" portion of a "bait and switch" claim.[20]

To avoid the risk of "bait and switch," some agencies require personnel to sign the resumes they submit and require the contractor to agree to a statement that if the company wins the contract, the people specified will actually work on the contract for a minimum period of time. See Figure 7-3 for an example.

When a company submits a proposal, it typically states the date after which the proposal is no longer effective—i.e., the *validity period* of the proposal. For example, an agency may write in the solicitation, "Proposals in response to this solicitation will be valid for the number of days specified on the solicitation cover sheet (unless a different period is proposed by the offeror)."

Letters of Commitment: Key Personnel (Oct. 2000)

1. All proposed key personnel require written, signed (by employee/ contingency hire), and dated letters of commitment. The Offeror shall provide letters of commitment from current employees that state they: (1) will remain employed by the Offeror; and (2) will work full time, or the percentage of time designated in the RFP, for at least one year on the resultant contract if awarded to the Offeror.

2. Letters of commitment must be submitted for contingency hires, defined as persons not currently employed but who have executed a binding letter of commitment for employment with the Offeror, if the Offeror receives award under subject solicitation. The letter of commitment must reflect agreement on salary, benefits and position. New hires may not be proposed for key personnel. (A new hire is defined as specified or unspecified persons to fill an empty position who are neither identified as a current employee of the Offeror (or proposed subcontractor) nor as a contingency hire)

3. For those key personnel designated by the Contracting Officer, a binding signed employment contract between the key person(s) and the employer/offeror contingent upon the Department of Labor (DOL) awarding the employer/offeror the resultant contract must be provided with the proposal in order for the proposal to be considered responsive or technically acceptable. The employment contract must: (1) be for at least one year from the date of the award of the contract by DOL to the employer/offeror; (2) state that the employee will work full time, or the percentage of time designated in the RFP, on the resultant contract if awarded to the employer/offeror; and (3) the employment contract must address salary, benefits, and position.

Confirmation of Proposed Key Personnel (Oct. 2000)

The following certificate shall be provided upon request by the Contracting Officer should discussions be required and revisions and/or best and final offers be requested.

> I certify that the proposed key personnel are still available for performance under any contract resulting from this solicitation, and that the letters of commitment are still valid. I base this certification on written and/or oral confirmation which I received, within the past 30 days, from each individual proposed to fill the Key Personnel requirements. I further certify that I possess copies of written confirmations I received from each individual, and/or a memorandum to the file documenting oral confirmation of that individual's availability. I further promise to immediately inform the Government of any changes in the availability of any proposed key personnel.

Date of Certification

By (Name and signature of company president)

Figure 7-3 Key Personnel Commitments[21]

Contracting officers should note that the key personnel provisions are subject to the validity period stated in the proposal. If the agency awards the contract after the proposal's validity period, the key personnel provision will have expired, and the personnel proposed may not be available. Thus, offerors should carefully consider which key personnel will be included in the proposal. It is advisable to make sure they will actually be available before using their skill set in a proposal. This caution is particularly relevant when a long time elapses between identifying the personnel, the proposal due date, and contract award. It is possible that a person named in the proposal will have another job, either within the company or at another company. Companies that have key personnel committed and ready to go upon contract award have a smooth transition, especially when subcontractors are also supplying key personnel.

After contract award, the contract may require that the contractor comply with special requirements regarding the use and retention of key personnel on the contract. Figure 7-4 provides examples of contract clauses applicable to key personnel. Agencies may have their own format for these clauses. The text is typically placed in

---

Sample 1: Addition or Substitution of Personnel

   a. A requirement of this contract is to maintain stability of personnel proposed in order to provide quality services. The Contractor shall assign only those key personnel listed in the Attachment whose resumes were approved and who are necessary to fulfill the requirements of the effort. The Contractor shall assign to any effort requiring non-key personnel only personnel who meet or exceed the applicable labor category descriptions.

   b. No key personnel substitutions or additions will be made unless necessitated by compelling reasons including, but not limited to, an individual's illness, death, termination of employment, declining an offer of employment (for those individuals proposed as contingent hires), or maternity leave. In such an event, the Contractor shall promptly provide the information required by paragraph c below to the Contracting Officer for approval prior to the substitution or addition of key personnel. Proposed substitutions of key personnel shall meet or exceed the qualifications of personnel for whom they are proposed to replace. Fully compliant requests for substitutions or additions shall be submitted, in writing, to the Contracting Officer for approval at least 15 working days in advance of the proposed change.

   c. Requests for key personnel changes shall provide a detailed explanation of the circumstances necessitating the proposed substitutions or additions, a complete resume of the proposed change in accordance with the Attachment (resume format), information regarding the full financial impact of the change, and any other information requested by the Contracting Officer.

   d. Any addition or substitution of key personnel made pursuant to this clause shall result in no increase in the fully burdened hourly rate for the subject category set forth in Section B. However, such rate may be subject to downward negotiation if the addition or substitution results in a decrease to the rate for the category in which the substitution was made.

   e. Noncompliance with the provisions of this clause will be considered a material breach of the terms and conditions of the contract for which the Government may seek any and all appropriate remedies including Termination for Default pursuant to the Termination clause.

Sample 2: Substitution or Addition of Personnel

   a. The offeror agrees to assign to the contract those persons whose resumes, personnel data forms or personnel qualification statements were submitted as required in Section L to fill the requirements of the contract.

   b. The offeror agrees that during the contract performance period; no personnel substitutions will be permitted unless such substitutions are necessitated by an individual's sudden illness, death or termination of employment. In any of these events, the contractor shall promptly notify the Contracting Officer and provide the information required by paragraph (d) below.

   c. If personnel for whatever reason become unavailable for work under the contract for a continuous period exceeding 30 working days, or are expected to devote substantially less effort to the work than indicated in the proposal, the contractor shall propose a substitution of such personnel, in accordance with paragraph (d) below.

Figure 7-4 Contract Clauses on Substitution or Addition of Personnel[22]

d. All proposed substitutions shall be submitted, in writing, to the Contracting Officer at least 15 days prior to the proposed substitution. Each request shall provide a detailed explanation of the circumstances necessitating the proposed substitution, a complete resume for the proposed substitute and any other information required by the Contracting Officer. All proposed substitutes shall have qualifications equal to or higher than the qualifications of the person being replaced.

e. In the event a requirement to increase the specified level of effort for a designated labor category, but not the overall level of effort of the contract occurs, the offeror shall submit to the Contracting Officer a written request for approval to add personnel to the designated labor category. The information required is the same as that required for paragraph (d) above. The additional personnel shall have qualifications greater than or equal at least one of the individuals proposed for the designated labor category.

f. The Contracting Officer shall evaluate requests for substitution and addition of personnel and promptly notify the offeror, in writing, of whether the request is approved or disapproved.

g. If the Contracting Officer determines that suitable and timely replacement of personnel who have been reassigned, terminated or have otherwise become unavailable to perform under the contract is not reasonably forthcoming or that the resultant reduction of productive effort would impair the successful completion of the contract or the delivery order, the contract may be terminated for default or for the convenience of the Government. Alternatively, if the Contracting Officer finds the contractor to be at fault for the condition, the Contracting Officer may equitably adjust (downward) the contract price or fixed fee to compensate the Government for any delay, loss or damage.

Sample 3: Key Personnel

a. The Contractor agrees to assign to the contract tasks those persons whose resumes were submitted with its proposal and who are necessary to fulfill the requirements of the contract as "key personnel". No substitutions may be made except in accordance with this clause.

b. The Contractor understands that during the first 90 days of the contract performance period, no personnel substitutions will be permitted unless these substitutions are unavoidable because of the incumbent's sudden illness, death or termination of employment. In any of these events, the Contractor shall promptly notify the Contracting Officer and provide the information described in paragraph (c) below. After the initial 90 day period, the Contractor must submit to the Contracting Officer all proposed substitutions, in writing, at least 15 days in advance (120 days if security clearance must be obtained) of any proposed substitution and provide the information required by paragraph (c) below.

c. Any request for substitution must include a detailed explanation of the circumstances necessitating the proposed substitution, a resume for the proposed substitute, and any other information requested by the Contracting Officer. Any proposed substitute must have qualifications equal to or superior to the qualifications of the incumbent. The Contracting Officer or his/her authorized representative will evaluate such requests and promptly notify the Contractor in writing of his/her approval or disapproval thereof.

d. In the event that any of the identified key personnel cease to perform under the contract and the substitute is disapproved, the contract may be immediately terminated in accordance with the Termination clause of the contract.

The following are identified as key personnel: (list names)

....

....

....

Figure 7-4   *(Continued)*

section H of the RFP (Special Contract Requirements). (Section H is where agencies insert requirements that are not included in section I [Contract Clauses] or in other sections of the uniform contract format.[23])

SUBCONTRACTING IMPLICATIONS

Few large, complex contracts are completed without subcontracts. Despite their prevalence, some companies do not pay close attention to the subcontracts themselves. Yet a subcontractor can make the difference between contract success and contract disputes. So it's a good idea to fine-tune the subcontract before the problems surface. First, let's look at subcontract relationships.

One of the unique aspects of contracting with the federal government is the requirement for the government to give its consent before the prime contractor issues subcontracts. If the contractor does not have an approved purchasing system, it must get the contracting officer's consent before entering into cost-reimbursement, time-and-materials, labor-hour, or letter contracts. If the prime contractor has an approved purchasing system, the contracting officer may require consent to subcontract to protect the government because of the type, complexity, or dollar value of the subcontract.[24] In some cases, under cost-reimbursement contracts, the prime contractor must notify the contracting officer of certain subcontract awards, as required by FAR 44.201.

Understanding Privity of Contract

A prime contractor has a contract with the federal government, which may, in turn, award one or more subcontracts to complete performance of that contract. These subcontractors may also have suppliers or, if it's a larger effort, may award their own subcontracts to another company or companies. Thus, there may be multiple levels of subcontracts. The level of a subcontractor is frequently referred to as a *tier*. For example, if the prime contractor is company A, the companies that supply the prime contractor directly (companies B and C) are first-tier subcontractors. Companies B and C may award subcontracts to companies D and E, which are second-tier subcontractors. Figure 7-5 illustrates these tiers.

Privity of contract refers to a direct contractual relationship between the parties that allows the parties to enforce contractual rights and seek remedies.[25] If there isn't an arrow connecting two parties in Figure 7-5, there isn't privity of contract. For example, if company E (a second-tier sub) is late delivering supplies to company C (a first-tier sub), then company A (the prime contractor) cannot penalize company

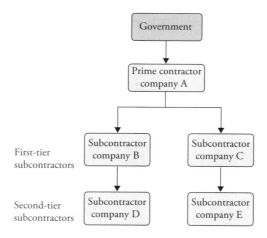

Figure 7-5   Subcontract Tiers and Privity

E for making company C late in its delivery, because there is no privity of contract between company A and company E. Company C is responsible for managing its own subcontract and ensuring a timely delivery despite problems it may have with company E. Company A has no recourse against company E for being late. The only appropriate course of action for company A is to pursue its remedies against company C, its own subcontractor, with whom it has privity of contract. It is unlikely to excuse company C's failure to perform because of its subcontractor, company E's, delayed delivery.

Understanding Flow-Down Clauses

Despite the lack of privity between the government and subcontractors, however, the government still has an influence on subcontracts through *flow-down clauses*. The FAR identifies flow-down clauses and the tier and dollar value of subcontracts to which they apply. Contract managers (including purchasing professionals and subcontract managers) must review not only the relevant clause itself, but the prescribing text as well. For example, FAR 9.409 states that the contracting officer shall insert the clause at 52.209-6 (Protecting the Government's Interest When Subcontracting with Contractors Debarred, Suspended, or Proposed for Debarment) in solicitations and contracts when the contract value exceeds $30,000. Readers will note that FAR 52.209 starts with the phrase, "As *prescribed* in 9.409(b), insert the following clause." Thus, FAR 9.409 is called a *prescription* because it prescribes when to use the clause at 52.209-6.

Contract managers must review both the prescription and the clause to determine whether the clause should apply to subcontractors and at what tier. Figure 7-6

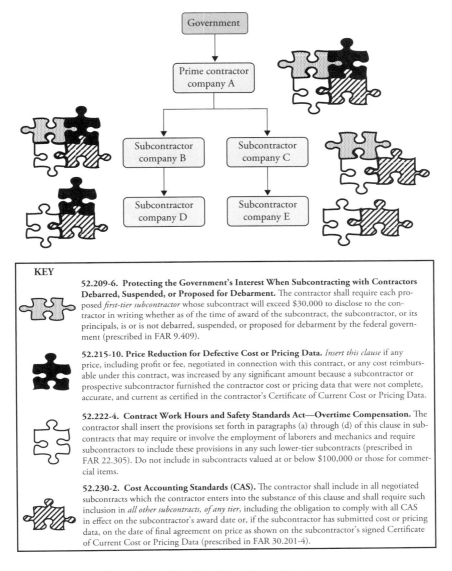

Figure 7-6 Puzzling Flow-Down Requirements

illustrates how flow-down clauses work. In this example, the prime contract is for $10 million, and the prime contractor has two subcontracts with company B and company C. These subcontractors each have one subcontract. Company B's subcontract is with company D, and company C's subcontract is with company E.

The prime contractor has the following clauses in its contract:

- FAR 52.209-6 (Protecting the Government's Interest When Subcontracting with Contractors Debarred, Suspended, or Proposed for Debarment)
- FAR 52.215-10 (Price Reduction for Defective Cost or Pricing Data)

- FAR 52.222-4 (Contract Work Hours and Safety Standards Act)
- FAR 52.230-2 (Cost Accounting Standards).

Company B's subcontract is for $2 million. It is a negotiated subcontract for which the company submitted certified cost or pricing data. Company C's subcontract is for $500,000 and is a negotiated subcontract, but it is not for a commercial item.

The contract manager must determine which clauses to flow down to which subcontract. Both companies are first-tier subcontractors with subcontracts of more than $30,000, so FAR 52.209-6 applies to both. This is illustrated by the gray puzzle piece in Figure 7-6.

In addition, both companies have negotiated subcontracts of more than $100,000 but are not supplying commercial items. Thus, FAR 52.222-4 applies to both subcontracts. This situation illustrates another kind of a flow-down clause, one that the FAR requires subcontractors to flow down to lower-tier subcontracts based on dollar value. For example, FAR 52.222-4 (Contract Work Hours and Safety Standards Act) requires subcontractors to include the clause in any lower-tier subcontracts. But contract managers must read the prescription at FAR 22.305 to learn that it does not apply to subcontracts valued at or below $100,000 or for commercial items. This situation is illustrated by the white puzzle piece in Figure 7-6.

FAR 15.408 prescribes the use of FAR 52.215-12 (Subcontractor Cost or Pricing Data) when the subcontract exceeds the cost or pricing data threshold defined at FAR 15.403-4 and when the prime believes cost or pricing data will be required from any subcontractor. Because only company B submitted certified cost or pricing data, only company B has FAR 52.215-10 (Price Reduction for Defective Cost or Pricing Data) in its subcontract. This situation is illustrated by the black puzzle piece in Figure 7-6.

If a subcontractor submits defective cost or pricing data to the prime, then it is responsible for the resultant price reduction. If a company (prime or subcontractor) does not make this clause part of its subcontract, then it cannot reduce the subcontractor's contract price if the subcontractor submits defective cost or pricing data that causes a price reduction in the prime's contract. Many prime contractors and subcontractors choose to include this clause in subcontracts to protect themselves in the event that the subcontractor submits defective cost or pricing data. Thus, even when the government does not require clauses to be flowed from the prime contract to subcontracts to protect its own interests, they sometimes *should* be flowed to the subcontractor to protect the interests of the higher-tier contractor.

Finally, other flow-down clauses apply based on the contract type or method of acquisition. For example, FAR 52.230-2 (Cost Accounting Standards) applies to all negotiated subcontracts and subcontracts of any tier. This situation is illustrated by the striped puzzle piece in Figure 7-6.

Companies B and C must determine which clauses to flow down to their own sub-contractors. FAR 52.209-6 does not apply to company D or company E because they are second-tier subcontractors. That is why the gray puzzle piece is not shown beside the second-tier subcontracts. Because FAR 52.230-2 applies to *all* negotiated subcontracts, contract managers for company B and company C know to include that clause in their subcontracts, as illustrated by the striped puzzle piece.

The contract manager at company B must determine if FAR 52.215-10 applies to company D's subcontract. Company D has a negotiated subcontract for $750,000, and it submitted certified cost or pricing data. So the contract manager flows FAR 52.215-10 down to the subcontract. This is illustrated by the black puzzle piece. Because company D's contract exceeds $100,000 and is not for a commercial item, FAR 52.222-4 applies, too, as shown by the white puzzle piece.

Company E has a $150,000 contract with company C. Because company C does not have FAR 52.215-10 in its contract, it cannot flow down to company E. FAR 52.222-4 applies, and the contract manager flows it down to company E's subcontract.

As readers can see, there are various requirements for determining if a clause flows down to a first- or second-tier subcontractor. Unfortunately, some companies simply copy the terms and conditions from the prime contract, then state that the prime contractor's name should be substituted for *government* and the subcontractor's name for *contractor*. Accepting these clauses could increase costs for subcontractors, which may have to pay for additional compliance and documentation, and can increase their risk if they accept a clause that isn't mandatory or applicable to their subcontracts.

It's good practice to read not only the clause but also the prescription so that the prime contractor and subcontractors all know what's required. This is why analyzing the RFP is important. The prime contractor needs to understand what the government requires of it before it can pass the requirements down to the subcontractors.

ANALYZING THE RFP

Before beginning to write a proposal, a company should prepare an RFP compliance matrix that outlines the RFP's requirements. This matrix maps the SOW requirements to the evaluation criteria and proposal preparation instructions. Then the company uses this compliance matrix as a guiding document throughout the proposal-writing process to ensure that it is meeting the RFP's requirements. Some agencies call the compliance matrix a *requirements traceability matrix,* but the intent is the same.[26] It's important to remember to revise the matrix if the contracting officer issues RFP amendments.

Some agencies actually require offerors to submit a compliance matrix with their proposal. This matrix shows where in its proposal the offeror addresses each SOW requirement and section L requirement. The contracting officer may include a cross-reference RFP matrix in section L of the solicitation.

Many companies use the compliance matrix as a starting point for proposal preparation. The matrix helps the proposal authors build the outline on which they will base the proposal. The sample matrix shown in Table 5-3 appears again as Table 7-1, with columns added for the offeror's use. The offeror can list the proposal page on which each requirement is addressed and the name of the author of that part of the proposal. This information helps the company's proposal manager make sure all of the requirements have been addressed and tells the proposal manager who to contact if he or she has questions.

Table 7-1 RFP Compliance Matrix[27]

Requirement	Section L Paragraph	Section M Paragraph	Proposal Page	Author
Volume I: Executive Summary	3.0	N/A		
	3.1	N/A		
	3.2	N/A		
Volume II: Mission Capability	4.0	N/A		
	4.1	N/A		
	4.2	N/A		
Subfactor 1: Key system requirements	4.2.2	N/A		
Subfactor 2: System integration and software	4.2.3	N/A		
Subfactor 3: Logistics	4.2.4	N/A		
	4.2.4.2	2.2.3		
Manpower and personnel	4.2.4.3	N/A		
Supportability	4.2.4.5	2.2.3		
	4.2.4.5.1	2.2.3		
Data management	4.2.4.6	2.2.3		
Supply support	4.2.4.7	N/A		
Training	4.2.4.9	2.2.3		

Table 7-1 (*Continued*)

Requirement	Section L Paragraph	Section M Paragraph	Proposal Page	Author
Subfactor 4: Program management	4.2.5	N/A		
	4.2.5.1	2.2.4		
SOW	4.2.5.2	2.2.4		
Integrated master plan	4.2.5.3	2.2.4		
Integrated master schedule	4.2.5.4	2.2.4		
Cost reporting	4.2.5.6	2.2.4		
Integrated risk management	4.2.5.7	2.2.4		
Small business	4.2.5.8	2.2.4		
Manufacturing and subcontract management	4.2.5.9	N/A		
Test and evaluation	4.2.5.10	2.2.4		
Subfactor 5: Tech maturity and demonstration	4.2.6	2.2.5		
Proposal risk	4.3	2.3		
Volume III: Past Performance	5.	2.4		
	5.1	2.4		
	5.2	2.4		
	5.3	2.4		
	5.4	2.4		
	5.5	2.4		
Volume IV: Cost	6.	2.5		
	6.1	2.5		
Volume VI: Contract Documentation	8.0	N/A		
	8.1	N/A		
	8.2	N/A		
	8.3	N/A		
Volume VII: Oral Presentation	9.0			

PROPOSAL PREPARATION

How does a company start writing a proposal? It's always a good idea to start by addressing the evaluation factors and subfactors with the highest priority or weighting, as identified in section M of the solicitation.[28] Make clear that the company understands the agency's needs, and explain how the company will meet the agency's requirements by providing specific details. Illustrations and graphics are effective ways to explain processes, cause-and-effect relationships, and management structure.

- Questionable or inadequate understanding of the agency's requirements or needs
- Incomplete response to the solicitation, or critical sections are missing from the proposal
- Noncompliance with or misinterpretation of requirements
- Insufficient resources, such as personnel, funds, time to accomplish the requirements
- Poor proposal organization; correlating proposal content to the solicitation is confusing
- Failure to show relevance of past performance to the current requirement
- Unsubstantiated or unconvincing rationale for proposed approaches or solutions
- Repeating requirements without discussing how they will be performed (i.e., quoting or paraphrasing the requirements, but not proposing a specific solution for them).

Figure 7-7   Typical Proposal Weaknesses[29]

How can companies avoid the weaknesses that cause evaluators to downgrade their proposals? Figure 7-7 identifies typical proposal weaknesses.

A successful proposal not only responds to the requirements set forth in the RFP, but convinces the agency that it has done so better than any other proposal. When writing a proposal, the authors need to keep the customer and its requirement in mind at all times. Some agencies let or recommend evaluators quickly skim the proposal before doing a detailed evaluation. The company must show the evaluator during this quick read that the proposal is clear, concise, organized, and easy to evaluate. Successful companies know that it is important to make the evaluators' job easy, and there are different ways to accomplish this.

Proposal Development Methods

There are four typical methods for proposal preparation. Some companies may combine approaches as needed.

1. **Compliance.** The main purpose of this method is to show that the proposal complies with the requirements. The RFP may require the offeror to explain how proposed products or services satisfy the requirement and to substantiate the response.
2. **Positioning.** The positioning method is based on differentiating a company's supplies or services from others in the marketplace. It's helpful to refer to the capture plan assessment when writing the proposal. The company should highlight its differences from its competitors by emphasizing its strengths and neutralizing its weaknesses (while pointing out its competitors' weaknesses and neutralizing their strengths) and showing how its solutions are more meaningful and valuable to the customer.[30] This proposal-writing technique is also called *ghosting*.
3. **Storyboarding.** The storyboarding method helps to organize the proposal, section by section, into a logical sequence following the RFP's requirements. Companies

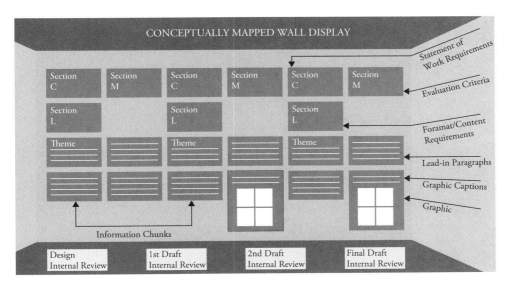

Figure 7-8   Storyboarding[31]

that use this approach literally cut up the RFP and tack sections onto a wall. They may have a structured format for authors to use when writing responses to the requirements. See Figure 7-8 for a storyboard illustration and Figure 7-9 for an example of a proposal input page that can be used in a storyboard.

4. **Evaluation outlining.** This method organizes the proposal using the RFP's evaluation factors. This approach focuses on the evaluation scoring methodology. For example, if the RFP states that the technical approach is weighted 50 percent; the management approach, 30 percent; and past performance, 20 percent, technical, management, and past performance become main headings in the proposal outline.[32] Some companies use the weighting to help them determine the amount of content, too. For example, under the weightings above, approximately 50 percent of the proposal volume's page count would address the technical approach, and 30 percent of the proposal volume's page count would address the management approach.

No matter what proposal development strategy an offeror chooses, the proposal should not only meet the RFP's requirements, but also be:

• Clearly written, or the evaluators will not understand the company's win strategy

• Well organized, or the evaluators will not know where to find important information

• Concisely written, or the evaluators' eyes will glaze over in confusion

• Supported with credible statements, or the evaluators will not believe the company's solution will work.[33]

Author	Phone/Extension	Proposal Page	Title

Compliance (RFP requirements from sections L, M; other directions)

Relevant global win themes

Customer issues/concerns

Our issues/concerns (why we should win/how we could lose)

Win strategy for this module

Approach and rationale

Features and benefits

Win theme for this module

Key topics and bullets

Relevant experience/past performance and other noteworthy information

Figure 7-9   Proposal Input Page

Colorful Reviews

Another important element of proposal preparation is conducting a critical review of the proposal before submitting it to the customer. Many companies call a critical review a *red team* review. Critical review teams may consist of upper management, legal counsel, and consultants. Members of the review team should read and understand the RFP before reading the proposal so that they are familiar with the requirements. Effective reviews not only highlight problems but also suggest improvements. Simply stating that a section is weak is not helpful; the reviewer needs to suggest a way to make it better.

Some companies assign other color designations, such as the colors on a traffic light, to indicate the level or type of review conducted. The first review is green, the second amber, and the final review is red. Other companies just have two types of review: pink and red. A pink review precedes the red team review and identifies discrepancies and deficiencies in a proposal. Preliminary reviews assess the proposal's readability and clarity and answer two questions:

- Are the points made clearly and concisely?
- Do the graphics help make the point?

It's important to note that all companies do not use the same system. In some companies, colors designate the content under review rather than the order. For example, the technical review is a red review; the preliminary technical solution review, pink; the cost review, blue; and the combined technical and cost review (done if time permits), purple. Because the cost volume or pricing review is not only proprietary but also closely held within the company, it has a very limited audience and may not be reviewed as widely as the other volumes.

A red team review is the final and most comprehensive proposal review. It includes not only the technical and management volumes but also the cost volume and pricing strategy. The most productive red team reviews are conducted by those who have not participated in previous reviews and have never before seen the proposal. The red team may act as a mock source selection team and evaluate the proposal against the stated evaluation criteria, grading it accordingly.

Conducting critical reviews is an important quality assurance check in the proposal preparation process. Proposal managers must allow enough time, however, to incorporate recommendations from the reviewers in order for the review to be meaningful and effective. Expecting the red team reviewers to simply rubber-stamp the proposal does not help improve it. Similarly, asking senior executives to review a proposal when there's not enough time in the schedule to incorporate their suggestions is a waste of time. After the proposal team incorporates the red team reviewers' comments, the company prints and binds the proposal.

Proposal Submission Tips

After many weeks spent writing the proposal, the last thing the contract manager wants is for small errors to cause the company to lose the contract. Here are some helpful hints and tips for successful proposal submission:

- Pay attention to due dates and times.
- Pay attention to any special hand-delivery or mailing provisions set forth in the RFP.
- Review the solicitation website daily for posting of amendments, news, and other related items that may affect the company's proposal, and update the compliance matrix. If a significant amendment is issued, consider requesting an extension of the proposal preparation period.
- Have an independent party within the company compare the proposal submission against the compliance matrix.
- Carefully review the proposal, especially the cost volume, for mathematical errors or inconsistencies.
- Use rounding formulas in all calculations.
- Ensure that someone other than the price proposal writers prints and reviews the price proposal and rechecks the entire price proposal on a calculator. (Formula errors can creep into spreadsheets, especially when they are used repeatedly.)
- For hand-delivered offers, prepare a delivery receipt and obtain signature, date, and time of delivery from the government agency receiving the proposal.
- For e-mail submission, use your email software's "read" receipt notification tool.
- For online submission:
  - Ensure the company is registered and able to post its proposal at the designated website.
  - Don't wait until the last minute, as websites can get tied up, and posting can take longer than anticipated.
  - After submission, print out a copy of the website delivery notification receipt.[34]

CHAPTER SUMMARY

Chapter 7 explores industry's side of the acquisition process: preparing a proposal. A company uses capture planning to evaluate its understanding of the agency and the agency's objectives. Capture planning helps win new business by creating mutually beneficial offers that solve the customer's problems and meet the company's profitability and risk requirements. Companies then assess their strengths and weaknesses as well as their competitors' strengths and weaknesses.

Next, after making a bid/no-bid decision, the company needs to make sure the entire proposal team understands the requirements and works toward meeting them. Important steps in the proposal preparation process include establishing teaming arrangements, determining key personnel, and considering subcontracting implications.

Contractor teaming arrangements may be desirable from both a government and industry standpoint, to enable the companies involved to complement each other's unique capabilities and offer the government the best combination of performance, cost, and delivery for the solicited system or product. Please note that some companies look for or expect exclusive teaming partners, and some agencies prohibit such exclusive arrangements.

If the RFP requires the identification of key personnel, companies must make sure that personnel they're proposing are available to work on the effort. Some agencies require personnel to sign the resumes they submit and require the contractor to agree to a statement that if the company wins the contract, the people specified will actually work on the contract for a specified period.

One of the most important subcontracting considerations is determining which clauses to flow down to subcontractors. Despite the lack of privity between the government and subcontractors, the government still has an influence on subcontracts through *flow-down clauses*. The FAR identifies flow-down clauses and the tier and dollar value of subcontracts to which they apply. Contract managers (including purchasing professionals and subcontract managers) must review not only the relevant clause itself but also the prescribing text.

The proposal preparation process begins with analyzing the RFP and writing the proposal. A company should prepare an RFP compliance matrix that outlines the RFP's requirements. This matrix maps the SOW requirements to evaluation criteria and proposal preparation instructions. Then the company uses this compliance matrix as a guiding document throughout the proposal-writing process to ensure that it is meeting the RFP's requirements.

A successful proposal not only responds to the requirements set forth in the RFP but also convinces the agency that its responses are better than any other proposal. When writing a proposal, the authors need to keep the customer and its requirement in mind at all times.

Conducting critical reviews is an important quality assurance check in the proposal preparation process.

While companies prepare proposals, the agency can prepare for proposal evaluations. This is the topic covered in Chapter 8.

NOTES

1 Daniel M. Jacobs, *The Program/Contract Definition Document* (Warrenton, VA: Federal Market Group, 1999), 1.

2 Gregory A. Garrett and Reginald J. Kipke, "The Capture Management Life Cycle," *Contract Management* 43 (Ashburn, VA: National Contract Management Association, June 2003), 8.

3 Adapted with permission from Daniel M. Jacobs, *The Program/Contract Definition Document* (Warrenton, VA: Federal Market Group, 1999), 4–8.

4 Garrett and Kipke, 10.

5 Federal Acquisition Regulation (FAR) 9.505-1.

6 FAR 9.505-2.

7 FAR 9.505-3.

8 Gregory A. Garrett, "Bid/No-Bid Decision-Making Tools and Techniques," *Contract Management* 47 (Ashburn, VA: National Contract Management Association, April 2007), 22–24.

9 Michael O'Guin, "How Capture Teams Win," *Contract Management* 42 (Ashburn, VA: National Contract Management Association, August 2002), 29.

10 Ibid., 28.

11 FAR 9.601.

12 FAR 9.602.

13 John W. Chierichella and Douglas E. Perry, "Negotiating Teaming Agreements," *Acquisition Issues* 1 (1991), 3.

14 FAR 9.603.

15 Chierichella and Perry, 4–5.

16 *EG&G Inc. v. the Cube Corp*, Va. Cir. Ct., Chancery no. 178996 (2002).

17 Robert G. Fryling and Edward J. Hoffman, "Teaming Agreements: Proceed with Caution," *Contract Management* 43 (Ashburn, VA: National Contract Management Association, December 2003), 58.

18 National Reconnaissance Office, *NRO Acquisition Manual*, clause N15.215-020, "Exclusive Teaming Prohibition" (Chantilly, VA: National Reconnaissance Office, April 2004).

19 FAR 9.604.

20 U.S. Government Accountability Office, "Ann Riley & Associates, Ltd.—Reconsideration B-271741.3" (Washington, DC: U.S. Government Accountability Office, March 10, 1997).

21 U.S. Department of Labor, Division of Contract Services, RFP no. DCS-00-36 (July 14, 2000); amendment 2 (November 2, 2000), http://www.doleta.gov/sga/rfp/rfp00-36-amend2.htm (accessed January 22, 2009).

22 William A. John, *Service Contracting: A Desk Guide to Best Practices* (Arlington, VA: Navy Acquisition Reform Office, 1998).

23 FAR 14.201-2.

24 FAR 44.201-1.

25 Margaret G. Rumbaugh, *Desktop Guide to Basic Contracting Terms* (Ashburn, VA: National Contract Management Association, 2006), 193.

26 Readers may wish to review Thomas Reid, "How to Construct a Contract Compliance Matrix," *Contract Management* 44 (Ashburn, VA: National Contract Management Association, January 2004), 40.

27 Adapted from U.S. Air Force/Air Force Materiel Command, RFP no. FA8625-07-R-6470, Section L, Attachment 1 (Wright-Patterson Air Force Base, OH: U.S. Air Force/Air Force Materiel Command, January 30, 2007).

28 Beverly A. Arviso, "How to Maximize Your Success," *Contract Management* 46 (Ashburn, VA: National Contract Management Association, October 2006), 10.

29 Daniel M. Jacobs, Janice M. Menker, and Chester P. Shinaman, *Building a Contract: Solicitations/Bids and Proposals* (Ashburn, VA: National Contract Management Association, 1990), 117.

30 Ibid., 132–133.

31 Joseph T. Nocerino, "Selling 'Best Value' in the New Commercial Government Market," *Contract Management* 47 (Ashburn, VA: National Contract Management Association, July 2007), 11. Reprinted with permission from the National Contract Management Association.

32 Jacobs, Menker, and Shinaman, 134.

33 Ibid., 138.

34 Arviso, 12.

Chapter 8

Preparing for Proposal Evaluations

While offerors are preparing proposals, agencies should train the proposal evaluators. The best time to conduct source selection training is after the final RFP is released, while the offerors prepare their proposals. This training and orientation gives the source selection managers and evaluators the background and information necessary to conduct a fair and effective evaluation, including the agency's objectives, the evaluation factors, and the requirements each offeror's proposal must meet. The evaluators will develop a common understanding of what to look for and how to interpret what they find and will learn the procedures for documenting their findings.[1]

It's important to remember that the evaluators may or may not be the same people as those involved in writing the acquisition plan, evaluation criteria, and statement of work. This is why the evaluators need training regarding the source selection's objectives, including the acquisition plan, RFP elements, and evaluation procedures. Scheduling the training for after the RFP release and before proposal submission gives the agency sufficient time to let the evaluators practice using the forms and software, if they are going to use an electronic tool.

In this chapter, we'll explain the considerations for selecting evaluators and what to include in the evaluators' training and orientation session. In addition, the time between RFP release and proposal receipt is the perfect time to determine what facilities and security are needed for the evaluation process. Finally, we'll discuss the process of receiving proposals and assigning them to the evaluators.

SELECTING EVALUATORS

Selecting proposal evaluators is an important part of the source selection. They need to have technical expertise in the topics they evaluate and the ability to discuss the relative strengths and weaknesses of each proposal in a consensus session with their peers.

Agencies should not assume that evaluators intuitively understand how to evaluate competitive proposals.[2] Even if they have participated in a previous source selection, they may have forgotten how the process works, or it may have been so long ago that the process has changed. That's why it's important to have a training and orientation session before the proposals arrive.

Evaluators are government personnel who:

- Analyze proposals based on the RFP's evaluation criteria
- Apply the source selection plan's standards
- Rate the proposals
- Develop risk scores
- Participate in consensus sessions.

CASE STUDY: CHALLENGING THE EVALUATORS' QUALIFICATIONS

Although the government has the discretion to choose evaluators, in this case, two unsuccessful offerors questioned the evaluators' qualifications. IMLCORP LLC and Wattre Corporation protested the award of a contract to American Technology Corporation (ATC) under a U.S. Navy request for proposals for acoustic hailing devices. According to the Government Accountability Office (GAO) decision on the protest, the device in question was a "rugged and lightweight loudspeaker system with very high directivity that is intended for long-range hailing and warning" used on Navy vessels to warn other vessels that they are entering the Navy's 500-yard exclusion zone.

The RFP stated the Navy would award a contract based on a cost/technical trade-off and required the offerors to submit a product sample and "any optional accessories or upgrades that provide claimed improvements in functionality, performance, or additional capabilities." The GAO decision states that offerors were informed that:

> The product sample shall be tested in a non-destructive manner by Government personnel. Product sample testing is planned to occur in a laboratory and field environment at [the Naval Surface Weapons Center in Crane, Indiana]. The Government may test the product sample against the technical requirements set forth in the Performance Specification contained in this solicitation.

Award was made to ATC, based upon that firm's higher technical rating and lowest evaluated price.

The protesters

> complain[ed] that the Navy's evaluators were not trained, experienced, "operational military personnel" and that the hearing of these evaluators was not tested before [they

conducted the product sample tests].... The Navy responds that the solicitation did not require them to use operational military personnel or identify any other experience requirements for these evaluators ... [Furthermore,] the Source Selection Evaluation Board chair is an electrical engineer with significant experience with acoustic hailing devices. The Navy also asserts that there was no requirement that the evaluators' hearing be tested before the product sample evaluation and that the evaluators reflected the average hearing that would be expected of actual users of the shipboard devices.

[The GAO ruled that] the protesters' speculative challenges to the qualifications of the Navy's evaluators gave them no basis to question the agency's product sample evaluation.... Moreover, [the GAO has always held] that the selection of individuals to serve as evaluators is a matter within the discretion of the agency, and [it does] not review allegations such as these concerning the evaluators' qualifications or the composition of evaluation panels absent a showing of possible fraud, conflict of interest, or actual bias on the part of evaluation officials, none of which have been alleged or shown here.

The protest was denied.[3]

This case shows that the agency has the discretion to select evaluators and that the GAO will not question that selection without evidence of fraud, conflict of interest, or bias on the part of the evaluator.

Now that readers understand the evaluator's role, let's look at the factors that should be considered when conducting a training and orientation session.

TRAINING AND ORIENTATION

After the government releases the RFP, the government can conduct training and orientation for evaluators and managers. The next section describes what is typically included in the evaluators' and managers' training.

Evaluator Training

The training should explain the agency's objectives for the acquisition, the statement of work, the evaluation criteria, and the source selection process. Before training begins, some agencies give evaluators copies of the RFP, acquisition plan, source selection plan, and rating scale to read before the training session. Becoming familiar with these documents gives them an opportunity to formulate questions ahead of time so the training class is more productive.

The training should include an overview of these documents and the source selection process, with specific training on how to properly document each proposal's strengths, weaknesses, and risks.[4] The information evaluation team members receive at training usually includes:

- An overview of the source selection process, including a schedule.
- The acquisition plan and objectives.
- The source selection plan and the source selection evaluation guide, if one was prepared, including:
  - The evaluation criteria
  - The evaluation standards.
- The guidelines for evaluating the technical and management proposals.
- A statement of the evaluators' responsibilities, including:
  - Safeguarding data from unauthorized disclosure
  - Factually supporting their determinations and conclusions and documenting them
  - Basing decisions regarding proposals' technical acceptability or merit on the RFP requirements alone.
- The forms to be used in the evaluation.
- A description of the scoring or rating scale and applicable definitions.
- An explanation of how to determine the intensity of strengths and weaknesses.
- Guidance on writing narratives.
- The risk assessment scales and definitions.
- A demonstration of how to use source evaluation software tools. There are many automated tools that help organize and document source selections. If the agency will use one of these tools, it is important for evaluators to be trained in using the software before the proposals arrive.
- A reminder to have on record procurement integrity certificates, nondisclosure forms, and financial disclosures applicable to the acquisition.[5]

The agency may hold a practice session before the actual training class to conduct a mock source selection exercise. This exercise gives evaluators practice in using the forms and applying the RFP's standards and evaluation factors.

The instructions to the evaluators may be formal and written or informal and verbal. In addition to written instructions, the contracting officer may present a short briefing to the team members and may answer their questions. Specific instructions to evaluators depend on the nature of the solicitation, but there are certain instructions which should be included in any case. A sample is provided in Figure 8-1.

Orientation and training can include the rules of conduct for the source selection. The following is an example of typical rules of conduct for the source selection process:

Goal of This Technical Evaluation

The goal of this technical evaluation process is to determine which offer(s) is (are) most favorable to the government. This will be done by providing the source selection authority (SSA) the maximum flexibility to make a selection based on a complete and documented technical evaluation.

Guidelines for Evaluating Proposals

1. Each technical evaluator will read each technical/management proposal separately and completely.

2. Each evaluator will apply the evaluation factor and subfactors only against the established standards.

3. Each proposal will be evaluated only against the evaluation criteria. Proposals will not be evaluated against one another.

4. If any clarification is necessary, the technical evaluators will reread all proposals and reapply the technical evaluation criteria to all proposals. If discussions are held, each evaluator will read each proposal revision and reapply the technical evaluation criteria to each proposal revision.

5. Any findings on technical acceptability or merit must be based solely on provisions and clauses of the RFP. Any determinations and conclusions must be factually supported.

6. All evaluations will be recorded only on the worksheets and forms provided for that purpose.

7. Each evaluator is personally responsible for safeguarding the information in the offerors' proposals. The information in the proposals will not be given to anyone outside the source selection evaluation board (SSEB). All proposals will be handled in accordance with the markings thereon. For example, offerors typically put a statement on the cover or title page of the proposal which states:

   Use and Disclosure of Data: This proposal includes data that shall not be disclosed outside the Government and shall not be duplicated, used, or disclosed—in whole or in part—for any purpose other than to evaluate this proposal. However, if a contract is awarded to this offeror as a result of—or in connection with—the submission of these data, the Government shall have the right to duplicate, use, or disclose the data to the extent provided in the resulting contract. This restriction does not limit the Government's right to use information contained in these data if they are obtained from another source without restriction. The data subject to this restriction are contained in Sheets [insert numbers or other identification of sheets].[6]

8. The technical evaluation team will provide a technical evaluation report to the contracting officer (CO) or SSEB at the conclusion of the evaluation. The report will include, at a minimum:
   - Determinations and conclusions, including the acceptability of each proposal
   - Recommendations for further fact-finding, as appropriate
   - Any other recommendations or conclusions.

9. Evaluators must have procurement integrity certificates and nondisclosure forms on record for this acquisition.

10. The due date for delivery of the technical evaluation report to the contracting officer is _____.[7]

Figure 8-1   Sample Instructions to Technical Evaluators[8]

- The contracting officer must control all exchanges with offerors after receiving proposals.
- Refer any inquiries pertaining to the source selection from sources other than the evaluation team members or advisors to the contracting officer.
- The evaluators must avoid the appearance of actual or potential improprieties or conflicts of interest with any offeror or proposed subcontractor or vendor that may have a potential interest in the award.

- Any unauthorized disclosure that is discovered must be brought to the contracting officer's and source selection authority's attention.[9]

Although conducting evaluator training may be time consuming, remember that the evaluators' effectiveness depends on quality training because none of this is intuitive. Training will make the source selection run more efficiently; the evaluators will understand how to apply the evaluation criteria and standards. They will know how to assess and score risk and apply the weights established in the RFP to the criteria.

Management Training

In addition to training evaluators before the source selection begins, agencies may also train the source selection team's managers, such as the source selection authority; personnel in an authority position, like the source selection advisory council; and board or panel chiefs. In addition to training on the agency's evaluation process and the RFP, management training should include the following topics:

- Team-building and facilitation skills
- Communicating effectively within the source selection team
- Reaching consensus
- Developing documentation
- Conducting the cost-technical trade-off.

It's important for the source selection team to function as a team. The managers must have the skills to facilitate discussions, work through disagreements, and reach consensus. Sometimes source selection team managers are selected for their technical skills, not their interpersonal skills, but both sets of skills are necessary for an effective source selection. Training can help close that gap, giving managers the tools they need to work through the issues that inevitably come up and make meetings more productive.

Throughout the source selection process, agencies typically conduct regular status and progress report meetings between individual evaluators and their team leaders and between team leaders and the SSA. These sessions are a valuable part of the process. They allow team leaders to assess the evaluators' progress and provide feedback to them on whether they are correctly following the RFP's requirements and the source selection plan (SSP). These meetings foster open communication and identify any issues or concerns early in the process. Thus, team-building and communication training will help the source selection proceed efficiently and effectively.

FACILITIES AND SECURITY

Before receiving proposals, agencies must also determine where they will evaluate the proposals and how they will secure the source selection information. The source selection evaluation team needs a secure work area and associated storage space. The work area should be large enough to seat all members of the evaluation team and consultants or advisors and to store the proposals and other reference materials. Don't underestimate the size of the space required. Look at section L of the RFP to see how many copies of each proposal the contracting officer requested and what the page limit is. To make sure there is enough space to safely store all of the proposals, the contracting officer might put together a blank "proposal" to determine how much space is required to store one offeror's submission and should then look at the pre-proposal conference attendee list to determine the potential number of offerors. At a minimum, there should be lockable file cabinets to store proposals and all evaluation materials, and the room itself should be lockable with strictly limited access.[10]

Another factor to consider is the facility's location. Sites too close to the workplace may tempt evaluators to go back to their offices to catch up on work during the evaluation period. This can distract them from focusing on the evaluation. On the other hand, choosing a site too far from the workplace may cause a logistical problem for evaluators who carpool.

The facility should also have desks, file cabinets, conference tables, computers, copy machines, telephones, and other supplies available to meet the needs of the evaluation team members. If space permits, it's nice to have a break room with snacks and drinks so that evaluators don't need to leave the facility for a snack to tide them over during the long hours of the source selection process.

Finally, the source selection team should determine the hours of operation for the facility. Will the evaluation sessions be of the same duration as a standard work day? What time is the earliest team members can arrive and the latest they can stay?

Figure 8-2 summarizes key points to remember regarding the source selection facility.

It's important for the facility to have adequate security to protect the source selection information from improper disclosure. The contracting officer usually establishes the procedures for protecting proprietary and source selection information. The CO also ensures that everyone associated with the source selection is aware of the need to protect the sensitive source selection information. Remember that the Procurement Integrity Law prohibits any person from disclosing procurement information before the award of any federal agency procurement.

- The evaluation area should be away from regular working areas, because distractions from everyday work will slow the evaluation process.
- Establish separate evaluation rooms for each panel or proposal volume, such as
  - Cost
  - Technical
  - Management
  - Past performance.
- Provide a secure storage area for proposals.
- Identify one or more conference rooms for meetings and consensus sessions.

Figure 8-2   Source Selection Facility Key Points

Only the CO may release *contractor proposal information*, which is information submitted with a proposal, if that information has not been previously made available to the public or disclosed publicly. Unauthorized releases could jeopardize the integrity of a source selection. Examples of contractor proposal information include cost or pricing data, indirect costs and direct labor rates, proprietary information about manufacturing processes, and information marked by the company as "contractor proposal information" in accordance with applicable law or regulation.[11]

Source selection information is information developed by the government for the purpose of evaluating proposals that has not been previously disclosed publicly. Examples of source selection information includes source selection plans, technical evaluations of proposals, competitive range determinations, rankings of proposals and reports, and evaluations of source selection panels, boards, or advisory councils. The head of the agency or the CO may also designate any information as source selection information if its release would jeopardize the integrity or successful completion of the procurement to which the information relates.[12] The key concern is that all offerors be treated fairly.

It is recommended that the source selection team members work in a totally isolated facility using totally isolated writing and communication tools—such as a separate computer system and not a networked system for email and printing—but this is not usually possible. In many cases, evaluators prepare documents and store them on an open computer network that has a wide variety of uses and users. This means that the source selection team members must diligently protect procurement information on an open network.

The CO should consider restricting the procurement information to specific access-controlled directories on the network. He or she can structure directories to restrict access to specific folders. For example, technical evaluators require access to only those documents they will need to do their evaluations, so their access should be restricted to folders or files that contain sections L and M of the RFP, the source selection plan, and the source selection evaluation guide. As part of the access control procedures, the CO should maintain a record of individuals who have access to the secure network directories and should ensure that no unauthorized access occurs.

Most open networks have several printers in common areas. The CO should ensure that the source selection team members understand that it can be risky to send sensitive documents to a common area and should ask them to promptly retrieve them from the printer. Team members should be just as diligent when sending electronic documents to fellow members. It is easy to address an email message to "Smith," only to later find a reply from an unknown "Smith" asking what should be done with the sensitive document she just received.

Some would argue that open networks should not be used at all, but the reality is that electronic documents must be developed and stored somewhere, and it is often too expensive to operate and maintain a separate network. The security risk of an open network can be managed by simply being careful and documenting how the risks are mitigated. For example, the contracting officer should require all source selection team members to promptly retrieve such documents from their printers due to the sensitivity of sending documents to a common area.[13]

In more complex, highly competitive, or politically sensitive source selections, it may be necessary to go a step further and establish procedures for ensuring the security of the source selection physical facilities. These may include:

- Requiring identification, such as a badge, to access the source selection area and requiring authorized visitors (e.g., maintenance and service personnel) to sign in and out
- Ensuring access points to the facilities are either manned at all times by a representative of the source selection team or are kept locked (with appropriate key or password control procedures)
- Establishing procedures for approving visitors to the facilities
- Conducting security inspections and spot checks.

All source selection team members are responsible for the security of source selection information. For more complex source selections, it may be beneficial to designate certain members of the source selection team to oversee and perform security control functions. These duties may be collateral duties or full-time duties.

The source selection authority should ensure that all source selection team personnel attend a security briefing that emphasizes that each member:

- Is responsible for the security of the evaluation and proposal materials and other source selection and proprietary information related to the procurement
- Must be knowledgeable of, and adhere to, security procedures and regulations
- Not discuss any matters related to the source selection with anyone not assigned to the source selection, unless authorized, and then only within appropriately secure areas
- Challenge the presence of any apparently unauthorized individual in the source selection facility.[14]

RECEIVING PROPOSALS

Offerors deliver their proposals to the location designated in the RFP by the date and time specified in the RFP. The agency must record the date and time they were received and ensure that the unopened proposals are properly safeguarded from unauthorized disclosure throughout the source selection process.[15] Some companies may want to deliver their proposals early; the agency should be prepared to receive early proposals by having the delivery address staffed and able to provide receipts for proposals delivered on or before the date and time specified in the RFP. Figure 8-3 offers advice for receiving and protecting proposals.

After receipt, proposals must be handled carefully so that they are not misplaced or, worse, lost. The following case study illustrates the importance of safe proposal receipt.

Case Study: Lost Proposal

Project Resources, Inc., (PRI) protested the failure of the U.S. Army Corps of Engineers to evaluate its proposal for environmental remediation services. PRI contended that the agency lost its proposal and requested that the agency evaluate its proposal.

- Safeguard proposals, other proprietary information, and source selection information against unauthorized disclosure.
- Establish a system to track and continue safeguarding the proposals during evaluation.
- Establish an effective, easy-to-understand system to:
  - Identify the proposals received, the firms that submitted them, and the items included with each proposal.
  - Mark each proposal for tracking purposes, especially when there are multiple copies of a proposal.
  - Establish a system to identify who currently has each copy of the proposal and retain that information to permit identification of everyone who has had access during the evaluation.

Figure 8-3   Proposal-Receipt Tips[16]

According to GAO decision B-297968,

> The RFP required that proposals be submitted to the Department of the Army at the office of the Sacramento District Corps of Engineers, in Sacramento, California, no later than 2 p.m. on October 12, 2005. PRI shipped its proposal via FedEx, and the FedEx tracking slip shows that the package was received by the agency at 9:38 a.m. on October 12. The agency acknowledges timely receipt of the proposal (as evidenced by the FedEx receipt), but apparently the agency lost the proposal before it was evaluated.

On January 31, the agency made award to five firms, but not PRI. "After PRI informed the agency post-award that it had submitted a proposal, the agency searched for PRI's proposal and [was] unable to locate it."

PRI protested the failure of the agency to evaluate its proposal. It provided a copy of its proposal, which it stated was an exact duplicate of the original proposal that was submitted on time and lost, and it asked the GAO to direct the agency to evaluate it.

Per the GAO decision,

> Agencies have a fundamental obligation to have procedures in place to receive submissions for competitors under a solicitation, to reasonably safeguard submissions received, and to fairly consider all submissions received. As a practical matter, however, even with appropriate procedures in place, an agency may lose or misplace a submission, and such occasional loss, even if through agency negligence, generally does not entitle an aggrieved competitor to relief.

> This arguably harsh result is justified by the unique circumstances arising in protests concerning lost information. The only means generally available to establish the content of lost information is for the protester to reconstruct that information. However, allowing an offeror to establish the content of its lost proposal after the closing date has passed would be inconsistent with maintaining a fair competitive system.

> Here, the only evidence of the content of the information that the protester may have submitted prior to closing is a copy of that information produced by PRI during this protest process. The record does not contain any pre-closing evidence of the content of PRI's proposal that the agency properly could evaluate.

GAO ruled that it would not "disturb the agency's decision not to reopen the competition to evaluate PRI's proposal."

The GAO

> has recognized a limited exception to the rule that negligent loss of proposal information does not entitle the offeror to relief. The exception generally applies

where the loss was not an isolated act of negligence, but was the result of a systemic failure resulting in multiple or repetitive instances of lost information.... However, the exception does not apply here. There is no evidence that the agency, for example, lost the proposal information submitted by other offerors in this procurement or that the agency previously lost proposal information.

The protest was denied.[17]

This case illustrates the offeror's responsibility in delivering the proposal to the agency and confirming receipt. Although the offeror did exactly that in this case, the agency lost the proposal. As a result, the offeror's proposal was not evaluated. Because the agency did not demonstrate a systemic failure in losing proposals, GAO ruled that this was an isolated act of negligence, and the offeror suffered as a result. If it's a "must-win" scenario for the offeror, that company may want to consider the added expense of delivering the proposal in person to make sure it gets to the right place on time.

Determining Conflicts of Interest

After receiving all proposals, the contracting officer should compile a complete list of all offerors and team members (subcontractors) so that each evaluation team member can reaffirm that he or she has no potential conflict of interest with any of the potential contractors or subs. Although not required by statute, it is a good idea for every member of the source selection team to sign a source selection information briefing certificate that includes nondisclosure and conflict of interest agreements. The source selection information briefing certificate (see Figure 8-4) documents that each member of the source selection team understands the responsibility to protect procurement information and to avoid even the appearance of conflicts of interest.

The CO should personally brief the source selection team members before they sign the certificate. The briefing is a good opportunity to discover whether any source selection team members have a conflict of interest—for example, if a member holds stock in one of the companies or has a spouse who works for an offeror's company. Team members should fully disclose any potential conflicts, no matter how trivial they may seem, before they are allowed access to source selection material. To determine if a conflict exists, the CO should simply ask, "Can this person benefit in any way, real or perceived, by influencing the outcome of this source selection decision?"[18] Keep in mind that if an unsuccessful offeror protests the agency's source selection decision, and an appearance of impropriety exists, the agency's decision will generally be overturned if the protester can present evidence that an evaluator actually influenced the award of the contract.

If any member of the source selection team refuses to sign the certificate due to a conflict of interest, the source selection authority should ask the member to delegate

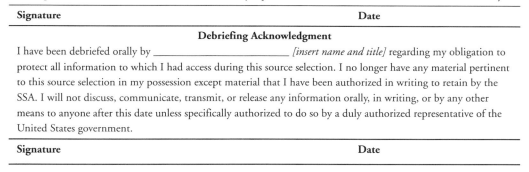

Last name	First name	Job title
Organization	Source selection description	

Briefing Acknowledgment

1) I acknowledge that I have been assigned to the source selection described above. I am aware that unauthorized disclosure of contractor proposal information or source selection information could damage the integrity of this procurement and that the transmission or revelation of such procurement information to unauthorized persons could subject me to prosecution under the Procurement Integrity laws or other disciplinary action.

2) I agree that I will not divulge, publish, or reveal by word, conduct, or other means such procurement information or knowledge, except as necessary in the performance of my official duties related to this source selection and in accordance with the laws of the United States, unless specifically authorized in writing in each and every case by a duly authorized representative of the United States government. I make this agreement freely, without any mental reservation or purpose of evasion, and in the absence of duress.

3) I acknowledge that the procurement information I receive will be given only to persons specifically granted access to the information and may not be further divulged without specific prior written approval from an authorized individual.

4) If, at any time during the source selection process, my participation might result in a real, apparent, possible, or potential conflict of interest, I will immediately report the circumstances to the source selection authority.

Signature	Date

Debriefing Acknowledgment

I have been debriefed orally by _____ *[insert name and title]* regarding my obligation to protect all information to which I had access during this source selection. I no longer have any material pertinent to this source selection in my possession except material that I have been authorized in writing to retain by the SSA. I will not discuss, communicate, transmit, or release any information orally, in writing, or by any other means to anyone after this date unless specifically authorized to do so by a duly authorized representative of the United States government.

Signature	Date

Figure 8-4   Source Selection Information Briefing Certificate[19]

his or her authority accordingly. The SSA and CO must ensure that all personnel fully understand their responsibilities when it comes to protecting procurement information. If, during the source selection process, the SSA discovers that a source selection team member has a conflict of interest or bias, the SSA must decide whether the member's conflict will require remedial action.

Receiving Electronic Proposals

The FAR states that the federal government shall use electronic commerce whenever practicable or cost effective[20] and that electronic commerce may be used to issue RFPs and to receive proposals. In negotiated acquisitions, the RFP must specify the electronic commerce method offerors may use to submit proposals.[21] If any portion of an electronic or facsimile proposal is unreadable, the CO must immediately notify the offeror and permit resubmission of the unreadable portion. The CO must prescribe a required method and time for resubmission after consulting the offeror and must document this requirement in the file.[22]

If the RFP requests both electronic and hard-copy proposal submissions, the RFP must state the order of precedence for electronic versus hard-copy submittals for evaluation purposes in the proposal preparation instructions.[23]

During evaluation, precise correlation between the electronic and paper versions of a proposal is very important. Evaluators prepare proposal comments that refer to volume and page numbers; if both versions of the proposal are identical, then the contracting officer can avoid a great deal of frustration. Before distributing the proposals to evaluators, the CO must compare each offeror's electronic proposal submission with the offeror's paper copy. The CO should conduct a page-by-page, graphic-by-graphic comparison to ensure that the electronic submission matches the paper submission exactly.

If the electronic and paper page counts are different, then it is likely that the printer driver the offeror used to generate the paper copy is different from the printer driver the CO uses. One way to avoid this discrepancy is to instruct the offeror in the solicitation to provide the printer driver as part of the electronic proposal submission. The CO may also recommend that offerors use specific software and file formats that are known to alleviate such discrepancies (e.g., Adobe Acrobat). Discrepancies should be resolved by treating the paper copy as the official proposal, or by any other manner specified in the RFP.

If the CO cannot synchronize the page numbers between the paper copy submission and the electronic submission, the source selection evaluation team (SSET) chairperson should be notified. The SSET chairperson may decide to direct the evaluators to use only the paper submission for page references.

After the CO validates the electronic proposals, they can be distributed to the evaluators by loading them on a common source selection network. Offerors should send electronic proposals as read-only files to protect the content from inadvertent deletion or alteration. It is very important that the system administrator saves all proposal files as read-only on the network. The system administrator will then restrict access to the proposal files to the source selection evaluation team members as authorized by the SSET chair.[24]

Determining Ineligibility, Debarment, or Suspension Status

The contracting officer must check the Excluded Parties List System (EPLS) to determine if any of the offerors that have submitted proposals are on the list. The electronic listing is available online at https://www.epls.gov/ and is updated daily. If an offeror is on the list, its proposal should not be opened and, in accordance with FAR 9.405, cannot be evaluated. The contracting officer should notify the source selection authority and the legal counsel.

Some agencies will not evaluate a proposal from a firm known to be debarred, suspended, or proposed for debarment unless the agency head or a designee determines, in writing, that there is a compelling reason to do so. However, if the period of ineligibility expires or is terminated before contract award, the contracting officer may, but is not required to, consider a proposal from that company.[25]

Reviewing RFP Compliance

After checking an offeror's eligibility status, the contracting officer must conduct a thorough RFP compliance review to make sure all offerors complied with the proposal preparation instructions. The CO unpacks the proposals in a manner that ensures an accurate inventory, organizes each offeror's proposal volumes into coherent groups, and checks the offeror's master packing list to verify that the agency received all required copies and volumes.

If the acquisition is complex, the RFP may require offerors to include a master packing list and all electronic proposals in the first box of its submission. The master packing list should identify all proposal volumes by copy number and box number. After opening the boxes and logging in the proposals, the contracting officer determines if the proposals comply with the RFP's requirements and handles instances of noncompliance in accordance with the relevant RFP provision. If the solicitation specifies a page count limitation for proposal volumes, then the CO counts those volumes' pages before accepting and distributing them to evaluators. The CO should pay particular attention to ploys to circumvent the page count limit. For example, an offeror could number pages 24, 24a, and 24b, which, of course, is three pages, but an offeror may consider this just one page. Further, if the solicitation specifies a page count limitation for the technical volume, the CO must ensure that additional technical information is not included in other proposal volumes, such as the management or cost volume.[26]

The contracting officer must document whether any material is missing and contact the offeror if it is. However, offerors cannot correct many problems after the proposal due date. Contracting officers should consult the agency's legal counsel before sending pages back or requesting missing data.[27] Any case in which the proposal exceeds established page limitations must be documented and dealt with as stated in the RFP.

Identifying Initially Unacceptable Proposals

The next step in the RFP compliance review is identifying proposals that will not receive further consideration. How does the contracting officer do this? First, the CO must require strict compliance with the RFP's proposal preparation instructions. The CO also must apply applicable law and regulation. For example, the CO would not give further consideration to a proposal:

- That does not meet the minimum standards for acceptability established in the solicitation.
- From large business concerns if the award is set aside for small business concerns. (The CO should obtain an SBA determination before challenging to a firm's representation that it is a small business concern.)
- When there is specific evidence or other reasonable basis to suspect misrepresentation or violation of the covenant against contingent fees.[28] A contingent fee is a commission, percentage, brokerage, or other fee that is conditional upon the success of a person or business securing a government contract.[29]

In addition to the above criteria, contracting officers at the National Aeronautics and Space Administration (NASA) may reject a proposal for one or more of the following reasons:

- It does not represent a reasonable initial effort to address the essential requirements of the RFP or clearly demonstrates that the offeror does not understand the requirements.
- In research and development acquisitions, a substantial design drawback is evident in the proposal, and sufficient correction or improvement that would allow the proposal to be considered acceptable would virtually require an entirely new technical proposal.
- It contains major deficiencies, omissions, or out-of-line costs which discussions with the offeror could not reasonably be expected to cure.

The contracting officer shall document the rationale for discontinuing the initial evaluation of a proposal. Any determination to discontinue evaluation of a proposal generally requires legal review, and the SSA must be notified of the determination. If the decision is made to discontinue evaluation of a proposal, the offeror must be notified in writing, and it is recommended that this notification provide a complete explanation for the determination of initial unacceptability.[30]

Let's look at a case in which the agency rejected a noncompliant proposal.

Case Study: An Unacceptable Proposal

This case shows what can happen when an offeror submits a proposal that exceeds the page limit stated in an RFP. Mathews Associates, Inc., protested the rejection of its proposal submitted in response to an RFP issued by the Department of the Army's Communications-Electronics Life Cycle Management Command to procure loudspeakers and battery boxes for use in the Single Channel Ground and Airborne Radio System. According to GAO decision B-299305, Mathews argued "that the Army unreasonably rejected its proposal after concluding that every page of the proposal exceeded the solicitation's specified margin limitations."

> The [proposal preparation] instructions limited proposals to 25 pages, specified the margin settings and font sizes to be used, and required that proposals be submitted electronically.... In addition, the RFP advised that "pages that exceed the margin, font, or total page limit will not be evaluated." The proposal submitted by Mathews, and a proposal submitted by another offeror, were removed from consideration as a result of this screening; thus, they were never evaluated by the Source Selection Evaluation Board (SSEB).

The agency advised Mathews that its proposal would not be evaluated because it was not prepared in accordance with the margin requirements specified in the solicitation. Specifically, the agency concluded that the proposal submitted by Mathews violated the solicitation's limitations, as shown in Table 8-1.

"After Mathews asked the agency to reconsider its decision, and after the agency advised it would not, Mathews filed a protest with [the GAO.]" Mathews argued "that the Army position is unreasonable." It noted that

> since the proposal was submitted electronically, it would have been a simple matter for Mathews—or the Army—to change the margin settings in the proposal. Mathews point[ed] out that if the proposal, as reformatted, exceed[ed] the 25-page limit, the Army could [have] reasonably refuse[d] to read any portion of the proposal that exceed[ed] the page limit. In addition, Mathews argue[d] that the public policy

Table 8-1 Mathews Protest

Solicitation's margin requirements		Margins in the Mathews proposal
Top	1"	0.87"
Bottom	1"	0.5"
Left	1"	1"
Right	1"	1"
From edge:		
-- Header	0.5"	0.28"
-- Footer	0.5"	0.18"

rationale for including margin, page, and font limitations in solicitations is to create a level playing field for competition; thus, in Mathews' view, while enforcement of page limitations serves to provide equal competitions, no discernible public policy end is served by upholding the Army's decision not to allow reformatting of this proposal.

As the Army note[d], there is no dispute here that every page of the protester's proposal exceeded the margin limitations in the solicitation, and that the solicitation clearly advised that no page that exceeded the margin, font, or page limitations would be read. In addition, while conceding the relative technical ease with which reformatting could be accomplished, the Army raise[d] several concerns about the impact of a decision holding that it was required to reformat the protester's proposal, or [to] allow the protester to do so.

The Army was concerned about the potential dispute between it and Mathews about how the reformatting should be accomplished. In the Army's view, any reformatting should only [have] involve[d] a change to the margin settings in the electronic document, which, it claim[ed], would add four pages to the proposal. In the protester's view, the Army should not only [have] change[d] the margins in its submission, but should [have made] some additional changes to spacing and headings that would [have] allow[ed] the proposal to meet the 25-page limit. Alternatively, the protester argue[d] that the Army should [have] change[d] the margins and simply not read the portion of the proposal that exceed[ed] the page limitation.

[The proposal Mathews submitted] did not contain a single page that complied with the solicitation's margin requirements. Simply put, [the GAO] know[s] of no reason why an agency should be required to allow an offeror to reformat its proposal when the solicitation's requirements were so clear. While the protester asserted that reformatting—or allowing the protester to reformat—its proposal does not appear to pose a significant risk of unfairness to other offerors, that view does not translate into a requirement that the agency take such action, given the RFP's clear instructions regarding formatting and the consequences of not complying with those instructions.

In addition, the GAO stated that the record supported "the agency's contention that the approach urged by Mathews raises the possibility of further disputes about the manner in which the reformatting is accomplished." In the GAO's opinion, "the agency should not [have been] forced to assume the risk of such potential disruptions to the procurement due to the reformatting made necessary by Mathews' failure to comply with the unequivocal requirements of the RFP." The GAO ruled that "there is nothing unfair, or unduly burdensome, about requiring offerors to assume the risks associated with submitting proposals that do not comply with clearly stated solicitation formatting requirements." The protest was denied.[31]

This case illustrates the importance of offerors complying with the proposal preparation instructions in the RFP and the CO's duty to enforce them upon proposal-receipt. Proposal preparation requires a substantial effort; in this case, it was a wasted effort because the proposal could not be evaluated. On the other hand, if the company can't follow clearly stated proposal preparation instructions, how can the agency trust them to follow contract requirements?

Special Compliance Considerations

After reviewing proposals for compliance, the contracting officer must consult the Office of Federal Contract Compliance Programs (OFCCP) National Pre-Award Registry at http://www.dol-esa.gov/preaward/pa_reg.html to verify that all offerors are listed as Equal Employment Opportunity (EEO) compliant. In the event an offeror is not listed, an EEO compliance review must be initiated in accordance with agency procedures.

Per FAR 22.13, a contracting officer must not obligate or expend funds with a contractor that has not submitted a required annual VETS-100 Report in the preceding fiscal year if the contractor was subject to the reporting requirements of 38 USC 4212(d) for that fiscal year. The contracting officer (or designee) must verify that all offerors have submitted current VETS-100 Reports by querying the Department of Labor's VETS-100 online database at https://vets100.vets.dol.gov, using the validation code *vets* to proceed with the search. If an offeror states that it has submitted the VETS-100 Report but is not listed in the database, the CO or designee can contact the VETS-100 Reporting Systems via email at verify@vets100.com for confirmation.

Verifying Central Contractor Registration

Next, the contracting officer needs to check whether each offeror has registered with the Central Contractor Registration (CCR) database (see Chapter 2 for a detailed discussion of the CCR database). In accordance with FAR 4.1102, unless an enumerated exception applies, a contract may not be awarded to a prospective contractor that has not registered in the CCR database. Per FAR 4.1104, the contracting officer must verify that each prospective contractor is registered in the CCR database and should use the offeror's DUNS number or, if applicable, the DUNS+4 number to verify registration. The verification may be done online at http://www.ccr.gov or by phone (toll-free, 1-888-227-2423; commercial, 269-961-5757).

Reviewing Representations and Certifications

The final check the contracting officer makes before distributing proposals to the evaluators is to review the completed representations and certifications. These are found in section K of the RFP, and the offeror's annual representations and certifications should be on the Online Representations and Certifications Application (ORCA) website, https://orca.bpn.gov.[32]

The CO conducts this review to determine if there is any reason, based on an offeror's representations and certifications, that may preclude awarding the contract to that offeror (for example, the company certifies that it is a large business, but the solicitation is for a small business set-aside). Any significant problem indicated by this review must be brought to the attention of the legal counsel and the source selection authority. In accordance with FAR 4.1201, prospective offerors shall complete electronic annual representations and certifications and certify them as current, per FAR provision 52.204-8.

Finally, after all of this is done, the CO can release the proposals to the evaluators, but what happens if a late proposal arrives? Let's explore that possibility in the next section.

Late Proposals

Any proposal received after the deadline stated in the RFP is considered a late proposal and "will not be considered unless it is received before award is made, the contracting officer determines that accepting the late proposal would not unduly delay the acquisition, and:

- If it was transmitted through an electronic commerce method authorized by the solicitation, it was received at the initial point of entry to the government infrastructure not later than 5:00 p.m. one working day prior to the date specified for receipt of proposals; or
- There is acceptable evidence to establish that it was received at the government installation designated for receipt of proposals and was under the government's control prior to the time set for receipt of proposals; or
- It was the only proposal received."[33]

If an emergency or unanticipated event interrupts normal government processes so that proposals cannot be received at the government office designated for receipt of proposals by the exact time specified in the solicitation, and urgent government requirements preclude amending the solicitation closing date, the time specified for receipt of proposals will be extended to the same time of day specified in the solicitation on the first workday on which normal government processes resume. [34]

Contracting officers may consult their agency's legal advisor before rejecting a proposal as late.

Case Study: Late Proposal

Sector One Security Solution, of Franklin, Virginia, protested the rejection as late of its proposal submitted in response to a Department of State RFP. According to GAO decision B-400728, Sector One argued "that the agency should have accepted its proposal because the protester sent it by United States Postal Service (USPS) Express Mail and because the protester believe[d] the USPS carrier attempted to deliver the proposal before the closing time for receipt."

The RFP instructed offerors to submit their proposals by 3 p.m. local time on September 11, 2008, to a particular address if mailed or to another address if hand-carried. Offerors planning to hand-carry their submissions were to "pre-coordinate drop-off with the Contracting Officer."

The RFP incorporated FAR 52.215-1, "which provides that late proposals generally will not be considered for award if they do not reach the designated government office by the time specified in the solicitation." The protestor

> used United States Postal Service (USPS) Express Mail to send its proposal to the address in the RFP for hand-carried submissions. The agency report[ed] that the USPS does not deliver mail to office annex buildings of the Department of State such as the one in which the Office of Acquisition is located.... For this reason, the RFP provided a post office box address for mailing and required that any hand-carried proposal be coordinated with the contracting officer.

> Sector One's proposal was returned to it unopened with a notation that it was refused; the protester subsequently contacted the agency and claim[ed] it was advised that the proposal was returned because it had been misaddressed. However, the agency report[ed] that it never received Sector One's proposal.

> Sector One assert[ed] that it sent its proposal by express mail to the address in the RFP for hand-delivery or courier. The protester ... provided the USPS Express Mail label from the package indicating that it had the correct hand-carried address provided by the RFP and that USPS made two attempts to deliver the package, one of which was after the date and time for submission of proposals. The protester argue[d] that express mail is delivered by courier and that someone at the agency marked "refused" in the employee signature box.

> [GAO asserted that it is] the responsibility of each firm to deliver its proposal to the proper place at the proper time, and late delivery generally requires rejection of the

submission.... Where late receipt results from the failure of a vendor to reasonably fulfill its responsibility for ensuring timely delivery to the specified location, the late offer may not be considered.... An offer that arrives late may only be considered if it is shown that the paramount reason for late receipt was improper government action, and where consideration of the proposal would not compromise the integrity of the competitive procurement process.

The agency denie[d] receiving or rejecting the Sector One proposal submission that was the subject of the alleged delivery attempt by the USPS carrier. As explained above, since USPS does not deliver mail to the building where the Office of Acquisition is located, the RFP contained a P.O. box for mailed proposals, and allowed for hand-carried proposals provided delivery was coordinated with the contracting officer. By its own admission, the protester did not follow the instructions in the RFP for submission of its proposal in that it made no arrangements with the contracting officer for hand-carried delivery.

[GAO ruled that] the evidence submitted by the protester did not establish that the agency actually received the protester's submission or that there was an attempt to deliver the proposal to the agency before the closing time established in the solicitation. As explained above, the record ... only demonstrate[d] that the USPS carrier attempted to deliver the protester's submission to some [Department of State] location and does not specifically demonstrate whether anyone there refused to accept delivery. The record show[ed] that the paramount reason for the nonreceipt of the protester's submission is the protester's failure to follow the solicitation instructions to either mail its proposal to the designated P.O. box number or make the proper arrangements for hand-carried delivery. In short, there is nothing in the record showing that any affirmative government action deprived the protester of the ability to make a proper delivery of its proposal.

The protest was denied.[35]

This case illustrates the importance of following the RFP instructions exactly. It is not prudent to make assumptions about proposal delivery. Some companies hand-deliver their proposals early. If the first attempt doesn't arrive as expected, they have a backup ready and waiting to be delivered by the time required in the RFP. Whoever delivers the first copy should call his or her company to let them know the proposal was successfully delivered and that a signed proposal receipt was received. If the company does not receive this phone call by a predetermined time, then someone else takes the backup copy in time to arrive by the time stated in the RFP.

This kind of proposal-delivery arrangement works best if the company is located in commuting distance to the agency. It can also be done from a hotel if the company is willing and able to incur the travel expenses. This delivery arrangement is usually conducted for only large-revenue or must-win opportunities. It requires advance planning, and it is helpful if the company has offices near the delivery site. If the company is across the country from the delivery site, then it is prudent to use a mail-delivery method with a tracking system.

Assigning Proposals to Evaluators

After the contracting officer checks all of the proposals to ensure that they're compliant with the RFP requirements and that the offerors are eligible for contract award, it's time to distribute the proposals to the evaluators. The contracting officer retains the original of each proposal volume for the official file. The contracting officer or contract specialist sequentially numbers each remaining copy of the proposal for tracking purposes. The source selection board chairperson or contracting officer typically assigns a copy or a specific volume to each evaluator. When a numbered copy is assigned to an individual evaluator, the number should be recorded, and the evaluator should sign a receipt with the understanding that he or she is personally responsible for safeguarding that copy within the designated source selection area.

Note that proposals should never be taken from the source selection facility without a very good reason. Even then, they should be taken out only if appropriate safeguards are in place to prevent them from being seen by or accessed by unauthorized personnel. The source selection board chairperson or contracting officer must grant specific approval for a team member to take a copy of a proposal out of the facility.[36]

CHAPTER SUMMARY

Chapter 8 explains the steps necessary to prepare for proposal evaluations, including selecting evaluators and conducting training for both evaluators and managers. Evaluators need to have technical expertise in the topics they evaluate, and they need to be able to discuss the relative strengths and weaknesses of each proposal in a consensus session with their peers. Evaluators are government personnel who analyze proposals based on the RFP's evaluation criteria; apply standards from the source selection plan; rate the proposals; develop risk scores; and participate in consensus sessions.

Agencies should train their evaluators before proposal evaluations begin. The training should explain the agency's objectives for the acquisition, the statement of work, the evaluation criteria, and the source selection process. Some agencies give evaluators copies of the RFP, acquisition plan, source selection plan, and rating scale to read before the training session. Training should also include an overview of these documents and the source selection process, and it should explain how to properly document each proposal's strengths, weaknesses, and risks.

In addition to training evaluators before the source selection begins, agencies may also train the source selection team's managers, such as the source selection authority; personnel in an authority position, such as the source selection advisory council; and board or panel chiefs.

Ensuring adequate facilities exist is important not only to conduct the evaluation, but also to secure the sensitive information relevant to the source selection. The source selection evaluation team needs a secure work area and associated storage space. The work area should be large enough to seat all members of the evaluation team and consultants or advisors and to store the proposals and other reference materials. The facility should also have desks, file cabinets, conference tables, computers, copy machines, telephones, and other supplies available to meet the needs of the evaluation team members.

Another factor to consider is the facility's location. Sites too close to the workplace may tempt evaluators to go back to their offices to catch up on work during the evaluation period. This can distract them from focusing on the evaluation. On the other hand, choosing a site too far from the workplace may cause a logistical problem for evaluators who carpool.

Contracting officers play a pivotal role in this stage by receiving proposals and determining their eligibility for evaluation. Any noncompliant proposals are returned to the offeror and not evaluated. The agency must record the date and time proposals were received and ensure that the unopened proposals are properly safeguarded from unauthorized disclosure throughout the source selection process. In addition, the contracting officer should compile a complete list of all offerors and team members (subcontractors) so that each evaluation team member can reaffirm that he or she has no potential conflict of interest with any of the potential contractors or subcontractors.

Electronic proposal submissions presents additional considerations. In negotiated acquisitions, the RFP must specify the electronic commerce method offerors may use to submit proposals. If any portion of an electronic or facsimile proposal is unreadable, the CO must immediately notify the offeror and permit resubmission of the unreadable portion. If the RFP requests both electronic and hard-copy proposal submissions, then the RFP must state the order of precedence for electronic versus hard-copy submittals for evaluation purposes in the proposal preparation instructions.

After checking an offeror's eligibility status, the contracting officer must conduct a thorough RFP compliance review to make sure all offerors complied with the proposal preparation instructions. The contracting officer shall document the rationale for discontinuing the initial evaluation of a proposal. Any determination to discontinue evaluation of a proposal generally requires legal review, and the SSA must be notified of the determination.

Once the proposals are submitted and the government has prepared for evaluations, the process of evaluating the proposals begins. This is the subject of Chapter 9.

NOTES

1 Peter S. Cole, *How to Evaluate and Negotiate Government Contracts* (Vienna, VA: Management Concepts, 2001), 219.

2 Ibid.

3 U.S. Government Accountability Office, "IMLCORP LLC; Wattre Corporation," B-310582; B-310582.2; B-310582.3; B-310582.4; B-310582.5 (Washington, DC: U.S. Government Accountability Office, January 9, 2008).

4 Defense Information Systems Agency, *Source Selection Deskbook* (Arlington, VA: Defense Information Systems Agency, May 2003), 22.

5 Federal Acquisition Institute, *Source Selection Text Reference* (Washington, DC: Federal Acquisition Institute, 1993), 4–7; National Reconnaissance Office, *Source Selection Manual* N87 (Chantilly, VA: National Reconnaissance Office, 2008), 29.

6 Federal Acquisition Regulation (FAR) 15.609.

7 Federal Acquisition Institute, *Source Selection Text Reference*, 4–7.

8 Federal Acquisition Institute, "Receiving Quotations and Proposals," *Contract Specialist Training Blueprints*, Unit 30 (Washington, DC: Federal Acquisition Institute, September 2002).

9 Harold V. Hanson, *NAVSEA Source Selection Guide* (Washington, DC: U.S. Naval Sea Systems Command, 2001), 21.

10 Ibid.

11 FAR 3.104-1.

12 FAR 2.101.

13 *NRO Source Selection* N87, 12.

14 Defense Information Systems Agency, 39–40.

15 FAR 15.207.

16 Federal Acquisition Institute, "Receiving Quotations and Proposals."

17 U.S. Government Accountability Office, "Project Resources, Inc.," B-297968 (Washington, DC: U.S. Government Accountability Office, March 31, 2006).

18 *Source Selection Manual* N87, 12.

19 National Reconnaissance Office, *Source Selection Manual* (Chantilly, VA: National Reconnaissance Office, April 2000), A-385.

20 FAR 4.502.

21 FAR 15.203.

22 Federal Acquisition Institute, "Receiving Quotations and Proposals."

23 *Source Selection Manual* N87, 11.

24 *Source Selection Manual*, 134.

25 Federal Acquisition Institute, "Receiving Quotations and Proposals."

26 *Source selection manual, 133.*

27 National Aeronautics and Space Administration, *Source Selection Guide* (Washington, DC: National Aeronautics and Space Administration, June 2007), 36.

28 Federal Acquisition Institute, "Receiving Quotations and Proposals."

29 FAR 3.401

30 National Aeronautics and Space Administration, *NASA FAR Supplement* 1815.305-70 (Washington, DC: National Aeronautics and Space Administration).

31 U.S. Government Accountability Office, "Matthews Associates, Inc.," B-299305 (Washington, DC: U.S. Government Accountability Office, March 5, 2007).

32 National Aeronautics and Space Administration, *Source Selection Guide*, 36–37.

33 FAR 15.208(b).

34 FAR 15.208(d).

35 U.S. Government Accountability Office, "Sector One Security Solution," B-400728 (Washington, DC: U.S. Government Accountability Office, December 10, 2008).

36 National Aeronautics and Space Administration, *Source Selection Guide*, 36–37.

PART III

Evaluating Proposals and Making the Award Decision

This is the stage of the source selection process that everyone has been preparing for: proposal evaluation and contract award.

The proposal evaluation process can be very lengthy and complicated depending on the nature of the RFP and evaluation criteria. Upon receipt of proposals, the contracting officer (CO) reviews them for compliance with the stated proposal preparation instructions and distributes them to evaluators. The evaluators must evaluate the proposals in accordance with the stated evaluation criteria. It is important to note that several months may have elapsed since writing the RFP, and it is critical that all the evaluators fully understand how to apply the evaluation standards and criteria. In some situations, new personnel on the evaluation team might not have participated in writing the RFP or evaluation factors. The proposal manager must ensure that the new personnel are properly trained *before* reading any proposals.

CHAPTER 9   EVALUATING PROPOSALS

Chapter 9 explains the proposal evaluation process and the issues that evaluators consider while evaluating technical/management proposals, past performance, cost, and oral presentations. Case studies illustrate the topics discussed in each section.

Once the offerors have submitted their proposals and the contracting officer has determined if the proposals are acceptable for evaluation, the evaluators read and assess the proposals in accordance with the RFP's evaluation criteria and the agency's procedures, which are sometimes documented in a source selection plan or a source selection evaluation guide.

At this stage in the source selection process, the initial evaluations are complete, and the SSA must determine if award without discussions is appropriate or if holding discussions will provide the best value to the government.

CHAPTER 10   AWARDING WITHOUT DISCUSSIONS

Chapter 10 takes the reader through the decision-making process for making award without conducting discussions, highlighting important factors to consider and presenting relevant case studies.

Awarding without discussions is a way to streamline the source selection process and entails selecting a proposal based on the initial evaluation findings and accepting that proposal as-is, including its weaknesses and at the contract value proposed. Agencies need to consider the cost of conducting discussions (e.g., the hours that take evaluators away from their normal work) and decide if that cost might offset the potentially lower prices or increased quality that may occur after discussions.

If the agency thinks that the apparent winner's proposed price is reasonable and the quality meets their requirements, then it may be appropriate to award based on initial proposals. Before doing so, the source selection authority (SSA) should ask the following questions:

• How much better can the proposals get?
• Is it worth the time to achieve that additional value? In other words, will discussions significantly lower costs or increase quality?

If the SSA determines that the government will get the best value by having discussions, the next step in the process is for the SSA to establish the competitive range of the highest proposal ratings. An agency cannot conduct discussions without first establishing a competitive range of the most highly rated offerors.

CHAPTER 11   ESTABLISHING THE COMPETITIVE RANGE

Chapter 11 explains how to determine a competitive range and includes case studies that illustrate the ways this process can go wrong.

The contracting officer determines which proposals are in the competitive range based on the evaluated price and other evaluation factors included in the RFP. The contracting officer may also limit the number of proposals in the competitive range to the greatest number that will permit an efficient competition among the most highly rated proposals. If at any time during the negotiations an offeror is no longer among the most highly rated, the agency may eliminate that company from the competitive range.

After the SSA has established the competitive range, the evaluation team must get ready to begin the negotiation process.

CHAPTER 12   DISCUSSIONS, NEGOTIATIONS, AND PROPOSAL REVISIONS

Chapter 12 begins by distinguishing between *discussions* and *negotiations*. Then the chapter explains things to consider before beginning discussions, such as preparing the negotiation plan and determining the method or place for conducting negotiations. Next the chapter covers what to discuss during a negotiation and restrictions on discussions. The chapter concludes with a section on proposal revisions.

Discussions—also called *negotiations*—are conducted by the contracting officer. The primary objective of discussions is to maximize the government's ability to obtain the best value based on the requirement and the evaluation factors set forth in the solicitation.

Negotiations may include bargaining. Bargaining involves persuading; altering assumptions and positions when the other party explains its position; and compromising; and may apply to the proposed contract's price, schedule, technical requirements, type, terms and conditions, or other elements. At a minimum the contracting officer must indicate proposal deficiencies, significant weaknesses, and adverse past performance information to each offeror still being considered for award, to give the offeror an opportunity to respond to these concerns.

The contracting officer is also encouraged to discuss other aspects of the offeror's proposal that could be altered or enhanced to increase the offeror's potential for award. The CO is not required, however, to discuss every opportunity for improvement. Instead, the CO must ensure only that the scope and extent of discussions meet the definition of "meaningful" as described in a variety of GAO decisions.

Although the CO has discretion about the scope and extent of discussions, he or she must also consider certain restrictions. For example, the CO may not engage in conduct that:

- Favors one offeror over another
- Reveals an offeror's technical solution, including unique technology, innovative and unique uses of commercial items, or any information that would compromise an offeror's intellectual property to another offeror

- Reveals an offeror's price without that offeror's permission
- Reveals the names of individuals providing reference information about an offeror's past performance
- Knowingly furnishes source selection information.

A proposal revision is a change to a proposal made after the solicitation closing date as a result of negotiations. The revision is made at the request of or as allowed by a contracting officer, who may request or allow proposal revisions to clarify and document understandings reached during negotiations.

CHAPTER 13   MAKING TRADE-OFF DECISIONS

At this stage in the competitive source selection process, the evaluators have assessed the final proposal revisions and are ready to brief the source selection authority (SSA). The SSA makes the contract award decision based on a comparative assessment of the proposals against the source selection criteria stated in the RFP. Chapter 13 walks through each step of this decision-making process, including comparing proposals, exercising independent judgment, and documenting the decision.

Although the SSA may use reports and analysis prepared by the evaluators, the final source selection decision must represent the SSA's independent judgment. The numerical, color, or adjectival ratings the evaluation teams assigned are merely labels and not the sole basis for comparing proposals. The evaluation rating alone does not determine the successful offeror. Rather, the SSA bases the source selection decision on a trade-off analysis that compares the strengths and weaknesses of the competing proposals against the RFP's evaluation criteria. The SSA documents the rationale for its decision in the source selection decision document.

Chapter 9

Evaluating Proposals

Once the offerors have submitted their proposals, and the contracting officer (CO) has determined if the proposals are acceptable for evaluation, the evaluators read and assess the proposals in accordance with the RFP's evaluation criteria and the agency's procedures, which are sometimes documented in a source selection plan or a source selection evaluation guide.

It's important to note that although the evaluators score the proposals, that score does not make the source selection decision. Scores must not be used as the primary justification for contract award. Rather, the evaluators' written narratives, which identify the proposal strengths, weaknesses, and risks upon which the scores are based, are the primary justification for contract award.[1]

Evaluators should keep in mind what they learned during training and orientation (covered in detail in Chapter 8), as well as the following four tips while reading and evaluating the proposals:

1. Evaluate only what is actually written in the proposal.
2. Follow the evaluation criteria stated in the RFP.
3. Document specific strengths, weaknesses, and risks of each proposal.
4. Do not make comparisons between proposals.[2]

This chapter explains the proposal evaluation process and the issues that evaluators consider while evaluating technical/management proposals, past performance, cost, and oral presentations. We'll present case studies that illustrate the topics discussed in each section.

THE PROPOSAL EVALUATION PROCESS

Proposal evaluation involves assessing the content of a proposal against established evaluation factors and determining whether the offeror will be able to perform the prospective contract successfully. Evaluators identify the relative strengths, deficiencies, significant weaknesses, and risks in each proposal and document their assessments.[3] In so doing, evaluators must assess only what each offeror submits in its proposal. Judgments may not be based on other factors, such as personal knowledge of a company's capabilities. When evaluating multiple proposals, evaluators must not compare the proposals against each other, but must evaluate each proposal on its own merits as if it were the only proposal received. This helps ensure objectivity in the initial evaluation. Comparing and ranking proposals occurs at the end of the process, after the evaluators assess all of the proposals.[4]

The proposal evaluation phase is probably the most visible part of the source selection process and the part most susceptible to criticism. Not only is there time pressure to award the contract on schedule, but there is also scrutiny that comes from outside the agency: from offerors at the debriefing; from the GAO, if there's a protest; or, if the acquisition is highly visible, from Congress.

Thus, it is essential that the agency properly manage the evaluation process. Typically, the contracting officer or the source selection evaluation team (SSET) chairperson manages the evaluation process. For complex acquisitions, different panels may evaluate different proposal volumes.[5] For example, a technical panel, a management panel, a past performance panel, and a cost panel might evaluate those respective volumes of the proposals. Some agencies have a separate group that evaluates contractual issues; others combine cost and contracts into one panel.

Regardless of how a source selection is organized, completing the evaluation in a timely manner requires planning, coordination, and leadership by the contracting officer or the SSET chairperson. Agencies must establish procedures to govern the source selection. Some agencies rely on a source selection plan (discussed in detail in Chapter 2) or a source selection evaluation guide. Source selection procedures guide evaluators in:

- Evaluating proposals and preparing narrative reports identifying strengths, weaknesses, deficiencies, and risks based on the evaluation criteria stated in the RFP
- Rating each proposal based on standards established in the source selection plan or source selection evaluation guide
- Making recommendations to the source selection authority (SSA).[6]

The agency should tailor the procedures for each source selection to the circumstances and to the source selection organizational structure that it is using.

As evaluators read each proposal, they should note anything that could be a problem on the appropriate documentation form, along with the offeror's name and the proposal page number. If problems are documented in order, it will be easier for evaluators to find references to them during consensus sessions. Generally, problems in proposals are categorized as deficiencies, significant weaknesses, or weaknesses. The source selection plan or source selection evaluation guide should define these terms, and the evaluators must apply them consistently when reviewing all of the proposals.

Assessing Deficiencies

A *deficiency* is a material failure of a proposal to meet a government requirement, or a combination of significant weaknesses that increases the risk of unsuccessful contract performance to an unacceptable level.[7] A deficiency is typically a substantive problem, such as proposing materials, equipment, or personnel that do not meet the statement of work (SOW) requirements. A deficiency may also exist if an offeror does not address an issue in enough detail for an evaluator to determine whether the offeror's approach is acceptable. Evaluators should not only identify deficiencies but also note their impact on the program if they are not corrected.[8]

Assessing Significant Weaknesses

The Federal Acquisition Regulation (FAR) defines a *significant weakness* as "a flaw that appreciably increases the risk of unsuccessful contract performance."[9] Generally, a significant weakness affects a proposal's score more than a minor weakness. After reading the proposal, an evaluator may determine that a number of minor weaknesses become a significant weakness when combined. Similarly, a number of significant weaknesses may rise to the level of a deficiency.

Assessing Minor Weaknesses

According to the FAR, a *weakness* is "a flaw in [a] proposal that increases the risk of unsuccessful contract performance." [10] Note that the difference between a weakness and a significant weakness is how "appreciable" the weakness is. Unfortunately, the FAR does not explain how to determine this. It is the individual evaluator's job to determine how appreciable a weakness is, and they must do so in a consistent manner.

Offering staffing below the level stated in the standard, or proposing a tried and true approach rather than an innovative one if the evaluation criteria state a preference for innovation, might be considered minor weaknesses.[11]

Proposal Evaluation Steps

The proposal evaluation process comprises four general steps.

1. **Identify and document proposal uncertainties**, such as:
   - Ambiguous language
   - Sections in which the offeror didn't provide sufficient information to determine whether:
     - The proposal should be in the competitive range; or
     - The offeror should win the contract, if the agency doesn't anticipate conducting discussions.

   The contracting officer may ask an offeror to provide additional information to help the government better understand its proposal. Initial ratings reflect the proposal as submitted, but these ratings may be revised when the offeror responds to the clarification request.

2. **Identify and document proposal strengths, weaknesses, risks, and deficiencies.** These will be discussed during negotiations, if applicable.

3. **Assign ratings for non-cost evaluation factors (when using the trade-off process).** Source selection team members independently evaluate each offeror's past performance and technical/management and cost/price proposals. After the individual evaluations, each team convenes to discuss the evaluator's assessment of the proposal's strengths, weaknesses, risks, and deficiencies relative to the evaluation factor(s) or subfactor(s). Then the panel determines a final consensus rating for each factor and subfactor. We discuss the consensus process in more detail later in this chapter.

4. **Prepare a summary evaluation report.** Once evaluators finish assessing each proposal, the SSET chairperson prepares a summary report that includes the evaluated price, the final rating for each evaluation factor and subfactor, and a discussion of the strengths, weaknesses, deficiencies, and risks of each proposal.[12] Documenting the evaluation is discussed in more detail later in this chapter.

EVALUATING TECHNICAL/MANAGEMENT PROPOSAL VOLUMES

Some agencies designate a single panel to evaluate technical and management proposal volumes; others require separate proposal volumes and separate evaluation teams. We'll combine the two in our discussion, because many of the issues evaluation panels encounter when assessing these volumes are similar.

A technical/management proposal evaluation is challenging to conduct because it may involve a large number of people with diverse levels of expertise and experience.

The technical/management panel chairperson should conduct regular meetings with the evaluators and advisors to monitor accomplishments and coordinate ongoing activities. Maintaining good communication within and among the evaluation team and panels and establishing a schedule of expected milestones are essential for a successful evaluation. If everyone is kept informed, the evaluation process will proceed with minimal disruption and should meet expected milestones.

The SOW identifies the agency's needs, and the offeror's technical proposal should explain how it will fulfill those needs. The offeror should fully address all of the SOW requirements in its proposal. Evaluators assess how well the proposal meets the SOW requirements. This evaluation typically covers:

- The soundness of the technical approach
- The validity of the proposed methodology or techniques
- The likelihood of success
- The performance risks associated with the offeror's proposed approach.[13]

Managing the Evaluation Panel

Many source selections involve collaborative teams of evaluators or advisors, and managing the evaluation panel is an important part of keeping the source selection process on task and on schedule.

For complex acquisitions, the panel chairperson may appoint a lead person to manage each evaluation factor for that proposal volume. For example, if there are four technical evaluation factors, there would be four technical factor leads or managers in charge of those factor evaluations. Factor managers should have strong leadership skills and strong technical knowledge about the topic evaluated.

Although they must be familiar with each proposal's content, factor managers don't actually evaluate proposals. If they did, their assessments might influence other evaluators during the factor consensus session. Factor managers make sure that the evaluators have a clear and common understanding of:

- The evaluation criteria
- The standards
- The factor scoring definitions
- The proposal risk rating definitions
- Strength and weakness intensity ratings.

Sometimes an agency assigns evaluators to a source selection on a full-time basis, while others with specific expertise participate only on an as-needed basis. It is prudent for agencies to relieve full-time evaluators of their normal job responsibilities during the source selection. To facilitate this, some agencies issue formal source selection appointment letters to evaluators and their supervisors. The appointment letter states how long the assignment period is estimated to last and emphasizes that the assignment carries full-time responsibilities. Such advance notice allows the evaluator's supervisor to delegate the evaluator's regular workload during the source selection evaluation process. If mission requirements preclude full-time participation, each evaluator should be tasked at a level to which he or she can commit. The source selection facility operating hours may need to be extended if evaluators are not available during normal business hours.

The technical/management panel chairperson should assign the workload such that evaluators can simultaneously complete project tasks. Allowing long periods of unproductive time to elapse while evaluators wait for input from another panel or for others to complete their own evaluations is inefficient. To fill the time, some evaluators may want to return to the office to catch up on work. This is understandable, but it increases the likelihood that an evaluator will inadvertently release sensitive source selection information to coworkers who ask, "How's the source selection going?" or "What are you doing back at the office?" Keeping evaluators focused on the source selection not only helps to avoid the risk of their disclosing sensitive information, but also helps to keep the process on schedule.[14]

Many agencies prohibit technical evaluators from seeing the cost proposal and cost evaluators from seeing the technical proposal. But sometimes situations arise in which the panels need to communicate with each other. For example, the technical evaluation team must see the basis of estimate, which is generally part of the cost volume. Using interpanel communication forms—or a simple memo—protects the cost proposal while allowing the technical evaluators to get the information they need. For more complex acquisitions, the SSET chairperson may consider appointing technical liaisons to the cost panel. The cost panel technical liaison must be familiar with the special technical inputs required in the cost models and helps facilitate the information exchange between the cost panel and the technical panel.

In addition to the evaluators, some agencies may use advisors, who may be government or contractor personnel. *Advisors* are subject matter experts who provide technical expertise and advice to the evaluators. Advisors may read the proposal, document their findings, and make recommendations to the evaluators. Advisors offer specific input in their area of expertise and may only be asked to evaluate a limited subset of evaluation factors.

Agencies usually restrict contractor employees' involvement in a source selection to advisory or support roles, and they may not rate or rank proposals without special permission from the SSA. However, FAR 9.503 states that the agency head may waive the rule about organizational or consultant conflict of interest if following it would not be in the government's interest.[15]

Conducting the Evaluation

Specific evaluation processes and tasks vary between agencies and source selections, but the basic objective remains constant: to provide the source selection authority with sufficient information to make an informed and reasoned selection. To this end, the evaluators identify deficiencies, strengths, weaknesses, clarifications, and uncertainties applicable to each proposal.

The technical/management panel may begin with a quick read of the proposals, skimming them to get familiar with the format and content. No assessment, judgment, or evaluation is done at this time. After the quick read, the evaluators read the technical/management volumes of the proposal to get a thorough understanding of the proposed approach. They conduct an in-depth, systematic evaluation of the proposals against the evaluation factors and subfactors in the RFP, which they must apply consistently. In accordance with the applicable evaluation standards, evaluators conduct an equitable, impartial, and comprehensive evaluation of each proposal against the solicitation requirements. The evaluators should also review the offeror's basis of estimate to understand the proposed staffing levels and overall technical/management approach.[16]

The contracting officer uses evaluators' assessments to establish a competitive range when discussions are necessary and shares the evaluation of each proposal with the offeror that submitted it during clarifications or discussions. Thus, it is important to establish an orderly method for identifying, reporting, and tracking each deficiency, strength, and weakness. Using an automated evaluation tool can ease the administrative burden associated with these tasks.

Using Evaluation Forms

Based on the evaluation narratives they write while assessing proposals, evaluators prepare individual evaluation reports. They may also have to complete other forms if they encounter problems or have questions about a proposal. Evaluators use these additional forms to document parts of a proposal that are weak, deficient, or require additional information.

The requests and reports an agency sends to offerors depend on the phase of the source selection process. For example, once the agency decides to begin discussions, it is too late to send out clarification requests to offerors. Evaluation forms are used during the last phase, discussions. This is the phase in which offerors are given an opportunity to review their proposals. Figure 9-1 shows three distinct phases in the source selection process:

1. Clarifications
2. Communications
3. Discussions.

Evaluation forms vary between agencies but typically include the following, although they may have different names.

- **Clarification requests (CRs).** Evaluators complete a CR when the agency anticipates making the contract award without discussions, or to clarify the relevance of the offeror's past performance information, adverse past performance information to which the offeror has not had an opportunity to respond, and minor or clerical errors.
- **Information requests (IRs).** Evaluators complete an IR when they encounter a part of a proposal that is not complete for evaluation or in which evaluators find contradictory statements. IRs may be used during two phases:
  - Before establishing the competitive range, in order to request information to enhance the government's understanding of the proposal, to allow reasonable interpretation of proposals, or to facilitate the government's evaluation process

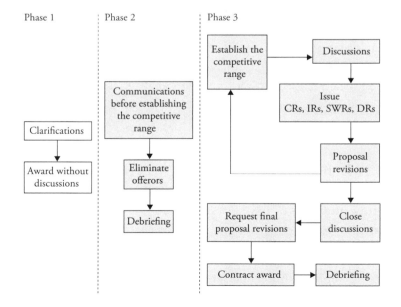

Figure 9-1   The Evaluation Process[17]

- During discussions, to request additional information from offerors on aspects of their proposals that, if altered or explained, could materially enhance the proposal's potential for award.
- **Significant weakness reports (SWRs).** Evaluators prepare an SWR for any part of a proposal that has a significant weakness.
- **Deficiency reports (DRs).** Evaluators prepare an DR for any part of a proposal that does not satisfy a requirement of the solicitation, or for a combination of significant weaknesses that increases the risk of performance to an unacceptable level.

Evaluators may also use the SWR and DR as a form of discussions after determining the competitive range. Figure 9-2 provides samples of these evaluation forms.

The following case study illustrates the importance of consistency when conducting an evaluation.

Case Study: Evaluation Consistency

Systems Research and Applications Corporation (SRA) and Booz Allen Hamilton, Inc. (BAH), protested the award of a contract to Jacobs Technology under a request for proposals issued by the Department of the Air Force for engineering and technology acquisition support services (ETASS) for the agency's Electronic Systems Center (ESC).

The RFP explained that the agency would award the contract on a "best value" basis and stated the following evaluation factors and subfactors:

- Mission capability factor
  - Subfactor 1: Technical approach
  - Subfactor 2: Transition planning
  - Subfactor 3: Personnel
  - Subfactor 4: Management practices
- Proposal risk factor
  - Subfactor 1: Technical approach
  - Subfactor 2: Transition planning
  - Subfactor 3: Personnel
  - Subfactor 4: Management practices
- Past performance factor
- Cost/price factor.

The mission capability, proposal risk, and past performance factors were of equal weight, and each, individually, was more important than the cost/price factor. The subfactors within the mission capability and proposal risk factors were of equal importance.

Individual Evaluation

Offeror _____

Evaluator _____

Item _____

Factor _____

Proposal Evaluation

Standard number _____

Proposal page number _____

Evaluation of standard (whether it meets the standard; strengths, weaknesses)

_____

_____

_____

_____

_____

_____

_____

_____

Score

_____

_____

Risks

_____

_____

_____

_____

_____

Risk rating:

_____

_____

Figure 9-2 Sample Proposal Evaluation Forms

Clarification Request

Offeror _____

Item _____

Factor _____

Date _____

Proposal page number and paragraph _____

Explain exactly what must be clarified.

_____
_____
_____
_____
_____
_____
_____
_____
_____
_____
_____
_____
_____

Information Request

Offeror _____

Item _____

Factor _____

Date _____

Proposal page number and paragraph _____

Specify the information requested, and explain why it is needed and what the offeror must provide.

_____
_____
_____
_____
_____
_____
_____
_____
_____
_____
_____

Figure 9-2   (*Continued*)

Significant Weakness Report

Offeror _____

Item _____

Factor _____

Date _____

Proposal page number and paragraph _____

State the nature of the weakness. Specify the part of the proposal that is weak, and explain why it is weak.

_____
_____
_____
_____
_____
_____
_____
_____
_____
_____
_____
_____
_____

Deficiency Report

Offeror _____

Item _____

Factor _____

Date _____

Proposal page number and paragraph _____

State the nature of the deficiency. Clearly explain why it is considered a deficiency, and specify the requirement that has not been met.

_____
_____
_____
_____
_____
_____
_____
_____
_____
_____
_____

Figure 9-2   *(Continued)*

According to the Government Accountability Office (GAO) decision regarding the protest, the agency's evaluators "individually reviewed and rated the offerors' proposals, and then met as a team to discuss their individual ratings and to agree to consensus ratings for the offerors' proposals under each subfactor."

After conducting discussions and receiving revised proposals, the SSET evaluated the final proposals as shown in Table 9-1:

Table 9-1   Evaluation of Jacobs Technology, Systems Research and Applications Corporation, and Booz Allen Hamilton, Inc., Proposals

	Jacobs	SRA	BAH
1. Mission capability			
Technical approach	Green/acceptable	Green/acceptable	Green/acceptable
Transition	Green/acceptable	Green/acceptable	Green/acceptable
Personnel	Green/acceptable	Green/acceptable	Green/acceptable
Management practices	Blue/exceptional	Green/acceptable	Green/acceptable
2. Proposal risk			
Technical approach	Low	Low	Low
Transition	Low	Low	Low
Personnel	Low	Low	Low
Management practices	Low	Low	Low
3. Past performance	High confidence	Significant confidence	Significant confidence
4. Price (proposed)	$260.0 million	$[deleted]	$[deleted]

Per the GAO decision,

> The green/acceptable/low risk ratings assessed for the protesters' and awardee's proposals under most of the subfactors of the mission capability factor and proposal risk factor reflected the SSET's judgment that, although the firms proposed differing approaches, their proposals were merely acceptable, meeting requirements, and presented low proposal risk.

> For example, under the technical approach subfactors of the mission capability and proposal risk factors, the SSET found that the protesters and awardee demonstrated a clear understanding of the ESC [statement of objectives], proposed adequate approaches to controlling systems engineering processes, and tailored their respective approaches for each task order. In short, the evaluators found that all of the offerors presented proposals that, although they proposed a "different path" to systems engineering improvement, would improve the ESC systems engineering processes.

> Unlike the other management capability/proposal risk subfactors, the SSET found that Jacobs's proposal merited a higher rating under the management practices subfactors

than did SRA's and BAH's. Specifically, the SSET found that "Jacobs's proposal for Management Practices [was] EXCEPTIONAL (Blue), and exceeded the requirements, and [was] significantly better than all the other Offerors' proposals." ... The SSA concluded that Jacobs's proposal reflected the best value to the government.

With respect to SRA's proposal, the SSA concluded that Jacobs's higher ratings under the management practices subfactor of the mission suitability factor and the past performance factor outweighed SRA's lower proposed price. With respect to BAH's proposal, the SSA noted that BAH's proposal, which had a higher evaluated price than Jacobs's, presented no advantages over Jacobs's proposal.

The record also indicates that the SSET's risk assessment was based upon a material factual error, given that Jacobs's proposal identified, as major transition experience, only two contracts of similar scale to the ETASS contract (that is, more than 700 personnel transitioned); the remainder of the contracts identified provided for transitioning many fewer personnel.... Thus, the statements in the [proposal analysis report] and Source Selection Decision that "Jacobs has applied its transition processes to successful transitions in over a dozen large organizations of the scale of ESC (personnel >700)" appear to be factually inaccurate.... Moreover, as the protesters note, the record does not show that the evaluators considered the relevance of Jacobs's past transition experience in terms of whether it involved similar transition plans or techniques.

Furthermore, the SSET's final evaluation found, with regard to Jacobs's transition planning, that considerable government time and manpower could be needed to bring the contractor "up to speed," even after application of the identified risk mitigators.... Nevertheless, the SSET's final evaluation found Jacobs's proposal to be low risk under the proposal risk transition planning subfactor.... This appears to be inconsistent with the definition of "low" risk contained in ... [the RFP], which defined low proposal risk as reflecting a proposal that had "little potential to cause disruption of schedule, increased cost or degradation of performance. Normal contractor effort and normal government monitoring will likely be able to overcome any difficulties." In sum, the record [did] not demonstrate the reasonableness of Jacobs's green/low risk rating under the transition planning subfactors.

As noted above, ultimately the proposals of SRA, BAH, and Jacobs all received the same green/acceptable with low risk rating under the transition planning subfactor. Although the SSA was informed of the weakness identified in Jacobs's proposal with respect to its lack of current program knowledge as it related to transition planning, the record does not establish that the agency considered the differences in the firms' proposals for transition planning. That is, based on the record, SRA's and BAH's proposals appeared to provide superior approaches to transition planning to that offered by Jacobs, but the SSET ultimately concluded, applying its narrow interpretation of what it considered a strength, that all of the firms' proposals merely met the agency's requirements.... Absent from the record [was] any meaningful explanation from the agency as to why the firms' differing transition approaches (which were admittedly based largely upon differing amounts of incumbent staff and program knowledge) should not have been considered under these evaluation subfactors. Based on this record, [the GAO found that] the agency did not reasonably evaluate the offerors' proposals under these subfactors.

Given that the RFP informed offerors that the agency would evaluate the 'degree to which the offeror presents a clear understanding and an innovative approach to fulfill all the objectives outlined in the ETASS' [indefinite delivery/indefinite quantity statement of objectives] under these subfactors, [the GAO found] no support in the record for the SSET's conclusion that BAH's demonstration of its clear and detailed understanding of the ETASS objectives should not have been reported as a strength or considered in the agency's assessment of the merits of the firms' proposals. Rather, although the evaluators found that BAH proposed a "clear understanding of the [ETASS] objectives" and strong approach to satisfying them, the record does not explain why the SSET found that BAH's approach would merely satisfy the agency's requirements.

Further, the Air Force ... failed to persuasively rebut BAH's contention that Jacobs did not similarly demonstrate a clear understanding and approach to fulfilling all of the ETASS objectives. Specifically, BAH contend[ed] that Jacobs's technical approach proposal presented a generic, standard systems engineering methodology that did not specifically address how the firm would satisfy the ETASS objectives.

The GAO sustained the protests "because the record [did] not show that the agency qualitatively assessed the differences in the offerors' proposals, as required by the RFP." The GAO recommended "that the Air Force perform a new evaluation consistent with this decision, reopen discussions, if necessary, and make a new source selection decision."[18]

This case illustrates the importance of consistently applying the RFP's stated evaluation factors and standards to each proposal and documenting the basis for each strength, significant weakness, and deficiency. When finalizing the documentation, the rating definitions and all documentation must be carefully screened to ensure evaluation consistency. In this case, the lack of documentation specifically explaining how the SSET and SSA arrived at the scores influenced the GAO's decision.

EVALUATING PAST PERFORMANCE

The past performance panel evaluates the past performance information each offeror submits. This evaluation helps determine how the offeror might fulfill the current solicitation's requirements, based on previous demonstrated performance.

By reviewing relevant contracts the offeror has performed, the panel can determine the degree of performance risk associated with awarding that offeror the contract. This evaluation is subjective, and evaluators must consider all relevant facts and circumstances to reach a conclusion. These typically include the following factors:

- The contractor's record of conforming to contract requirements and standards of good workmanship
- The contractor's record of forecasting and controlling costs
- The contractor's adherence to contract schedules, including the administrative aspects of performance
- The contractor's history of reasonable and cooperative behavior and commitment to customer satisfaction
- The contractor's record of integrity and business ethics
- The contractor's businesslike concern for the interest of the customer.[19]

The past performance information each offeror submits in its proposal must be similar to what the RFP requires for the evaluation to be effective. In other words, the offeror should follow instructions in the RFP for submitting past performance information, and the projects for which the offeror provides past performance information should be similar to the new project in terms of scope and price. The agency considers the currency and relevance of the information, the source of the information, the context of the data, and general trends in the contractor's performance. The evaluation should take into account past performance information regarding predecessor companies, key personnel who have relevant experience, or subcontractors that will perform major or critical aspects of the requirement (when such information is relevant to the instant acquisition).

Typically, *experience* describes how long a company has performed similar work. For example, a company can have ten years' experience in computer programming. *Past performance*, on the other hand, evaluates *how well* that company performed the work. If the agency intends to evaluate experience and past performance separately, each must be clearly defined in the solicitation to avoid evaluating the same information twice, under the two different factors.

The evaluation for any large business should also include the past performance of offerors in complying with subcontracting plan goals for small disadvantaged business (SDB) concerns, reaching monetary targets for SDB participation, and complying with the notification requirement in FAR 19.1202-4(b).

If an offeror does not have a record of relevant past performance, or information on the offeror's past performance is not available, the offeror may not be evaluated favorably or unfavorably on past performance.[20] In a negotiated competitive procurement, past performance is evaluated on a graduated scale; how it affects an offeror's opportunity for contract award depends on how heavily the government weights the evaluation factor.

The RFP instructions should state if the agency will evaluate a company's past performance differently from, or in addition to, personnel past performance. For example, if an offeror is a new company but has hired several experienced people, the past performance of the company may be minimal, but the staff members' past performance could be extensive. It's prudent for agencies to consider both personnel and corporate past performance.

Note that this assessment of past performance information is separate from the responsibility determination required by the FAR. A *responsibility determination* is a broad pass/fail assessment of an offeror's capability and capacity to perform the contract. FAR 9.104 requires the contracting officer to determine responsibility before contract award by analyzing an offeror's competency, experience, capacity, credit, integrity, perseverance, tenacity, and limitations on subcontracting.

Unlike a pass/fail responsibility determination, a comparative past performance evaluation conducted using the trade-off process is a very specific task that identifies the degree of risk associated with each competing proposal. *Proposal risk* is the evaluated risk associated with the offeror's proposed approach to meeting the requirements of the current solicitation. Rather than asking if a company can do the work, the question becomes, "Will the company perform successfully?" In short, the evaluation establishes the government's degree of confidence in the offeror's likelihood of success by relying on past demonstrated success. Note, though, that if a contractor has a history of performing well on high-risk projects, its performance risk is low, but the proposal risk associated with the proposed approach may still be high.

The past performance panel should not limit its past performance inquiry to the company submitting the proposal if other corporate divisions, contractors or subcontractors will perform a critical element of the proposed effort. Evaluators should also assess the performance record of those organizations, in accordance with the solicitation.[21]

Before gathering additional past performance information, such as that regarding key employees, evaluators independently assess the relevance of each offeror's past performance information. This relevancy assessment is necessary to permit valid comparisons between the prior contracts and the work required in the RFP.

Evaluators look at the offeror's work experience and compare it to what is required in the current solicitation's SOW. If experience and current expectations closely match, the past performance is considered relevant. For example, the expertise required to install computer *equipment* in an office building is not same as the expertise required to install a computer *network* in an office building.

Next, evaluators consider the size of the past work efforts and compare it to the current requirements. Managing a multimillion-dollar contract requires a different set of skills than managing a contract valued at $50,000. Frequently, the RFP will state a dollar range for past performance references. If a dollar range is not specified, it's prudent for offerors to provide references in the same dollar range as their current proposal.

Researching Additional Past Performance Information

After assessing the relevance of past performance information submitted by each offeror, the next step is to check the offerors' references and research other sources of past performance information. The past performance evaluation is unique in the source selection process because the past performance panel does not just rely on the information the offeror submits. The panel may also gather data from external sources. Section L of the RFP should state that the government may use past performance information obtained from sources other than those identified by the offeror, and that the information obtained will be used for both the responsibility determination and the best value decision.

The data submitted by the offeror is the primary source of past performance information, but the past performance panel may use other public and private references, such as

- Dun and Bradstreet reports
- Other commercial sources
- SEC filings
- Data from other government agencies
- Data from organizations that give awards of excellence or vendor quality certifications, such as the International Organization for Standardization (for ISO 9000 quality management certification).

To ensure accuracy, evaluators should verify information received from all sources, and the verification must identify supporting rationale for any evaluation report; performance evaluations must always rely on supportable data.

Some agencies require offerors to submit their past performance information before the other proposal volumes so that the past performance panel can complete the initial evaluation by the time the rest of the source selection evaluation team is done with its initial proposal evaluations. Another advantage of requesting this information early is that it allows the agency to find out earlier which companies will submit proposals and learn about their teaming arrangements and the subcontractors they will use.

The past performance panel should proceed with a broad assessment of all the relevant past performance references and should tailor the assessment after the offerors submit the technical, management, and cost proposal volumes. Tailoring the assessment after reviewing the proposals involves determining what risks are associated with the current solicitation and comparing past performance references to see how offerors have handled similar risks in the past. Evaluating past performance information can be a time-consuming task, and when establishing the source selection schedule, agencies should consider how much data the evaluators should collect.

Some agencies include a questionnaire in the RFP for offerors to send out to references. Agencies can use the same questionnaire as an interview form for gathering additional information from references they find independently. Standardized questionnaires are useful for gathering consistent data from all interviewees. Figure 9-3 suggests sample past performance interview questions an agency may use.

Some evaluators find that it is easier to make contact with references if they begin by calling each reference to schedule an interview. The evaluator should provide a copy of the questionnaire to the reference in advance and should call again on an agreed-upon date and time to conduct the interview. This procedure allows the reference to become familiar with the questions and increases the likelihood of receiving thoughtful responses. The evaluator should record each interviewee's specific answers to the questions and try to determine through further inquiry exactly what happened during performance of the contract in question.

Recording each interviewee's answers is especially important with award fee contracts because the contractor's award fee rating is subjectively determined by the government agency. An award fee rating is the amount that the contractor earns during contract performance, as determined by the government's evaluation of the contractor's performance in terms of the criteria stated in the contract.[23] When evaluators receive award fee rating information from other agencies in response to past performance requests, the evaluator should ask about that agency's general philosophy on award fee.

For example, an award fee rating of 70 percent may be appropriate in one agency for the same level of performance that would earn a 90 percent award fee rating in another agency. It is important, then, for the evaluator to get detailed information about the offeror's performance from the other agency to help put the award fee rating in context.[24]

- Confirm the following data from the offeror's proposal:
  - Contract number
  - Contractor's name and address
  - Type of contract
  - Complexity of work
  - Description and location of work (e.g., products, services, and tasks)
  - Contract dollar value
  - Date of award
  - Contract completion date (including extensions)
  - Type and extent of subcontracting
- Verify any past performance data to which you may have access.
- If the award amount or delivery schedule changed during performance, find out why.
- Ask what role the reference played (e.g., contracting officer's representative, contract specialist, administrative contracting officer) and for how long.
- If a problem surfaced, ask what the government and contractor did to fix it.
- Ask for a description of the skills and expertise of the personnel the contractor used and an assessment of the overall quality of the contractor's team. Did the company appear to use personnel with the appropriate skills and expertise?
- Ask how the contractor performed, considering technical performance or quality of the product or service, schedule, cost control (if applicable), business relations, and management.
- Ask whether the contractor was cooperative in resolving issues.
- Ask whether there were any particularly significant risks involved in performance of the effort.
- Ask if the company appeared to apply sufficient resources (personnel and facilities) for the effort.
- If the company used subcontractors, ask:
  - What was the relationship between the prime and the subcontractors?
  - How well did the prime manage the subcontractors?
  - Did the subcontractors perform the bulk of the effort or just add depth in particular technical areas?
  - Why were the subcontractors chosen to work on specific technical areas, what were those areas, and why did the subcontractors, rather than the prime, perform that work?
- If a problem is revealed, but the reference is unfamiliar with it, ask who might have more information about the problem.
- Ask if this firm has performed other contract work for that agency or company.
- Ask about the company's strong points or what the reference liked best about its work.
- Ask whether the reference has any reservations about recommending the company receive a future contract award.
- Ask whether the reference knows of anyone else who might have past performance information on the offeror.

Figure 9-3   Sample Past Performance Interview Questions[22]

Upon completing the reference check, the past performance panel should review trends to determine the risks of choosing each offeror to perform the current contract. When checking private-sector references, they should consider whether there is potential for any conflict of interest between the offeror and the reference.[25] This is particularly important if the reference is currently competing against that company as a prime contractor or subcontractor to another offeror.

Collecting all of the relevant past performance information, including data submitted by the offeror and data evaluators obtained from other sources, is just the beginning of the process. The past performance panel still must evaluate this information fairly, consistently, and in accordance with the evaluation criteria in the RFP.

Evaluating Past Performance Information

The past performance panel should validate the offeror's past contract information as part of the overall evaluation process, then assign a performance risk rating as stated in the source selection plan. Performance risk assessments should consider:

- The number and severity of problems
- The demonstrated effectiveness of corrective actions taken (not just planned or promised)
- The overall work record.

Evaluators should note instances of good or poor performance, particularly indications of excellent or exceptional performance in the areas most critical to past requirements, and relate that performance history to the current solicitation requirement. Evaluators should also take into consideration the role the government may have played in any performance problems. For example, if the company made a late delivery because government-furnished property was late, that's not really the contractor's fault. Keep in mind that all programs experience some problems, so expecting a perfect past performance record is unrealistic. Instead, consider how the contractor resolved the problems as a measure of its merit.

The source selection team first evaluates how well each offeror performed, then rates the relevancy of that performance. A significant achievement in, problem with, or lack of relevant data for any aspect of the requirement can become an important consideration in the source selection process. A negative finding may result in an overall high performance risk rating, depending upon the significance placed on that aspect of the requirement by the source selection team. Evaluators should relate their ratings to the solicitation requirements, explain any strengths or weaknesses they identify, and determine whether the government may have contributed to a weakness, and, if so, to what extent.

The past performance panel evaluators must consider all past performance data collected on each offeror. When making an overall judgment on an offeror's past performance, evaluators should consider:

- The number and severity of an offeror's problems, in relation to the offeror's overall work record.
- The age and relevance of past performance information.

- Any potential bias on the part of any given interviewee.
- The extent to which poor performance by an offeror on a past contract may have been caused by external influences.
- Any differences in requirements between the current solicitation and contracts being evaluated (e.g., differences in the level of technical and performance risk).
- The extent to which the offeror has taken measures to correct past problems.
- The effect of predecessor companies. (To determine the relevancy of contracts held by a predecessor or an affiliate, the effect of the workforce, management, facilities, or other resources of the predecessor/affiliate on contract performance must be assessed.)
- The subcontractors that will perform major or critical aspects of the proposed effort.
- The key personnel who have relevant experience.

If evaluators receive adverse past performance information about a particular offeror, the agency must share the information with the offeror and give it an opportunity to respond if it has not already done so.[26] The offeror may have had an opportunity to comment on the negative past performance assessment during the agency's performance assessment of the completed contract. The FAR requires that agencies evaluate contractor performance for all contracts that exceed the simplified acquisition threshold.[27] Agencies must give contractors an opportunity to comment on the government's evaluation of contractor's performance.[28]

Giving an offeror an opportunity to respond to adverse past performance evaluations does not mean the government's past performance panel must investigate every single negative remark received. A good rule of thumb: If adverse past performance is significant enough to affect the offeror's standing in the competition, the agency should pursue it with the offeror. Furthermore, even after the offeror has had the opportunity to respond to negative information, the government is free to use reasonable discretion when evaluating its impact. Evaluators should exercise good judgment and common sense.

The FAR requires agencies to communicate with offerors if information about their past performance is the determining factor preventing them from being placed within the competitive range. Such communications should address adverse past performance information to which an offeror has not had a prior opportunity to respond.[29] When the agency contemplates making an award without discussions, the past performance panel must request clarification of adverse past performance data if the offeror has not previously had an opportunity to respond to the adverse information. These clarification requests do not constitute discussions but are a limited form of information exchange intended to permit the offeror to respond to negative past performance reports without permitting other changes to the proposal.

After the evaluators review and consider all of the data, they individually score each factor for each of the offerors' past performance. The past performance panel then convenes to reach consensus on each offeror's strengths, weaknesses, and factor ratings. In cases in which an offeror or its proposed key personnel have no record of relevant previous performance, or past performance information is not available, the parties cannot be evaluated either favorably or unfavorably, per FAR 15.305(a)(2)(iv).[30] This rule can actually be favorable to companies with no past performance record. For example, one offeror might have an extensive but marginal past performance record; another offeror might have no record of past performance. The company with no past performance record could receive a higher score because the other company's extensive experience yielded negative performance assessments.

Please note that even if an offeror is new, or new to the business area, it is likely that the key personnel proposed for the contract have some relevant experience. All solicitations should, therefore, indicate that the offeror must provide a list of references indicating similar contracts on which key personnel have worked. An evaluation of the performance of the proposed key personnel on relevant contracts can be used, as appropriate, as part or all of the past performance evaluation, unless this is precluded by the evaluation scheme in the RFP.

For many evaluators, it is difficult to determine what color or numerical rating to assign a proposal if past performance data is not available. Accordingly, if none of an offeror's key personnel have relevant experience (a rare situation), the offeror's lack of past performance could be treated as an unknown performance risk: essentially neutral. Some agencies assign an offeror with no past performance information a moderate rating. For example, if the solicitation uses a five-point evaluation scheme, the offeror is given the middle rating, such as "3," "good," or "satisfactory/green." The GAO has upheld this approach because "it most closely conforms to a neutral rating."[31] In any case, the contracting officer must decide before issuing the solicitation what approach to use and must state the chosen approach in the solicitation.

If the offeror has performance history on non-relevant contracts, (i.e., it has a proven government or commercial performance record, but the record does not pertain to the type of work currently being solicited), the agency could use this information to demonstrate management potential and reduce concerns about risk.

Teaming relationships can reduce offerors' performance risk, depending on the relationships that exist within the teaming arrangement. If subcontractors will perform critical aspects of the work, evaluators should assess the past performance of these subcontractors. Agencies must be aware that evaluating subcontractor past performance poses unique concerns because the government may not disclose past performance information about a subcontractor to the prime contractor without a subcontractor's consent. So it is advisable to obtain this consent in advance. There are different ways to get the subcontractor's consent; a common approach is to include a requirement in the RFP for the prime to submit its principal subcontractors' consent with its proposal. [32] The past performance panel should carefully consider the proposed subcontractors' contribution to the overall proposed effort and the likely impact of each subcontractor on the prime's ultimate success.

After the evaluation is complete, the past performance panel members document their findings and determinations regarding each offeror's performance risk.[33] Let's review a case in which past performance experience was a determining factor in contract award.

Case Study: Past Performance

Aegis Defense Services Limited protested that the Army Corps of Engineers misevaluated the relevance of the proposals submitted by the awardee, Global Strategies Group (Integrated Security), Inc. (GSG-IS), and Aegis. Aegis stated that the Corps downgraded Aegis' past performance based on its limited experience in Afghanistan and gave GSG-IS credit for its subcontractors' experience, including contracts performed in Afghanistan.

According to the GAO decision regarding the protest,

> First, Aegis complain[ed] that it was downgraded by the Corps under the experience factor simply because its references were for contracts in Iraq, rather than Afghanistan. Aegis argue[d] that the experience that it identified in Iraq is very similar to the services required under this contract, and that the Corps had made an unreasonable distinction between experience in Iraq and experience in Afghanistan.

> The Corps respond[ed] that its evaluators concluded that the differences in the security situation between Iraq and Afghanistan were sufficiently different that it was reasonable to distinguish between them in evaluating experience and past performance. The Corps explain[ed] that Iraq is outside the Afghanistan Engineer District, the two countries have different geography, the people have different cultural practices, and [there are] different causes of unrest.

> Therefore, the Corps explained that even though Aegis had high-rated past performance in performing similar services in Iraq, given the different conditions in Afghanistan, the Corps had a reasonable basis to give Aegis a rating of 'good,' rather than a rating of "excellent," under the experience factor because the experience in Iraq was less relevant.

It is important to note that

> the RFP reasonably informed offerors that the Corps would consider the geographic location of experience in determining its relevance, and it follows that contracts performed in Afghanistan would be more relevant than contracts performed elsewhere.

In denying the protest, GAO asserted that

> the Corps could treat contracts performed in areas outside the Afghanistan Engineer District (including Iraq) as slightly less relevant based on the Corps's understanding of the differences in the operational environment in Afghanistan …. The Corps could reasonably value more highly experience in Afghanistan than experience in Iraq. [There was] nothing unreasonable about the Corps's decision to rate Aegis as 'good' under the experience factor.[34]

This case illustrates that offerors should pay close attention to the evaluation factors before determining which past performance references to use. In this case, the RFP stated a clear preference regarding the kind of experience the agency desired, and the protestor submitted references that were less relevant than the winning offeror's.

Evaluating Price or Cost

Recall from Chapter 3 that cost or price must be evaluated in every source selection.[35] Normally, competition establishes price reasonableness, and when contracting on a firm fixed-price or fixed-price with economic price adjustment basis, comparing the proposed prices should satisfy the price analysis requirement, so a detailed cost analysis isn't necessary.

The cost panel is responsible for evaluating the proposed cost or price of the proposals and establishing price reasonableness. The panel looks for inconsistencies, math errors, logic errors, unsupported assertions, and inappropriate estimating methodologies in each cost proposal.[36] See Figure 9-4 for an illustration of the cost panel's evaluation process.

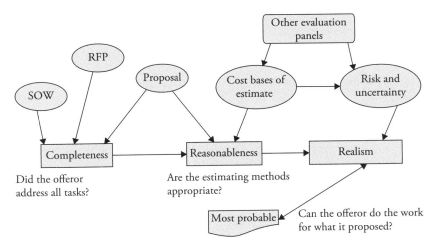

Figure 9-4   The Cost Evaluation Process[37]

When contracting on a cost-reimbursement basis, evaluators must perform a *cost realism* analysis to determine what the government should realistically expect to pay for the proposed effort, how well each offeror understands the work, and whether each offeror is able to perform the contract.

The contracting officer documents the results of the cost or price analysis.[38] The cost panel should coordinate with the non-cost evaluators as necessary to ensure consistency between the proposed costs and other proposal volumes. Coordination between cost and technical panels benefits both the non-cost and cost evaluators. For example, if evaluators find a deficiency in the technical proposal, it can reveal a weakness in the cost proposal. Cost evaluators may find that the staffing levels an offeror proposed in its cost volume don't match what it proposed in the management volume.

Although communication between evaluation panels is important, the evaluation team must protect the cost data to avoid unintentional bias on the part of the technical evaluators. In most cases, the cost panel does not disclose cost information to the non-cost evaluators. Communications may be limited to specific questions about staffing levels and equipment proposed or the corresponding costs of those elements. Some agencies permit all evaluators to access the cost proposal; others do not. For example:

- The EPA acquisition regulation states, "In accordance with FAR 15.305 (a)(4), the contracting officer may release the cost/price proposals to those members of the evaluation team who are evaluating proposals at his/her discretion."[39]

- The U.S. Special Operations Command FAR supplement states:

  The Source Selection Authority (SSA) may allow access to cost information to all source selection evaluation team members. If access to cost data is to be limited or denied to the technical team or others, describe the limitations and rationale for it in the SSP [Source Selection Plan].[40]

- The Navy Marine FAR supplement puts restrictions on sharing cost information with technical evaluators:

  The sharing of cost information with the technical evaluation team, and any limitations on the timing and extent of such sharing, should be addressed during the planning for the source selection. [Heads of the contracting activity] may establish specific procedural requirements for approving, documenting and/or varying from plans related to such sharing.[41]

- The Army lets the SSA determine if technical evaluators can access the cost proposal. "The SSA shall determine whether cost information will be provided to the technical evaluators, when and what information shall be provided, and under what conditions."[42]

Agency personnel should consult their FAR supplement or other agency regulations regarding technical team access to the cost proposal. Limitations may be set on what information may be shared. Keep in mind that cost information includes elements beyond just the total proposed cost, such as overhead and general and administrative rates.

Analyzing Price

Price analysis is the examination and evaluation of a proposed price without evaluating its separate cost elements and proposed profit or fee. Price analysis is used when cost or pricing data are not required.[43] (See Chapter 1 and FAR 15.404-3 for cost or pricing data submission requirements.) The level of price analysis will vary depending on the specific circumstances of each acquisition. For fixed-price contracts, the evaluation could be as simple as comparing the offered prices to ensure the contract price is fair and reasonable.

The government may use various price analysis techniques and procedures to ensure a fair and reasonable price. Examples of such techniques include, but are not limited to, the following:

- Comparing proposed prices received in response to the solicitation
- Comparing previously proposed prices and previous government and commercial contract prices with current proposed prices for the same or similar items, if doing so can establish both the validity of the comparison and the reasonableness of the previous price(s)
- Using parametric estimating methods or applying rough yardsticks (such as dollars per pound or per horsepower, lines of computer code, or other units) to highlight significant inconsistencies that warrant additional pricing inquiry
- Comparing proposed prices against competitive published price lists, published market prices of commodities, similar indices, and discount or rebate arrangements
- Comparing proposed prices with independent government cost estimates
- Comparing proposed prices with prices obtained through market research for the same or similar items
- Analyzing pricing information provided by the offeror.

The FAR states that the first two techniques are preferred, but if the contracting officer determines that information on competitive proposed prices or previous contract prices is not available or is insufficient to determine whether the price is fair and reasonable, the contracting officer may use any of the remaining techniques, as appropriate to the circumstances.

Value analysis involves objectively evaluating a product's function and its related cost to give insight into the product's worth. A contracting officer may use value analysis in conjunction with the price analysis techniques listed above.[44]

Price analysis cannot be performed for cost-reimbursement and level-of-effort contracts. In these situations, the agency must analyze costs for completeness, reasonableness, and realism.

Analyzing Cost

Evaluators use cost analysis to determine the reasonableness of individual cost elements when cost or pricing data are required. Agencies may also use cost analysis to evaluate information other than cost or pricing data to determine cost reasonableness or cost realism. Such information may include pricing information, sales information, or cost information, and includes cost or pricing data for which certification is determined inapplicable after submission.[45]

Cost analysis involves reviewing and evaluating the separate cost elements and profit or fee in an offeror's proposal (including cost or pricing data or information other than cost or pricing data), then applying reasoned judgment to determine how well the proposed costs represent what the cost of the contract should be, assuming reasonable economy and efficiency.

The government may use various cost analysis techniques and procedures to ensure a fair and reasonable price, given the circumstances of the acquisition. Such techniques and procedures include the following:

- Verifying cost or pricing data and evaluation of cost elements, including:
  - The necessity for, and reasonableness of, proposed costs, including allowances for contingencies
  - A projection of the offeror's cost trends, on the basis of current and historical cost or pricing data
  - The reasonableness of estimates generated by appropriately calibrated and validated parametric models or cost-estimating relationships
  - The application of audited or negotiated indirect cost rates, labor rates, and cost of money or other factors.
- Evaluating the effect of the offeror's current practices on future costs. In conducting this evaluation, the contracting officer shall ensure that the effects of inefficient or uneconomical past practices are not continued in the future. The company should learn to improve practices, not continue uneconomical ones. For example, a painting company using rollers rather than sprayers to paint a large area will

take longer to complete the task, thereby increasing costs. Therefore, the government should project future costs by estimating the time it would take to paint the area using a sprayer.

- When pricing production of recently developed complex equipment, the contracting officer should perform a trend analysis of basic labor and materials, even in periods of relative price stability.
- Comparing costs proposed by the offeror for individual cost elements with the:
  - Actual costs previously incurred by the same offeror
  - Previous cost estimates from the offeror or from other offerors for the same or similar items
  - Other cost estimates received in response to the government's request
  - Independent government cost estimates made by technical personnel
  - Forecasts of planned expenditures.
- Verifying that the offeror's cost submissions are in accordance with the contract cost principles and procedures in FAR part 31 and, when applicable, the requirements and procedures in the Cost Accounting Standards.
- Reviewing the cost proposal to determine if any cost or pricing data necessary to make the contractor's proposal accurate, complete, and current have not been submitted or identified in writing by the contractor. If there are such data, the contracting officer shall attempt to obtain them and negotiate, either using the data or making satisfactory allowance for the incomplete data.
- Analyzing the results of any make-or-buy program reviews in evaluating subcontract costs.[46] A make-or-buy program review identifies major items that the prime contractor will provide (make) and major items that a subcontractor will provide (buy).[47] Subcontract cost detail may be provided directly to the government by the subcontractor, and the prime contractor may not have access to that data. Sometimes the subcontractor prohibits the prime contractor from seeing this data because the prime could be a competitor on another solicitation.

Reviewing Historical Cost Information

The cost panel reviews the available files from an offeror's contracts with a particular firm to learn about the offeror's pricing practices, the quality of historical pricing information provided by the offeror, and any precedents established in past negotiations. Evaluators should, however, be cautious about using historical information on contract costs. They should always consider differences between the past and the current contracting situations.

Identifying problems that may have affected previous proposals or past contracts and how they were resolved can give the contracting officer insight into the accuracy of current estimates. The contracting officer can ask and answer these questions when reviewing historical information:

- Does the offeror have a history of problems controlling costs?
  - **Issue:** Did the offeror experience cost overruns attributable to historical problems that do not or should not exist today?
  - **Impact:** If the contracting officer does not look at historical cost projections critically and carefully, he or she could miss or overlook the offeror's inflated contract cost estimates.
- Does the offeror have a history of not providing adequate cost estimate support?
  - **Issue:** Proposal errors can seriously affect the contracting officer's ability to perform an effective cost analysis.
  - **Impact:** If a firm has a track record of problems in a certain area, the contracting officer should take care to ensure that similar problems do not exist in the current proposal.
- Does the offeror have a history of over- or underestimating costs?
  - **Issue:** How accurate have this offeror's proposal estimates been in the past?
  - **Impact:** Historical proposal tendencies may help the contracting officer identify proposed costs that require special scrutiny.
- What were the major cost-related problems and negotiation points in past contract negotiations?
  - **Issue:** The price negotiation memorandum (PNM) should identify cost-related problems and major points that came up during fact-finding and negotiation. These same issues may come up in the current proposal.
  - **Impact:** Referring to past PNMs can help the contracting officer identify key areas of analysis and explain how they were handled.
- How did the negotiated price compare with the proposed price?
  - **Issue:** The PNM should explain the differences between the proposed price, the government objectives, and the price negotiated.
  - **Impact:** These differences may give the contracting officer insight into potential weaknesses in the firm's current proposal.
- Were any pricing precedents established during previous negotiations that may affect the current negotiations?
  - **Issue:** Is there a history of dealing with this offeror?
  - **Impact:** Past negotiations may have included an agreement on how to handle a specific type of cost in specific situations. Such agreements may establish a precedent that the contracting officer should consider in the current analysis. However, be careful; do not blindly accept precedents that do not make sense in the current situation.[48]

In addition to the above questions, evaluators should identify any differences between the contracting situations of the past and the current contracting situation. These differences may help the contracting officer identify cost elements requiring special attention during cost analysis. At a minimum, consider the following questions:

- Have there been any changes in production methods?
  - **What:** Changes in the production methods.
  - **Why:** If the offeror has improved production methods, leading to reductions in costs (e.g., labor, material, or scrap), those improvements must be reflected in projected costs.
- Have there been any changes in the offeror's make-or-buy program?
  - **What:** If the offeror has changed component sources, those changes should be considered in cost estimates. Producing previously subcontracted items in house will normally increase in-house costs and reduce subcontract costs.
  - **Why:** Give special attention to the effect such changes have on total cost. If such a change increases total cost, offeror make-or-buy decision criteria require further examination.
- Have contract requirements changed?
  - **What:** Changes in government requirements documents or business terms will likely affect costs.
  - **Why:** For example, if a tolerance has been relaxed or a specific process or inspection is no longer required, projected costs should change accordingly.
- Have the offeror's accounting practices changed?
  - **What:** If the offeror has changed procedures for classification or accumulation of a particular cost, projected costs may be affected.
  - **Why:** For example, if a particular type of cost was previously classified as a direct cost and is now classified as an indirect cost, expect changes in the totals for both cost groupings. Oversight agencies such as the Defense Contract Audit Agency document approved changes in accounting practices.
- Have business or general economic conditions changed?
  - **What:** Have economic conditions changed?
  - **Why:** Changes in business or general economic conditions will also affect costs. The contracting officer must adjust historical costs to consider these changes. The most obvious example is inflation/deflation. [49]

In addition to conducting a cost analysis, many agencies also evaluate cost-reimbursement and level-of-effort contracts for completeness, reasonableness, and realism.

Assessing Completeness

The cost panel assesses a cost proposal's completeness by reviewing it to ensure that the offeror submitted all of the information required by the RFP. The cost panel prepares the necessary reports as appropriate to identify any deficient, missing, inconsistent, or ambiguous information.

Next, the cost panel reviews the cost proposal for consistency. The panel traces cost buildups described in the basis of estimate (BOE) through all of the summary sheets. Again, the evaluators note inconsistencies, weaknesses, and discrepancies in the appropriate report.

The cost panel prepares a cost report that the contracting officer uses to help determine the competitive range if the agency decides to enter discussions. The last step in the completeness evaluation is verifying that the assumptions in and scope of the cost proposal are consistent with the assumptions and scope presented in the other volumes of the offeror's proposal. Technical liaisons have a critical role in this evaluation. After finishing the completeness assessment, the cost panel moves on to determine cost reasonableness.

Assessing Reasonableness

The cost panel determines the reasonableness of the offeror's cost-estimating methods by first assessing the appropriateness of each offeror's basis of estimate against the proposed item. In other words, the panel considers the degree to which the supporting data and logic the offeror provides explain the estimate.

If an offeror proposes delivering a product or service it has many years of experience delivering, its proposal should include actual cost data from similar contract work. Can the costs proposed be independently calculated using the historical cost information provided? Is the conclusion the offeror presents what one could reasonably expect?

Evaluators assess how well offerors applied the estimating method. Here the cost panel may find math errors, errors in logic, or unsupported assertions; the cost panel prepares the appropriate documentation when it finds such problems. This reasonableness determination gives the cost panel a thorough understanding of the offeror's cost-estimating method. A reasonable cost-estimating method is the first indicator that an offeror prepared a realistic cost proposal. Evaluating cost realism is the next step.

Assessing Realism

According to FAR 15.404-1(d)(1), cost realism analysis is "the process of independently reviewing and evaluating specific elements of each offeror's proposed cost estimate to determine if the estimated proposed cost elements are realistic for the work proposed; reflect a clear understanding of the requirements; and are consistent with the unique methods of performance and materials described in the offeror's technical proposal."[50]

The FAR requires agencies to conduct a cost realism analysis on "cost-reimbursement contracts to determine the probable cost of performance for each offeror. The probable cost may differ from the proposed cost and should reflect the government's best estimate of the cost of any contract that is most likely to result from the offeror's proposal. The agency uses probable cost to determine the best value."[51]

An agency may also perform a cost realism analysis on a competitive fixed-price incentive contract or, in exceptional cases, on other competitive fixed-price type contracts if offerors may not understand new requirements, there are quality concerns, or past experience indicates that contractors' proposed costs have resulted in quality or service shortfalls. Evaluators may use the resulting analysis when assessing performance risk and making a responsibility determination. However, the agency must evaluate the proposals using the criteria in the solicitation, and the offered prices shall not be adjusted as a result of the analysis.[52]

Cost realism can be the most important element of any source selection decision because it forms the basis for the offeror's evaluated cost. The manner in which cost realism is determined is a function of several considerations, including:

- The nature of the item being procured (e.g., a systems engineering/technical assistance contract versus a major system design and procurement)
- The size of the procurement
- The importance of cost relative to non-cost considerations.

Because proposals do not always provide the type of cost information needed to verify realism, the cost panel may prepare a most probable cost (MPC) assessment using an independent cost estimate. For acquisitions that lead to selecting a program development and production contractor, the MPC includes the life cycle cost to the government (as defined in the solicitation). The cost panel performs a quantitative assessment of cost risk to assure that they present all alternatives at the same cost risk level (e.g., 50 percent confidence level).

Another component of determining whether a cost proposal is realistic is verifying that the offeror prepared the cost estimate in accordance with the proposed scope of work. The cost panel determines the realism of the offeror's cost estimate by:

1. Establishing that the offeror competently applied a reasonable methodology to the scope of work; or

2. Showing a comparable cost result by preparing an independent cost estimate based on verifiable, empirical cost data; or

3. Using a combination of (1) and (2) above.

Most often, it is necessary to rely on an MPC derived by an independent cost estimate. Some agencies use cost estimating models based as much as possible on actual experience. It is important for the cost and technical panels to communicate with each other during this process.

The cost realism analysis enables the cost panel to determine the most probable cost (MPC) of performance for each offeror. The MPC represents the most likely cost to be incurred by the offeror should that firm be awarded the contract. This precludes an award decision based upon overly optimistic cost estimates by offerors where risks of an overrun may be significant.

The MPC should reflect the cost panel's best estimate of the cost of the contract likely to result from the offeror's proposal. This estimate is determined by adjusting each offeror's proposed cost and fee up or down, as appropriate based upon the cost realism assessment. These adjustments can be made for inconsistencies, math errors, logic errors, unsupported assertions, or inappropriate estimating methodologies in the offeror's cost proposal.

The MPC estimates developed for each offeror are used to evaluate and compare proposals and ultimately to select the proposal expected to result in the best value to the government. The MPC is used only in making the best value determination and not for setting the contract price.[53]

When using the trade-off process, identifying proposal strengths, weaknesses, risks, and deficiencies is crucial, because the contracting officer considers these items when determining the competitive range, and specific information on the relative strengths and weaknesses form the basis for trade-off analysis and the source selection decision.[54] The agency indicates in the RFP if a most probable cost analysis will be used in the trade-off process. In complex or high-dollar-value acquisitions, the scope proposed by the offerors can vary, and the MPC can more accurately reflect the true cost to the government of each offeror's proposal.

Evaluators determine the *probable cost* of a proposal by adjusting each offeror's proposed cost (and fee, when appropriate) to reflect any additions or reductions in cost elements to realistic levels based on the results of the cost realism analysis. For example, if the offeror proposes using a certified professional senior project manager with twenty years' experience, is the proposed hourly rate realistic for that level of experience? If the technical proposal suggests using advanced technical processes and materials, does the cost proposal adequately cover all of the elements proposed? Any inconsistencies may indicate that the offeror does not fully understand the requirement and might not be able to perform what it promised in the technical proposal.[55]

Many agencies use an independent government cost estimate (IGCE) to help with the cost analysis process, but the IGCE should not determine cost reasonableness, realism, or completeness. The individual evaluators must make independent determinations of these factors in comparison with the technical and management proposals.

Now, let's look at a case regarding an agency's reliance on its independent cost estimate when conducting a most probable cost assessment.

Case Study: The Role of the Independent Cost Estimate in Cost Assessment

Honeywell Technology Solutions, Inc., and Wyle Laboratories, Inc., protested the award of a contract to Sverdrup Technology, Inc., under a National Aeronautics and Space Administration (NASA) RFP for test operations services at the John C. Stennis Space Center and George C. Marshall Space Flight Center. The protesters argued that the agency's cost realism evaluation of proposals was unreasonable. According to the GAO decision on the protest, the RFP specified that the agency would evaluate proposals for cost realism and noted that because

> "the proposed cost of the work (and rates proposed) may be a significant indicator of an offeror's understanding and ability to perform the PWS," the proposals' "Mission Suitability scores may be adjusted for lack of cost realism."

> The RFP included a table detailing the point deductions that would be made to mission suitability scores based on the percentage difference between the proposed costs and the most probable costs as calculated by the agency (e.g., an adjustment of 6 to 10 percent to an offeror's proposed costs to arrive at a most probable cost as calculated by the agency would result in a deduction of 50 points from the proposal's mission suitability score).

The protesters argued

> that the agency's cost realism evaluation was unreasonable. They argue[d] that the [independent government staffing estimate was] unreasonable and that the agency used the IGSE in an overly mechanical manner, with the result being that the offerors' proposed staffing levels were adjusted upwards to approximate the IGSE, with concomitant increases in the most probable costs associated with their proposals, even though the protesters' proposed staffing levels were reasonable and consistent with the RFP.

The GAO determined that the written record, as well as testimony of three members of the source evaluation board (SEB), was

> inconsistent or incomplete to such an extent that [they could not] find the agency's evaluation of proposals to be reasonable. Specifically, the SEB found in the technical evaluation of Honeywell's proposal that its proposed staffing level was appropriate and warranted a "strength," and then determined in the cost realism evaluation that Honeywell's proposed staffing level was significantly inadequate.

GAO asserted that the agency

> did not reasonably reconcile this anomaly in the contemporaneous record or at the hearing. Moreover, the record raise[d] serious questions concerning the reasonableness of the agency's development and use of the IGSE in the cost evaluation to determine the reasonableness of the offerors' proposed staffing levels.

> Regarding Honeywell's proposed staffing, the SEB identified nine "strengths" in Honeywell's proposal and one "weakness" in evaluating Honeywell's proposal under the technical performance subfactor paragraph relating to the staffing plans.... Based upon [the SEB's] review of two exhibits in Honeywell's proposal pertaining to its proposed staffing plan (detailing Honeywell's staffing by, among other things, [performance work statement] section, skill category, number of personnel, and minimum qualification standards proposed), the SEB found that one exhibit "demonstrates that Honeywell has thought through the critical skill mix required to operate the [centers]," and that the other exhibit "further demonstrates a strong knowledge of the qualification standards required by each permanent member of the [contract work team]." ... Honeywell's proposal received an overall rating of "excellent" under the technical performance subfactor.

During its cost realism evaluation of Honeywell's proposal, however,

> "the same SEB found that the proposal had 'limited supporting rationale for being 45 [full time equivalents] below the government estimate from day one.'" ... The contemporaneous documentation of the agency's cost realism evaluation of Honeywell's proposal with regard to proposed staffing is two pages long, with only one page actually addressing the agency's "rationale" for the adjustments made. On this page, the agency identified each of the specific skill categories where adjustments were found to be necessary in the proposed staffing, typically concluding in each case, with little further elaboration, that Honeywell had not provided "sufficient rationale" for its proposed staffing. This evaluation resulted in a significant increase in the evaluated most probable cost of Honeywell's proposal, as well as a significant deduction from the proposal's mission suitability score, such that Honeywell's proposal score fell from the 'excellent' range to the "very good" range.

The record, however, did not

discuss or attempt to reconcile the SEB's conclusions in the cost evaluation, where Honeywell's staffing plan was deemed "inadequate" by 43 FTEs, with the evaluation of the staffing plan under the technical performance subfactor, where Honeywell's plan was found to contain "strengths" and an "appropriate" number of proposed personnel. Thus, the ... record provide[d] no basis to conclude whether the SEB's evaluation of Honeywell's proposed staffing under the technical performance subfactor or with regard to cost realism, or either, was reasonable.

The Chairperson of the SEB conceded that the evaluation record was inconsistent with regard to Honeywell's staffing plan.... He also testified that "the Honeywell staffing was not unreasonable." ... The Chairperson added later in his testimony, however, that Honeywell's proposed staffing level was inadequate, and that the SEB ultimately concluded that Honeywell "could not do the job without risk with the number that they proposed."

Given the inability of the agency to credibly explain the apparent inconsistency between its evaluation of Honeywell's staffing plan under the technical performance subfactor and its cost realism evaluation, [the GAO] could not find the agency's determinations to be reasonable with regard to either its technical performance subfactor evaluation or its cost realism evaluation.

[T]he record also raises serious questions as to both the development of the IGSE and its use during the evaluation process.... The IGSE was used in what appears to be a mechanical way in the cost realism evaluation. A reasonably derived estimate of labor hours and material costs can provide an objective standard against which the realism of proposed costs can be measured.... However, an agency may not mechanically apply that estimate to determine the most probable costs associated with proposals, without regard to the individual proposal's technical approach.

This is so because in some instances an estimate has limited applicability to a particular proposal due to, for example, the skill of the labor force or innovative work methods proposed. In those cases, any rigid reliance on the government estimate could have the effect of arbitrarily and unfairly penalizing (or rewarding) one firm and depriving the government of the benefit available from the different approaches of the various offerors. Accordingly, in order to undertake a proper cost realism evaluation, the agency must independently analyze the realism of an offeror's proposed costs based upon its particular approach, personnel, and other circumstances.

The record does not indicate that the agency engaged in an absolutely rigid application of the IGSE to the offerors' proposals. There do appear to be instances where the agency accepted proposed staffing for a particular function or labor category that was less than that reflected in the IGSE, and in other instances, the agency made adjustments to an offeror's proposed staffing that put the probable staffing associated with the proposal at a level between that set forth in the proposal and that provided by the agency in its IGSE.

Nevertheless, the record also reflects that in the vast majority of instances where an offeror proposed a staffing level that differed from the IGSE, the staffing level was adjusted during the cost evaluation to the IGSE staffing level, with the primary documented reason by the agency being that the proposal did not provide 'sufficient rationale' for the proposed staffing, with little further elaboration.

The SEB adjusted the staffing levels proposed by all five offerors to within 4 FTEs of the IGSE of 293.... This, along with the sparse evaluation documentation, suggests that the IGSE was used in a mechanical way in the cost realism evaluation, notwithstanding the encouragement in the RFP for proposing innovative approaches. That the agency used the IGSE in the cost realism evaluation in a mechanical way was supported by other evidence in the record.

[Using] the IGSE as a "baseline" to which the offerors' staffing levels were adjusted for cost realism analysis purposes appears inconsistent with the view of the SEB member who prepared the Stennis [Space Center] estimate that the total number of positions listed by the incumbent contractor (182) was "pretty close" to his estimate of 223 positions .... It seems incongruous that the SEB member who prepared this estimate was not troubled by its significant variance from the incumbent's staffing estimate, yet when the estimate was used in the evaluation, proposals with different staffing levels were adjusted to approximate the IGSE.

Of most significance in showing that the IGSE was used in a mechanical way [was] the fact that Honeywell's proposed staffing was characterized as "appropriate" during the evaluation of its proposal under the technical performance subfactor, but was then adjusted upwards by 43 FTEs to within 2 FTEs of the IGSE during the cost realism evaluation.

GAO found the agency's cost realism evaluation "unreasonable."[56]

This case illustrates the importance of documenting the basis for any cost realism adjustments and not mechanically applying adjustments based upon the independent government cost or staffing estimate. To support the agency cost realism assessment, the evaluators must explain how and why any adjustments were made. Adjusting proposals by comparison to an IGSE essentially levels the cost proposals of all the offerors. In addition, using an FTE analysis alone is not a good measure unless the evaluators also look at the skill mix of the positions.

For additional resources on conducting cost or price analysis, readers may consult the Contract Pricing Reference Guides. The Air Force Institute of Technology (AFIT) and the Federal Acquisition Institute (FAI) jointly prepared this five-volume set of contract pricing reference guides. The titles include:

- Price Analysis
- Quantitative Techniques for Contract Pricing
- Cost Analysis
- Advanced Issues in Contract Pricing
- Federal Contract Negotiation Techniques.

These references provide detailed discussions and examples of applying pricing policies to pricing problems. They are intended to instruct and offer professional guidance and are available online at http://www.acq.osd.mil/dpap/cpf/contract_pricing_reference_guides.html.[57]

EVALUATING ORAL PRESENTATIONS

Agencies may ask offerors to give oral presentations to streamline the source selection process or to allow the SSET to get a better understanding of each offeror's technical approach or past performance. Oral presentations may be given at any time in the acquisition process; their timing and content are subject to the same restrictions as written information. Such elements as an offeror's capability, past performance, work plans or approaches, staffing resources, transition plans, or sample tasks (or other types of tests) may be suitable topics for oral presentations. One effective way of evaluating the offeror's experience and problem-solving skills, for example, is by giving a "pop quiz" where evaluators ask the offeror what it might do in a particular situation and give the offeror a time limit to answer.

When the RFP requires an oral presentation, it provides offerors with guidance on preparing the presentation. It should state:

- The types of information that must be presented orally and the associated evaluation factors that will be used.
- Whether prime or subcontractor personnel are required to give the oral presentations, or if a hired consultant who will not work on the contract may do so instead, and whether any or all the offeror's key personnel must attend.
- The requirements regarding, and any limitations or prohibitions on, using written material or other media to supplement the oral presentations.
- The location, date, and time oral presentations will be given.
- The restrictions governing the time permitted for each oral presentation.
- The scope and content of exchanges that may occur between the evaluators and the offeror's representatives as part of the oral presentations.

It is important to know whether the government intends to conduct discussions during oral presentations. If the solicitation does not permit discussions during oral presentations, the CO must be careful to monitor questions and answers to ensure that they do not cross the line and become discussions. The distinction between clarifications, communications, and discussions is discussed in more detail in Chapter 10.

When an oral presentation includes information that the parties intend to incorporate in the contract as material terms or conditions, the CO must document that information in writing so it can be incorporated into the contract. It is important to note that the agency may not incorporate oral statements by reference into the contract.[58]

Contracting officers should schedule presentations promptly after receipt of proposals, determine the sequence of the presentations, and inform the offerors of the schedule. All oral presentation panel evaluators should attend each presentation. In the rare instance an evaluator cannot attend, the presentation should be recorded on video. Encourage the source selection authority to attend as well.

Some agencies use a lottery to determine the sequence of presentations by offerors. The time between the first and the last presentation should be as short as practical to minimize any advantage to the later presenters. It's important to allow adequate time between presentations for evaluators to document their observations and assessments.[59]

The RFP should contain clear and concise instructions on the amount of material to be presented, and the contracting officer must strictly enforce these requirements. Typically, agencies regulate the following elements of an oral presentation:

- The number of presentation charts
- The font size used in the charts
- The time allotted for the presentation
- The content
- The number of participants
- The due date for the oral presentation charts (often due to the government on the same date the other proposal volumes are due).

The agency should have a dedicated facility for conducting and evaluating the oral presentations. It is important to video-record oral presentation sessions, including all remarks and instructions made by government personnel. These video recordings can be referred to later by the evaluators (individually or as a group) if necessary. It is also a good practice to give a copy of the recording to the offeror, as well, so that all parties have identical records of the presentation. If oral presentations take place before the competitive range is established, evaluators must be careful to avoid entering into discussions with the offerors, although offerors may ask clarification questions.

Once the oral presentations are complete, the evaluators should treat the presentation charts, their notes from the presentation sessions, and the video recordings just like any other part of the proposal. That is, they should compare the material against the evaluation criteria, develop findings accordingly, and protect the information as source selection sensitive data. Generally, evaluators should not consider presentation style or demonstrated public speaking ability in developing findings. The evaluators should focus their evaluations on the content of the presentation, not the style or flair with which it is delivered. [60]

SCORING EVALUATIONS

By this point in the evaluation process, the evaluators have identified the strengths and weaknesses of each proposal. The next steps are to assign degrees of strength or weakness, then to give adjectival, color, or numeric ratings to the proposal, all based on the criteria in the source selection plan or source selection evaluation guide. Table 9-2 shows an example of degrees of strength and weakness.

Evaluators must document and justify proposal strengths and weaknesses for each factor based on the stated evaluation standards. If a proposed approach exceeds the relevant evaluation standard, the evaluator records it as a strength and assigns a degree of strength. Likewise, if a proposed approach is below standards, the evaluator records a weakness and assigns the appropriate degree of weakness. If a proposed approach meets the government's expectations, evaluators assign a "meets standards" rating; this rating does not necessarily require justification.

Determining the degree of a strength or weakness is subjective and is left to each evaluator's experienced judgment, but part of the evaluators' training should include instruction in calibrating the degrees of strengths and weaknesses for each of the evaluation standards.

Table 9-2 Sample Degrees of Strength and Weakness

Strength		Weakness	
+	Slightly above standards/expectations	–	Slightly below standards/expectations
++	Clearly above standards/expectations	– –	Clearly below standards/expectations
+++	Significantly above standards/expectations	– – –	Significantly below standards/expectations

Identifying specific strengths and weaknesses gives the SSA the information he or she needs to make a reasonable and rational basis for the selection decision. Detailed information on strengths and weaknesses is also needed by contracting officials to debrief unsuccessful offerors, as required by FAR 15.506(d), as well as by contracting and legal personnel in order to defend against any protests that might be filed with the agency, GAO, or the U.S. Court of Federal Claims.[61]

All evaluators must be especially thorough in writing the narratives that support their evaluation and rating scores because the agency uses them for several important purposes:

- Explaining individual evaluations during the factor group consensus process
- Preparing panel reports
- Developing SSA briefings that are used to determine the competitive range and ultimately the successful offeror
- Preparing debriefings for unsuccessful offerors.

The supporting narrative also helps ensure that the evaluators consistently applied the criteria. This is particularly important when using a numeric scoring system, because it is too easy to rely on the numeric rating as opposed to the actual strengths or weaknesses of the proposal to determine the proposal's attributes.[62] Thus, it is critical that all evaluators' narratives be specific, clear, concise, and contain supportable statements.

After determining the degrees of strength and weakness for each proposal, the evaluators need to score the proposals, as defined in the source selection plan or source selection evaluation guide. Table 9-3 illustrates a sample scoring scheme.

Next, let's look at a case in which a protester questioned an agency's application of the scoring methodology.

CASE STUDY: SCORING METHODOLOGY

Wackenhut Services, Inc., protested the award of a contract to Coastal International Security, Inc., under an RFP issued by NASA for providing agency-wide protective services. Wackenhut challenged NASA's technical evaluation and source selection decision.

According to the GAO decision in response to the protest, the RFP set forth three evaluation factors: mission suitability, past performance, and price. The RFP indicated that the mission suitability factor was more important than the past performance factor, and that when these two factors were combined, they were "significantly more important than the Price factor."

Table 9-3   Sample Numerical/Adjectival/Color Scoring Scheme[63]

Numerical	Adjectival	Color	Definition or standard
10	Excellent	Blue	The proposal demonstrates an excellent understanding of requirements and has an approach that significantly exceeds performance or capability standards. It has exceptional strengths that will significantly benefit the government.
8	Good	Green	The proposal demonstrates a good understanding of requirements, and the approach exceeds performance or capability standards. It has one or more strengths that will benefit the government.
5	Satisfactory	Yellow	The proposal demonstrates an acceptable understanding of requirements, and the approach meets performance or capability standards. The solution is acceptable. There are few or no strengths.
3	Marginal approach	Amber	The proposal demonstrates a shallow understanding of requirements and only marginally meets performance or capability standards necessary for minimal but acceptable contract performance.
0	Unsatisfactory	Red	The proposal fails to meet performance or capability standards. Requirements can only be met with major changes to the proposal.

The mission suitability factor comprised the four following subfactors, scored according to the following weights:

- Technical approach (425 points)
- Management approach (375 points)
- Small business participation approach (100 points)
- Safety and health approach (100 points).

According to the protest decision,

> The agency established a source evaluation board (SEB) and based upon the findings of the SEB, the source selection authority (SSA) decided to establish a competitive range for the purpose of holding discussions limited to Coastal and Wackenhut. After receiving Coastal's and Wackenhut's responses to discussion questions and clarifications, and considering oral presentations, the SEB's final evaluation findings reflected [the results shown in Table 9-4.]

The decision continues,

> Overall, for the mission suitability factor, the SEB evaluated Wackenhut as having nine significant strengths as compared to five for Coastal. Wackenhut and Coastal were found to have 20 and 21 "regular strengths" and [seven and four] "regular weaknesses," respectively. Neither offeror's proposal was evaluated as having any significant weaknesses.

Table 9-4 Wackenhut Protest Scoring Summary

	Coastal		Wackenhut	
	Adjectival rating	Points	Adjectival rating	Points
Mission suitability	Very good	880	Very good	901
• Technical approach	Excellent	387	Excellent	395
• Management approach	Very good	338	Excellent	356
• Small business	Good	70	Good	51
• Safety and health	Very good	85	Very good	85
Past performance	Very good		Very good	
Price	$1.186 billion		$[deleted]	

As relevant to the protest, in rating Wackenhut's proposal as excellent under the technical approach subfactor, with 395 points, the SEB found that Wackenhut's proposal included ... four significant strengths. In rating Coastal as excellent under the technical approach subfactor, with 387 points, the SEB identified and documented two significant strengths.

In scoring Wackenhut's proposal as excellent under the management approach subfactor, with 356 points, the SEB identified and documented four additional significant strengths .... In rating Coastal as very good under this same subfactor, with 338 points, the SEB identified two significant strengths.

In his source selection statement, the SSA stated:

> Assessing the importance of the strengths Offerors received was more revealing to me than the number of strengths each offeror received. I recognized Coastal had customized its proposal to achieve the goals of the [NASA protective services contract] with a continuous improvement plan and its intended web portal. Based upon the value of this customization, I found the Mission Suitability proposal from Coastal was basically equal to the Mission Suitability proposal submitted by Wackenhut.

GAO's decision continues,

> In assigning ratings and scores, the SEB Chairperson explained that, with respect to significant strengths, it was the content of the offerors' proposals, as reflected in the specific findings, which was used to rate and score offerors. The SEB Chairperson stated that the process of assigning ratings and scores was not merely a "numbers game" driven by the mere number of significant strengths identified in an offeror's proposal.

GAO found the agency's evaluation process "unobjectionable":

> At the core, Wackenhut [sought] a mathematical or mechanical consideration of the number of significant strengths in determining the evaluation ratings and attributing

points to the offerors' proposals. Adjectival ratings and point scores, [noted GAO,] are mere tools in the evaluation and selection process and should not be mechanically derived or applied. Rather, it is the agency's qualitative findings in connection with its evaluation of proposals—in this case the documented written narratives underlying and justifying the SEB's findings of particular significant strengths—that govern the reasonableness of an agency's assessment of offerors' proposals.

Here, the offerors' proposals were evaluated independently against the RFP's evaluation criteria and the evaluation ratings and scores simply served as an expression of the agency's exercise of its discretion in making its qualitative findings. As a consequence, there is nothing *per se* improper with Coastal and Wackenhut receiving similar ratings and scores under the mission suitability factor, and related subfactors, notwithstanding the fact that Wackenhut's proposal had more significant strengths as compared to the proposal submitted by Coastal.

While Wackenhut argues that its greater number of significant strengths should have been the dispositive discriminator, rendering the SSA's finding of equivalence unreasonable, as noted above, what is important is not the number of significant strengths, but rather the qualitative findings underlying these significant strengths. In this regard, the SSA's determination that the proposals were essentially equal qualitatively was entirely consistent with the SEB's evaluation results, which, notwithstanding Wackenhut's greater number of significant strengths, reflected only a slim advantage.

GAO denied the protest.

This case illustrates the importance of the narrative documentation in the source selection process (the evaluators had to refer to their notes to respond to the protest) and of consistently applying the chosen scoring methodology to proposals. It also indicates that an agency's discretion and judgment won't be second-guessed by the GAO in the event of a protest. This is usually the case. As long as the agency followed its process as stated in the RFP and/or SSP, then GAO typically doesn't second-guess the agency. If the agency doesn't follow the RFP and/or SSP, then GAO typically sustains the protest but doesn't specify which company should win the contract. On a rare occasion, GAO overturns an award.

The next section details how evaluators can properly document their assessments.

DOCUMENTING EVALUATIONS

Proper documentation of the entire source selection process is a critical aspect of source selection with a major impact on the success of the procurement. While the evaluators rate proposals only against the RFP's evaluation criteria, the source selection authority bases his or her decision on a comparative assessment of proposals against all source selection criteria in the solicitation. Thus, the source selection process requires proper documentation that can help the SSA understand the rationale the evaluation team used. The documentation may also give the SSA confidence that the findings of the source evaluation board are consistent with the stated evaluation criteria and scoring plan.

While the SSA may use reports and analyses prepared by others, the source selection decision must represent the SSA's independent judgment. The SSA must document the source selection decision and the rationale for any business judgments and trade-offs he or she made or relied on, including benefits associated with additional costs, though he or she need not quantify the trade-offs that led to the decision.[64]

Why Document?

Evaluation documentation can also demonstrate to any third-party forum, such as GAO, that the evaluation was performed in a fair and honest manner consistent with the solicitation. A properly documented record will greatly assist those called on to justify the selection decision.

Although the SSA has significant discretion in making the source selection decision, the SSA must first understand the evaluations. For this reason, evaluators should present the SSA with sufficient information on each of the competing offerors and their proposals for the SSA to make a comparative analysis and arrive at a rational, fully supportable selection decision. Narrative statements serve as the most important part of the documentation supporting the decision. They communicate specific information concerning relative advantages or disadvantages of proposals to the SSA that ratings alone (whether adjectival, color, or numerical) obviously cannot.

The documentation need not be lengthy, as long as it effectively conveys the basis for the evaluator's assessment. Proposals receiving the same rating can still have distinctions, requiring evaluators to assess each offeror's ability to accomplish the task, and these distinctions could have a direct impact on the source selection decision. Preparing narrative statements forces evaluators to justify their ratings and use the stated evaluation criteria consistently. Keep in mind that preparing proposals is expensive, and offerors want to be assured that the evaluation was fair and impartial. Protests often arise when offerors believe that this was not the case.[65]

What to Document

Recall that the most important aspect of a valid proposal evaluation is that it conforms to the criteria and weightings in the solicitation. Evaluators must, therefore, provide sufficient detail so the SSA can clearly understand the evaluation and how it relates to the stated evaluation criteria. Such detailed information helps the SSA appreciate distinctions among proposals and the relative significance of those distinctions for making a trade-off decision.[66]

In addition to the source selection decision, the agency uses evaluators' documentation to support the debriefing of unsuccessful offerors. The evaluators' narrative reports can provide details of the evaluation for the oral debriefing, or written excerpts from the report can be given to individual offerors as a part of a written debriefing. Consider that the evaluation report may be reviewed by a third party, e.g., GAO or a court, and the conclusions reached and the basis for such conclusions must be very definitive.[67]

Evaluators' comments should be concise but sufficiently detailed to support their position. They must also include specific references (e.g., page or paragraph numbers) to proposal content that supports their ratings. Evaluator comments should address all of the following issues:

- How well the proposal, as submitted, meets the requirements for each criterion.
- The strengths, weaknesses, and deficiencies that had a bearing upon the rating:
  - What the offeror proposed.
  - The government's assessment—good or bad, strong or weak.
  - Why it is good or bad; what is the effect of what is proposed?
  - How it relates to the evaluation criteria.[68]
- What would be required to remedy any deficiencies and significant weaknesses.
- The impact the deficiencies and any needed correction to them have on the quality of the offeror's proposal (e.g., the deficiencies are fatal errors that cannot be corrected; the weaknesses may be correctable through discussions and proposal revision).

When in doubt about which rating to assign for a given criterion, evaluators should make a best assessment based upon the content of the proposal. Issues in doubt should be addressed during the consensus session of the proposal ratings. After completing the rating sheets, evaluators assign an overall rating to the proposal. The overall rating is based on the ratings assigned to the individual criterion, as described in the source selection plan.[69]

Evaluators should write their findings and supporting rationale clearly and logically so that if they are read by someone unfamiliar with the source selection, the reader would be able to understand it. GAO has consistently held that agencies have broad discretion in the evaluation process, but evaluations (findings) must be able to withstand scrutiny regarding their reasonableness and must be made in accordance with the RFP's stated evaluation criteria. Agency decisions have been overturned if their evaluations are irrational, arbitrary, not based on evidence in the record, or simply not clearly articulated. Each finding approved by the SSET should, therefore, capture the team's collective reasoning and not merely paraphrase or provide excerpts from the proposal. For this reason, the evaluators should avoid merely identifying a proposal element as a strength, weakness, or deficiency without clearly documenting the logic or rationale for designating it as such.

Similarly, evaluators should explain their logic or rationale for assigning increased significance to any individual finding designated as a significant strength, significant weakness, or deficiency. For example, each technical finding should be clearly tied to a specific technical evaluation factor. The technical findings should reference the proposal page number(s) from which each finding originated. This will help the voting members of the technical panel during consensus discussions.

Electronic Documentation Issues

The computer age in which we work requires that agencies take additional record-keeping measures. Some agencies use electronic media for storing source selection records. But in light of the rapid changes in information technology, agencies must consider whether that media will be readable in five or ten years. For example, some agencies may still have data stored on 5.25-inch floppy disks that computers today can't read. Thus, all critical documents (source selection statements, SEB reports, approvals, protest decisions, etc.) should be kept in hardcopy in the official contract file. Emails and electronic approvals also should be printed and stored in the official contract file.

The electronic age has also revolutionized the way we do business and raises concerns about safeguarding and protecting procurement sensitive data. When transmitting procurement sensitive data electronically, the agency must take adequate precautions to ensure the data does not end up in the wrong hands.[70]

In addition, when using a computer-based system for evaluation, evaluators should back up and save their data often, at least daily, to minimize data loss in the event of a system crash or power loss.[71]

Case Study: The Importance of Documentation

Carahsoft Technology Corporation and Allied Technology Group protested the decision not to include services for compensation management in the award of a Federal Supply Schedule (FSS) contract by the General Services Administration

(GSA) for human resources and equal employment opportunity services worldwide. According to the GAO decision on the protest, the protesters objected because "GSA unreasonably excluded compensation management services from their contracts based on flawed evaluations."

The RFP stated that those offerors "whose written proposals were evaluated as acceptable were then provided instructions for a 'technical and functional operational capability demonstration (OCD).' ... GSA concluded that both firms had submitted satisfactory written proposals." There was, however,

> no contemporaneous documentation of the demonstration process: GSA did not record audio or video of the demonstration, and the evaluation record is incomplete. GSA "acknowledge[d] that not all of the OCD [demonstration] evaluation documents were retained because the final product of the evaluators' decisions was the 107-page final technical evaluation panel (TEP) report."

> The TEP report ... recommended that Carahsoft and Allied receive an award ... for personnel action processing and benefits management services, ... and all non-core services.... While the TEP report omitted compensation management from the award recommendation for the protesters, the report did not provide any reasons for the exclusion.

GSA explained to the offerors:

> "The reason that the TEP recommended that your firm not be awarded Compensation Management is that Carahsoft, and its subcontractors Avue and Ceridian, failed to properly complete the functional Operational Capabilities Demonstration (OCD) for the payroll portion as required in the Functional OCD instructions."

Because there was no documentation of the protestors performing the payroll demonstration, the TEP concluded that "there was a high degree of risk" if either firm were awarded the compensation management part of the contract. In response,

> the protesters point[ed] to the TEP final report, showing that despite the written notes of the TEP meeting and in the final evaluation consensus, the protesters received a yellow rating (the second highest rating) for their functional capability and approach, which encompasses compensation management.

GAO stated that for its office

> to perform a meaningful review, the record must contain adequate documentation showing the bases for the evaluation conclusions and source selection decision.... Where an agency fails to document or retain evaluation materials, it bears the risk that there may not be adequate supporting rationale in the record for [GAO] to conclude that the agency had a reasonable basis for the source selection decision.

GAO stated that the record in this case was "inadequately documented to show the reasonableness of GSA's decision to exclude compensation management from the protesters' awards."

GAO asserted that

> while the TEP's conclusions are fairly general, [it did] not assign the protesters a "high risk," a "red" rating, or any other rating indicating technical unacceptability for any aspect of compensation management. In addition, there is no record that the contracting officer arrived at a reasoned independent judgment regarding rating, risk, or acceptability of the protesters' proposals under the RFP criteria after [receiving the] TEP report, which assigned a rating of "yellow" and "moderate risk" to these proposals. The TEP report itself is otherwise silent on the basis for implicitly excluding compensation management from the awards.

GAO sustained the protests and recommended that

> GSA reevaluate the protesters' proposals… and make a new award decision for each of the protesters, adequately documenting the agency's conclusions on these points. In doing so, GSA should ensure that its evaluation takes into account the content of both the written proposal and the demonstration provided, as measured against the instructions provided in the RFP, and the evaluation criteria. If the failure to retain documentation of the earlier demonstration leads GSA to conclude that an additional partial demonstration is needed in order to determine technical acceptability, it should promptly arrange one.[72]

This case illustrates the importance of documenting the basis for the evaluation scores and the source selection decision. In this case, GSA did not document or retain evaluation materials that were necessary for a rational award decision. We see that not only does the SSA rely on the documentation for the source selection decision, but the GAO also relies on it in the event of a protest.

At this stage in the source selection process, the evaluators have completed and documented the initial evaluations. Now it's time for the evaluators from each panel to meet to discuss their evaluations and reach a consensus decision on the strengths and weaknesses of and the score for each proposal.

REACHING CONSENSUS

Consensus means an opinion or position reached by a group as a whole.[73] It does not mean that the majority rules or that individual dissenting opinions don't matter. It's important to note that simply averaging the individual evaluation results does not constitute consensus. Reaching consensus requires a meeting of the minds on the assigned ratings and associated deficiencies, strengths, weaknesses, and risks.[74] Consensus discussions on a particular finding should continue until all panel members reach a consensus or the panel members agree to disagree and the dissenter(s) prepare a minority opinion. The latter rarely happens, but the fact that the option exists underscores the importance of reaching consensus on all findings.

The source selection evaluation team chairperson is responsible for ensuring that each voting member has the opportunity to express his or her opinion on each proposal attribute of interest to the government. It is very important to clearly identify these attributes and to document the reasoning or rationale for determining them to be strengths, weaknesses, or deficiencies.

Evaluation panels must fully document all of the findings used to reach consensus that were considered during the rating and scoring process. Thorough, clearly explained findings that clearly communicate the benefits or risks associated with each proposal will help the SSA make the selection decision. The panel should note the specific parts of the proposal (such as the proposal volume, page numbers, illustrations, or figure numbers) that pertain to each finding. These proposal citations will enable traceability for the SSET, SSA, or others, who will be able to quickly locate any particular finding in the report when necessary.[75]

The Consensus Process

After the evaluators finish their individual assessments, the panel chairperson (or factor manager) convenes a consensus meeting to assemble the evaluators assigned to that panel or factor. The purpose of the meeting is to reach consensus on the strengths, weaknesses, factor rating, and factor proposal risk assessment.

Evaluators explain their individual evaluations before the group and review the other evaluators' assessments and advisors' opinions, if appropriate. (Consensus evaluation is a government function, and advisors do not normally participate in this session unless the evaluators need specific technical clarification.) Hearing the presentations and reviewing others' assessments allow the evaluators to get different perspectives and new insight into the proposals.

The evaluators then document the results of this consensus session in a report that forms the basis of the panel's collaborative evaluation.

Consensus sessions typically follow a six-step process:

1. **Distribute evaluator and advisor comments.** The factor managers provide evaluators with copies of all of the comments made by the individual evaluators and advisors before the meeting. This allows the evaluators time to review the narratives and prepare questions or comments for the consensus session.

2. **Establish a set of ground rules (rules of conduct).** The factor managers establish rules of conduct at the initial session and enforce them throughout the consensus process to ensure orderly meetings. For example, the panel should be polite, respectful, and professional during the consensus session.

3. **Consolidate strengths and weaknesses relative to the standards.** Evaluators review and discuss strengths and weaknesses, combine them when appropriate, and summarize them for the consensus evaluation report. Displaying evaluators' narratives using an overhead projector or computer helps the group reconcile its ideas and write the collaborative report.

4. **Review and consolidate the various reports.** The evaluation team discusses all of the significant weakness and/or deficiency reports and develops a consolidated set. At this point, several minor weaknesses may be combined into a significant weakness, or several significant weaknesses may become a deficiency. Occasionally, a weakness perceived by one evaluator is explained away by other evaluators. Alternatively, a weakness identified by only one evaluator may be included in the consensus report, even though the other evaluators didn't initially identify the weakness.

5. **Determine the factor consensus rating and proposal risk assessment factor by factor.** Evaluators discuss the rationale for their individual scores and reach consensus. They may reach agreement in a variety of ways, from a simple vote-by-voice poll to computer-based voting tools. If the group cannot reach a consensus on a single score or rating, the panel should record the minority opinion (and rating) in the report. The panel chair should inform the SSET chair (who may wish to consult with the contracting officer and legal counsel) if the group does not reach a consensus.

6. **Prepare the consensus evaluation report and cover sheet.** The factor manager prepares a cover sheet for the panel chair that identifies the evaluators and states the date the consensus took place. The factor manager signs this cover sheet after each evaluator signs it.

Evaluators repeat the group consensus process for each evaluation factor until they complete all factors for the proposal. The evaluators should not proceed to evaluating the next proposal until the SSET chair and/or the contracting officer concurs with the consensus result.[76]

The GAO's overriding concern with regard to consensus findings is not whether the final ratings are consistent with earlier, individual ratings, but whether they reasonably reflect the relative merits of the proposals. The consensus evaluation record should document the differences in the firms' proposals or explain why seemingly warranted strengths identified by the evaluators were not adopted by the SSET. And the evaluators' assessments of strengths and weaknesses must be documented for the contract file. White boards are a useful tool for capturing the positive and negative aspects of proposals during a consensus session, but they are not a permanent method of documentation.[77]

For example, if all of the evaluators identify a particular attribute of the proposal as a strength, it follows logically that the SSET would similarly identify that attribute as a strength. If it does not, then the SSET needs to explain why and document that decision.

Now that readers understand the consensus evaluation process, let's examine a case in which the consensus evaluation report was relevant to a protest.

Case Study: Consensus Evaluation Report

Smart Innovative Solutions (SIS) of Columbia, Maryland, protested the exclusion of its proposal from the competitive range under an RFP issued by the Department of Labor for administration of the Job Corps National Call Center. SIS argued that excluding its proposal from the competitive range was improper.

According to GAO decision B-400323.3, "The RFP anticipated award to the offeror whose proposal presented the best value after evaluation in accordance with the stated factors." SIS argued that

> the agency's technical evaluation was flawed because the [technical evaluation panel] failed to produce a consensus report and because weaknesses noted in the evaluation report appeared to conflict with statements on the scoring sheets of an individual TEP member.

GAO stated that there is

> no statute or regulation that requires an agency to create a consensus report in evaluating proposals, nor is there any requirement that every individual evaluator's scoring sheet track to the final evaluation report.

> A consensus score need not be the same score as initially scored by the individual evaluators. In short, these matters alone [did] not lead [the GAO] to conclude that there was an impropriety in the agency's evaluation or a violation of procurement law or regulation.

Further, GAO reviewed the record and determined that there was "support for the weaknesses the agency noted in the protester's technical proposal." The protest was denied.[78]

CHAPTER SUMMARY

Chapter 9 discusses the heart of source selection: the evaluation process. Proposal evaluation involves assessing the proposal and the offeror's ability to perform the prospective contract successfully. Agencies evaluate the competitive proposals and assess their relative qualities based only on the factors and subfactors specified in the

RFP. Evaluators identify the relative strengths, deficiencies, significant weaknesses, and risks and document their assessments.

The chapter covers the essential elements of evaluating technical, management, past performance, and price or cost information, as well as oral presentations. Evaluators need to evaluate only what is actually written in the proposal; follow the evaluation criteria stated in the RFP; document specific strengths, weaknesses, and risks of each proposal; and not make comparisons between proposals.

As evaluators read the proposal, they should note anything that could be a problem. Generally, such problems are categorized as deficiencies, significant weaknesses, or weaknesses. The source selection plan or source selection evaluation guide should define these terms in the way evaluators intend to apply them.

The technical/management panel may begin with a quick read to skim the proposals just to get familiar with the format and content. No assessment, judgment, or evaluation is done at this stage; it's just a familiarization process. After the quick read, evaluators read the relevant volumes of the proposal to thoroughly understand the proposed approach. This step avoids documenting presumed "missing" information in the beginning of the proposal, only to find it later in the proposal.

Evaluators use forms to document areas of the proposal that are weak, deficient, or that require additional information. Typical forms include clarification requests (CRs), information requests (IRs), significant weakness reports (SWRs), and deficiency reports (DRs).

After the evaluations, the agency scores and documents the assessments of the individual proposals. Properly documenting the entire source selection process is critical and has a large impact on the success of the procurement. While the evaluators rate proposals only against the RFP's evaluation criteria, the source selection authority bases its decision on a comparative assessment of proposals against all source selection criteria in the solicitation.

While the SSA may use reports and analyses prepared by others, the source selection decision must represent the SSA's independent judgment. The SSA must document the source selection decision, and the documentation must include the rationale for any business judgments and trade-offs made or relied on by the SSA, including the benefits associated with additional costs.

Once the individual scoring and documentation is complete, the evaluators reach a consensus as a group. *Consensus* means an opinion or position reached by a group as a whole.[79] It does not mean the majority rules or that individual dissenting opinions don't matter. It's important to note that simply averaging the individual evaluation results does not constitute consensus. Consensus requires a meeting of the minds on the assigned rating and associated deficiencies, strengths, weaknesses, and risks.

Now that the evaluations are complete, the SSA determines if award without discussions is appropriate. That's what we'll discuss in the next chapter.

NOTES

1   Peter S. Cole, *How to Evaluate and Negotiate Government Contracts* (Vienna, VA: Management Concepts, 2001), 125.

2   Cole, 224–225.

3   Federal Acquisition Regulation (FAR) 15.305.

4   Cole, 224.

5   These groups are called a variety of names, including *source evaluation committee* (SEC), *source evaluation panel* (SEP), and many others. The names should not be a source of confusion because the role of each group, regardless of its name, is to assist in the evaluation of proposals.

6   Harold V. Hanson, *NAVSEA Source Selection Guide* (Washington, DC: U.S. Naval Sea Systems Command, 2001), 22.

7   FAR 15.001.

8   Cole, 223.

9   FAR 15.001.

10 Ibid.

11 Cole, 234–235.

12 Defense Information Systems Agency, *Source Selection Deskbook* (Arlington, VA: Defense Information Systems Agency, May 2003), 22–23.

13 Cole, 226.

14 National Reconnaissance Office, *Source Selection Manual* (Chantilly, VA: National Reconnaissance Office, 2000), 141.

15 FAR 9.503.

16 *Source Selection Manual*, 139–143.

17 Adapted from *Source Selection Manual*, 397–400.

18 U.S. Government Accountability Office, "Systems Research and Applications Corporation; Booz Allen Hamilton, Inc.," B-299818; B-299818.2; B-299818.3; B-299818.4 (Washington, DC: U.S. Government Accountability Office, September 6, 2007).

19 FAR 42.1501.

20 FAR 15.305.

21 FAR 15.305(a)(2).

22 Office of Federal Procurement Policy, *Best Practices for Collecting and Using Current and Past Performance Information* (Washington, DC: Office of Federal Procurement Policy, May 2000), 36.

23 FAR 16.405-2(a)(2).

24 *Source Selection Manual*, 155.

25 Office of Federal Procurement Policy, 22–23.

26 FAR 15.306 (b)(4).

27 FAR 42.1502.

28 FAR 42.1503.

29 FAR 15.306(b).

30 FAR 15.305(a)(2)(iv).

31 U.S. Government Accountability Office, "Oceaneering International, Inc.," B-278126; B-278126.2 (Washington, DC: U.S. Government Accountability Office, December 31, 1997).

32 Johnnie E. Wilson, *Best Value Source Selection* 715-3 (Alexandria, VA: Army Materiel Command, 1998), D13.

33 *Source Selection Manual*, 157–158.

34 U.S. Government Accountability Office, "Aegis Defense Services Limited," B-400093.4; B-400093.5 (Washington, DC: U.S. Government Accountability Office, October 16, 2008).

35 FAR 15.304(c)(1).

36 National Reconnaissance Office, *NRO Source Selection* N87 (Chantilly, VA: National Reconnaissance Office, 2008), N87.403, 38–39.

37 *NRO Source Selection* N87, N87.403,39.

38 FAR 15.305.

39 U.S. Environmental Protection Agency, *EPA Acquisition Regulation* 1515.305-72 (Washington, DC: Environmental Protection Agency).

40 U.S. Special Operations Command, *USSOCOM FAR Supplement* 5615.305 (MacDill Air Force Base, FL: U.S. Special Operations Command).

41 Department of the Navy, Office of the Assistant Secretary, Research, Development and Acquisition, *Navy Marine Corps Acquisition Regulation Supplement* 5215.305 (Washington, DC: Department of the Navy, February 14, 2005).

42 Department of the Army, *Army Federal Acquisition Regulation Supplement* 5115.305 (Washington, DC: Department of the Army, October 2001).

43 FAR 15.404-1(a)(2).

44 FAR 15.404-1.

45 Defense Contract Audit Agency, *DCAA Contract Audit Manual*, Section 9.202 (Fort Belvoir, VA: Defense Contract Audit Agency, June 30, 2009), 922.

46 FAR 15.404.

47 FAR 2.101.

48 Adapted from Federal Acquisition Institute and the Air Force Institute of Technology, "Cost Analysis," *Contract Pricing Reference Guide*, vol. 3 (Washington, DC: Federal Acquisition Institute, 1998), 132–133.

49 Ibid., 133–134.

50 FAR 15.404-1(d)(1).

51 FAR 15.404-1(d)(2).

52 FAR 15.404-1(d).

53 *Source Selection Manual*, 40.

54 Defense Information Systems Agency, 22–23.

55 Cole, 241.

56 U.S. Government Accountability Office, "Honeywell Technology Solutions, Inc.; Wyle Laboratories, Inc.," B-292354; B-292388 (Washington, DC: U.S. Government Accountability Office, September 2, 2003).

57 FAR 15.404-1.

58 FAR 15.102.

59 U.S. Air Force Materiel Command, *Guide for the Use of Oral Presentations in Contracting by Negotiation* (Wright-Patterson Air Force Base, OH: Air Force Materiel Command, May 1999), 6.

60 National Aeronautics and Space Administration, *Source Selection Guide* (Washington, DC: National Aeronautics and Space Administration, June 2007), 44–45.

61 U.S. Department of Energy, *Source Selection Guide* (Washington, DC: U.S. Department of Energy, 2005), 14–15.

62 Ibid., 12.

63 *NRO Source Selection* N87, 32.

64 FAR 15.308.

65 U.S. Department of Energy, 53–56.

66 Frequently, technical personnel work well with numbers and concepts but are not the most articulate writers. If necessary, the contracting officer might consider offering personnel specific training in writing skills to improve the quality of the source selection documentation.

67 U.S. Department of Energy, 47–48.

68 Ibid., 48.

69 U.S. Department of State, *Contracting Officer's Representative Handbook,* vol. 14, Handbook 2, 14 FAH-2 H-360 (Washington DC: U.S. Department of State, December 2005), 10.

70 U.S. Department of Energy, 53–56. Chapter 1 of this text offers details about the protection of sensitive source selection data in its discussion of the Procurement Integrity Act and regulatory guidance found in FAR part 3.

71 *Source Selection Manual*, 143–145.

72 U.S. Government Accountability Office, "Carahsoft Technology Corporation; Allied Technology Group," B-311241; B-311241.2 (Washington, DC: U.S. Government Accountability Office, May 16, 2008).

73 *The American Heritage Dictionary*, 4th ed. (New York: Houghton Mifflin Company, 2006), 391.

74 Claude M. Bolton, Jr., *Army Source Selection Manual* (Washington, DC: Office of the Assistant Secretary of the Army for Acquisition, Logistics and Technology, 2007), 29.

75 National Aeronautics and Space Administration, 38–39.

76 *Source Selection Manual*, 146–148.

77 U.S. Government Accountability Office, "Systems Research and Applications Corporation; Booz Allen Hamilton, Inc.," B-299818; B-299818.2; B-299818.3; B-299818.4 (Washington, DC: U.S. Government Accountability Office, September 6, 2007).

78 U.S. Government Accountability Office, "Smart Innovative Solutions," B-400323.3 (Washington, DC: U.S. Government Accountability Office, November 19, 2008).

79 *The American Heritage Dictionary,* 391.

Chapter 10

Awarding without Discussions

At this stage in the source selection process, the initial evaluations are complete, and the source selection authority (SSA) must determine if award without discussions is appropriate or if holding discussions will provide the best value to the government. Of course, awarding without discussions is an option only if the RFP contained the Federal Acquisition Regulation (FAR) provision 52.215-1, which notifies potential offerors of the possibility. To preserve the option of awarding without discussions, many contracting officers (CO) routinely include this clause in all solicitations they issue.

Even if the agency will award the contract without conducting discussions, offerors may be given the opportunity to resolve minor or clerical errors or to clarify certain aspects of their proposals, such as:

- The relevance of their past performance information
- Adverse past performance information to which the offeror has not previously had an opportunity to respond.[1]

Unfortunately, the FAR does not offer much more guidance about when it's appropriate to award without discussions or when "clarifications" become so extensive as to constitute "discussions." This chapter discusses some factors to consider before awarding without discussions and highlights relevant case studies. First, we'll put the decision on whether to hold discussions into perspective by going back to the beginning of the acquisition process: the source selection plan, writing the RFP, and the impact of these documents on the proposals received.

Recall from Chapter 2 that the source selection plan (SSP) addresses the approach for soliciting and evaluating proposals. Awarding without discussions is one approach for a competitive source selection and can save weeks of discussions and proposal revisions (which can be very expensive for the offerors), allowing the agency to streamline the process and award a contract sooner. Let's review the process of deciding whether to award with or without discussions step by step.

STATING AN INTENTION TO AWARD WITHOUT DISCUSSIONS

Before issuing the RFP, the agency determines if it intends to award the contract without discussions and documents the desired acquisition approach in the SSP. Before making this decision, the agency should consider whether or not holding discussions will yield the best value to the government. Award without discussions is most likely to result in best value when the requirements are clear, and the marketplace is very competitive. This is where market research plays a pivotal role. The agency must know the marketplace and must be able to clearly state the requirements in the RFP so that discussions won't be required.[2]

When the source selection plan incorporates the possibility of awarding without discussions, the RFP must, as mentioned earlier, include the provision from FAR 52.215-1. The agency should consider the following key points if it is contemplating award without discussions:

- Evaluation factors must be specific to the needs of the program and to the statement of work in the solicitation. Don't use generic evaluation factors that can be applied to many different types of procurements.
- Information that offerors are required to submit for evaluation must be related to the evaluation factors.
- Solicitation instructions for submitting information must be specific and sufficiently detailed so that proposals submitted have all of the information the evaluators need to determine each proposal's strengths, weaknesses, and risks.
- The solicitation should state that any proposed deviation from the terms and conditions in the solicitation may make the offer unacceptable for award without discussions and that the government may make an award without discussions to another offeror that did not take exception to the terms and conditions of the solicitation.[3]

The following is an example of RFP language to emphasize the agency's intent to award without discussion:

> The government intends to evaluate proposals and award a contract without discussions with offerors. The government reserves the right to conduct discussions if the CO later determines discussions to be necessary. Any exceptions or deviations by the offeror to the terms and conditions stated in this solicitation for inclusion in the resulting contract may make the offer unacceptable for award without discussions. If an offeror proposes exceptions to the terms and conditions of the contract, the government may make an award without discussions to another offeror that did not take exception to the terms and conditions of the contract.[4]

PROPOSAL WEAKNESSES AND AWARDING WITHOUT DISCUSSION

It's important for agencies to know that offerors can't submit excellent proposals if the RFP is marginal. If you want quality proposals, you need to prepare a quality RFP. As previous chapters have made clear, that takes planning and review time. Once an agency puts together a high-quality RFP, it is the offerors' responsibility to submit high-quality initial proposals.

An offeror's initial proposal must contain sufficient information to demonstrate that it can do the work for the price proposed without requiring discussions. An offeror that fails to do so runs the risk of not getting the contract award. Offerors must be aware that an agency is not obligated to enter discussions merely because one unacceptable initial proposal could be made acceptable through discussions.[5]

Thus, agencies may award contracts to an offeror with a weak proposal despite the problems or weaknesses in the proposal. Some agencies hesitate to do this, but the agency doesn't need to have a perfect proposal in hand to make contract award. Receiving contract award doesn't necessarily mean that the company has a perfect proposal; rather, the proposal meets the government's needs in accordance with the evaluation criteria at a fair and reasonable price. The evaluators may discover weaknesses in the proposal, but that does not preclude the agency from awarding without discussions.

There is no such thing as a perfect RFP, a perfect proposal, or a perfect contract. Agencies must be willing to accept inherent reasonable weaknesses in proposals in order to award without discussions. An agency should, however, in all cases, strive for a clear and concise RFP so as to receive clear and concise proposals, increasing the possibility that award can be made based on initial proposals with minimal risk to either party.

Evaluators play an important role in the decision to award without discussions. Their initial evaluation essentially becomes the determinant evaluation. It must be consistent with the source selection criteria and be properly documented from the beginning, as discussed in Chapter 9.[6]

SPECIAL CONSIDERATIONS

When determining whether awarding without discussions will provide the best value, agencies should consider the probable benefits of holding discussions based on two criteria: how well the apparent successful proposal fulfills the prenegotiation objectives, and the cost in time and money of conducting negotiations. It makes no sense to spend thousands of dollars in labor costs for agency employees' time to save a couple of dollars by having discussions.[7] Also, proposals are extremely expensive endeavors for each of the offerors. Because only one will ultimately win the contract, it is best for everyone involved if agencies do not put particular offerors through the unnecessary expense of proposal revisions if their proposal isn't competitive.

The source selection authority should award contracts without discussions when the appropriate conditions exist:

- A clear winner has been identified.
- The initial evaluation was fair and complete, and the evaluation procedures were followed.
- All offerors understood the requirements of the solicitation; that is, there were no requirements in the solicitation that were ambiguous and misinterpreted by one or more offerors. Solicitation ambiguities may exist if several offerors have deficiencies for the same reason in a single evaluation standard. This situation may reflect a flawed solicitation, not the incompetence of the offerors.
- The government perceives no appreciable advantage to open discussions.
- No sustainable grounds for protest appear to exist.[8]
- The apparent winning proposal:
  - Contains no deficiencies or significant weaknesses that require correction before contract award
  - Contains no proposed exceptions to contract clauses that are unacceptable to the agency
  - Includes a proposed contract value that is realistic, reasonable, and within any budgetary/funding limitations or constraints.[9]

Making award without discussions entails selecting a proposal based on the initial evaluation findings and accepting that proposal as-is, including weaknesses and at the contract value proposed. If it is clear that the cost of conducting discussions would not offset the potentially lower prices or increased functionality resulting from discussions, then it may be appropriate to award based on initial proposals.[10]

The SSA should ask the following questions:

- How much better can the proposals get?
- Is it worth the time to get that additional value? In other words, will discussions significantly lower costs or increase quality?

If the agency has already received good proposals, going into discussions isn't likely to provide more value. It's not a good practice to conduct discussions to lower offerors' prices when initial offers are fair and reasonable. Therefore, the agency should consider awarding without discussions if there is a clearly superior proposal.

The SSA must be involved early in the decision to award without discussions, and the initial evaluation findings presented to the SSA must be in sufficient detail to permit the SSA to choose a source without discussions or to direct the contracting officer to make a competitive range determination in preparation for discussions. (The level of preparation for this presentation should be commensurate with that for a final evaluation presentation.) If the SSA's final decision is to conduct discussions, but the evaluation panels have not begun to prepare for them, there may be a significant delay in completing the evaluation process and awarding a contract.[11]

The contracting officer can avoid this delay by instructing evaluators to prepare documentation for making a competitive range determination in the event that the SSA decides to conduct discussions. This documentation can be used for debriefings even if the SSA decides to award without discussions, so the evaluators would not be wasting their time by preparing ahead.

STREAMLINING THE SOURCE SELECTION PROCESS

Awarding without discussions streamlines the source selection process by omitting the following steps in the source selection process:

- Making the competitive range determination
- Conducting discussions
- Requesting final proposal revisions
- Evaluating final proposal revisions.

Conducting discussions can add weeks, even months, to the source selection schedule. In some instances the "final" proposal revisions offerors submit after discussions lead to more questions, even further discussions, and another round of "final" proposal revisions. The additional time needed to conduct discussions can impose a burden on personnel who have other work to do. The SSA must balance the value of staffers' time and their need to tend to other work against the value of the lower price or increased technical capability discussions would allow.

CONSIDERING PRECEDENTS

From the offerors' perspective, conducting discussions increases their costs: They need to keep the proposal team together to address discussion questions and prepare a revised proposal. Subcontractor or vendor prices may increase as well. Some companies, however, plan to reduce prices during proposal revisions to improve their competitive position.

This is especially common when offerors submit proposals to agencies that have never awarded without discussions. These agencies set a precedent, suggesting that offerors wait to submit their best proposals. Offerors may hold back a technical improvement or cost reduction, then offer them during the proposal revision phase. If an agency wants to get the best proposals in the initial submission, it must have a high-quality RFP, then actually make contract award on initial proposals.

Next, let's examine a case study in which an unsuccessful offeror protested the agency's decision to award without discussions.

CASE STUDY: AWARDING WITHOUT DISCUSSIONS

NV Services (NVS) protested the award of a contract to LB&B Associates, Inc., under an RFP issued by the National Aeronautics and Space Administration (NASA) for facilities operation and maintenance services at the Goddard Space Flight Center in Greenbelt, Maryland. NVS argued that NASA had improperly failed to conduct discussions concerning the cost proposals.

> According to Government Accountability Office (GAO) decision B-284119.2, Based upon the evaluation results, the SSA concluded that discussions were not necessary.... From her review of the evaluated proposal strengths and weaknesses and probable costs of performance of the offerors, the SSA determined that only NVS and LB&B had a reasonable chance of receiving award.... Weighing the relative merits of NVS's and LB&B's proposals, the SSA concluded that LB&B's proposal reflected the best value to the government, given its probable cost advantage ... and higher past performance rating.

Specifically, the SSA stated:

> The difference in mission suitability scores between NVS and LB&B was so slight as to be negligible. LB&B had a moderately lower probable cost and a higher rating for Relevant Experience and Past Performance than NVS.

Therefore, the SSA concluded that LB&B's was the superior proposal.

NVS argued that "NASA should not have made award on initial proposals to LB&B, but rather should have conducted discussions with LB&B concerning its proposed [Other Direct Costs] and with both offerors concerning their proposed award fee."

GAO noted,

> There is generally no obligation [for] a contracting agency [to] conduct discussions where, as here, the RFP specifically [informs] offerors of the agency's intent to award a contract on the basis of initial proposals. While the contracting officer's discretion in deciding not to hold discussions is not unfettered, it is quite broad.

The scope of GAO's review of "the exercise of such discretion is solely to ensure that it was reasonably based on the particular circumstances of the procurement." This does not require the decision to be obvious or universally agreed to. It doesn't even have to be proven "right" in any objective sense. It need only have a reasonable basis. In this case, GAO determined that

> NASA reasonably exercised its discretion to make award on the basis of initial proposals, as provided for by the RFP. It is true that the agency found that LB&B understated its proposed costs and [GAO's] review found a number of errors in the agency's cost realism evaluation of LB&B's proposal; [GAO] also found, however, that the firms' relative cost standing was unaffected by NASA's and [GAO's] probable cost adjustments. Under the circumstances, the agency had no reasonable doubt as to which offer represented the best value to the government and could make award on initial proposals.

The protest was denied.[12]

It's important to remember when awarding without discussions that the agency may clarify information in an offeror's proposal, but the contracting officer must be careful not to cross the line and conduct discussions.

CLARIFYING PROPOSAL INFORMATION WITHOUT DISCUSSIONS

So what does the agency do if it has a quality proposal, but it is not sure about the relevance of a past performance reference? The agency may clarify that information with the offeror. Because clarifying a past performance reference does not change the technical or management proposal or change the cost, it does not constitute discussions.

The FAR permits limited exchanges with offerors when necessary to "clarify certain aspects of proposals." As noted earlier in this chapter, an agency may ask about the relevance of an offeror's past performance or adverse past performance information or may allow the offeror to resolve minor clerical errors.[13] Note the FAR's discretionary language: When award without discussions is anticipated, the government *may* conduct clarifying exchanges. Thus, the agency need not conduct exchanges if there's nothing to clarify. Nevertheless, contracting officers should clarify all ambiguities in a proposal but should consult legal counsel before doing so, just to make sure the question and answer do not cross the line into discussions.

Contracting officers must make their intentions clear at the outset and maintain rigid control of the conversation so that the offeror is unable to turn a clarification into a discussion. If this line is crossed with one offeror, and the offeror claims a right to revise its proposal, then all other offerors must also be afforded the same opportunity to participate in discussions and revise their proposals.[14] If clarifications turn into discussions, the contracting officer must establish a competitive range and conduct discussions with everyone in the range—and the agency will not realize the benefits of awarding without discussions.

Distinguishing between clarifications, communications, and discussions can be difficult. *Clarifications* help an agency understand what an offeror proposed or help it discern a company's capability to perform based on past performance references. It's important to remember that offerors cannot revise their proposals simply because the agency asks clarification questions. This is the easiest way to distinguish clarifications from discussions: Proposal revisions are not permitted in clarifications.

Exchanges between the agency and the offeror begin with clarifications if the agency anticipates awarding without discussions. If the agency needs more information to make a competitive range determination, the next step is *communications*. The last step is *discussions*, which allow offerors to make proposal revisions. Simply stated, the contracting officer receives more information as he or she goes through the process, as illustrated in Figure 10-1.

Table 10-1 details:

- When exchanges between the agency and the offeror occur
- The scope of information exchanged
- The purpose of each type of exchange
- Examples of topics the contracting officer may introduce
- Whether the offeror may revise its proposal.

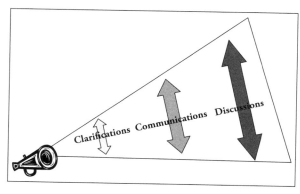

Figure 10-1   Scope of Information Received through Clarifications, Communications, and Discussions

Table 10-1 Clarifications, Communications, and Discussions[15]

	Clarifications	Communications	Discussions/ negotiations
When it's done	When the agency anticipates award without discussions	Before establishing the competitive range if the agency anticipates award with discussions	After establishing the competitive range. Note: the term negotiation applies to both competitive and noncompetitive acquisitions. In competitive acquisition, negotiation is also called discussion.
Scope of information exchanged	Most limited	Somewhat limited	Most detailed
Purpose	To clarify certain aspects of a proposal	Addresses issues to help the agency determine if a particular proposal should be in the competitive range	To maximize the government's ability to obtain best value
Examples of topics covered	• Relevance of past performance information • Adverse past performance information • Resolving minor or clerical errors	• Adverse past performance information • Relevance of past performance ambiguities • Errors, omissions, or mistakes	• Past performance information • Weaknesses • Significant weaknesses • Deficiencies
Can offeror revise proposal?	No	No	Yes

The communications and discussions columns will be explained in later chapters. Here, they are shown for comparison purposes.

When conducting clarifications with an offeror, the contracting officer should ask only those questions necessary to understand the proposal and make the award decision. Information the contracting officer receives during clarifications may not be used to revise a proposal, correct any deficiencies or material omissions, or change any technical or cost elements of a proposal. A clarification allows an offeror to correct a minor math error or a certification or acknowledge a nonmaterial amendment. These minor points of information are not defined as a discussion.[16]

It is important to remember that clarifications are *limited* exchanges. The contracting officer may use clarifications to give an offeror an opportunity to make clear and obvious key points about the proposal as originally submitted. The offeror may not revise, expand (by adding new information that enhances the proposal), or amplify its proposal. The intent of clarifications is to remove obvious ambiguity, not to permit an offeror to improve its position by drawing inferences from the government's questions and using those inferences to alter the meaning of the original proposal so that it becomes more attractive and more beneficial to the government.[17]

CASE STUDY: CLARIFICATIONS VERSUS DISCUSSIONS

Colson Services Corporation protested the award of a contract to Retirement System Group, Inc., (RSG) under an RFP issued by the Small Business Administration (SBA) for Fiscal and Transfer Agent (FTA) services for the secondary market program of SBA's 7(a) Guaranteed Loan program. Colson argued that the SBA's proposal evaluation was unreasonable and that the agency improperly failed to conduct discussions with the firm.

Per the GAO decision on the protest,

The purpose of the RFP at issue … [was] to facilitate the receipt and recording of guaranteed interests in loan payments from lending institutions participating in the 7(a) Guaranteed Loan program and to conduct a primary and secondary market in the individual loans and certificates guaranteed by the SBA.

[The RFP permitted] the contractor to collect various service fees from lenders as compensation for the services that it furnishes under the contract; it also authorize[d] the contractor to collect and retain float income on any loan payment funds in its possession.... In lieu of prices, the RFP asked offerors for proposed "rebate" amounts; that is, it asked offerors for the amounts (of the income that they make under the contract) that they will remit to the government.

Before making the award,

the contracting officer determined that she should clarify with each offeror whether the rebate amounts that it had proposed were on a monthly or an annual basis. As a consequence, she sent identical e-mail messages to the two offerors requesting this information.... "I wanted to clarify the rebate amount in your proposal. Is it on a monthly or an annual basis?"

The protester argue[d] that the agency's request for clarification of the basis for the offerors' rebate amounts constituted discussions because this information was necessary to determine their proposed prices, and that the SBA's initiation of discussions in one area obligated the agency to conduct discussions regarding all significant weaknesses in offerors' proposals.

[As noted,] the contracting officer asked both offerors to clarify whether their rebate amounts were on a monthly or an annual basis, but did not otherwise communicate with them regarding the content of their proposals. The contracting officer sought clarification of the basis for the rebate amounts after being advised by the chairperson of the technical evaluation team that since the RFP included language providing that "[t]he rebate will be made to SBA monthly,"… the rebate amounts entered by the offerors on their price schedules should be considered monthly amounts. The contracting officer apparently questioned whether the two offerors had indeed interpreted the RFP in this manner.

GAO ruled that "the exchanges here did not constitute discussions because neither offeror was given the opportunity to revise its proposal; rather, each was merely given the opportunity to clarify the basis on which it had understood the RFP to be requesting pricing." The protest was denied.[18]

This case study illustrates how to correctly use clarifications when awarding without discussions and should help readers better understand the distinction between clarifications and discussions.

DOCUMENTING THE AWARD DECISION

The source selection authority must carefully document the award decision when awarding without discussions in a source selection decision document (SSDD).[19] The rationale and justification for business decisions and cost/technical trade-off determinations must be reasonable, consistent with evaluation factors listed in the solicitation, and adequately documented. "Adequately documented" means that the SSA should compare the solicitation's source selection criteria with the winning proposal, point by point. The document may include specific references, including page and paragraph numbers, from the successful offeror's proposal.

The rationale must include a comparative analysis of the offerors' relative strengths and weaknesses in all factors and subfactors and the advantages or disadvantages of each proposal to the government. There is no requirement to give credit for special features of a proposal if evaluators determined and documented that such features would not make a meaningful contribution or better satisfy government needs.

The final SSDD will, therefore, document the key differences between or among the offerors, including strengths and weaknesses, and the perceived benefit or lack of benefit to the government as independently determined by the SSA, which is *not* required to agree with the evaluators' assessments. This integrated assessment of the offers details the benefits of any cost/price trade-off and the rationale for selecting the awardee over the other offerors, and it must be consistent with the source selection criteria in the solicitation.

The SSDD need not be a lengthy document, but it must:

- Describe the solicited requirement.
- Specify the number of proposals and name them.
- List non-cost evaluation factors and subfactors and their relative importance, as cited in the solicitation.
- List each offeror's overall factor ratings, subfactor ratings, and cost/price.
- Provide a narrative comparing the non-cost rating of each proposal, including its strengths and weaknesses.
- Describe the business justification and/or cost-benefit analysis of the best value decision.[20]

NOTIFYING UNSUCCESSFUL OFFERORS

Within three days of making the contract award, the contracting officer must provide written notification to each offeror whose proposal was not selected for award. The notice must include:

- The number of offerors solicited.
- The number of proposals received.
- The name and address of each offeror receiving an award.
- The items, quantities, and any stated unit prices of each award. If the number of items or other factors makes listing stated unit prices impracticable at the time of notification, only the total contract price must be furnished in the notice.

The notice should also include, in general terms, the reason(s) the offeror's proposal was not accepted, unless the price information readily reveals the reason. In no event shall an offeror's cost breakdown, profit, overhead rates, trade secrets, manufacturing processes and techniques, or other confidential business information be disclosed to any other offeror.

If the agency receives a written request for a postaward debriefing from an offeror within three days after the date on which that offeror received notification of contract award, the agency must fulfill the offeror's request by explaining the basis for the selection decision and contract award.[21] Chapter 14 explains the debriefing process.

CHAPTER SUMMARY

Chapter 10 discusses the importance of planning to award without discussions by including the specific FAR provision in the source selection plan and RFP. Conducting market research plays a pivotal role in awarding without discussions because the government needs to know the marketplace and state the requirements clearly in the RFP so that discussions won't be required.

Offerors need to have a clear and concise RFP in order to submit clear and concise proposals. Awarding without discussions means that the agency awards the contract including the imperfections inherent in any proposal. Perfect proposals don't exist any more than a perfect RFP does. If you're waiting for a perfect proposal before awarding without discussions, you'll have to wait a long time!

The SSA should consider the following before awarding without discussions:

- Is a clear winner identified?
- Was the initial evaluation fair and complete?
- Were all evaluation procedures followed as planned?
- Do all offerors understand the requirements of the solicitation?
- Does the government perceive any appreciable advantage to open discussions?
- Are there any sustainable grounds for protest?
- Does the apparent winning proposal include any deficiencies or significant weaknesses that require correction before contract award?
- Does the apparent winning proposal include any exceptions to contract clauses that are unacceptable to the agency?
- Does the apparent winning proposal include a proposed contract value that is realistic, reasonable, and within any budgetary or funding limitations or constraints?

If it is clear that the cost of conducting discussions would not offset the potentially lower prices or increased functionality resulting from discussions, then it may be appropriate to award on initial proposals.

Chapter 10 also explains the distinction between clarifications, communications, and discussions and the importance of those distinctions in awarding without discussions. The FAR permits the government to conduct limited exchanges with offerors when it is necessary to "clarify certain aspects of proposals." For example, to resolve minor clerical errors or inquire about the relevance of an offeror's past performance; e.g., by asking an offeror about adverse past performance information. Distinguishing between clarifications, communications, and discussions may be difficult, and contracting officers should ensure that seeking clarifications does not turn into discussions.

Finally, the chapter also explains how to document the award decision and offer a debriefing to the unsuccessful offeror. The rationale and justification for business decisions and cost or technical trade-off determinations must be reasonable, consistent with the evaluation factors listed in the solicitation, and adequately documented.

The SSDD will document the key differences among the offerors, including strengths and weaknesses, and the perceived benefit or lack of benefit to the government as independently determined by the SSA.

If the agency does not award without discussions, it needs to establish the competitive range before conducting discussions. This is the topic of Chapter 11.

NOTES

1 Federal Acquisition Regulation (FAR) 15.306(a)(2).

2 Claude M. Bolton, Jr., *Army Source Selection Manual* (Washington, DC: Office of the Assistant Secretary of the Army for Acquisition, Logistics and Technology, 2007), 33.

3 U.S. Department of Energy, *Source Selection Guide* (Washington, DC: U.S. Department of Energy, 2005), 45–46.

4 U.S. Department of Energy, RFP no. DE-RP09-06SR22470 (Washington, DC: U.S. Department of Energy, June 6, 2007).

5 U.S. Government Accountability Office, "Century Elevator, Inc.," B-283822 (Washington, DC: U.S. Government Accountability Office, December 20, 1999).

6 National Aeronautics and Space Administration, *Source Selection Guide* (Washington, DC: National Aeronautics and Space Administration, June 2007), 41.

7 Federal Acquisition Institute, "Award without Discussions," *Contract Specialist Training Blueprints*, Unit 39 (Washington, DC: Federal Acquisition Institute, September 2002).

8 National Reconnaissance Office, *NRO Source Selection* N87 (Chantilly, VA: National Reconnaissance Office, 2008), 46.

9 National Aeronautics and Space Administration, 41.

10 Johnnie E. Wilson, *Best Value Source Selection* 715-3 (Alexandria, VA: Army Materiel Command, 1998), 21.

11 National Aeronautics and Space Administration, 47–48.

12 U.S. Government Accountability Office, "NV Services," B-284119.2 (Washington, DC: U.S. Government Accountability Office, February 25, 2000).

13 FAR 15.306(a).

14 National Aeronautics and Space Administration, 46.

15 Adapted from Bolton, 33.

16 Defense Information Systems Agency, *Source Selection Deskbook* (Arlington, VA: Defense Information Systems Agency, May 2003), 26–27.

17 U.S. Department of Energy, *Source Selection Guide*, 35–36.

18 U.S. Government Accountability Office, "Colson Services Corporation," B-310971; B-310971.2; B-310971.3 (Washington, DC: U.S. Government Accountability Office, March 21, 2008).

19 Some agencies refer to this as the *source selection statement* (SSS), and other agencies use different terms. What is important to remember is that it is a formal document that explains the decision.

20 Defense Logistics Agency, *Defense Logistics Agency FAR Supplement* 15.308 (Fort Belvoir, VA: Defense Logistics Agency).

21 Federal Acquisition Regulation (FAR) 15.306(c)(z).

Chapter 11

Establishing the Competitive Range

After the source selection authority (SSA) determines that the agency will get the best value by having discussions, the next step in the process is establishing the competitive range. The FAR states that based on the ratings of each proposal against all evaluation criteria, the contracting officer shall establish a competitive range comprising all of the most highly rated proposals, unless the range is further reduced for purposes of efficiency.[1]

The FAR offers no guidance on *how* to determine the competitive range beyond this definition. This lack of guidance gives the agencies a lot of flexibility and, again, underscores the importance of the individual evaluators' documentation of the proposal evaluations. Note that the contracting officer bases the competitive range determination on the ratings of each proposal against the evaluation criteria—in other words, the evaluators' documentation.

This chapter explains how to make a competitive range determination and includes case studies that illustrate ways in which this process can go wrong.

DEFINING THE COMPETITIVE RANGE

Which proposals are included in the competitive range, which are not, and why? To answer these questions, we'll walk step-by-step through the FAR definition of the competitive range. The definition begins by stating that the decision to include proposals in the competitive range is "based on the ratings of each proposal against all evaluation criteria." These ratings come from the evaluators' documentation or consensus sessions, depending on the agency's evaluation process. The contracting officer (CO) reviews the scoring plan and notes which proposals fall into each scoring range. It may be apparent from looking at the rankings which offerors are the most highly rated. For example, if there are three proposals with excellent ratings and three that are marginal, the three with excellent ratings are the most highly rated and would be in the competitive range.

The contracting officer determines which proposals are within the competitive range based on the evaluated price and other evaluation factors included in the RFP. He or she may limit the number of proposals in the competitive range to the greatest number that will permit an efficient competition among the most highly rated proposals[2]. In such a case, the RFP must clearly state that the government reserves the right to limit the competitive range for the purposes of efficiency. The agency should, however, not establish predetermined cutoff ratings or identify a predetermined number of offerors that may be in the competitive range. Rather, the CO should make the competitive range determination using prudent business judgment based on the specifics of the RFP criteria and the source selection plan.[3]

COMMUNICATING WITH OFFERORS BEFORE ESTABLISHING THE COMPETITIVE RANGE

If the initial proposal evaluations do not make obvious which proposals should fall into the competitive range, then the agency may communicate with the offerors to help it decide which proposals should be in the competitive range. Recall from the last chapter that the FAR identifies three types of exchanges: clarifications, communications, and discussions. We explained that clarifications are used when the agency intends to award without discussions. An agency uses communications when it needs more information from an offeror to make the competitive range determination. Offerors may not revise their proposals as a result of these communications.

Table 11-1, Clarifications, Communications, and Discussions, illustrates the distinctions between the different types of exchanges. The clarifications column was discussed in the last chapter, and the discussions column will be discussed in the next chapter. In this chapter, we'll focus on communications.

Communications are exchanges held between the government and offerors to establish a competitive range after receipt of proposals.[4] Communications are authorized only when an offeror is not clearly in or clearly out of the competitive range and are used to determine whether an offeror has a reasonable chance for award—in other words, whether it should be included in the competitive range. Information obtained during communications may also be used to:

- Amend the solicitation
- Prepare or revise negotiation objectives
- Support documentation of prenegotiation objectives.[5]

Table 11-1   Clarifications, Communications, and Discussions[6]

	Clarifications	**Communications**	**Discussions/negotiations**
When it's done	When the agency anticipates award *without* discussions	Before establishing the competitive range if the agency anticipates award *with* discussions	After establishing the competitive range. Note: the term *negotiation* applies to both competitive and noncompetitive acquisitions. In competitive acquisition, negotiation is also called *discussion*.
Scope of information exchanged	Most limited	Somewhat limited	Most detailed
Purpose	To clarify certain aspects of a proposal	Addresses issues to help the agency determine if a particular proposal should be in the competitive range	To maximize the government's ability to obtain best value
Examples of topics covered	• Relevance of past performance information • Adverse past performance information • Resolving minor or clerical errors	• Adverse past performance information • Relevance of past performance Ambiguities • Errors, omissions, or mistakes	• Past performance information • Weaknesses • Significant weaknesses • Deficiencies
Can offeror revise proposal?	No	No	Yes

It's important to note that conducting communications with one offeror does not require the contracting officer to hold communications with all offerors. Communications should not be held with those offerors the agency has no questions to ask. The contracting officer should conduct communications only with offerors:

• Whose past performance information is the determining factor preventing them from being placed within the competitive range
• Whose exclusion from, or inclusion in, the competitive range is uncertain.

Communications should identify information needed to:

• Enhance the government's understanding of the proposal
• Allow reasonable interpretation of the proposal
• Facilitate the government's evaluation process.

The contracting officer should never use communications to:

- Cure proposal deficiencies or material omissions
- Materially alter the technical or cost elements of the proposal
- Otherwise revise the proposal.[7]

If a CO permits an offeror to revise its proposal, then it has crossed the line into discussions. The contracting officer must then hold discussions with *all* offerors in the competitive range. For all practical purposes, this contracting officer has established a competitive range consisting of all offerors that were part of the competitive range at the time communications started. This is why it is important not to let communications related to the establishment of the competitive range stray into discussions.

In order to avoid any confusion over which form of exchanges the agency is conducting, the CO may consider explaining what phase of exchanges the agency and offeror are in. For example, the Army FAR supplement states, "All exchanges with offerors after receipt of proposals must clearly identify the types of exchanges, i.e., clarifications, communications or discussions."[8] Another agency requires the contracting officer to document the decision to conduct communications with offerors before establishing the competitive range.[9]

As with all elements of the source selection process, the contracting officer must carefully document communications to ensure they meet regulatory requirements and are not actually discussions. The nature and extent of the exchanges must be clearly defined for the record.[10]

After completing communications, the contracting officer must make the competitive range determination. The contracting officer and the SSA should continually reassess the competitive range as discussions and evaluations continue to ensure that neither the government nor the offerors waste resources by keeping proposals in the competition that are no longer contenders for award.

Next, let's examine a case in which an offeror protested an agency's competitive range determination.

CASE STUDY: MAKING A COMPETITIVE RANGE DETERMINATION

Arc-Tech, Inc., protested the exclusion of its proposal from the competitive range under an RFP issued by the Department of Health and Human Services (HHS) for custodial services at National Institutes of Health buildings. The solicitation stated that HHS would make contract award to the offeror whose proposal represented the best value to the government, technical, cost/price, and past performance factors considered. According to Government Accountability Office (GAO) decision B-400325.3, the protester argued that "the agency's evaluation of its proposal was unreasonable and that the agency improperly failed to consider price in its competitive range determination.

> The determination of whether a proposal is in the competitive range is principally a matter within the reasonable exercise of discretion of the procuring agency.... In reviewing an agency's evaluation of proposals and subsequent competitive range determination, [the GAO] will not evaluate the proposals anew in order to make [its] own determination as to their acceptability or relative merits; rather, [it] ... examine[s] the record to determine whether the evaluation was reasonable and consistent with the evaluation criteria.

"Arc-Tech contend[ed] that the agency failed to consider price in determining the competitive range and instead based its determination as to which proposals were included on an arbitrary technical cut-off score." Its proposal was excluded from the competitive range, Arc-Tech argued, "not because it was technically unacceptable, but because it was not among the most highly rated proposals technically.

> While the competitive range determination and the technical evaluation panel report ... both labele[d] the protester's proposal "unacceptable," neither of those documents provide[d] any explanation for such a [conclusion], and [GAO could find] no support for it anywhere else in the record.... "The results [of the individual technical evaluations] were averaged to provide a total score to determine whether the company was in the competitive range or not." [Thus,] the evaluators used the offerors' technical scores to determine whether their proposals should be included in the competitive range, and ... proposals excluded from the competitive range based on their technical scores were, simply as a consequence of their exclusion, labeled unacceptable.

> Further, there [was] no indication in the record that the agency considered the protester's proposed price as part of the competitive range determination.

Citing a general rule, GAO stated:

> An agency may not exclude a technically acceptable proposal from the competitive range without taking into account the relative cost of that proposal to the government .... That is, an agency may not exclude a technically acceptable proposal from the competitive range simply because the proposal received a lower technical rating than another proposal or proposals, without taking into consideration the proposal's price.

Because the agency's decision to exclude the protester's proposal from the competitive range was based on its technical score alone—without consideration of its relative cost to the government and without a documented finding that the proposal was unacceptable—the decision was improper, and on that basis the GAO sustained Arc-Tech's protest.[11]

This case illustrates the importance of following the evaluation criteria when making the competitive range determination. Arbitrary cutoff scores should not be used. Also, because cost is a required evaluation factor, the contracting officer must consider cost when making the competitive range determination.

LIMITING THE COMPETITIVE RANGE

In some situations, it may be appropriate to limit the size of the competitive range to allow for an efficient competition. For example, if an agency received 25 proposals, and 15 were highly rated, the source selection authority might determine that a further reduction was necessary, as it would take significant agency resources to evaluate 15 final proposal revisions. Though the FAR permits agencies to limit the number of proposals in the competitive range, it does not provide guidance on *how* to limit the competitive range, so individual agencies have the flexibility to develop their own procedures.

Generally, the following factors should be considered when attempting to identify the greatest number of proposals that will permit an efficient competition:

- The expected dollar value of the award
- The total number of highly rated offerors
- The complexity of the acquisition and the variety and complexity of offered solutions, in terms of how the chosen proposals are likely to affect the breadth and depth of the discussions
- The resources available to conduct discussions vs. the expected variable administrative costs of discussions
- The impact on lead time for award vs. the need for timely delivery
- The extent to which discussions with additional offerors would likely provide diminishing returns.[12]

One author has suggested that one efficient and effective way to further limit the competitive range is to examine the top-rated proposals to see if there is a logical break in the ranking that justifies dropping lower-rated proposals that have no reasonable chance of receiving contract award.[13] It's interesting to note that the National Aeronautics and Space Administration FAR supplement recommends that no more than three proposals be included in the competitive range.[14]

Now that readers understand the essential elements of making an efficient competitive range determination, let's look at a case in which an agency made an efficient competition determination that resulted in a protest.

CASE STUDY: EFFICIENT COMPETITION DETERMINATION

Computer & Hi-Tech Management, Inc., (CHM) protested the exclusion of its proposal from the competitive range under a request for proposals issued by the Department of Commerce (DOC) for information technology services. CHM contended that exclusion of its proposal was based on the agency's improper evaluation. Unfortunately, this case does not indicate the number of proposals in the efficient competitive range, but it gives us insight into the agency's decision-making process.

According to GAO decision B-293235.4,

> The RFP provided that the procurement would be conducted in three phases and may encompass several competitive range determinations.... Phase I [was] a down-select process in which DOC intend[ed] to select the offerors that [would] proceed to the next phase of the competition. In Phase II, qualified offerors [would] submit a more detailed technical and price proposal in accordance with the Phase II solicitation instructions.

Under Phase III (which was optional), offerors were invited to make oral presentations.

The decision continues:

> In order to determine which proposals should be included in the competitive range, the contracting officer reviewed the technical and price evaluation results and determined that the competitive range would be limited to the ... proposals assigned an overall blue rating.

According to the agency,

> This determination was made based on the fact that those offerors were substantially stronger in areas where the government believed its requirements would be met, [and to allow for] an adequate amount of competition within each tier. If offerors that [were rated] "green" had been included in the competitive range, the agency would have had to evaluate [too many] proposals, effectively precluding fair and timely evaluations. If those with an overall "yellow" rating had been included, effective and timely evaluations would have been impossible.

"CHM protest[ed] that its proposal was improperly excluded from the competitive range on the basis of an improper evaluation." The protestor also argued that it "and other offerors were impermissibly excluded from the competitive range for purposes of efficiency."

"The record shows that, while CHM submitted an acceptable proposal, its proposal was not among the ... most highly rated ones." GAO saw no basis to question the agency's determination of how many proposals constituted an efficient competitive range. "Indeed, [the GAO believes] the agency had the discretion to establish a smaller competitive range." GAO determined that the agency reasonably excluded CHM's proposal from the competitive range. The protest was denied.[15]

This case shows that agencies have broad discretion to determine how many proposals constitute an efficient competitive range and can determine the criteria by which to make that determination. Next, let's look at a case in which the agency received a protest after revising the competitive range.

CASE STUDY: A REVISED COMPETITIVE RANGE

Cambridge Systems, Inc., of Chantilly, Virginia, protested the decision by the Department of the Army, Space and Missile Defense Command (SMDC), to establish a revised competitive range under an RFP "issued as a small business set-aside for installation and testing of an integrated commercial intrusion detection system-IV (ICIDS-IV)," per the GAO protest decision. Cambridge, the apparent awardee, was determined ineligible for award under the applicable small business size standard. Cambridge challenged the agency's decision to establish a revised competitive range, rather than cancel and reissue the solicitation on an unrestricted basis.

> Seven offerors, including Cambridge, submitted proposals by the original extended closing date. The agency's source selection evaluation board (SSEB), evaluated proposals using adjectival ratings of excellent, good, satisfactory, marginal, or unsatisfactory for the technical factor and subfactors.... After reviewing the SSEB evaluation findings, the contracting officer determined that only Cambridge's proposal, the most highly rated, would be included in the competitive range.
>
> The agency sent letters to the other offerors informing them that their proposals were excluded from the competitive range and would not be considered further for award.... The agency conducted discussions with Cambridge, received and evaluated its revised proposal and determined that Cambridge's proposal represented the best value to the government. Notice of intent to make award to Cambridge was sent to the six offerors whose proposals had been excluded from the competitive range.
>
> Sim-G filed a timely protest regarding Cambridge's size status with the contracting officer, who forwarded it to the Small Business Administration (SBA).... SBA ... determined Cambridge to be other than small under the applicable size standard for this procurement and thus ineligible for award.... As a result of the SBA's determination, the agency notified Cambridge it was no longer eligible for award.
>
> The agency then decided to establish a revised competitive range consisting of the remaining most highly rated proposals. After again reviewing the initial evaluation results of the other six offerors, including the associated strengths

and weaknesses of the proposals, the contracting officer determined that the proposals submitted by Chugach and Sim-G, would be included in the revised competitive range.

Cambridge alleges that the agency impermissibly reopened the competitive range to conduct discussions with Chugach and Sim-G, whose initial proposals were previously determined technically marginal overall.... It asserts that since the proposals of the remaining small business offerors received evaluation ratings that were not acceptable, i.e., satisfactory, the set-aside should be withdrawn and the procurement recompeted on an unrestricted basis.... The decision to establish a competitive range and the determination whether a proposal should be included therein is principally a matter within the sound judgment of the procuring agency.

FAR 15.306(c)(1) requires the contracting officer

> "to establish a competitive range comprised of all of the most highly rated proposals based on the 'ratings of each proposal against all evaluation criteria." ... As mentioned previously, of the remaining small business offerors, [the agency determined that] the initial proposals submitted by Chugach and Sim-G were ... the most highly rated based on the overall technical rating of marginal. That is, the agency evaluators concluded that any errors or deficiencies in the proposals could be corrected through discussions without a major rewrite or major revision of proposals.

The protester maintained "that the agency impermissibly reopened the competitive range despite a FAR provision prohibiting it to do so." Specifically, FAR 15.306(c)(3) states: "'If an offeror's proposal is eliminated or otherwise removed from the competitive range, no further revisions to that offeror's proposal shall be accepted or considered.'

"Under this provision, the contracting agency is prohibited from accepting further proposal revisions from an offeror where the offeror's proposal is excluded from the competitive range." The GAO stated, however, that this provision does not address a situation in which, as here, the agency decides to establish a new or revised competitive range:

> It would be unreasonable to interpret this provision to effectively deprive the agency of the discretion to establish a new and/or revised competitive range, to conduct discussions with competitive range offerors, or to evaluate revised proposals. In fact, FAR part 15 specifically recognizes the authority to make successive competitive range determinations albeit generally with the intent of narrowing the competitive range. [Since GAO has] consistently upheld the agency's authority to establish successive competitive ranges, [the protest was denied].[16]

This case illustrates the flexibility the FAR affords contracting officers in making competitive range determinations. The FAR also gives contracting officers flexibility in determining how many proposals should be in the competitive range.

What happens if only one of two proposals has any chance of being selected for award? If the SSA determines that award without discussions is too risky because the agency must receive revised proposals before awarding the contract, can the agency establish a competitive range of one, or must it include the offeror with a poor proposal? The following case study shows what can happen when only one proposal comprises the competitive range.

CASE STUDY: A COMPETITIVE RANGE OF ONE

General Atomics Aeronautical Systems, Inc., (GA) protested the exclusion of its proposal from the competitive range under an RFP issued by the U.S. Army Communication-Electronics Command (CECOM). According to the GAO decision on the protest, GA asserted "that the determination to exclude its proposal from the competitive range failed to reasonably account for the performance of its proposed [synthetic aperture radar/ground moving target indicator] SAR/GMTI system in the flight test conducted as part of the evaluation."

The solicitation stated that "award was to be made to the offeror whose proposal was determined to be the most beneficial to the government ('best value') when evaluated under four factors:"

1. Technical
2. Performance risk
3. Price/cost
4. Small business participation.

Overall, the technical factor was significantly more important than performance risk, which was slightly more important than price/cost, which was significantly more important than small business participation. The non-price/cost factors combined were significantly more important than price/cost.

The RFP stated that the technical evaluation would consider:

1. Adequacy of response
2. Understanding of the requirement
3. Feasibility of the approach
4. The results of a scheduled two- or three-day flight test to be performed as part of the proposal process.

Regarding the required flight test, the solicitation stated:

"The Flight Test will be used to aid in the assessment of the Offeror's ability to produce the system as proposed. The Flight Test will be evaluated to help to determine the level of confidence provided the Government with respect to the Offeror's methods and approach in successfully completing the proposed tasks and technical requirements within the proposed schedule.... Failure to successfully demonstrate [the flight test] will be deemed a deficiency and will result in a Technical Factor rating of Unacceptable. Offerors are cautioned that they will be provided only one flight test session. Accordingly, Offerors will not be afforded an opportunity to correct any deficiencies received in the Flight Test."

[The agency] received offers from GA and Northrop Grumman Corporation (NG). Both GA and NG demonstrated SAR/GMTI systems during the required source selection flight tests in October 2007 that were evaluated as demonstrating sufficient capability in the four required areas to pass the flight test. However, analysis of the source selection flight test data resulted in GA's SAR/GMTI system receiving only a moderate confidence rating with respect to meeting proposed SAR performance, and a low confidence rating with respect to meeting proposed GMTI performance.

While GA's system passed the flight test, its proposal was rated unacceptable under the technical factor. In this regard, the source selection evaluation board ... evaluated GA's proposal as having nine deficiencies under the technical solution subfactor.... In addition to the nine deficiencies, GA's proposal was evaluated as having 13 significant weaknesses and 32 weaknesses under the technical solution subfactor.

The source selection authority ... determined that, given the evaluated major deficiencies in GA's proposal and the SSEB's conclusion that a major rewrite of the proposal would be required to make it acceptable, a rating of unacceptable under the technical solutions subfactor was consistent with the rating definitions in the source selection evaluation plan.... The source selection evaluation plan provided that an "unacceptable" rating was warranted where a proposal "contains a major error(s), omission(s) or deficiency(ies) that indicates a lack of understanding of the problems or an approach that cannot be expected to meet requirements or involves a very high risk; and none of these conditions can be corrected without a major rewrite or revision of the proposal."

The SSEB also rated GA's proposal unacceptable under the schedule/production capability subfactor (on the basis of [eight] deficiencies, 12 significant weaknesses, and [four] weaknesses) and under the supportability subfactor (on the basis of [three] deficiencies and [five] weaknesses).

The SSA determined that, in light of the fact that GA's proposal was evaluated as unacceptable (with major deficiencies) under the technical factor, and would require a major rewrite to become acceptable, it was not one of the most highly rated proposals, and on that basis excluded it from the competitive range. This resulted in a competitive range consisting only of NG's proposal....

[In summary, the GAO found that] the agency reasonably determined both that GA had failed to substantiate the compliance of its GMTI mode with the mandatory … requirements, and that the information in GA's proposal reasonably called into question whether it would in fact meet those requirements.…

[GAO asserted that] it is an offeror's responsibility to submit a well-written proposal, with adequately detailed information, that clearly demonstrates compliance with the solicitation requirements and allows a meaningful review by the procuring agency.… Where, as here, an offer does not affirmatively demonstrate compliance with mandatory requirements, the offeror risks rejection of its proposal.

[GAO concluded] that the Army reasonably determined that GA's proposal failed to substantiate compliance with, and/or took exception to[,] the required levels of performance with respect to significant mandatory … requirements. Further, given the significant deficiencies in GA's proposal, and the reasonable determination on the part of the agency that some of these deficiencies resulted from fundamental limitations on the performance of GA's proposed system, or otherwise would require a major rewrite to correct, the agency reasonably excluded GA's proposal from the competitive range.

The protest was denied.[17]

This case illustrates the importance of submitting a high-quality initial proposal. Although discussions might have improved the company's evaluation, the company was not afforded an opportunity to revise its proposal. Offerors should strive to submit the best proposals they can from the outset in order to be included in the competitive range. Those excluded from the competitive range are not entitled to participate in discussions.

PREAWARD DEBRIEFING

The contracting officer should notify offerors promptly in writing when their proposals are excluded from the competitive range or otherwise eliminated from the competition. The notice to each offeror must state the basis for excluding or eliminating its offer and that the agency will not consider a revision of its offer.[18]

The agency should then strive to conduct preaward debriefings as soon as possible to provide feedback to unsuccessful offerors. The contracting officer may refuse to provide preaward debriefings if, for compelling reasons, it is not in the best interest of the government to conduct them at that time. The CO must document the rationale for delaying the debriefing in the contract file. The debriefing must still be provided to earlier-excluded competitors no later than the time postaward debriefings are given to the other competitors.

Alternatively, an offeror may request to delay the debriefing until after contract award. By delaying the debriefing, the offeror gets more information about the competition, but obviously must wait until after contract award to get it. We'll discuss the differences between preaward and postaward debriefings in Chapter 14.

If the debriefing is delayed until after award, it must include all information normally provided in a postaward debriefing. Refer to Table 11-2 for an overview of what to include and exclude in a preaward debriefing.

Table 11-2 Preaward Debriefing Summary[19]

Preaward Debriefing	
Who is entitled to a debriefing?	Offerors excluded from the competitive range or otherwise excluded from the competition before award.
When must the government conduct the debriefing?	As soon as practical after receiving a timely written request from an offeror. The contracting officer or the offeror may ask to postpone the preaward debriefing until after contract award. When delayed, the debriefing shall include all the information provided in a postaward debriefing. This debriefing must be done within the timeframe established for postaward debriefings.
What is a *timely request*?	A request received by the contracting officer within three calendar days after the offeror received the notice of exclusion from the competition. Do not count the day the offeror received the notice; start with the next day. Consider sending the notice of exclusion by mail with return receipt requested or electronically (by fax or email) with immediate acknowledgment requested so that the contracting officer can easily establish the date the offeror received it.
What cannot be disclosed?	• The number of offerors. • The identity of other offerors. • The content of other offerors' proposals. • The ranking of other offerors. • How other offerors were evaluated. • Any of the information prohibited from disclosure by FAR 15.506(e) or FAR 24.202, including trade secrets; privileged or confidential information, e.g., manufacturing processes and techniques, commercial and financial information, and cost data; and the names of individuals who have provided past performance information. It does not include information otherwise available without restriction to the government or public. • A point-by-point comparison with other proposals.
What should be discussed?	• The agency's evaluation of significant elements in the offeror's proposal. If the element was significant enough to eliminate the offeror from the competitive range, it is significant for debriefing purposes. Discuss both positive and negative elements of the offeror's proposal to help it submit better proposals in the future. • A summary of the rationale for eliminating the offeror from the competition. • Reasonable responses to relevant questions about whether source selection procedures contained in the solicitation, applicable regulations, and other applicable authorities were followed in the process of eliminating the offeror from the competition.

A poorly prepared debriefing is the surest way to lose the confidence of the off-eror and increase the prospects of a protest. Because debriefings are time sensitive, preparation must begin before proposal evaluation is complete. The extent of preparation necessary varies considerably with the complexity of each acquisition. Sometimes, merely preparing debriefing charts with the help of source selection team members is sufficient. Other times, writing a script and holding dry-run rehearsals may be beneficial. Finally, the contracting officer must brief all government personnel who will attend the debriefing on their roles and expected demeanor during the debriefing.[20]

Whether conducting a preaward or postaward debriefing, the contracting officer should:

- Ensure that the debriefing includes all required information
- Make sure none of the information that cannot be disclosed in a debriefing is presented (see Table 11-2)
- Keep the Q&A session relatively unstructured, so that it supports a frank and open exchange of information
- Include an official summary of the debriefing in the contract file, as well as copies of any visual aids and the presentation script.[21]

CHAPTER SUMMARY

Chapter 11 explains how to make a competitive range determination. The FAR states that, based on the ratings of each proposal against all evaluation criteria, the contracting officer shall establish a competitive range composed of all the most highly rated proposals, unless the range is further reduced for purposes of efficiency.

The CO reviews the ratings from the evaluator's documentation and/or consensus sessions depending on the agency's evaluation process. The CO determines which proposals are within the competitive range based on the evaluated price and other evaluation factors included in the RFP.

The CO uses communications to determine the competitive range. If the competitive range isn't obvious after initial proposal evaluations, the agency may communicate with offerors to help it decide which proposals to include. Communications are authorized only when the offeror is not clearly within or outside the competitive range. Information obtained during communications may also be used to amend the solicitation; prepare or revise negotiation objectives; or support documentation of pre-negotiation objectives.

Contracting officers may wish to limit the competitive range. The FAR permits limiting it to the greatest number of proposals needed to support efficient competition among the most highly rated proposals. The CO may examine the most highly rated proposals to see if there is a logical break in the ranking, to justify dropping the lower rated proposals that have no reasonable chance of receiving contract award.

Certain factors are involved in conducting preaward debriefings. The contracting officer should promptly notify offerors in writing when their proposals are excluded from the competitive range or otherwise eliminated from the competition. The agency should strive to conduct preaward debriefings as soon as possible to provide feedback to unsuccessful offerors.

The CO may refuse to provide a preaward debriefing when the competitive range is established, however, if compelling reasons suggest it is not in the best interests of the government to conduct a debriefing at that time. If that happens, the CO must document the rationale for delaying the debriefing in the contract file. The agency is required to conduct a debriefing with excluded competitors no later than scheduled postaward debriefings are provided to other competitors.

Chapter 12 discusses the next step in the source selection process: conducting meaningful discussions and receiving proposal revisions.

NOTES

1 Federal Acquisition Regulation (FAR) 15.306(c).

2 FAR 15.306(c)(2).

3. Claude M. Bolton, Jr., *Army Source Selection Manual* (Washington, DC: Office of the Assistant Secretary of the Army for Acquisition, Logistics and Technology, 2007), 34–35.

4. FAR 15.306(b).

5 Federal Acquisition Institute, "Communications," *Contract Specialist Training Blueprints*, no. 40 (Washington, DC: Federal Acquisition Institute, September 2002).

6 Adapted from Bolton, 33.

7 See note 3.

8 Department of the Army, *Army Federal Acquisition Regulation Supplement* 5115.305 (Washington, DC: Department of the Army, October 2001).

9 U.S. Special Operations Command, *USSOCOM FAR Supplement* 5615.306 (MacDill Air Force Base, FL: U.S. Special Operations Command).

10 U.S. Department of Energy, *Source Selection Guide* (Washington, DC: U.S. Department of Energy, 2005), 36–37.

11 U.S. Government Accountability Office, "Arc-Tech, Inc.," B-400325.3 (Washington, DC: U.S. Government Accountability Office, February 19, 2009).

12 Federal Acquisition Institute, "Competitive Range," *Contract Specialist Training Blueprints*, no. 41 (Washington, DC: Federal Acquisition Institute, September 2002).

13 Peter S. Cole, *How to Evaluate and Negotiate Government Contracts* (Vienna, VA: Management Concepts, 2001), 351.

14 National Aeronautics and Space Administration, *NASA FAR Supplement* 1815.306 (Washington, DC: National Aeronautics and Space Administration).

15 U.S. Government Accountability Office, "Computer & High-Tech Management, Inc.," B-293235.4 (Washington, DC: U.S. Government Accountability Office, March 2, 2004).

16 U.S. Government Accountability Office, "Cambridge Systems, Inc.," B-400680; B-400680.3 (Washington, DC: U.S. Government Accountability Office, January 8, 2009).

17 U.S. Government Accountability Office, "General Atomics Aeronautics Systems, Inc.," B-311004; B-311004.2 (Washington, DC: U.S. Government Accountability Office, March 28, 2008).

18 Federal Acquisition Institute, "Competitive Range."

19 Adapted from Johnnie E. Wilson, *Best Value Source Selection* 715-3 (Alexandria, VA: Army Materiel Command, 1998), F1–F4.

20 Bolton, 48.

21 Federal Acquisition Institute, "Debriefings," *Contract Specialist Training Blueprints*, no. 47 (Washington, DC: Federal Acquisition Institute, September 2002).

Chapter 12

Discussions, Negotiations, and Proposal Revisions

At this stage in the competitive acquisition process, the source selection authority (SSA) has established the competitive range, consisting of the most highly rated proposals, and the evaluation team must get ready to begin the negotiation process. We're now halfway through the competitive source selection process. In this chapter, we'll talk about discussions and proposal revisions.

First, we will distinguish between discussions and negotiations. Then we'll explain some considerations and decisions that must be made before beginning discussions, such as preparing the negotiation plan and determining the method or place for conducting negotiations. Next, we'll talk about what to discuss during a negotiation, and finally, limits on discussions.

DISTINGUISHING BETWEEN DISCUSSIONS AND NEGOTIATIONS

The Federal Acquisition Regulation (FAR) makes a distinction between discussions and negotiations, but in practice, the terms are used interchangeably. *Negotiations* are exchanges, in either a competitive or sole source environment, between the government and offerors that an agency conducts with the intent of allowing the offeror to revise its proposal. Negotiations may include bargaining. Bargaining includes:

- Persuading
- Altering assumptions and positions
- Compromising.

Bargaining may apply to the contract's:

- Price
- Schedule

- Technical requirements
- Type
- Terms and conditions
- Other elements.[1]

Negotiations conducted after establishing the competitive range are called *discussions*. The contracting officer (CO) tailors these discussions to each proposal within the competitive range. Per the FAR, "The primary objective of discussions is to maximize the government's ability to obtain best value, based on the requirement and the evaluation factors set forth in the solicitation."[2]

PLANNING NEGOTIATIONS

Before negotiations even begin, the agency must address important preliminary matters, such as identifying a location for the negotiation and preparing a negotiation plan. Negotiations may be held via:

- Telephone conference
- Letter
- Email
- Videoconference/web conference
- Conference at the government facility
- Conference at the offeror's facility.[3]

Today, face-to-face negotiations are not as common as they used to be because videoconferencing has become more prevalent.

Once the parties know where the negotiation will occur, the next step is for each party to draft a negotiation plan. The contents may vary, but each party's plan should cover:

- The background of the acquisition (contract description, agency, contractor, negotiation history with that company/agency, purpose of the requirement, relationship to other requirements, and constraints that suggest nonnegotiable elements)
- Major and minor negotiation issues and objectives (both price and non-price)
- The party's negotiation priorities and positions on key issues, established in a range of possibilities, including minimum, objective, and maximum positions (e.g., the maximum amount the agency is willing to pay for the product or service; the minimum technical capability the agency needs to meet the requirement; or the best combination of the minimum technical quality and maximum price they're willing to accept; the highest technical solution the company can

offer for the proposed price; the minimum price the company can accept for the level of quality proposed; or the best combination of quality and price they would like to achieve)
- Negotiation approach.

The prenegotiation objectives establish the initial negotiation position. They help the contracting officer determine whether a proposed price is fair and reasonable and should be based on the results of the contracting officer's analysis of the offeror's proposal, taking into consideration all pertinent information, including pricing assistance from the field, audit reports and technical analysis, fact-finding results, independent government cost estimates, and price histories. A company may base its initial negotiation position on profit goals, a corporate business plan forecast, and its contractual history with the agency.

The contracting officer establishes prenegotiation objectives before negotiating any pricing action. The scope and depth of the analysis supporting the objectives should be directly related to the dollar value, importance, and complexity of the pricing action. When the evaluation requires cost analysis, the contracting officer documents the pertinent issues to be negotiated, the cost objectives, and a profit or fee objective.[4]

Before a negotiation, it's a good practice to review the negotiation plan with key negotiation team members. Everyone participating in the negotiation should be aware of objectives and levels of flexibility from one negotiated topic to another.

- Present the plan to the team.
- Encourage others on the team to identify weaknesses and alternatives.
- Revise the plan as necessary.
- Define the role each team member will play in putting the plan into action.
- Ensure positions and the overall plans are fair and reasonable.[5]

From these negotiation plans, both parties can develop an agenda for the negotiation session. One of the more difficult tasks during a negotiation is to confine the discussion to the important topics while avoiding irrelevant subjects or those slated to be discussed later. Setting an agenda for both sides to follow can help promote a productive and efficient discussion. The CO may want to prepare a draft agenda for the company review before starting negotiations. This professional courtesy gives the company an idea of what is most important to the agency and an opportunity to recommend changes to the agenda. Some negotiators prefer to wait until the start of negotiations to present the agenda, but this approach may lengthen negotiations because the parties will take time at the beginning to review the agenda.[6]

IDENTIFYING TOPICS FOR DISCUSSION

The most important step in the process for the contracting officer is determining what to discuss with each offeror. Remember that the primary objective of discussions is to maximize the government's ability to obtain the best value based on the requirement and the evaluation factors in the RFP.[7] At a minimum, the contracting officer must discuss with each offeror still being considered for award deficiencies, significant weaknesses, and adverse past performance information to which the offeror has not yet had an opportunity to respond. The contracting officer also is encouraged to discuss other aspects of the offeror's proposal that could, in the CO's opinion, be altered or explained to materially enhance the proposal's potential for award.

The contracting officer is not required, however, to discuss every way in which the proposal could be improved. The scope and extent of discussions are a matter of the CO's judgment, but they must meet the definition of *meaningful*, as described in a variety of GAO decisions.[8]

The government may, in situations in which the solicitation states that evaluation credit will be given for technical solutions exceeding any mandatory minimums, negotiate with offerors for increased performance beyond any mandatory minimums. Also, the government may, if it is in its best interest, suggest to offerors that have exceeded any mandatory minimums (in ways that are not integral to the design) that their proposals would be more competitive if the excesses were removed and the offered price decreased.[9]

The CO may use the consolidated reports from evaluator consensus sessions to develop questions to ask the offerors. In addition, the government may disclose its rating for each factor in the offeror's proposal. If the agency provides this information, the CO should state that the ratings are not subject to negotiation and are being disclosed for informational purposes only. In other words, an offeror cannot change its rating, but the rating may help it determine what parts of its proposal should be revised.

Identifying Significant Weaknesses

A *significant weakness* in a proposal is a flaw that appreciably increases the risk of unsuccessful contract performance. A *weakness* is a flaw in a proposal that increases the risk of unsuccessful contract performance.[10]

If a proposal contains a significant weakness, the CO must disclose it to the offeror, explaining what part of the proposal is affected by the weakness. For example, an offeror should be told that personnel it has proposed appear only minimally qualified in the skills required for contract performance. The CO should not merely restate the solicitation requirements. This will not help the offeror identify the proposal weakness and may even be a basis for a protest.

Agencies do not need to discuss every minor weakness or aspect of a proposal that receives less than the maximum possible rating. However, they may not conduct prejudicially unequal discussions. They must take a balanced approach to discussing weaknesses. For example, they may not discuss every minor weakness with one offeror and only significant weaknesses with another. In addition, agencies should never offer suggestions on how to correct any weakness. However, they should emphasize the importance of correcting significant weaknesses.

Identifying Deficiencies

A *deficiency* is a material failure of a proposal to meet a government requirement or a combination of significant weaknesses in a proposal that increases the risk of unsuccessful contract performance to an unacceptable level.[11]

If a proposal contains a deficiency, it must be revealed during discussions so that the offeror can correct it. For example, if the proposed project manager's qualifications do not meet minimum contract requirements, point that out to the offeror. As with weaknesses, the agency must not offer suggestions on how to correct a deficiency. In addition, the agency must emphasize to the offeror that unless proposal deficiencies are corrected, the proposal evaluation will reflect the unacceptable level of performance risk associated with the deficiencies.

In addition to significant weaknesses and deficiencies, the agency also should identify other aspects of the proposal that could be improved to enhance the offeror's chance of receiving the contract award.[12] At the same time, the agency must be extremely careful to not engage in *technical transfusion*, which is the intentional or inadvertent disclosure to one competitor of a solution or approach taken by another competitor. This is discussed more fully later in this chapter.

Identifying Other Items for Possible Improvement

Because the objective of discussions is to maximize the government's ability to obtain the best value, it makes sense to also discuss other aspects of the offeror's proposal that could be changed or explained. For example:

- As mentioned previously, if the solicitation states that evaluation credit will be given for technical solutions exceeding mandatory minimums, the contracting officer may:

- Negotiate for performance that exceeds the minimums; or
- Suggest that an offeror remove excesses that aren't integral to the design and decrease the price to make a proposal more competitive.[13]
- If the contracting officer's analysis indicates that the proposed cost or price is unreasonably high or is unrealistically low for the work required, tell the offeror this and support the assessment.
- For cost-reimbursement proposals, remind the offeror that the proposed cost may be adjusted for evaluation based on the most probable cost to the government.
- For fixed-price proposals, remind the offeror that an unrealistically low price may be considered a performance risk.[14]

We'll discuss the offeror's responses to discussion items later in this chapter.

After discussions begin, the contracting officer may determine that a particular proposal is no longer among the most highly rated and may eliminate the proposal from the competitive range. Remember, the contracting officer is not required to discuss all material aspects of such a proposal with the offeror or to provide the offeror with an opportunity to revise its proposal before eliminating it from the competitive range. Once a contracting officer eliminates a proposal from the competitive range, he or she must not request or accept any further proposal revisions from the offeror.[15]

Limits on Discussions

Although the scope and extent of discussions are determined by the contracting officer, there are limits to what a CO can discuss.[16] The FAR states that government personnel involved in an acquisition shall not engage in conduct that:

- Favors one offeror over another.
- Reveals an offeror's technical solution, including unique technology, innovative and unique uses of commercial items, or any information that would compromise an offeror's intellectual property, to another offeror.
- Reveals an offeror's price without that offeror's permission. The contracting officer may, however, inform an offeror that its price is considered by the government to be too high or too low, and he or she may reveal the results of the analysis supporting that conclusion. It is also permissible, at the government's discretion, to indicate to all offerors the cost or price that the government's price analysis, market research, and other reviews have identified as reasonable.
- Reveals the names of individuals providing reference information about an offeror's past performance.
- Knowingly furnishes source selection information in violation of FAR 3.104.[17]

A contracting officer should never mislead an offeror into submitting a final proposal revision (FPR) that fails to address the concerns identified during the initial proposal evaluation. For example, a CO should not suggest an offeror review its proposal for additional cost savings if the proposed price already appears unrealistically low. Such discussions could mislead the offeror into submitting a FPR that reduces price without addressing cost realism. That FPR would likely be evaluated as offering less value to the government than the original proposal.[18]

Now that readers understand the essential elements of conducting discussions, let's examine a case study that explains what the GAO considers "adequate discussions."

Case Study: Adequate Discussions

Comprehensive Health Services, Inc., (CHS) protested the award of a contract to Logistic Health, Inc., (LHI) under an RFP issued by the Department of the Army. CHS challenged the adequacy of the discussions.

According to Government Accountability Office (GAO) decision B-310553, "The RFP sought proposals to support the Reserve Health Readiness Program (RHRP), under which reserve military personnel are provided medical and dental support services." The proposals were to be evaluated for "best value" on the basis of five factors (the first three of which included subfactors):

1. Technical approach for periodic health assessments (PHA)
2. Technical approach for postdeployment health reassessments (PDHRA)
3. Corporate and management capabilities
4. Past performance
5. Price.

Per the GAO decision,

> Factors 1 and 2 were of equal weight and were considered more important than factors 3 and 4, which were of equal weight. The non-price factors were rated on an adjectival basis (exceptional, good, acceptable, marginal, unacceptable, or, for past performance only, neutral) and, combined, were significantly more important than price. [See Table 12-1.] Price was to be evaluated for completeness, reasonableness, and to ensure offerors understood the RFP's scope of work.

After the initial evaluation, only CHS's and LHI's proposals were included in the competitive range, and discussions were conducted with both.

Based on the SSEB's evaluation report, the source selection advisory council (SSAC) recommended award to LHI as the best value based on its technically superior

Table 12-1 Army Case Study Evaluation Results

	CHS	LHI
Factor 1: Technical approach, PHA	**Good**	**Good**
General requirements	Good	Good
Individual medical readiness	Good	Exceptional
Additional services	Acceptable	Good
Factor 2: Technical approach, PDHRA	**Acceptable**	**Exceptional**
Understanding requirements	Acceptable	Exceptional
General requirements	Acceptable	Exceptional
Factor 3: Corporate/management	**Acceptable**	**Exceptional**
Program management	Acceptable	Exceptional
Quality control plan	Good	Exceptional
Transition plan	Acceptable	Good
Factor 4: Past performance	**Acceptable**	**Good**
Overall rating	**Acceptable**	**Good**
Factor 5: Price	$706,953,207	$784,474,334

proposal. After reviewing and independently analyzing the various evaluation reports and the SSAC's award recommendation, the source selection authority ... concluded that the benefits offered by LHI's proposal indeed outweighed its higher price. The agency thus made award to LHI. After a written debriefing, CHS filed this protest

GAO's decision continues:

> CHS assert[ed] that the agency failed to provide it with meaningful discussions regarding weaknesses under factor 1, technical approach PHA. It maintains that the agency's discussion questions ... did not reasonably alert the firm to the specific issues of concern to the agency.

> When an agency engages in discussions with an offeror, the discussions must be meaningful, that is, must lead the offeror into the areas of its proposal that require correction or amplification.... An agency need not "spoon-feed" an offeror as to each and every item that must be revised or addressed to improve the submission....

> [GAO ruled that] the discussions here were meaningful. For example, the agency asked CHS to describe its processes for minimizing vaccine waste and cost. CHS state[d] that it understood the agency's area of concern to be the treatment of expired vaccines, and assert[ed] that the agency was required to clearly state that its concern was with recovery of unused vaccines....

[GAO disagreed, stating,] The recovery of unused vaccines clearly is directly related to the agency's discussion question focusing on minimizing vaccine waste and cost.

As another example, the [performance-based statement of work] PBSOW established requirements for cardiovascular screening based on various parameters, such as screening for all service members age 40 and above in the Army Reserve and National Guard ..., and for Navy and Marine Reserve personnel, screening for males at age 35 and females at age 45.

CHS's initial proposal did not adequately address all of these requirements, so the agency asked CHS "to more fully explain its proposed program for cardiovascular screening. In its [final proposal revision], CHS failed to address the differing Navy and Marine requirements.

In light of the specific identification of the differing requirements for cardiovascular screening among the different [service components] in the RFP, and CHS's responsibility for addressing all PBSOW requirements in its proposal, [GAO ruled that] the agency's discussion question was sufficient to draw the firm's attention to the area of its proposal needing amplification.

The protest was denied.[19]

This case illustrates the importance of an offeror's responding adequately and completely to an agency's inquiries regarding its proposal weaknesses and deficiencies. Also, as the GAO stated, it is not necessary for the agency to specify each and every item that must be revised or addressed to improve the offeror's submission.

CONDUCTING NEGOTIATIONS

According to the Federal Acquisition Institute and Air Force Institute of Technology *Contract Pricing Reference Guide,*

Negotiation is a process of communication by which two parties, each with its own viewpoint and objectives, attempt to reach a mutually satisfactory result on a matter of common concern.

In negotiation, a mutually satisfactory result is vital, because even though the parties may have opposing interests they also are dependent on each other. Labor and management, for example, need each other to produce products efficiently and effectively. Likewise, buyers and sellers need each other to transact business. Both sides must be willing to live with the result.

Negotiation is not one party dictating or imposing terms on another. When that happens, the outcome will rarely produce mutual satisfaction.... While negotiation is often a process of mutual sacrifice, it should also be a process of finding ways whereby both parties will have their interests optimized under the circumstances. Negotiations should not just be aimed at how to split the pie. Instead they should be aimed at finding optimal solutions—ways to make the pie larger for both parties.[20]

The result of a negotiation can be mutually satisfactory only if the parties consider both differences and common interests. To reach an agreement, one party must generally give up something in order to get something in return. In other words, negotiators have to give to get. But as long as the anticipated benefit is greater than the sacrifice, the negotiator benefits from the agreement. A party reaches its limit on giving when it believes that the concessions cost more than the benefits received.

Negotiations are more likely to end successfully, with both parties satisfied about the result, when both parties plan for a fair outcome by making fair concessions.[21] The likelihood of a successful negotiation decreases, however, when either party is poorly motivated or acts unfairly. Achieving negotiation success is particularly difficult when one party is unwilling to compromise or show any flexibility.[22]

Negotiation Skills

Those who are new to the acquisition profession tend to be nervous about their first negotiation sessions. Although this is understandable, they should keep in mind that they've been negotiating since childhood; they just didn't call it that. For example, surely they've negotiated for one more cookie or were successful at getting the car keys on both Friday and Saturday nights. The skills needed to get what they wanted then can apply now to formal negotiation situations. For example, asking for a cookie right before dinner probably didn't work, but it was possible to get one after school. This was effective planning. And when asking for the car keys, they knew which parent was more likely to hand them over.

Both government and industry personnel benefit from strong negotiation skills. The best negotiators:

- **Plan carefully.** Planning begins with requirement development and continues through negotiation. It includes market research, solicitation preparation, and proposal evaluation. A negotiator must know the product, the alternatives, and the objectives.
- **Have management support.** Management support is vital to success as a negotiator. If the other party knows that management does not support the negotiation team, the other party may simply tolerate the negotiators until they can escalate the negotiation to management. Make sure negotiators have management support before beginning the negotiation.

- **Effectively apply bargaining techniques.** Good negotiators use effective bargaining techniques. Bargaining involves persuading; altering assumptions and positions when the other party explains its position; and compromising; and may apply to the contract's price, schedule, technical requirements, type, or other elements.[23]
- **Communicate effectively.** A good negotiator:
  - Sells others on his or her bargaining position by speaking in an articulate, confident, and businesslike manner.
  - Disagrees with others in a cordial and non-argumentative manner.
  - Listens effectively. Many otherwise good negotiators begin concentrating on their own answer almost as soon as the other party begins speaking. As a result, they miss the true meaning of what the other party is saying.
- **Tolerate conflict while searching for agreement.** Most contract negotiations involve some conflict. After all, no two people on earth agree on everything all the time. Consider the results of three different negotiation styles:
  - A successful negotiator who can agree to disagree in a polite, respectful manner is able to search for ways to achieve a mutually satisfactory outcome.
  - Negotiators who will give anything to avoid conflict are often not able to secure satisfactory results for their side.
  - Negotiators who tend to argue increase conflict and make a satisfactory outcome more difficult to attain.
- **Project honesty.** Good negotiators are honest, and they make others believe that they are honest. Securing trust is vital to securing a mutually satisfactory outcome. It's difficult to get concessions from the other side if it does not trust the negotiators.
- **Foster team cooperation.** All members of the negotiation team may not agree on every issue, but the lead negotiator or team leader must resolve disagreements in a manner that fosters team cooperation and gives the appearance of team unity during contract negotiations.
- **Apply good business judgment.** Good negotiators are able to evaluate every change in a negotiating position based on how the change affects the chances of attaining a mutually satisfactory result.[24]

Negotiation Styles

Negotiation styles are simply different ways to meet an organization's objectives. In general, there are three negotiation styles: win/win, win/lose, and lose/lose. Negotiators who take a long-term view and want a good working relationship with the other party have a win/win negotiation style. Conversely, some negotiators have a "win at all costs," or a win/lose attitude, which may alienate coworkers and the other team. The organization might attain its goal this time, but this attitude may have a negative effect on the next negotiation. Any negotiation can succeed or fail, but the negotiation style may make one or the other more likely.

Win/Win

A *win/win* outcome happens when both sides achieve long-term satisfaction with the negotiation results. Negotiations emphasize developing a mutually beneficial agreement. For example, awarding a contract at a fair and reasonable price is in the best interest of both the offeror and the government.

Companies emphasize win/win negotiations because long-term business relationships are increasingly important. Each side has a vested interest in mutual long-term satisfaction. Any short-term advantage achieved by wringing out every last concession is usually not as important as a long-lasting business relationship.

There are several important reasons government negotiators also should strive for win/win outcomes. The FAR paves the way for a mutually satisfactory result by emphasizing negotiation guidelines such as best value, fair and reasonable pricing, equitable adjustments, and fair compensation for work performed. The following FAR citations illustrate the importance of fairness:

- FAR 15.101: The best value continuum
- FAR 15.402(a): Pricing policy
- FAR 43.103(a): Bilateral contract modifications
- FAR 49.201(a): Contract termination settlement.

All of these FAR guidelines make clear that the government should not win at the expense of the offeror or contractor. The reasons are simple:

- The government has a vested interest in the long-term success and survival of its suppliers.
- High-quality companies that provide goods and services at reasonable prices are essential to government operations.
- A company's success enhances competition by encouraging more firms to do business with the government, and increased competition reduces contract prices and improves quality.

Thus, win/win negotiators often achieve better outcomes. A negotiator is less likely to be giving and trusting if the other party's negotiator displays selfishness and mistrust. The genuine concern demonstrated by win/win negotiators is frequently reciprocated by the other party. Win/win negotiations are typically much less confrontational and tend to foster better long-term relationships. Finally, win/win negotiations are characterized by much higher levels of trust and cooperation, which facilitate the negotiation process.

Agencies and offerors can establish a positive win/win environment by:

- Greeting the other team cordially
- Taking time to introduce participants
- Helping participants feel at ease
- Briefly reviewing background information
- Emphasizing the goal of a win-win outcome
- Reviewing the negotiation agenda.[25]

Win/Lose

A *win/lose* outcome happens when one side has a better result at the expense of the other. This type of negotiation tends to be highly competitive, with a lot of mistrust on both sides.

In commercial business, win/lose outcomes often occur when the negotiators don't anticipate getting more business beyond the initial transaction. Thus, there is no motivation to ensure long-term satisfaction for the other side. There are many win/lose outcomes in everyday life—for example, home and auto sales. The negotiators generally don't plan to have more transactions with the other party.

What happens when a win/lose negotiation occurs?

- Because of the competitiveness and mistrust that characterized the negotiation, both sides may feel as if they lost.
- The losing side might feel good at the conclusion of the negotiation, initially believing that it got the best deal possible under the circumstances.
- In the long run, the losing party often regrets the agreement after discovering that the deal wasn't a good one after all.
- The losing party becomes even more mistrustful of the other party and is reluctant to continue any sort of business relationship.[26]

Some contracting officers might argue that the government is in a superior bargaining position because it is the only customer in certain situations. While this may be true, it doesn't justify a win/lose negotiation strategy. In some government contracts a *monopsony* exists: The government is the only buyer. In this situation, the government could achieve many short-term wins to the detriment of contractors by dictating unfavorable contract terms. But according to the *Contract Pricing Reference Guide*, "win/lose outcomes may have the following negative long-term consequences:

- Suppliers on the losing end of win/lose negotiations may be forced out of business.
- High-quality suppliers may no longer be willing to do business with the government.

- Contracts with the remaining suppliers may have a greater risk of poor-quality or overpriced deliverables."[27]

Clearly, these outcomes are not in the best interest of the government in the long run.

Lose/Lose

When there is a deadlock, the negotiating outcome is called *lose/lose*. A deadlock happens when the parties can't reach a final agreement. The contractor side may lose more than just the profit projected for the lost government contract. For example,

- "Any contribution income (i.e., the difference between revenue and variable cost) that could have been used to help absorb the company's fixed costs may be lost. As a result, all fixed costs must be absorbed by the other business of the firm. The resulting cost increases for those items may reduce company profits and may even contribute to overall company losses."
- The company may no longer need the direct labor associated with the proposed contract. As a result, the contractor may be forced to lay off employees. A layoff may affect labor management relations. It might also increase direct labor costs for other contracts, because layoffs typically affect lower-paid employees first.[28]

Now, let's take a look at the steps that follow negotiations: the possibility of another competitive range determination and the receipt of proposal revisions.

REVISING PROPOSALS

A *proposal revision* is a change to a proposal made after the solicitation closing date, at the request of, or as allowed by, a contracting officer as the result of negotiations.[29] The contracting officer may request or allow proposal revisions to clarify ambiguities or document understandings reached during negotiations. Proposal revisions may occur on an interim basis and/or at the end of the process. The FAR requires only final proposal revisions, so offerors may not have the opportunity to submit interim proposal revisions.

Interim Proposal Revisions

The contracting officer should not require offerors to submit more information than necessary for discussions and proposal evaluation. Normally, this means agencies use offerors' initial proposals during discussions. The contracting officer may, however, request or allow a proposal revision during discussions to clarify an offeror's position for further discussion.[30]

If the agency is expecting a written response from an offeror, it's a good idea for the contracting officer to establish a page limit and a format for the offeror's response to the agency's questions. The evaluation team should follow a structured approach to reviewing the offeror's response, just as it did during the initial proposal evaluations. The evaluators must determine whether the offeror provided an adequate response to the agency's questions. An adequate response:

- Reflects the offeror's clear understanding of the agency's need for additional information.
- Provides requested information.
- Does not reveal a previously unknown deficiency. If the offeror creates a deficiency, the agency may create a new deficiency report or revise the competitive range.

If the evaluators determine that the offeror did not provide an adequate response, the evaluation team will document any parts of the offeror's response that indicate the offeror misunderstood or failed to address the agency's concerns. The evaluation team then develops a recommendation for either reducing the competitive range or issuing new questions to continue the discussions.[31]

Final Proposal Revisions

When the CO determines that the discussions are complete, and the government has notified offerors of their proposals' deficiencies and significant weaknesses and maximized its ability to obtain best value, the CO closes discussions by requesting final proposal revisions. He or she must give each offeror still in the competitive range an opportunity to submit an FPR.

The request for FPRs should be made in writing. This written request serves as the formal notice to the offeror that discussions have concluded. The request should state that offerors must document changes identified during discussions in their final proposal revisions. It also should:

- Include preparation and formatting instructions for FPRs
- Establish a common cutoff date for receipt of FPRs from all offerors still in the competitive range
- Advise each offeror that:
  - Its FPR must be in writing
  - Clarity is essential
  - The government intends to make award without obtaining further revisions.[32]

The CO can set the FPR due date based on the date of its discussion with the last offeror. All offerors should be given adequate time for FPR preparation.

Depending on the extent of discussions and resulting proposal revisions, the contracting officer may require offerors to submit changed pages, revised proposal volumes, or a completely revised proposal. The contracting officer should direct offerors to trace changes to the initial proposal and to any revisions made during discussions and should also direct each offeror to fully substantiate changes to its cost proposal. The CO must notify offerors that the agency may not accept unsupported cost changes.

The contracting officer may require offerors to highlight text changes and might suggest a method for doing this. For example, text change bars could be placed in the page margins of the final proposals, or offerors could indicate changes in redline, bold, strikeout, or italicized text. FPRs should also include an index of changed pages. Requiring offerors to specifically identify proposal changes makes it easier for evaluators to distinguish information from the different proposal versions.

The contracting officer may also request that offerors use a different color binder for the FPR to make the revised proposal readily distinguishable from earlier versions. Page limitations established in the solicitation for initial proposals can also be applied to FPRs. (Note that if the CO asks offerors to use strikeout notation for deleted or replaced material, the CO can still verify adherence to page limitations by hiding or turning off the strikeout feature.)

Regardless of the method selected, offerors should prepare their FPRs in a manner that allows evaluators to quickly determine the purpose and extent of the changes.[33]

Case Study: Misleading Discussions and the Final Proposal Revision

The final proposal revision is the last opportunity for the offeror to communicate its understanding of the agency's requirements. But how can an offeror do this if the agency misled it during the discussion process? Let's review a case in which that happened.

Cygnus Corporation protested the award of a contract by the Department of Health and Human Services, National Institutes of Health (NIH), to The Hill Group (THG). Cygnus challenged the evaluation of proposals and asserted that the agency failed to conduct meaningful discussions.

According to the GAO decision on the protest,

> Award was to be made to the responsible contractor whose offer was determined to provide the best overall value to the government. The best value proposal was to be

determined based on cost and the technical evaluation factors, including past performance [and two technical evaluation criteria: personnel capabilities and organizational capability]. The RFP provided that past performance was not to be scored, but indicated that past performance would be "highly influential" in determining the relative merits of the proposals. Overall, the technical proposal was to receive "paramount consideration" in the selection of the contractor, and all evaluation factors other than cost were, when combined, significantly more important than cost.

NIH opened technical and cost discussions with offerors in the competitive range by letter.... Based upon offerors' responses to the letters ..., NIH ... requested additional cost information. The NIH contracting officer, project officer[,] and contract specialist conducted site visits ... in which they met offerors' key personnel and toured offerors' facilities. After then conducting oral discussions with offerors, NIH ... requested final proposal revisions.... Subsequently..., as a result of a delay in the expected award date, NIH afforded offerors an opportunity to submit a second FPR.

Based upon its evaluation of the FPRs, NIH determined that THG's offer was technically superior overall. Specifically, the [source selection document] explained that while, as a result of negotiations, all offerors were "qualified," THG's proposal was superior to Cygnus's under several of the technical subcriteria and with respect to past performance.

[In its protest,] Cygnus assert[ed] that NIH failed to advise it during discussions of perceived weaknesses in its proposal and, where [NIH] did raise other matters during discussions, affirmatively misled [Cygnus] into believing that such other matters had been satisfactorily resolved during discussions.

[GAO stated that] discussions must be meaningful, equitable, and not misleading.... Discussions cannot be meaningful unless they lead a firm into those weaknesses, excesses[,] or deficiencies in its quote or proposal that must be addressed in order for it to have a reasonable chance of being selected for contract award.

[GAO held that] NIH's discussions with Cygnus did not comply with the requirement that discussions be meaningful.... In explaining why THG's proposal was superior to Cygnus's proposal..., notwithstanding the significantly lower cost of Cygnus's proposal, THG's proposal represented the best value to the government, the source selection authority cited a number of weaknesses in Cygnus's proposal.... NIH, however, failed to raise several of these weaknesses during the discussions with Cygnus.

Thus, the agency failed to advise Cygnus that the agency had found what it perceived to be a major weakness under the most important technical evaluation subcriterion. GAO further noted that

in conducting discussions with Cygnus, the agency was [minimally] required to discuss [this concern], since the agency indisputably viewed it as [a] major weakness.

Moreover, while NIH did raise other matters of concern during discussions, the record indicates that the agency misled the protester as to the results of those discussions, advising Cygnus that it had successfully addressed the agency's concerns when this in fact does not appear to have been the case.

[W]hen the agency afforded Cygnus and the other offerors ... an opportunity to submit a second FPR, it advised Cygnus in its letter that "discussions ... resulted in agreement of all technical and cost issues raised during negotiations." ... According to the sworn declarations of Cygnus's president and Cygnus's comptroller, when asked whether the agency had any remaining unresolved concerns with Cygnus's proposal, the agency representatives responded in the negative.... While NIH was not required to advise Cygnus as to the results of the discussions, it was improper for the agency to mislead Cygnus in this regard. In summary, the record clearly establishe[d] that the agency conducted inadequate and misleading discussions with Cygnus.

The protest was sustained.[34]

This case illustrates the importance of disclosing significant weaknesses and deficiencies to the offeror before requesting final proposal revisions. If there are any outstanding or unresolved issues remaining, the CO must advise the offeror about those issues so the offeror can address them in the FPR. Conducting misleading discussions is improper and will result in a sustained protest.

DOCUMENTING THE NEGOTIATION

When the negotiation is complete, the CO must document the results for the record. Although the FAR requires the CO to document the negotiation, there is no corresponding regulatory requirement for the offeror to do the same. Nonetheless, it's still a good idea for companies to document the negotiation for their own records. The documentation will be useful during contract performance if the offeror wins the contract, but even if it does not, the information is a useful addition to the offeror's capture planning file cabinet (discussed in Chapter 7). Although much of the following is directed to agencies, contractors can also apply it to their own documentation.

The contracting officer's primary concern is the overall price the government will actually pay. A price negotiation memorandum (PNM) is a detailed summary of a contract's technical, business, contractual, and pricing (including price reasonableness) elements, as well as other negotiated elements of the contract and the methodology and rationale used to arrive at the final negotiated agreement.[35]

The CO's objective is to negotiate a contract of a type and with a price that will give the contractor the greatest incentive for efficient and economical performance. Contract type and price negotiations are related and should be considered along with the level of risk and uncertainty to the contractor and the government. The contracting officer should not become preoccupied with any single element and should balance the contract type, cost, and profit or fee negotiated to achieve a total result—a price that is fair and reasonable to both the government and the contractor.[36]

The contracting officer is required by the FAR to document the principal elements of the negotiated agreement in the contract file. This documentation, *including the PNM*, shall include the following:

1. The purpose of the negotiation.
2. A description of the acquisition, including appropriate identifying numbers (e.g., the RFP number).
3. The name, position, and organization of each person representing the contractor and the government in the negotiation.
4. The current status of any contractor systems (e.g., purchasing, estimating, accounting, and compensation) that affected and were considered in the negotiation.
5. If cost or pricing data were not required in the case of any price negotiation exceeding the cost or pricing data threshold, the exception used and the basis for it.
6. If cost or pricing data were required, whether the contracting officer:
   6.1. Relied on the cost or pricing data submitted and used them in negotiating the price;
   6.2. Recognized as inaccurate, incomplete, or noncurrent any cost or pricing data submitted; the action taken by the contracting officer and the contractor as a result; and the effect of the defective data on the price negotiated; or
   6.3. Determined that an exception applied after the data were submitted; the data were no longer considered *certified* cost or pricing data.
7. A summary of the contractor's proposal; any field pricing assistance recommendations, such as those obtained from a DCAA Field Audit Office, including the reasons for any pertinent variances from the recommendations; the government's negotiation objective; and the negotiated position. If the determination of price reasonableness was based on cost analysis, the summary shall address each major cost element. When determination of price reasonableness was based on price analysis, the summary shall include the source and type of data used to support the determination.

8. The most significant facts or considerations controlling the establishment of the prenegotiation objectives and the negotiated agreement, including an explanation of any significant differences between the two positions.

9. To the extent such direction has a significant effect on the action, a discussion and quantification of the impact of direction given by Congress, other agencies, and higher-level officials (i.e., officials who would not normally exercise authority during the award and review process for the contract action).

10. The basis for the profit or fee prenegotiation objective and the profit or fee negotiated.

11. Documentation of fair and reasonable pricing.

12. Whenever field pricing assistance has been obtained, the contracting officer shall forward a copy of the negotiation documentation to the office(s) that provided assistance. When appropriate, information on how advisory field support can be made more effective should be provided separately.[37]

CHAPTER SUMMARY

Chapter 12 explains discussions, negotiations, and the proposal revision process. The FAR makes a distinction between discussions and negotiations, but in practice, the terms are used interchangeably. Negotiations may include bargaining, which involves persuading; altering assumptions and positions when the other party explains its position; and compromising; and may apply to the contract's price, schedule, technical requirements, type, terms and conditions, or other elements.

Certain considerations apply to preliminary matters, such as determining where and how negotiations will occur and developing a negotiation plan. Once the parties know where the negotiation will occur, each party should draft a negotiation plan. The negotiation plan includes major and minor negotiation issues and objectives (both price and non-price) and the party's negotiation priorities and positions on key issues.

Agencies must disclose certain information during negotiations. The primary objective of discussions is to maximize the government's ability to obtain the best value based on the requirement and the evaluation factors stated in the RFP. At a minimum, the CO must discuss with each eligible offeror any proposal deficiencies, significant weaknesses, and adverse past performance information to which the offeror has not yet had an opportunity to respond.

The CO is also encouraged to discuss other aspects of the offeror's proposal that the company could alter or explain to materially enhance its potential for award. The contracting officer is not required, however, to discuss every opportunity to improve the proposal. The scope and extent of discussions are a matter of the CO's judgment, as long as the discussions prove meaningful.

Other considerations applying to the negotiation include the negotiator's abilities and different negotiation styles (e.g., win/win, win/lose, and lose/lose). The objective should be to conduct a win/win negotiation. A win/win outcome happens when both sides achieve long-term satisfaction with the negotiation results. Negotiations emphasize developing a mutually beneficial agreement. For example, awarding a contract at a fair and reasonable price is in the best interest of both the offeror and the government.

The proposal revision process includes interim proposal revisions and final proposal revisions. A proposal revision is a change to a proposal made after the solicitation closing date, at the request of or as allowed by a contracting officer as a result of negotiations.[38] The CO may request or allow proposal revisions to clarify ambiguities or document understandings reached during negotiations. Proposal revisions may occur on an interim basis and/or at the end of the process. The FAR requires the opportunity for only final proposal revisions, so offerors may not have an opportunity to submit interim proposal revisions.

After the negotiations, the CO must document negotiation results for the record. Although the FAR requires the CO to document the negotiation, there is no corresponding regulatory requirement for the offeror to do the same. Nevertheless, it's still a good idea for offerors to document the negotiation for their own records. The documentation will be useful during contract performance, but even if the offeror does not win the contract, the information will be useful for future planning during similar solicitations.

At this stage in the source selection process, evaluators need to review the final proposal revisions just as they did during initial proposal evaluations, applying the same standards and criteria as before. Afterward, the source selection authority reviews their evaluations and makes a trade-off decision. Chapter 13 discusses trade-off decisions.

NOTES

1 Federal Acquisition Regulation (FAR) 15.306(d).

2 Ibid.

3 Federal Acquisition Institute, "Conducting Discussions," *Contract Specialist Training Blueprints*, no. 43 (Washington, DC: Federal Acquisition Institute, September 2002).

4 FAR 15.406-1.

5   Federal Acquisition Institute, "Negotiation Strategy," *Contract Specialist Training Blueprints*, no. 42 (Washington, DC: Federal Acquisition Institute, September 2002).

6   Federal Acquisition Institute and the Air Force Institute of Technology, "Negotiation Techniques," *Contract Pricing Reference Guide*, vol. 5 (Washington, DC: Federal Acquisition Institute, 2005), 57, 60.

7   FAR 15.306(d)(2).

8   FAR 15.306(d)(3).

9   FAR 15.306(d)(4).

10   FAR 15.001.

11   Ibid.

12   FAR 15.306(d)(3).

13   FAR 15.306(d)(4).

14   Federal Acquisition Institute and the Air Force Institute of Technology, 140.

15   FAR 15.306(d)(5).

16   FAR 15.306(d)(3).

17   FAR 15.306(e).

18   Federal Acquisition Institute and the Air Force Institute of Technology, 141

19   U.S. Government Accountability Office, "Comprehensive Health Services, Inc.," B-310553 (Washington, DC: U.S. Government Accountability Office, December 27, 2007).

20   Federal Acquisition Institute and the Air Force Institute of Technology, 2.

21   Ibid., 5.

22   Ibid.

23   FAR 15.306(d).

24   Federal Acquisition Institute and the Air Force Institute of Technology, 6–7.

25   Federal Acquisition Institute, "Conducting Discussions."

26   Federal Acquisition Institute and the Air Force Institute of Technology, 9.

27   Ibid.

28   Ibid., 9.

29   FAR 15.001.

30   Federal Acquisition Institute and the Air Force Institute of Technology, 141.

31   National Reconnaissance Office, *NRO Source Selection* N87 (Chantilly, VA: National Reconnaissance Office, 2008), 53–54.

32   Federal Acquisition Institute and the Air Force Institute of Technology, 142.

33   National Reconnaissance Office, *Source Selection Manual* (Chantilly, VA: National Reconnaissance Office, 2000), 204–205.

34   U.S. Government Accountability Office, "Cygnus Corporation, Inc.," B-292649.3; B-292649.4 (Washington, DC: U.S. Government Accountability Office, December 30, 2003).

35   National Aeronautics and Space Administration, *NASA FAR Supplement* 1815.406-3 (Washington, DC: National Aeronautics and Space Administration).

36   FAR 15.405.

37   FAR 15.406-3.

38   FAR 15.001.

Chapter 13

Making Trade-Off Decisions

At this stage in the competitive source selection process, the evaluators have assessed the final proposal revisions and are ready to brief the source selection authority (SSA). The SSA makes the contract award decision based on a comparative assessment of the proposals against the source selection criteria stated in the RFP. Although the SSA may use reports and analysis prepared by the evaluators, the final source selection decision must represent the SSA's independent judgment.

The selection decision must not only identify the differences between proposals, but also their strengths, weaknesses, and risks relative to the stated evaluation factors. The SSA documents the rationale for any business judgments and trade-offs, including the benefits associated with higher cost, if applicable, in the source selection decision document (SSDD).[1] If the RFP states that the contract will be awarded to the lowest price technically acceptable offeror, then this trade-off decision-making process will not occur. The SSA would make contract award to the company offering the lowest-priced technically acceptable solution. But if the RFP states that the contract will be awarded using trade-offs to determine the best value, then the SSA needs to make the trade-off determination, which is the subject of this chapter.

It is important to note that the numerical, color, or adjectival ratings the evaluation teams assigned are merely labels and should not be the sole basis for comparing proposals. The SSA bases the source selection decision on the trade-off analysis, which compares the strengths and weaknesses of the competing proposals against the RFP's evaluation criteria.[2] The rating does not determine the successful offeror.

In this chapter, we'll walk through each step of making the trade-off decision:

- Comparing proposals
- Exercising independent judgment
- Documenting the decision.

COMPARING PROPOSALS

The SSA may ask the source selection panels to prepare a briefing that summarizes the evaluation process, especially for complex or high-visibility acquisitions. This briefing might include the following topics, though it is not limited to these.

- **Introduction or background.**
  - Include information from the acquisition plan about the background of the requirement, its risks, and funding.
  - Include information from the source selection plan, such as the basis for award, evaluation factors, subfactors, and source selection team structure.
  - Provide a summary of the solicitation requirements, the number of offerors solicited, the number that responded, those in the competitive range, and any unusual events that may have occurred, such as late submissions or protests.
- **Evaluation results.** Summarize the evaluators' assessments of each offeror's proposal. List strengths, weaknesses, and each proposal's non-cost rating and final evaluated cost.
- **Preliminary comparative proposal analysis.**
  - Compare both cost and non-cost factors of the proposals.
  - Discuss each proposal's fulfillment of the evaluation factors and subfactors, first individually, then comparatively.
  - Include preliminary results of the technical trade-off analysis and potential justification for paying a price premium, if applicable.
- **Risk assessment.** Discuss the overall impact of significant risks associated with each proposal within the competitive range, including performance risks and the source selection team's degree of confidence in the realism of the proposed cost or price.
- **Summary.** Briefly summarize the comparative analyses and the issues that may help guide the SSA's decision.[3]

The evaluation teams must present the SSA with sufficient information on each of the proposals for the SSA to make a comparative analysis and arrive at a rational, fully supportable selection decision. The narrative statements prepared during the evaluation become an integral part of the documentation supporting the source selection decision. Narrative statements communicate specific information about the relative advantages or disadvantages of proposals that a rating scheme alone cannot.[4]

When conducting a cost/technical trade-off, the SSA assesses the relative value and impact of the cost and technical differences between proposals. This process is a subjective or qualitative, rather than a quantitative, analysis of cost or price. The cost evaluation team's cost realism analysis should be factored into the SSA's decision. It's important to note that the SSA bases the cost/technical trade-off decision on the evaluated cost or price, not the proposed cost or price.

The cost/technical trade-off focuses on the differences between the proposals and attempts to measure the value to the agency of those differences. The SSA uses this information to determine if award to a higher-priced proposal with a high technical score is worth the price premium. Of course, a cost/technical trade-off could also result in award being made to a company that did not submit the highest-rated technical proposal, even if the RFP stated that technical factors were more important than price.[5]

The trade-off analysis is a subjective process that requires the SSA to exercise reasonable, prudent business judgment. The SSA analyzes the differences between the proposals in light of the relative importance of each evaluation factor. This process is summarized in four steps below:

1. Identify the proposal differences that surfaced during evaluations.
2. Analyze their impact on the acquisition objectives with regard to the relative importance of the evaluation factors.
3. Compare proposals against the evaluation criteria.
4. Assess the best mix of cost or price and non-cost benefits to determine whether the strengths of a higher-rated proposal merit the price premium.[6]

It is important to note that the evaluators' ratings are merely guides for decision-making. Harold V. Hanson writes,

> The source selection authority is responsible for independently determining whether non-cost advantages are worth the cost/price that might be associated with a higher[-] rated proposal. The decisive element is not the difference in ratings, but the SSA's rational judgment of the significance of that difference, based on an integrated comparative assessment of proposals.[7]

The SSA bases his or her decision solely on the facts and circumstances of each acquisition. His or her assessment, like those of the evaluators, must be consistent with the solicitation to ensure that the source selection decision is a disciplined process.

Unfortunately, there is no magic formula for making the cost/technical trade-off decision, but there are some basic elements to the trade-off decision that the SSA should consider, such as:

• The proposals' total evaluated prices or costs.

- Each proposal's strengths, weaknesses, risks, and deficiencies and the significance of the non-cost differences between proposals. The SSA should look for areas of difference that are important to the agency's objectives, as stated in the acquisition plan. What discriminators will affect (positively or negatively) the agency's mission?[8]
- The strengths, weaknesses, risks, and deficiencies for each factor, in light of the relative importance of each factor.
- An assessment of whether any perceived benefits are worth the associated price premium (if any) and why.[9] An award decision that requires the agency to pay a price premium must be justified, regardless of the superiority of the winning proposal's rating.[10]

Now, let's look at a case in which the SSA selected a lower-rated, lower-priced item for award under one line item and a higher-rated, higher-priced item for award under another.

CASE STUDY: MAKING A COST/TECHNICAL TRADE-OFF COMPARISON

Freedom Lift Corporation protested the award of three line items to Bruno Independent Living Aids, Inc., under a request for proposals issued by the National Acquisition Center of the Department of Veterans Affairs (VA) for wheelchair lifts and carriers and scooter lifts.

According to Government Accountability Office (GAO) decision B-298772.2, "The solicitation explained that after the product literature and technical proposals had been evaluated to determine compliance with the specifications, a 'subjective technical evaluation' of the lifts and carriers would be performed." Four subfactors, listed in descending order of importance, were to be considered in the evaluation:

- Safety and stability
- Performance
- Number of warranty years
- Dealer network.

The RFP provided that in addition to these technical subfactors, proposals would be evaluated on the basis of the offeror's:

- Price
- Past performance and reputation for quality
- Small disadvantaged business participation targets.

According to GAO's decision,

> The solicitation advised that all factors other than price, when combined, were somewhat more important than price. The solicitation further advised that the government intended to award one contract per line item to the offeror whose proposal was determined most advantageous to the government, price and other factors considered.

In determining that Bruno's proposal represented the best value to the government under line item 2 (a power-operated wheelchair carrier for manual wheelchairs), "the contracting officer concluded that '[a]lthough Freedom Lift had some desirable features that earned them a rating of "Very Good" vs. Bruno's "Good" rating, VA is not willing to pay a significantly higher price for them.'

> In determining that Harmar's proposal, which had received a technical rating of superior as compared with the protester's rating of good, represented the best value under item 8, [the CO] concluded that "the enhanced safety feature of the automatic lock down 'hands free' feature [of the Harmar lift], which makes the lift easier to use, as well as the better dealer network, would offset paying a higher price."

> In other words, the contracting officer determined that the technical advantages associated with the lift offered by Harmar under item 8 were worth a price premium of 35 percent, but that those associated with the lift offered by Freedom Lift under item 2 were not worth a price premium of 30 percent.

> [The GAO did not] think that the fact that in one instance the contracting officer concluded that the technical advantages of a higher-rated product were worth a higher price, while in another instance conclud[ed] that they were not, demonstrates inconsistent treatment on her part; it simply demonstrate[d] that the tradeoff considerations in the two cases were distinct.

> [The GAO held that] the propriety of a price/technical tradeoff decision turns not on the difference in the technical scores or ratings per se, but on whether the selection official's judgment concerning the significance of the difference was reasonable and adequately justified in light of the RFP's evaluation scheme.

> [Although] the solicitation provided that non-price factors would be somewhat more important than price in the determination of best value, the GAO state[d] that it was neither unreasonable nor inconsistent with the solicitation for the contracting officer to determine that what she regarded as the slight technical advantage of Freedom Lift's proposal was not worth a 30 percent increase in price.

The protest was denied.[11]

This case illustrates the flexibility the SSA has when making a cost/technical trade-off. In this case, one line item was worth the price premium, but another line item was not. What is important here is that the SSA explained the distinction between the line items in the source selection decision document with sufficient detail related to the offeror's proposals.

EXERCISING INDEPENDENT JUDGMENT

Aside from the requirement to comply with the evaluation factors and process described in the RFP and source selection plan, the SSA has a lot of discretion in making the source selection decision. As discussed earlier in this chapter, he or she uses rational, prudent, and independent judgment based on a comparative analysis of the proposals to decide which proposal offers the government the best value. There are three possible basic outcomes of the SSA's comparative analysis:

• The lowest-priced proposal is found to be superior in terms of non-cost factors.
• There are no meaningful distinctions between the non-cost portions of the proposals.
• The lowest-priced proposal is not found to be superior in terms of non-cost factors.

In the first two outcomes, it is fairly clear that the SSA should award to the lowest-priced offeror. In the case of the third outcome, however, the decision is not as obvious. The SSA must consider whether or not the benefits of the non-cost strengths warrant the additional price premium. This is accomplished by conducting a trade-off analysis among the competing proposals.

Figure 13-1 is a decision model that an SSA may use to determine the successful offeror(s). While the decision model appears simple, the process is far from simple. The evaluation, proposal comparison, and trade-off analysis process require a great deal of subjectivity and judgment.

Just because an agency stated it would use the trade-off process in the RFP, it still may select the lowest-priced proposal as the one that provides the best value. In fact, writes Claude Bolton,

> [selecting a] higher-priced offer always [necessitates] ... document[ing] the rationale for concluding that paying a higher price is justified by a proportionate superiority in non-cost factors. If the superior technical proposal is not selected, it is also important that the rationale for its non-selection be documented.[12]

If the SSA has doubts about the evaluation findings and analysis or believes they are not sufficiently detailed, he or she may require the evaluators to reevaluate some or all of the proposals or factors. The SSA also has the authority to assemble a new evaluation team or to personally conduct an independent evaluation.[13] In some circumstances, the SSA may not agree with the evaluators' assessment or recommendation.

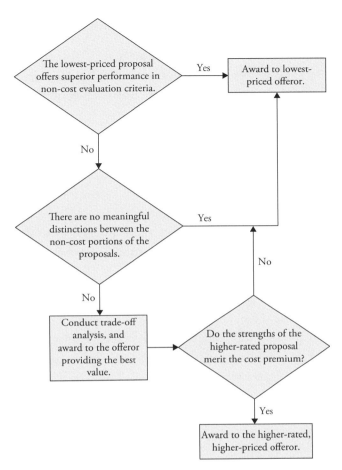

Figure 13-1 Trade-Off Decision Model[14]

Disagreeing with the Evaluators' Recommendation

The SSA should document disagreements with evaluators in the source selection decision document, explaining the difference in opinion and the reasons the SSA didn't follow the evaluator's recommendation each time there is a disagreement. The National Aeronautics and Space Administration *Source Selection Guide* suggests,

> The basis for the disagreement should describe any differences regarding the perceived consequences to the agency and the reasons why the SSA believes his or her perception should [prevail]. This explanation of a disagreement usually [involves] differences regarding business or technical judgment. In addition, any disagreement should be explained in relation to the evaluation scheme in the solicitation and, when appropriate, [should] include specific proposal references to support the ... conclusion.[15]

Let's review a case in which the SSA disagreed with the evaluator's recommendation, and an unsuccessful offeror protested the decision.

Case Study: The SSA Disagrees with the Evaluators' Recommendation

TruLogic, Inc., protested the award of a contract to Command Technology, Inc., (CTI) under an RFP issued by the Department of the Air Force. TruLogic challenged the agency's technical and price evaluation and contended that the source selection authority was biased.

According to GAO decision B-297252.3,

> The RFP stated that award would be made on a "best-value" basis, considering mission capability (including two equally weighted subfactors for program management and technical performance), proposal risk, past performance, and price. The first three factors were stated to be of equal importance and combined were "significantly more important than price; however, price will contribute substantially to the selection decision."

> The RFP [also] stated that each of the mission capability subfactors would receive one of four adjectival ratings (blue, green, yellow, or red) based on the assessed strengths and proposal inadequacies within each offeror's proposal.... In addition, the RFP provided that each of these subfactors would be assessed risk ratings of high, moderate, or low risk. The RFP further advised that in evaluating risk, the agency would focus on "risks and weaknesses associated with an offeror's proposal approach," including an assessment of the "potential for disruption of schedule, increased cost, degradation of performance, and the need for increased Government oversight, as well as the likelihood of unsuccessful performance."

> Once initial evaluations were complete, the [source selection evaluation team (SSET)] members developed "Evaluation Notices" (EN) that were sent to the offerors regarding technical and price issues. After several rounds of ENs, the entire SSET met to evaluate the responses.

> With regard to the technical performance subfactor of the mission capability factor, the SSET members agreed that TruLogic's proposal demonstrated that its proposed ... system provided "basic functionalities and several enhancements [that were] fully developed and available for immediate incorporation," was "extremely user-friendly," and presented a low risk solution.

> The SSET members also agreed that there were no "inadequacies" in CTI's proposal under the technical performance subfactor. [But the majority of the SSET] determined that there remained "uncertainties" whether CTI's proposal met some of the functionality requirements of the SOW.... The majority view that CTI's proposal had "significant system uncertainties" was based on their belief that CTI's demonstration disk did not fully demonstrate these capabilities, and reflected the

majority's concern that the screen appearance and layout of some of the features were not "user-friendly" and thus would require "system improvement with Government direction."

The minority of members disagreed, noting that CTI fully explained how it met the functionality requirements of the SOW in its EN responses, and that ease of use was not an RFP requirement; rather appearance, formatting, and layout could be worked out during the initial "Guidance Conference" after award.

The majority SSET members drafted a final evaluation report, and the minority SSET members drafted a separate evaluation report documenting their disagreement. The resulting reports (both of which were presented to the SSA) reflected different ratings for CTI under the technical performance subfactor of the mission capability factor. In all other respects, the members agreed.... The proposal ratings assigned by the majority and minority SSET members were as [shown in Table 13-1]:

The majority SSET report recommended TruLogic for award based on TruLogic's superior technical rating.... The minority SSET report recommended CTI for award, finding that CTI's proposal met the requirements of the RFP and was the "better value," given the firm's lower cost and essentially "equal" past performance.

The SSA (who was also the contracting officer) ... agreed with the SSET's evaluation and "blue" rating of TruLogic's proposal under the technical performance subfactor

Table 13-1 TruLogic Case Study Evaluation Results

	TruLogic		CTI		
	Majority score	Minority score	Majority score	Minority score	SSA
Mission capability					
• Program management	Green/low	Green/low	Green/low	Green/low	Green
• Technical performance	Blue/low	Blue/low	Yellow/moderate	Green/moderate	Green
Proposal risk	Low	Low	Low/moderate	Low/moderate	Low
Past performance	High confidence	High confidence	Significant confidence	Significant confidence	
Price	$4,163,946		$3,283,235		

of the mission capability factor, and with the assessment that TruLogic's proposal was technically superior to CTI's under this subfactor. In so doing, he set forth the various strengths in TruLogic's proposal that supported that rating.

[The SSA, however,] did not concur [with] the majority SSET's yellow rating of CTI's proposal under this subfactor and instead adopted the minority SSET views that CTI's proposal met the requirements of the RFP in all areas identified by the majority SSET members as "uncertainties" and that it should be rated "green" under this subfactor.... In addition, he found a number of strengths in CTI's proposal that were overlooked by the majority SSET members in their report.... Accordingly, the SSA rated CTI's proposal green under the technical performance subfactor of the mission capability factor.

Under the program management subfactor of the mission capability factor, the SSA found that both of these offerors had excellent management structures and described the strengths of each proposal that supported this determination. He also stated that while TruLogic had "more experience in Air Force Technical Order [TO] sustainment than CTI," this was "balanced by" CTI's experience with the Navy and its "extensive commercial experience" with building [the required systems], as well as the fact that CTI's team members were "highly experienced" with Army, Navy, Air Force, and commercial entities. The SSA also determined that the personnel teams of each offeror were "equal." Based on the foregoing, the SSA rated both proposals green under the program management factor.

Under the proposal risk factor, the SSA found that TruLogic's proposal presented the "least risk to the schedule and performance" because of the firm's experience on Air Force TO systems. However, the SSA found that CTI's proposal also deserved a low risk rating, rather than the moderate risk rating assigned by the majority SSET members under the technical performance subfactor, because, in his view, CTI's proposal did not contain the "uncertainties" identified by the majority SSET members in their report, and thus there was "little doubt" as to CTI's ability to perform.

The SSA selected CTI for award, based on his belief that that "CTI will successfully perform the requirement, and at a significantly lower price" than TruLogic and that CTI's proposal provided the "best overall value" to the Air Force. The strengths identified in TruLogic's proposal, in the SSA's opinion, did not "offer sufficient advantage over the features proposed by CTI such as to merit a 27 percent price premium."

TruLogic first argue[d] that the SSA failed to act with "impartiality." It assert[ed] that the SSA unreasonably ignored the SSET majority view, instead relying on the minority view, and "manipulated" the evaluation to support his selection of CTI for award.

TruLogic further contend[ed] that the SSA either ignored or only mentioned in a cursory way TruLogic's proposal strengths, while dedicating several paragraphs of the SSD to emphasize CTI's proposal strengths.

[GAO stated that the record showed] a well-documented, reasoned evaluation and award decision without evidence of bias. Despite TruLogic's insistence that the SSA should have adopted the majority view, source selection officials are not bound by the evaluation judgments of lower level evaluators; they may come to their own reasonable evaluation conclusions. [GAO held that] the SSA reasonably concluded that the minority view was a more accurate assessment of CTI's proposal.

The SSA did not "manipulate" the evaluation, as alleged, but documented in detail his disagreement with the majority of the SSET. To the extent that TruLogic complains that the SSD contains more paragraphs discussing CTI's proposal than TruLogic's, the agency explains that this was because the SSA was explaining his disagreement with the majority of the SSET, not because the SSA was ignoring the benefits of TruLogic's approach or over-emphasizing CTI's proposal strengths.

[GAO determined] that the SSA fairly considered the benefits and drawbacks of both TruLogic's and CTI's proposal features, and reasonably concluded that CTI's proposal provided the better value.

The protest was denied.[16]

This case illustrates several important points. First, minority dissenting opinions are acceptable, and evaluators must document dissenting opinions should they be expressed during the consensus session. Second, the SSA may disagree with the majority opinion; that's acceptable, too. In this case, the SSA documented the disagreement and made a well-reasoned cost/technical trade-off decision. Finally, this case illustrates the importance of a well-documented trade-off decision.

DOCUMENTING THE SOURCE SELECTION DECISION

Properly documenting the entire source selection process is a critical part of source selection that will help agencies avoid protests. Proper documentation helps the SSA understand the evaluators' rationale and establishes that the evaluators' findings were consistent with the stated evaluation criteria and rating plan. It also demonstrates to any third-party forum (such as GAO) that the agency conducted the evaluation fairly, impartially, and consistently.[17]

The SSA documents his or her rationale for selecting the successful offeror(s) in an independent, standalone document called the SSDD by many agencies.[18] The source selection decision document explains how the successful proposal compares with other proposals, based on the evaluation factors and subfactors in the solicitation, and discusses the SSA's reasoning for making any trade-offs.

The document should be written in the first person; for example, it should state "I concluded," or "I decided." For example, an SSDD should include language such as, "I decided that offeror A's approach to factor X was better than offeror B's (or all other offerors') because offeror A proposed the following: [state the discriminators]." Figure 13-2 shows the structure and style of a typical source selection decision document.

When an SSA determines that the best-value proposal is not the lowest-priced one, the document should justify paying a price premium, regardless of how superior the proposal's non-cost rating is. The justification must clearly state what benefits or advantages the agency receives for the added price and why it is in the agency's

---

SOURCE SELECTION DECISION STATEMENT

As the source selection authority for this acquisition, I have determined that the _____ (*product/ service*) proposed by offeror _____ provides the best overall value to satisfy agency needs. This selection was made based on the factors and subfactors established in the solicitation and my integrated assessment and comparison of the strengths, weaknesses, and risks of the proposals submitted in response to the solicitation. This memorandum documents the basis for my decision.

The SSA should provide the following information:

1. Brief description of the product/service being procured.
2. Brief description of the basis for award (as set forth in the RFP), including the factors and subfactors against which proposals were measured and their relative order of importance.
3. A list of offerors in the competitive range.
4. The rationale for the business judgments and trade-offs made. *Include the following points*:

   • Succinct comparison of all proposals, focusing on key proposal differences (strengths, weaknesses, and risks) that surfaced in the evaluation and their impact on the acquisition.
   • Explanation of specific trade-offs that led to the decision.
   • Explanation of specific benefits offered by the technically superior proposals(s) and why they are or are not significant enough to warrant any additional cost.

SUMMARY

In summary, based on my integrated assessment of all proposals in accordance with the specified evaluation factors and subfactors, it is my decision that offeror _____'s proposal provides the best overall value.

Figure 13-2   Sample Source Selection Decision Document[19]

interest to spend the additional money. This justification is prudent even when the solicitation indicates that non-cost factors are more important than cost (or price). Or, when the SSA determines the non-cost benefits offered by the higher-priced, technically superior proposal are not worth the price premium, a statement explaining why should be included.

The SSDD must stand alone to support the SSA's decision, consistent with the stated evaluation criteria, and each conclusion or decision in the SSDD should be directly linked to the stated evaluation criteria. The specific criteria that allowed for discrimination between offerors should be discussed, especially the extent to which the criteria affected the cost-benefit analysis.

The SSA should include all pertinent information in the SSDD, even if it's proprietary information. It is important to be specific about proposal strengths and weaknesses, their significance to the program, and their relationship to the source selection decision.[20] The SSDD should contain source selection information to the extent it is pertinent to the SSA's decision. For example, the agency may disclose the proposals' relative ranking at debriefings. The SSDD should include and support those rankings. Typically, the SSDD reflects the debate between or among the merits of two or three proposals.

If there's a protest, the SSDD may be released to the GAO and other parties authorized to receive proprietary and source selection information. The contracting officer must redact the sensitive or proprietary information before releasing it to anyone not authorized to receive proprietary and source selection information. Merely because certain information may have to be redacted is not a justification for excluding that information from the SSDD.

In summary, the SSDD is the single most important document created in the source selection. The SSA's key duties are to first select the best proposal based on the evaluation criteria in the solicitation, and then to explain in writing why he or she selected that proposal.[21]

Next, let's examine a case in which the SSDD was critical in deciding the outcome of a protest.

CASE STUDY: DOCUMENTING THE SOURCE SELECTION DECISION

Fedcar Company, Ltd., protested the award of a lease contract to Duke Realty Limited Partnership by the General Services Administration (GSA) under a solicitation for offers for the construction and lease of a dedicated campus facility in Indianapolis, Indiana, for use by the Federal Bureau of Investigation (FBI).

According to the GAO decision on the protest,

> The procurement was to be conducted in two separate phases; Phase I required offerors to submit proposals that included information on the offeror's technical approach and qualifications, while Phase II addressed design concepts and cost proposals. After the evaluation of the Phase I proposals, the agency would select the qualified offerors that would advance to Phase II.

The Phase II technical evaluation was based upon four evaluation factors listed in descending order of importance:

- Facility design
- Building system
- Exterior/interior design
- Management plan.

The decision continues, "Price was to be evaluated based upon the 'present value' ANSI/BOMA [American National Standards Institute/Building Owners and Managers Association] office area per square foot cost of the offers.

> Award was to be made to the offeror whose offer "conforms to the solicitation and is most advantageous to the Government" based upon both the technical and price evaluations.... The technical evaluation factors, when combined, were to be significantly more important than price; however, the [solicitation] noted that price would become more important in the best value tradeoff decision as the technical proposals became more equal.

> [Fedcar asserted] that the agency's price evaluation was unreasonable because the agency inserted incorrect numbers into the price evaluation spreadsheet, which resulted in an error in favor of Duke's present value ANSI/BOMA office area per square foot price. In its report, the agency admits that it erred in calculating the present value of the rent being offered by Duke.... The agency dismisse[d] this mistake, [however], as inconsequential and assert[ed] that Fedcar [was] not prejudiced by the error because the solicitation stated that "the technical evaluation factors, when combined, are significantly more important than price."

GAO asserted that "if the award decision were ... based on this revised price difference, price under the [solicitation's] evaluation scheme could reasonably [have] become more important and change[d] the award decision."

> The technical evaluation of Duke's and Fedcar's proposals was relatively close:

> While it is true that the technical evaluation factors were said to be significantly more important than price, the [Solicitation for offers] also stated, "[a]s proposals become more equal in their technical merit, the evaluation of price becomes more important."

While the agency argue[d] that the outcome of the SSA's cost/technical tradeoff would be the same regardless of the re-calculated price, [the GAO] afford[ed] little weight to an agency's post-protest arguments that are based on judgments the agency asserts it would have made because such judgments made in the heat of litigation and based on facts that were not previously considered that are materially different from those on which the agency relied in making the original decision may not represent the fair and considered judgment of the agency.

[The GAO further] give[s] little weight to the agency's assertion that the outcome would have been the same, given that Fedcar now has a significantly greater price advantage than found by the agency when it made its source selection decision. Where a source selection authority bases his or her source selection decision on figures that do not reasonably represent the differences in costs to be incurred under competing proposals, the source selection is not reasonably based.

Moreover, as noted by Fedcar, the source selection document selecting Duke for award set forth the strengths found in Duke's proposal, but did not discuss that proposal's weaknesses or the strengths found in Fedcar's proposal.... An agency which fails to adequately document its source selection decision bears the risk that [the GAO] may be unable to determine whether the decision was proper.

[In this case, where] the source selection decision [was] devoid of any substantive consideration of the relative merits of the proposals that would justify whether a higher[-]rated, higher[-]priced proposal was a better value to the government than a lower rated, lower priced proposal, the cost/technical tradeoff decision is not reasonably justified.

The protest was sustained.[22]

This case illustrates the importance of thoroughly documenting the source selection decision. Without adequate documentation about the decisions made, GAO cannot determine if the decision was in accordance with the solicitation and regulations.

CHAPTER SUMMARY

Chapter 13 explains the factors to consider when making a trade-off decision. The SSA makes the contract award decision based on a comparative assessment of the proposals against the source selection criteria stated in the RFP. The numerical, color, or adjectival ratings assigned by the evaluation teams are merely labels and should not be the sole basis for comparing proposals. The SSA bases the source selection decision on a trade-off analysis, comparing the proposals' strengths and weaknesses against the RFP's evaluation criteria. The proposal rating does not solely determine the successful offeror.

The evaluation teams must present the SSA with sufficient information on each of the proposals for the SSA to make a comparative analysis and arrive at a rational, fully supportable selection decision. The narrative statements prepared during the evaluation become an integral part of the documentation supporting the source selection decision. When conducting a cost/technical trade-off, the SSA assesses the relative value and impact of the cost and technical differences between proposals. This process is a subjective or qualitative, rather than a quantitative, analysis of cost or price.

The SSA analyzes the differences between the proposals in light of the relative importance of each evaluation factor. This process is summarized in the following four steps:

- Identify the proposal differences surfaced during evaluations
- Analyze the impact of those differences on acquisition objectives with regard to the relative importance of the evaluation factors
- Compare proposals against the evaluation criteria
- Assess the best mix of cost or price and non-cost benefits to determine whether the strengths of a higher-rated proposal merit the price premium.

The SSA may disagree with the evaluators' recommendation. If this occurs, the SSA should document disagreements with evaluators in the SSDD, explaining the difference in opinion and the reasons for each disagreement.

Properly documenting the entire source selection process is a critical part of source selection that will help agencies avoid protests. Proper documentation helps the SSA understand the evaluators' rationale and establishes that the evaluators' findings were consistent with the stated evaluation criteria and rating plan.

At this point in the source selection process, the SSA has made the contract award decision and needs to advise the offerors about the decision. In that notification the agency lets the offerors know that they may receive a debriefing of the evaluation results. Chapter 14 discusses these debriefings.

NOTES

1 Federal Acquisition Regulation (FAR) 15.308.

2 Claude M. Bolton, Jr., *Army Source Selection Manual* (Washington, DC: Office of the Assistant Secretary of the Army for Acquisition, Logistics and Technology, 2007), 37.

3 Adapted from Bolton, 38.

4 U.S. Department of Energy, *Source Selection Guide* (Washington, DC: U.S. Department of Energy, 2005), 54.

5 Peter S. Cole, *How to Evaluate and Negotiate Government Contracts* (Vienna, VA: Management Concepts, 2001), 445.

6 Adapted from Bolton, 41.

7   Harold V. Hanson, *NAVSEA Source Selection Guide* (Washington, DC: U.S. Naval Sea Systems Command, 2001), 30.

8   Cole, 447.

9   Hanson, 30.

10 Ibid., 30–31.

11 U.S. Government Accountability Office, "Freedom Lift Corporation," B-298772.2 (Washington, DC: U.S. Government Accountability Office, January 25, 2007).

12 Bolton, 40–41.

13 Adapted from Bolton, 40.

14 Defense Information Systems Agency, *Source Selection Deskbook* (Arlington, VA: Defense Information Systems Agency, May 2003), 31–32.

15 National Aeronautics and Space Administration, *Source Selection Guide* (Washington, DC: National Aeronautics and Space Administration, June 2007), 56.

16 U.S. Government Accountability Office, "TruLogic, Inc.," B-297252.3 (Washington, DC: U.S. Government Accountability Office, January 30, 2006).

17 U.S. Department of Energy, 53.

18 Another common name is *source selection statement* (SSS).

19 Bolton, 42.

20 Usually, none of the evaluators' documentation is released under FOIA because it is pre-decisional. The SSDD, on the other hand, *is* the decision and therefore is usually released to the public. To the degree possible, SSDDs should be drafted without proprietary data unless the proprietary information is a key determinant in the SSA's decision.

21 National Reconnaissance Office, *Source Selection Manual* (Chantilly, VA: National Reconnaissance Office, 2000), 227–228.

22 U.S. Government Accountability Office, "Fedcar Company, Ltd.," B-310980; B-310980.2; B-310980.3 (Washington, DC: U.S. Government Accountability Office, March 25, 2008).

PART IV

Completing the Source Selection Process

Part IV explains the end of the source selection process. At this stage in the process, the source selection authority (SSA) makes a contract award decision, and the agency notifies all the offerors. In the award announcement, the contracting officer gives offerors an opportunity to receive a debriefing, where the agency provides each offeror a summary of its proposal evaluation. Once notified, offerors have a limited amount of time to protest the award decision.

CHAPTER 14   CONDUCTING DEBRIEFINGS

Debriefing is the final step in the source selection process, provided none of the offerors protest the selection decision. At this point, the SSA has announced the contract award, notified the unsuccessful offerors of its award decision, and offered to conduct debriefings.

All offerors should take advantage of the available debriefing by requesting a debriefing in a timely manner. This is an excellent opportunity to learn about the strengths and weaknesses in their proposals so they can improve future proposal submissions. The debriefings also provide an opportunity to confirm that the agency did, in fact, award the contract based on the evaluation factors stated in the solicitation.

Chapter 14 begins by comparing preaward and postaward debriefings, and it explains how, why, and when to conduct debriefings. Then the chapter explains what can and cannot be discussed at a debriefing, and it concludes with a brief discussion of the protest clock, which is discussed at greater length in Chapter 15.

CHAPTER 15 FILING AND RESPONDING TO PROTESTS

Sometimes, unsuccessful offerors decide to file a protest after attending the debriefing. Protesting a government contract source selection is a specialized legal field, and readers are advised to seek legal counsel if they find themselves in a protest situation. Although the contents of this book should not be considered legal advice, Chapter 15 does provide an overview of how the protest process works and elements for both government and industry contracting personnel to consider.

Like earlier stages of source selection, the protest process is structured with specific timelines that both government and private industry must follow. Once offerors are made aware of any problems with the solicitation, they have ten calendar days to protest. For example, if an offeror wants to protest an aspect of the RFP, it has to do so within ten calendar days of receiving the RFP. The offeror cannot wait to see which company wins the contract before protesting the RFP.

Chapter 15 defines protests and explains the protest process, including the avenues available to unsuccessful offerors, and the common reasons companies file protests. The chapter describes why, when, and how to file a protest, and it gives tips for avoiding protest situations.

Chapter 14

Conducting Debriefings

Debriefing is the final step in the source selection process, provided none of the offerors protest the selection decision. At this point, the source selection authority (SSA) has announced the contract award, notified the unsuccessful offerors of the award decision, and offered to conduct debriefings. In this chapter, we begin by comparing preaward and postaward debriefings, and we explain how, why, and when debriefings are done. Then, we will explain what can and cannot be discussed at a debriefing. We conclude with a brief discussion of the protest clock, which Chapter 15 discusses in greater detail.

There are two types of debriefings: preaward and postaward. Each unsuccessful offeror is entitled to one debriefing. Table 14-1 outlines when each type of debriefing is appropriate and the information that may and may not be disclosed at each. There are more restrictions on what may be disclosed to an unsuccessful offeror at a preaward debriefing because the procurement is still ongoing at the time. Because of these restrictions, some offerors prefer to wait until the postaward debriefing to get more information.

Table 14-1   Comparison of Pre- and Postaward Debriefings[1]

	Preaward debriefing	Postaward debriefing
Who receives the debriefing?	Offerors excluded from the competitive range or otherwise excluded from the competition before award.	Any unsuccessful offeror that has not had a preaward debriefing.
When is it done?	As soon as practical after receiving a timely written request. However, the contracting officer (CO) may refuse the request for a preaward debriefing if it isn't in the government's best interest to conduct a preaward debriefing.[2]	Within five days, to the maximum extent practical, after receiving a timely written request for a debriefing.[3]

Table 14-1   (*Continued*)

	Preaward debriefing	Postaward debriefing
What's a *timely request*?	A request received by the contracting officer within three calendar days after the offeror received the notice of exclusion from the competition.[4]	A request received by the contracting officer within three calendar days after the offeror received notice of contract award.[5]
What should be discussed?	• The agency's evaluation of significant elements in the offeror's proposal.[6] • A summary of the rationale for eliminating the offeror from the competition. • Reasonable responses to relevant questions about whether source selection procedures contained in the solicitation, applicable regulations, and other applicable authorities were followed in the process of eliminating the offeror from the competition.	• The government's evaluation of the significant weaknesses or deficiencies in the offeror's proposal, if applicable • The overall evaluated cost or price (including unit prices) and technical rating, if applicable, of the successful offeror and the debriefed offeror, and past performance information on the debriefed offeror • The overall ranking of all offerors if any ranking was developed by the agency during the source selection • A summary of the rationale for award • For acquisitions of commercial items, the make and model of the item to be delivered by the successful offeror • Reasonable responses to relevant questions about whether source selection procedures contained in the solicitation, applicable regulations, and other applicable authorities were followed • Other information, as appropriate.
What cannot be disclosed?	• The number of offerors • The identity of other offerors • The content of other offerors' proposals • The ranking of other offerors • How other offerors were evaluated • A point-by-point comparison of the debriefed offeror's proposal with other proposals • Information prohibited from disclosure by FAR 24.202 or information exempt from release under the Freedom of Information Act.[7]	• Point-by-point comparisons of a debriefed offeror's proposal with other proposals. • Information prohibited from disclosure by FAR 24.202, or information exempt from release under the Freedom of Information Act.[8]

This chapter explains the basics of conducting debriefings, including why debriefing is required and what to discuss with the offeror during a debriefing. Keep in mind that debriefings aren't held only for unsuccessful offerors. Sometimes the winning company wants a debriefing, too.

WHY CONDUCT DEBRIEFINGS?

As readers may recall from Chapter 1, the Federal Acquisition Streamlining Act requires timely debriefings. Because each offeror puts considerable resources into preparing and submitting a proposal, it's important that the agency promptly debrief offerors and explain why a proposal was unsuccessful. Timely and thorough debriefings:

* Increase competition
* Encourage offerors to continue to invest resources in the government marketplace
* Enhance the government's relationship and credibility with industry.

Thus, not only is conducting timely debriefings a statutory requirement, it also makes good business sense.

WHEN TO CONDUCT DEBRIEFINGS

The government must conduct a debriefing for an unsuccessful offeror if:

* The offeror makes a written request for a debriefing; and
* The request is received by the contracting activity within three days after the offeror received notice of exclusion from the competition or contract award.

The days required by the FAR are calendar days, not working days. Contracting officers must include weekends and legal holidays in the calculation, but the day the offeror received the notice should not be counted; the next day is day one. For example, if the offeror received the notice on Tuesday, the first day is Wednesday, the second day is Thursday, and the third day is Friday. Thus, the contracting officer must receive the request for the debriefing no later than close of business on Friday in order for it to be timely.

Establishing the date the offeror received the notice may be difficult if the notice is sent by regular mail. Contracting officers should therefore consider sending the notice by mail with a request for a return-receipt or by fax or email requesting immediate acknowledgment of receipt. Remember, every day of delay in notifying the offeror usually extends by one day the time during which it may file a protest.

Recall from Chapter 11 that an offeror excluded from the competitive range may request a preaward debriefing, and the contracting officer shall make every effort to debrief the unsuccessful offeror as soon as possible. If there are compelling reasons why it is not in the government's best interest to conduct a debriefing before award, the contracting officer can delay it but no later than the time he or she conducts the postaward debriefings. In such cases, the contracting officer must document in the contract file the rationale for the delay. The delayed preaward debriefing is then done as a postaward debriefing. The contracting officer must conduct postaward debriefings within five days, to the maximum extent possible, after receiving a timely written request.[9]

It is very important that the contracting officer schedule the debriefing for the earliest possible date and inform the offeror of the scheduled date in writing. If the offeror is not available on the scheduled date and requests a later date, the contracting officer should mandate that the company acknowledge in writing that it was offered an earlier date but requested the later date instead. This precaution will protect the government's interests if the company subsequently files a protest. If the offeror rejects the government's offered date and specifies another date, the company is still required to file a protest within five days of the offered debriefing date to stop performance of the contract.[10]

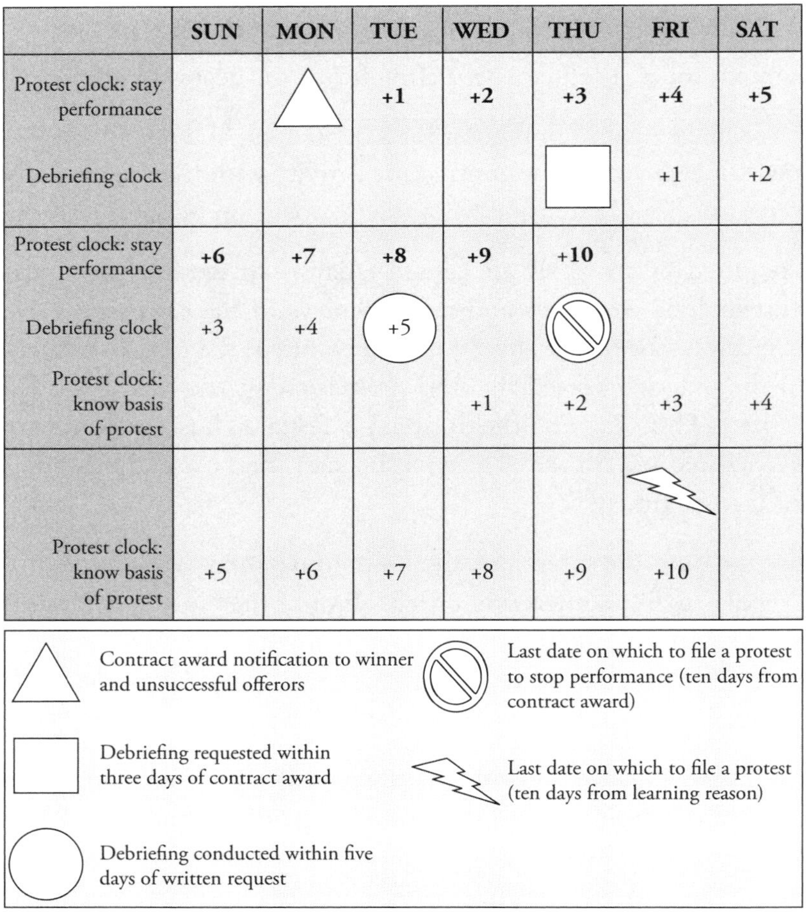

	SUN	MON	TUE	WED	THU	FRI	SAT
Protest clock: stay performance		△	+1	+2	+3	+4	+5
Debriefing clock					□	+1	+2
Protest clock: stay performance	+6	+7	+8	+9	+10		
Debriefing clock	+3	+4	◯ +5		⊘		
Protest clock: know basis of protest				+1	+2	+3	+4
						⚡	
Protest clock: know basis of protest	+5	+6	+7	+8	+9	+10	

△ Contract award notification to winner and unsuccessful offerors

⊘ Last date on which to file a protest to stop performance (ten days from contract award)

□ Debriefing requested within three days of contract award

⚡ Last date on which to file a protest (ten days from learning reason)

◯ Debriefing conducted within five days of written request

Figure 14-1 The Debriefing Timeline

If an offeror submits an untimely request for debriefing—that is, the request is received more than three days after notice of elimination from the competition or contract award—the contracting officer is not obligated to conduct a debriefing.[11] The contracting officer should conduct the debriefing if it's feasible, but should inform the offeror that the request is untimely. The CO may schedule the debriefing when it is convenient for him or her. If this occurs, the offeror must file its protest within ten days of award to stop performance, but it will have little information on which to base the protest.

Figure 14-1 illustrates the debriefing timeline. In this illustration, the contract award announcement is made to the successful and unsuccessful offerors on the same day, Monday. This announcement is represented by a triangle in the illustration. The offeror requests a debriefing on Thursday, which is the last possible day to make the

	SUN	MON	TUE	WED	THU	FRI	SAT
Protest clock: stay performance		△	+1	+2	+3	+4	+5
Debriefing clock					□	◯ +1	
Protest clock: know basis of protest							+1
Protest clock: stay performance	+6	+7	+8	+9	+10 ⊘		
Protest clock: know basis of protest	+2	+3	+4	+5	+6	+7	+8
Protest clock: know basis of protest	+9	+10 ⚡					

△ Contract award notification to winner and unsuccessful offerors	⊘ Last date on which to file a protest to stop performance (ten days from contract award)
□ Debriefing requested within three days of contract award	⚡ Last date on which to file a protest (ten days from learning reason)
◯ Debriefing conducted within five days of written request	

Figure 14-2   Alternate Debriefing Timeline

request because it's the third day after the offeror received the notification. This event is noted by a square. The contracting officer now has five calendar days to conduct the debriefing. A very well-prepared contracting officer could do the debriefing on the very next day (Friday) or wait until the next week, as long as it's done within five days.

In this illustration, the contracting officer conducts the debriefing on Tuesday represented by the circle. The conclusion of the debriefing starts another ten-day protest clock. But using that clock, the offeror does not have the opportunity to stay contract performance. The details of this consideration are discussed further in Chapter 15.

Of course, this is just one scenario. The contracting officer can speed up the process by conducting the debriefing as soon as possible. For example, Figure 14-2 shows an alternate debriefing timeline. In this scenario, the CO conducts the debriefing the day after receiving the written request and, as a result, moves up the last day on which the offeror can file a protest. This demonstrates the important role the debriefing's timing has on the protest clock. By delaying the debriefing, contracting officers give unsuccessful offerors more time to file a protest because the clock starts on the date the offeror learns about whatever it is that becomes the basis for the protest.

HOW TO CONDUCT DEBRIEFINGS

A debriefing explains to an unsuccessful offeror how the agency conducted the source selection and gives the offeror information that will help it submit a better or more competitive offer in the next competition.

Perceptions often mean a lot in a debriefing. If the contracting officer goes into the debriefing prepared, organized, and professional, then the offerors will think the source selection was conducted in an organized and professional manner. If, however, the contracting officer is unprepared, sloppy, and disorganized, then the unsuccessful offerors will think that the source selection was conducted in a sloppy, disorganized manner.

An effective debriefing can often deter a protest. It demonstrates that the government conducted a thorough, fair evaluation and made a sound decision according to the evaluation methodology established in the solicitation.

Being unprepared when conducting a debriefing increases the prospects of a protest. Of course, the amount of preparation necessary varies considerably with the complexity of each acquisition. Sometimes just a few charts are all that is needed. Other times, the contracting officer may prepare a written script and conduct dry-run rehearsals.[12]

Because debriefings are time sensitive, the contracting officer must begin preparing for them while the proposals are being evaluated. An organized contracting officer may set up a filing system by offeror to collect information to use in the debriefings. For example, if company A is eliminated from the competitive range, an organized contracting officer would already have set up a file containing evaluators' narratives on A's proposal. The CO would do the same for each offeror eliminated from the competition.

Debriefing Methods

The contracting officer should debrief one unsuccessful offeror at a time and may conduct the meeting in person, in writing, by telephone, electronically via video teleconference or webcam, or by any other method acceptable to the contracting officer. Travel costs may make it difficult for an offeror to attend in person, and the agency should take this into consideration. Likewise, if some of the government personnel involved are located at a location other than where the debriefing will be conducted, they may participate by telephone or videoconference. Face-to-face debriefings or those involving video should be held in a professional and distraction-free environment.

The contracting officer normally chairs all debriefing sessions held. The individuals who conducted the evaluations shall provide support.[13] Evaluation team members may help the contracting officer prepare debriefing charts and should attend the debriefings to help answer questions. It is important to ensure that appropriate government personnel attend so the agency can provide a meaningful debriefing. The contracting officer may rely on evaluation team members to address particular parts of the proposals, and he or she might not be able to answer certain questions if the appropriate evaluators aren't there. The contracting officer's legal counsel also may help prepare or review the debriefing and usually attends the debriefing, especially if the offeror's legal counsel is there.[14]

The contracting officer should discuss with government attendees their roles and expected demeanor during the debriefing. Defensive or overly compassionate behavior is not appropriate. The agency should let the unsuccessful offeror know why it lost without arguing or apologizing. Presentations should be positive and straightforward.

The contracting officer may elect to provide an advance copy of the debriefing materials to the offeror and may allow the offeror to submit written questions for the government to review before the debriefing.

Debriefing Materials

Debriefing materials are prepared by the CO and normally consist of briefing charts, handouts, and notes. The contracting officer is not required to provide any written material, but doing so is a common practice. The materials should:

- Explain the rationale for the offeror's exclusion from the competition or why it was not chosen for award
- Instill confidence in the offeror that it was treated fairly
- Assure the offeror that appropriately qualified personnel evaluated its proposal in accordance with the RFP and applicable laws and regulations
- Identify strengths and weaknesses in the offeror's proposal so the offeror can prepare better proposals for future government acquisitions
- Reduce misunderstandings and the risk of protests
- Give the offeror an opportunity to provide feedback on the RFP, discussions, evaluation, and the source selection process.[15]

The contracting officer may want to give the unsuccessful offeror a copy of the SSDD at its debriefing. The contracting officer should redact the SSDD to remove information that discusses other unsuccessful offerors and information that is exempt under the Freedom of Information Act (FOIA).[16]

Figure 14-3 illustrates a sample debriefing agenda.

For a less complex source selection, an abbreviated debriefing format might be more appropriate. The agency would share with the offeror relevant parts of the:

---

1. Introduce government and industry attendees.
2. Explain the purposes of the debriefing.
3. Announce the ground rules.
4. Summarize the source selection process.
5. State the proposal evaluation factors and subfactors.
6. Explain the rating definitions.
7. Reveal the evaluation results for the offeror to be debriefed:
    7.1. The significant advantages of the unsuccessful offeror's proposal
    7.2. The significant weaknesses of the unsuccessful offeror's proposal
    7.3. The evaluation ratings of the unsuccessful offeror's proposal to the subfactor level
    7.4. The government's total evaluated cost/price for the unsuccessful offeror's proposal.
8. Reveal the awardee's evaluation results:
    8.1. The significant advantages of the awardee's proposal
    8.2. The significant weaknesses of the awardee's proposal
    8.3. The evaluation ratings of the awardee's proposal to the subfactor level
    8.4. The government's total evaluated cost/price for the awardee's proposal.
9. Summarize the rationale for the contract award decision.
10. Reveal the overall ranking of all proposals, if overall rankings were made during source selection; other unsuccessful offerors should not be identified by name.
11. Answer relevant questions about how the agency followed the source selection procedures set forth in the solicitation, applicable regulations, and other authorities.

Figure 14-3   Sample Debriefing Agenda[17]

- Evaluation criteria
- Proposal preparation instructions
- Statement of work
- Offeror's proposal
- Source selection decision document.

Comparing the unsuccessful offeror's proposal with the evaluation criteria and statement of work illustrates how the offeror's proposal did or did not address the requirements. The awardee's proposal should be compared in the same manner, without disclosing proprietary or confidential information. Excerpts from the SSDD show how the SSA made the award decision.

The following references should be available during the debriefing:

- A copy of the RFP
- The debriefed offeror's proposal
- Consensus evaluation reports and the debriefed offeror's score
- The source selection decision document.

Do not have other offerors' proposals or evaluation reports pertaining to other offerors' proposals in the room.

Debriefing Attendance

Although the contracting officer is responsible for chairing the debriefing, this doesn't mean that the contracting officer must conduct the entire debriefing. In fact, contracting officers often rely on technical and cost/price personnel to present the portions of the debriefing that address those specialized parts of the offeror's proposal. The contracting officer selects the debriefing team members based on the pertinent issues in each offeror's proposal. The key is ensuring that someone who knows the issues and can answer questions is at the debriefing.

Some agencies ask the offeror to be debriefed to identify in advance all individuals by name and position who will attend the debriefing. This helps the agency identify a government counterpart for each offeror attendee. For example, if the company's vice president will attend, the SSA or program manager may wish to attend as well. If the SSA can't be there for the entire session, it may be appropriate for him or her to make a brief statement at the beginning. The presence of the SSA is recommended if high-level officials were substantially involved in the acquisition, or the acquisition received extensive high-level visibility or scrutiny.

Normally, an agency should not limit how many people an offeror brings to the debriefing. For example, major subcontractors may wish to attend along with offeror personnel. If there are space limitations at the agency's facility, however, the agency may restrict the number of offeror personnel invited to attend. Contracting officers should not impose restrictions unless they have determined that larger facilities are not available.[18]

Responding to Questions

Most questions received from an offeror can be answered right away, unless these questions concern material that is restricted from disclosure under the Freedom of Information Act, or concern material that is proprietary or confidential. The contracting officer can ask each offeror to submit written questions in advance to give the government the time to prepare a thorough answer. This also gives the contracting officer time to determine if the agency can answer the questions given the FOIA restrictions.

An offeror may ask about the evaluation factors that were used, such as why a particular technical evaluation factor was considered more important than another. The contracting officer should not, however, disclose proprietary or confidential information about the trade-off decisions made by the SSA in the final source selection decision. For example, the contracting officer could state that the SSA selected the successful offeror because it presented a more suitable or superior technical proposal, without discussing the details or content of the winning proposal.[19]

During both preaward and postaward debriefings, the offeror being debriefed is permitted to ask relevant questions about

- The source selection procedures
- The RFP
- The applicable regulations.

The contracting officer must make every effort to provide reasonable responses to those questions but must be careful not to inadvertently disclose other offerors' proprietary information when answering the questions.

If an offeror asks a question that the contracting officer can't answer right away, the contracting officer should get the answer immediately after the debriefing and promptly provide it to the offeror. Asking for written questions in advance will help the CO avoid this scenario, but even then, the offeror may ask new questions based on the information shared in the debriefing.

Describing the Source Selection Process and Explaining Evaluation Results

When conducting a postaward debriefing, the contracting officer may name the source selection authority; the SSA's identity is usually withheld in a preaward debriefing. The contracting officer doesn't typically reveal evaluator identities, except, of course, for those evaluators present at the debriefing. The objective should be to convey to the offeror that the proposals were evaluated by qualified personnel.

The contracting officer should explain the process used to evaluate proposals, establish the competitive range, and select the awardee. At a minimum, the contracting officer discloses the following information:

- **The deficiencies and significant weaknesses of the debriefed offeror's proposal.** When is a weakness significant? If the weakness was of enough concern to warrant its discussion during the negotiation phase of the acquisition, it is probably significant for debriefing purposes as well. If it wasn't significant enough to warrant discussion, it is not significant for debriefing purposes either, unless, of course, the weakness appeared in the final proposal revision. It is also a good practice to discuss the significant advantages of the debriefed offeror's proposal.
- **The evaluation ratings for the debriefed offeror's and awardee's proposals.** Identify the evaluation rating or score for both proposals. This may include the subfactor ratings, but be careful about releasing any more details of the awardee's evaluation; this could violate the statutory prohibition against point-by-point comparisons of proposals.[20] Detailed ratings for the debriefed offeror's proposal may be revealed if necessary to explain the rationale for the award decision. Be prepared to explain the rationale for the ratings.
- **The government's total evaluated cost/price for the debriefed offeror's proposal** for each contract line item. Explain any significant cost realism adjustments at the major cost element level.
- **The total evaluated cost/price of the awardee's proposal.** But don't disclose the awardee's total proposed and evaluated cost/price for each contract line item or the specific government cost/price adjustments to the awardee's proposed cost/price.
- **Overall ranking of all proposals.** If the source selection authority ranked the proposals, the overall ranking of all proposals ("first," "second," "third") must be revealed, but don't reveal the identities of the other unsuccessful offerors. Instead, call the other offerors company "X," "Y," or "Z."
- **Rationale for award decision.** The government must summarize the rationale for the contract award decision. The rationale is contained in the source selection decision document, which may be redacted and released at the debriefing.
- **The significant advantages of the awardee's proposal in general terms,** without revealing confidential proprietary information contained in the awardee's proposal.
- **The make and model of any commercial end items proposed by the awardee.** If the awardee's proposal includes a commercial item that is an end item under the contract, the make and model of the item must be disclosed.[21]

The government should keep in mind that one of the reasons unsuccessful offerors protest an award decision is that they left their debriefings not fully understanding why the government did not select their proposals. Make sure that the debriefing is thorough to avoid protest. Of course, some companies attend a debriefing looking for a basis to file a protest. Next, we examine the perspective of offerors in the debriefing process.

ATTENDING DEBRIEFINGS

It's very hard for a company to spend so much time and money putting together what it thinks is a winning proposal, only to find out that it lost the contract. Corporate executives will be angry; layoffs may even ensue as a result of the loss.

Most of this chapter is targeted to contracting officers because they lead the debriefing session. But the unsuccessful offeror also needs to know what to expect from a debriefing and should prepare an agenda listing what it wants to learn. First, and foremost, a debriefing is an opportunity for an offeror to learn about the strengths and weaknesses of its proposal. Offerors should take advantage of this time with the agency to learn more about its needs and how the company can fulfill them. Recall from Chapter 7 that knowing the customer and understanding the program are important elements in capture planning. Offerors can use this information in future proposals with the agency.

Figure 14-4 lists questions companies can ask at debriefings.

Offerors should keep in mind that debriefings do not provide a point-by-point comparison between their proposals and the awardee's, and they will not be able to see the awardee's technical solution or cost proposal. However, offerors may look for irregularities that could become a basis for pursuing a protest. Consider the following questions before pursuing a protest:

- **Did the source selection follow the evaluation criteria listed in the RFP?** Focus on the strengths and weaknesses the agency identified in your proposal and the awardee's proposal. Was the award made in accordance with the stated criteria?
- **Did the evaluators create undisclosed evaluation criteria?** For example, does the source selection decision document mention considerations in the trade-off evaluation that are not evaluation criteria in the RFP?
- **Did the SSA consider cost in the award decision?** Even if another evaluation factor is more important than cost, cost must be considered in every source selection.[22]
- **Did the contracting officer advise your company of deficiencies and significant weaknesses during discussions?** Offerors should not learn about deficiencies or significant weaknesses for the first time in a debriefing. The discussions could be considered misleading if deficiencies and significant weaknesses are not

1. *Technical proposal*
   1.1 Did our proposal reflect a good understanding of the government's requirements?
   1.2 Was our proposal organized in a way that let the evaluators easily track our responses to each RFP requirement?
   1.3 Did we fail to respond to any of the RFP's requirements? If so, which ones? In what ways did this affect the evaluation?
   1.4 Were there any inconsistencies in our proposal that made evaluators question our understanding of the work required?
   1.5 Did any statements in our proposal seem unrealistic or unsubstantiated?
   1.6 What were the deficiencies and significant weaknesses in our proposal?
2. *Cost proposal*
   2.1 Did the agency conduct a price realism assessment? What adjustments were made to our proposal and why?
   2.2 Did our cost proposal reflect a misunderstanding of the RFP's requirements?
   2.3 Was our price realistic and reasonable?
3. *Cost/technical trade-off*
   3.1 Did the agency conduct a cost/technical trade-off?
   3.2 What were the discriminators among the proposals? How do these discriminators relate to the agency's program objectives?
   3.3 Did the agency perceive any risks in making an award to our company?
4. *Source selection process*
   4.1 What was the agency's source selection process?
   4.2 What recommendations did the evaluators make to the source selection authority?
   4.3 Did the SSA follow the recommendations of the evaluation team?
5. *How can we improve future proposals?*
   5.1 Did we explain our technical solution clearly?
   5.2 What was the weakest aspect of the proposal?
   5.3 Did our past performance references provide good feedback?
   5.4 Could we have improved our rating by teaming with another company?
6. *What were the strengths in the proposal we should retain in the future?*
   6.1 Were the key personnel qualified?
   6.2 Was the technical solution excellent?

Figure 14-4　Postaward Debriefing Questions

mentioned. Remember, though, that the contracting officer does not have to discuss every part of the proposal that could be improved.[23]

- **Did your company have the opportunity to address negative past performance information?**

DOCUMENTING DEBRIEFINGS

After the debriefings are finished, the contracting officer must document the file with a debriefing memorandum, an official summary, for each debriefing.[24] A debriefing memorandum should include:

- A list of everyone who attended the debriefing.
- A summary of the information disclosed during the debriefing. The most efficient way to do this is to list the charts used at the debriefing and attach a copy of them to the memorandum.
- The substance of all questions and answers discussed at the debriefing. Include answers provided to the offeror after the debriefing.[25]

A good debriefing memorandum is essential if the acquisition is reopened or resolicited as a result of a protest, or for another reason, within one year of the contract award date. In such a case, the law requires the contracting agency make available to all offerors information disclosed at the debriefings regarding the original awardee's proposal. This requirement is designed, in part, to allow all offerors to compete on a level field.[26]

THE PROTEST CLOCK

At the end of a debriefing, the contracting officer should definitively state, "This concludes the debriefing," so that both parties know when the protest clocks start to run. One clock limits the period of time in which an offeror may file a protest. The second clock determines whether the agency will have to stay the award of the protested contract or suspend performance on the protested contract.[27] Figures 14-1 and 14-2 illustrate these two clocks and the impact the debriefing has on the protest clock.

If there are outstanding questions, the debriefing will not end until the government has satisfactorily responded to the offeror's questions. This does not mean, however, that an offeror can extend the debriefing end date by continuing to ask questions.

CASE STUDY: AN UNTIMELY PROTEST

New SI, LLC, protested the National Geospatial-Intelligence Agency's (NGA) award of a contract to Orbimage, Inc., for commercial satellite imagery services. According to the Government Accountability Office's (GAO) decision on the protest,

> On September 30, 2004, New SI was notified of the award to Orbimage. Later that day, New SI submitted a written request to the agency for a debriefing. NGA provided a debriefing on October 6, during which New SI was advised of the agency's evaluation process, the ratings and scores on the factor and subfactor level for New SI's proposal, and the weaknesses, strengths and risk assessments for New SI's proposal. In addition, the agency answered a number of questions asked by New SI. The next day, October 7, New SI submitted written questions to the agency. The agency furnished a response on October 15. On October 20, New SI filed its protest with [the GAO].

NGA requested that the GAO

> dismiss the protest as untimely, since it was filed 14 days after New SI's debriefing session on October 6. New SI responded that October 6 should not be the point from which timeliness is measured, since the debriefing did not provide the information on which its protest is based.

The protester asserted that "the debriefing was not complete until October 15, when the agency provided responses to the protester's October 7 questions."

The GAO's "Bid Protest Regulations contain strict rules for the timely submission of protests. Under these rules, [protests] ... must be filed not later than 10 days after the protester knew, or should have known, of the basis for protest." GAO agreed with the agency that "New SI's protest was not filed with [GAO] until more than 10 days after the debriefing session concluded, it is untimely."

GAO noted in its analysis that "contrary to New SI's assertion, it is clear from the October 7 written questions that the protester was made aware of the basis for its October 20 protest during the October 6 debriefing.

> Further, GAO did not agree that the debriefing was essentially ongoing pending the agency's answering the protester's October 7 questions.... The record indicates that NGA did not answer all of New SI's questions at the debriefing session, and New SI maintains that there was "no statement by any NGA representative that the debriefing process was concluded at the end of the October 6, 2004 meeting."
>
> [However,] the source selection authority ... state[d] that the contracting officer informed New SI at the beginning of the debriefing that "if it had any remaining questions *after the debriefing was finished* ... New SI could submit written questions to the [CO] after the debriefing." ... It is clear from this statement that the agency considered the debriefing 'finished' at the conclusion of the October 6 session, notwithstanding that it was willing to answer further questions the protester might have.
>
> Given the absence of any affirmative indication from the agency that the debriefing would remain open after the scheduled session, [the GAO considered] it to have concluded at the end of that session. The fact that New SI may not have been satisfied with all aspects of the debriefing, and that it continued to pursue certain questions with the agency, did not extend the time for filing a bid protest based on the information provided during the debriefing.

GAO dismissed the protest.[28] This case illustrates the importance of establishing a definitive end date for a debriefing so that both parties know when the clock for filing a protest starts and ends.

CHAPTER SUMMARY

Chapter 14 explains why, when, and how a debriefing is done. There are two types of debriefings: preaward and postaward. Each unsuccessful offeror is entitled to one debriefing—by requesting one either within three calendar days after the offeror received the notice of exclusion from the competition or within three calendar days after the offeror received notice of contract award.

In a preaward debriefing, the agency discusses its evaluation of significant elements in the offeror's proposal. The agency also gives a summary of the rationale for eliminating the offeror from the competition. Finally, the agency offers reasonable responses to relevant questions about whether source selection procedures contained in the solicitation, applicable regulations, or other applicable authorities were followed in the process of eliminating the offeror from the competition.

In a postaward debriefing the contracting officer explains the government's evaluation of the significant weaknesses or deficiencies in the offeror's proposal; the overall evaluated cost or price (including unit prices) and technical rating, if applicable, of the successful offeror and the debriefed offeror; and past performance information of the debriefed offeror. The CO also explains the overall ranking of all offerors if any ranking was developed by the agency during the source selection and a summary of the rationale for its award. As in a preaward debriefing, the CO will also consider reasonable responses to relevant questions about whether source selection procedures contained in the solicitation, applicable regulations, and other applicable authorities were followed.

Although the contracting officer is responsible for chairing the debriefing, this doesn't mean that the contracting officer must conduct the entire debriefing. In fact, contracting officers often rely on technical and cost/price personnel to present their specialized review of relevant parts of the offeror's proposal. The contracting officer selects the debriefing team members based on the pertinent issues in each offeror's proposal.

Offerors should understand that, first and foremost, a debriefing is an opportunity for them to learn about the strengths and weaknesses of their proposals. Offerors should take advantage of this time with the agency to learn more about the customer's needs and how the company can fulfill them. Offerors should keep in mind that debriefings do not provide a point-by-point comparison between their proposals and the awardee's, and they will not be able to see the awardee's technical solution or cost proposal. However, offerors may look for irregularities that could become a basis for pursuing a protest.

It is important to document debriefings. A debriefing memorandum should include a list of everyone who attended the debriefing and a summary of the information disclosed during the debriefing. The CO should also describe all questions and answers discussed at the debriefing. At the end of a debriefing, the contracting officer should definitively state, "This concludes the debriefing," so both parties know when the protest clocks start to run.

Chapter 15 discusses protests in detail.

NOTES

1 Adapted from Claude M. Bolton, Jr., *Army Source Selection Manual* (Washington, DC: Office of the Assistant Secretary of the Army for Acquisition, Logistics and Technology, 2007), 46.

2 The offeror may request the debriefing be delayed until after contract award. When delayed, the debriefing should include all the information typically provided in a postaward debriefing. When either the government or the offeror delays the debriefing, the contracting officer must provide the debriefing within the timeframe established for postaward debriefings.

3 If an offeror submits an untimely request for a debriefing, the contracting officer should nonetheless conduct a debriefing if feasible. In such cases, the offeror should be informed that the request is untimely.

4 Do not count the day the offeror received the notice; start with the next day. Consider sending the notice by mail with a request for a return receipt or electronically by fax or email with a request for immediate acknowledgment. This way, the contracting officer can easily establish the date the offeror received notice.

5 Ibid.

6 If the element was significant enough to eliminate the offeror from the competitive range, it is significant enough to discuss in the debriefing. Include both positive and negative elements of the offeror's proposal to help the offeror improve future proposals.

7 The Freedom of Information Act (FOIA) restricts releasing trade secrets; privileged or confidential information, e.g., manufacturing processes and techniques, commercial and financial information, cost data; and the names of individuals providing past performance information. FOIA does not restrict releasing information otherwise available without restriction to the government or public.

8 Ibid.

9 FAR 15.505(b).

10 National Reconnaissance Office, *Source Selection Manual* (Chantilly, VA: National Reconnaissance Office, 2000), 244.

11 Federal Acquisition Regulation (FAR) 15.506(a)(4).

12 Bolton, 48.

13 FAR 15.506(c).

14 Bolton, 47.

15 Ibid., 45.

16 Ibid., 42.

17 Johnnie E. Wilson, *Best Value Source Selection* 715-3, Appendix F (Alexandria, VA: Army Materiel Command, 1998), 73.

18 Ibid., 68.

19 Federal Acquisition Institute, *Source Selection Text Reference* (Washington, DC: Federal Acquisition Institute, 1993), 289.

20 FAR 15.506(e).

21 Wilson, 71–72.

22 FAR 15.304(c)(1).

23 FAR 15.306(d)(3).

24 FAR 15.506.

25 Bolton, 42.

26 Defense Information Systems Agency, *Source Selection Deskbook* (Arlington, VA: Defense Information Systems Agency, May 2003), 38.

27 FAR 33.104.

28 U.S. Government Accountability Office, "New SI, LLC," B-295209; B-295209.2; B-295209.3 (Washington, DC: U.S. Government Accountability Office, November 22, 2004).

Chapter 15

Filing and Responding to Protests

At this stage in the acquisition cycle, the source selection authority has made the contract award decision, and the contracting officer has conducted debriefings. After being debriefed, offerors sometimes believe that the agency didn't conduct the source selection in accordance with the RFP or required statutes or regulations. Before filing a protest, however, both parties must make their best effort to quickly resolve concerns raised by an interested party at the contracting officer level through open, frank discussions.[1] Speed is important, because there is a very limited window of time in which an offeror has the right to protest. If the parties can't resolve the issues, the company may file a protest. This chapter explains the protest process, including the avenues available to unsuccessful offerors, and the common reasons companies file protests.

KEY DEFINITIONS

Let's start with a few definitions so that we can understand all of the dynamics involved in a protest. A *protest* is a written objection by an interested party to:

- A solicitation or other request by an agency for offers for a contract for the procurement of property or services
- The cancellation of the solicitation or other request
- An award or proposed award of the contract
- A termination or cancellation of an award of the contract, if the written objection contains an allegation that the termination or cancellation is based in whole or in part on improprieties concerning the award of the contract.[2]

An *interested party* for the purpose of filing a protest is defined by the FAR as "an actual or prospective bidder or offeror whose direct economic interest would be affected by the award of a contract or by the failure to award a contract."[3]

When a protest is filed, it is not simply a matter between the protestor and the agency. The prospective awardee, as well as other offerors that may have participated in the procurement, may also have an interest to protect. These parties are called *interveners*. The *Code of Federal Regulations* defines the term *intervener* as "an awardee if the award has been made or, if no award has been made, all bidders or offerors who appear to have a substantial prospect of receiving an award if the protest is denied."[4]

Another important term is adverse agency action*,* which the *Code of Federal Regulations* defines as "any action or inaction by a contracting agency which is prejudicial to the position taken in a protest filed with the agency, including a decision on the merits of a protest; the opening of bids or receipt of proposals, the award of a contract, or the rejection of a bid or proposal despite a pending protest; or contracting agency acquiescence in continued and substantial contract performance."[5]

It is important to note that adverse agency action is defined as both an affirmative action as well as inaction by an agency. In other words, doing nothing can also be considered an adverse action. Given the extremely narrow timeframe in which a protest must be filed, a protestor has to determine very quickly whether the agency's inaction has triggered the start of the protest clock.

For example, if the company requests a postaward debriefing and the agency doesn't respond, the protest clock nevertheless continues to run. Waiting for the agency to respond will not prevent the Government Accountability Office (GAO) from throwing a protest out as untimely. The company initiated an action that *should* have generated a response; the agency ignoring the company is inactive and thereby committing an adverse agency action. Sometimes the agency might complain that it was preparing a response and the company jumped the gun. But if the company didn't protest in such a situation, it might never hear from the agency and lose that opportunity.

Given the extremely narrow timeframe in which a protest must be filed, a protestor has to determine very quickly whether to file a protest. With that in mind, a protestor must be very aware of how GAO counts days. *Days* are, first and foremost, calendar days. GAO explains that

> the day from which the period begins to run is not counted, and when the last day of the period is a Saturday, Sunday, or Federal holiday, the period extends to the next day that is not a Saturday, Sunday, or Federal holiday. Similarly, when the GAO, or another Federal agency where a submission is due, is closed for all or part of the last day, the period extends to the next day on which the agency is open.[6]

Timing is very critical. There are situations in which an agency is required to forebear on awarding a contract if not yet awarded or suspend performance of an awarded contract. If the agency receives notice of the protest before the contract has been awarded, the contract "may not be awarded" while the protest is pending,[7] unless the head of the agency makes a written finding that "urgent and compelling circumstances which significantly affect interests of the United States will not permit waiting for the decisions of the Comptroller General."[8] Similarly, if notice of the protest is received within ten days after award of the contract, the agency "shall… immediately direct the contractor to cease performance under the contract and to suspend any related activities that may result in additional obligations being incurred by the United States" while the protest is pending.[9] The head of the agency may authorize performance of the contract during this period only if he finds that "urgent and compelling circumstances" will not permit waiting for the decision of the Comptroller General or that "performance of the contract is in the best interests of the United States."[10]

A successful protest may result in the agency's:

- Issuing a stop work order to suspend performance
- Reevaluating proposals
- Awarding proposal preparation and protest filing costs to the successful protester
- Terminating the awarded contract and re-soliciting the requirement.[11]

The GAO does not have a pot of money to pay for proposal preparation and protest filing costs. The agency pays these costs with its own procurement funds.[12]

DECIDING WHETHER TO FILE A PROTEST

Filing a protest against a contract award is a decision companies do not make lightly. A company must have a realistic case before filing a protest. Not only will the protestor have to pay filing fees and legal expenses, but it may also be concerned about risking its business relationship with a potential or existing customer.

Why, then, might an unsuccessful offeror file a protest? It may believe, for example, that the agency did not follow the evaluation criteria or did not consider cost in the award decision. The offeror can decide whether to protest the decision by asking three questions:

- Was the procurement legally flawed?
- Was the company prejudiced?
- Is there an adequate business case for filing a protest?

Identifying Legal Flaws

The offeror's first step is to determine whether the agency's award decision was legally flawed. All protests must have a *basis*. This means that the protestor has to cite the rule, regulation, or statute that the agency failed to follow. The protestor cannot simply disagree with the decision. It must determine whether there was something procedurally wrong with the agency's evaluation. Keith R. Szeliga suggests that an offeror considering a protest try to answer the following questions:

- "Did the agency evaluate factors or require capabilities not disclosed in the solicitation?
- Did the agency downgrade your proposal based on inaccurate information or incorrect assumptions regarding what you actually proposed?
- Did the agency disclose all significant weaknesses, deficiencies, and adverse past performance information during discussions?
- Did the agency evaluate your cost/price based on the technical solution you actually proposed?
- Did the agency ignore your competitor's failure to meet a minimum mandatory solicitation requirement?
- Did the agency fail to analyze whether your competitor may have an organizational conflict of interest?
- Did the agency consider all of the disclosed evaluation factors, and only the disclosed evaluation factors, in conducting its cost/technical trade-off?
- Did the agency fail to adequately document its award determination?"[13]

This list of questions identifies some of the reasons the GAO sustains protests. The company's legal counsel will help determine if the agency may have made any errors during the source selection. If the agency's source selection decision was not legally flawed, then filing a protest is not recommended. If, on the other hand, the agency made fundamental errors in the source selection, it's time to move on to step two: determining whether the company was prejudiced by the flaws in the agency's evaluation.[14]

Identifying Prejudice

To win a protest, the company "must be able to show that the agency's errors prevented [the] firm from having a reasonable chance to win the contract."[15] Szeliga writes, "Competitive prejudice is an essential element of every protest. If the record does not demonstrate that the protestor would have had a reasonable chance of receiving award but for the agency's actions,"[16] the GAO will not sustain a protest, even if there are deficiencies in the procurement process.[17] In other words, if a company had no chance of winning the contract anyway, the agency's errors won't help it at this point in the process.

The requirement for proving prejudice is basically a "no harm, no foul" rule, but this requirement can be difficult to meet.[18] Not all errors affect the outcome of a source selection; even when they do, it is possible that another company would have won the contract regardless. The company should consider the agency's errors alongside the company's proposal and ask: "If the agency had not made the errors, would we have had a good chance to win the award?" If not, there's no point in protesting the award.[19]

Ensuring an Adequate Business Case

If the company is still considering filing a protest, it must determine if there is an adequate business case for doing so. Even if the agency made errors in source selection, and the company can establish that it was prejudiced, there are other questions to answer, such as:

- **How important is the contract to the company?** Consider not only the size of the contract and profit to be earned, but also if winning this contract would help the company enter a new market. Could this contract lead to follow-on work? Is winning this contract necessary to maintain a particular line of business?[20]
- **How will a protest affect the company's relationship with the customer?**[21] Consider the strength of the existing customer relationship. Does the agency rely on the company for products or services it can't get elsewhere? How much time will pass until the company submits its next proposal with this agency?
- **What is the likelihood the company will win the protest?**[22] The published sustain rate for GAO bid protests in fiscal year 2008 was 21 percent.[23] Of course, every protest is different. Szeliga writes,

  Protests challenging an agency's technical and best-value judgments rarely prevail. On the other hand, if the agency's errors were so fundamental that [the company was] denied a fair opportunity to compete for the contract, [its] probability of success will be greater.[24]

- **What is the likelihood the company will win the contract?** Szeliga writes,

  The most common bid protest remedies (in addition to reimbursement of a portion of [the company's] attorneys' fees) include the re-evaluation of proposals and/or solicitation of revised proposals. Thus, winning a protest does not guarantee that [the company] will win the contract; it merely gives [it] another bite at the apple.[25]

If a company believes, based on its debriefing, that its proposal is competitive or can be revised to be more advantageous to the government, then a second bite at the apple can be a very valuable opportunity. If, on the other hand, the agency seems unlikely to award [the] company the contract under any circumstances, then a successful protest may be a hollow victory.

Ironically, the most common bases for winning protests involve procedural irregularities, such as formulaic cost evaluations or departures from stated evaluation criteria. [The company] need[s] to consider whether, in the end, [its] remedy will be nothing more than a revised solicitation or re-evaluation of proposals that corrects these types of procedural errors, but leads to the same result (i.e., an award to [a] competitor). In short, there is no reason to fight the battle if you know you will lose the war.[26]

Now that you have a basic understanding of the decision-making process for filing a protest, let's explore some of the common reasons for protest.

COMMON CAUSES FOR PROTEST

Although there are many causes for protest, the most typical include:

- Improper agency evaluation
- A lack of meaningful discussions
- Defective solicitations
- Improper exclusion from the competitive range
- A lack of cost realism
- Agency bias or bad faith.

Improper Agency Evaluation

Although agencies have a great deal of flexibility when preparing RFPs, when evaluating proposals, they must follow the evaluation criteria set forth in the RFP and the regulations stated in the FAR. An evaluation may be improper if the agency:

- Relaxes the RFP's evaluation criteria
- Imposes additional, unannounced criteria
- Fails to follow existing criteria
- Conducts an improper cost/technical trade-off analysis.

A Lack of Meaningful Discussions

In a negotiated procurement, federal agencies must hold meaningful discussions with all offerors within the competitive range. During these discussions, the agency must point out to the offeror deficiencies and significant weaknesses in its proposal.

If the agency fails to do so, the discussions aren't meaningful. Keep in mind, however, that an agency is not obligated to point out every weakness or area where a proposal could be improved.[27]

Defective Solicitations

Examples of solicitation defects include ambiguities in the RFP or overly restrictive requirements that reduce competition. A protest alleging that a solicitation is defective must be filed prior to the date for submission of the bids or proposals.[28] This tighter timeline benefits agencies: Once the deadline for proposal submission comes and goes, competitors may not raise defects in the solicitation as an issue.

Improper Exclusion from the Competitive Range

The competitive range consists of the most highly rated proposals. The determination of which proposals fall into the range must be based on the evaluation criteria in the RFP.[29] A competitive range consisting of only one offeror is acceptable as long as it is justified. If an offeror believes it was improperly excluded from the competitive range, it must file a protest within ten days of learning (or within ten days of the date it should have learned) the agency's reason for excluding it.

A Lack of Cost Realism

The offeror would learn about the cost realism evaluation during the debriefing. When contracting on a cost-reimbursement basis, evaluations shall include a cost realism analysis to determine:

- What the government should realistically expect to pay for the proposed effort
- The offeror's understanding of the work
- The offeror's ability to perform the contract.

The contracting officer is required to document the cost or price evaluation. One GAO decision, for example, defines an agency's responsibilities in determining cost realism:

> An agency's cost realism analysis need not achieve scientific certainty; rather, the methodology employed must be reasonably adequate and provide some measure of confidence that the agency's conclusions about the most probable costs under an offeror's proposal are reasonable and realistic in view of other cost information reasonably available to the agency as of the time of its evaluation.[30]

When the analysis is done in a mechanical manner with little or no independent analysis, however, GAO will review the cost analysis and determine its appropriateness in the event of a protest. In one case, the protestor, Metro Machine Corporation,

> challenge[d] the Navy's cost realism analysis on the ground that the Navy simply assumed all offerors could perform the notional work items at the government-estimated labor hours and material costs without considering whether those estimates were consistent with each offeror's technical approach or how the offeror's technical capability affected these cost elements in determining the offeror's total evaluated cost. According to Metro, this mechanical application of the government estimates was inconsistent with the requirements of FAR § 15.404-1(d), which states in part that a cost realism analysis is the process of evaluating whether an offeror's cost elements 'are consistent with the unique methods of performance and materials described in the offeror's technical proposal.'[31]

The GAO sustained the protest, stating that,

> [w]hile an agency can utilize a reasonably derived estimate of labor hours based on the government's experience as an objective standard to measure realism of proposed costs, an agency may not mechanically apply its own estimates for labor hours or costs—effectively normalizing cost elements of an offeror's proposal to government estimates—without considering the offeror's unique technical approach.[32]

This case illustrates how a faulty cost realism analysis can result in a sustained protest.

Agency Bias or Bad Faith

Protests brought on the basis of agency bias or bad faith require evidence of specific and malicious intent. The GAO will not accept unsupported allegations by a protester that may be disappointed in the results of a particular procurement as evidence of bias or bad faith.

If a firm decides to pursue a protest after following the three-step process outlined above (determining whether the acquisition was legally flawed, proving prejudice, and determining whether there is an adequate business case for protest), it's important to keep the protest clock in mind. Protesters have five days from the offered debriefing date to file a protest to suspend contract performance.

FILING PREAWARD OR POSTAWARD PROTESTS

This chapter focuses on protests filed after award, but for the sake of completeness, we'll briefly touch on protest before award. The rest of this section and chapter will cover postaward protests.

Preaward Protests

If a company finds an apparent impropriety in the RFP, it must file a protest by the proposal due date. In all other cases, protests must be filed no later than 10 days after the basis of protest is known or should have been known, whichever is earlier. The agency may consider the merits of any protest that is not filed on time:

- For good cause shown; or
- When it determines that a protest raises issues significant to the agency's acquisition system.

As noted earlier in this chapter, agencies can, in certain circumstances, make an award in the face of a protest, but those are clearly intended to be the exception to the rule. Further, if the agency makes the award, and GAO later determines the award to be improper, that will have no bearing on GAO's decision, and the increased cost to the agency of rescinding the award will be borne solely by the agency.

Postaward Protests

If an offeror requests a postaward debriefing after being eliminated from the competitive range, the date the offeror was notified of its exclusion from the competition is considered the date the offeror knew or should have known the basis for a protest.[33]

Per FAR 33.103(f)(3),

> Upon receipt of a protest within ten days after contract award or within five days after a debriefing date offered to the protester under a timely debriefing request… the contracting officer shall immediately suspend performance, pending resolution of the protest within the agency, including any review by an independent higher level official.[34]

The agency may state in writing why continuing performance is justified for urgent and compelling reasons or is in the best interest of the government. This justification or determination must be approved at a level above the contracting officer or by another official, pursuant to agency procedures.[35]

The FAR provision continues, "Pursuing an agency protest does not extend the time for obtaining a stay of performance at GAO. Agencies may include, as part of the agency protest process, a voluntary suspension period when agency protests are denied and the protester subsequently files at GAO."[36]

PROTESTING TO THE AGENCY OR THE GAO

An unsuccessful offeror has two primary avenues available to file a protest: with the agency or with GAO. The U.S. Court of Federal Claims is also an option, but is not used as often as the GAO, so we won't discuss it in this text.[37] The agency should provide for inexpensive, informal, procedurally simple, and expeditious resolution of protests. Some agencies may use alternative dispute resolution techniques, third party neutrals, or another agency's personnel to resolve protests.[38]

Even if the company decides to file with GAO, it must still furnish a copy of its complete protest to the person designated in the RFP or to the contracting officer if the RFP does not provide a name. The agency must receive the protest no later than one day after the protest is filed with GAO.[39]

Protesting to the Agency

Protesting to the agency is a less expensive, less structured, and less time-consuming process than protesting to the GAO. Companies and agencies may also use alternative dispute resolution techniques.[40] In fact, the FAR recommends that parties should use their best efforts to resolve their concerns at the contracting officer level through open discussions before submitting a protest.[41] The objective of agency-level protest is to "build confidence in the Government's acquisition system, and to reduce protests outside of the agency."[42]

Protests to an agency must be concise, logical, and include the following information:

- Name, address, and fax and telephone numbers of the protester
- Solicitation or contract number
- Detailed statement of the legal and factual grounds for the protest, including a description of resulting prejudice to the protester
- Copies of relevant documents
- Request for a ruling by the agency
- Statement as to the form of relief requested
- All information establishing that the protester is an interested party for the purpose of filing a protest
- All information establishing the timeliness of the protest.

If any of the above required information is not included in the protest, the agency may dismiss the protest.[43]

Interested parties may request an independent review of their protest at a level above the contracting officer; solicitations should advise potential bidders and offerors that this review is available. Agency procedures should state whether this independent review is available as an alternative to consideration by the contracting officer of a protest or as an appeal of a contracting officer's decision on a protest. Officials designated to conduct the independent review should not have had previous personal involvement in the procurement. If there is an agency appellate review of the contracting officer's decision on the protest, it will not extend GAO's timeliness requirements. Therefore, any subsequent protest to the GAO must be filed within ten days of knowledge of initial adverse agency action.[44]

Per FAR 33.103(g) and (h),

> Agencies shall make their best efforts to resolve agency protests within 35 days after the protest is filed. To the extent permitted by law and regulation, the parties may exchange relevant information. Agency protest decisions shall be well-reasoned, and explain the agency position. The protest decision shall be provided to the protester using a method that provides evidence of receipt.[45]

The following case demonstrates that an agency's protest review does not extend GAO's timeliness requirements.

Case Study: Protesting Adverse Agency Action

In this case, the Navy eliminated a company called RTI from competition by means of a letter dated January 20, 2009. The Navy claimed that RTI's proposal was unacceptable due to (at least) a noncompliant pricing matrix, and the problems with the proposal could be corrected only with discussions. Since the agency intended to award without discussions, it eliminated RTI's proposal from the competition.

On January 21, 2009,

> RTI sent a letter to the contracting officer requesting that the agency reconsider the decision and reinstate RTI's proposal in the final evaluation for award. In this letter, RTI argued that the assertedly noncompliant pricing matrix was the result of a 'clerical error' by RTI that could be addressed through clarifications and would not require the agency to reopen discussions. The contracting officer denied RTI's request on January 22, reiterating the position that the government could not determine RTI's intended pricing, and further explaining that the alleged error in RTI's pricing matrix could not be corrected without reopening discussions.

In response, RTI sent an email to the contracting officer on January 23,

> advising that it intended on submitting a preaward protest later that day. Instead of filing a protest, however, RTI, on that same date, requested a debriefing, and advised the contracting officer that it would withhold filing a protest until after the debriefing. The agency provided RTI a debriefing on January 27, which provided RTI with essentially the same information that the agency provided on January 22. RTI then filed [a] protest with [GAO] on February 3, challenging the agency's decision to eliminate

its proposal from the competition and arguing that the clerical error could have been resolved through clarifications.

The Navy argued

that RTI's protest to [the GAO was] untimely because it was filed…more than 10 days after the agency denied RTI's request for reconsideration, which the agency argues constituted initial adverse agency action in response to an agency-level protest by RTI. RTI argues that its request for reconsideration was not an agency-level protest and that since it obtained a debriefing, it could file its protest within 10 days of the debriefing and be considered timely.

GAO agreed with the Navy, stating

Bid Protest Regulations contain strict rules for the timely submission of protests. Where a protest first has been filed with a contracting activity, any subsequent protest to [GAO], to be considered timely, must be filed within 10 calendar days of 'actual or constructive knowledge of initial adverse agency action.' 4 C.F.R. § 21.2(a)(3) (2008)....

The initial adverse agency action in response to this agency-level protest was the agency's January 22 letter refusing to reconsider its decision to eliminate RTI's proposal from the competition. RTI's protest to [GAO] was filed on February 3, more than 10 days from when RTI learned of the initial adverse agency action on its agency-level protest. Therefore, RTI's protest to [GAO] is untimely filed under our Bid Protest Regulations, 4 C.F.R. § 21.2(a)(3).

On whether RTI's January 21 request for reconsideration constituted an agency-level protest, the GAO stated that

even if a letter to the agency does not explicitly state that it was intended to be a protest and even if the letter was not intended to be a formal bid protest, we will nevertheless consider the letter to be a protest, where it conveys an expression of dissatisfaction and a request for corrective action.

On RTI's argument that its protest to GAO was timely because it was filed within 10 days of the required debriefing, GAO denied the exception was applicable in this case

because RTI elected to file an agency-level protest, which is covered by 4 C.F.R. § 21.2(a)(3), which contains no exception to our timeliness rules based upon the request and receipt of a required debriefing. M2 Global Tech., Ltd., supra. That is, a debriefing, required or not, does not toll the requirement that a protest be filed within 10 days of adverse action on an agency-level protest. Because RTI did not learn any more information at the debriefing, given that the basis on which it has challenged the agency's action is essentially the same as that in its agency-level protest, its protest to [GAO] is untimely filed under our Bid Protest Regulations.

The protest was dismissed.[46]

This case illustrates the importance of the timelines involved in filing a protest. Even though RTI did not consider its communication with the agency as a formal protest, the agency and GAO did. Clearly, the GAO strictly adheres to the rule of filing ten days from the adverse agency action.

Protesting to the GAO

Many companies decide to file their protests with GAO. Provided the company meets the required filing deadlines, protests filed at GAO receive an automatic stay of performance, which prohibits the agency from proceeding with contract performance until GAO resolves the protest.[47] Szeliga writes, "While such an automatic stay is also available with an agency-level protest, the likelihood of a successful challenge at the agency is low."[48] Also,

> An agency may override GAO's automatic stay of performance if it determines that there are urgent and compelling circumstances or that doing so would be in the best interest of the government. Although override decisions are rare, they do occasionally occur.[49]

When an agency receives notice of a protest from GAO within ten days after contract award or within five days after a debriefing date offered to the protester, the contracting officer shall immediately suspend performance or terminate the awarded contract.[50]

The contracting officer must file a statement of facts, accompanied by a memorandum of law that explains to GAO, the protestor, and other intervening parties the rationale behind the agency's actions. Typically GAO contacts the agency and requests the documents within a day of receiving the protest. The agency has 30 days to submit the report.

When a protest is filed with GAO, and an actual or prospective offeror asks for reasonable access to the protest file (whether or not it has filed with GAO as an intervener), the agency must provide it.[51] If GAO dismisses the protest before the agency submits the statement of facts and memorandum of law to GAO, then the agency doesn't have to provide the parties a copy of the protest file. The protest file shall include an index, and, as appropriate:

- The protest.
- The proposal submitted by the protester.

- The proposal being considered for award or being protested.
- All relevant evaluation documents.
- The solicitation, including the specifications or portions relevant to the protest.
- The abstract of offers or relevant portions. (The abstract of offers [standard form 1409] is a form that summarizes the offers by name, business size [large or small], prices, delivery time, and acceptance period.)
- Any other documents that the agency determines are relevant to the protest, including documents specifically requested by the protester.[52]

Information exempt from disclosure under 5 USC 552 may be redacted from the protest file.

In accordance with agency procedures, the head of the contracting activity may authorize contract performance, notwithstanding the protest, upon a written finding that:

- Contract performance will be in the best interest of the United States; or
- Urgent and compelling circumstances that significantly affect the interests of the United States will not permit waiting for GAO's decision.

The agency may not authorize contract performance until it has notified GAO of this written finding.[53]

AVOIDING A PROTEST

The agency should anticipate the possibility of protest early in the acquisition cycle. This approach makes it easier to avoid or defend a protest. An agency can try to avoid a protest by making certain that:

- The evaluation criteria focus on the truly important discriminators for what is being purchased.
- The process described in the source selection plan and RFP is followed exactly and consistently across all proposals.
- The winning proposal complies with the solicitation requirements, including section L of the RFP and the statement of work.
- The evaluators evaluate all proposals consistently, use the "what, why, and impact" format for writing their comments, give credit where possible, and address weaknesses when necessary.
- The evaluators ensure that they understand each proposal and use clarification requests to allow offerors to make their proposals clear.
- The evaluation documentation supports the proposal scores and award decision.

- The RFP adequately describes the evaluation criteria, including any absolute performance requirements that are necessary to meet the standard, and evaluators follow the evaluation criteria in section M.
- The evaluators don't use extraneous information from outside the proposals (except past performance information).
- The discussions, if conducted, are inclusive, practical, and meaningful.
- The cost evaluation is sound and includes a most probable cost/price analysis.
- The source selection authority's best value trade-off analysis is reasonable and adequately supported.
- The source selection decision document explains, in a comparative manner, the relative merits of the competing proposals. It should not recite the merits and faults of each proposal in a structured fashion, but should clearly explain how the winning proposal is superior with regard to the key discriminators and how it will enable the agency to fulfill its mission.
- The debriefings provide offerors with positive, constructive, and comprehensive feedback, demonstrating that the government is interested in their future success. Offerors feel as if they've gotten the "complete story" about their evaluation.

No one can prevent a protest from being filed. Having a well-prepared plan for each source selection and following it will go a long way toward minimizing perceived grounds for protest. Being prepared to defend against a protest offers the best chance of having the protest dismissed. It will be easier for an agency to defend its decision if:

- The agency has a roster of all source selection personnel and advisors, complete with contact information so the agency can contact them to support the protest as necessary.
- The agency has established a logical system for indexing all source selection documents.
- The source selection evaluation team uses standard software to generate documents; responding to a protest is made easier if the protest response team can copy and paste from existing documents.
- The electronic documents are labeled with a file name that indicates the nature of each document. This is important because the protest response team must review every document related to the source selection to determine whether it must be provided to the opposing party. Opening and reviewing each document adds time to the protest process.
- The documents track from one to another (e.g., from the source selection panel reports to the award recommendation briefs to the offeror debriefing documents).
- Source selection team members are aware that they must never have any conversations with any offeror at any time regarding the source selection or the protest.[54]

Readers interested in an in-depth case study may wish to read Appendix 2, which provides a detailed analysis of the Boeing Tanker protest.

CHAPTER SUMMARY

Chapter 15 discusses protests, including why, when, and how to file a protest. A very strict timeline applies to filing a protest. If a protest is filed within ten days of contract award, the agency must immediately tell the contractor to stop performance and suspend any related activities that may result in additional obligations incurred by the agency. A successful protest may result in the agency's issuing a stop-work order to suspend performance; reevaluating proposals; awarding proposal preparation and protest filing costs to the successful protester; or terminating the awarded contract and re-soliciting the requirement.

The offeror can decide whether to file a protest by asking whether the procurement was legally flawed; the company was prejudiced; or the company has an adequate business case for filing. Although there are many causes for protest, the most typical include an improper agency evaluation; a lack of meaningful discussions; defective solicitations; an improper exclusion from the competitive range; a lack of cost realism; or agency bias or bad faith.

Unsuccessful offerors predominately file protest with either the agency or with the GAO. Protesting to the agency is a less expensive, less structured, and less time-consuming process than protesting to the GAO. Companies and agencies may also use alternative dispute resolution techniques. Many companies choose to file with the GAO because such protests cause an automatic stay of performance, prohibiting the agency from proceeding with contract performance until GAO resolves the protest. When filing with the GAO, the company must meet all required filing deadlines.

No one can prevent a protest from ever being filed. Following a well-prepared plan for each source selection will go a long way, however, toward minimizing potential grounds for protest. Being prepared to defend against a protest will give agencies the best chance of having protests dismissed when they do occur.

NOTES

1 Federal Acquisition Regulation (FAR) 33.103.

2 FAR 33.101.

3 Ibid.

4 U.S. Government Accountability Office, "Bid Protest Regulations," *Code of Federal Regulations*, Title 4, §21.0(b)(1) (Washington, DC: U.S. Government Accountability Office, June 9, 2008).

5 Ibid., §21.0(f).

6 Ibid., §21.0(e).

7 31 *U.S. Code* 3553(c)(1).

8 31 *U.S. Code* 3553(c)(2)(A).

9 31 *U.S. Code* 3553(d)(1).

10 31 *U.S. Code* 3553(d)(2).

11 FAR 52.233-3, 33.103, and 33.104.

12 FAR 33.104(h).

13 Keith R. Szeliga, "So You Lost: Now What? A Vacationer's Guide to GAO Bid Protests," *Contract Management* 48 (Ashburn, VA: National Contract Management Association, November 2008), 35.

14 Ibid.

15 Ibid.

16 Ibid.

17 Ibid.

18 Ibid.

19 Ibid.

20 Ibid

21 Ibid.

22 Ibid., 37.

23 U.S. Government Accountability Office, "Bid Protest Statistics for Fiscal Years 2004–2008," B-158766 (Washington, DC: U.S. Government Accountability Office, December 22, 2008).

24 Szeliga, 37.

25 Ibid.

26 Ibid.

27 FAR 15.306(d)(3).

28 U.S. Government Accountability Office, "Bid Protest Regulations," *Code of Federal Regulations*, Title 4, §21.2(a)(1).

29 FAR 15.306(c)(1).

30 U.S. Government Accountability Office, "Information Ventures, Inc.," B-297276.2; B-297276.3; B-297276.4 (Washington, DC: U.S. Government Accountability Office, March 1, 2006).

31 U.S. Government Accountability Office, "Metro Machine Corporation," B-297879.2 (Washington, DC: U.S. Government Accountability Office, May 3, 2006).

32 Ibid.

33 Johnnie E. Wilson, *Best Value Source Selection* 715-3 (Alexandria, VA: Army Materiel Command, 1998), 67.

34 FAR 33.103(f)(3).

35 Ibid.

36 FAR 33.103(f)(4).

37 Interested readers may consult the Court of Federal Claims rules, available at http://www.uscfc.uscourts.gov/sites/default/files/court_info/rules_071309_v7.pdf (accessed August 20, 2009).

38 FAR 33.103(c).

39 FAR 33.104(a).

40 Readers interested in learning more about alternative dispute resolution may consult FAR 33.214.

41 FAR 33.103(b).

42 FAR 33.103(d).

43 Ibid.

44 U.S. Government Accountability Office, "Bid Protest Regulations," *Code of Federal Regulations*, Title 4, §21.2(a)(3).

45 FAR 33.103(g) and (h).

46 U.S. Government Accountability Office, "RTI Technologies, LLC," B-401075 (Washington, DC: U.S. Government Accountability Office, April 15, 2009).

47 35 *U.S. Code* 3553(d)(3).

48 Szeliga, 34.

49 Szeliga, 39.

50 FAR 33.104(c).

51 FAR 33.104(a)(ii).

52 FAR 33.104(a).

53 FAR 33.104(c).

54 National Reconnaissance Office, *Avoiding and Defending Protests Resulting from Source Selections*, pamphlet version 1.8 (Chantilly, VA: National Reconnaissance Office, May 2008).

Appendix I

Sample Proposal Preparation Instructions (Section L)

Appendix I provides a sample template for writing proposal preparation instructions in section L. Although this template comes from the Defense Acquisition University, it can be applied to civilian requests for proposals (RFPs) as well because it is not DoD-specific.[1] Readers can use this template to identify key topics an offeror needs to know to prepare a high-quality proposal.

L-1. GENERAL

The offeror shall submit documentation illustrating its approach for satisfying the requirements of this solicitation. The offeror shall describe its proposal through the use of graphs, charts, diagrams, and narrative. The proposal must be clear, coherent, and prepared in sufficient detail for the government to understand and evaluate the nature of the approach against the evaluation criteria.

The proposal shall cover all aspects of this solicitation and shall include the offeror's approach for integration and program management activities. The proposal must clearly demonstrate how the offeror intends to accomplish the project and must include convincing rationale and substantiation of all claims.

Unnecessarily elaborate brochures or other presentations beyond what is needed to present a complete, effective response to the solicitation are not desired. The government is seeking substance, not gloss.

In its evaluation and confidence assessment of each proposal, the government will consider the degree to which the offeror substantiated its proposed approach in the proposal volumes and in response to any discussions.

All correspondence in conjunction with this solicitation should be directed to the government's point of contact (POC) identified below:

{POC name}

Phone: *{POC phone number}*

Fax: *{POC fax number}*

Email: *{POC email address}*

L-2. REQUIREMENTS FOR PROPOSAL VOLUMES

The proposal shall be accompanied by a cover letter (letter of transmittal) prepared on the company's letterhead stationery. The cover letter (letter of transmittal) shall identify all enclosures being transmitted and shall be used only to transmit the proposal and shall include no other information. The first or title page shall be in accordance with FAR 52.215-1(c)(2).

The following are further descriptions of the information that shall be provided with the proposal.

{Complete the following table to summarize the organization of the proposal, page limits, authorized page sizes, and number of copies required for hard copy and electronic copy.}

Volume	Section title (subfactor)	Section L reference	Electronic copies	Paper copies	Page limit
I. Executive summary		L-x	1	Original plus y copies	z
II. Factor title	Subfactor title	L-x	1	Original plus y copies	z
	Subfactor title	L-x	1	Original plus y copies	z
	Subfactor title	L-x	1	Original plus y copies	z
III. Factor title	Subfactor title	L-x	1	Original plus y copies	z
	Subfactor title	L-x	1	Original plus y copies	z
	Subfactor title	L-x	1	Original plus y copies	z
	Subfactor title	L-x	1	Original plus y copies	z plus supporting documents
IV. Cost		L-x	2	Original plus y copies	No limit
V. Contract information		L-x	1	Original plus y copies	No limit

L-2.1. Page limitations. The cover letter, title page, table of contents, table of figures, list of tables, and glossary of abbreviations and acronyms do not count against page count limitations. Proposal contents that exceed the stated page limitations will be removed from the proposal by the contracting officer before the proposal is turned over to the government evaluation teams and will not be considered in the evaluation.

L-2.2. Format. {*Identify the required physical format requirements for the proposals to include paper size, font size, etc. For example*:}

Text shall be single-spaced, on 8½ x 11 inch paper (except as specifically noted), with a minimum one-inch margin all around. Pages shall be numbered consecutively. A page printed on both sides shall be counted as two pages. Submitting double-sided pages and copying on recycled paper is encouraged. Fold-out pages sized 11" x 17" may be used for tables, charts, graphs, or pictures that cannot be legibly presented on 8½" x 11" paper. An 11" x 17" sheet is equivalent to two pages with regard to the page count limitations.

Print shall be of a minimum 12-point font size or a maximum 10 characters per inch (10-pitch, pica) spacing. Bolding, underlining, and italics may be used to identify topic demarcations or points of emphasis. Graphic presentations, including tables, while not subject to the same font size and spacing requirements, shall have spacing and text that is easily readable.

Each volume in the proposal shall include a copy of the cover letter (letter of transmittal), title page, and table of contents. The table of contents shall list sections, subsections, and page numbers. Each volume shall contain a glossary of all abbreviations and acronyms used. Each acronym used shall be spelled out in the text the first time it appears in each proposal volume.

In addition to submitting the required number of paper copies, the offeror shall submit all proposal information in electronic format on a CD. Text and graphics portions of the electronic copies shall be in a format readable by {*insert the electronic format requirement, such as*:} Microsoft (MS) Office 20XX, MS Word 20XX. Data submitted in spreadsheet format shall be readable by MS Office 20XX, MS Excel 20XX. Materials for oral presentations (if conducted) shall be readable by MS Office 20XX, MS PowerPoint 2000.

In case of conflict between the paper copy and the electronic copy of a proposal, the paper copy shall take precedence.

Each paper volume shall be bound separately in hard-sided three-ring binders (e.g., Section L-5.4: Executive Summary shall be placed in a binder and L-5.5.1: Factor Title in another binder).

All CDs shall be in read-only format and formatted for Microsoft Windows 7, Windows VISTA, or Windows XP, with one exception. The Volume IV (Cost) volume shall be submitted in at least two CDs: one read-only and the other read/write. The spreadsheets submitted in read/write cost disk shall not be linked to any other spreadsheets or other files. The other disk may contain links, but only to documents/spreadsheets that have been submitted as part of the proposal.

L-2.3. Submission address. All copies of the proposals shall be sent or hand-carried to:

> {Organization name}
>
> ATTN {POC name}
>
> RFP: {RFP number}
>
> {Address proposals are to be delivered to}

{If electronic proposals are to be submitted in lieu of paper copies, a paragraph such as the following may be included:}

Offerors shall submit electronic versions of volume _____ to {POC name} at {POC email}. Offerors must identify the RFP number in the subject line of the email and should include "# of #" if multiple emails are required for submission of the entire proposal. Offerors may consider sending more than one email to ensure size limitations will not hinder transmission. Offerors are advised to submit electronic documents early and confirm successful transmission/receipt. The government POC will provide a return response signifying receipt of the transmissions.

L-2.4. Submission due dates. {*This paragraph should specifically identify the time and date that proposals are due. If offerors are required to submit different parts of the proposal at different times, specify which part is due at which time.*} As discussed in chapter 5, the CO may want to require the past performance volume to be delivered before the cost, technical and management volumes. The following paragraph illustrates how to identify this requirement.

The {*factor name*} volume referenced in section L-*x.x* must be received prior to 12:00 noon EST, {*date*}. All other volumes must be received prior to 12:00 noon EST, {*date*}. The government POC will provide a receipt showing the time and date of delivery. Late submissions will not be accepted.

L-2.5. Restriction of disclosure/proprietary information. If the offeror wishes to restrict the disclosure or use of its proposal, use the legend permitted by FAR 52.215-1(e). Individual subcontractor/vendor proprietary information may be submitted in separate binders or CDs. The information contained in these binders/CDs must be referenced (by binder title, page, and section number, as appropriate) within the main proposal where the information would have been included if it were not proprietary to the subcontractor/vendor. The information in these separate binders/CDs is subject to all other requirements of the RFP and must be well marked to clearly indicate any special handling instructions.

L-2.6. Cross-referencing. Each volume, other than the cost volume, shall be written to the greatest extent possible on a standalone basis so that its content may be evaluated with a minimum of cross-referencing to other volumes of the proposal. Cross-referencing within a proposal volume is permitted where its use would conserve space without impairing clarity. Hyperlinking of cross-references is permissible. Information required for proposal evaluation that is not found in its designated volume or cross-referenced is assumed to have been omitted from the proposal.

L-2.7. Oral presentations. {*If oral presentations or proposals will be used as part of the evaluation, rules for the oral presentations should be stated here. For example:*}

   a. Time limit. The offeror's oral presentation shall not exceed {*number*} hours. The contracting officer reserves the right to terminate the presentation if it overruns the *x*-hour limit.

   b. Questions. During the presentation, the source selection evaluation board (SSEB) members will not interrupt the offeror to ask questions (except to request the repetition of inaudible words or statements or the explanation of terms that are unknown to them) or otherwise engage the offeror in any dialogue. A question-and-answer period will follow and may cover the entire proposal. These questions will not constitute "discussions" as defined in FAR 15.306.

   c. Offeror attendees. A maximum of {*number*} presenters will be allowed into the presentation room at any one time.

   d. Topics. The offeror's oral presentation will address the following:

Topic	Applicable subfactor	Specific instructions
Topic	Subfactor title	Section L-*x.x* of the solicitation
Topic	Subfactor title	Section L-*x.x* of the solicitation
Topic	Subfactor title	Section L-*x.x* of the solicitation
Topic	Subfactor title	Section L-*x.x* of the solicitation

   e. Presentation media. Offerors are free to structure their oral presentations using 8½" x 11" view graphs (slides, transparencies) or computer-generated media. If the offeror chooses to use an electronic projection, it must provide its own equipment. An overhead projector will be available at the oral presentation site. The number of view graphs (or other media) should be reasonable for the stated time limits for the presentation. Use of these visual aids is at the offeror's discretion.

f. Paper and electronic copies. The offeror shall submit a preliminary version of its planned oral presentation materials as part of its written submission. {*Number*} printed color copies of the final presentation shall be provided to the government when the offeror begins its presentation. The offeror shall also provide an electronic copy of the final presentation.

g. Recording the presentation. Oral presentations will be videotaped by the government, will be available to the SSEB for its review during the source selection, and will be maintained as part of the source selection record.

h. Scheduling. Oral presentations will be scheduled as soon as practicable after proposal receipt. The contracting officer will arrange scheduling with the offerors. The government reserves the right to reschedule presentations at the sole discretion of the contracting officer.

i. Location. The oral presentation site will be arranged conference style; an overhead projector and screen will be provided. The location will be {*location*} or another announced location. The government reserves the right to change the oral presentation site at the sole discretion of the contracting officer.

A visit to the presentation room may be arranged when the contracting officer schedules each offeror's oral presentation.

L-2.8. Electronic submission of proposals

(a) When submitting a proposal on electronic media, the offeror must ensure that the submission is readable using the software specified in the solicitation and has been verified as free of computer viruses. Prior to any evaluation, the government will check all files for viruses and ensure that all information is readable. In the event that any files are defective (unreadable), the government may only evaluate the readable electronic files. However, if the defective (unreadable) media renders a significant deficiency in the offeror's proposal, the government may consider the proposal incomplete and eliminate such proposals from further evaluation.

(b) The offeror must ensure that:
   (1) The electronic and paper copies of its proposal submitted in response to the solicitation are identical.
   (2) It has verified that its electronic proposal is readable using the operating system and software specified{*specify format*}.
   (3) Using standard commercial antivirus software, it has verified that its electronic proposal is free of computer viruses.

(c) A proposal that fails to conform to the requirements of paragraphs (a) and (b) above may be subject to interception or delay at governmental electronic communications portals. This interception or delay may result in the proposal being lost, deleted, destroyed, or forwarded in such a manner that the proposal arrives at the target destination past the time and date of the deadline for submission established in the solicitation. In the event that a proposal is lost, deleted, or destroyed due to the offeror's failure to conform to the requirements of paragraphs (a) and (b) above, such proposal will be considered to have never been delivered to the government. In the event that a proposal is delayed due to the offeror's failure to conform to the requirements of paragraphs (a) and (b) above, the proposal will be treated as late in accordance with the provision of this solicitation entitled Late Submissions, Modifications, and Withdrawals of Proposals.

L-3. COMMUNICATION WITH THE CONTRACTING OFFICE

Solicitation information and amendments will be posted to the Federal Business Opportunities website at https://www.fbo.gov.

Offerors may email written questions requesting clarification of the RFP to the government via the contract specialist, {*POC name*}, at {*POC email address*}. The government will answer questions received up to {*insert date*}. Questions received after this date may not be answered.

Only proposals submitted in accordance with Section L-2 (Requirements for Proposal Volumes) of this solicitation will be accepted.

L-4. EXECUTIVE SUMMARY FACTOR VOLUME REQUIREMENTS (VOLUME I)

{*If an executive summary is to be included as part of the proposal, insert limitations, topics, and other requirements for submission.*}

L-5. {FACTOR NAME} FACTOR REQUIREMENTS (VOLUME II)

The {*factor name*} volume shall be organized as follows:

Subfactor 1: {Subfactor name} (Section 1)

Subfactor 2: {Subfactor name} (Section 2)

Subfactor 3: {Subfactor name} (Section 3)

L-5.1. Subfactor 1. {Subfactor name} (Section 1). The offeror shall {*insert submission requirements. The submission requirements should match those included in the source selection plan.*}

L-5.2. Subfactor 2 {Subfactor name} (Section 2). The offeror shall {*insert submission requirements. The submission requirements should match those included in the source selection plan.*}

L-5.3. Subfactor 3 {Subfactor name} (Section 3). The offeror shall {*insert submission requirements. The submission requirements should match those included in the source selection plan.*}

L-6. {FACTOR NAME} FACTOR REQUIREMENTS (VOLUME III)

The {factor name} volume shall be organized as follows:

> Subfactor 1: {Subfactor name} (Section 1)
> Subfactor 2: {Subfactor name} (Section 2)

L-6.1. Subfactor 1. {Subfactor name} (Section 1). The offeror shall {*insert submission requirements. The submission requirements should match those included in the source selection plan.*}

L-6.1.1. Master project list.

L-6.2. Subfactor 2. {Subfactor name} (Section 2). The offeror shall {*insert submission requirements. The submission requirements should match those included in the source selection plan.*}

L-7. COST FACTOR REQUIREMENTS (VOLUME IV)

{Insert submission instructions for the cost/price proposal.}

L-8. CONTRACT INFORMATION VOLUME REQUIREMENTS (VOLUME V)

This volume must include a completed SF33 {*or whichever form the agency uses*}, the information required to complete sections B, F, G, H, J, and K, and any other information required to complete the contract. {*This volume shall also include the offeror's subcontracting plan, if the subcontracting plan is not being evaluated as part of another factor.*}

---

[1]   Adapted from Defense Acquisition University, "Annex F – Sample RFP – sections L & M," https://acc.dau.mil/communitybrowser.aspx?id=25170&lang=en-us (accessed December 12, 2008).

Appendix ⏺ II

Case Study: Boeing Tanker Protest

The Boeing tanker protest is a significant protest case not only because of the visibility and dollar value of the acquisition, but also because of the lessons learned from the effort. This section will review the attempted acquisition from planning through protest and resolicitation.

THE HISTORY

The KC-135 aircraft is crucial to the core mission of the U.S. Air Force (USAF). The aircraft's main purpose is to provide aerial refueling for fighter and attack aircraft of the USAF, Navy, and Marine Corps. The Air Force, Navy, and Marine Corps operate almost 900 tanker aircraft, most of which are derivatives of cargo or commercial aircraft. Their history goes back over half a century.

In 1955, the USAF chose the Boeing plane over its Lockheed competitor. It received the first KC-135 delivery in June 1957 and the last one in 1965. Thus, even the newest one is more than 40 years old. David W. Thornton writes,

> Since their initial deployment, the original KC-135A models have undergone substantial upgrades, most notably replacement of the original Pratt & Whitney... engines with quieter and more fuel-efficient [ones].... Other modifications included replacing the "skin" surface under the wings, and enhancing the avionics and navigation systems.[1]

Although these upgrades kept the KC-135s operating effectively over the years, in the mid-1990s, the USAF, Department of Defense (DoD), and Congress began to consider replacing the fleet.[2]

Modernizing or replacing the Air Force tanker fleet has been a point of contention for more than a decade. In 1996, the General Accounting Office (GAO; now Government

Accountability Office) asserted that the long-term viability of the KC-135 fleet was questionable and advocated studying replacement options. DoD countered that KC-135 airframe hours were low and that the Air Force could sustain the fleet for another 35 years.[3]

Between 2002 and 2004, the Air Force attempted to lease Boeing KC-767 aircraft to replace some of the older models. This lease agreement used the new commercial item acquisition procedures, which was a controversial decision. Meanwhile, the misconduct of the lead negotiator for the Air Force led to criminal charges. William Knight and Christopher Bolkcom write,

> On April 20, 2004, Darleen A. Druyun, the former lead Air Force negotiator on the tanker lease program, pleaded guilty to one charge of criminal conspiracy. Ms. Druyun admitted to secretly negotiating an executive job with the Boeing Company while still overseeing the $23 billion deal between the Air Force and Boeing.[4]

In September 2006, the Air Force's Aeronautical Systems Center (ASC) released to industry a draft request for proposal (RFP) for the KC-X program. The final RFP was issued on January 30, 2007. It provided for the award of a contract with cost-reimbursement and fixed-price contract line items. Offerors were informed that, although the agency would procure up to 179 KC-X aircraft over a 15- to 20-year period, the initial contract would be for the system development and demonstration (SDD) of the KC-X aircraft and the procurement of up to 80 aircraft, beginning with the delivery of four SDD aircraft and two low rate initial production (LRIP) aircraft. Offerors were also informed that the agency was contemplating receiving an existing commercial transport aircraft, certified by the Federal Aviation Administration (FAA) or the equivalent, and modified to meet the agency's requirements.[5]

Both Boeing and a consortium of Northrop Grumman and European Aeronautic Defense and Space Company (EADS, which is the parent company of Airbus) participated in the competition for the KC-X tanker aircraft. Boeing offered a variation of its 767-200, while the Northrop Grumman consortium proposed a version of the Airbus 330-200. On February 29, 2008, the Air Force awarded the KC-X contract to Northrop Grumman. On March 11, 2008, Boeing protested the Air Force's decision to GAO, which sustained the protest.

THE RFP

Per the executive summary of the RFP, "As the initial phase of a comprehensive aerial refueling recapitalization strategy, the KC-X program [was intended to] replace approximately one[-]third of the warfighting capability provided by the current aerial refueling fleet."[6]

The Air Force planned to acquire 179 new commercial off-the-shelf airliners modified to accomplish air refueling missions.[7] The RFP outlined nine primary key performance parameters:

- Air refueling capability
- Fuel offload and range at least as great as the KC-135
- Compliant Communication, Navigation, Surveillance/Air Traffic Management (CNS/ATM) equipment
- Airlift capability
- Ability to take on fuel while airborne
- Sufficient force protection measures
- Ability to network into the information available in the battle space
- Survivability measures (such as defensive systems, electromagnetic pulse [EMP] hardening, chemical/biological protection)
- Provisioning for a multipoint refueling system to support Navy and allied aircraft.[8]

EVALUATION FACTORS

The RFP read:

> This is a capability[-]based, best value source selection conducted in accordance with Federal Acquisition Regulation (FAR) 15.3, Source Selection, as supplemented by the Defense Federal Acquisition Regulation Supplement (DFARS), Air Force Federal Acquisition Regulation Supplement (AFFARS), dated June 2006, and the Air Force Materiel Command Federal Acquisition Regulation Supplement (AFMCFARS).

> The Government will select the best overall offer, based upon an integrated assessment of:

- Mission capability
- Proposal risk
- Past performance
- Cost/price
- Integrated Fleet Aerial Refueling Assessment (IFARA).

Contract(s) may be awarded to the offeror who is deemed responsible in accordance with the FAR, as supplemented, whose proposal conforms to the solicitation's requirements (to include all stated terms, conditions, representations, certifications, and all other information required by Section L of this solicitation) and is judged, based on the evaluation factors and subfactors, to represent the best value to the Government. The Government seeks to award to the offeror who gives the [Air Force] the greatest confidence that it will best meet, or exceed, the requirements. This may result in an award to a higher[-]rated, higher[-]priced offeror, where the decision is consistent with the evaluation factors and the Source Selection Authority (SSA) reasonably determines that the technical superiority and/or overall business approach and/or superior past performance, and/or the IFARA of the higher priced offeror outweighs the cost difference.

The SSA will base the source selection decision on an integrated assessment of proposals against all source selection criteria in the solicitation. While the Government source selection evaluation team and the SSA will strive for maximum objectivity, the source selection process, by its nature, is subjective and, therefore, professional judgment is implicit throughout the entire process.[9]

Award will be made to the offeror submitting the most advantageous proposal to the Government based upon an integrated assessment of the evaluation factors and subfactors described below. The Mission Capability, Proposal Risk, and Past Performance evaluation factors are of equal importance and individually more important than either Cost/Price or IFARA evaluation factors individually. The IFARA is equal in importance to Cost/Price. Within the Mission Capability factor, the five (5) subfactors are listed in descending order of relative importance from 1 to 5. In accordance with FAR 15.304(e), the Mission Capability, Proposal Risk, Past Performance, and IFARA evaluation factors, when combined, are significantly more important than Cost/Price; however, Cost/Price will contribute substantially to the selection decision.[10]

The RFP listed the factors and subfactors as follows:

- Factor 1: Mission capability
  - Subfactor 1: Key system requirements
  - Subfactor 2: System integration and software
  - Subfactor 3: Product support
  - Subfactor 4: Program management
  - Subfactor 5: Technology maturity and demonstration
- Factor 2: Proposal risk
- Factor 3: Past performance
- Factor 4: Cost/price
- Factor 5: Integrated Fleet Aerial Refueling Assessment (IFARA)[11]

Factor 1: Mission Capability

The RFP continued, "The Mission Capability evaluation provides an assessment of the offeror's capability to satisfy the Government's requirements. Mission Capability subfactors 1–5 will receive one of the color ratings described in Table [A2-1]: Mission Capability Ratings."[12]

Table A2-1   Mission Capability Ratings1[13]

Color	Rating	Description
Blue	Exceptional	Exceeds specified minimum performance or capability requirements in a way beneficial to the government; a proposal must have one or more strengths and no deficiencies to receive a blue.
Green	Acceptable	Meets specified minimum performance or capability requirements delineated in the request for proposal; a proposal rated green must have no deficiencies but may have one or more strengths.
Yellow	Marginal	Does not clearly meet some specified minimum performance or capability requirements delineated in the request for proposal, but any such uncertainty is correctable.
Red	Unacceptable	Fails to meet specified minimum performance or capability requirements; the proposal has one or more deficiencies. Proposals with an unacceptable rating are not awardable.

Factor 2: Proposal Risk

The RFP read:

> The proposal risk evaluation focuses on the weaknesses associated with an offeror's proposed approach and includes an assessment of the potential for disruption of schedule, increased cost, degradation of performance, and the need for increased Government oversight, as well as the likelihood of unsuccessful contract performance.

The mission capability subfactors (1–4) will receive one of the proposal risk ratings described in Table A2-2: Proposal Risk Ratings.[14]

Table A2-2   Proposal Risk Ratings[15]

Rating	Description
High	Likely to cause significant disruption of schedule, increased cost, or degradation of performance. Risk may be unacceptable even with special contractor emphasis and close government monitoring.
Moderate	Can potentially cause disruption of schedule, increased cost, or degradation of performance. Special contractor emphasis and close government monitoring will likely be able to overcome difficulties.
Low	Has little potential to cause disruption of schedule, increased cost, or degradation of performance. Normal contractor effort and normal government monitoring will likely be able to overcome any difficulties.

Factor 3: Performance Confidence Assessment

Regarding past performance, the RFP read:

> Under the past performance factor, the Performance Confidence Assessment represents the evaluation of an offeror's present and past work record to assess the Government's confidence in the offeror's probability of successfully performing as proposed. The Performance Confidence Assessment will be assessed at the overall factor level after evaluating aspects of the offeror's recent past performance, focusing on performance that is relevant to the mission capability subfactors 1–4 only and cost or price. Each offeror will receive one of the following confidence ratings described in [Table A2-3] below:[16]

Factor 4: Cost/Price

Regarding cost/price evaluation, the RFP read:

> The Cost Panel will evaluate the offeror's cost proposal against the following criteria:

> - **Realism.** Each offeror's proposed costs are realistic when the proposed costs are evaluated and found to be realistic for the work to be performed; reflective of a clear understanding of the requirements; and consistent with the unique methods of performance and materials described in the offeror's technical proposal.
> - **Reasonableness.** For a price to be reasonable, it must represent a price to the Government that a prudent person would pay when consideration is given to prices in the market. Normally, price reasonableness is established through cost and price analysis techniques as described in FAR 15.404. For additional information see FAR 31.201-3.

Table A2-3 Performance Confidence Assessments[17]

Rating	Description
High confidence	Based on the offeror's performance record, the government has high confidence the offeror will successfully perform the required effort.
Significant confidence	Based on the offeror's performance record, the government has significant confidence the offeror will successfully perform the required effort.
Satisfactory confidence	Based on the offeror's performance record, the government has confidence the offeror will successfully perform the required effort. Normal contractor emphasis should preclude any problems.
Unknown confidence	No performance record is identifiable.
Little confidence	Based on the offeror's performance record, substantial doubt exists that the offeror will successfully perform the required effort.
No confidence	Based on the offeror's performance record, extreme doubt exists that the offeror will successfully perform the required effort.

The government will also check the factors proposed for all lots of the Variation in Quantity provision to ensure they are reasonable and based on reasonable methodology.

- **Cost/price risk rating.** A cost/price risk evaluation [is] applicable to the cost/price evaluation factor. This risk rating will characterize the Government's evaluation of the offeror's proposed cost/price when compared to the corresponding portions of the independently computed Government most probable cost/price.... This evaluation also considers the extent to which the offeror's cost/price is realistic for the work to be performed.

- **Most probable life cycle cost (MPLCC).** The MPLCC is an independent government estimate, adjusted for technical, cost, and schedule risk, to include all contract, budgetary, and other government costs (OGCs) associated with all phases of the entire weapon system life cycle (SDD, PD, and Operations and Support (O&S)). The independent government estimate will be done by work breakdown structure.[18]

Factor 5: Integrated Fleet Aerial Refueling Assessment

The RFP read:

> The Government will use modeling and simulation to provide an integrated assessment of the utility and flexibility for a fleet of the offeror's proposed KC-X by evaluating the number of aircraft required to fulfill the peak demand of the aerial refueling elements evaluated in the 2005 Mobility Capability Study (MCS). In the context of this evaluation scenario, the Government will determine the proposed KC-X's fleet effectiveness in relation to a KC-135R fleet.[19]

> Offerors are required to meet all solicitation requirements including terms and conditions, representations/certifications, and technical requirements in addition to the factors/subfactors identified. Failure to meet a solicitation requirement may result in an offeror being ineligible for award.[20]

The RFP included a detailed system requirements document (SRD) that presented the technical performance requirements for the KC-X aircraft. The SRD identified the minimum and desired performance/capability requirements for the aircraft.[21] The minimum performance capabilities of the aircraft were identified in nine key performance parameters (KPP), which the Air Force summarized and are presented in Table A2-4.

THE PROPOSALS

Boeing proposed as its KC-X aircraft the KC-767 Advanced Tanker, a derivative of its commercial 767-200 LRF (long range freighter) aircraft, and Northrop Grumman and European Aeronautic Defense and Space Company collaboratively

Table A2-4   Key Performance Parameters[13]

KPP	Parameter	Required Performance
1	Tanker air refueling capability	Air refueling of all current and programmed fixed-wing receiver aircraft
2	Fuel offload and range	Fuel, offload, range chart equivalent to KC-135
3	Communications, navigation, surveillance/air traffic management	Worldwide flight operations at all times in all civil and military airspace
4	Airlift capability	Carry passengers, palletized cargo, and/or aeromedical patients on entire main deck
5	Receiver air refueling capability	Refueled in flight from any boom-equipped tanker aircraft
6	Force protection	Operate in chemical/biological environments
7	Net-ready	Meet enterprise-level joint critical integrated architecture requirements
8	Survivability	Operate in hostile environments (night vision and imaging systems, electromagnetic pulse, defensive systems: infrared detect and counter, radio frequency detect, no counter)
9	Multipoint refueling	Multipoint drogue refueling

proposed the KC-30 aircraft, which was a derivative of the Airbus A330-200 commercial aircraft.

The Boeing KC-767 was composed of elements of a number of Boeing commercial aircraft, including the 767-200ER, 767-300F, 767-400 ER, 737, and 777 models. Boeing's proposed production plan for its SDD and production KC-X aircraft was to build the 767-200 LRF baseline aircraft at the Everett, Washington, facility of its commercial division, Boeing Commercial Airplanes (BCA), and then fly the aircraft to its Wichita, Kansas, facility for installation of military equipment and software by its military division, Integrated Defense Systems (IDS).[23]

Knight and Bolkcom write,

> Boeing touted its entrant, a version of the Boeing 767-200[,] as the "right-sized" tanker. Proponents of the KC-767 argue that it is most similar in size and offload capacity to the KC-135. [Further,] proponents stated that the KC-767's smaller "footprint" compared to the competing KC-30 might enable it to better utilize potentially limited ramp space in forward operating locations. Additionally, proponents believed the smaller KC-767 to be potentially more fuel efficient due to its lower gross weight[,] leading to less fuel being burned in transit. [24]

According to the GAO decision on the protest, the KC-30 proposal from Northrop Grumman contained a production plan that provided for a number of changed locations for the production, assembly, and modification of its SDD and LRIP aircraft. For the first SDD aircraft, Northrop Grumman proposed to build the commercial A330 aircraft in sections in various European locations, then assemble the aircraft in Toulouse, France, add the cargo door in Dresden, Germany, and complete militarization of the aircraft in Madrid, Spain. For the second and third SDD aircraft, Northrop Grumman proposed using its own Melbourne, Florida[,] facility, in place of EADS's Madrid facility, to complete militarization. For the last SDD aircraft, Northrop Grumman proposed replacing its Melbourne facility with a new facility it proposed to build in Mobile, Alabama.

For the first LRIP aircraft, Northrop Grumman proposed to have the Toulouse facility not only assemble the commercial baseline aircraft but also install the cargo door, and the Mobile facility would complete the militarization of the aircraft. Beginning with the second LRIP aircraft, and thereafter through the production phase, Northrop Grumman proposed to build the A330 baseline aircraft in sections at various locations in Europe and then ship those sections to the Mobile facility, which would assemble the aircraft, install the cargo door, and complete militarization of the aircraft.[25]

Knight and Bolkcom write that Northrup Grumman believed the KC-30 offered a superior value in comparison to the KC-767 because of its larger size. KC-30 proponents espoused the aircraft's potentially greater fuel offload capability and larger airlift capacity in terms of weight, pallet positions[,] and passengers when compared to the KC-767. As a result, KC-30 proponents believed their aircraft would reduce the number of aircraft required to meet some potential operational scenarios.[26]

PROPOSAL EVALUATIONS

According to the GAO decision,

> The proposals were evaluated by the agency's SSET, which initiated discussions with the offerors by issuing evaluation notices (EN). After evaluating the offerors' EN responses, the SSET provided a "mid-term" evaluation briefing to the SSAC and SSA. Because there were "concerns regarding how to properly show that all SRD requirements had been evaluated," the SSET prepared and provided another briefing to the SSA that detailed how each offeror's proposal was evaluated against each SRD requirement.... Following the SSA's approval of the mid-term briefing, the SSET provided mid-term briefings to Boeing and Northrop Grumman, at which each offeror was provided with the agency's evaluation ratings of their respective proposals....[27]

> Extensive discussions were conducted with each offeror, after which a "pre-final proposal revision" briefing was provided to the SSAC and SSA by the SSET that presented updated evaluation ratings of Boeing's and Northrop Grumman's proposals and

discussion responses. Following approval of this briefing by the SSA, the SSET again provided to each offeror the agency's evaluation ratings of their respective proposals.[28]

"Final revised proposals" were received from the offerors. Although intended by the agency to be the final proposal revisions, shortly after receipt of these proposals, the Air Force reopened discussions with the offerors in response to the enactment of the National Defense Authorization Act for [fiscal year] 2008…. As a part of these discussions, the Air Force provided offerors with additional information concerning the firms' respective IFARA evaluations and with a "clarified chart on Airlift Efficiency."… Subsequently, the agency received the firms' final proposal revisions.

The protester's and awardee's final proposal revisions were evaluated by the SSET as [shown in Table A2-5].

The protest decision continues:

As indicated by the nearly identical evaluation ratings received by both firms' technical proposals and the nearly identical evaluated MPLCCs, the competition was very close, and, as evaluated, both firms' proposals were found to be advantageous to the government. Ultimately, the SSAC concluded, however, that Northrop Grumman's proposal was more advantageous to the agency than Boeing's under the mission capability, past performance, cost/price, and IFARA factors; the two firms were found to be essentially equal under the proposal risk factor.

Table A2-5   Evaluation Results

	Boeing	Northrop Grumman
Mission capability/proposal risk		
Key system requirements	Blue/low	Blue/low
System integration/software	Green/moderate	Green/moderate
Product support	Blue/low	Blue/low
Program management	Green/low	Green/low
Technology maturity/demonstration	Green	Green
Past performance	Satisfactory confidence	Satisfactory confidence
Cost/price (MPLCC)	$108.044 billion	$108.010 billion
Cost risk		
SDD phase/production and deployment phase	Moderate/low	Low/low
IFARA fleet effectiveness value	1.79	1.9

SSAC Mission Capability Factor Evaluation

According to the protest decision,

> Northrop Grumman's evaluated advantage under the mission capability factor was largely based upon the firm's perceived superiority under the key system requirements and program management subfactors; the two firms were found essentially equal under the remaining three subfactors....

The SSAC assigned both firms' proposals, under the key system requirements subfactor (the most important mission capability subfactor), blue, low risk ratings, noting:

> Both Offerors proposed to meet all Key Performance Parameters (KPP) Thresholds. Both Offerors proposed capability beyond KPP Thresholds and offered significant trade space Key System Attribute (KSA) capability. Additionally, both offered numerous non-KPP/KSA trade space capabilities deemed beneficial to the Government.[29]

The SSAC concluded, largely based upon Northrop Grumman's evaluated advantages in the aerial refueling and airlift areas, that Northrop Grumman's proposal was superior to Boeing's under the key system requirements subfactor. Specifically, the SSAC noted:

> While [the] KC-767 offers significant capabilities, the overall tanker/airlift mission is best supported by the KC-30. [The] KC-30 solution is superior in the core capabilities of fuel capacity/offload, airlift efficiency, and cargo/passenger/aeromedical carriage. These advantages in core capabilities outweigh the flexibility advantages of the attributes which Boeing offered.

Under the program management subfactor, the SSAC assigned both offerors green, low risk ratings, identifying no strengths, deficiencies, or uncertainties in either firm's proposal. Nevertheless, the SSAC concluded that Northrop Grumman's program management approach was superior to that of Boeing, finding:

> Northrop Grumman's approach of providing four 'green' aircraft for use early in SDD, by leveraging the existing A330 commercial production line, is deemed to be of benefit to the Government by reducing program risk. Northrop Grumman's approach adds value for the Government through increased confidence in overall program management.

Cost/Price Evaluation

According to the protest decision:

> The Air Force calculated a MPLCC for each offeror, which, as noted above, was intended to be an independent government estimate of each proposal, adjusted for

technical, cost[,] and schedule risk and including all contract, budgetary[,] and other government costs associated with all phases of the aircraft's entire life cycle….

With respect to Boeing's proposal, the Air Force made a number of adjustments in Boeing's proposed costs in calculating its MPLCC…. The Air Force also made a number of adjustments in Northrop Grumman's proposed costs, including upwardly adjusting the proposed SDD costs….[30] The Air Force calculated a MPLCC for Boeing of $108.044 billion and a MPLCC for Northrop Grumman of $108.010 billion.

In comparing the firms' evaluated costs, the SSAC noted that Northrop Grumman had a lower evaluated MPLCC, but that the firms' evaluated MPLCCs were within $34 million of each other (approximately a .03-percent difference). The SSAC noted, however, that Boeing's slightly higher evaluated MPLCC was "driven" primarily by the firm's much higher SDD costs, "which reflected Boeing's more complex design, development, and integration activities."… In addition, the SSAC accepted the SSET's evaluation that Boeing's proposal presented a moderate cost risk for SDD. Northrop Grumman's proposal was assessed as a low cost risk for SDD costs. The SSAC viewed this difference in cost risk for the SDD phase to be the discriminator under this factor.[31]

THE SOURCE SELECTION DECISION

Regarding the contract award, the protest decision stated:

Ultimately, the SSAC recommended to the SSA that [the SSA] select Northrop Grumman's proposal for award, because the SSAC concluded that Northrop Grumman's proposal was more advantageous under the mission capability, past performance, cost/price, and IFARA evaluation factors. With respect to cost/price, the SSAC noted that, although the difference between the two proposals' MPLCC was "negligible," Northrop Grumman's risk rating under this factor (low risk) for the SDD phase was lower than that assigned to Boeing's proposal (moderate cost/price risk) for the SDD phase….

The SSA agreed with the SSAC's recommendation that Northrop Grumman's proposal reflected the best value to the agency, and [the SSA] identified Northrop Grumman's evaluated superiority under the mission capability, past performance, cost/price, and IFARA factors as supporting this conclusion; [the SSA] also concluded that neither offeror had an advantage under the proposal risk factor.

With respect to the mission capability factor, the SSA emphasized that Northrop Grumman's evaluated superiority in the aerial refueling and airlift areas of the key system requirements subfactor were key factors in [the SSA's] decision…. Although not key to [the SSA's] determination that Northrop Grumman's proposal was more advantageous than Boeing's under the key system requirements subfactor, the SSA noted Boeing's evaluated superiority in the survivability area; [the SSA] also noted that neither offeror had an advantage in the operational utility area....[32]

In sum, the SSA selected Northrop Grumman's proposal for award, finding:

> Northrop Grumman's proposal was better than Boeing's proposal in four of the five factors evaluated and equal in one. Northrop Grumman's offer was clearly superior to that of Boeing's for two areas within KC-X's Mission Capability factor: aerial refueling and airlift. Additionally, Northrop Grumman's KC-30's superior aerial refueling capability enables it to execute the IFARA scenario described in the RFP with [Deleted] fewer aircraft than Boeing's KC-767—an efficiency of significant value to the Government. [The SSA was] confident that Northrop Grumman [would] deliver within the cost, schedule, and performance requirements of the contract because of [its] past performance and the lower risk of [its] cost/price proposal.[33]

On February 29, 2008, the Air Force awarded the KC-X contract to Northrop Grumman. Knight and Bolkcom write,

> The initial $12.1 billion KC-X contract provide[d] for the purchase the first 68 KC-45s of the anticipated 179 aircraft. Air Force officials debriefed both Boeing and Northrop Grumman officials on how their respective bids were scored in March 2008. On March 11, 2008, Boeing protested the Air Force's decision to the GAO.[34]

After the protest was filed, the Air Force issued the following press release:

> Proposals from both offerors were evaluated thoroughly in accordance with the criteria set forth in the Request for Proposals. The proposal from the winning offeror is the one Air Force officials believe will provide the best value to the American taxpayer and to the warfighter. Air Force members followed a carefully structured process, designed to provide transparency, maintain integrity[,] and promote fair competition. Air Force members and the offerors had hundreds of formal exchanges regarding the proposals throughout the evaluation process. Air Force officials provided all offerors with continuous feedback through discussions on the strengths and weaknesses of their proposals. Several independent reviews assessed the process as sound and thorough.[35]

THE PROTEST DECISION

After "review of the extensive record, including a hearing," GAO concluded:

> The Air Force had made a number of significant errors that could have affected the outcome of what was a close competition between Boeing and Northrop Grumman.

The errors included not assessing the relative merits of the proposals in accordance with the evaluation rules and criteria identified in the solicitation, not having documentation to support certain aspects of the evaluation, conducting unequal and misleading discussions with Boeing, and having errors or unsupported conclusions in the cost evaluation.

Accordingly, GAO sustained Boeing's protest.[36]

According to testimony on the protest:

First, although the solicitation identified the relative order of importance of the requirements and features of the aircraft solicited by the Air Force, the record did not show that the Air Force, in its evaluation and source selection decision, applied the identified relative weighting in assessing the merits of the firms' proposals. In comparing Boeing's assessed advantages against Northrop Grumman's assessed advantages, the Air Force did not account for the fact that many of Boeing's assessed advantages were derived from requirements and features of the aircraft which the solicitation identified as being more important than those from which Northrop Grumman's assessed advantages were derived. Moreover, the solicitation requested that offerors propose to satisfy as many of the solicitation's desired aircraft features and performance as possible, but the record did not show that the Air Force in its evaluation or source selection decision credited Boeing with satisfying far more of these features and functions than did Northrop Grumman.

Second, [GAO] found that a key discriminator relied upon by the Air Force in its selection of Northrop Grumman's proposal for award was not consistent with the terms of the solicitation. Specifically, the Air Force credited Northrop Grumman for proposing to exceed a solicitation key performance parameter objective for fuel offload versus unrefueled range (that is, the amount of fuel a tanker could offload to a receiver aircraft at a given distance of flight by the tanker without itself refueling) to a greater extent than Boeing proposed, but the solicitation plainly provided that no consideration would be given for proposing to exceed key performance parameter objectives.

Third, [GAO] found that the record did not show that the Air Force reasonably determined that Northrop Grumman's proposed aircraft could refuel all current Air Force fixed-wing, tanker-compatible aircraft using current Air Force procedures, as was required by the solicitation. During the procurement, the Air Force twice informed Northrop Grumman that the proposed maximum operating velocity for that firm's proposed aircraft would not be sufficient under current Air Force procedures to achieve overrun speeds for various Air Force aircraft. (In aerial refueling operations, if a receiver aircraft overruns the tanker during the final phase of rendezvous, the tanker and receiver pilots are directed to adjust to specified overrun speeds, and after overtaking the receiver aircraft, the tanker will decelerate to a refueling airspeed.) In response to the Air Force's concerns, Northrop Grumman promised a solution to allow its aircraft to achieve the required overrun speeds. The record did not show that the Air Force reasonably evaluated the capability of Northrop Grumman's proposed aircraft to achieve the necessary overrun speed in accordance with current Air Force procedures.

In addition, [GAO] found that the Air Force did not reasonably evaluate the capability of Northrop Grumman's proposed aircraft to initiate emergency breakaway procedures, consistent with current Air Force procedures, with respect to a current fixed-wing, tanker-compatible Air Force aircraft. A breakaway maneuver is an emergency procedure that is done when any tanker or receiver aircraft crewmember perceives an unsafe condition that requires immediate separation of the aircraft. In such a situation, the tanker pilot is directed to accelerate, and if necessary to also climb, to achieve separation from the receiver aircraft.

Fourth, [GAO] found that the Air Force conducted misleading and unequal discussions with Boeing. The agency informed Boeing during the procurement that it had fully satisfied a key performance parameter objective relating to operational utility. Later, the Air Force decided that Boeing had not fully satisfied this particular objective, but did not tell Boeing this, which would have afforded Boeing the opportunity to further address this. GAO concluded that it was improper for the Air Force, after informing Boeing that it had fully met this objective, to change this evaluation conclusion without providing Boeing the opportunity to address this requirement in discussions. In contrast, Northrop Grumman, whose proposal was evaluated as only partially meeting this requirement, received continued discussions addressing this same matter during the procurement.

Fifth, [GAO] found that the Air Force improperly accepted Northrop Grumman's proposal, even though that firm took exception to a material solicitation requirement. Specifically, the solicitation required offerors to plan and support the agency to achieve initial organic depot-level maintenance within [two] years after delivery of the first full-rate production aircraft. Northrop Grumman was informed several times by the Air Force that the firm had not committed to the required [two]-year timeframe, but Northrop Grumman refused to commit to the required schedule. GAO concluded that Northrop Grumman's refusal to do so could not be considered an "administrative oversight[,]" as was found by the Air Force in its evaluation.

Sixth, [GAO] found that the Air Force did not reasonably evaluate military construction costs in evaluating the firms' cost proposals. The solicitation provided that the Air Force would calculate a most probable life cycle cost estimate for each offeror. A most probable life cycle cost estimate reflects the agency's independent estimate of all contract, budgetary, and other government costs associated with all phases of the aircraft's life cycle[,] from system development and demonstration through production and deployment and operations and support; military construction costs were specifically identified as a cost that the agency would evaluate in calculating the firms' most probable life cycle costs. Because the agency believed that its anticipated requirements could not be reasonably ascertained, the Air Force established a notional (hypothetical) plan, identifying a number of different types of airbases, to provide for a common basis for evaluating military construction costs. GAO found that, in addition to four errors related to military construction costs that the Air Force conceded during the protest, the record otherwise showed that the agency's military construction cost evaluation was flawed, because the agency's evaluation did not account for the offerors' specific proposals and because the record did not otherwise support the reasonableness of the agency's notional plan.

Seventh, [GAO] found that the Air Force improperly increased Boeing's estimated non-recurring engineering costs in calculating that firm's most probable life cycle cost. Specifically, the Air Force assigned a moderate risk to Boeing's system development and demonstration costs, because, despite several efforts to obtain support from Boeing for its proposed non-recurring engineering costs, Boeing had not sufficiently supported its estimate. Although the GAO found the Air Force's assignment of a moderate cost risk reasonable, GAO also found that the Air Force unreasonably increased Boeing's estimated non-recurring engineering costs in calculating the firm's most probable life cycle cost where the Air Force did not find that Boeing's estimated costs were unrealistic or not probable.

Finally, [the GAO] found unreasonable the Air Force's use of a simulation model to determine the amount by which Boeing's non-recurring engineering costs should be increased in calculating that firm's most probable life cycle cost. Although such simulation models can be useful evaluation tools, here the Air Force used as data inputs in the model the percentage of cost growth associated with weapons systems at an overall program level, and there was no indication that these inputs would be a reliable predictor of anticipated growth in Boeing's non-recurring engineering costs.[37]

LESSONS LEARNED

Although the circumstances surrounding this case study are unique—the congressional oversight, ethics violations, and a planning cycle that began more than ten years before the RFP was released—we can take away critical lessons learned from this case study:

- The importance of following the RFP when evaluating proposals
- The importance of accurate cost evaluations.

The first lesson learned is the importance of following the RFP when evaluating proposals. GAO found that the Air Force had improperly accepted Northrop Grumman's proposal, even though that firm did not fulfill a material solicitation requirement. Northrop Grumman was informed several times by the Air Force that it had not committed to the mandated timeframe (within two years after delivering the first full-rate production aircraft) for achieving "initial organic depot-level maintenance," but Northrop Grumman refused to commit to the required schedule. GAO concluded that Northrop Grumman's refusal to do so could not be considered an "administrative oversight," as the Air Force called it in its evaluation.

In addition, the Air Force did not comply with the solicitation's order of importance or weighting. They did not credit Boeing for meeting more of the higher rated requirements than Northrop Grumman did. They also gave Northrop Grumman "extra credit" for exceeding a key performance parameter, but the solicitation did not state that this would occur.

Next, the Air force conducted misleading and unequal discussions with Boeing by not telling them that they did not fully satisfy a key performance parameter while continuing discussions with Northrop Grumman on the same matter.

The second lesson learned is the importance of accurate cost proposal evaluations. Remember that cost is a required evaluation factor.[38] The government may use various cost analysis techniques and procedures to ensure a fair and reasonable price, given the circumstances of the acquisition.[39]

THE AIR FORCE RE-COMPETE SOLICITATION

On September 25, 2009, the Air Force released a draft RFP for the tanker modernization program and requested comments by October 26, 2009. The Air Force will post responses to questions and comments on the FedBizOpps website. Before a KC-X request for proposals is released, a notice of contract action will be published at least 15 days prior to such release.

Requirements and Acquisition Strategy

FedBizOpps gives the Air Force's requirements and acquisition strategy:

Requirements. The Air Force presently operates a nearly 50-year old fleet of KC-135 aerial refueling tanker aircraft which requires replacement. The KC-X tanker modernization program is the first step in this process. Key performance capabilities to be provided by the KC-X include: (1) aerial refueling of all current and programmed fixed-wing receiver aircraft; (2) range payload at least as good as the KC-135R; (3) same sortie boom and drogue capability as well as simultaneous drogue, multi-point refueling capability; (4) tanker receiver capability to enhance KC-X fleet effectiveness; (5) airlift capability to carry palletized cargo, passengers, and/or medical patients on the entire main cargo deck, (6) the ability to operate anywhere, anytime with global communication, navigation, and air traffic management; (7) survivability features allowing operation in low to medium threat environments including: detection and defeat of infrared missiles, covert lighting to enable refueling in hostile airspace, and electro-magnetic hardening to protect the aircrew and aircraft; (8) crew and passenger protection from chemical and biological environments; and (9) net centric information exchange with joint services. The primary KC-X mission is to provide aerial refueling support to joint and allied forces engaged in homeland defense, global air-bridge deployments and theater conflicts. The KC-X will also augment existing transport aircraft by providing an enduring cargo capability for sustained materiel, passenger, medical/humanitarian aid transportation.

Acquisition Strategy. This procurement will be conducted in accordance with Federal Acquisition Regulation (FAR) Part 15, as supplemented. As the initial phase of a comprehensive aerial refueling recapitalization strategy, the KC-X Program will begin replacement of the warfighting capability provided by the current aerial refueling fleet. This program will develop and acquire up to 179 modern aerial refueling tanker aircraft based on existing commercial aircraft designs; a production rate targeted at 15 aircraft per year is anticipated. Five years of interim contractor support will also be procured in support of the long term goal of standing up a completely organic government repair capability. The contractor will ensure the aircraft acquired, including integrated military systems, are certified as flight worthy by the FAA (or foreign equivalent) during the Engineering and Manufacturing Development phase of the program.[40]

Now that readers understand the basic overview of the acquisition requirements and strategy, let's look at the details of the draft RFP and compare them to the previous solicitation.

Evaluation Factors

The government will base its source selection decision on an assessment of mission capability, cost/price, and, if necessary, non-mandatory technical requirements in the solicitation. This is a best-value competition and not a low-price, technically acceptable approach. The new evaluation factors are more objective and less subjective than the previous solicitation. Section M of the draft RFP states that

> while the Government source selection evaluation team and the Source Selection Authority (SSA) will strive for maximum objectivity, the source selection process, by its nature is subjective and, therefore, professional judgment is implicit throughout the entire process.[41]

The RFP lists three primary evaluation factors: (1) mission capability (mandatory requirements); (2) cost/price; and (3) non-mandatory technical requirements.

Factor 1: Mission Capability (Mandatory Requirements)

The RFP continues,

This evaluation provides an assessment of the offeror's proposed capability to satisfy the Government's mandatory technical requirements. Offerors must receive acceptable ratings for all subfactors (1.1 - 1.6) to be eligible for award. Subfactors 1.1 - 1.5 will be rated acceptable when all Measures of Acceptability (MOAs) in each of those subfactors are rated acceptable. Factor 1 has six subfactors:

- Subfactor 1.1: Key System Requirements
- Subfactor 1.2: Systems Engineering
- Subfactor 1.3: Product Support
- Subfactor 1.4: Program Management
- Subfactor 1.5: Technology Maturity
- Subfactor 1.6: Past Performance

The Government will evaluate the Mission Capabilities Factor (Factor 1) to determine technical acceptability. The Mission Capability subfactors … will not be weighted and each subfactor will be rated as being acceptable or unacceptable. An unacceptable rating in any subfactor will render the entire proposal unacceptable and ineligible for award.[42]

Factor 2: Cost/Price

The offerors must propose prices for most of the contract line items, including engineering and manufacturing development, live-fire assets, and operations and maintenance, for a fixed price incentive contract type. Other line items such as data licenses, training, and low-rate initial production are on a firm fixed price contract type. The previous solicitation was primarily a cost plus incentive fee contract type.

To calculate an offeror's total evaluated price (TEP), the government will first validate that an offeror has correctly calculated its total proposed price (TPP) in discounted present value dollars—TPP (PV). Then the government will subtract from an offeror's TPP (PV) any adjustments from the three elements below:

- Element 1: Integrated Fleet Aerial Refueling Assessment (IFARA)
- Element 2: Fuel Usage Rate Assessment (FURA)
- Element 3: Military Construction (MILCON) Assessment.

The proposed price will not by itself determine the winner. The government will evaluate the wartime effectiveness of each offered airplane as well as the cost of ownership, including fuel use and MILCON requirements. The acquisition prices will be adjusted to take these factors into account. If the adjusted prices are very close (within one percent of the overall adjusted acquisition price), the government will consider other non-mandatory features.

At this point the proposals must go through the TEP gate. The government will calculate the TEP gate after it receives the final proposal revisions (FPR) by multiplying the lowest acceptable proposed TEP by 101 percent. If only one acceptable proposal has a TEP less than or equal to the TEP gate, then the contract will be awarded to that offeror without consideration of the factor 3 evaluation scores. If there is more than one acceptable offeror with a TEP less than or equal to the TEP gate, the government will consider the offerors' factor 3 scores for non-mandatory technical requirements.

Factor 3: Non-Mandatory Technical Requirements

Next the government will evaluate each of the 93 non-mandatory technical requirements, scoring each of the requirements as met or not met—no partial credit will be granted. For non-mandatory requirements proposed by the offeror which are deemed to have been met, the government will assign a point value for that requirement. The proposal with the highest non-mandatory point score by more than one point wins. If the offerors' non-mandatory scores are within one point of one another, the contract will be awarded to the offeror with the lower TEP.[43]

COMPARING THE ORIGINAL AND NEW SOLICITATIONS

The Air Force's new draft RFP imposes more risk on the contractor by changing the contract type from cost-plus-incentive-fee to fixed-price-incentive-fee. In addition, the source selection process is much less subjective than the process stipulated in the previous RFP.

Another distinction is the new possibility of two contract awards. The previous solicitation noted that "The Government intends to award one contract for the KC-X Program. However, based on cost and other considerations, the Government reserves the right not to award a contract at all."[44] The new draft RFP states that "The Government intends to award one contract. However, the Government reserves the right to award multiple contracts or not to award a contract at all."[45]

The previous solicitation had 808 requirements, of which only 37 were mandatory. These requirements left a large trade space that gave the offerors too many options. This caused confusion because the offerors didn't know which options were the most important. *Trade space* is the degree of flexibility in trading performance objectives against one another to achieve the best value. The new draft RFP gives 373 mandatory requirements and 93 non-mandatory, trade-

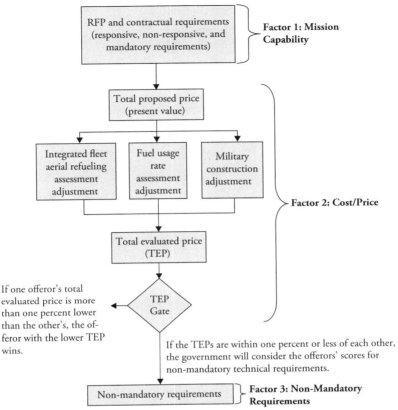

Figure A2-1 Tanker Evaluation Process[46]

space requirements. Fulfilling any of the 93 non-mandatory requirements would provide additional capability to the Air Force, but not to such an extent that the agency would be willing to pay a significant amount more than it would without those capabilities.

Table A2-6 highlights changes to the new draft RFP. [47]

The Air Force's draft RFP further states that the source selection team is composed of an SSA who is a senior Air Force official, an advisory council, and 14 separate evaluation and independent review teams to assess the source selection process and proposal evaluations. The independent review teams will ensure connectivity between the RFP, requirements document, evaluation process, and source selection decision.[48]

The Air Force has addressed the issues of the previous source selection and made changes to the contract type, mandatory and non-mandatory requirements, basis

Table A2-6 A Summary of Changes to the New Draft RFP

Solicitation Requirement	2007 RFP	2009 Draft RFP	Analysis of Change
Contract type	CPIF/CPAF/FPIF/FFP	FPIF/FFP	Eliminates cost-reimbursement contract types. This reduces government risk and increases contractor risk.
Mandatory requirements	37	373	Increases mandatory requirements. An unacceptable rating in any subfactor will render the entire proposal unacceptable and the contractor ineligible for award.
Non-mandatory technical requirements (trade space)	771	93	Reduces trade space, making the RFP less confusing to offerors. The previous RFP's large trade space gave offerors too many options without stating which options were most important to the government.
Basis for award	The government will select the best overall offer, based upon an integrated assessment of mission capability, proposal risk, past performance, cost/price, and the IFRAA.	The government will select a source based upon an assessment of mission capability and cost/price. It will make a comparative assessment of non-mandatory technical requirements only if the initial assessment doesn't present a clear awardee. If the offerors' non-mandatory scores are within one point of one another, the contract will be awarded to the offeror with the lower TEP.	Changes the basis of source selection decisions. The decision is now based primarily on meeting mandatory requirements and cost. Non-mandatory elements are considered only if it's a close competition.

Table A2-6 (*Continued*)

Solicitation Requirement	2007 RFP	2009 Draft RFP	Analysis of Change
Evaluation factors	1 Mission capability 1.1 Key system requirements 1.2 System integration and software 1.3 Product support 1.4 Program management 1.5 Technology maturity and demonstration 2 Proposal risk 3 Past performance 4 Cost/price 5 IFARA	1 Mission capability 1.1 Key system requirements 1.2 System integration and software 1.3 Product support 1.4 Program management 1.5 Technology maturity 1.6 Past Performance 2 Cost/Price 2.1 IFARA 2.2 FURA 2.3 MILCON assessment 3 Non-mandatory technical requirements	Reduces the number of evaluation factors. Combines past performance into a subfactor of mission capability, and combines IFARA into cost element.
Number of awards	One contract, with the right not to award any contract	One contract, with the right to award multiple contracts or no contract at all	Introduces the possibility of multiple contract awards.
Cost/price evaluation factor	Evaluated on realism, reasonableness, and most probable life-cycle cost; assessments of technical, cost, and schedule risks for the entire most-probable life-cycle cost estimate based upon the offeror's proposal	Calculate an offeror's TEP by validating offeror's TPP (PV) calculations and then subtracting any IFARA, FURA, and MILCON adjustments	Makes closer cost associations to offerors' specific proposals; necessitates more support for the reasonableness of estimated costs, especially the most probable life-cycle cost.
Source selection process	Subjective assessment of proposals against evaluation factors	Subjective and objective assessment of proposals against evaluation factors; comparison of offerors' TEPs; comparison of 93 non-mandatory technical requirements for only close competitions	Focuses more on mandatory requirements and cost. Non-mandatory trade-space requirements are considered for only close competitions.

for and number of awards, evaluation factors, and source selection process. At the time of this writing, the draft RFP is still in the comment process. The Air Force will require proposals 60 days after the final RFP is released and will allow a subsequent 120 days for proposal evaluation. The agency anticipates making contract award sometime during the summer of 2010.

NOTES

1 David W. Thornton, "Replacing the KC135 Stratotanker: The Politics of a Flawed Procurement Policy," panel paper presented at the Transatlantic Studies Association 7th Annual Conference, Dundee, Scotland, July 7–10, 2008, 3.

2 Ibid., 4.

3 U.S. General Accounting Office, *U.S. Combat Air Power: Aging Refueling Aircraft Are Costly to Maintain and Operate,* GAO/NSIAD-96-160 (Washington, DC: U.S. General Accounting Office, August 8, 1996).

4 William Knight and Christopher Bolkcom, *Air Force Air Refueling: The KC-X Aircraft Acquisition Program* (Washington, DC: Congressional Research Service, April 4, 2008), 45.

5 U.S. Government Accountability Office, "The Boeing Company," B-311344; B-311344.3; B-311344.4; B-311344.6; B-311344.7; B-311344.8; B-311344.10; B-311344.11 (Washington, DC: U.S. Government Accountability Office, June 18, 2008).

6 U.S. Air Force/AFMC Aeronautical Systems Center (ASC), KC-X Executive Summary to RFP no. FA8625-07-R-6470 (Wright-Patterson Air Force Base, OH: U.S. Air Force/AFMC Aeronautical Systems Center (ASC), January 30, 2007).

7 Knight and Bolkcom, 6.

8 Ibid., 24.

9 U.S. Air Force/AFMC Aeronautical Systems Center (ASC), RFP no. FA8625-07-R-6470, M001: Source Selection, M-1.

10 Ibid., M-2.

11 Ibid., M-3.

12 Ibid.

13 Ibid.

14 Ibid., M-9.

15 Ibid.

16 Ibid., M-10.

17 Ibid.

18 Ibid., M-12–M-13.

19 Ibid., M-14–M-15.

20 Ibid., M-15.

21 U.S. Air Force/AFMC Aeronautical Systems Center (ASC), RFP no. FA8625-07-R-6470.

22 U.S. Government Accountability Office, "The Boeing Company."

23 Ibid.

24 Knight and Bolkcom, 27–28.

25 U.S. Government Accountability Office, "The Boeing Company."

26 Knight and Bolkcom, 27–28.

27 U.S. Government Accountability Office, "The Boeing Company," 15.

28 Ibid.

29 Ibid., 17.

30 Ibid., 23.

31 Ibid.

32 Ibid., 24.

33 Ibid., 25.

34 Knight and Bolkcom, 2.

35 Knight and Bolkcom, 32.

36 U.S. Government Accountability Office, *Air Force Procurement: Aerial Refueling Tanker Protest*, Testimony of Daniel I. Gordon, Deputy General Counsel, GAO-08-991T (Washington, DC: U.S. Government Accountability Office, July 10, 2008).

37 Ibid.

38 Federal Acquisition Regulation (FAR) 15.304(b)(1).

39 FAR 15.404-1(c).

40 Federal Business Opportunities, *KC-X Tanker Modernization Program*, announcement of Draft RFP no. FA8625-10-R-6600, September 25, 2009, https://www.fbo.gov/index?s=opportunity&mode=form&id=cced18cd9f21580ef249e74e64e947dd&tab=core&_cview=1 (accessed October 14, 2009).

41 U.S. Air Force/AFMC Aeronautical Systems Center (ASC), Draft RFP no. FA8625-10-R-6600 (Wright-Patterson Air Force Base, OH: U.S. Air Force/AFMC Aeronautical Systems Center (ASC), September 25, 2009), M-1.

42 Ibid.

43 Ibid.

44 U.S. Air Force/AFMC Aeronautical Systems Center (ASC), RFP FA8625-07-R-6470, M-2.

45 William J. Lynn, Michael B. Donley, and Ashton B. Carter, *Moving Forward*, Refueling Tanker Briefing, (Washington, DC: U.S. Department of Defense, September 24, 2009), 7–8.

46 U.S. Air Force/AFMC Aeronautical Systems Center (ASC), RFP FA8625-10-R-6600, M-2.

47 U.S. Air Force/AFMC Aeronautical Systems Center (ASC), RFP FA8625-07-R-6470, M-2; U.S. Air Force/AFMC Aeronautical Systems Center (ASC), RFP FA8625-10-R-6600, M-2.

48 DefenseLink News Transcript, "DoD News Briefing with Deputy Secretary of Defense William Lynn, Under Secretary of Defense Ashton Carter, and Secretary of the Air Force Michael Donley," September 24, 2009, http://www.defenselink.mil/transcripts/transcript.aspx?transcriptid=4484 (accessed October 1, 2009).

Acronyms

BOE	Basis of estimate
B&P	Bid and proposal
CAIV	Cost as an independent variable
CAS	Cost accounting standards
CER	Cost estimating relationships
CFE	Contractor-furnished equipment
CFR	Code of Federal Regulations
CICA	Competition in Contracting Act
CO	Contracting officer
COC	Certificate of competency
COTR	Contracting officer's technical representative
COTS	Commercial-off-the-shelf
CPAF	Cost-plus-award-fee
CPFF	Cost-plus-fixed-fee
CPIF	Cost-plus-incentive-fee
CR	Clarification request
DCAA	Defense Contract Audit Agency
D&F	Determination and findings
DR	Deficiency report
EEO	Equal Employment Opportunity
EFT	Electronic funds transfer
FAR	Federal Acquisition Regulation

FCCM	Facilities capital cost of money
FFP	Firm fixed-price
FOB	Free on board
FPIF	Fixed-price-incentive-fee
FPR	Fixed-price redeterminable
FSS	Federal Supply Schedule
FTE	Full-time equivalents
GFE	Government-furnished equipment
GFP	Government-furnished property
IDIQ	Indefinite-delivery indefinite-quantity
ILS	Integrated logistics support
IR&D	Independent research and development
J&A	Justification and approval
LOE	Level of effort
MOA	Memorandum of agreement
MOU	Memorandum of understanding
NDI	Nondevelopmental item
NTE	Not to exceed
OCI	Organizational conflict of interest
ODC	Other direct costs
OFPP	Office of Federal Procurement Policy
PALT	Procurement administrative lead time
PBA	Performance-based acquisition
PCO	Procuring contracting officer
P&L	Profit and loss
PM	Program manager

PNM	Price negotiation memorandum
PO	Purchase order
PR	Purchase request; purchase requisition
PRAG	Performance risk assessment group
PWS	Performance work statement
QA	Quality assurance
QASP	Quality assurance surveillance plan
QBL	Qualified bidders list
QC	Quality control
R&D	Research and development
RFP	Request for proposals
ROI	Return on investment
ROM	Rough order of magnitude
SADBUS	Small and Disadvantaged Business Utilization specialist
SBA	Small Business Administration
SF	Standard Form
SSA	Source selection authority
SSAC	Source selection advisory council
SSEB	Source selection evaluation board
SSP	Source selection plan
TEP	Total evaluated price
TINA	Truth in Negotiations Act
T&M	Time-and-materials
TPP (PV)	Total proposed price present value
Ts and Cs	Terms and conditions
UCF	Uniform contract format

VE Value engineering

VECP Value engineering change proposal

WBS Work breakdown structure

WGM Weighted guidelines method

Glossary

A	
Acquisition	Acquiring by contract, with appropriated funds, supplies or services (including construction) by and for the use of the federal government through purchase or lease, whether the supplies or services are already in existence or must be created, developed, demonstrated, and evaluated. Acquisition begins at the point when agency needs are established and includes the description of requirements to satisfy agency needs, solicitation and selection of sources, award of contracts, contract financing, contract performance, contract administration, and those technical and management functions directly related to the process of fulfilling agency needs by contract (FAR 2.101).
Acquisition planning	The process by which the efforts of all personnel responsible for an acquisition are coordinated and integrated through a comprehensive plan for fulfilling the agency need in a timely manner and at a reasonable cost. It includes developing the overall strategy for managing the acquisition (FAR 2.101).
Acquisition risk	The chance that some element of an acquisition program will produce an unintended result with an adverse effect on system effectiveness, suitability cost, or availability for deployment.
Acquisition strategy	The acquisition strategy is the program manager's overall plan for satisfying the mission need in the most effective, economical and timely manner. The acquisition strategy can be prepared as a briefing and/or as a written document. The strategy integrates the business, technical and management concepts used to achieve the program objectives within the imposed program constraints (e.g., technical, budget, schedule, and political). It provides a framework for managing the entire program, addresses all program phases, and identifies the resources needed to execute the program. The acquisition strategy addresses the entire acquisition life cycle and includes a schedule of significant program milestones.
Acquisition streamlining	Any effort that results in more efficient and effective use of resources to design and develop or produce quality systems. This includes ensuring that only necessary and cost-effective requirements are included, at the most appropriate time in the acquisition cycle, in solicitations and resulting contracts for the design, development, and production of new systems, or for modifications to existing systems that involve redesign of systems or subsystems (FAR 7.101).
Acquisition team	A team consisting of all participants in government acquisition, including not only representatives of the technical, supply, and procurement communities, but also the customers they serve and the contractors who provide the products and services. The role of each member of the acquisition team is to exercise personal initiative and sound business judgment in providing the best value product or service to meet the customer's needs. In exercising initiative, government members of the acquisition team may assume that if a specific strategy, practice, policy, or procedure is in the best interest of the government and is not addressed in the FAR, nor prohibited by law (statute or case law), executive order, or other regulation, the strategy, practice, policy, or procedure is a permissible exercise of authority (FAR 1.102).

Amendment	A change in a solicitation made by the contracting officer when, either before or after receipt of proposals, the government changes its requirements or terms and conditions.
	Amendments issued before the established time and date for receipt of proposals shall be issued to all parties receiving the solicitation.
	Amendments issued after the established time and date for receipt of proposals shall be issued to all offerors that have not been eliminated from the competition (FAR 15.206).
Assessment criteria	Areas of consideration common to more than one evaluation factor.
Award	The furnishing of an executed contract or other notice of award to a successful offeror by a contracting officer (FAR 15.504).

B	
Best value	The expected outcome of an acquisition that, in the government's estimation, provides the greatest overall benefit in response to the requirement (FAR 2.101).
Bid and proposal costs (B&P)	Costs incurred in preparing, submitting, and supporting bids and proposals (whether or not solicited) on potential government or nongovernment contracts.
Business evaluation factors	Elements used to assess performance of the offerors. Examples: relevant experience, past performance, management plan, company resources, or quality of product/service.
Buying in	Submitting an offer below anticipated costs, expecting to:
	• Increase the contract amount after award (e.g., through unnecessary or excessively priced change orders); or
	• Receive follow-on contracts at artificially high prices to recover losses incurred on the buy-in contract (FAR 3.501-1).

C	
Central Contractor Registration (CCR) database	The primary government repository for contractor information required for the conduct of business with the government (FAR 2.101).
Clarifications	Limited exchanges between the government and offerors that may occur when award without discussions is contemplated. If award will be made without conducting discussions, offerors may be given the opportunity to clarify certain aspects of their proposals (e.g., the relevance of an offeror's past performance information and adverse past performance information to which the offeror has not previously had an opportunity to respond) or to resolve minor or clerical errors (FAR 15.306).
Clarification request (CR)	Written communication that is issued by the source selection evaluation board through the contracting officer for the purpose of eliminating minor irregularities, informalities, or apparent clerical mistakes in a proposal. A CR does not give the offeror an opportunity to revise or modify its proposal.
Commercial item	1. Any item, other than real property, that is of a type customarily used by the general public or by nongovernmental entities for purposes other than governmental purposes, and:

    i. Has been sold, leased, or licensed to the general public; or

    ii. Has been offered for sale, lease, or license to the general public.

2. Any item that evolved from an item described in paragraph (1) of this definition through advances in technology or performance and that is not yet available in the commercial marketplace, but will be available in the commercial marketplace in time to satisfy the delivery requirements under a government solicitation.

3. Any item that would satisfy a criterion expressed in paragraphs (1) or (2) of this definition, but for:

    i. Modifications of a type customarily available in the commercial marketplace; or

    ii. Minor modifications of a type not customarily available in the commercial marketplace made to meet federal government requirements. *Minor modifications* means modifications that do not significantly alter the nongovernmental function or essential physical characteristics of an item or component or change the purpose of a process. Factors to be considered in determining whether a modification is minor include the value and size of the modification and the comparative value and size of the final product. Dollar values and percentages may be used as guideposts, but are not conclusive evidence that a modification is minor.

4. Any combination of items meeting the requirements of paragraphs (1), (2), (3), or (5) of this definition that are of a type customarily combined and sold in combination to the general public.

5. Installation services, maintenance services, repair services, training services, and other services if:

    i. Such services are procured for support of an item referred to in paragraph (1), (2), (3), or (4) of this definition, regardless of whether such services are provided by the same source or at the same time as the item; and

    ii. The source of such services provides similar services contemporaneously to the general public under terms and conditions similar to those offered to the federal government.

6. Services of a type offered and sold competitively in substantial quantities in the commercial marketplace based on established catalog or market prices for specific tasks performed or specific outcomes to be achieved and under standard commercial terms and conditions. For purposes of these services:

    i. *Catalog price* means a price included in a catalog, price list, schedule, or other form that is regularly maintained by the manufacturer or vendor, is either published or otherwise available for inspection by customers, and states prices at which sales are currently, or were last, made to a significant number of buyers constituting the general public; and

    ii. *Market prices* means current prices that are established in the course of ordinary trade between buyers and sellers free to bargain and that can be substantiated through competition or from sources independent of the offerors.

7. Any item, combination of items, or service referred to in paragraphs (1) through (6) of this definition, notwithstanding the fact that the item, combination of items, or service is transferred between or among separate divisions, subsidiaries, or affiliates of a contractor; or

8. A nondevelopmental item, if the procuring agency determines the item was developed exclusively at private expense and sold in substantial quantities, on a competitive basis, to multiple state and local governments (FAR 2.101).

Communications	Exchanges, between the government and offerors, after receipt of proposals, leading to establishment of the competitive range.
	
	If a competitive range is to be established, these communications shall be held with offerors whose past performance information is the determining factor preventing them from being placed within the competitive range. Such communications shall address adverse past performance information to which an offeror has not had a prior opportunity to respond. They:
	
	• May only be held with those offerors whose exclusion from, or inclusion in, the competitive range is uncertain.
	• May be conducted to enhance government understanding of proposals; allow reasonable interpretation of the proposal; or facilitate the government's evaluation process. Such communications shall not be used to cure proposal deficiencies or material omissions, materially alter the technical or cost elements of the proposal, and/or otherwise revise the proposal. Such communications may be considered in rating proposals for the purpose of establishing the competitive range.
	• Are for the purpose of addressing issues that must be explored to determine whether a proposal should be placed in the competitive range. Such communications shall not provide an opportunity for the offeror to revise its proposal, but may address:
	   • Ambiguities in the proposal or other concerns (e.g., perceived deficiencies, weaknesses, errors, omissions, or mistakes); and
	   • Information relating to relevant past performance; and
	• Shall address adverse past performance information to which the offeror has not previously had an opportunity to comment (FAR 15.306).

Competition in Contracting Act (CICA)	A 1984 congressional act designed to foster competition and promote cost savings; requires the use of advance procurement planning and market research, as well as the use of commercial products whenever practicable.
Competitive range	A highly rated group of proposals chosen by the contracting officer, based on the ratings of each proposal against all evaluation criteria. The competitive range consists of all of the highest-rated proposals, unless the range is further reduced for purposes of efficiency (FAR 15.306).
Contract	• A mutually binding legal relationship obligating the seller to furnish the supplies or services (including construction) and the buyer to pay for them. • Contracts include all types of commitments that obligate the government to an expenditure of appropriated funds and that, except as otherwise authorized, are in writing. In addition to bilateral instruments, contracts include (but are not limited to) awards and notices of awards; job orders or task letters issued under basic ordering agreements; letter contracts; orders, such as purchase orders, under which the contract becomes effective by written acceptance or performance; and bilateral contract modifications (FAR 2.101).
Contracting officer (CO)	A person with the authority to enter into, administer, and/or terminate contracts and make related determinations and findings. The term includes certain authorized representatives of the contracting officer acting within the limits of their authority, as delegated by the contracting officer (FAR 2.101).

Contracting officer's technical representative (COTR)	A person provided to assist the contracting officer in matters related to inspection, acceptance, and other duties; a person without specific authority acting as an extension of the contracting officer at a specific duty station.
Contractor bid or proposal information	Any of the following information submitted to a federal agency as part of or in connection with a bid or proposal to enter into a federal agency procurement contract, if that information has not been previously made available to the public or disclosed publicly: • Cost or pricing data (as defined by 10 USC 2306a(h)) with respect to procurements subject to that section, and section 304A(h) of the Federal Property and Administrative Services Act of 1949 (41 USC 254b(h)), with respect to procurements subject to that section • Indirect costs and direct labor rates • Proprietary information about manufacturing processes, operations, or techniques marked by the contractor in accordance with applicable law or regulation • Information marked by the contractor as "contractor bid or proposal information" in accordance with applicable law or regulation • Information marked in accordance with FAR 52.215-1(e) (FAR 3.104-1).
Contractor team arrangement	An arrangement in which two or more companies form a partnership or joint venture to act as a potential prime contractor, or a potential prime contractor agrees with one or more other companies to have them act as its subcontractors under a specified government contract or acquisition program (FAR 9.601).
Cost analysis	The review and evaluation of the separate cost elements and profit in an offeror's or contractor's proposal (including cost or pricing data or information other than cost or pricing data), and the application of judgment to determine how well the proposed costs represent what the cost of the contract should be, assuming reasonable economy and efficiency (FAR 15.404-1).
Cost or pricing data	All facts that, as of the date of price agreement or, if applicable, an earlier date agreed upon between the parties that is as close as practicable to the date of agreement on price, prudent buyers and sellers would reasonably expect to affect price negotiations significantly. Cost or pricing data require certification, in accordance with FAR 15.406-2. Cost or pricing data are factual, not judgmental, and are verifiable. While they do not indicate the accuracy of the prospective contractor's judgment about estimated future costs or projections, they do include the data forming the basis for that judgment. Cost or pricing data are more than historical accounting data; they are all the facts that can be reasonably expected to contribute to the soundness of estimates of future costs and to the validity of determinations of costs already incurred. They include such factors as: • Vendor quotations • Nonrecurring costs • Information on changes in production methods and in production or purchasing volume • Data supporting projections of business prospects and objectives and related operations costs • Unit-cost trends, such as those associated with labor efficiency • Make-or-buy decisions • Estimated resources to attain business goals • Information on management decisions that could have a significant bearing on costs (FAR 2.101).

Cost or price evaluation factors	Information used to evaluate what the proposed offer will most likely cost the government. Examples: cost/price reasonableness, cost/price realism, life cycle cost, and cost risk. Cost/price itself should not be scored or rated (FAR 2.101).
Cost realism	Means that the costs in an offeror's proposal: • Are realistic for the work to be performed; • Reflect a clear understanding of the requirements; and • Are consistent with the various elements of the offeror's technical proposal (FAR 2.101).
Cost realism analysis	The process of independently reviewing and evaluating specific elements of each offeror's proposed cost estimate to determine whether the estimated proposed cost elements are realistic for the work to be performed; reflect a clear understanding of the requirements; and are consistent with the unique methods of performance and materials described in the offeror's technical proposal. Cost realism analyses shall be performed on cost-reimbursement contracts to determine the probable cost of performance for each offeror (FAR 15.404-1).
Cost reasonableness	Situation in which the cost of a contract does not exceed what would be incurred by a prudent person in the conduct of competitive business (FAR 31.101-3).
Cost-plus-award-fee contract	A cost-reimbursement contract that provides for a fee consisting of (1) a base amount fixed at inception of the contract, if applicable and at the discretion of the contracting officer, and (2) an award amount that the contractor may earn in whole or in part during performance and that is sufficient to provide motivation for excellence in the areas of cost, schedule, and technical performance (FAR 16.405-2).
Cost-plus-fixed-fee contract	A cost-reimbursement contract that provides for payment to the contractor of a negotiated fee that is fixed at the inception of the contract. The fixed fee does not vary with actual cost, but may be adjusted as a result of changes in the work to be performed under the contract. This contract type permits contracting for efforts that might otherwise present too great a risk to contractors, but it provides the contractor only a minimum incentive to control costs (FAR 16.306).
Cost-plus-incentive-fee contract	A cost-reimbursement type of contract with provision for a fee that is adjusted by a formula in accordance with the relationship between total allowable costs and target costs (FAR 16.304).
Cost risk	An assumption of possible monetary loss or gain in light of the job or work to be done; an element to be considered in the negotiation of a fair and reasonable price, as well as in the determination of contract type. Cost risk measures the degree of cost responsibility and associated risk assumed as a result of the contract type contemplated considering the complexity and duration of the contract (FAR 15.404(d).
D	
Debriefing	An explanation given by the contracting officer that states why an offeror's proposal was not successful. Debriefing may be pre- or postaward. See FAR 15.505 and 15.506.
Defective cost or pricing data	Certified cost or pricing data subsequently found to have been inaccurate, incomplete, or non-current as of the effective date of the certificate.
Deficiency	A material failure of a proposal to meet a government requirement, or a combination of significant weaknesses in a proposal that increases the risk of unsuccessful contract performance to an unacceptable level (FAR 15.001).
Deficiency report (DR)	Written communication that is issued by the source selection evaluation board through the contracting officer for the purpose of identifying portions of a proposal that, when compared with the pertinent standard, fail to meet the government's minimum level of compliance.

Design specification	A purchase description that establishes precise measurements, tolerances, materials, in-process and finished product tests, quality control, inspection requirements, and other specific details of the deliverable.
Determination and findings	A document signed by an authorized government official justifying a decision to take a certain action, expressed in terms of meeting the regulatory requirements of the situation.
Discussions	When negotiations are conducted in a competitive acquisition, they take place after establishment of the competitive range and are called discussions. Discussions must be conducted by the contracting officer with each offeror within the competitive range and are tailored to each offeror's proposal.
	The primary objective of discussions is to maximize the government's ability to obtain best value, based on the requirement and the evaluation factors set forth in the solicitation.
	At a minimum, the contracting officer must indicate to, or discuss with, each offeror still being considered for award deficiencies, significant weaknesses, and adverse past performance information to which the offeror has not yet had an opportunity to respond. The contracting officer is also encouraged to discuss other aspects of the offeror's proposal that could, in the opinion of the contracting officer, be altered or explained to enhance materially the proposal's potential for award. However, the contracting officer is not required to discuss every area where the proposal could be improved. The scope and extent of discussions are a matter of contracting officer judgment.
	In discussing other aspects of the proposal, the government may, in situations where the solicitation stated that evaluation credit would be given for technical solutions exceeding any mandatory minimums, negotiate with offerors for increased performance beyond any mandatory minimums. The government may also suggest to offerors that have exceeded any mandatory minimums (in ways that are not integral to the design) that their proposals would be more competitive if the excesses were removed and the offered price decreased (FAR 15.306).

E

Evaluation factors	Factors that will be considered in evaluating proposals and that have an impact on the source selection decision. Evaluation factors are tailored to each acquisition, but price or cost to the government and quality shall be included as an evaluation factor in every source selection. Quality may be expressed in terms of technical excellence, management capability, personnel qualifications, prior experience, past performance, and schedule compliance. Any other relevant factors, such as cost realism, may also be included.
	Evaluation factors and significant subfactors must represent the key areas of importance and emphasis to be considered in the source selection decision and must support meaningful comparison and discrimination between and among competing proposals (FAR 15.304).
Evaluation standards	A predetermined level of merit against which proposals are measured. Standards are usually a statement of the minimum level of compliance with a requirement a proposal must offer for it to be considered acceptable.
Exchanges	Communications between the government and potential offerors intended to improve offerors' understanding of government requirements and industry capabilities, thereby allowing them to judge whether or how they can satisfy the government's requirements. Exchanges also enhance the government's ability to obtain quality supplies and services, including construction, at reasonable prices, and increase efficiency in proposal preparation, proposal evaluation, negotiation, and contract award (FAR 15.201).

F	
Fact finding	The process of identifying and obtaining information necessary to complete the evaluation of proposals. This may include fact-finding sessions with offerors.
Fair and reasonable price	A price that is fair to both parties, considering the agreed-upon conditions, promised quality, and timeliness of contract performance. Although a fair and reasonable price is generally a function of the law of supply and demand, there are statutory, regulatory, and judgmental limits on the concept.
Federal Technical Data Solution (FedTeDS)	A web application integrated with the governmentwide point of entry (GPE) and the Central Contractor Registration (CCR) system for distribution of information related to contract opportunities. It is designed to enhance controls on the access and distribution of solicitation requirements or other documents when controls are necessary, according to agency procedures. FedTeDS is available at https://www.fedteds.gov (FAR 2.101).
Firm fixed-price contract	A contract that provides for a price that is not subject to any adjustment by reason of costs experienced by the contractor in the performance of the contract (FAR 16.202-1).
Fixed-price contract	Fixed-price types of contracts provide for a firm price or, in appropriate cases, an adjustable price. Fixed-price contracts providing for an adjustable price may include a ceiling price, a target price (including target cost), or both. Unless otherwise specified in the contract, the ceiling price or target price is subject to adjustment only by operation of contract clauses providing for equitable adjustment or other revision of the contract price under stated circumstances (FAR 16.201).
Fixed-price incentive (FPI) contract	A type of contract that provides for adjusting profit and establishing the final contract price by application of a formula based on the relationship of total final negotiated cost to total target cost. The final price is subject to a price ceiling, negotiated at the outset. There are two types of FPI contracts: firm target and successive targets (FAR 16.204 and FAR 16.4).
Fixed-price redeterminable contract	A fixed-price type of contract that contains provisions for subsequently negotiated adjustment, in whole or in part, of the initially negotiated base price.
Flow-down	The transference of prime contract requirements to subcontracts.
Full and open competition	A competition for contract award in which all responsible sources are permitted to participate.
G	
Government-furnished property	Property in the possession of or acquired by the government and subsequently delivered or otherwise made available to the contractor (FAR 45.101).
Governmentwide point of entry (GPE)	The single point where government business opportunities exceeding $25,000, including synopses of proposed contract actions, solicitations, and associated information, can be accessed electronically by the public. The GPE is located at http://www.fedbizopps.gov (FAR 2.101).
I	
Incentive arrangement	A negotiated pricing arrangement that structures a series of relationships designed to motivate and reward the contractor for performance in accordance with the contract specifications; involves target costs, fees, and/or profits; in the case of award fee arrangements, it involves the payment of a fee tied to negotiated incentive criteria (FAR 16.401).

Ineligible	Excluded from government contracting and subcontracting pursuant to statutory, executive order, or regulatory authority other than the FAR (FAR 2.101).
Inherently governmental function	A function that, as a matter of policy, is so intimately related to the public interest as to mandate performance by government employees. This definition is a policy determination, not a legal determination.

Inherently governmental functions include activities that require either the exercise of discretion in applying government authority, or the making of value judgments in making decisions for the government.

Governmental functions normally fall into two categories: the act of governing, i.e., the discretionary exercise of government authority, and monetary transactions and entitlements. An inherently governmental function involves, among other things, the interpretation and execution of the laws of the United States so as to:

- Bind the United States to take or not to take some action by contract, policy, regulation, authorization, order, or otherwise
- Determine, protect, and advance United States economic, political, territorial, property, or other interests by military or diplomatic action, civil or criminal judicial proceedings, contract management, or otherwise
- Significantly affect the life, liberty, or property of private persons
- Commission, appoint, direct, or control officers or employees of the United States
- Exert ultimate control over the acquisition, use, or disposition of the property, real or personal, tangible or intangible, of the United States, including the collection, control, or disbursement of federal funds.

Inherently governmental functions do not normally include gathering information for, or providing advice, opinions, recommendations, or ideas to, government officials. They also do not include functions that are primarily ministerial and internal in nature, such as building security, mail operations, operation of cafeterias, housekeeping, facilities operations and maintenance, warehouse operations, motor vehicle fleet management operations, or other routine electrical or mechanical services (FAR 2.101).

L

Life cycle cost	The total cost to the government of acquiring, operating, supporting, and (if applicable) disposing of the items being acquired (FAR 7.101).
Limits on exchanges	A proscription against government personnel involved in an acquisition engaging in conduct that:

- Favors one offeror over another;
- Reveals an offeror's technical solution, including unique technology, innovative and unique uses of commercial items, or any information that would compromise an offeror's intellectual property to another offeror;
- Reveals an offeror's price without that offeror's permission. However, the contracting officer may inform an offeror that its price is considered by the government to be too high or too low and may reveal the results of the analysis supporting that conclusion. It is also permissible, at the government's discretion, to indicate to all offerors the cost or price that the government's price analysis, market research, and other reviews have identified as reasonable;
- Reveals the names of individuals providing reference information about an offeror's past performance; or
- Knowingly furnishes source selection information in violation of FAR 3.104 (FAR 15.306).

Lowest price technically acceptable	A source selection process that is appropriate when best value is expected to result from selecting the technically acceptable proposal with the lowest evaluated price.

When using the lowest price technically acceptable process, the following apply:

- The evaluation factors and significant subfactors that establish the requirements of acceptability shall be set forth in the solicitation. Solicitations shall specify that award will be made on the basis of the lowest evaluated price of proposals meeting or exceeding the acceptability standards for non-cost factors. If the contracting officer documents the file pursuant to FAR 15.304(c)(3)(iii), past performance need not be an evaluation factor in lowest price technically acceptable source selections. If the contracting officer elects to consider past performance as an evaluation factor, it shall be evaluated in accordance with FAR 15.305. However, the comparative assessment in FAR 15.305(a)(2)(i) does not apply. If the contracting officer determines that a small business's past performance is not acceptable, the matter shall be referred to the Small Business Administration for a certificate of competency determination, in accordance with the procedures contained in FAR 19.6.
- Trade-offs are not permitted.
- Proposals are evaluated for acceptability but not ranked using the non-cost/price factors.
- Exchanges may occur (FAR 15.101-2).

M	
Market research	Collecting and analyzing information about capabilities within the market to satisfy agency needs (FAR 2.101).
Mistakes	Mistakes in a contractor's proposal that are disclosed after award shall be processed substantially in accordance with the procedures for mistakes in bids at FAR 14.407-4, which states:

When a mistake in a contractor's bid is not discovered until after award, the mistake may be corrected by contract modification if correcting the mistake would be favorable to the government without changing the essential requirements of the specifications (FAR 15.508 and 14.407-4).

N	
Negotiations	Exchanges, in either a competitive or sole source environment, between the government and an offeror that are undertaken with the intent to allow the offeror to revise its proposal.

Negotiations may include bargaining. Bargaining includes persuasion, alteration of assumptions and positions, and give-and-take, and may apply to price, schedule, technical requirements, type of contract, or other terms of a proposed contract.

When negotiations are conducted in a competitive acquisition, they take place after establishment of the competitive range and are called discussions (FAR 15.306).

O	
Offer	A response to a solicitation that, if accepted, would bind the offeror to perform the resultant contract.

Responses to invitations for bids (sealed bidding) are offers called *bids* or *sealed bids*; responses to requests for proposals (negotiation) are offers called *proposals*; and responses to requests for quotations (simplified acquisition) are *quotations*, not offers (FAR 2.101).

Oral presentations	Presentations by offerors that may substitute for, or augment, written information when requested by the government. Oral presentations as a substitute for portions of a proposal can be effective in streamlining the source selection process. Oral presentations may occur at any time in the acquisition process and are subject to the same restrictions as written information regarding timing (see FAR 15.208) and content (see FAR 15.306).

Oral presentations provide an opportunity for dialogue among the parties. Prerecorded videotaped presentations that lack real-time interactive dialogue are not considered oral presentations for the purposes of this section, although they may be included in offeror submissions when appropriate (FAR 15.102). |
| **Organizational conflict of interest** | A situation in which, because of his or her other activities or relationships with other persons:

• A person is unable or potentially unable to render impartial assistance or advice to the government
• The person's objectivity in performing the contract work is or might be impaired
• A person has an unfair competitive advantage (FAR 2.101). |

P

Participating personally and substantially	Active and significant involvement of an official in any of the following activities directly related to that procurement:

• Drafting, reviewing, or approving the specification or statement of work for the procurement

• Preparing or developing the solicitation
• Evaluating bids or proposals or selecting a source
• Negotiating price or terms and conditions of the contract
• Reviewing and approving the award of the contract.

Participating personally means participating directly and includes the direct and active supervision of a subordinate's participation in the matter.

*Participating substan*tially means that the official's involvement is of significance to the matter. Substantial participation requires more than official responsibility, knowledge, perfunctory involvement, or involvement on an administrative or peripheral issue. Participation may be substantial even though it is not determinative of the outcome of a particular matter.

A finding of substantiality should be based not only on the effort devoted to a matter, but on the importance of the effort. While a series of peripheral involvements may be insubstantial, the single act of approving or participating in a critical step may be substantial.

However, the review of procurement documents solely to determine compliance with regulatory, administrative, or budgetary procedures does not constitute substantial participation in a procurement (FAR 3.104-1). |

Past performance evaluation	One indicator of an offeror's ability to perform the contract successfully. The currency and relevance of the information, source of the information, context of the data, and general trends in contractor's performance shall be considered. This comparative assessment of past performance information is separate from the responsibility determination required under FAR 9.1.
	The solicitation shall describe the approach for evaluating past performance, including evaluating offerors with no relevant performance history, and shall provide offerors an opportunity to identify past or current contracts (including federal, state, local government, and private) for efforts similar to the government requirement. The solicitation shall also authorize offerors to provide information on problems encountered on the identified contracts and the offeror's corrective actions. The government shall consider this information, as well as information obtained from any other sources, when evaluating the offeror's past performance. The source selection authority shall determine the relevance of similar past performance information.
	The evaluation should take into account past performance information regarding predecessor companies, key personnel who have relevant experience, or subcontractors that will perform major or critical aspects of the requirement when such information is relevant to the instant acquisition.
	In the case of an offeror without a record of relevant past performance or for whom information on past performance is not available, the offeror may not be evaluated favorably or unfavorably on past performance.
	The evaluation should include the past performance of offerors in complying with subcontracting plan goals for small disadvantaged business (SDB) concerns, monetary targets for SDB participation, and notifications submitted under FAR 19.1202-4(b). (FAR 15.305).
Performance-based acquisition	An acquisition structured around the results to be achieved, as opposed to the manner by which the work is to be performed (FAR 2.101).
Preaward in-use evaluation	Supplies may be evaluated under comparable in-use conditions without a further test plan, provided offerors are so advised in the solicitation. The results of such tests or demonstrations may be used to rate the proposal, to determine technical acceptability, or otherwise to evaluate the proposal (FAR 11.801).
Prenegotiation objectives	Objectives that are used to establish the government's initial negotiation position. They help the contracting officer determine a fair and reasonable price. They should be based on the results of the contracting officer's analysis of the offeror's proposal, taking into consideration all pertinent information, including field pricing assistance, audit reports and technical analysis, fact-finding results, independent government cost estimates, and price histories.
	The contracting officer shall establish prenegotiation objectives before the negotiation of any pricing action. The scope and depth of the analysis supporting the objectives should be directly related to the dollar value, importance, and complexity of the pricing action.
	When cost analysis is required, the contracting officer shall document the pertinent issues to be negotiated, the cost objectives, and a profit or fee objective (FAR 15.406-1).
Price	Cost plus any fee or profit applicable to the contract type (FAR 15.401).
Price analysis	The process of examining and evaluating a proposed price without evaluating its separate cost elements and proposed profit (FAR 15.407).

Pricing	The process of establishing a reasonable amount or amounts to be paid for supplies or services (FAR 2.101).
Procuring activity	A component of an executive agency having a significant acquisition function and designated as such by the head of the agency. Unless agency regulations specify otherwise, the term *procuring activity* is synonymous with *contracting activity* (FAR 2.101).
Profit	A representation of that element of the potential total remuneration that contractors may receive for contract performance over and above allowable costs.
	This potential remuneration element and the government's estimate of allowable costs to be incurred in contract performance together equal the government's total prenegotiation objective. Just as actual costs may vary from estimated costs, the contractor's actual realized profit or fee may vary from negotiated profit or fee, because of such factors as efficiency of performance, incurrence of costs the government does not recognize as allowable, and the contract type.
	It is in the government's interest to offer contractors opportunities for financial rewards sufficient to stimulate efficient contract performance, attract the best capabilities of qualified large and small business concerns to government contracts, and maintain a viable industrial base.
	Both the government and contractors should be concerned with profit as a motivator of efficient and effective contract performance. Negotiations aimed merely at reducing prices by reducing profit, without proper recognition of the function of profit, are not in the government's interest. Negotiation of extremely low profits, use of historical averages, or automatic application of predetermined percentages to total estimated costs do not provide proper motivation for optimum contract performance (FAR 15.404-4).
Proposal analysis	An assessment intended to ensure that the final agreed-to price is fair and reasonable (FAR 15.404-1).
Proposal evaluation	An assessment of the proposal and the offeror's ability to perform the prospective contract successfully.
	An agency shall evaluate competitive proposals and then assess their relative qualities solely on the factors and subfactors specified in the solicitation. Evaluations may be conducted using any rating method or combination of methods, including color or adjectival ratings, numerical weights, and ordinal rankings.
	The relative strengths, deficiencies, significant weaknesses, and risks supporting proposal evaluation shall be documented in the contract file (FAR 15.305).
Proposal modification	A change made to a proposal before the solicitation closing date and time, or made in response to an amendment, or made to correct a mistake at any time before award (FAR 15.001).
Proposal revision	A change to a proposal made after the solicitation closing date, at the request of or as allowed by a contracting officer, as the result of negotiations (FAR 15.001).
	The contracting officer may request or allow proposal revisions to clarify and document understandings reached during negotiations. At the conclusion of discussions, each offeror still in the competitive range shall be given an opportunity to submit a final proposal revision. The contracting officer is required to establish a common cutoff date only for receipt of final proposal revisions.
	Requests for final proposal revisions shall advise offerors that final proposal revisions must be made in writing and that the government intends to make award without obtaining further revisions (FAR 15.307).

Proposal risk	Proposal risk is the uncertainty associated with an offeror's proposed approach to accomplishing the requirements of the solicitation.

Q

Qualification requirement	A government requirement for testing or other quality assurance demonstration that must be completed before award of a contract (FAR 2.101).

R

Rating/scoring instructions	Instructions given to each evaluator on how to rate or score evaluation factors.
Rating/scoring method	A method of rating or scoring an evaluation factor in relationship to its corresponding standard, such as numerical, adjectival, or color.
Rejecting proposals	The source selection authority may reject all proposals received in response to a solicitation, if doing so is in the best interest of the government (FAR 15.305).
Request for proposals (RFPs)	Document used in negotiated acquisitions to communicate government requirements to prospective contractors and to solicit proposals. RFPs for competitive acquisitions shall, at a minimum, describe the: • Government's requirement; • Anticipated terms and conditions that will apply to the contract: • The solicitation may authorize offerors to propose alternative terms and conditions, including the contract line item number (CLIN) structure; and • When alternative CLIN structures are permitted, the evaluation approach should consider the potential impact on other terms and conditions or the requirement; • Information required to be in the offeror's proposal; and • Factors and significant subfactors that will be used to evaluate the proposal and a statement of their relative importance (FAR 15.203).
Responsibility standards	Standards that measure whether an offeror is able to provide the required supplies or services. FAR 9.103 requires a determination of responsibility. The go/no-go decisional rule applies.

S

Should-cost review	A specialized form of cost analysis. Should-cost reviews differ from traditional evaluation methods because they do not assume that a contractor's historical costs reflect efficient and economical operation. Instead, these reviews evaluate the economy and efficiency of the contractor's existing workforce, methods, materials, equipment, real property, operating systems, and management. Should-cost reviews are accomplished by a multifunctional team of government contracting, contract administration, pricing, audit, and engineering representatives. The objective of should-cost reviews is to promote both short- and long-range improvements in the contractor's economy and efficiency in order to reduce the cost of performance of government contracts. In addition, by providing rationale for any recommendations and quantifying their impact on cost, the government will be better able to develop realistic objectives for negotiation (FAR 15.407-4).
Significant subfactor	The breakdown of an evaluation factor. A subfactor must be rated to be significant.
Significant weakness	A significant weakness in the proposal is a flaw that appreciably increases the risk of unsuccessful contract performance (FAR 15.001).

Solicitation	Any request to submit offers or quotations to the government. Solicitations under sealed bid procedures are called *invitations for bids*. Solicitations under negotiated procedures are called *requests for proposals*.
	Solicitations under simplified acquisition procedures may require submission of either a quotation or an offer (FAR 2.101).
Solicitation provision or provision	A term or condition used only in solicitations and applying only before contract award (FAR 2.101).
Source selection decision	The selection of a proposal for contract award by a source selection authority (SSA).
	The decision shall be based on a comparative assessment of proposals against all source selection criteria in the solicitation. While the SSA may use reports and analyses prepared by others, the source selection decision shall represent the SSA's independent judgment.
	The source selection decision shall be documented, and the documentation shall include the rationale for any business judgments and trade-offs made or relied on by the SSA, including benefits associated with additional costs. Although the rationale for the selection decision must be documented, that documentation need not quantify the trade-offs that led to the decision (FAR 15.308).
Source selection evaluation board	Any board, team, council, or other group that evaluates bids or proposals (FAR 3.104-1).
Source selection information	Any of the following information that is prepared for use by an agency for the purpose of evaluating a bid or proposal to enter into an agency procurement contract, if that information has not been previously made available to the public or disclosed publicly:
	• Bid prices submitted in response to an agency invitation for bids, or lists of those bid prices before bid opening • Proposed costs or prices submitted in response to an agency solicitation, or lists of those proposed costs or prices • Source selection plans • Technical evaluation plans • Technical evaluations of proposals • Cost or price evaluations of proposals • Competitive range determinations identifying proposals that have a reasonable chance of being selected for award of a contract • Rankings of bids, proposals, or competitors • Reports and evaluations of source selection panels, boards, or advisory councils • Other information marked as "source selection information—see FAR 2.101 and 3.104," based on a case-by-case determination by the head of the agency or the contracting officer that its disclosure would jeopardize the integrity or successful completion of the federal agency procurement to which the information relates (FAR 2.101).
Statement of objectives (SOO)	A government-prepared document incorporated into a solicitation that states the overall performance objectives. SOOs are used when the government intends to provide the maximum flexibility to each offeror to propose an innovative approach (FAR 2.101).
Subcontract	A contract between a buyer and a seller in which a significant part of the supplies or services being obtained is for eventual use in a government (prime) contract.

T	
Technical analysis	A process that at a minimum examines the types and quantities of material proposed by an offeror, the need for the types and quantities of labor hours, and the labor mix. Any other data that may be pertinent to an assessment of the offeror's ability to accomplish the technical requirements or to the cost or price analysis of the service or product being proposed should also be included in the analysis.
	The contracting officer may request that personnel having specialized knowledge, skills, experience, or capability in engineering, science, or management perform a technical analysis of the proposed types and quantities of materials, labor, processes, special tooling, equipment, real property, the reasonableness of scrap and spoilage, and other associated factors set forth in the proposal(s) in order to determine the need for and reasonableness of the proposed resources, assuming reasonable economy and efficiency (FAR 15.404-1).
Technical evaluation	An assessment of each offeror's ability to accomplish the technical requirements and a summary, matrix, or quantitative ranking, along with appropriate supporting narrative, of each technical proposal using the evaluation factors. This must be included in the source selection records when trade-offs are performed (FAR 15.305).
Technical evaluation factors	Descriptions of the technical aspects of an offer used to evaluate the merit of the proposed technical approach and/or work to be performed. Examples: technical approach, understanding of the requirement, and compliance with requirement.
Trade-off process	A process that is used to select an offeror for contract award when it may be in the best interest of the government to consider award to other than the lowest priced offeror or other than the highest technically rated offeror.
	When using a trade-off process, the following apply:
	• All evaluation factors and significant subfactors that will affect contract award and their relative importance shall be clearly stated in the solicitation; and • The solicitation shall state whether all evaluation factors other than cost or price, when combined, are significantly more important than, approximately equal to, or significantly less important than cost or price.
	This process permits trade-offs among cost or price and non-cost factors and allows the government to accept other than the lowest priced proposal. The perceived benefits of the higher priced proposal shall merit the additional cost, and the rationale for trade-offs must be documented in the file in accordance with FAR 15.406 (FAR 15.101-1).
U	
Unbalanced pricing	Pricing that may increase performance risk and could result in payment of unreasonably high prices. Unbalanced pricing exists when, despite an acceptable total evaluated price, the price of one or more contract line items is significantly over- or understated, as indicated by the application of cost or price analysis techniques.
	The greatest risks associated with unbalanced pricing occur when:
	• Startup work, mobilization, first articles, or first article testing are separate line items; • Base quantities and option quantities are separate line items; or • The evaluated price is the aggregate of estimated quantities to be ordered under separate line items of an indefinite-delivery contract.

All offers with separately priced line items or subline items shall be analyzed to determine if the prices are unbalanced. If cost or price analysis techniques indicate that an offer is unbalanced, the contracting officer shall:

- Consider the risks to the government associated with the unbalanced pricing in determining the competitive range and in making the source selection decision; and
- Consider whether award of the contract will result in paying unreasonably high prices for contract performance.

An offer may be rejected if the contracting officer determines that the lack of balance poses an unacceptable risk to the government (FAR 15.404-1).

Unsolicited proposal	A written proposal for a new or innovative idea that is submitted to an agency on the initiative of the offeror for the purpose of obtaining a contract with the government, and that is not in response to a request for proposals, Broad Agency Announcement, Small Business Innovation Research topic, Small Business Technology Transfer Research topic, Program Research and Development Announcement, or any other government-initiated solicitation or program (FAR 2.101).

W

Warranty	A promise or affirmation given by a contractor to the government regarding the nature, usefulness, or condition of the supplies or performance of services furnished under a contract (FAR 2.101).
Weakness	A flaw in a proposal that increases the risk of unsuccessful contract performance. A significant weakness in a proposal is a flaw that appreciably increases the risk of unsuccessful contract performance (FAR 15.001).

Bibliography

Air Force, "Source Selection," *Mandatory Procedure* MP5315.3 (Washington, DC: U.S. Air Force, March 2009).

Air Force Materiel Command, *Guide for the Use of Oral Presentations in Contracting by Negotiation* (Wright-Patterson Air Force Base, OH: Air Force Materiel Command, May 1999).

———. *Source Selection Plan Guide* (Wright-Patterson Air Force Base, OH: Air Force Materiel Command, March 2005).

———. RFP no. FA8625-07-R-6470 (Wright-Patterson Air Force Base, OH: U.S. Air Force/Air Force Materiel Command, January 30, 2007).

———. Draft RFP no. FA8903-09-R-8374 (Wright-Patterson Air Force Base, OH: U.S. Air Force/Air Force Materiel Command, March 3, 2009).

———. Aeronautical Systems Center (ASC), Draft RFP no. FA8625-10-R-6600 (Wright-Patterson Air Force Base, OH: U.S. Air Force/AFMC Aeronautical Systems Center (ASC), September 25, 2009).

Allen, Rand, and Scott M. McCaleb, "E-Contracting in the USA Agency Purchases Are Increasingly Paperless Transactions," February 28, 2000, http://www.wiley-rein.com/publications.cfm?sp=articles&id=614 (accessed May 15, 2009).

Army, *Army Federal Acquisition Regulation Supplement* 5115.305 (Washington, DC: Department of the Army, October 2001).

Arviso, Beverly A. "How to Maximize Your Success," *Contract Management* 46 (Ashburn, VA: National Contract Management Association, October 2006), 10.

Bennett, Deanna J. "A Program Manager Talks: What Contractors Should Know," *Acquisition Review Quarterly* (Fort Belvoir, VA: Defense Acquisition University, Fall 1997).

Bolton, Jr., Claude M. *Army Source Selection Manual* (Washington, DC: Office of the Assistant Secretary of the Army for Acquisition, Logistics and Technology, 2007).

Central Contractor Registration, *Central Contractor Registration Handbook* (Washington, DC: Central Contractor Registration, September 2008), 1.

Central Contractor Registration website, http://www.ccr.gov/Default.aspx (accessed October 10, 2008).

Chierichella, John W., and Douglas E. Perry, "Negotiating Teaming Agreements," *Acquisition Issues* 1 (June 1991).

Cibinic, Jr., John, and Ralph C. Nash, Jr., *Formation of Government Contracts* (Washington, DC: George Washington University, 1982).

Cole, Peter S. *How to Evaluate and Negotiate Government Contracts* (Vienna, VA: Management Concepts, 2001).

Court of Federal Claims, *Rules of the United States Court of Federal Claims*, July 13, 2009, http://www.uscfc.uscourts.gov/sites/default/files/court_info/rules_071309_v7.pdf (accessed November 24, 2009).

Defense Acquisition University, *Risk Management Guide for DoD Acquisition*, 5th ed. (Washington, DC: Defense Acquisition University, June 2003), B-5.

———. "Annex F – Sample RFP – sections L & M," https://acc.dau.mil/communitybrowser.aspx?id=25170&lang=en-us (accessed December 12, 2008).

Defense Contract Audit Agency, *DCAA Contract Audit Manual*, Section 9.202 (Fort Belvoir, VA: Defense Contract Audit Agency, June 30, 2009).

Defense Information Systems Agency, *Source Selection Deskbook* (Arlington, VA: Defense Information Systems Agency, May 2003), 12.

DefenseLink News Transcript, "DoD News Briefing with Deputy Secretary of Defense William Lynn, Under Secretary of Defense Ashton Carter, and Secretary of the Air Force Michael Donley," September 24, 2009, http://www.defenselink.mil/transcripts/transcript.aspx?transcriptid=4484 (accessed October 1, 2009).

Defense Logistics Agency, *Defense Logistics Agency FAR Supplement* 15.308 (Fort Belvoir, VA: Defense Logistics Agency).

Defense Systems Management College, *Introduction to Defense Acquisition Management*, 3rd ed. (Fort Belvoir, VA: Defense Systems Management College Press, 1996).

Department of Defense, General Services Administration, and the Administrator for the National Aeronautics and Space Administration, *Federal Acquisition Circular* 90-32 (Washington, DC: U.S. Department of Defense, General Services Administration, and the Administrator for the National Aeronautics and Space Administration, September 18, 1995).

———. *Federal Acquisition Circular* 97-2, 62 RF 51224 (Washington, DC: U.S. Department of Defense, General Services Administration, and the Administrator for the National Aeronautics and Space Administration, September 30, 1997).

Department of Energy, *Source Selection Guide* (Washington, DC: U.S. Department of Energy, 2005).

———. RFP no. DE-RP09-06SR22470 (Washington, DC: U.S. Department of Energy, June 6, 2007).

Department of Health and Human Services, *DHHS Project Officers' Contracting Handbook* (Washington, DC: U.S. Department of Health and Human Services, 2003).

Department of Labor, Division of Contract Services, RFP no. DCS-00-36 (July 14, 2000)

———. Amendment no. 2 to RFP no. DCS-00-36, November 2, 2000, http://www.doleta.gov/sga/rfp/rfp00-36-amend2.htm (accessed January 22, 2009).

Department of State, *Contracting Officer's Representative Handbook,* vol. 14, Handbook 2, 14 FAH-2 H-360 (Washington DC: U.S. Department of State, December 2005).

EG&G Inc. v. the Cube Corp, Va. Cir. Ct., Chancery no. 178996 (2002).

Environmental Protection Agency, *EPA Acquisition Regulation* 1515.305-70 (Washington, DC: U.S. Environmental Protection Agency).

———. *EPA Acquisition Regulation* 1515.305-72 (Washington, DC: Environmental Protection Agency).

Federal Acquisition Institute, *Source Selection Text Reference* (Washington, DC: Federal Acquisition Institute, 1993).

———. "Solicitation Preparation," *Contract Specialist Training Blueprints*, no. 20 (Washington, DC: Federal Acquisition Institute, September 2002).

———. "Communications," *Contract Specialist Training Blueprints*, no. 40 (Washington, DC: Federal Acquisition Institute, September 2002).

———. "Competitive Range," *Contract Specialist Training Blueprints*, no. 41 (Washington, DC: Federal Acquisition Institute, September 2002).

———. "Negotiation Strategy," *Contract Specialist Training Blueprints*, no. 42 (Washington, DC: Federal Acquisition Institute, September 2002).

———. "Conducting Discussions," *Contract Specialist Training Blueprints*, no. 43 (Washington, DC: Federal Acquisition Institute, September 2002).

———. "Debriefings," *Contract Specialist Training Blueprints*, no. 47 (Washington, DC: Federal Acquisition Institute, September 2002).

———. "Defective Cost or Pricing Data," *Contract Specialist Training Blueprints*, no. 64 (Washington, DC: Federal Acquisition Institute, September 2002).

———. "Receiving Quotations and Proposals," *Contract Specialist Training Blueprints*, Unit 30 (Washington, DC: Federal Acquisition Institute, September 2002).

———. "Award without Discussions," *Contract Specialist Training Blueprints*, Unit 39 (Washington, DC: Federal Acquisition Institute, September 2002).

———. "Pre-Quote/Pre-Bid/Pre-Proposal Conferences," *Contract Specialist Training Blueprints*, Unit 22 (Washington, DC: Federal Acquisition Institute, October 2003).

Federal Acquisition Institute and the Air Force Institute of Technology, *Contract Pricing Reference Guide*, vol. 1, "Price Analysis" (Washington, DC: Federal Acquisition Institute, 2005).

———. "Cost Analysis," *Contract Pricing Reference Guide*, vol. 3 (Washington, DC: Federal Acquisition Institute, 2005).

———. "Negotiation Techniques," *Contract Pricing Reference Guide*, vol. 5 (Washington, DC: Federal Acquisition Institute, 2005).

Federal Acquisition Regulation (FAR).

———. FAR 1.102, "Statement of guiding principles for the Federal Acquisition System."

———. FAR 2.101, "Definitions of Words and Terms, Definitions."

———. FAR 3.104-1, "Procurement Integrity, Definitions."

———. FAR 3.401, "Contingent Fees, Definitions."

———. FAR 4.502, "Electronic Commerce in Contracting, Policy."

———. FAR 4.1102, "Central Contractor Registration, Policy."

———. FAR 5.002, "Synopses of Proposed Contract Actions, General."

———. FAR 5.101, "Methods of disseminating information."

———. FAR 5.102, "Availability of solicitations."

———. FAR 5.201, "Synopses of Proposed Contract Actions, General."

———. FAR 5.203, "Publicizing and response time."

———. FAR 6.102, "Use of competitive procedures."

———. FAR 6.301, "Other Than Full and Open Competition, Policy."

———. FAR 6.302-1, "Only one responsible source and no other supplies or services will satisfy agency requirements."

———. FAR 6.302-2, "Unusual and compelling urgency."

———. FAR 6.302-3, "Industrial mobilization; engineering, developmental, or research capability; or expert services."

———. FAR 6.302-4, "International agreement."

———. FAR 6.302-5, "Authorized or required by statute."

———. FAR 6.302-6, "National security."

———. FAR 6.302-7, "Public interest."

———. FAR 6.401, "Sealed bidding and competitive proposals."

———. FAR 7.105, "Contents of written acquisition plans."

———. FAR 7.108, "Additional requirements for telecommuting."

———. FAR 9.503, "Organizational and Consultant Conflicts of Interest, Waiver."

———. FAR 9.505-1, "Providing systems engineering and technical direction."

————. FAR 9.505-2, "Preparing specifications or work statements."

————. FAR 9.505-3, "Providing evaluation services."

————. FAR 9.601, "Contractor Team Arrangements, Definition."

————. FAR 9.602, "Contractor Team Arrangements, General."

————. FAR 9.603, "Contractor Team Arrangements, Policy."

————. FAR 9.604, "Contractor Team Arrangements, Limitations."

————. FAR 10.001, "Market Research, Policy."

————. FAR 10.002, "Market Research, Procedures."

————. FAR 11.002, "Describing Agency Needs, Policy."

————. FAR 11.101, "Order of precedence for requirements documents."

————. FAR 12.101, "Acquisition of Commercial Items—General, Policy."

————. FAR 12.301, "Solicitation provisions and contract clauses for the acquisition of commercial items."

————. FAR 12.302, "Tailoring of provisions and clauses for the acquisition of commercial items."

————. FAR 12.603, "Streamlined solicitation for commercial items."

————. FAR 13.002, "Simplified Acquisition Procedures, Purpose."

————. FAR 13.004, "Simplified Acquisition Procedures, Legal effect of quotations."

————. FAR 13.106-2, "Evaluation of quotations or offers."

————. FAR 14.101, "Elements of sealed bidding."

————. FAR 14.104, "Types of contracts."

————. FAR 14.201-2, "Solicitation of Bids, Part I—The Schedule."

————. FAR 14.207, "Pre-bid conference."

————. FAR 14.301, "Responsiveness of bids."

————. FAR 14.408-1, "Opening of Bids and Award of Contract, Award, General."

————. FAR 15.001, "Contracting by Negotiation, Definitions."

————. FAR 15.101-1, "Tradeoff process."

————. FAR 15.101-2, "Lowest price technically acceptable source selection process."

————. FAR 15.203, "Requests for proposals."

————. FAR 15.204-1, "Uniform contract format."

————. FAR 15.205, "Issuing solicitations."

————. FAR 15.206, "Amending the solicitation."

————. FAR 15.207, "Handling proposals and information."

———. FAR 15.208, "Submission, modification, revision, and withdrawal of proposals."

———. FAR 15.302, "Source selection objective."

———. FAR 15.303, "Responsibilities."

———. FAR 15.304, "Evaluation factors and significant subfactors."

———. FAR 15.305, "Proposal evaluation."

———. FAR 15.306, "Exchanges with offerors after receipt of proposals."

———. FAR 15.308, "Source selection decision."

———. FAR 15.403, "Obtaining cost or pricing data."

———. FAR 15.403-1, "Prohibition on obtaining cost or pricing data."

———. FAR 15.403-3, "Requiring information other than cost or pricing data."

———. FAR 15.404, "Proposal analysis."

———. FAR 15.404-1, "Proposal analysis techniques."

———. FAR 15.405, "Price negotiation."

———. FAR 15.406-1, "Prenegotiation objectives."

———. FAR 15.406-3, "Documenting the negotiation."

———. FAR 15.407-2, "Make-or-buy programs."

———. FAR 15.407-4, "Should-cost review."

———. FAR 15.506, "Postaward debriefing of offerors."

———. FAR 15.605, "Content of unsolicited proposals."

———. FAR 15.609, "Limited use of data."

———. FAR 16.101, "Selecting Contract Types, General."

———. FAR 16.102, "Selecting Contract Types, Policies."

———. FAR 16.103, "Selecting Contract Types, Negotiating contract types."

———. FAR 16.104, "Factors in selecting contract types."

———. FAR 16.202, "Firm-fixed-price contracts."

———. FAR 16.203, "Fixed-price contracts with economic price adjustment."

———. FAR 16.301, "Cost-Reimbursement Contracts, General."

———. FAR 16.306, "Cost-plus-fixed-fee contracts."

———. FAR 16.405-2, "Cost-plus-award-fee contracts."

———. FAR 19.1202-3, "Small Disadvantaged Business Participation Program, Evaluation factor or subfactor, Considerations in developing an evaluation factor or subfactor."

———. FAR 33.101, "Protests, Definitions."

———. FAR 33.103, "Protests to the agency."

———. FAR 33.104, "Protests to GAO."

———. FAR 33.214, "Alternative dispute resolution (ADR)."

———. FAR 37.104, "Personal services contracts."

———. FAR 37.602, "Performance work statement."

———. FAR 42.1501, "Contractor Performance Information, General."

———. FAR 42.1502, "Contractor Performance Information, Policy."

———. FAR 42.1503, "Contractor Performance Information, Procedures."

———. FAR 44.201-1, "Consent to Solicitations, Consent requirements."

———. FAR 46.401, "Government Contract Quality Assurance, General."

———. FAR 52.233-3, "Protest after Award."

The Federal Acquisition Reform Act, Public Law 104-106 §4101 (February 10, 1996).

The Federal Acquisition Streamlining Act of 1994, Public Law 103-355 §1091.

Federal Business Opportunities, *KC-X Tanker Modernization Program*, announcement of Draft RFP no. FA8625-10-R-6600, September 25, 2009, https://www.fbo.gov/index?s=opportunity&mode=form&id=cced18cd9f21580ef249e74e64e947dd&tab=core&_cview=1 (accessed October 14, 2009).

Federal Procurement Regulations §1-1.301-1.

Fenster, Herbert L. "The A-12 Legacy: It Wasn't an Airplane—It Was a Train Wreck." *U.S. Naval Institute Proceedings* 125 (February 1999).

Fryling, Robert G., and Edward J. Hoffman, "Teaming Agreements: Proceed with Caution," *Contract Management* 43 (Ashburn, VA: National Contract Management Association, December 2003), 58.

Garrett, Gregory A. "Bid/No-Bid Decision-Making Tools and Techniques," *Contract Management* 47 (Ashburn, VA: National Contract Management Association, April 2007).

Garrett, Gregory A., and Reginald J. Kipke, "The Capture Management Life Cycle," *Contract Management* 43 (Ashburn, VA: National Contract Management Association, June 2003).

General Accounting Office, *Federal Regulations Need To Be Revised to Fully Realize the Purposes of the Competition in Contracting Act of 1984*, GAO/OGC-85-14 (Washington, DC: U.S. General Accounting Office, August 1985).

———. *U.S. Combat Air Power: Aging Refueling Aircraft Are Costly to Maintain and Operate*, GAO/NSIAD-96-160 (Washington, DC: U.S. General Accounting Office, August 8, 1996).

———. *Year End Spending: Reforms Under Way but Better Reporting and Oversight Needed*, GAO/AIMD-98-185 (Washington, DC: U.S. General Accounting Office, July 1998).

————. *Obstacles to Implementing the Federal Acquisition Computer Network*, GAO/NSIAD-97-26 (Washington, DC: U.S. General Accounting Office, January 1997).

General Services Administration, *A Guide: How to Market to the Federal Government,* June 2009, http://www.gsa.gov/Portal/gsa/ep/contentView.do?contentType=GSA_DOCUMENT&contentId=17212&noc=T (accessed August 20, 2009).

Government Accountability Office, "Ann Riley & Associates, Ltd.—Reconsideration," B-271741.3 (Washington, DC: U.S. Government Accountability Office, March 10, 1997).

————. "Oceaneering International, Inc.," B-278126; B-278126.2 (Washington, DC: U.S. Government Accountability Office, December 31, 1997).

————. "Century Elevator, Inc.," B-283822 (Washington, DC: U.S. Government Accountability Office, December 20, 1999).

————. "NV Services," B-284119.2 (Washington, DC: U.S. Government Accountability Office, February 25, 2000).

————. "Mnemonics, Inc.," B-290961 (Washington, DC: U.S. Government Accountability Office, October 28, 2002).

————. "Colmek Sys Eng'g," B-291931.2 (Washington, DC: U.S. Government Accountability Office, July 9, 2003).

————. "Honeywell Technology Solutions, Inc.; Wyle Laboratories, Inc.," B-292354; B-292388 (Washington, DC: U.S. Government Accountability Office, September 2, 2003).

————. "Cygnus Corporation, Inc.," B-292649.3; B-292649.4 (Washington, DC: U.S. Government Accountability Office, December 30, 2003).

————. "Base Technologies, Inc.," B-293061.2; B-293061.3 (Washington, DC: U.S. Government Accountability Office, January 28, 2004).

————. "Computer & High-Tech Management, Inc.," B-293235.4 (Washington, DC: U.S. Government Accountability Office, March 2, 2004).

————. "Chapman Law Firm, LPA," B-293105.6; B-293105.10; B-293105.12 (Washington, DC: U.S. Government Accountability Office, November 15, 2004).

————. "New SI, LLC," B-295209; B-295209.2; B-295209.3 (Washington, DC: U.S. Government Accountability Office, November 22, 2004).

————. "Trajen, Inc.; Maytag Aircraft Corporation," B-296334; B-296334.2; B-296334.3; B-296334.4 (Washington, DC: U.S. Government Accountability Office, July 29, 2005).

————. "Information Ventures, Inc.," B-297276.2; B-297276.3; B-297276.4 (Washington, DC: U.S. Government Accountability Office, March 1, 2006).

———. "Project Resources, Inc.," B-297968 (Washington, DC: U.S. Government Accountability Office, March 31, 2006).

———. "Metro Machine Corporation," B-297879.2 (Washington, DC: U.S. Government Accountability Office, May 3, 2006).

———. "eFedBudget Corporation," B-298627 (Washington, DC: U.S. Government Accountability Office, November 15, 2006).

———. "Freedom Lift Corporation," B-298772.2 (Washington, DC: U.S. Government Accountability Office, January 25, 2007).

———. "Matthews Associates, Inc.," B-299305 (Washington, DC: U.S. Government Accountability Office, March 5, 2007).

———. "Systems Research and Applications Corporation; Booz Allen Hamilton, Inc.," B-299818; B-299818.2; B-299818.3; B-299818.4 (Washington, DC: U.S. Government Accountability Office, September 6, 2007).

———. "Comprehensive Health Services, Inc.," B-310553 (Washington, DC: U.S. Government Accountability Office, December 27, 2007).

———. "Gap Solutions, Inc.," B-310564 (Washington, DC: U.S. Government Accountability Office, January 4, 2008).

———. "IMLCORP LLC; Wattre Corporation," B-310582; B-310582.2; B-310582.3; B-310582.4; B-310582.5 (Washington, DC: U.S. Government Accountability Office, January 9, 2008).

———. "Colson Services Corporation," B-310971; B-310971.2; B-310971.3 (Washington, DC: U.S. Government Accountability Office, March 21, 2008).

———. "Fedcar Company, Ltd.," B-310980; B-310980.2; B-310980.3 (Washington, DC: U.S. Government Accountability Office, March 25, 2008).

———. "General Atomics Aeronautics Systems, Inc.," B-311004; B-311004.2 (Washington, DC: U.S. Government Accountability Office, March 28, 2008).

———. "Carahsoft Technology Corporation; Allied Technology Group," B-311241; B-311241.2 (Washington, DC: U.S. Government Accountability Office, May 16, 2008).

———. "Bid Protest Regulations," *Code of Federal Regulations*, Title 4, §21.0(b) (1) (Washington, DC: U.S. Government Accountability Office, June 9, 2008).

———. "Bid Protest Regulations," *Code of Federal Regulations*, Title 4, §21.0(f) (Washington, DC: U.S. Government Accountability Office, June 9, 2008).

———. "Bid Protest Regulations," *Code of Federal Regulations*, Title 4, §21.0(e) (Washington, DC: U.S. Government Accountability Office, June 9, 2008).

———. "Bid Protest Regulations," *Code of Federal Regulations*, Title 4, §21.2(a) (1) (Washington, DC: U.S. Government Accountability Office, June 9, 2008).

———. "Bid Protest Regulations," *Code of Federal Regulations*, Title 4, §21.2(a) (3) (Washington, DC: U.S. Government Accountability Office, June 9, 2008).

————. "The Boeing Company," B-311344; B-311344.3; B-311344.4; B-311344.6; B-311344.7; B-311344.8; B-311344.10; B-311344.11 (Washington, DC: U.S. Government Accountability Office, June 18, 2008).

————. *Air Force Procurement: Aerial Refueling Tanker Protest*, Testimony of Daniel I. Gordon, Deputy General Counsel, GAO-08-991T (Washington, DC: U.S. Government Accountability Office, July 10, 2008).

————. "ASRC Research & Technology Solutions, LLC," B-400217; B-400217.2 (Washington, DC: U.S. Government Accountability Office, August 21, 2008).————. "Fintrac, Inc.," B-311462.2; B-311462.3 (Washington, DC: U.S. Government Accountability Office, October 14, 2008).

————. "Aegis Defense Services Limited," B-400093.4; B-400093.5 (Washington, DC: U.S. Government Accountability Office, October 16, 2008).

————. "Smart Innovative Solutions," B-400323.3 (Washington, DC: U.S. Government Accountability Office, November 19, 2008).

————. "Sector One Security Solution," B-400728 (Washington, DC: U.S. Government Accountability Office, December 10, 2008).

————. "Bid Protest Statistics for Fiscal Years 2004–2008," B-158766 (Washington, DC: U.S. Government Accountability Office, December 22, 2008).

————. "Cambridge Systems, Inc.," B-400680; B-400680.3 (Washington, DC: U.S. Government Accountability Office, January 8, 2009).

————. "Arc-Tech, Inc.," B-400325.3 (Washington, DC: U.S. Government Accountability Office, February 19, 2009).

————. *Federal Register* 74.166 (August 28, 2009).

Hanson, Harold V. *NAVSEA Source Selection Guide* (Washington, DC: U.S. Naval Sea Systems Command, 2001).

Ireton, Donna S., and Ronald L. Smith, *Acquisition Reform 1996* (Vienna, VA: National Contract Management Association, 1996).

Jacobs, Daniel M. *The Program/Contract Definition Document* (Warrenton, VA: The Federal Market Group, 1999).

————. *Capture Planning Briefing.* (Warrenton, VA: The Federal Market Group, 1999).

Jacobs, Daniel M., Janice M. Menker, and Chester P. Shinaman, *Building a Contract: Solicitations/Bids and Proposals* (Ashburn, VA: National Contract Management Association, 1990).

John, William A. *Service Contracting: A Desk Guide to Best Practices* (Arlington, VA: Navy Acquisition Reform Office, 1998).

Knight, William, and Christopher Bolkcom, *Air Force Air Refueling: The KC-X Aircraft Acquisition Program* (Washington, DC: Congressional Research Service, April 4, 2008).

Lynn, William J., Michael B. Donley, and Ashton B. Carter, *Moving Forward*, Refueling Tanker Briefing, (Washington, DC: U.S. Department of Defense, September 24, 2009).

McDonnell Douglas Corp. v. United States of America, 35 Fed. Cl. 358 (1996).

McDonnell Douglas Corp. and General Dynamics Corp. v. United States of America, no. 91-1204C (Fed. Cl. 1998).

Nagle, James F. *A History of Government Contracting*, 2nd ed. (Washington, DC: George Washington University Press, 1999).

National Aeronautics and Space Administration, *Source Selection Guide* (Washington, DC: National Aeronautics and Space Administration, June 2007).

———. *NASA FAR Supplement* 1815.300-70(a)(1)(ii) (Washington, DC: National Aeronautics and Space Administration).

———. *NASA FAR Supplement* 1815.304-70 (Washington, DC: National Aeronautics and Space Administration).

———. *NASA FAR Supplement* 1815.305-70 (Washington, DC: National Aeronautics and Space Administration).

———. *NASA FAR Supplement* 1815.306 (Washington, DC: National Aeronautics and Space Administration).

———. *NASA FAR Supplement* 1815.406-3 (Washington, DC: National Aeronautics and Space Administration).

National Reconnaissance Office, *Source Selection Manual* (Chantilly, VA: National Reconnaissance Office, 2000).

———. *NRO Acquisition Manual*, clause N15.215-020, "Exclusive Teaming Prohibition" (Chantilly, VA: National Reconnaissance Office, April 2004).

———. *Avoiding and Defending Protests Resulting from Source Selections*, pamphlet version 1.8 (Chantilly, VA: National Reconnaissance Office, May 2008).

———. *Source Selection Manual* N87 (Chantilly, VA: National Reconnaissance Office, 2008).

Navy, Office of the Assistant Secretary, Research, Development and Acquisition, *Navy Marine Corps Acquisition Regulation Supplement* 5215.305 (Washington, DC: Department of the Navy, February 14, 2005).

Naval Air Systems Command, RFP no. N00421-08-R-0042 (April 21, 2008).

Nocerino, Joseph T. "Selling 'Best Value' in the New Commercial Government Market," *Contract Management* 47 (Ashburn, VA: National Contract Management Association, July 2007).

Office of Federal Procurement Policy, *Best Practices for Collecting and Using Current and Past Performance Information* (Washington, DC: Office of Federal Procurement Policy, May 2000).

Office of Management and Budget, "Value Engineering," *OMB Circular* A-131 (Washington, DC: Office of Management and Budget, May 21, 1993).

―――. "Performance of Commercial Activity," *OMB Circular* A-76, May 29, 2003.

―――. "Federal Participation in the Development and Use of Voluntary Consensus Standards and in Conformity Assessment Activities," *OMB Circular* A-119.

O'Guin, Michael. "How Capture Teams Win," *Contract Management* 42 (Ashburn, VA: National Contract Management Association, August 2002), 29.

Reid, Thomas. "How to Construct a Contract Compliance Matrix," *Contract Management* 44 (Ashburn, VA: National Contract Management Association, January 2004).

―――. "Exactly Who Is the Government Customer?" *Contract Management* 46 (Ashburn, VA: National Contract Management Association, December 2006).

―――. "Scared Speechless." *Contract Management* 47 (November 2007).

Rumbaugh, Margaret G. *Desktop Guide to Basic Contracting Terms* (Ashburn, VA: National Contract Management Association, 2006).

Rumbaugh, Margaret G., and Mark J. Lumer, *The Brave New World of Market Research* (Vienna, VA: National Contract Management Association, 1996).

Small Business Administration, *Opening Doors: Small Business Opportunities in Federal Government Contracting*, http://www.sba.gov/idc/groups/public/documents/sba_homepage/serv_pub_contracting.pdf (accessed August 20, 2009).

Special Operations Command, *USSOCOM FAR Supplement* 5615.305 (MacDill Air Force Base, FL: U.S. Special Operations Command).

―――. *USSOCOM FAR Supplement* 5615.306 (MacDill Air Force Base, FL: U.S. Special Operations Command).

Szeliga, Keith R. "So You Lost: Now What? A Vacationer's Guide to GAO Bid Protests," *Contract Management* 48 (Ashburn, VA: National Contract Management Association, November 2008).

Thornton, David W. "Replacing the KC135 Stratotanker: The Politics of a Flawed Procurement Policy," panel paper presented at the Transatlantic Studies Association 7th Annual Conference, Dundee, Scotland, July 7–10, 2008.

The Truth in Negotiations Act, Public Law 87-653, §2304 (September 10, 1962).

United States Code. 10 *U.S. Code* 2306a, "Cost or pricing data: truth in negotiations."

―――. 31 *U.S. Code* 3553, "Review of protests; effect on contracts pending decision."

―――. 41 *U.S. Code* 253a, "Planning and solicitation requirements."

―――. 41 *U.S. Code* 253b, "Evaluation and award."

———. 41 *U.S. Code* 254b, "Cost or pricing data: truth in negotiations."

———. 41 *U.S. Code* 401, "Repealed."

———. 41 *U.S. Code* 423, "Restrictions on disclosing and obtaining contractor bid or proposal information or source selection information."

———. 15 *U.S. Code* 4724, "Trade shows."

Whalen, Tim. "Providing High-Quality Technical Resumes for Technical Proposals." *Contract Management* 47 (March 2007): 20.

Wilson, Johnnie E. *Best Value Source Selection* 715-3 (Alexandria, VA: Army Materiel Command, 1998).

Index

A

accounting system, 80
acquisition history, contractor, 80
acquisition planning
  acquisition streamlining, 45
  budgeting and funding, 45–46
  commercial items, 71–72
  competition, 45
  conditions affecting acquisition, 43
  considerations, 45
  contract administration, 48
  contract types, 72
  contracting by negotiation, 67, 70–71
  contractor versus government performance, 46
  cost, 44
  delivery or performance period requirements, 44
  environmental and energy conservation
    objectives, 47–48
  government-furnished information, 47
  government property, 47
  importance of, 37, 43
  inadequate planning case study, 57–58
  inherently governmental functions, 46
  logistics considerations, 47
  make or buy, 46–47
  management information requirements, 46
  marketing plan, 66–67
  milestones, 48–49
  other considerations, 48
  plan of action, 45
  priorities, allocations, and allotments, 46
  product or service description, 46
  required capabilities or performance
    characteristics, 44
  requirements, 43
  risks, 44–45
  sealed bidding, 67, 69–70
  security considerations, 48
  simplified acquisition procedures, 67–69
  source selection authority, 51–53
  source selection plan, 49–51
  source selection procedures, 45
  sources, 45
  statement of need, 43
  strategy, 53–57
  test and evaluation, 47
  trade-offs, 44
acquisition strategy
  common elements, 56–57
  importance of, 53
  lowest price technically acceptable, 53–55
  trade-off approach, 55–56
acquisition streamlining, 45
acts, 2
adjectival rating system, 114, 129–130
adverse agency action, 414
agency bias or bad faith, 420
agenda, debriefings, 402
allocations, 46
allotments, 46
Armed Service Procurement Regulation (ASPR), 3
Armed Services Procurement Act of 1947, 1
Army Corps of Engineers, 244–246, 288–289
ASPR. See Armed Service Procurement Regulation
assistance awards, 59
average annual receipts, 61
average number of employees, 60–61
awarding without discussions
  case study, 328–329
  clarifications, 329–332
  clarifications versus discussions case study,
    332–333
  documenting decision, 333–334
  ensuring offeror can begin work, 325
  importance of, 323
  notifying unsuccessful offerors, 334
  precedents, 327–328
  special considerations, 325–327
  stating intention, 324
  streamlining source selection process, 327

B

bait and switch, 215
basis, 416
basis of estimate (BOE), 296
best value continuum, 71
bidder's conference. See pre-proposal conference
BOE. See basis of estimate
brainstorming, evaluation factors, 102

budgeting and funding, 45–46
business case, 417–418
business start date, 60
buying in, 123

C

CAGE. See Commercial and Government Entity
    Code
calendar days, 415
case studies
    adjectival rating system, 130–134
    averaging adjectives, 134–135
    awarding without discussions, 328–329
    challenging evaluator's qualifications, 236–237
    competitive range, 340–342
    competitive range of one, 346–348
    consensus evaluation report, 317
    cost/technical trade-off comparison, 378–380
    deficient scoring plan, 145–148
    disagreeing with evaluators, 382–385
    documentation, 309–312
    efficient competition determination, 343–344
    evaluation consistency, 273–279
    evaluation factors, 97–99
    inadequate planning, 57–58
    inconsistently applied scoring, 141–145
    independent cost estimate, 299–303
    late proposals, 255–257
    lost proposals, 244–246
    misleading discussions and final proposal
        revisions, 368–370
    past performance, 288–289
    protesting adverse agency action, 423–425
    revised competitive range, 344–346
    risk, 118–119
    scoring methodology, 306–309
    source selection decision document, 387–389
    subcontractor teaming, 211–212
    unacceptable proposal, 250–253
CBD. See Commerce Business Daily
CCR. See Central Contractor Registration
CDC. See Centers for Disease Control and
    Prevention
CECOM. See Communications-Electronics
    Command
Centers for Disease Control and Prevention (CDC),
    145–148
Central Contractor Registration (CCR)
    average annual receipts, 61
    average number of employees, 60–61
    business start date, 60
    Commercial and Government Entity Code, 61
    Data Universal Numbering System number, 60
    doing business as name, 60
    Employer Identification Number, 60

exceptions, 59
fiscal year end date, 60
importance of, 59
legal business name, 60
North American Industry Classification System
    code number, 60–61
U.S. Federal Tax Identification Number, 60
verifying, 253
CICA. See Competition in Contracting Act
clarification request (CR), 272
clarifications, 339
Clinger-Cohen Act. See Federal Acquisition
    Reform Act
CMR. See commercial marketing representative
CO. See contracting officer
color coding rating system, 136–138
colorful reviews. See critical reviews
Commerce Business Daily (CBD), 10, 30, 63
Commercial and Government Entity Code
    (CAGE), 61
commercial items, 25–26, 71–72
commercial marketing representative (CMR), 65
communications, 338–340
Communications-Electronics Command
    (CECOM), 346
competition, 45
Competition in Contracting Act (CICA)
    cost or price factors, 92
    full and open competition, 10–11
    impact on source selection, 13–14, 27
    importance of, 3, 9
    planning, solicitation requirements, and protests,
        11–13
    requirements, 10
competitive range
    case study, 340–342
    communicating with offerors before establishing,
        338–340
    communications, 338–340
    competitive range of one case study, 346–348
    defining, 337–338
    efficient competition determination case study,
        343–344
    importance of, 337
    limiting, 342
    preaward debriefing, 348–350
    revised competitive range case study, 344–346
competitive source selection process, 2
completeness, 296
completion form, cost-plus-fixed-fee contracts, 75
completion statement of work, 163–164
compliance method, 226
concurrent contracts, 80
conditions affecting the acquisition, 43
conflicts of interest, 246–247

Congress, role of, 1–2
consensus, 314–317
consensus evaluation report, 317
contract administration, 48
contract administration data, uniform contract
   format (section G), 155
contract clauses, uniform contract format
   (section I), 155
contract types
   cost-reimbursement contracts, 74–75
   fixed-price contracts, 73–74
   incentive contracts, 75–77
   overview, 72
   risk ranking, 78
   selecting, 77–81
   time-and-materials contract, 77
contracting by negotiation, 67, 70–71
contracting officer (CO), 3, 85, 133, 153, 186–187
contractor library, 190
contractor versus government performance, 46
contractual approach, 161
cost, 44, 113
cost analysis, 79, 93, 292–295
cost and price information, 92–95, 171–172, 289–291
cost-plus-award-fee (CPAF) contract, 76–77
cost-plus-fixed-fee (CPFF) contract, 74–75
cost-plus-incentive-fee (CPIF) contract, 75
cost-reimbursement contracts, 74–75
CPAF. See cost-plus-award-fee contract
CPFF. See cost-plus-fixed-fee contract
CPIF. See cost-plus-incentive-fee contract
CR. See clarification request
critical reviews, 228–229

D

Data Universal Numbering System (DUNS), 60
DBA. See doing business as name
debarment, 248–249
debriefings
   agenda, 402
   attendance, 403–404, 406–407
   documenting, 407–408
   evaluation results, explaining, 404–406
   how to conduct, 400–402
   importance, 395
   materials, 401–403
   methods, 401
   postaward, 395–396
   preaward, 395–396
   protest case study, 408–409
   purpose, 397
   responding to questions, 404
   source selection process, explaining, 404–406
   timeline, 399
   when conducted, 397–399

defective solicitations, 419
Defense Priorities and Allocations System (DPAS), 46
deficiencies, 267
deficiency report (DR), 273
deliverables, 158
deliveries or performance, uniform contract format
   (section F), 155
delivery or performance period requirements, 44
Department of Commerce (DOC), 343–344
Department of Defense (DoD), 1
Department of Energy (DOE), 140
Department of Health and Human Services (HHS),
   340–342, 368–370
Department of Housing and Urban Development
   (HUD), 134–135
Department of Labor, 317
Department of State (DOS), 57–58, 255–257
Department of Veterans Affairs (VA), 378–380
description/specifications/statement of work,
   uniform contract format (section C), 154
design-to-cost, 44
detailed design-oriented requirements document, 162
detailed technical requirements, 158
discriminators, 96
discussions. See also negotiations
   adequate discussions case study, 359–361
   competitive range, 339
   deficiencies, 357
   improvements, 357–358
   limits, 358–359
   misleading discussions and final proposal
     revisions case study, 368–370
   significant weaknesses, 356–357
   topics, 356
documentation
   awarding without discussions, 333–334
   case study, 309–312, 312–314
   debriefings, 407–408
   detailed design-oriented requirements, 162
   evaluating proposals, 309–312, 312–314
   market research, 41–43
   negotiations, 370–372
   performance-oriented requirements, 162
   source selection decision document, 387–389
DoD. See Department of Defense
DOE. See Department of Energy
doing business as name (DBA), 60
DOS. See Department of State
DPAS. See Defense Priorities and Allocations
   System
DR. See deficiency report
draft request for proposals (DRFP),
   173–176, 188
DUNS. See Data Universal
   Numbering System

E

EEO. See Equal Employment Opportunity
efficient competition, 24
EIN. See Employer Identification Number
electronic funds transfer (EFT), 60
electronic proposals, 247–248
Electronic Systems Center (ESC), 273–279
Employer Identification Number (EIN), 60
engineering and technology acquisition support
   services (ETASS), 273–279
environmental and energy conservation objectives,
   47–48
EPLS. See Excluded Parties List System
Equal Employment Opportunity (EEO), 243
ESC. See Electronic Systems Center
ETASS. See engineering and technology acquisition
   support services
ethical behavior rules, 14–15
evaluating proposals. See also past performance
   completeness, 296
   conducting evaluation, 271
   consensus, 314–317
   consensus evaluation report case study, 317
   cost analysis, 292–295
   cost and price information, 289–291
   deficiencies, 267
   documentation, 312–314
   documentation case study, 309–312
   evaluation consistency case study, 273–279
   evaluation forms, 271–273
   evaluation panel, 269–271
   importance of, 265
   independent cost estimate case study, 299–303
   minor weaknesses, 267
   oral presentations, 303–305
   price analysis, 291–292
   process, 266–268
   realism, 296–299
   reasonableness, 296
   scoring, 305–306
   scoring methodology case study, 306–309
   significant weaknesses, 267
   technical/management proposal volumes,
      268–269
   value analysis, 292
evaluation criteria model, 103
evaluation criteria structure, 101
evaluation factors. See also risk
   brainstorming, 102
   case study, 97–99
   cost and price, 92–95
   evaluation criteria model, 103
   evaluation criteria structure, 101
   grouping, 103–105
   importance of, 85–86

   key personnel, 90–91
   limiting, 108–109
   management, 89–90
   mandatory, 86–88
   narrative statements, 120
   numerical weighting, 120–124
   problems, 124
   relative importance, 120
   security, 91–92
   selecting, 99–102
   subfactors, 96–97
   technical, 88–89
   work breakdown structure, 104–107
   writing, 109–112
evaluation factors for award, uniform contract
   format (section M), 155
evaluation forms, 271–273
evaluation outlining method, 227
evaluation panel, 269–271
evaluation results, explaining, 404–406
Excluded Parties List System (EPLS), 248

F

FAC. See Federal Acquisition Circular
facilities and security, 241–244
FACNET. See Federal Acquisition Computer
   Network
FAR. See Federal Acquisition Regulation
FARA. See Federal Acquisition Reform Act
FASA. See Federal Acquisition Streamlining Act
FBI. See Federal Bureau of Investigation
FedBizOpps (FBO), 62
Federal Acquisition Circular (FAC), 20
Federal Acquisition Computer Network
   (FACNET), 19–20
Federal Acquisition Reform Act (FARA)
   commercial items, 25–26
   efficient competition, 24
   impact on source selection, 26–28
   importance of, 2, 23–24
   preaward debriefing, 24–25
   Procurement Integrity Act, 26
Federal Acquisition Regulation (FAR), 4
Federal Acquisition Streamlining Act (FASA)
   best value acquisitions, 21–22
   commercial contracting methods, 17–18
   Federal Acquisition Computer Network, 19–20
   impact on source selection, 23, 28
   importance of, 2, 15–17
   offerors, notifying and debriefing, 22–23
   past performance, 19
   Truth in Negotiations Act, 20–21
Federal Bureau of Investigation (FBI), 387–389
Federal Procurement Data Center (FPDC), 61–62
Federal Procurement Data System (FPDS), 61
Federal Property and Administrative Services Act, 1

Federal Supply Schedules. See GSA Schedule
   Program
final proposal revisions (FPR), 135
Fiscal Transfer Agent (FTA), 356–357
fiscal year end date, 60
fixed-price contracts, 73–74
FPDC. See Federal Procurement Data Center
FPDS. See Federal Procurement Data System
FPR. See final proposal revisions
FTA. See Fiscal Transfer Agent
full and open competition, 10–11

G

GAO. See Government Accountability Office
General Accounting Office. See Government
   Accountability Office
General Services Administration (GSA), 61,
   312–314, 387–389
ghosting. See positioning method
Government Accountability Office (GAO)
   adequate discussions case study, 359–361
   averaging adjectives case study, 134–135
   awarding without discussions case study,
      328–329
   challenging evaluators' qualifications case study,
      236–237
   clarifications versus discussions case study,
      332–333
   competitive range determination case study,
      340–342
   competitive range of one case study, 346–348
   consensus evaluation report case study, 317
   cost/technical trade-off comparison case study,
      378–380
   deficient scoring plan case study, 145–148
   deviating from designated adjectival rating
      system case study, 133–134
   disagreeing with evaluators case study, 382–385
   documentation case study, 312–314
   efficient competition determination case study,
      343–344
   evaluation consistency case study, 273–279
   inadequate planning case study, 57–58
   inconsistently applied scoring methodology case
      study, 141–145
   independent cost estimate case study, 299–303
   late proposal case study, 255–257
   lost proposal case study, 244–246
   misleading discussions and final proposal
      revisions case study, 368–370
   past performance case study, 288–289
   protesting adverse agency action case study,
      423–425
   protests case study, 408–409
   revised competitive range case study, 344–346
   scoring methodology case study, 306–309

source selection decision document case study,
   387–389
unacceptable proposal case study, 250–253
unstated evaluation factors case study, 97–99
government-furnished information, 47
government property, 47
GSA. See General Services Administration
GSA Schedule Program
   GSA Advantage!, 63–64
   GSA Marketing Partnership, 64
   GSA SmartPay logos, 64
   GSA Starmark logos, 64
   importance of, 63–64
   small business opportunities, 65–66

H

HHS. See Department of Health and Human
   Services
HUD. See Department of Housing and Urban
   Development

I

ICIDS-IV. See integrated commercial intrusion
   detection system-IV
IGCE. See independent government cost estimate
improper agency evaluation, 418
improper exclusion from competitive range, 419
independent government cost estimate (IGCE), 299
ineligibility, 248–249
information request (IR), 272–273
inherently governmental functions, 46
initially unacceptable proposals, 250
inspection and acceptance, uniform contract
   format (section E), 155
instructions, conditions, and notices to offerors
   or respondents, uniform contract format
   (section L), 155
integrated commercial intrusion detection system-IV
   (ICIDS-IV), 344
interested party, 413
interveners, 414
invitation for bid (IFB), 69
IR. See information request

K

key personnel evaluation factors, 90–91

L

lack of cost realism, 419–420
lack of meaningful discussions, 418–419
late proposals, 254–255
laws, summary of, 27–28
legal business name, 60
legal flaws, 416
level of confidence assessment rating (LOCAR),
   116–117
life-cycle cost, 44

list of attachments, uniform contract format
(section J), 155
LOCAR. See level of confidence assessment rating
logistics considerations, 47
Long Range Acquisition Estimate (LRAE), 63
lowest price technically acceptable (LPTA), 53–55

M

make or buy, 46–47
management evaluation factors, 89–90
management information requirements, 46
mandatory evaluation factors, 86–88
market research
   data, 38–40
   documenting, 41–43
   importance of, 37–38
   sources, 40–41
marketing plan, 66–67
master packing list, 170
materials, debriefing, 401–403
milestones, 48–49
military installations, 63
minor weaknesses, 267
most probable cost (MPC), 297–298
Multiple Award Schedules. See GSA Schedule
Program

N

NAICS. See North American Industry
Classification System code number
National Aeronautics and Space Administration
(NASA), 1, 139–141, 299–303, 306–309, 328–329
National Geospatial-Intelligence Agency (NGA),
408–410
National Institute of Health (NIH), 368–370
negotiations
   competitive range, 339
   conducting, 361–362
   disagreeing with evaluators, 381
   disagreeing with evaluators case study,
    382–385
   discussion, compared to, 353–355
   documenting, 370–372
   independent judgment, 380–381
   lose/lose, 366
   skills, 362–363
   styles, 363–364
   win/lose, 365–366
   win/win, 364–365
NGA. See National Geospatial-Intelligence Agency
NIH. See National Institute of Health
North American Industry Classification System
code number (NAICS), 61
numerical rating system, 139
numerical weighting, 120–124

O

Office of Federal Contract Compliance Programs
(OFCCP), 253
Office of Management and Budget (OMB), 46, 61
Online Representations and Certifications
Application (ORCA), 254
oral presentations, 303–305
oral proposals, 170–171
ORCA. See Online Representations and
Certifications Application

P

packaging and marking, uniform contract format
(section D), 155
page and formatting limits, 170
past performance
   case study, 288–289
   evaluating, 285–288
   importance of, 279–282
   information, 172–173
   researching, 282–284
   sample interview questions, 284
PCR. See procurement center representative
performance confidence assessment technique,
   115–117
performance-oriented requirements document, 162
performance risk, 113–114
performance work statement (PWS), 156,
   163, 180
period of performance, 80
plan of action, 45
positioning method, 226
postaward debriefings, 395–396
postaward protests, 421
pre-proposal conference
   government considerations, 188–191
   importance of, 185
   industry considerations, 191–194
   planning, 188
   purpose, 185–186
   RFP release, 195
   tips for government participants, 191
   topics, 187
preaward debriefing, 24–25, 348–350, 395–396
preaward protests, 421
prejudice, 416–417
preparing proposals
   bid/no-bid decision, 204–207
   capture planning, 199–200
   competition information, 201–202
   compliance method, 226
   critical reviews, 228–229
   customer folder, 200–201
   evaluating strengths and weaknesses, 202–204
   evaluation outlining method, 227

flow-down clauses, 220–223
importance of, 199
key personnel, 215–219
positioning method, 226
privity of contract, 219–220
program description, 201–202
proposal input page, 228
RFP compliance matrix, 223–225
storyboarding method, 226–227
subcontractor teaming case study, 211–212
subcontracts, 219
submission tips, 229–230
team agreements, 209–214
team restrictions, 214–215
weaknesses, 226
win strategy, 207–209
price analysis, 79, 291–292
price competition, 79
priorities, 46
probable cost, 298
procurement center representative (PCR), 65
Procurement Integrity Act
  amendments, 26
  ethical behavior rules, 14–15
  impact on source selection, 15, 27
  importance of, 3, 14
product or service description, 46
project objectives, 158
proposal evaluation, preparing for
  assigning proposals to evaluators, 257
  Central Contractor Registration, 253
  challenging evaluator's qualifications case study, 236–237
  conflicts of interest, 246–247
  debarment, 248–249
  electronic proposals, 247–248
  facilities and security, 241–244
  importance of, 235
  ineligibility, 248–249
  initially unacceptable proposals, 250
  late proposals, 254–255
  late proposals case study, 255–257
  lost proposal case study, 244–246
  receiving proposals, 244
  representations and certifications, 254
  RFP compliance, 249
  selecting evaluators, 235–236
  special compliance considerations, 253
  suspension, 248–249
  training and orientation, 237–240
  unacceptable proposal case study, 250–253
proposal input page, 228
proposal revisions
  final, 367–368
  importance of, 366

interim, 366–367
  misleading discussions and final proposal revisions case study, 368–370
proposal risk, 113
protests
  adverse agency action, 414
  to agency, 421–423
  agency bias or bad faith, 420
  avoiding, 426–428
  basis, 416
  business case, 417–418
  calendar days, 415
  common causes, 418
  debriefings, 408–409
  deciding whether to file, 415
  defective solicitations, 419
  definition, 413
  filing with GAO, 425–426
  improper agency evaluation, 418
  improper exclusion from competitive range, 419
  interested party, 413
  interveners, 414
  lack of cost realism, 419–420
  lack of meaningful discussions, 418–419
  legal flaws, 416
  postaward, 421
  preaward, 421
  prejudice, 416–417
  protesting adverse agency action case study, 423–425
  timing, 415
PWS. See performance work statement

Q

QASP. See quality assurance surveillance plan
QC. See quality control
qualitative standards, 109
quality assurance surveillance plan (QASP), 163
quality control (QC), 90
quantitative standards, 109

R

rating system. See scoring plan
realism, 296–299
reasonableness, 296
red team reviews. See critical reviews
references, 159
reporting schedule, 158–159
representations, certifications, and other statements of offerors or respondents, uniform contract format (section K), 155
request for proposals (RFP)
  draft, 173–176
  final review, 176–180
  government requirements, communicating, 153–154

request for proposals (RFP) (*cont.*)
  importance of, 33–34
  market research, 38
  uniform contract format, 154–155
required capabilities or performance
  characteristics, 44
requirements
  acquisition plan, 43
  full and open competition, 10
  specifying, 162–163
  statement of work, 160–161
  type and complexity, 79–80
  urgency, 80
requirements traceability matrix. See RFP
  compliance matrix
Reserve Health Readiness Program (RHRP),
  359–361
RFP. See request for proposals
RFP compliance, 249
RFP Compliance Matrix, 179–180, 223–225
risk
  acquisition plan, 44–45
  adjectival scale, 114
  case study, 118–119
  cost, 113
  evaluating, 112
  mitigating, 115
  performance, 113–114
  performance confidence assessment technique,
    115–117
  proposal, 113
  schedule, 113
  technical, 113

S

SAR/GMTI. See synthetic aperture radar/ground
  moving target indicator
schedule risk, 113
scope of work, 158
scoring, 305–306
scoring plan
  adjectival rating system, 129–130
  adjectival rating system case study, 130–134
  averaging adjectives case study, 134–135
  color coding rating system, 136–138
  combining approaches, 139–141
  deficient scoring plan case study, 145–148
  definition, 34–35
  inconsistently applied scoring case study, 141–145
  narrative descriptions, 148–149
  numerical rating system, 139
SDB. See small disadvantaged business
sealed bidding, 67, 69–70
section A, uniform contract format, 154
section B, uniform contract format, 154

section C, uniform contract format, 154
section D, uniform contract format, 155
section E, uniform contract format, 155
section F, uniform contract format, 155
section G, uniform contract format, 155
section H, uniform contract format, 155
section I, uniform contract format, 155
section J, uniform contract format, 155
section K, uniform contract format, 155
section L, uniform contract format
  cost/price information, 171–172
  draft RFP, 174–176
  final RFP, 176–177, 179–180
  importance of, 155
  master packing list, 170
  oral proposals, 170–171
  organizing, 169–170
  page and formatting limits, 170
  past performance information, 172–173
  preparing, 168–169
  technical/management information, 171
section M, uniform contract format, 155, 169,
  174–177
security considerations, 48
security evaluation factors, 91–92
selecting evaluators, 235–236
service-disabled veteran-owned small business, 65
should cost analysis, 44
SIC. See Standard Industrial Classification system
significant weakness report (SWR), 273
significant weaknesses, 267
simplified acquisition procedures, 67–69
Small Business Administration (SBA)
  clarifications versus discussions case study,
    332–333
  commercial marketing representatives, 65
  procurement center representatives, 65
  service-disabled veteran-owned small business, 65
  Small Disadvantaged Business Certification, 65
  special contracting opportunities, 65
  Subcontracting Assistance Program, 65
  veteran-owned small business, 65–66
  woman-owned small business, 66
small disadvantaged business (SDB), 65, 87–88
SMDC. See Space and Missile Defense Command
solicitation, 35–36, 153
solicitation/contract form, uniform contract format
  (section A), 154
source selection authority (SSA), 51–53, 95,
  119, 133
source selection decision document (SSDD)
  case study, 387–389
  importance of, 375, 385
  writing, 386–387
Source Selection Decision Statement, 386

source selection plan (SSP), 49–51

source selection procedures, 45

source selection process, explaining, 404–406

sources, 45

SOW. See statement of work

Space and Missile Defense Command (SMDC), 244–246

special compliance considerations, 253

special contract requirements, uniform contract format (section H), 155

SSA. See source selection authority

SSDD. See source selection decision document

SSP. See source selection plan

Standard Form 33, 178

Standard Industrial Classification system (SIC), 61

standards, 109

statement of need, 43

statement of work (SOW)

    background, 157–158

    completion, 163–164

    confusing elements, 166–168

    contractual approach, 161

    deliverables, 158

    detailed technical requirements, 158

    importance of, 33–34, 85, 155–157

    outlining, 164–165

    phasing contracts, 164

    planning, 159

    project objectives, 158

    proposal preparation instructions, 168–169

    references, 159

    reporting schedule, 158–159

    requirements, 160–161

    revising, 165

    scope of work, 158

    section L, 168–173

    special considerations, 159

    specifying requirements, 162–163

    term, 163–164

    writing, 166

storyboarding method, 226–227

strategy, 53–57

Subcontracting Assistance Program, 65

submission tips, 229–230

supplies or service and prices/costs, uniform contract format (section B), 154

suspension, 248–249

SWR. See significant weakness report

synopsis, 71

synthetic aperture radar/ground moving target indicator (SAR/GMTI), 346

T

technical capability, 80

technical evaluation factors, 88–89

technical/management information, 171

technical/management proposal volumes, 268–269

technical risk, 113

term form, cost-plus-fixed-fee contracts, 75

term statement of work, 163–164

test and evaluation, 47

time-and-materials (T&M) contract, 77

timeline, debriefings, 399

TIN. See U.S. Federal Tax Identification Number

TINA. See Truth in Negotiations Act

T&M. See time-and-materials contract

trade-offs

    acquisition plan, 44

    cost/technical trade-off comparison case study, 378–380

    proposal comparison, 376–378

    source selection decision document, 375

training and orientation, 237–240

Truth in Negotiations Act (TINA)

    adequate price competition, 5–6

    amendments, 20–21

    competitive range, 7

    cost and pricing data, 3–5

    defective pricing, 6–7

    impact on source selection, 7–9, 27

    overview, 3

U

uniform contract format (UCF), 154–155

United States Agency for International Development (USAID), 141–144

United States Postal Service (USPS), 255–257

U.S. Air Force, 273–279, 382–385

U.S. Army, 97–99, 250–253, 344–348, 359–361

U.S. Army Corps of Engineers, 244–246

U.S. Coast Guard, 1

U.S. Federal Tax Identification Number (TIN), 60

U.S. Navy, 118–119, 236–237, 423–425

USPS. See United States Postal Service

V

VA. See Department of Veterans Affairs

value analysis, 292

veteran-owned small business, 65–66

VETS-100 Report, 253

volumes, 95

W

woman-owned small business, 66

work breakdown structure (WBS), 85, 104–107

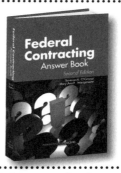

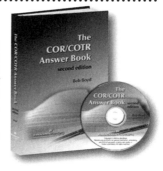

Federal Acquisition ActionPacks

Federal Acquisition ActionPacks are designed for busy professionals who need to get a working knowledge of government contracting quickly—without a lot of extraneous detail. This ten-book set covers all phases of the acquisition process, grounds you firmly in each topic area, and outlines practical methods for success, from contracting basics to the latest techniques for improving performance.

Each spiral-bound book contains approximately 160 pages of quick-reading information—simple statements, bulleted lists, questions and answers, charts and graphs, and more. Each topic's most important information is distilled to its essence, arranged graphically for easy comprehension and retention, and presented in a user-friendly format designed for quick look-up.

Or order the single titles that are most important to your role in the contracting process. Either way, this is the most effective, affordable way for both buyers and sellers to get a broad-based understanding of government contracting—and proven tools for success.

Earned Value Management Gregory A. Garrett ISBN 978-1-56726-188-2 Product Code B882 173 Pages	**Best-Value Source Selection** Philip E. Salmeri ISBN 978-1-56726-193-6 Product Code B936 178 Pages
Performance-Based Contracting Gregory A. Garrett ISBN 978-1-56726-189-9 Product Code B899 153 Pages	**Government Contract Law Basics** Thomas G. Reid ISBN 978-1-56726-194-3 Product Code B943 175 Pages
Cost Estimating and Pricing Gregory A. Garrett ISBN 978-1-56726-190-5 Product Code B905 161 Pages	**Government Contract Basics** Rene G. Rendon ISBN 978-1-56726-195-0 Product Code B950 176 Pages
Contract Administration and Closeout Gregory A. Garrett ISBN 978-1-56726-191-2 Product Code B912 153 Pages	**Performance Work Statements** Philip E. Salmeri ISBN 978-1-56726-196-7 Product Code B967 151 Pages
Contract Formation Gregory A. Garrett and William C. Pursch ISBN 978-1-56726-192-9 Product Code B929 163 Pages	**Contract Terminations** Thomas G. Reid ISBN 978-1-56726-197-4 Product Code B974 166 Pages